Great Ideas in the History of Surgery

IN nomine ſancte & indiuidue trinitatis laquale creo tutte le coſe:& ciaſcuna coſa doto di propria uirtute: &dallaquale ogni ſapientia eidata a ſaui & laſcientia a ſaputi: opera comincio ſopra le forze mie cõfidandomi dellaiuto di colui ſi come per noi p iſtrumiento adopera lopere ſue tutte: laqle

A

THIRTEENTH

CENTURY

SURGERY

Woodcut from: Petrus Hispanus: *Thesaurus pauperum* [Tesoro dei poveri, translated by Zucchero Bencivenni, Florence, Bartolommeo di Libri, ca. 1497]. Petrus Hispanus (ca. 1220–1277), who became Pope John XXI in 1276, was a Portuguese physician, surgeon, and man of letters. His "Treasury of the Poor," from which this illustration is taken, was one of the most popular and influential textbooks for three centuries. *Courtesy of the Historical Library, Yale University School of Medicine.*

Great Ideas in
the History of Surgery

LEO M. ZIMMERMAN, M.D.

Professor and Chairman, Department of Surgery,
Chicago Medical School;
Attending Surgeon, Michael Reese Hospital

ILZA VEITH, M.A., Ph.D.

Professor and Vice-Chairman,
Department of the History of Health Sciences,
University of California,
San Francisco Medical Center

Second Revised Edition

DOVER PUBLICATIONS, INC., NEW YORK

This Dover edition, first published in 1967, is an unabridged and corrected republication of the work originally published in a clothbound edition in 1961 by The Williams & Wilkins Company. The illustrations opposite pages 56 and 58, which were reproduced in color in the original edition are here reproduced in black and white.
This edition is published by special arrangement with The Williams & Wilkins Company, Baltimore, Maryland 21202.

Library of Congress Catalog Card Number: 67-14872

Manufactured in the United States of America
Dover Publications, Inc.
180 Varick Street
New York, N.Y. 10014

PROLOGUE

Surgery and medicine are inseparably fused today as essential parts of the art of healing. Such, of course, has not always been the case. Indeed, it was but a short time ago that this union took place. Over the millennia of recorded history, medicine and surgery have followed separate and largely independent evolutionary patterns, with only brief and infrequent periods of convergence of the two streams. It is a curious fact that, whenever the gap between the two has been closed, both halves have prospered as by a form of cross-fertilization, each giving as well as taking from the other. The modern period, in which the medical sciences have flourished more rapidly than ever before, coincides with the final welding of the two into an indivisible whole.

The story of the evolution of medicine has received considerable attention from both physicians and historians; that of surgery, by contrast, very little. Most of the available references emphasize the ignorance of the early surgeons, their mendacity, coarseness, and brutality. That such existed, there can be no doubt, inasmuch as some of the most vitriolic denunciations have come from surgeons themselves. Yet these characterizations form but part of the picture. In all periods there have been intelligent, high-minded, and sincere men who observed and recorded, building up fact-by-fact the imposing structure of modern surgical knowledge. Their need for basic scientific information compelled them to investigate successively the normal anatomy and physiology, and then the morphology and altered function brought on by disease. These researches not only served the purposes of surgery but also enriched medicine and the sciences as a whole to a degree that has not been generally appreciated. Thus the debt which surgeons owe to the other disciplines has been, and continues to be, repaid in kind.

The contributions of these surgical pioneers have extended into two additional directions, namely, into ethics and education. Jealous of the reputation of their craft, and distressed by the injury done to it and to the public by unscrupulous and unskilled practitioners, they have endeavored to control the training requirements as well as the ethical behavior from within the profession. By precept, by caustic exposures in their writings, by attempts to limit privileges to the competent, and by pressure on governments to exercise the power of license, they have elevated the status of surgery from a craft that enjoyed scant esteem to its present respected place in the healing profession.

It has often been stressed that surgeons lacked education. And, indeed, it is entirely true that for many centuries in most countries the universities were closed to students of surgery. But to a largely unrecognized degree bedside and clinical training, which is now considered to be the essence of medical education, has grown out of schools set up by surgeons, first as private ventures, and later as hospital centers for training. This process of evolution in educational methods and institutions will be indicated in the successive chapters of this book.

The present manifest interest in its history is perhaps a criterion of the maturation of modern medicine; and particularly striking is the growing attention given to the history of surgery which never before had received its full due. Surgery, indeed, had a proud history, and its exploration is a gratifying experience. An unexpected wealth of interesting fact, of commanding personalities, and of fascinating literature is encountered. Our aim in this book is to make a portion of this treasure available to the reader, and particularly to the surgeon who is the professional descendant and the modern counterpart of the great figures of the past. The reading of the history of surgery, we believe, should provide more than avocational pleasure. Surgery, like every other cultural stream, is a continuum, and an awareness of its past enables the practitioner of the present to sense his linkage with what has gone before and, also, what will come afterward.

This book is neither a complete nor a conventional history of surgery. It is rather an attempt to convey a feeling for the growth of surgery by presenting its leading personalities from the beginning of literary records to the present time. In quoting from their writings, particular effort has been made to retain the *flavor* of their original style. Much of the charm lies therein, although this may entail sacrifice of some ease in reading. We have used original English texts or contemporary translations when they were available. All other translations (with a few indicated exceptions) are our own, and the sources have been designated in each instance.

The plan followed in the presentation of this material has been consistent throughout. An introductory biographical sketch of each of the authors has been given, with brief commentary on the medical climate of the period to provide orientation in time and place. Their contributions to surgery have been described and then follow the verbatim extracts from their writings, preserving, in so far as we have been able, the quality of the original. A pithy epigrammatic statement has been selected from the works of each which usually expresses a philosophical or ethical thought rather than a scientific one. Illustrations have been used when available, especially if they convey some of the drama and the background of contemporary surgery. Although some portraits have been included this has been far from the rule.

It is obvious that in a work such as this it would be impossible to include all of the figures, or even the names, of those who have significantly con-tributed to the art or science, the education, or the professional status of surgery. The numbers who have done so are far too vast. A certain amount of arbitrary selection was therefore necessary, although we recognize that inherent in such choice is the possibility that there may be objections to the inclusion of some among the great and the omission of others. This dilemma arises particularly when dealing with the recent past, in which so many have done so much in so short a time. Lacking as yet a historical perspective, the relative significance of the legion of contributions cannot yet be assessed with assurance. Such omissions, therefore, are of lesser significance because the more recent writings are easily available to those who might desire to read them. For this last, hectic period we have selected a few of the major subdivisions of surgery and have presented as the protagonist of each that individual who in our opinion has played the most important role in bringing it to its present status; and brief mention has been made of a few others who have carried the work onward. In any event, we have tried to avoid chauvinistic imbalance, and we hope that we will be credited with having made our choice delib-erately rather than because of unawareness of those who have been omitted. Moreover, despite our admiration of the great men of the past who have made the history of surgery, we have attempted to avoid hero worship; we have pre-sented their weaknesses as well as their virtues, and have tried to evoke as their image the same human qualities that are possessed by their descendants in the profession to this day.

ACKNOWLEDGMENTS

We acknowledge gratefully the kindness of the authors and publishers who granted us their permission to quote passages and to reproduce illustrations from the following publications:

The Oriental Institute of the University of Chicago and the University of Chicago Press for quotations and illustrations from *The Edwin Smith Surgical Papyrus*, published in facsimile and hieroglyphic transliterations with translation and commentary, by James Henry Breasted, 2 Vols., Chicago, University of Chicago Press, 1930.

J. B. Lippincott Company for quotations from the article on "Hippocratic Surgery" by Fred B. Lund, *Annals of Surgery*, Vol. 100, 1935.

Dr. George W. Corner for excerpts from his translation of Sudhoff's text of Roger in "The Rise of Medicine at Salerno in the Twelfth Century," *Annals of Medical History*, 3 (N.S.), 1931.

Appleton-Century-Crofts, Inc., and the New York Academy of Medicine for illustration and text from *The Surgery of Theodoric* by Eldridge Campbell and James Colton, 2 Vols., New York, 1955 and 1960.

Johann Ambrosius Barth for permission to translate the Galen text: Aus Klassiker der Medizin Band 21: *Galenos*, Über die Krankhaften Geschwülste (zwischen 169 and 180 n. Chr.) übersetzt und eingeleitet von Paul Richter, Leipzig, Johann Ambrosius Barth, 1913.

Scholars' Facsimiles and Reprints and Dr. DeWitt Starnes for excerpts from *A Profitable and Necessarie Booke of Observations*. . . . by William Clowes. Reprint edited by DeWitt Starnes and Chauncey D. Leake, New York, 1945.

Dr. Jerome P. Webster for quotations and illustrations from *The Life and Times of Gaspare Tagliacozzi* by Martha Teach Gnudi and Jerome Pierce Webster, New York, Herbert Reichner Publishing Company, 1950.

E. & S. Livingstone, Ltd., for illustrations from *The Life and Work of Astley Cooper* by R. C. Brock, Edinburgh, 1952; and *Sir Charles Bell, His Life and Times* by Sir Gordon Gordon-Taylor and E. W. Walls, Edinburgh, 1958.

Dr. Michael L. Mason for his translation from Paracelsus' *Grosse Wundartzney* which was published in the *Quarterly Bulletin*, Northwestern University Medical School, Vol. 30, 1956.

Unless otherwise designated, the illustrations used were taken with permission from the Frank Webster Jay and Charles B. Pike print collections of the University of Chicago.

To the Bayer-Werke, Leverkusen, Pharmazeutisch-Wissenschaftliche Abteilung we are particularly grateful for their extraordinary generosity in supplying us with the two color pages which were published by them and which first appeared in *Medizin in Tibet* by Ilza Veith, Leverkusen [1961].

TABLE OF CONTENTS

PART I

THE BEGINNINGS

CHAPTER 1

Egyptian Surgery:
The *Edwin Smith Surgical Papyrus*

"If thou examinest a man having a gaping wound in his head, penetrating to the bone, thou shouldst lay thy hand upon it and thou shouldst palpate his wound. If thou findest his skull uninjured, not having a perforation in it, thou shouldst say regarding him: 'One having a gaping wound in his head. An ailment which I will treat.'"[1]

The earliest scientific document ever brought to light is a treatise on surgery![2] This work, the *Edwin Smith Papyrus*, was conceived in ancient Egypt almost 5000 years ago, and is one of the most remarkable books in the entire history of surgery. Compiled by an unknown author at a time when medicine was magico-religious, when the vocabulary of science had not yet been created, and when the first groping steps in inductive reasoning were being taken, this volume is as logical as a modern textbook in surgery. In addition to its description of clinical methods then in use, it contains astonishingly accurate observations in anatomy, physiology, and pathology. Magic and mysticism are almost entirely absent. Many inferences as to medical practice in this ancient period may be drawn from this unique document.

The *Edwin Smith Papyrus* is named for the pioneer American Egyptologist who purchased the scroll in 1862 from a native dealer in Luxor, Egypt. Although he was unable at the time to decipher the manuscript, Smith, nevertheless, was apparently aware of its extraordinary significance. After the death of its purchaser, the papyrus was presented by his heirs to the New-York Historical Society in the library of which it now reposes. Permission was given by the present owners to the renowned Orientalist, James Henry

1. *The Edwin Smith Surgical Papyrus*, published in facsimile and hieroglyphic transliteration with translation and commentary in two volumes by James Henry Breasted, Chicago, University of Chicago Press, 1930, "Consecutive Translation" of the Surgical Treatise, Case 2, Vol. I, p. 431.
2. *Ibid.*, p. xiii.

FIG. 1. A portion of the *Edwin Smith Papyrus* in the original hieratic script. From: *The Edwin Smith Surgical Papyrus*, translated by James Henry Breasted, Chicago, University of Chicago Press, 1930.

Breasted, of the University of Chicago, to study its contents. This work was aided by Dr. Arno B. Luckhardt, Professor of Physiology at the same institution and an ardent student of medical history, who lent his valuable medical knowledge in the interpretation of the text. Two preliminary accounts which were published in 1922 created sensational interest among Egyptologists, who eagerly awaited the publication of the entire text. The completed translation,

FIG. 2. Transcription into hieroglyphics from which the translation was made. From: *The Edwin Smith Surgical Papyrus, loc. cit.*

with facsimile reproductions, commentary, and glossary, appeared in two magnificent volumes in 1930, and furnished a totally new concept of early Egyptian surgery.

The original text of this surgical treatise dates back to the early part of the Old Kingdom (3000–2500 B.C.). It was copied some centuries later, presumably by another surgeon, at a time when many of the terms originally used had become obsolete and incomprehensible. Fortunately, that writer added a series of "glosses" or explanations, which interpret the meaning of the original and serve to bridge the span of years and obsolescence. The present copy was made much later, about 1700 B.C., by a scribe who was obviously not a surgeon, and whose unfamiliarity with the material is indicated by his many errors, corrections, and omissions. He transcribed the book but left it incomplete, stopping abruptly with an unfinished sentence in the middle of a description of a clinical case. The unfinished portion has remained forever lost.

The text of the *Edwin Smith Papyrus* differs importantly from the other medical papyri so far discovered. It is the oldest in date of origin, and is the only one that deals primarily with surgery. The others consist essentially of a jumble of prayers, incantations, and fanciful prescriptions. This one describes a series of cases, logically arranged, beginning at the head and progressing downward. In the papyrus the more superficial injuries are described first, followed by the progressively more severe ones. A definite pattern is followed in the presentation of each case. Each is headed by a "Title," usually beginning with the word "Instructions," which is followed by a designation of the type and location of the injury or disease, such as, "Instructions concerning a gaping wound in his head, penetrating to the bone and splitting his skull." This is followed by the "Examination" which includes interrogation of the patient, inspection, palpation, and the observation of movements executed at the direction of the surgeon. On the basis of these clinical findings, the "Diagnosis" is reached, usually introduced by the words, "Thou shouldst say concerning him." These are followed by a description of the ailment. Included herewith is the "Verdict," a statement of the surgeon's decision regarding treatment. He can pronounce one of the following judgments:

1. "An ailment which I will treat." (This he considers curable.)
2. "An ailment with which I will contend." (In this manner he records his doubts about the curability although, at the same time, he institutes his therapeutic measures.)
3. "An ailment not to be treated." (With this verdict he emphasizes the seriousness of the case, thus relieving himself of personal responsibility in the event of a fatal outcome. He refrains from immediate therapy and restricts himself to watchful waiting and thorough observation of the patient. The inclusion of these cases, even though they are not to be treated, bespeaks a scientific interest in placing them on record.)

The final section in each case deals with "Treatment." Included herewith are mechanical, medicinal, postural, and dietary instructions.

The material dealt with in this textbook consists of forty-eight surgical cases, most of which are injuries. These include the following:

Wounds of the head   twenty-seven cases
Injuries:
    Throat and neck   six cases

Clavicle	two cases
Humerus	three cases
Chest and breast (including tumors and abscesses)	eight cases
Shoulder	one case
Thoracic spine	one case (incomplete)

The book offers us a glimpse of the state of scientific knowledge in that early period. The primitive anatomical observations are remarkably descriptive, and terms are created to designate the structures seen. For the first time in any language, the word "brain" appears. Its convoluted surface is likened to the corrugations that form on cooling slag from molten copper. The pulsations imparted to the examining fingers exploring the exposed brain in compound fractures are compared to the "throbbing and fluttering under thy fingers like the weak place of an infant's crown before it becomes whole." The membranes of the brain (meninges) and the contained cerebrospinal fluid are mentioned, and the sutures of the skull are recognized.

Other skeletal structures mentioned are the mandible, including the "ligaments at the end of the ramus which are fastened to the temporal bone," and the temporo-mandibular joint. The vertebrae, collar bones (clavicles), sternum, ribs, and shoulder blades are among the bones discussed. The ramus of the mandible is described, its articular end being compared to the claw of a two-toed bird which clasps the temporal bone.

Physiological observations of astounding discernment are made and recorded by this earliest known natural scientist. The pulse is recognized and counted, antedating the Hippocratic observations by 2500 years. The significance of the pulse as an indication of the clinical condition of the patient is described, ". . . like measuring the ailment of a man, in order to know the action of the heart." The heart is known to be the center from which pulsating vessels lead to all parts of the body; thus a knowledge of the circulation is foreshadowed.

Astute observations are made, too, of the function of the nervous system. The influence of the brain on the action of remote structures is recognized. Paralysis of the lower extremities in injuries of the brain is noted, and there is an awareness of the relation between the location of the cranial injury and the side of the body involved. In a similar fashion, motor and sensory impairments in crushing injuries of the cervical vertebrae are noted.

The clinical evaluation of the cases described bespeaks careful objective examination. Symptoms are observed and physical findings obtained by inspection, by palpation, and even by smell. The ability of patients to execute motions, as directed by the surgeon, further completes the clinical picture.

Treatment is, in the main, logical. Expectancy, in the Hippocratic manner, is the keynote of management. The use of sutures or adhesive tape approximation of soft-tissue wounds, the employment of splints and bandages, and the application of dressings follow logical concepts. Fresh meat is the usual dressing for the first day, perhaps for its hemostyptic value. Later, soothing and protective substances are applied. Both heat and cold are used for logically indicated conditions. Dislocation of the mandible is reduced in a manner identical with that employed today.

Of particular interest are the pathological manifestations of injury and disease. In wounds involving the meninges or brain, meningeal irritation is noted, in the form of "stiffness" of the neck or the inability of the patient to "look at his shoulders." Bleeding from the ears and nostrils is regularly described accompanying skull fractures, and "shuffling" gait after brain damage, even in the absence of scalp laceration. The complications of wounds, including infection, tetanus, and "exhaustion," are all described. And in fractures of the mid-cervical vertebrae, priapism, seminal emission, and involuntary urination are noted, with appropriately poor ultimate prognosis.

In addition to the direct statements contained in this surgical pioneering work, interesting inferences may be drawn from this contemporary record of medical practice. The gulf between physicians and surgeons is revealed. Of the surviving Egyptian papyri, only one deals with surgery. Whether this proportion is accidental or indicative of the relative illiteracy of the Egyptian surgeons cannot be stated with certainty. More striking, however, are the differences between this surgical text and the other manuscripts. Egyptian medicine was deistic, its votaries priestly. Illness was the result of divine ill will, or possession by malign spirits. Healing was achieved by invoking more powerful supernatural assistance, by propitiating outraged gods, and by exorcising evil spirits. The writings are a chaotic and meaningless jumble of prayers, incantations, exorcisms, and recipes consisting of a multitude of medicaments, many of which are bizarre and disgusting, and few of which, if any, are of any real therapeutic value. Clinical observation, scientific recording of fact, anatomy, physiology—these have no place in the prevailing philosophy of medicine of the time. Finally, the priest-physician stands as the mediator of divine assistance. What votary could so belittle the powers of his gods as to declare that an ailment is not to be treated? This strongly suggests that the surgeon-author of the *Edwin Smith Papyrus* was not a member of the priestly class.

In this connection Breasted's remarks on the connotations of the word "Treatment" assume specific interest. He points out that, in most of the case histories presented, surgical manipulation is directed under the heading of "Examination" and only medicinal applications are considered under "Treatment." This is doubtless indicative of the difference in esteem accorded to the manipulative techniques of the surgeon as contrasted with the use of medicinal preparations of the physicians.

𝕤𝕖 𝕤𝕖 𝕤𝕖
𝕤𝕖 𝕤𝕖 𝕤𝕖

CASE SIX.[3] A GAPING WOUND IN THE HEAD WITH COM-
POUND COMMINUTED FRACTURE OF THE SKULL AND
RUPTURE OF THE MENINGEAL MEMBRANES

Title

Instructions concerning a gaping wound in his head, penetrating to the bone, smashing his skull, (and) rending open the
brain of his skull.

Examination

If thou examinest a man having a gaping wound in his head,
penetrating to the bone, smashing his skull, (and) rending open
the brain of his skull, thou shouldst palpate his wound. Shouldst
thou find that smash which is in his skull (like) those corrugations which form in molten copper, (and) something therein
throbbing (and) fluttering under thy fingers, like the weak
place of an infant's crown before it becomes whole—when it
has happened there is no throbbing (and) fluttering under thy
fingers until the brain of his (the patient's) skull is rent open—
(and) he discharges blood from both his nostrils, (and) he
suffers with stiffness in his neck, (conclusion in diagnosis).

Diagnosis

(Thou shouldst say concerning him): "An ailment not to be
treated."

Treatment

Thou shouldst anoint that wound with grease. Thou shalt
not bind it; thou shalt not apply two strips upon it: until thou
knowest that he has reached a decisive point.

CASE SEVEN: A GAPING WOUND IN THE HEAD PENETRAT-
ING TO THE BONE AND PERFORATING THE SUTURES

Title

Instructions concerning a gaping wound in his head, penetrating to the bone, (and) perforating the sutures of his skull.

Examination

[If thou examinest a man having a gaping wound in his
head, penetrating to the bone, (and) perforating the sutures
of his skull], thou shouldst palpate his wound, (although) he

3. *Ibid.*, pp. 431–453.

shudders exceedingly. Thou shouldst cause him to lift his face; if it is painful for him to open his mouth, (and) his heart beats feebly; if thou observe his spittle hanging at his two lips and not falling off, while he discharges blood from both his nostrils (and) from both his ears; he suffers with stiffness in his neck, (and) is unable to look at his two shoulders and his breast, (conclusion in diagnosis).

First Diagnosis

Thou shouldst say regarding him: "One having a gaping wound in his head, penetrating to the bone, (and) perforating the sutures of his skull; the cord of his mandible is contracted; he discharges blood from both his nostrils (and) from both his ears, while he suffers with stiffness in his neck. An ailment with which I will contend."

First Treatment

Now as soon as thou findest that the cord of that man's mandible, his jaw, is contracted, thou shouldst have made for him something hot, until he is comfortable, so that his mouth opens. Thou shouldst bind it with grease, honey, (and) lint, until thou knowest that he has reached a decisive point.

Second Examination

If, then, thou findest that the flesh of that man has developed fever from that wound which is in the sutures of his skull, while that man has developed ty' from that wound, thou shouldst lay thy hand upon him. Shouldst thou find his countenance is clammy with sweat, the ligaments of his neck are tense, his face is ruddy, his teeth and his back [—], the odor of the chest of his head is like the *bkn* (urine) of sheep, his mouth is bound, (and) both his eyebrows are drawn, while his face is as if he wept, (conclusion in diagnosis).

Second Diagnosis

Thou shouldst say regarding him: "One having a gaping wound in his head, penetrating to the bone, perforating the sutures of his skull; he has developed ty', his mouth is bound, (and) he suffers with stiffness in his neck. An ailment not to be treated."

Third Examination

If, however, thou findest that that man has become pale and has already (shown exhaustion).

Third Treatment

Thou shouldst have made for him a wooden brace padded with linen and put into his mouth. Thou shouldst have made for him a draught of *w'h*-fruit. His treatment is sitting, placed between two supports of brick, until thou knowest he has reached a decisive point.

CASE THIRTY-ONE: DISLOCATION OF A CERVICAL VERTE-BRA

Title

Instructions concerning a dislocation in a vertebra of (his) neck.

Examination

If thou examinest a man having a dislocation in a vertebra of his neck, shouldst thou find him unconscious of his two arms (and) his two legs on account of it, while his phallus is erected on account of it, (and) urine drops from his member without his knowing it; his flesh has received wind; his two eyes are blood-shot; it is a dislocation of a vertebra of his neck extending to his backbone which causes him to be unconscious of his two arms (and) his two legs. If, however, the middle vertebra of his neck is dislocated, it is an *emissio seminis* which befalls his phallus.

Diagnosis

Thou shouldst say concerning him: "One having a dislocation in a vertebra of his neck, while he is unconscious of his two legs and his two arms, and his urine dribbles. An ailment not to be treated."

CASE TWELVE: A BREAK IN THE NASAL BONE

Title

Instructions concerning a break in the chamber of his nose.

Examination

If thou examinest a man having a break in the chamber of his nose, (and) thou findest his nose bent, while his face is disfigured, (and) the swelling which is over it is protruding, (conclusion in diagnosis).

Diagnosis

Thou shouldst say concerning him: "One having a break in the chamber of his nose. An ailment which I will treat."

Treatment

Thou shouldst force it to fall in, so that it is lying in its place, (and) clean out for him the interior of both his nostrils with two swabs of linen until every worm of blood which coagulates in the inside of his two nostrils comes forth. Now afterward thou shouldst place two plugs of linen saturated with grease and put into his two nostrils. Thou shouldst place for him two stiff rolls of linen, bound on. Thou shouldst treat him afterward with grease, honey, (and) lint every day until he recovers.

Gloss A

As for: "A break in the chamber of his nose," it means the middle of his nose as far as the back, extending to the region between his two eyebrows.

Gloss B

As for: "His nose bent, while his face is disfigured," it means his nose is crooked and greatly swollen throughout; his two cheeks likewise, so that his face is disfigured by it, not being in its customary form, because all the depressions are clothed with swellings, so that his face looks disfigured by it.

Gloss C

As for: "Every worm of blood which coagulates in the inside of his two nostrils," it means the clotting of blood in the inside of his two nostrils, likened to the 'n'r·t-worm, which subsists in the water.

CASE TWENTY-FIVE: A DISLOCATION OF THE MANDIBLE

Title

Instructions concerning a dislocation in his mandible.

Examination

If thou examinest a man having a dislocation in his mandible, shouldst thou find his mouth open (and) his mouth cannot close for him, thou shouldst put thy thumb(s) upon the ends of the two rami of the mandible in the inside of his mouth, (and) thy two claws (meaning two groups of fingers) under his chin, (and) thou shouldst cause them to fall back so that they rest in their places.

Diagnosis

Thou shouldst say concerning him: "One having a dislocation in his mandible. An ailment which I will treat."

Treatment

Thou shouldst bind it with *ymrw*, (and) honey every day until he recovers.

CHAPTER 2

Hippocrates
(Fifth to Fourth Century B.C.)

"The physician must be able to tell the antecedents, know the present, and foretell the future—must meditate these things, and have two special objects in view with regard to diseases, namely, to do good or to do no harm. The art consists in three things—the disease, the patient, and the physician. As to diseases, make a habit of two things—to help, or at least to do no harm. The art has three factors, the disease, the patient, the physician. The physician is the servant of the art, and the patient must cooperate with the physician in combating the disease."[1]

The figure of Hippocrates looms large against the background of early medical history. None has been so revered as has been the "Father of Medicine," and none has so influenced the evolution of the healing art. Scientific medicine begins with the Hippocratic writings and the history of medicine for 2000 years is largely the struggle to regain the peaks which were attained during the Golden Age of Greece, 400 years before the Christian era.

Little is known about the actual life of Hippocrates. He was born about 460 B.C. on the island of Cos and he died in Thessaly about 377 B.C. Whether this long life span is a compliment to the skill of the great physician or a historical fact will never be known. Contemporaries relate that he traveled widely and studied man in his natural environment. Posterity acclaimed him as the greatest physician of his time and attributed to his authorship a great number of medical writings the influence of which has never been equalled.

The more than seventy books which bear his name are called the *Corpus Hippocraticum*. The many commentators and translators of this work agree that these books do not stem from his pen alone, but represent the collective efforts of his successors and disciples as well. There is no agreement, however, concerning certain volumes, as to which are the "genuine" books of the great Hippocrates and which were written by others. For the purposes of this chapter we speak of Hippocrates in the traditional manner as the sole author of

1. *Epidemics* I, xi, in *Hippocrates* with an English translation by W. H. S. Jones (Loeb Classical Library), London, William Heinemann, 1923, Vol. I, p. 165.

the *Corpus* without making any attempt to separate the genuine from the spurious.

The eminent medical historian, Fielding H. Garrison, succinctly summarizes the achievements of Hippocrates as follows: "He dissociated medicine from theurgy and philosophy, crystallized the loose knowledge of the Coan and Cnidian schools into systematic science, and gave physicians the highest moral inspiration they have." By freeing medicine from religion and speculation, and directing attention to careful clinical observation of the patient, Hippocrates laid the basis for scientific medicine. The accuracy of his bedside observations and the vividness of his descriptions have set the pattern for all who have come after him. The well-known picture of the "Hippocratic Facies" remains a classic. The "Aphorisms" are nuggets of medical wisdom that have been quoted for centuries. The "Oath" of Hippocrates, whether originally composed by him or not, is still acknowledged as containing the essential maxims of medical ethics throughout most parts of the world.

When the causes of illness were removed from the supernatural and were sought in the constitution of the individual and the influences of his environment, the artificial separation of physicians and surgeons disappeared, and both disciplines became welded into one. Medicine and surgery are both dealt with in the *Corpus*, and there is little doubt that the Hippocratic physician practiced both forms of treatment. Indeed, it is quite generally agreed that the surgical books belong to the "genuine" writings of Hippocrates, and they are among the most lucid and brilliant sections of the entire work. Comprising these are "The Physicians' Establishment" or "Surgery," "On Injuries of the Head," "Fractures," "On the Articulations," "The Instruments of Reductions (Mochlichus)," "Ulcers," "Fistulas," and "Hemorrhoids."

Anatomy, in general, is rather sketchily treated in the *Corpus*. Indeed, a precise knowledge of human structure and function was of little real significance in general medicine because of the predominantly "humoral" concept of health and disease. A proper balance of the four humors, blood (warm-dry), yellow bile (cold-dry), black bile (warm-moist), and mucus (moist-cold) implied a state of good health. Illness resulted from a disturbed balance of these essential fluids, and treatment was directed toward attempting to restore the normal balance.

In the surgical writings, by contrast, the anatomical knowledge appears detailed and accurate and the descriptions are clear and precise. Such information was essential in recognizing and reducing fractures and dislocations, and was vital if injury to important structures during operations was to be avoided.

The book "On the Surgery" deals in detail with the operating room, the lighting, personnel, instruments, positioning of the patient, and techniques of bandaging and splinting. The practical instructions given bespeak wide experience in actual surgical manipulation. "The things relating to surgery are

—the patient; the operator; the assistants; the instruments; the light, where and how; how many things, and how; where the body, and the instruments; the time; the manner; the place." The surgeon's hands are discussed. "The nails should be neither longer nor shorter than the points of the fingers. . . . One should practice all sorts of work with either of them, and with both together (for they are both alike), endeavoring to do them well, elegantly, quickly, without trouble, neatly, and promptly."

In general, Hippocrates favored the "dry" treatment of wounds, with, at most, the application of wine as a dressing. However, in badly contused or infected wounds, he attempted to promote suppuration by the use of ointments, as a means of lessening inflammation and preventing complications. He thus foreshadowed the dispute which raged for many later centuries as to the relative merits of the dry method which strove to prevent infection and led to primary union, and the encouragement of suppuration ("laudable pus") in all wounds. The indications for either method, as used by Hippocrates, seem entirely logical.

Fistula-in-ano is well described in the Hippocratic writings, and the use of the seton employed for its cure. This operation consisted in threading a ligature through the fistula and out through the anus. It was tied gradually tighter until it cut through by pressure necrosis, thus laying the tract completely open. Whereas the author mentions "cutting, excising, sewing, binding, applying putrefacient means to the anus" for the relief of hemorrhoids, he describes in detail the use of the actual cautery. As an alternative method he suggests that the operator should position "the anus to protrude as much as possible, foment with hot water, and then cut off the extremities of the hemorrhoids." Condylomata were removed with the finger.

The treatise "On Injuries of the Head" begins with a fairly accurate description of the skull. Five types of cranial injuries are described: (1) simple fractures or fissures of various kinds or sizes; (2) contusion, without fracture or depression; (3) depressed fractures; (4) fractures of the outer table alone; and (5) *contrecoup* fractures. Trepanning was an important feature in the management of head injuries, but the indications for the operation may seem strange to us from the vantage point of modern knowledge and practice. The operation was recommended for contusion of the skull, fissure, and indentation (fracture of the outer table only), if accompanied by contusion or fracture. For depressed fracture Hippocrates advises against trepanning. The technique of the procedure is described in detail.

The history of the injury is first ascertained, including the nature of the weapon inflicting it. "You should make inquiry as to all these particulars (for they are symptoms of a greater or lesser injury), whether the wounded person was stunned, and whether darkness was diffused over his eyes, and whether he had vertigo, and fell to the ground." The portion of the skull involved, whether thicker or thinner, is considered in arriving at a prognosis. Inspection of the wound then follows, and, if the bone is exposed, this may suffice for a determination of the diagnosis. The wound may be enlarged for better exposure of the skull. Scraping the surface with a raspatory may reveal fractures not detected by sight. Or the wound may be filled with ink (dissolved jet-black ointment) which will penetrate the fracture and delineate it.

Infection of the scalp wound, erysipelas, secondary necrosis of the bone, tetanus, and meningitis, all were known to Hippocrates as complications of head injuries, and their prognosis, prevention, and treatment are discussed. "And for the most part, convulsions seize the other side of the body; for if the wound be situated on the left side, the convulsions will seize the right side of the body; or if the wound be on the right side of the head, the convulsion attacks the left side of the body."

The three books dealing with the skeletal system, "On Fractures," "On Articulations," and "Mochlicus (Instruments of Reduction)," contain some of the most detailed and lucid descriptions in the entire *Corpus*. They reflect a profound practical knowledge and give evidence of a wide actual experience in the management of these conditions. The acquaintance with the anatomy of the parts involved is strikingly complete and accurate as compared with the general anatomical knowledge in the other books. Indeed, there is indication of a systematic study of human anatomy. Speaking of dislocations of the shoulder, for instance, Hippocrates writes, "But if one will strip the point of the shoulder of the fleshy parts, and where the muscle (*deltoid?*) extends, and also lay bare the tendon that goes from the armpit and clavicle to the breast (pectoral muscle?) the head of the humerus will appear to protrude strongly forward although not dislocated, for the head of the humerus naturally inclines forward, but the rest of the bone is turned outward."

The recognition and managment of the diseases and injuries of the skeletal structures is so astonishingly complete that it remained standard for 2000 years, and some of the methods described are in use today. In the treatment of fractures, reduction was accomplished by traction plus manual manipulation of the fragments. Bandages were applied initially, as the extension was being maintained, but splints were not incorporated until seven to eleven days had elapsed, perhaps to permit the swelling to subside. A variety of methods of reduction is presented, which exhibit great inventiveness and ingenuity. Instruments of considerable complexity are described, including small iron levers to pry otherwise irreducible fragments into place, in compound fractures with protruding bone.

Compound fractures are dealt with, as well as simple ones, and the complications of such injuries, including sepsis, tetanus, osteomyelitis, gangrene, and death, are described. It is of interest that the significance of the time element was emphasized. Thus, in compound fractures, ". . . for, in a word, at no time is it so little proper to disturb all kinds of wounds as on the third or fourth day; and all sort of probing should be avoided on those days on whatever other injuries are attended with irritation. For, generally, the third and fourth day in most cases of wounds, are those which give rise to exacerbations, whether the tendency be to inflammation, to a foul condition of the sore, or to fevers." Again, speaking of levers to effect reduction of bone fragments protruding from the wound, Hippocrates wrote, "The lever, along with extension, may be had recourse to on the day of the accident, or the next day, but by no means on the third, fourth or fifth. For if the limb is disturbed on these days, and yet fractured bones not reduced, inflammation will be excited, and this no less if they are reduced; for convulsions [tetanus] are more apt to occur if reduction takes place, than if the attempt should fail. . . . But when seven days have elapsed, or rather more, if there be no fever, and if the wound be not inflamed, then there will be less to prevent an attempt at reduction, if you hope to succeed. . . ." This is a good doctrine in terms of present day knowledge of contamination and infection. Early management of wounds is desirable, despite initial contamination, because there has been no opportunity for bacterial growth and infiltration. Once this opportunity is lost, no manipulation is permissible until an adequate period has elapsed to indicate the absence of infection.

The most complete and the most masterful descriptions are those of dislocations, particularly of the shoulder and the hip. Indeed, the grasp of these lesions exceeds that of most surgeons today who are not specifically expert in the field of orthopedics. Congenital as well as traumatic dislocations are accurately described, and the methods of reduction are not only logical, but some have not been improved upon to this day. Further sections deal with spinal deformities, and the association of gibbus with pulmonary tuberculosis is pointed out. The paragraph on congenital club-foot is close to being a masterpiece.

Two major omissions in surgical therapy are somewhat puzzling. These have to do with bladder stone and hernia. The specific injunction against cutting for stone in the "Oath" of Hippocrates has occasioned considerable speculation. The words are, "I will not cut persons laboring under the stone, but will this to be done by men who are practitioners of this work." Whether the hazards of the operation were too great to risk one's reputation by undertaking it, or whether the skill required was inadequate except in the hands of "specialists" trained in the field, even though "irregulars," cannot be stated positively.

The second omission concerns hernia. It is noteworthy that nowhere in the *Corpus Hippocraticum* is there discussion of this common and easily recognizable condition. Whether this omission is accidental and perhaps due to a loss of

parts of the treatise or whether this operation was also left to specialists can never be established with any certainty.

ᔓ   ᔓ   ᔓ   I. ON THE SURGERY[2]

ᔓ   ᔓ   ᔓ   1. It is the business of the physician to know, in the first place, things similar and things dissimilar; those connected with things most important, most easily known, and in any-wise known; which are to be seen, touched, and heard; which are to be perceived in the sight, and the touch, and the hearing, and the nose, and the tongue, and the understanding; which are to known by all the means we know other things.

2. The things relating to surgery, are—the patient; the operator; the assistants; the instruments; the light, where and how; how many things, and how; where the body, and the instruments; the time; the manner; the place.

3. The operator is either sitting or standing, conveniently for himself, for the person operated upon, for the light. There are two kinds of light, the common and the artificial; the common is not at our disposal, the artificial is at our disposal. There are two modes of using each, either to the light, or from the light (to the side?). There is little use of that which is from (*or* oblique to the light), and the degree of it is obvious. As to opposite the light, we must turn the part to be operated upon to that which is most brilliant of present and convenient lights, unless those parts which should be concealed, and which it is a shame to look upon; thus the part that is operated upon should be opposite the light, and the operator opposite the part operated upon, except in so far as he does not stand in his own light; for in this case the operator will indeed see, but the thing operated upon will not be seen. With regard to himself: when sitting, his feet should be raised to a direct line with his knees, and nearly in contact with one another; the knees a little higher than the groins, and at some distance from one another, for the elbows to rest upon them. The robe, in a neat and orderly manner, is to be thrown over the elbows and shoulders equally and proportionally. With regard to the part operated upon; we have to consider how far distant, and how near, above, below, on this side, on that side, or in the middle. The

2. *The Genuine Works of Hippocrates*, translated from the Greek with a Preliminary Discourse and Annotations by Francis Adams, New York, William Wood & Company, 1929, "On the Surgery," Vol. II, pp. 7–10.

measure as to distance and proximity is, that the elbows do not
press the knees before, nor the sides behind; that the hands be
not raised higher than the breasts, nor lower than so as that
when the breast reposes on the knees he may have the hands at
right angles with the arm: thus it is as regards the medium;
but as concerns this side or that, the operator must not be beyond his seat, but in proportion as he may require turning he
must shift the body, or part of the body, that is operated upon.
When standing, he must make his inspection, resting firmly
and equally on both feet; but he must operate while supporting
himself upon either leg, and not the one on the same side with
the hand which he makes use of; the knee being raised to the
height of the groins as while sitting; and the other measures in
like manner. The person operated upon should accommodate
the operator with regard to the other parts of his body, either
standing, sitting, or lying; so as that he may continue to preserve
his figure, avoid sinking down, shrinking from, turning away;
and may maintain the figure and position of the part operated
upon, during the act of presentation, during the operation, and
in the subsequent position.

4. The nails should be neither longer nor shorter than the
points of the fingers; and the surgeon should practice with the
extremities of the fingers, the index-finger being usually turned
to the thumb; when using the entire hand, it should be prone;
when both hands, they should be opposed to one another. It
greatly promotes a dexterous use of the fingers when the space
between them is large, and when the thumb is opposed to the
index. But it is clearly a disease when the thumb is impaired
from birth, or when, from a habit contracted during the time
of nursing, it is impeded in its motions by the fingers. One
should practice all sorts of work with either of them, and with
both together (for they are both alike), endeavoring to do them
well, elegantly, quickly, without trouble, neatly, and promptly

5. The instruments, and when and how they should be prepared, will be treated of afterwards; so that they may not im-
pede the work, and that there may be no difficulty in taking
hold of them, with the part of the body which operates. But if
another gives them, he must be ready a little beforehand, and
do as you direct.

6. Those about the patient must present the part to be
operated upon as may seem proper, and they must hold the

rest of the body steady, in silence, and listening to the commands of the operator.

II. ON WOUNDS[3]

No wounds should be moistened with anything except wine unless the wound is in a joint. Because dryness is more nearly a condition of health, and moisture more nearly allied to disease. A wound in moist and healthy tissue is dry. It is better to leave a wound unbandaged, unless a cataplasm is applied. Certain wounds ought not to have cataplasms applied. Fresh wounds are less suitable for cataplasms than old ones, and wounds in the joints. Restriction in the amount of food, and drinking nothing but water are most useful in all wounds, more especially in the recent than those which are old, or for some reason inflamed, or likely to become so; or when danger of necrosis exists, or inflamed wounds about the joints, or where there is danger of convulsions; also in wounds of the abdomen, but most of all in fractures of the skull and femur or any other bone. Standing erect does wounds the most harm, especially if the leg is the wounded part. Patients ought neither to walk about, or even be allowed the sitting position. Rest and quiet do the most good. Recent wounds, as well as the surrounding parts, will be less liable to inflammation, if one can induce suppuration as soon as possible, and not let the pus be blocked up in the opening of the wound, or if one can bring it about that it does not suppurate at all, except the little pus that necessarily appears, but keep it dry with some remedy that is not too harsh. For if it is dried to excess fever will come on, as indicated by chills and throbbing. For the wounds become inflamed when they are going to suppurate on account of the alteration and heating of the blood, till it softens and pus appears, in wounds of this sort at least. When you decide that a cataplasm is indicated, do not apply it to the wound, but to the surrounding parts, so that the pus may have free exit, and the tissues which are hardened rendered soft. In wounds made by the cut or thrust of a sharp weapon a remedy which will stop hemorrhage is indicated, as well as something which will prevent suppuration and dry up the wound. When the flesh has been lacerated and contused by the weapon, the wound should be treated in such a way as to produce suppuration as quickly as possible.

3. Fred B. Lund: "Hippocratic Surgery," *Annals of Surgery*, Vol. 102, No. 4, October 1935, pp. 537–538.

Because (if this is done) it will be less inflamed, and the tissues which have been contused and lacerated and putrid and purulent have to soften and come away. After that new tissue sprouts up. It is a good plan in fresh wounds, except those in the abdomen, to allow a lot of blood to escape, as much as you think is required for the purpose, both from the wound itself, and any lacerations of the surrounding parts, especially in wounds of the leg or fingers or toes. On account of the escape of blood the parts are drier, and less swollen. These conditions prevent the wound from becoming moist, indeed, for the most part suppuration results from the presence of blood, and the changes which take place in that blood. It helps after the escape of the blood to bandage over such wounds a piece of sponge, soft and thick, and cut to the appropriate size, preferably dry, rather than moist, or to place leaves of delicate texture over the sponge. Oil or softening or greasy remedies are not good for such wounds, unless they are already well on their way to a cure. Oil is not good for fresh wounds either, neither are greasy or fatty remedies good for them especially when the wound needs a lot of cleansing. To sum up, use oil only for anointing in both winter and summer, or for such conditions as is needed.

It is a good thing to move the bowels by enema in most wounds, especially in head injuries, and wounds of the abdomen and joints; also when there is danger of gangrene, in sutured wounds, in wounds which corrode, and undermine the tissues, and others which are slow to heal. But when you decide to bandage, do not smear on the ointment before you have thoroughly dried out the wound, then put it on; but sponge out the wound many times with a sponge, dry it with a clean dry fine linen cloth applying it many times. Having applied in this way the remedy which you think will be useful, either bandage it or not, as seems best. For most wounds warm weather is more favorable than winter except those in the head and abdomen. The equinoctial season is still better. These wounds which have been thoroughly cleansed as far as is necessary to make the granulations dry generally do not produce exuberant granulations. If a piece of bone has sloughed out on account of cauterization or trephining or any other cause, the scar resulting from the wound becomes concave and the cleansed wounds are reluctant to heal. They come together under compulsion, but not of their own accord. These in which the wound is surrounded by inflammation do not heal until the inflammation has ceased, nor are wounds likely to heal, in case the surrounding parts are blackened either from softened blood, or blood supplied by an adjoining varicosity and they won't heal at all until you get the surrounding parts into a healthy condition.

III. OPERATION FOR EMPYEMA[4]

When the duration of the disease becomes longer, the fever is severe and the cough is increasing, and the side is painful, and he cannot bear to lie upon the well side, but has to lie on the side of the disease, then the feet swell, and the hollows of the eyes. When the fifteenth day after the rupture arrives give him a profuse bath of hot water, sit him in a firm seat that he may not move, let an assistant hold his hands, while you shake his shoulder and listen to hear on which side the pus makes a splash. Hope it is on the left so that you can make your incision on that side, for it is less deadly. If on account of the thickness of the tissues and the fulness of the cavity it does not give out a sound, so that you cannot make out where it is, which sometimes occurs, make an incision on the side which is more swollen and painful, rather below and behind the swollen part, so that an easy outlet may be afforded for the pus. First incise the skin between the ribs with a broad knife, then wind the blade of the knife with a strip of linen leaving out the point to the breadth of a thumb nail, and push it in. Then when you have let out as much pus as you think best, stuff the wound with a drain of raw flax to which a thread is attached. Let out the pus once a day. On the tenth day when you have let out all the pus dress it with fine linen. Then introduce through a small tube a mixture of oil and wine, warm, so that the lung which has gotten used to the moisture of the pus may not be suddenly dried. Draw out the liquid which has been injected at night in the morning, and that injected in the morning at night. When the pus becomes thin like water, and feels slippery to the finger and is small in quantity put in a hollow tin tent. When the cavity is entirely dry, cut off the drains a little at a time and allow the incision to heal, till you take out the drain. An indication that the patient will recover: if the pus is white, clear, and has fibers of blood (like blood clot?) they generally get well. If on the first day the discharge is the color of egg yolk, and in the next thin and greenish with a bad odor, they die when the pus has run out.

4. *Ibid.*, p. 534.

IV. FRACTURE OF THE ARMS[5]

8. When the arm is broken, if one stretch the fore-arm and adjust it while in this position, the muscle of the arm will be bound while extended; but when the dressing is over, and the patient bends his arm at the elbow, the muscle of the arm will assume a different shape. The following, then, is the most natural plan of setting the arm: having got a piece of wood a cubit or somewhat less in length, like the handles of spades, suspend it by means of a chain fastened to its extremities at both ends; and having seated the man on some high object, the arm is to be brought over, so that the armpit may rest on the piece of wood, and the man can scarcely touch the seat, being almost suspended; then having brought another seat, and placed one or more leather pillows under the arm, so as to keep it a moderate height while it is bent at a right angle, the best plan is to put round the arm a broad and soft skin, or broad shawl, and to hang some great weight to it, so as to produce moderate extension; or otherwise, while the arm is in the position I have described, a strong man is to take hold of it at the elbow and pull it downward. But the physician standing erect, must perform the proper manipulation, having the one foot on some pretty high object, and adjusting the bone with the palms of his hands; and it will readily be adjusted, for the extension is good if properly applied. Then let him bind the arm, commencing at the fracture, and do otherwise as directed above; let him put the same questions and avail himself of the same signs to ascertain whether the arm be moderately tight or not; and every third day let him bind it anew and make it tighter; and on the seventh or ninth day let him bind it up with splints, and leave it so until after the lapse of more than thirty days. And if he suspect that the bone is not lying properly, let him remove the bandages in the interval, and having adjusted the arm, let him bind it up again. The bone of the arm is generally consolidated in forty days. When these are past, the dressing is to be removed, and fewer and slacker bandages applied instead of it. The patient is to be kept on a stricter diet, and for a longer space of time than in the former case; and we must form our judgment of it from the swelling in the hand, looking also to the strength of the patient. This also should be known, that the arm is naturally inclined outward; to this side,

therefore, the distortion usually takes place, if not properly treated; but indeed, all the other bones are usually distorted during treatment for fracture to that side to which they naturally incline. When, therefore, anything of this kind is suspected, the arm is to be encircled in a broad shawl, which is to be carried round the breast, and when the patient goes to rest, a

FIG. 3. Illustrations of the Hippocratic method of reducing dislocations. From: *Appolonius of Kitium* [first century B.C.] Illustrierter Kommentar zu der hippokratischen Schrift ΠΕΡΙ ΑΡΘΡΩΝ [*Peri Arthron*], Herausgegeben von Hermann Schöne, Leipzig, B. G. Teubner, 1896.

compress of many folds, or some such thing, is to be folded and placed between the elbow and the side, for thus the bending of the bone will be rectified, but care must be taken lest it be inclined too much inwards.

V. ON DISLOCATIONS OF THE HIP[6]

51. There are four modes of dislocation at the hip-joint: of which modes, dislocation inward takes place most frequently, outward, the most frequently of all the other modes; and it sometimes takes place backward and forward, but seldom. When, therefore, dislocation takes place inward, the leg appears longer than natural, when compared with the other leg, for two reasons truly; for the bone which articulates with the hip-joint is carried from above down to the ischium where it rises up to the pubes, upon it, then, the head of the femur rests, and the neck of the femur is lodged in the cotyloid foramen (*foramen thyroideum?*). The buttock appears hollow externally, from the head of the thigh-bone having shifted inward, and the extremity of the femur at the knee is turned outward, and the leg and foot in like manner. The foot then being turned outward, physicians, from ignorance, bring the sound leg to it and not it to the sound leg; on this account, the injured limb appears to be much longer than the sound one, and in many other cases similar circumstances lead to error in judgment. Neither does the limb at the groin admit of flexion as in the sound limb, and the head of the bone is felt at the perineum too prominent. These, then, are the symptoms attending dislocation of the thigh inward.

54. When the head of the femur is dislocated outward, the limb in these cases, when compared with the other, appears shortened, and this is natural, for the head of the femur no longer rests on a bone as in dislocation inward, but along the side of a bone which naturally inclines to the side, and it is lodged in flesh of a pulpy and yielding nature, and on that account it appears more shortened. Inwardly, the thigh about the perineum appears more hollow and flabby, but externally the buttock is more rounded, from the head of the thigh having slipped outward, but the nates appear to be raised up, owing to the flesh there having yielded to the head of the thigh-bone; but the extremity of the thigh-bone, at the knee, appears to be turned inward, and the leg and foot in like manner, neither

6. *Ibid.*, pp. 125–126, 130, 145–147.

does it admit of flexion like the sound limb. These, then, are the symptoms of dislocation outward.

70. Dislocation inward at the hip-joint is to be reduced in the following manner: (it is a good, proper, and natural mode of reduction, and has something of display in it, if any one takes delight in such ostentatious modes of procedure.) The patient is to be suspended by the feet from a cross-beam with a strong, soft, and broad cord, the feet are to be about four inches or less from one another; and a broad and soft leather collar connected with the cross-beam is to be put on above the knees; and the affected leg should be so extended as to be two inches longer than the other; the head should be about two cubits from the ground, or a little more or less; and the arms should be stretched along the sides, and bound with something soft; all these preparations should be made while he is lying on his back, so that he may be suspended for as short a time as possible. But when the patient is suspended, a person properly instructed and not weak, having introduced his arm between his thighs, is to place his fore-arm between the perineum and the dislocated head of the os femoris; and then, having joined the other hand to the one thus passed through the thighs, he is to stand by the side of the suspended patient, and suddenly suspend and swing himself in the air as perpendicularly as possible. This method comprises all the conditions which are natural; for the body being suspended by its weight, produces extension, and the person suspended from him, along with the extension, forces the head of the thigh-bone to rise up above the acetabulum; and at the same time he uses the bone of the fore-arm as a lever, and forces the os femoris to slip into its old seat. The cords should be properly prepared, and care should be taken that the person suspended along with the patient have a sufficiently strong hold.

CHAPTER 3

Celsus and the Alexandrians

"The third part of the Art of Medicine is that which cures by the hand, as I have already said, and indeed it is common knowledge. It does not omit medicaments and regulated diets, but does most by hand. The effects of this treatment are more obvious than any other kind; inasmuch as in diseases since luck helps much, and the same things are often salutary, often of no use at all, it may be doubted whether recovery has been due to medicine or a sound body or good luck. Besides, in cases where we depend chiefly upon medicaments, although an improvement is clear enough, yet it is often clear that recovery is in vain with them and gained without them: this can be seen for instance in treating the eyes, which after being worried by doctors for a long time sometimes get well without them. But in that part of medicine which cures by hand, it is obvious that all improvement comes chiefly from this, even if it be assisted somewhat in other ways."[1]

The turning wheel of political fortune saw the decline of Attic Greece after the Peloponnesian War at the close of the fifth century B.C., and the subjugation of all of Greece by the Macedonians a century later. But Greek culture lived on. Alexander the Great founded the city of Alexandria on the northern coast of Egypt, which perpetuated his name and became a monument to his achievements. There, under his reign and under those of the first two Ptolemys who succeeded him, was established a center of culture which attempted to gather and preserve not only the knowledge of Greece, but that of the rest of the world as well. Scholars were brought from all nations to translate and copy the books and manuscripts of all languages. A gigantic "Museum" was set up, and the library is said to have housed 700,000 scrolls.

In this benign environment and with the support of matchless wealth, art and science flourished. Much of modern learning had its roots in the school of Alexandria, particularly in the fields of mathematics, astronomy, and physics. Here, too, the medical sciences attained new heights, especially in the disciplines of anatomy, physiology, and surgery. For the first time, systematic dissection of human corpses was carried out, and later writers go so far as to

1. Celsus: *De Medicina* with an English Translation by W. G. Spencer, (The Loeb Classical Library) Cambridge, Harvard University Press, 1938, Vol. III, Book VII, p. 1.

report that actual human vivisections were done on condemned criminals. Much of our present day anatomical nomenclature stems from the Alexandrian school.

Of the many in Alexandria who worked and wrote on surgery and its ancillary sciences, two made lasting and significant contributions. They are Erasistratus and Herophilus. Unfortunately, only scraps and fragments of their original writings have survived the fires and destruction of conquering armies, and we are forced to depend on the citations of later writers, particularly of Celsus and Galen for a record of their discoveries. Because of the great importance of the two Alexandrians, even the fragmentary knowledge of their work must be recorded here.

Herophilus was born in Chalcedon, on the Asiatic side of the Bosporus, and lived in Alexandria sometime before 300 B.C. He was a pupil of Praxagoras, and a disciple of the Coan school. A physician of the Hippocratic type and an able surgeon, he is known to have written widely. He was the first to count the pulse with the aid of the water clock, and analyzed in detail its variations in rate, rhythm, and amplitude. His most important contributions were in the science of anatomy. He was particularly interested in the nervous system, and described the brain in detail, including the meninges, sinuses, and cranial nerves. The calamus scriptorius and the torquilar still bear his name. He established the brain as the center of awareness, and recognized both sensory and motor functions of the nerves. He also described the liver, pancreas, and salivary glands, and gave the duodenum its name. He studied the male and female genital organs, and noted the differences between nulliparous and parous uteri. He is the acknolwedged founder of anatomy.

Erasistratus was born somewhat later, on the island of Keos, and was a disciple of the Cnidian school. He, too, concerned himself primarily with the nervous system, but also studied and wrote on the heart and the lymphatics. In contrast to Herophilus, he was interested in function more than in structure, and experimented in the fields of digestion, metabolism, and circulation. In the latter system, he described the tricuspid and mitral valves, was aware of the cardiac contractions and dilatations, and foreshadowed the knowledge of the circulation. He further suggested that the entire body was made up of minute, discrete bodies, thus anticipating the discovery of cellular structure. As a surgeon he was renowned for his abdominal operations, for his draining of empyemas, and for his design of a catheter.

There were other Alexandrians who made significant contributions to surgery but all their writings have been lost and often even the identity of the discoverers is obscured. We know of them only through their procedures which are described in the writings of Celsus and other later commentators. Thus, the use of the ligature for the control of hemorrhage, lithotomy, hernia operations, opthalmic surgery, plastic repair of defects, methods for the reduction

of fractures and dislocations, tracheotomy, and, reputedly, the administration
of the juice of mandragora for anesthesia were all introduced during the period
of dominance of the Alexandrian school.

Aulus Cornelius Celsus who transmitted so much of our knowledge of
Alexandrian surgery also left to us the most lucid account of the status of
medicine and surgery in the Roman period. Celsus, who wrote *de Medicina* in
the first century of the Christian era, was probably not a physician. Rather,
historians believe that he was the first of the "Encyclopedists" who summarized the existing knowledge in all fields. With equal competence he wrote on
rhetoric, philosophy, agriculture, military science, and jurisprudence, as well
as on medicine. His work on the last subject, in eight books, is one of the great
Latin classics. It is the first complete and well-organized textbook, composed
in elegant style, and presenting to us the cumulative medical knowledge from
Hippocrates to the beginning of the Christian era. Perhaps, because he was
not a physician, Celsus' medical writings had little recognition in his own time.
They soon disappeared from view, and exerted little influence on early medicine. When rediscovered during the Renaissance, however, they were highly
esteemed for their informative value and literary beauty and went through
many editions.

Celsus considered surgery an integral part of medicine, and deplored the
tendency to separate them. All of medicine he divided into three parts, that
which could be treated by diet, that by medicine, and that by surgery. In the
Introduction to Book VII he writes:

> "The third part of the art of Medicine is that which cures by the
> hand, as I have already said, and indeed it is common knowledge.
> It does not omit medicaments and regulated diets, but does most
> by hand. The effects of this treatment are more obvious than any
> other kind; inasmuch as in diseases since luck helps much, and the
> same things are often salutary, often of no use at all, it may be
> doubted whether recovery has been due to medicine or a sound
> body or good luck. Besides, in cases where we depend chiefly
> upon medicaments, although an improvement is clear enough, yet
> it is often clear that recovery is sought in vain with them and gained
> without them: this can be seen for instance in treating the eyes,
> which after being worried by doctors for a long time sometimes get
> well without them. But in that part of medicine which cures by hand,
> it is obvious that all improvement comes chiefly from this, even if it
> be assisted somewhat in other ways."

The book begins with a Preface which presents a historical survey of the
growth of medicine from Hippocrates to the beginning of the Christian era.
The various "schools" of medical thought are described and critically evalu-
ated. There follows, in Book I, a complete discussion of diet and hygiene.

Book II deals in general with causes, symptoms, and management of disease. In the third and fourth books, diseases that are treated by dietetic and hygienic regimens are discussed, first the systemic illnesses, then the regional. Books V and VI include conditions that are treated primarily with medicines and Books VII and VIII those treated by surgery. Actually, the second half of the fifth book and all of the three last books deal with matter that is now generally considered to be surgical. However, our author differentiates between those conditions in which wounds are already present, and those in which the wound is made by the surgeon to effect a cure. The final book treats of fractures and dislocations.

"Now that I have recounted the properties of medicines, I shall mention the kinds of injury to which the body is liable. These are five; lesions from without, as in wounds; local corruptions internally, as in gangrene; local accretion, as in calculus of the bladder; enlargement of a vein, thus converted into a varix; and local defect, as when a part is maimed. . . .

"I shall arrange this department of treatment as I did a former one; first treating of those kinds which may befall any part of the body, and those which infest particular parts. I shall commence with wounds."

The symptoms and prognosis of wounds of the various viscera are described in vivid and graphic form.

"In a wound of the heart there is great hemorrhage; the vessels are collapsed, the complexion pale; there are cold dew-like sweats, of a disagreeable odor; and the extremities becoming cold, death soon follows.

"When the lung is wounded, the breathing is embarrassed; blood is discharged, frothy by the mouth, florid from the external wound, and with a sonorous puffing of air; the patient likes to lie on the wound; some rise up in a state of delirium: many are able to speak if lying on the wound; if on the opposite side, they remain dumb."

And so on with the other organs.

Two consequences are to be prevented: fatal hemorrhage and fatal inflammation. Packing of the wound and pressure are used to check bleeding. If ineffective, caustics are applied.

"But should these means fail also, the bleeding vessels should be taken up, and ligatures having been applied above and below the wounded part, the vessels are to be divided in the interspace; that thus they may retract, while their orifices yet remain closed."

If possible, wounds are closed by suture. Detailed instructions are given, including the aftercare and the management of complications. The general and regional surgical conditions discussed by Celsus cover an extremely wide range, including abscesses and infections of all types; fistulae in various regions; ulcers of many forms; benign and malignant tumors; herniae and hydroceles; diseases of the skin, of the eye, oral cavity, and ear; a section on the removal of missiles (military surgery); plastic surgery; lithotomy; and catheterization. The final chapter deals with skeletal afflictions, and includes amputations for gangrene. These various diseases and operations are presented with clarity and detail, and reveal an astonishing degree of skill and understanding. A few excerpts must suffice here to indicate not only the highly developed state of classic surgery, but also Celsus' superb literary style.

MUTILATIONS[2]

Mutilations then occur in these three parts and can be treated if they are small; if they are large, either they are not susceptible of treatment, or else may be so deformed by it as to be more unsightly than before. And indeed in the ear and nostrils the deformity is the only trouble; but in the case of the lips, if these have become too much contracted, there is also loss of a necessary function, because it becomes less easy both to take food and to speak plainly. Now new substance is not produced at the place itself, but it is drawn from the neighborhood; and when the change is small this hardly robs any other part and may pass unnoticed, but when large, it cannot do so. And again, this procedure is unsuited to the aged, to those in bad bodily condition, and to those whose wounds heal with difficulty; because there are no cases in which canker sets in more quickly, or is more difficult to get rid of.

The method of treatment is as follows: the mutilation is enclosed in a square; from the inner angles of this incisions are made across, so that the part on one side of the quadrilateral is completely separated from that on the opposite side. Then the two flaps, which we have freed, are brought together. If they cannot be sufficiently brought together, at each end beyond the original incisions semilunar cuts which only divide the skin are made with the horns pointing towards the incisions. This enables the edges to be brought together more easily. No force should be used, but the traction should be such that the edges easily approximate and, when left free, do not recoil much.

At times, however, if the skin has been drawn across from one side to a considerable extent, or even at all, it makes the part

2. *Ibid.*, VII, 9.

which it has left unsightly. In a case of that sort, leaving that side untouched, an incision should be made only on the other side. For instance we should not attempt to make traction upon the lobules of the ears, the bridge of the nose, the margins of the nostrils, or the corners of the lips. But we shall try traction from either side if anything is required for the upper part of the ears, the tip of the nose, the bridge of the nose, the skin between the nostrils, and the middle of the lips. At times the mutilation is in two places, but the method of treatment is the same. Cartilage if it projects into the incision is to be cut away; for it does not agglutinate nor is it safely transfixed by a needle. But it should not be much cut away lest pus collect on each side between the two margins of loose skin. Then the margins after being brought together are to be sutured by taking up from each skin only, and the earlier incisions are also to be sutured. In dry parts such as the nostrils, it is sufficient to spread on litharge. But into the more distant semilunar wounds lint is to be placed in order that flesh may grow and fill the wound; and it is clear that the greatest attention should be paid to what is thus sutured, from what I mentioned above about canker. Consequently every third day the part should be steamed, then dressed as before; and generally the wound has adhered by the seventh day. Then the sutures should be removed, and the wound allowed to heal.

STABWOUNDS OF THE ABDOMEN[3]

Sometimes the abdomen is penetrated by a stab of some sort, and it follows that the intestines roll out. When this happens we must first examine whether they are uninjured, and then whether their proper colour persists. If the smaller intestine has been penetrated, no good can be done, as I have already said. The larger intestine can be sutured, not with any certain assurance, but because a doubtful hope is preferable to certain despair; for occasionally it heals up. Then if either intestine is livid or pallid or black, in which case there is necessarily no sensation, all medical aid is vain. But if intestines have still their proper colour, aid should be given with all speed, for they undergo change from moment to moment when exposed to the external air, to which they are unaccustomed. The patient is to be laid on his back with his hips raised; and if the wound is too narrow, for the intestines to be easily replaced, it is to be cut until suffi-

3. *Ibid.*, VII, 16.

ciently wide. If the intestines have already become too dry, they are to be bathed with water to which a small quantity of oil has been added. Next the assistant should gently separate the margins of the wound by means of his hands, or even by two hooks inserted into the inner membrane: the surgeon always returns first the intestines which have prolapsed the later, in such a way as to preserve the order of the several coils. When all have been returned, the patient is to be shaken gently: so that of their own accord the various coils are brought into their proper places and settle there. This done, the omentum too must be examined, and any part that is black (dead) is to be cut away with shears; what is sound is returned gently into place in front of the intestines. Now stitching of the surface skin only or of the inner membrane only is not enough, but both must be stitched. And there must be two rows of stitches, set closer together than in other places, partly because they can be broken here more easily by the abdominal movement, partly because that part of the body is not specially liable to severe inflammations. Therefore two needles are to be threaded and one is to be held in each hand; and the stitches are to be inserted, first through the inner membrane, so that the surgeon's left hand pushes the needle from within outwards through the right margin of the wound, and his right hand through the left margin, beginning from one end of the wound. The result is that it is the blunt end of the needle which is always being pushed away from the intestines. When each margin has been once traversed, the hands interchange needles, so that into the right hand comes the needle which was in the left, and into the left the needle which was in the right; and again, after the same method they are to be passed through the margins; and when for the third and fourth time, the needles have changed hands the wound is to be closed. Afterwards the same threads and the same needles are now transferred to the skin, and stitches are to be inserted by a like method into this as well, always directing the needles from within outwards, and with the same change, between the hands. It is too obvious to need constantly repeating that agglutinants are then to be put on with the addition either of a sponge or of greasy wool, squeezed out of vinegar. Over this application the abdomen should be lightly bandaged.

INGUINAL HERNIA: ANATOMY[4]

Now I come to those lesions which are apt to arise in the genital parts around the testicles; and to explain them more easily, the nature of the said region must briefly be described first. The testicles then are somewhat like marrow, for they do not bleed and they lack all feeling; but the coverings by which they are enclosed give pain both when injured and inflamed. Now the testicles hang from the groins, each by a cord which the Greeks call the *cremaster* with each of which descends a pair of veins and a pair of arteries. And these are ensheathed in a tunic, thin, fibrous, bloodless, white, which is called by the Greeks *elytroides*. Outside this is a stronger tunic, which at its lowest part is closely adherent to the inner one; the Greeks call it *dartos*. Further, many fine membranes hold together the veins, and the arteries, and the cords aforesaid, and also in between the two tunics there are some fine and very small membranes, descending from the parts above. Thus far the coverings and supports belong to each testicle separately; next common to both and to all within is the pouch which is now visble to us; the Greeks call it *oscheon*, we the scrotum; and at its lowest part this is slightly connected with the middle coverings, higher up it is only surrounded by them. Now, underneath the scrotal covering many lesions are apt to occur, sometimes after the rupture of the coverings which, as I have said, begin from the groins, sometimes when they are uninjured. Since at times either owing to disease there is first inflammation, then afterwards a rupture from the weight; or after some blow there, there is a direct rupture of the covering which ought to separate the intestines from the parts below; then either omentum, or it may be intestine, rolls down by its own weight; this having found a way gradually from the groins into the parts below as well, there separates by its pressure the coverings which are fibrous and therefore give way. The Greeks call the condition *enterocele* and *epiplocele*, with us the ugly but usual name for it is hernia.

Now if omentum has come down, the tumour in the scrotum never disappears, either if the patient fasts, or if his body is turned from side to side, or lies in some special position; again, if the breath is held, it does not increase to any extent; to the touch it seems uneven and soft and slippery. But if intestine has also come down, this tumour is without inflammation, some-

4. *Ibid.*, VII, 18, 1–7.

times it diminishes, sometimes increases, and it is generally painless and soft. When the patient is quiescent or lying down, it
disappears, at times altogether; sometimes it becomes divided
so that very small remnants stay in the scrotum. But after shouting or over-eating, or if the patient has been strained by a
weight of any sort, it increases; under all kinds of cold it shrinks,
under heat it enlarges; then the scrotum becomes globular and
smooth to the touch; and within the scrotum the intestine slips
about, when pressed upon it reverts towards the groin, when
released it rolls down again with a sort of murmur. That is
what happens in slight cases; but at times, when faeces have
been taken in, it swells more largely, it cannot be forced back,
and it then brings on pain both in the scrotum and in groins
and abdomen. At times the stomach also becomes affected, and
there is an issue from the mouth, first of red, then of green, and
even in some of black bile.

INGUINAL HERNIA: SURGERY[5]

When these lesions have been recognized their treatment
must be discussed; in this some methods are common to all,
some peculiar to particular kinds. I shall discuss first what is
common to all. But I shall now speak of those cases demanding
the knife: for those which are incurable, or should be cared for
otherwise, will be mentioned as I come to the separate kinds.
Now sometimes the inguinal region has to be cut into, sometimes the scrotum. In either case the man for three days before
should drink water (only), and for the day before abstain also
from food: on the day itself he must lie on his back; next if the
groin has to be cut into, and if the pubes is already covered by
hair, this is to be shaved off beforehand: and then after stretching the scrotum, so that the skin of the groin is rendered tense,
the cut is made below the abdominal cavity, where the membranes below are continuous with the abdominal wall. Now the
laying open is to be done boldly, until the outer tunic, that of
the scrotum itself, is cut through, and the middle tunic reached.
When an incision has been made, an opening presents leading
deeper. Into this the index finger of the left hand is introduced,
in order that by the separation of the intervening little membranes the hernial sac may be freed.

Next the assistant grasping the scrotum with his left hand
should stretch it upwards, and draw it away as far as possible
from the groins, at first including the testicle itself until the sur-

5. *Ibid.*, VII, 19, 1–6.

geon cuts away with the scalpel all the fine membranes which
are above the middle tunic if he is unable to separate it with his
finger; then the testicle is let go in order that it may slip downwards, and show in the wound and then be pushed out by the
surgeon's finger, and laid along with its two tunics upon the
abdominal wall. There whatever is diseased is cut round and
away, in the course of which many blood vessels are met with;
the smaller ones can be summarily divided; but larger ones, to
avoid dangerous bleeding, must be first tied with rather long flax
thread. If the middle tunic be affected, or the disease has
grown beneath it, it will have to be cut away even as high as
the actual groin. Lower down, however, not all is to be removed: for at the base of the testicle there is an intimate connexion with the inner tunic, where excision is not possible without extreme danger: and so there it is to be left. The same is
to be done if the inner tunic is the seat of the disease. But the
cutting away cannot be done quite completely at the inguinal
end of the wound, but only somewhat lower down, lest the abdominal membrane be injured and set up inflammation. On
the other hand too much of its upper part should not be left
behind, lest subsequently there forms a pouch which continues
to be the seat of the same malady.

The testicle having been thus cleared is to be gently returned
through the incision along with the veins and arteries and its
cord; and it must be seen that blood does not drop down into
the scrotum, or a clot remain anywhere. This will be accomplished if the surgeon takes the precaution of tying the blood
vessels; the threads with which the ends of these are tied should
hang out of the wound; following upon suppuration they will
fall off painlessly. Through the margins of the wound itself two
pins are then passed, and over this an agglutinating dressing.
But it becomes necessary sometimes to cut away a little from
one or other of the edges of the skin-incisions in order to make a
broader and thicker scar. When this occurs the lint dressing
must not be pressed on but must be applied lightly, and over it
such things as repel inflammation, unscoured wool or sponge
soaked in vinegar: all the other treatment is the same as when
suppuratives have to be applied.

PTERYGIUM[6]

An *unguis* too, called *pterygium* in Greek, is a little fibrous membrane, springing from the angle of the eye which sometimes

6. *Ibid.*, VII, 7, 4B–D.

even spreads so as to block the pupil. Most often it arises from
the side of the nose, but sometimes from the temporal angle.
When recent it is not difficult to disperse by the medicaments
which thin away corneal opacities; if it is of long standing, and
thick, it should be excised. After fasting for a day, the patient
is either seated facing the surgeon, or turned away, so that he
lies on his back, his head in the surgeon's lap. Some want
him facing if the disease is in the left eye and lying down if in
the right. Now one eyelid must be held open by the assistant,
the other by the surgeon; but he holds the lower lid when seated
opposite the patient, and the upper when the patient is on his
back. Thereupon the surgeon passes a sharp hook, the point of
which has been a little incurved, under the edge of the pterygium and fixes the hook in it; next, leaving that eyelid also to
the assistant, he draws the hook towards himself thus lifting up
the pterygium, and passes through it a needle carrying a
thread; then having detached the needle, he takes hold of the
two ends of the thread, and raises up the pterygium by means
of the thread; he now separates any part of it which adheres to
the eyeball by the handle of the scalpel until the angle is reached;
next by alternately pulling and slackening the thread, he is
able to discover the beginning of the pterygium and the end of
the angle. For there is double danger, that either some of the
pterygium is left behind and if this ulcerates, it is hardly ever
amenable to treatment; or that with it part of the flesh is cut
away from the angle; and if the pterygium is pulled too strongly,
the flesh follows unnoticed, and when it is cut away a hole is left
through which there is afterwards a persistent flow of rheum;
the Greeks name it *rhyas*. Therefore the true edge of the angle
must certainly be observed; and when this has been clearly determined, after the pterygium has been drawn forward just
enough, the scalpel is to be used, then that little membrane is
to be so cut away as not to injure the angle in any way. After
that, lint soaked in honey is to be put on, and over that a piece
of linen, and either a sponge or unscoured wool; and for the
next few days the eye must be opened daily to prevent the eye-
lids uniting by a scar, for if that happens a third danger is
added; and the lint is to be put on again, and last of all one of
the salves applied which help wounds to heal.

CHAPTER 4

Galen of Pergamum
(129–199 A.D.)

"For it is only the wisest man who can know himself accurately."[1]

Galen, the most famous physician of the Graeco-Roman period, was next only to Hippocrates as the greatest physician of all of antiquity. Unlike the "Father of Medicine" who divulged almost nothing about his own life and personality, Galen interspersed his medical writings with much detailed auto-biographical information. And whereas there is great uncertainty as to the actual authorship of the seventy books attributed to Hippocrates, there is little doubt that the 400 separate treatises that bear Galen's name are actually from his pen. His interests knew no bounds and his work concerned itself with all phases of medicine including surgery, widening the horizons of its scientific aspects beyond anything that had been previously attempted. Within the range of his interests was the preparation of an anatomical treatise more complete than any previously attempted, together with observations and speculations as to function. His physiological views were based in significant part upon actual animal experimentation, and brought him additional fame as founder of experimental physiology. With his independent mind and great intellectual curiosity he had an abiding admiration only for the works of Hippocrates; and he revered only the personality of his father. Throughout his life he strove with varying success to live up to the pattern of these two men.

Galen was born in Greek Asia Minor in the city of Pergamum, which was famous for its temple to the healing God Aesculapius, for its medical teachers, and for its gladiators. In this surrounding, he relates:

"I was brought up by a father who, versed in the arithmetical, logical, and grammatical sciences, taught me these, as well as the other subjects of education. Then, when I was in my fifteenth year, he began to interest me in dialectic theory, his idea being that I

1. The epigram and the subsequent quotations in the introduction are taken from Galen's writings, translated and annotated by Arthur J. Brock in *Greek Medicine*, London, J. M. Dent & Sons, 1929.

should give attention to philosophy alone; then, however, when I was in my seventeenth year, he was impelled by vivid dreams to make me engage in medicine as well as philosophy."

His father, who taught him to despise reputation and honor and to feel reverence for truth alone, was a man of great erudition. Himself trained in geometry, arithmetic, architecture, and astronomy, he instructed his son not to proclaim himself in a hurry as belonging to any one school, but to "go on for a long time, learning and testing . . . striving after justice, moderation, courage, and intelligence."

Galen was most impressed, however, by his father's personal qualities which sharply contrasted with those of his mother.

"Now, personally I cannot say how I got my nature (physis). It was, however, my great fortune to have as my father a most good-tempered, just, efficient, and benevolent man. My mother, on the other hand, was so irascible that she would sometimes bite her serving-maids, and she was constantly shouting at my father and quarrelling with him, worse than Xantippe with Socrates. When I saw, then, the nobility of my father's conduct side by side with the shameful passions of my mother, I made up my mind to love and cleave to the former behaviour, and to hate and flee from the latter. And besides this enormous difference between my parents, I observed that he was never depressed over any affliction, while my mother became annoyed at the merest bagatelle. You yourself doubtless know that boys imitate what they are fond of, and avoid what they do not like to see."

But in spite of his father's magnificent example and the fact that he had been given the name Galenos, the Peaceful One, his writings reveal his own personality as contentious, argumentative, competitive, and proud. For pride, however, he had much cause. His intelligence was superb and the general and medical education he received was the best possible of his day. His studies with the medical teachers of Pergamum were followed by nine years of travel which took him over much of Asia Minor and the Greek mainland where he observed the diseases peculiar to each region. His final goal was Alexandria in Egypt, where the great scientific tradition of Herophilus and Erasistratus lingered on and where "the physicians . . . accompany the instructions they give to their students with opportunities for personal inspection (*autopsia*)."

He returned to Pergamum in 157 A.D. to accept an appointment as surgeon to the gladiators. After four years of this work which had given him tremendous opportunity for the practice of orthopedic and restorative surgery as well as general medicine, he sought the culmination of his career in the focal point

GALEN

FIG. 4. Bust of Galen. (Its authenticity is unconfirmed.)

of the Graeco-Roman empire, in Rome. Fortunate circumstances soon provided him with a distinguished patient, whose recovery established Galen's name almost at once. He was sought out by patients of high social rank and remunerated generously; he held public anatomical demonstrations, dissecting dogs and apes, which served to teach medical students and to amuse members of the aristocracy who attended this new diversion in large numbers. Throughout all this sudden success he remained thoroughly uncharitable towards his medical colleagues whom he had so quickly deprived of their most prominent patients and from whom he had taken the limelight almost overnight.

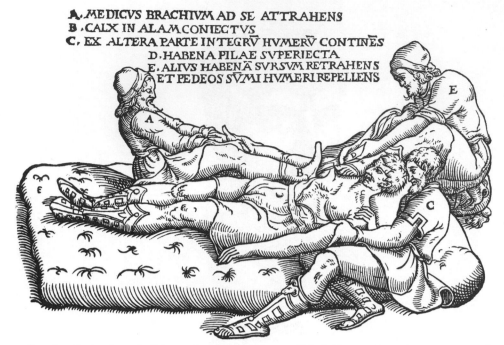

A. MEDICVS BRACHIVM AD SE ATTRAHENS
B. CALX IN ALAM CONIECTVS
C. EX ALTERA PARTE INTEGRV HVMERV CONTINES
D. HABENA PILAE SVPERIECTA
E. ALIVS HABENA SVRSVM RETRAHENS
ET PEDEOS SVMI HVMERI REPELLENS

FIG. 5.*a* Reduction of dislocated shoulder. From: *Galeni Pergameni omnia quae extant, in Latinum sermonem conversa*, Basel, Froben, 1562.

Except for one lengthy absence Galen remained in Rome for the rest of his life. This one absence casts a peculiar shadow on the character of the man and suggests that personal courage was not among his strongest attributes. It occurred after he had been in Rome but four years when the city was visited by a severe plague. Galen left Rome and took up practice in his home town, Pergamum. However, three years later when he was called back to Rome to the imperial court he accepted with avidity.

That he had matured in his three years' absence is borne out by his own words: "Then somehow, when I went to Rome the second time at the command of the Emperor. . . . I determined to do no more public teaching or demonstrating, as I had success greater than I could have hoped for in my practice. I knew how, when any doctor gets a reputation, his rivals envy him and call him a quack, and I would have liked to stitch up their spiteful tongues. In the presence of patients, however, I said nothing more than necessary. Nor did I teach or demonstrate to crowds as before; I merely showed by my practice how well acquainted I was with the science of medicine."

However, so far as his personal courage was concerned, Galen had changed little in his mature years. The emperor Antonius was involved in a campaign with the Germans, and in Galen's own words:

A:HOMO IN LATVS CVBĀS
B:VTER INTER FEMORA INIECTVS
C:ALTERAENEA FISTVLA VTREM INFLANS

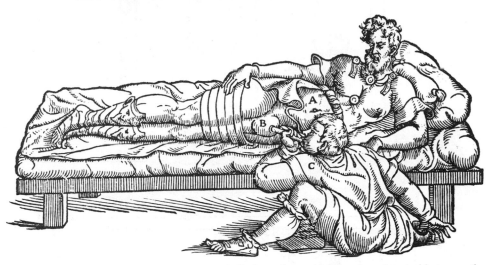

FIG. 5b. Reduction of dislocated hip by inflating a bag which has been inserted between the thighs. From: *Galeni Pergameni omnia quae extant, in Latinum sermonem conversa*, Basel, Froben, 1562. Galen's text reads as follows: "Thus an empty wine-skin is inserted between the thighs, in such a way so as to be placed as high as possible between the anus and the pudendum. Then the thighs are tied together by a strap beginning with the knee-cap and reaching half-way up the thigh. After this the wine-sack is inflated and distended by inserting a bronze tube into one of its legs which has been untied; and the patient lies on his side with the injured leg facing upward."

"He was extremely anxious to get me to go, but was persuaded to excuse me on being told that my family god Aesculapius commanded otherwise—he whose worshipper I declared myself to be since the time when he had saved me from a dangerous suppurative condition. The Emperor therefore worshipped the god, and bade me await his return (he hoped quickly to bring the war to a favourable conclusion). He himself went off, but left his son Commodus, a boy scarcely nine years old. He ordered his son's tutors to try and keep him in good health, and, if he ever should be ill, to call me in to treat him."

As it turned out the military campaign proved to be a lengthy one and Galen used the emperor's absence to complete his work "On the Utility of Parts" and "On the Principles of Hippocrates and Plato." The latter work attested to his devout admiration for the work of these men, although in gen-

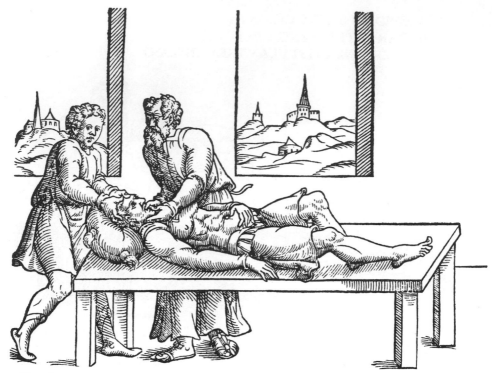

Fig. 6. Reduction of dislocated mandible. From: *Galeni Pergameni omnia quae extant, in Latinum sermonem conversa*, Basel, Froben, 1562.

eral Galen was proud of being an eclectic and of not adhering to any specific school of thought.

As an eclectic he selected freely from among the works of his medical and philosophical predecessors and was deeply influenced by Aristotle's teleological principles. His treatise "On the Utility of Parts" carries this principle to the utmost extreme where it closely resembles a religious dogma explaining that only a thoughtful Creator could have designed each part of the human body for the very function for which it was intended. Galen's tremendous posthumous influence which dominated medicine for more than fourteen centuries can be ascribed in large part to this very treatise. Although Galen was not a Christian, his belief in one supreme creative power was highly acceptable to the early church fathers. It thus came to pass that the medieval world accepted uncritically and as dogma all of the surviving works of Galen, although a number of his early writings, particularly those dealing with the movement of the blood, were later found to be based on erroneous ideas. Thus by perpetuating and declaring hallow all his works, including his misconceptions, the later world cast unjust aspersions upon Galen's perspicacity. The majority of his writings were scientifically sound and many far in advance of his day and of centuries to come. His anatomical observations were based wherever possible upon the study of the human body, and his frequent references to the *autopsia* he watched in Alexandria are matched by exhortation to look for accidental chances of studying the human body which Roman taboos had made unavailable for scientific study.

"Once also I examined the skeleton of a robber, lying on a mountain-side a short distance from the road. This man had been killed by some traveller whom he had attacked, but who had been too quick for him. None of the inhabitants of the district would bury him; but in their detestation of him they were delighted when his body was eaten by birds of prey; the latter, in fact, devoured the flesh in two days and left the skeleton ready, as it were, for anyone who cared to enjoy an anatomical demonstration.

"As regards yourself, then, even if you do not have the luck to see anything like this, still you can dissect an ape, and learn each of the bones from it, by carefully removing the flesh. For this purpose you must choose the apes which most resemble man.

. . . .

"The far-famed 'fortuitous anatomy' to which some physicians pay honour is not an adequate way of learning the nature of the parts visible. We must have plenty of leisure to inspect each of the parts first, so that, when suddenly seen, it may be recognised. And this should be done preferably with actual human beings, and, if not with them, then with animals like them."

It was for this reason that his surviving surgical works bespeak a competency that is met again in much more recent times only.

"Now, in the epidemic of carbuncle (anthrax) which occurred in many towns of Asia, a large number of the sufferers had parts of their body stripped of its skin, while others even lost the flesh itself. I was personally at this time still living in my own country, being taught by Satyrus. . . . Now, those of us who had seen Satyrus dissecting any of the denuded parts, readily recognised them and made a complete diagnosis, telling the patients to make some movement which we knew to be carried out by such and such a muscle, and sometimes diverting or drawing aside the muscles in order to observe an adjacent large artery, nerve, or vein. We saw that all the other physicians were like blind men, without any knowledge of the parts which were exposed, and that hence they did one or other of two things; either they lifted up and pushed about many parts of the muscles that had been stripped, thus giving the patients much distress and unnecessary annoyance, or else making no attempt at all to do anything. For those who were accustomed knew better how to tell the patient to move the part in the appropriate way.

"So I saw clearly from all this that to those who have had some previous instruction the inspection of wounds provides a confirmation of what they have learned, whereas to those with no previous knowledge it cannot teach anything at all."

Galen wrote widely on matters pertaining to surgery. These are diffused throughout his many treatises and are not summarized in a single volume. Perhaps his most significant contributions to surgical literature are his ideas of local pathology. These appeared in a brief treatise entitled *Tumors against Nature*. The views expressed therein sought an interpretation of the phenomena of inflammation and neoplasia on the basis of the prevailing humoral concepts. These views and the therapy implicit in them dominated the surgical literature until recent times. Because of the importance of this book it is quoted quite extensively below.

Galen enjoyed great professional success and the confidence of his imperial and highborn patients; but because of his personal traits he was less popular among his colleagues. He never married and rather decried the emotion of love. Little mention is found in his extensive writings of his home life or social position and we are left with the impression that he lived almost exclusively in his work.

Toward the end of his life, according to his own statements, he experienced two severe losses. The emperor, Marcus Aurelius, who had been his friend and protector throughout his entire Roman period, died in 180 A.D.; and sometime later a fire destroyed a number of Galen's manuscripts. Although he continued to serve as physician to the succeeding emperor, it seems that his chief interest during these years was the continuation of study and writing. He returned to Pergamum for his final years and died at the age of seventy at the very end of the second century of the Christian era, leaving neither heir or successor.

Galen's everlasting monuments were the remarkable scientific achievements and the large body of writings he left behind. These, as has been stated, became canonized in later centuries to the point where disagreement with them was tantamount to heresy; and the posthumous reverence extended to him far surpassed his contemporary fame. The concomitant arrest of all medical thinking to conform with the Galenical concepts seriously impeded scientific progress. When eventually thought again became free, Galen was unujstly blamed for the thrall, to the detriment of his place in history. Only in recent years, and as a result of unbiased studies, have accurate assessments been made of his true role in the evolution of medicine.

ᔓ ᔓ ᔓ   ON PATHOLOGICAL SWELLINGS[2]

ᔓ ᔓ ᔓ   The term tumor obviously describes one of the occurrences that takes place in the body; for the Greeks so designate changes in length, breadth and depth. At times they also designate as a tumor those enlargements which exceed the normal, which may even be present in those who enjoy health. For the obese show an enlargement in breadth and depth which goes beyond the normal, although they are not yet anywhere sick. As has been said repeatedly, there is a third condition in which bodies do not conform with Nature, which finds itself betwixt the healthy and diseased state; for the fat or the thin are not sick, but actually, the one exceeds the norm, while the latter is weaker than is healthy, but neither corresponds with Nature. But he who is swollen with dropsy or he who has become thin from emaciation, both of those are sick. Now in this book on the pathological swellings which befall the entire body and all its parts, we wish to examine those excesses of the non-natural[3] predisposition which are pathological. The dividing line for the excess is impairment of the ability to function. We will consider only those swellings which distinguish themselves from the norm according to the predisposition of the body and not only by their original character.

We will begin with *inflammation*. This term is generally used by the Greeks for more markedly swollen parts in which tension, resistance to pressure, throbbing pain, heat and redness are present. The cause, however, of these signs is not only unclear to the masses, but is even unknown to all doctors; for most of the latter do not attempt an orderly examination, but say whatever occurs to them at the moment. The reasoning, if one were to proceed in an orderly manner, would be the following: A larger swelling cannot arise in the body without its being attacked by one of the two following maladies, either that great heat radiates over it, or that something foreign were to penetrate into it.[4]

2. Galenos: *Über die krankhaften Geschwülste*, translated and introduced by Dr. Paul Richter, Leipzig, Johann Ambrosius Barth, 1913. In the interest of continuity and brevity, certain deletions were made without the usual indications therefor. Also, the seventeen chapters comprising this book are presented as a single running discussion without chapter divisions. The translation from the German was made by the authors.
3. Galen distinguished between the "non-natural" enlargements (such as obesity and pregnancy) and those "against nature," which are definitely pathological.
4. The pathological swellings, in the Galenic concept, are caused by accretions of one or more of the humors which may be either in their original or an altered state. The two factors

I have said earlier that in inflammations, when they cool, there is no reduction in size; for when the inflammation is maximal in strength and size, so that its flux is wedged in, and if one becomes ever so cold, there is no reduction in swelling. But if one makes the part blue-black and cold, one can change the ailment into a cancer. It is very easy to contract the flux and to push it back by cooling, before it is wedged in, especially when it is only insignificant. However, before it is firmly wedged in, no benefit can be achieved by bringing about contraction through cooling, but one must evacuate it. For this reason, the physicians have learned not only to soften it with hot compresses but also to evacuate something visible from the blood by making incisions into the skin. All of this furnishes significant signs that the inflamed part is filled with blood.

I believe that probably the skin, together with the swelling of the parts lying beneath, is elevated and stretched over it, and that eventually it takes up some of the flow as do also the walls of the vessels. Equally, the membranes covering inflamed limbs, as well as the nerves and tendons are gradually involved by the inflammation; sometimes, even, the malady makes its first appearance there, inasmuch as they have been lacerated or otherwise diseased. In the course of the inflammation, however, no part of the inflamed limbs that were formerly healthy remains undamaged, but together with the flesh, everything is involved by the exudate, even the bones, from the diseases of which they (the inflammations) often take their origin. Now in a healthy state the skin of the non-obese is loose, and the space upon which it rests is empty. Similarly, the spaces about the flesh, of which I spoke in detail in my anatomical lectures, are incidentally also empty, and especially those around the arteries in the region of their branchings. In inflammations, however, they are all filled with blood, that sweats out of the vessels through their walls and mixes like dew with all parts of the flesh. When, however, in the course of time, nature is victorious, when all the fluid is cooked, and pus is formed, then it is driven from the flesh by the powers which it [the flesh] possesses to evacuate that which is foreign. Where there are suitable natural pores, as a ditch for draining away superfluities, or where little room is available, a part of the pus evaporates and the rest visibly flows out. But where the skin is

---

mentioned which change the character of the body fluids are heat and the influence of a foreign element.

in firm and close apposition, as is the case on the body surface, pus is retained and it elevates the skin from the flesh lying beneath; but later, the pus eats its way through the skin by means of its corrosive nature and appears externally if one does not anticipate this event by incision.

If, however, Nature is overcome by the flow, then blood does not turn into pus, but into a dissimilar, variable mass which physicians designate by the generic term *abscess*, especially if it lies deeply. Some physicians prefer not to term all in this manner, but only those which are otherwise degenerated and not changed into the usually laudable pus.

When pus denudes [portions of] the body and removes and separates the covering layers from the underlying parts; when then, it [the pus] is removed in some fashion and the separated parts cannot return to their former condition, then we call the lesion a *sinus*. If one does not treat it soon, it will form in time a firm thickening that can no longer rejoin the parts beneath; but the opening may be covered over if one dries it up by medicines and diet, so that the part appears entirely healthy. Now, if one maintains a strict diet, the body will become really healthy and free from superfluous matter and the [margins of] the sinus remain firmly agglutinated; but if the superfluity is permitted to increase, then the cavity fills again, and there is, again, a swelling as there was in the beginning. And again, with proper treatment, it will be emptied, dried and agglutinated, and all this always happens more easily than with the original swelling. For the separated parts are not painful because they were previously separated, and they fill very quickly because the cavity accepts the influx easily, and it will also empty readily, since the way is paved for the outflow; however, they do pain again, after they have been agglutinated before the swelling breaks open again. But also, the so-called *fistula*, is a narrow, elongated cavity, which like the other cavities becomes closed over, and by the escape of superfluous matter, like the others, becomes elevated. Also, the *atheromata*, the *steatomata*, the *melicerides* (sebaceous cysts, lipomata and honey-like cysts) and similar conditions are placed by some into the group of elevations, but by others into another group. Their nature becomes apparent from their names, for one finds gruel-like matter in atheromata, tallow-like substance in the steatomata, honey-like substances in the melicerides, and frequently a membranous sac surrounds all such structures. Now these are all morbid swellings and to these also belong *carbuncle, wet gang-rene, herpes, erysipelas, scirrhi, edema, cancer* and *pneumatoceles*, about which the physician must not be ignorant, but must carefully seek their origin and nature.

Wet gangrene and *carbuncles* [anthrax] arise because the blood which, so to speak, is boiling burns the skin as does inflamma-tion.[5] Thereby arise crusts, and blisters precede the ulcers as in those burned by fire, and are accompanied by violent fever and grave danger to life. A deep black and ash-colored crust becomes visible on the ulcers and carbuncles, but the color of the surrounding inflammation is not red like in other inflamma-tions, but tends towards the black, but is different from those suffering from hemorrhages or freezing, since the swelling is not starkly blueblack as in the former, but has some fatty sheen, as does asphalt and pitch. That is an indication of the black bile, and from this arises also the malignancy of the ulcers ac-companying carbuncles, and it appears as if the blood, from the beginning, or from an excess of seething, becomes melan-cholic.

Cancers are produced by black bile without seething, and if the bile is more acrid, [it produces cancers] with ulceration which are blacker than the color of the inflamed portion and not very hot. However the veins in the latter are more filled and tenser than in inflammations; for the humor which gives rise to cancers, because of its viscosity, does not readily escape from the vessels into the surrounding flesh. Also, the veins are not red, as they are in inflammations, but they are similar to the disease-producing humor.

The violent inflammations are followed by the so-called *wet gangrene* which is mortification of the diseased part. If one does not treat it soon, the part suffering from it will readily die, and it [gangrene] affects the surrounding [structures] and kills the patient; because in the most violent inflammations the openings of the vessels are firmly closed and all the pores of the skin are deprived of their normal exhalation, thus the diseased parts die readily. First, the beautiful coloring which is present in in-flammations pales, then the pain and throbbing [pulsation] ceases, but not because the disease is ended, but because sensa-tion has died; inseparable, however, from the severest inflam-

---

5. The concept that the exudates themselves may possess irritating and even destructive quali-ties persisted in the literature for many centuries and is even to be found in the earlier writings of Lord Lister (1867).

mations is the pulsation; for thus the ancients generally designate the palpable motion of the arteries in the diseased part,
no matter whether it arises with or without pain. For this reason
some [doctors] also include the painful throbbing among the
signs of inflammation. Thus, there arises in the designation, a
contradiction; it would be better to neglect the designation and
to know the cause. Now in the healthy person the movement
of the arteries is not noticeable [subjectively] to us; in inflammations, however, it is noticeable, and there is simultaneously
pain. For the enlarged artery beats against the surrounding
flesh, and because of this beating we experience pain in inflammation. If, however, the walls of the arteries themselves
are inflamed, the walls also beat, and by their beating double
the pain. Of this we have said enough.

We must now discuss the biliary humors in sequence. Among
the doctors there predominates, I don't know why, the habit,
whenever they speak of biliary humor, to mean the yellow and
bitter, but not the acrid and black bile. Those physicians always talk about the latter with the special comment by adding
the color to the designation of the humor. If now, a biliary
outpouring has affected some one, then it always gives rise to
ulcers; but if it is mixed with watery lymph or blood, then it is
less acrid and more probably elevates the part in the nature of
a swelling rather than give rise to ulcers. The one is called
erysipelas, the other *herpes.* The color and the degree of warmth
of the lesion indicate the humor that is active within; according
to whether it is less or more acrid one should know that from
the more acrid arises *esthiomenous (corroding) herpes,* as it is called
by Hippocrates; the other, however, gives rise to the form which
Hippocrates called *miliary herpes,* because it produces elevations
in the skin resembling millet grains. It seems to me that in such
humor there must be an admixture of phlegm while the other
type arises from pure bile. For this reason, in the latter, the skin
is gnawed away and its continuity interrupted, from whence
the name of the disease arises. But if blood and bile are mixed
in equal parts, the disease in its appearance and nature is between erysipelas and inflammation; however, if one strongly
predominates, the disease is given the name of the noun and
the admixture the adjective. One calls it inflammatory erysipelas if bile predominates, and erysipeloid inflammation if
the blood predominates. The designation of other mixtures is
similar: indurated inflammations and inflammatory indura-

tions, inflammatory edema and edematous inflammation; for these four diseases, *erysipelas, edema, inflammation* and *induration* arise collectively from the influx of fluids so that in erysipelas the biliary humor predominates, in inflammation the blood, in edema thin phlegm, whereas the thick and tenacious phlegm causes one kind of induration while the other is caused by the sediment of the blood. This [sediment] also exists in two forms, namely, in one which is called "black" by Hippocrates, and the other which is also black, and has its own designation, is called "black bile;" the latter causes cancer, the other black humor causes a form of induration, but it is distinguished from the phlegmatic induration by its color; but common to both is a severely morbid, painless, hard swelling which is sometimes original, sometimes it has arisen from inflammation, from an erysipelas or edema which has become excessively cooled.

Resembling the indurations are the so-called *ecchymoses* and *bruises* which occur most often in old people because of the fragility of the blood vessels. As has been said before, some of these are black and they arise most frequently in the very aged from insignificant causes. Others are between red and black, or what is called livid. All these arise through hemorrhage from the blood vessels, and sometimes when the vessel coats are torn, they enlarge at their ends.

When the arteries are enlarged, the disease is called an *aneurysm*. If the artery is injured and the overlying skin is scarred over, the ulcer of the vessel persists and neither grows together, cicatrizes, or is covered with flesh. This disease can be recognized by the pulsations of the functioning arteries, and if one presses, the entire swelling disappears because its contents return to the arteries; those contents which we have shown in another place, are thin and yellow (biliary) because the blood is mixed with thin vapor. At the same time the blood is warmer than that in the veins, and if the aneurysm is injured, the blood gushes forth and it is difficult to staunch it. But even in edemas the underlying tissues yield if one presses upon them with the finger, and the part shows an indentation, but in this disease no pulsation is present and the color is whiter, and the edema is much flatter and larger than an aneurysm except in such cases where a blood clot which has come from an aneurysm causes *dry gangrene*; for so I designate any destruction of a solid body which also affects the bone, but not the flesh and the vessels. Wet gangrene is also death of solid parts, but it does not arise in the bones, and follows the severest inflammations; it is a form of dry gangrene that has a special as well as a general designation. This is now sufficiently defined and it is now time to speak of fluxes of black bile.

When black bile penetrates the flesh, it eats through the surrounding skin, since it is corrosive, and produces an *ulcer*. If it is moderate, it produces a *non-ulcerated cancer*. It has already been said above that it enlarges the veins more than inflammations do, and of which color its various forms assume. But not only cancerous ulcers, but many others are associated with swellings of the surrounding tissues, which are all the sequelae of a degeneration of the humors, be it a bitter-biliary or a black-biliary or another poisonous and useless one which was gradually nurtured by a strong putrefaction.

Whatever reaches out and attacks the surrounding healthy structures, is called "devouring" (*phagadena*), but that composed of both, namely, the ulcer itself and the surrounding swelling is called "devouring gangrene" (*cheironia*). Also herpes attacks the surrounding tissues and eats at it, but this is only a swelling of the skin; the "devouring gangrene," however attacks the skin *and* the underlying parts. It is superfluous to mention cheironic and telephish ulcers, it suffices to call them all malignant, also scabes and leprosy are black-biliary diseases exclusive to the skin, however if they arise in the veins or the flesh they are called cancer.

Elephantiasis [*leprosy*], also, is a melancholic (black bile) disease which arises originally from melancholic blood, but eventually black bile gains the upper hand over the blood, and because of this the patients become malodorous and disagreeable to look at. In some, there also arise ulcers. In the beginning the disease is called satyriasis because the patients' faces become similar to those of satyrs. Some doctors also designate it so because of the bone-like excrescences at the temples. But similar excrescences of the bones arise also in other parts, and some call them exostoses, as they also call the healthy but unremitting erection of the penis satyriasis, others again call it priapism.

But also *achor* (*wet eczema*) is a small ulcer in the scalp in which one might assume that it takes its origin from the salty, alkaline phlegm; for out of it flows neither a simple, watery lymph nor one which is as thick as honey, as is the case in the so-called *favus*. For also in this one there arises a certain swelling and numerous openings and a honey-like moisture flows out. In the latter, however, the swelling is small and it does not grow as large as it does in the achor. Regardless of this, small morbid swellings arise in the skin, such as *myrmicia* (flat warts), *achro-cordones*, *psydraces* and *epinytides* (*herpes zoster*). All of these are well-known diseases. No less familiar is *furuncle*, which is benign, so long as it is limited to the skin, but becomes malignant if it penetrates into the skin; for then it resembles an abscess and only through its hardness can such a furuncle be distinguished from an abscess, but both are inflammatory diseases. The third is a *bubo*, and the fourth we call a *suppurating bubo*, which can be distinguished by its heat and rapid origin from the other purulent swellings. Some say that only the inguinal gland swellings and axillary gland swellings lead to gland suppurations when the inflammations arise from glands. However, if they harden, the disease is called *struma*, as one uses the name sarcocele for indurations of the testicle, and as one speaks of *hydrocele* if a watery fluid has collected in the membranes of the testicle; and of *epiplocele* and *enterocele*, and in addition, when composed of both, and more than necessarily complicated, *entero-epiplocele*, while younger physicians use the designation *hernia* for all swellings about the testicles. Likewise, as each of the mentioned names indicates the disease of the part of which one speaks, so also the new name *varicocele* shows the disease of which we are speaking.

Varicose veins was the designation used by the older physicians for all venous enlargements. These varicose veins, however, arise in the thighs because of weakness of the blood vessels, and especially when the body is overfilled with thick blood. When, however, the peritoneum has been injured or torn, and does not grow together again, then a soft swelling appears at the site, and when they arise after some form of inguinal gland induration it is called an *inguinal hernia*; when it develops at the navel some physicians call those patients *umbilical hernia* sufferers. But none of these diseases is an illness of the abdominal wall itself, but also the aponeurosis of the muscles (the characteristics of which I have expounded in the anatomical lectures) must also have been totally damaged. Here we are dealing with a disease of the transverse muscles, but in inguinal hernia, with disease of the oblique muscles, whose aponeurosis, together with the peritoneal covering, is torn or stretched. Other swellings occur here, when one of the subjacent organs is pushed upward. The diseases which give rise to swellings here, as described above, are inflammations, indurations, detachments, etc. In the hydropic, there is an accumulation of fluid, for example, watery fluid in the ascitic, air-like in the tympanitic, and phlegm-like in those that are designated as *anasarca* and *leucophlegmatic*.

Several other swellings have individual names, even when they are not distinguished by anything special, such as *epulis* and *parulis thymi* and the other flesh-like growths; similarly the *uvae, paristhmia,* and the *tonsils* are nothing else than inflammations, namely the uvae of the uvula, tonsils of the glands which lie opposite one another at the beginning of the pharynx (fauces) and of the bodies which lie above the pharynx. Hippocrates, however, does not seem to call all inflammations of the uvula a uva, but only the kind in which the tip of the uvula becomes similar to a grape (acinus). But also *polyps* which rise from the nasal septum show something of inflammation, abscess or excrescence or however else one wishes to call it; for they are inflammatory and moist at the spot where they arise. Also the *encanthis* is a morbid swelling in the large angle of the eye, but it is not completely morbid. *Pterygium*, however, is an outgrowth of the membrane which covers the eye on its outside, which emanates from the periosteum and reaches to the iris. The so-called *staphylomata* are morbid swellings partly because of their position, partly because of their disposition. However, we have discussed all these eye diseases elsewhere, and it is now time to conclude this book here, since nothing of the morbid swellings has remained undiscussed.

CHAPTER 5

Surgery of the Orient
India: Sushruta

"A physician well versed in the principles of surgery, and experienced in the practice of medicine, is alone capable of curing distempers, just as only a two-wheeled cart can be of service in a field of battle."[1]

Medicine in ancient India reached a high level of development that was proportional to its other cultural achievements. As will be brought out subsequently, the dating of this intellectual flowering is very indefinite, and for that reason comparison with the levels of medical advance in other civilizations is difficult. It is significant that at the high point of Indian medicine the traditional rift between medicine and surgery was obliterated. It may be stated generally that in those periods in medical history in which medicine progressed rapidly there was an intimate fusion of these two major divisions of the healing art.

The traditional system of medicine of India is known as Ayurveda, which may be translated as the Science of Longevity, or the Science of Life. Originally it comprised what is now known as internal medicine in its broadest sense, which includes hygiene, preventive medicine, and the regimen that is conducive to health and longevity. Its age is not known, but it is generally believed that it came into being some centuries before the Christian era, and that its contents are derived from the wisdom of even earlier periods. They constitute the earliest Indian medical writings and, when they first appeared, did not include surgical subjects since the physicians were exclusively drawn from the Brahmin caste, among the members of which any contact with wounds, injuries, and death was considered defiling.

It is obvious that medical care could not have been complete without some surgery, and that the practitioners of the latter field were members of a lower caste who were illiterate, and who passed on their knowledge by oral tradition

---

1. Sushruta: *An English Translation of The Sushruta Samhita*, based on the original Sanskrit text, edited and published by Kaviraj Kunja Lal Bhishagratna 3 Vols., Calcutta, Wilkins Press, 1907, Vol. 1, p. 30.

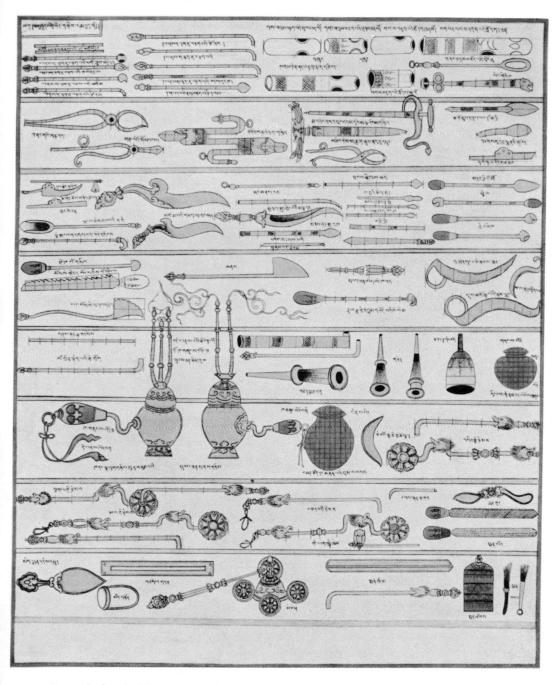

PLATE I. Surgical instruments similar to those described in the writings of Sushruta, as depicted in an ancient Tibetan medical scroll. Reproduced from paintings in the Far Eastern Library, University of California, Berkeley. (By permission.)

rather than in writing. This branch of medical skill did not become an accepted part of Hindu medicine until the first century A.D., but there is no doubt that it is of much greater age. The name for surgery was *Alya*, or "Arrow," after the most important weapon used in ancient Hindu warfare because, as in all other cultures, surgery advanced through the care of wounds sustained in battle. The bridging of the social and professional gulf between the war-born surgeons and the civilian Brahmin physicians was accomplished by the work of one personality, Sushruta, whose encyclopedic writings made surgery a vital part of the general art of healing. His collective work, the *Sushruta Samhita*, not only comprises a textbook of surgery but also systematizes and clarifies much of the earlier general medical thought as it had been previously recorded (by Charaka), and served as a basis in form and content for subsequent medical authors.

Neither Indian nor Western scholars have as yet succeeded in the accurate dating of any of the Indian medical classics. It is uncertain whether Charaka, the compiler of Ayurvedic medicine, and Sushruta, the author of the surgical text, were actual historical personages or simply legendary figures to whom these collective works were attributed. Sushruta's life has been placed in periods varying from the sixth century B.C. to the sixth century A.D. It is only certain that the *Sushruta Samhita* was written well before the eighth century A.D., for it then served as a model for another classical medical author, Vagbhata. In view of this uncertainty as to the dating of the work and its author, the Indian traditions which claim the greater antiquity concerning Sushruta must suffice, although in evaluating these beliefs the Oriental tendency of equating venerability with great age must be borne in mind. Thus we read in the most authoritative English translation and edition of his work that Sushruta was a disciple of the holy Dhanvantari, who was the first proponent of medical science, and that his style of writing proves him a contemporary of Buddha (about 600 B.C.). It is further stated in this book that "Sushruta was emphatically a surgeon, and the *Sushruta Samhita* is the only complete book we have which deals with the problems of practical surgery and midwifery. . . . To Sushruta may be attributed the glory of elevating the art of handling a lancet or forceps to the status of a practical science. . . ."[2]

With the *Sushruta Samhita* the development of Indian surgery reached its acme and its end. Beyond commentaries upon this text little, if anything, was added in the subsequent centuries. Thus in studying this one work we also analyze the totality of Indian surgery and, incidentally, the highest achievement of Indian medicine, for in this book surgery is considered the foremost branch of the entire healing art and appears as the first of the eight branches of Ayurveda. These are defined in the opening chapter of the *Sushruta Samhita* as:

2. *Ibid.*, p. xi.

1. Surgery—The scope of this branch of Medical Science is to remove (from an ulcer) any extraneous substance such as, fragments of hay, particles of stone, dust, iron or bone; splinters, nails, hair, clotted blood, or condensed pus (as the case may be), or to draw out of the uterus a dead foetus, or to bring about safe parturitions in cases of false presentation, and to deal with the principle and mode of using and handling surgical instruments in general, and with the application of fire (cautery) and alkaline (caustic) substances, together with the diagnosis and treatment of ulcers."[3]

Then follow the branches concerned with (2) diseases of the eyes, ears, mouth, and nose; (3) general (systemic) diseases, such as fever, dysentery, insanity, hysteria, leprosy, and unnatural discharges; (4) demoniacal diseases, incantation and exorcism; (5) management of children; (6) toxicology— elimination of natural or artificial poisons; (7) the science of rejuvenation and prolongation of life; and, finally, (8) the science of aphrodisiacs.

The primary importance of surgery among these eight branches of healing is stated succinctly:

"All hold this Tantram [branch] to be the most important of all the other branches of the Ayurveda, inasmuch as instantaneous actions can be produced with the help of such appliances as surgical operations, external applications of alkalis, cauterisation, etc., and secondly inasmuch as it contains all that can be found in the other branches of the science of medicine as well, with the superior advantage of producing instantaneous effects by means of surgical instruments and appliances. Hence it is the highest in value of all the medical Tantras. It is eternal and a source of infinite piety, imparts fame and opens the gates of Heaven to its votaries, prolongs the duration of human existence on earth, and helps men in successfully fulfilling their missions, and earning a decent competence in life."[4]

The great flowering of surgery in early Indian medical history is particularly significant in view of the obstacles that stood in the way of the study of anatomy. According to the Hindu tenets the human body is sacred in death. It may not by violated by dissection but, by the injunction of the Hindu *Shastras* [Laws], the corpses of all persons more than two years old must be cremated in their original condition. Contact with the corpse other than in the act of cremation would also have defiled the dissector himself. It is obvious, however, that Sushruta did have some anatomical knowledge, although of a vague and inexact nature. This was gained in two manners; one was to

3. *Ibid.*, p. 3.
4. *Ibid.*, pp. 7–8.

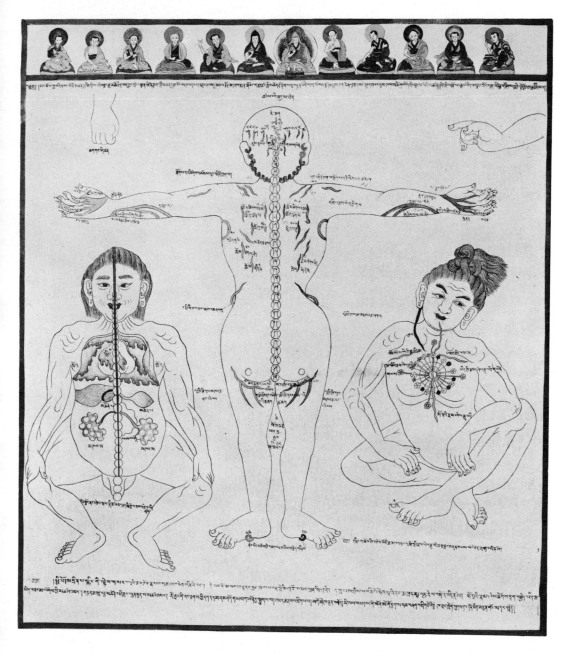

PLATE II. Indian and Tibetan concepts of anatomy and physiology as depicted on an ancient Tibetan medical scroll. The medical deities on the upper border are grouped around Baishajyaguru, the Buddha of the healing art. From paintings in the Far Eastern Library, University of California, Berkeley. (By permission.)

take the injunction concerning cremation literally and to confine dissection to bodies of children under two years of age. This custom probably accounts for the multitude of bones in the human skeleton which ranged between 300 to 360 in number because of the enumeration of the individual parts of bones which had not yet fused as they would appear in the adult body. The other way of obtaining anatomical knowledge was pursued secretly and only in cases where unclaimed bodies were found. These were left lying in a shallow running brook for seven days, then the macerated flesh was scraped off with whisk brooms and the exposed inner parts inspected, no hand ever actually touching the body. The resulting anatomical knowledge was far from accurate and was generally confined to an enumeration and classification of the constituent parts.

The physiological concepts underlying the *Sushruta Samhita* are even less suited than those of anatomy to furnish the basis of a rational surgical text. Like all other contributors to Ayurvedic medicine, Sushruta believed the body to be permeated and activated by three humoral elements—air, phlegm, and bile. Harmony in the elementary substances brought health; imbalance brought disease. But although he payed lip service to this system, Sushruta recognized other etiological factors as well. His definition of disease is actually quite broad when he says: "Man is the receptacle of any particular disease, and that which proves a source of torment or pain to him, is denominated as disease. There are four different types of disease such as, Traumatic, or of extraneous origin, Bodily, Mental, and Natural."[5] The "Bodily" diseases are related to food and drink, to the blood or the humors. Excessive hostility, joy, fear, or other emotions produce "Mental" diseases, whereas the "Natural" diseases are caused by physical wants and the process of aging.

Although it was considered the foremost of the medical arts, surgery was reserved as the last recourse in combating illness. Sushruta, the surgeon, was thus completely conversant with all other branches of therapy including diet and hygiene, which were greatly stressed, and pharmacology with its tremendous supply of vegetable, animal, and mineral medicaments. Sushruta lists 760 healing plants alone that were known to him. Of great and general medical importance, and of particular interest to modern readers was the selection and training of the physician-surgeon:

> ". . . The formal initiation of a pupil into the science of medicine
> . . . should be imparted to a student, belonging to one of the three
> twice-born castes such as, the Brahmana, the Kshatriya, and the
> Vaishya, and who should be of tender years, born of a good family,
> possessed of a desire to learn, strength, energy of action, content-
> ment, character, self-control, a good retentive memory, intellect,

5. *Ibid.*, p. 10.

courage, purity of mind and body, and a simple and clear comprehension, command a clear insight into the things studied, and
should be found to have been further graced with the necessary
qualifications of thin lips, thin teeth and thin tongue, and possessed
of a straight nose, large, honest intelligent eyes, with a benign con-
tour of the mouth, and a contented frame of mind, being pleasant in
his speech and dealings, and usually painstaking in his efforts. A
man possessed of contrary attributes should not be admitted into
(the sacred precincts of) medicine."[6]

Upon the extremely formal ritual of initiation the newly accepted disciple
was given the following solemn injunction by his preceptor:

"Then having thrice circumambulated the sacrificial fire, and
having invoked the firegod to bear testimony to the fact, the preceptor should address the initiated disciple as follows:—'Thou shalt re-
nounce lust, anger, greed, ignorance, vanity, egotistic feelings, envy,
harshness, niggardliness, falsehood, idleness, nay all acts that soil
the good name of a man. In proper season thou shalt pare thy nails
and clip thy hair and put on the sacred cloth, dyed brownish yellow,
live the life of a truthful, self-controlled anchorite and be obedient
and respectful towards thy preceptor. In sleep, in rest, or while
moving about—while at meals or in study, and in all acts thou
shalt be guided by my directions. Thou shalt do what is pleasant
and beneficial to me, otherwise thou shalt incur sin and all thy
study and knowledge shall fail to bear their wished for fruit, and
thou shalt gain no fame. If I, on the other hand, treat thee unjustly
even with thy perfect obedience and in full conformity to the terms
agreed upon, may I incur equal sin with thee, and may all my
knowledge prove futile, and never have any scope of work or display. Thou shalt help with thy professional skill and knowledge, the
Brahmanas, thy elders, preceptors and friends, the indigent, the
honest, the anchorites, the helpless and those who shall come to thee
(from a distance), or those who shall live close by, as well as thy
relations and kinsmen [to the best of thy knowledge and ability],
and thou shalt give them medicine [without charging for it any remuneration whatever], and God will bless thee for that. Thou shalt
not treat medicinally a professional hunter, a fowler, a habitual sin-
ner, or him who has been degraded in life; and even by so doing
thou shalt acquire friends, fame, piety, wealth and all wished for
objects in life and thy knowledge shall gain publicity'."[7]

6. *Ibid.*, p. 16.
7. *Ibid.*, pp. 18–19.

Diagnosis, although connected with the humoral theories in a general manner, was not restricted to speculations. Sushruta gave explicit instructions concerning inspection, palpation and auscultation, the use of taste and smell, the interpretation of dreams, and the interrogation of the patient and his family concerning the patient's habits, their deviation in disease, and all subjective symptoms. An indication of the detail into which the analysis of subjective manifestations went is the listing of the types of pain.

> "Pains of pricking, piercing, thrashing, cutting, expanding, gnawing, churning, shooting, tingling, burning, breaking, bursting, pinching, uprooting, uplifting, quivering, aching of different types, shifting, stuffing, benumbing, indurating, contracting, and pains of a spasmodic character are usually felt in ulcers. A pain, which comes on or vanishes without any apparent cause, or is varied and shifting in its character, should be ascribed to the effects of the deranged Váyu."[8]

Sushruta also touches upon the diagnosis of diabetes mellitus, first made in India, by pointing not only to the sweet taste of urine but also to the fact that the sweetness of the discharge could be inferred from its attracting flies and ants.

The importance of diagnosis was matched by that of prognosis, although the latter did not restrict itself to the rational ways of the former. Sushruta's chapters on prognosis are an amazing mixture of medical predictions and irrational portents. The observation of physical changes and symptoms presaging recovery or death was interchanged with a study of the messenger, omens, and dreams, all of which could augur well or badly for the patient's recovery. The emphasis on prognosis was not only for the benefit of the patient and his family but even more for the sake of the physician who was free, and even definitely advised by Sushruta, to cease treatment of an incurable disease in order to avoid the taint upon his reputation of a fatal outcome.

Sushruta divided surgical operations into eight categories: (1) *incision* for "ailment due to the lodgment of a foreign body in the flesh or a bone"; (2) *excision*, "in swellings in general diseases affecting the mammary organs . . . and diseases which are caused by suppuration in the local flesh or any soft part of the body (such as fistula-in-ano) as well as stone in the bladder and diseases due to a derangement of the fat"; (3) *scarification*; (4) *aspiration* to be used in connection with a vein, abdominal dropsy, hydroceles, and ulcers containing foreign matter; (5) *extraction* of morbid or foreign matter, bladder stones, feces from the constricted anus, or fetus from the uterus; (6) *secreting* or *evacuating measures*, to be employed in the case of pain or inflammatory

8. *Ibid.*, pp. 217–218.

swellings restricted to particular parts of the body, elephantiasis, blood poisoning, tumors, erysipelas, and so forth; (7) *probing* in fistulae; and (8) *suturing* with threads of flax, sinews, and hair. The needles for suturing were minutely described and graded in length and thickness according to the nature of the lesion.

> "The needle should not be pricked into a part too near, or too remote from the fissure, or the mouth of an ulcer [wound], as there might be the danger of the suture being broken off (at the least pressure or movement) in the first instance and of genesis of pain in the second. An ulcer, thus properly sutured, should be covered over with cotton and dusted over with a pulverised compound . . . or with the ashes of a burnt piece of Kshauma cloth, or with the powders of the Shallaki fruit. Then the ulcer should be properly bandaged, and measures and rules regarding the regimen of diet, and conduct previously laid down in the chapter on the nursing of an ulcer-patient should be adopted and observed."[9]

In the *Sushruta Samhita* 101 blunt and twenty sharp instruments are listed and described. Among the former are varieties of forceps, pincers, tubes, hooks, catheters, and sounds, as well as magnets for the extraction of foreign bodies. The hand, however, is considered the most important instrument, for without it no operation can be performed. The sharp instruments consist of lancets, knives, bistouries, scissors, needles, trocars, and saws. The instruments were made of steel, the manufacture of which was early understood by the Indians, and they were kept in wooden boxes.

Cauterization by escharotics and hot metal or boiling fluids was considered to be more effective than intervention by means of the knife. Red-hot needles were inserted into the parenchyma of the spleen in order to treat splenic enlargement. Fourteen different types of dressings were listed, made of a variety of materials including cotton, wool, silk, and linen. Splints were fashioned from bamboo, branches of other trees, and bark. Bleeding was arrested by compression, herbs, and hot oil. Facial wounds were sutured. A certain amount of anesthesia was achieved by means of alcoholic intoxication. Both alcohol and meat, normally forbidden to Hindus, were not only permitted but became important factors in the treatment and the diet of Indian patients.

The *Sushruta Samhita* makes it evident that surgery had achieved considerable mastery in diagnosis, operative intervention, and aftertreatment. Fractures, dislocations, the extirpation of tumors, the cauterization of fistulae, the removal of foreign bodies, and the performance of paracentesis were ration-

9. *Ibid.*, p. 242.

ally and intelligently described. Wounds were treated by methods considered best today, thorough cleansing "both of its inside and exterior" and closure by suture. Ophthalmic surgery was extensively described and the lens recognized as the seat of vision, but the description of the operation for cataract lacks the clarity of other operative procedures. It is noteworthy that the practice of gynecology and obstetrics fell into the surgical domain and explicit and highly intelligent directions were given for the regimen and diet of the mother during pregnancy and the lying-in period, as well as for the newborn child. Caesarian section after death and embryotomy in case of fetal death were also practiced. The most outstanding achievements of Indian surgery, however, are recorded in the chapters on lithotomy, laparotomy, and plastic surgery. The great stride in and need for this last-mentioned operation grew out of the practice of punishing many even slight offenses by the amputation of noses and ears. Although the question of reciprocal influences of Indian and Western medicine in general has never been completely answered, it is an established fact that Indian plastic surgery provided the basic pattern for Western efforts in this direction.

The influence of Sushruta as part of the totality of Ayurvedic medicine is clearly evident in the degree to which these teachings are used in present day India. Although Western medicine is being taught and practiced, the number of physicians so trained is totally inadequate to take care of the teeming population of the country. Because of this dearth of Western-trained doctors, practitioners of the ancient Ayurvedic art of healing have continued to flourish in large numbers; indeed, they are actually preferred by many Indian patients partly because of their faith in tradition and partly because the awakening nationalism in India puts increasing stress on its own cultural heritage. Thus the verities of Indian medicine span the millenia and still fulfill their original purpose.

ON THE TRAINING OF A SURGEON[10]

Now we shall discuss the Chapter which treats of practical instructions in surgical operations.

The preceptor should see that his disciple attends the practice of surgery even if he has already thoroughly mastered the several branches of the science of Medicine, or has perused it in its entirety. In all acts connected with surgical operations of incision, etc. and injection of oil, etc. the pupil should be fully instructed as regards the channels along or into which the operations or applications are to be made (Karma-patha). A

10. *Ibid.*, pp. 71–73.

pupil, otherwise well-read, but uninitiated into the practice (of medicine or surgery) is not competent (to take in hand the medical or surgical treatment of a disease). The art of making specific forms of incision should be taught by making cuts in the body of a Pushpaphalá (a kind of gourd), Alávu, water-melon, cucumber, or Erváruka. The art of making cuts either in the upward or downward direction should be similarly taught. The art of making excisions should be practically demonstrated by making openings in the body of a full water-bag, or in the bladder of a dead animal, or in the side of a leather pouch full of slime or water. The art of scraping should be instructed on a piece of skin on which the hair has been allowed to remain. The art of venesection (Vedhya) should be taught on the vein of a dead animal, or with the help of a lotus stem. The art of probing and stuffing should be taught on worm-eaten wood, or on the reed of a bamboo, or on the mouth of a dried Alávu (gourd). The art of extracting should be taught by withdrawing seeds from the kernel of a Vimbi, Vilva or Jack-fruit, as well as by extracting teeth from the jaws of a dead animal. The act of secreting or evacuating should be taught on the surface of a Shálmali plank covered over with a coat of bee's wax, and suturing on pieces of cloth, skin or hide. Similarly the art of bandaging or ligaturing should be prac-tically learned by tying bandages round the specific limbs and members of a full-sized doll made of stuffed linen. The art of tying up a Karna-sandhi (severed ear-lobe) should be prac-tically demonstrated on a soft severed muscle or on flesh, or with the stem of a lotus lily. The art of cauterising, or applying alkaline preparations (caustics) should be demonstrated on a piece of soft flesh; and lastly the art of inserting syringes and injecting enemas into the region of the bladder or into an ulcerated channel, should be taught (by asking the pupil) to insert a tube into a lateral fissure of a pitcher full of water, or into the mouth of a gourd (Alávu).

An intelligent physician who has tried his prentice hand in surgery (on such articles of experiment as gourds, etc., or has learnt the art with the help of things as stated above), or has been instructed in the art of cauterisation or blistering (ap-plication of alkali) by experimenting on things which are most akin, or similar to the parts or members of the human body they are usually applied to, will never lose his presence of mind in his professional practice.

RHINOPLASTIC OPERATIONS[11]

Now I shall deal with the process of affixing an artificial nose. First the leaf of a creeper, long and broad enough to cover fully the whole of the severed or clipped off part, should be gathered; and a patch of living flesh, equal in dimension to the preceding leaf, should be sliced off (from down upward) from the region of the cheek and, after scarifying it with a knife, swiftly adhered to the severed nose. Then the coolheaded physician should steadily tie it up with a bandage decent to look at and perfectly suited to the end for which it has been employed (Sádhu Vandha). The physician should make sure that the adhesion of the severed parts has been fully effected and then insert two small pipes into the nostrils to facilitate respiration, and to prevent the adhesioned flesh from hanging down. After that, the adhesioned part should be dusted with the powders of Pattanga, Yashtimadhukam and Rasánjana pulverised together; and the nose should be enveloped in Kárpása cotton and several times sprinkled over with the re-fined oil of pure sesamum. Clarified butter should be given to the patient for drink, and he should be anointed with oil and treated with purgatives after the complete digestion of the meals he has taken, as advised (in the books of medicine). Adhesion should be deemed complete after the incidental ulcer had been perfectly healed up, while the nose should be again scarified and bandaged in the case of a semi- or partial adhesion. The adhesioned nose should be tried to be elongated where it would fall short of its natural and previous length, or it should be surgically restored to its natural size in the case of the ab-normal growth of its newly formed flesh. The mode of bringing about the adhesion of severed lips is identical with what has been described in connection with a severed nose with the ex-ception of the insertion of pipes. The physician, who is well conversant with these matters, can be alone entrusted with the medical treatment of a King.

THE OPERATION OF LITHOTOMY[12]

The surgeon should use his best endeavours to encourage the patient and infuse hope and confidence in the patient's mind. A person of strong physique and unagitated mind should be first made to sit on a level board or table as high as the knee-

11. *Ibid.*, pp. 152–154.
12. *Ibid.*, 1911, Vol. 2, pp. 332–335.

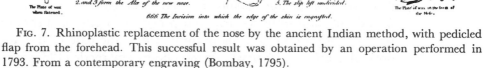

FIG. 7. Rhinoplastic replacement of the nose by the ancient Indian method, with pedicled flap from the forehead. This successful result was obtained by an operation performed in 1793. From a contemporary engraving (Bombay, 1795).

joint. The patient should then be made to lie on his back on the table placing the upper part of his body in the attendant's lap, with his waist on an elevated cloth cushion. Then the elbows and knee-joints (of the patient) should be contracted and bound up with fastenings (S'átaka) or with linen. After that the umbilical region (abdomen) of the patient should be well rubbed with oil or with clarified butter and the left side of the umbilical region should be pressed down with a closed fist so that the stone comes within the reach of the operator. The surgeon should then introduce into the rectum the second and third fingers of his left hand, duly anointed and with the nails well pared. Then the fingers should be carried upward towards the rope of the perineum *i.e.*, in the middle line so as to bring the stone between the rectum and the penis, when it should be so firmly and strongly pressed as to look like an elevated Granthi (tumour), taking care that the bladder remains contracted but at the same time even.

An operation should not be proceeded with nor an attempt made to extract the stone (Śalya) in a case where, the stone on being handled, the patient would be found to drop down motionless (*i.e.*, faint) with his head bent down, and eyes fixed in a vacant stare like that of a dead man, as an extraction in such a case is sure to be followed by death. The operation should only be continued in the absence of such an occurrence.

An incision should then be made on the left side of the raphe of the perineum at the distance of a barleycorn and of a sufficient width to allow the free egress of the stone. Several authorities recommend the opening to be on the right side of the raphe of the perineum for the convenience of the operation. Special care should be taken in extracting the stone from its cavity so that it may not break into pieces nor leave any broken particles behind (*i.e.*, inside the bladder), however small, as they would, in such a case, be sure to grow larger again. Hence the entire stone should be extracted with the help of an Agravaktra Yantra (a kind of forceps the points of which are not too sharp).

After the extraction of a stone, the patient should be made to sit in a Droni (cauldron) full of warm water and be fomented thereby. In doing so the possibility of an accumulation of blood in the bladder will be prevented; however if blood be accumulated therein, a decoction of the Kshira-trees should be injected into the bladder with the help of a Pushpanetra (urethral Syringe).

CHAPTER 6

Surgery of the Orient:
China and Japan

"Hence the Sages did not treat those who were already ill; they instructed those who were not yet ill."[1]

Compared with the surgical achievements of ancient India, those of the Far East, China and Japan, are meager indeed. In China, the Confucian tenets of the sacredness of the human body in life and in death early counteracted any tendency toward the development of anatomical studies and the practice of surgery. As a consequence, Chinese medicine placed its emphasis upon prevention of disease, which was taught in the form of detailed instruction for the physician and a code of ethical conduct for the people. In Japan it was the Shinto religion which considered any physical contact with death and sickness ritually defiling; the Japanese word for wound is *kega*, which also means impurity or defilement. When, in the sixth century A.D., Chinese medicine was adopted in Japan, the Confucian tenets were superimposed upon the Shinto rituals and thus the aversion toward anatomical studies and surgical treatment was doubly fortified.

In China, the first references to surgeons can be found in the *Annals* of the Chou Dynasty (1122–255 B.C.) but their ministrations were restricted to the treatment of swellings, ulcers, and wounds which were treated with plasters, scrapings, and cauterization. The treatment of fractures by means of splints is also mentioned. There are, however, no surgical texts from this period, nor indeed of any subsequent period, because the writings of Hua T'o, the one prominent surgeon of China's past, were destroyed at the time of his death. Although his works are no longer extant, his deeds were so extraordinary that they were recorded in the *Annals* of the Wei and Han Dynasties and in the *Chronicle* of the Three Kingdoms. From these sources which interweave fact and legend there comes to life the personality and achievements of this un-

1. Ilza Veith: *The Yellow Emperor's Classic of Internal Medicine*, Baltimore, Williams & Wilkins Company, 1949, p. 105.

68

usual figure who, flaunting religious proscription and social sensitivities, took up the profession of a surgeon and died for it.

Hua T'o was born around 190 A.D. and, according to legend, received the secret of the surgical art from two hermits upon whom he came in the course of his many wanderings. In permitting him to partake of their knowledge they pointed out the troublesome life of a surgeon, but they told him: "If you do not discriminate between the high and the low, the rich and the poor, the noble and the common, refuse bribery, be not afraid of hardships and be kind to the old as well as the young, you will get out of calamity eventually."

Like Sushruta, Hua T'o was a physician as well as a surgeon. It is recorded that he used but few drugs and these most carefully, that he was an excellent diagnostician, and that his prognoses were of an uncanny accuracy. He was the first Chinese to use hydrotherapy in fever and also the first to propose systematic exercise for the preservation of health.

Hua T'o's greatest fame, however, is attached to his skill in surgery and his discovery of the use of a potent anesthetic. It consisted of an effervescent powder which was added to wine, and it produced in his patients such numbness and insensibility that he could easily open the abdomen or the back, remove the diseased parts, suture the wound, and apply a healing salve. It is said that he returned his patients to health within a few months. These feats are recorded in the *Annals of the Later Han Dynasty*. The anesthesizing ingredient was designated as *ma-fei-san*, which literally translated means "bubbling drug medicine"; its composition, however, is unknown, although according to the interpretation of modern Sinologists it may well have been opium.

Hua T'o's surgical accomplishments are listed in numerous historical works and include a great variety of operations, ranging from venesection and acupuncture to laparotomy, excision of the spleen, intestines, and liver. One of his most celebrated operations he performed without the help of anesthetics. His patient was Kuan Kung, a famous general of the Three Kingdoms, later deified as God of War, who had been wounded in the arm by a poisoned arrow. The general who was playing chess at the time of Hua T'o's arrival declined to be anesthesized and continued his game without flinching as the surgeon with his great skill removed the arrow, scraped and cleansed the wound, and sutured the incision. Apparently, Hua T'o was also familiar with trepanation because it is said that he suggested this operation to a king to whom he had been called because of intolerable headaches. The king, however, declined this heroic intervention on the suspicion that such drastic means could only have been suggested to him at the behest of his enemies.

Hua T'o was the favorite physician of all the notables of his day and became personal physician to Ts'ao Ts'ao, King of Wei, who was a hot-tempered and irritable patient. Pleading illness in his own family, Hua T'o took leave from his difficult master, planning never again to return to court. The

FIG. 8. Ancient bas-relief depicting Hua T'o extracting an arrow from the arm of a general who continues to play chess during the operation. (Courtesy of the Welch Medical Library, The Johns Hopkins University School of Medicine.)

King, however, had him returned forcibly, arrested and thrown into prison, and later condemned to die. Before his death Hua T'o attempted to give his surgical writings to his prison warder in the hope that he would see to it that they were passed on to the medical profession. The warder, after some deliberation, decided that the possession of these papers was too dangerous, and returned them to Hua T'o who forthwith burnt all his manuscripts. According to legend, a few leaves were rescued from the ashes; they described the method of castration which was the only surgical procedure practiced by the Chinese until the introduction of Western medicine into that country.

Castration found its earliest mention in Chinese history almost a millenium B.C. Originally, it was adopted as a mode of punishment for especially grave offenses. Later on, however, the operation was used for the preparation of servants for the Imperial palaces and for the eight hereditary princes who, alone, beside the Imperial family, had the privilege of keeping eunuchs. The operation of castration was performed in a special establishment outside of the palace gates in Peking. This operation, although in strict contradiction to all tenets of Western medical ethics, is doubly so in China because it mutilates without a medical indication. However, because this operation and its voluntary victims, the eunuchs, have exerted such an important and pernicious influence upon China's social and political life, its original description is given here in full. It must further be stated that the operation of castration was not reserved for humans, but that the Chinese have castrated animals from earliest times. This was based on an early recognition that conception depended upon the presence of testicles and ovaries. Remarkable skill was attained in the castration of boars and cocks and in the spaying of sows.

"When about to be operated on, the patient is placed in a semi-supine position on a broad bench. One man squatting behind him grasps his waist, and another is told off to look after each leg. Bandages are fastened tightly round the hypogastric and inguinal regions, the penis and the scrotum are three times bathed in a hot decoction of pepper pods, and the patient, if an adult, is solemnly asked, whether he repents or will ever repent his decision. If he appears doubtful he is unbound and dismissed, but if his courage has held out, as it usually does, all the parts are swiftly swept away by one stroke of a sickle-shaped knife, a pewter-plug is inserted into the urethra, and the wound is covered with paper soaked in cold water and is firmly bandaged. The patient, supported by two men, is then walked about the room for two or three hours, after which he is permitted to lie down. For three days he gets nothing to drink nor is the plug removed from the urethra. At the end of this period the dressings are changed, and the accumulated urine is allowed to escape. The parts generally heal in about one hundred days. . . . About two per cent of all cases prove fatal, some by haemorrhage, some by extravasation, and some doubtless by sepsis. . . . For a long time there is incontinence of urine. . . ."[2]

As has been mentioned earlier, the initial Japanese aversion toward the performance of surgical operations even surpassed that of the Chinese and remained active for many centuries. As in China, so also in Japan, there were no surgical writings and one must assume that inevitable restorative surgery, such as the setting of fractures and the taking care of accidental wounds, received perfunctory attention by a class of manipulators who were not formally a part of the medical profession. It must be borne in mind that, for many

2. K. Chimin Wong and Wu Lien-Teh: *History of Chinese Medicine*, second edition, Shanghai, Mercury Press, 1936, p. 234.

centuries, Japan was free from internal and external strife and that war injuries did not constitute an incentive for the development of surgery.

In the eleventh century, however, the ancient and peaceful imperial rule was shaken by the newly evolved feudal system, which abruptly ended the tranquillity of the earlier period. Although Japan continued to remain aloof from foreign military involvements, internal warfare among the various clans fighting for superiority rent the peace of the country until the very end of the seventeenth century.

These wars and the resulting social upheaval brought about a deterioration of the medical profession, but the result was not entirely detrimental; for the period of unsettlement eradicated completely the imported and native prejudices which had prevented the development of surgery in Japan. With the decay of the medical schools the Confucian stigma attached to the practice of surgery, which had been adopted by the Japanese together with the Chinese medical system, fell into oblivion. The ancient Shinto tenets which considered the inflicting, receiving, and even touching of wounds as equally defiling were greatly modified with the growth of a socially prominent warrior class. Surgery, and especially battle surgery, became increasingly important during the centuries of internal strife. Although the medical history of this period suffers from a lack of great names, the history of surgery is rich with the reports of great endeavors. Indeed, some of the most outstanding surgeons were military men who made the transition from warrior to surgeon on the very field of battle.

Once the taboo against the caring for the wounded, the bleeding, and the dying was broken, and the profession of surgery had become socially and ritually acceptable, Japanese surgeons developed a great interest in the perfection of their art and in the study of the human body which had heretofore been forbidden to them. In this quest they were supported by the earliest Western influence which came to Japan in the persons of the Portuguese merchants and missionaries whose expeditions were accompanied by physicians and Jesuits with medical training. Their medical aid they extended also to the Japanese who were avid to study the surgical art of the *Nambanjin* or "Barbarians of the South." When in the early seventeenth century the Dutch established their trade settlement near Nagasaki, their physicians were among the best ambassadors of the Dutch East India Company. Medical supplies which formed part of the Dutch merchandise and the Dutch surgical methods were eagerly accepted by the Japanese medical profession and formed the core of the *Oranda-Ryu Geka,* or the Dutch Surgical School, which continued to be effective until the "Opening" of Japan in 1853. It was through the Dutch physicians that Western anatomical books and works, such as the writings of Ambroise Paré, found their way into Japan and became part of Japanese surgical practice hardly later than they did in the Western world.

A discussion of the surgical scene of China and Japan would hardly be complete without a mention of acupuncture and moxibustion, both of which, apart from medicines, diet, bathing, and massage, constituted practically the only traditional therapeutic intervention of the Far East. Neither of these procedures can be considered surgical, in the strict modern interpretation of the word, because they are not based on the type of rationale that normally determines surgical intervention. These forms of treatment are predicated on the belief that man's health depends on the harmonious interaction of a dual force, which stands for the positive and the negative, the male and the female, and a great many other opposites. Known by the names of Yin and Yang this dual force was held to permeate the body through twelve channels; its dyscrasia gave rise to disease. It was this dyscrasia which acupuncture and moxibustion were supposed to correct.

These treatments are of great antiquity and were first mentioned in the oldest Chinese medical work, the *Yellow Emperor's Classic of Internal Medicine*. Acupuncture, also known as "needling," consists of the insertion of needles of various materials and shapes into one or several of 365 specific points of the body. Moxibustion, or moxa treatment, is practiced by applying to the skin combustible cones of the powered leaves of *Artemisia vulgaris*; these cones are then ignited and a small blister forms. The points of acupuncture and moxibustion are distributed all over the body and represent strategic spots along the vessels believed to connect the various organs and to carry the pneuma and, with it, the Yin and the Yang. The effect of the insertion of the needle and the blistering of moxibustion is to create openings for the relief of congestion caused by amassed pneuma or a preponderance of Yin and Yang.

Acupuncture and moxibustion were applied for a vast variety of complaints, and especially for acute pain produced by rheumatic and neuralgic conditions, cramps, and colics. The Chinese and Japanese medical teachings included special classes for acupuncturists. Their course of study was based upon a lengthy Chinese treatise on acupuncture, *Ming T'ang Ching* (*i.e.*, the Japanese *Mei-dō-kiyo*), and lasted as long as the regular medical training.

It is of interest that both treatments are still widely practiced in the Far East. In Japan, the many practitioners of these measures are not part of the medical profession although they are tolerated without interference. In China, however, the People's Government has made acupuncture an important part of the medical armamentarium of all physicians and it is considered to be indispensable to the art of healing. Acupuncture has also found its way into European medicine; it is widely practiced in France and also has staunch adherents among the German physicians.

CHAPTER 7

Paul of Aegina (Seventh Century A.D.)

". . . Physicians have to act not only in cities, in the fields, and in desert places, but also at sea in ships, where such diseases sometimes suddenly break out as, in the event of procrastination, would occasion death, or at least incur the most imminent danger."[1]

The decline of the Western Empire in the fifth Century saw the passing of Roman might to the Eastern (Byzantine) Empire, with Constantinople its capital. The attenuation of Greek originality during this period, its admixture with the deism of Christianity, and the fatalism of the Orient led to stagnation of medical progress. Several surgeons made significant contributions after those of Galen. Of these, Antyllus was apparently the most original and he is quoted in the following excerpts. Little of importance was added to medicine or surgery during the ensuing millenium. Four encyclopedic writers of the first part of the Byzantine period, however, summarized and preserved for us the full achievements of Graeco-Roman medicine. These authors, Oribasius, Aetius of Amida, Alexander of Tralles, and Paul of Aegina, were translated into Arabic, and formed the basis of Arabic medical knowledge. Many of the highly significant advances made by earlier Greek and Roman physicians and surgeons, whose original writings have been lost, are known to us only through lengthy quotations in the books of these encyclopedists.

Paul of Aegina, the last of this quartet, who lived in the seventh century gave excellent descriptions of surgery of that period to which he added observations of his own. "On this account," he wrote, "I have compiled this brief collection from the works of the ancients, and have set down little of my own, except a few things which I have seen and tried in the practice of the art." Nevertheless, his descriptions indicate clearly a wide personal experience in the actual performance of surgical operations.

Little is known ot the life of Paul, other than that he studied and practiced in Alexandria up to the time of its actual conquest. From Arabic sources, we

---

1. *The Seven Books of Paulus Aegineta*, translated from the Greek by Francis Adams, London, 1844, printed for the Sydenham Society. From the author's Preface, Vol. 1, p. xviii.

learn how greatly he was esteemed by his contemporaries. His books were intended as a compend of Greek and Roman medicine because as he states,
"For being conversant with the most distinguished writers in the profession,
and in particular with Oribasius, who, in one work, has given a select view
of everything relating to health, I have collected what was best in them, and
have endeavored, if possible, not to pass by one distemper. For the work of
Oribasius, comprehending seventy books, contains indeed an exposition of
the whole art, but is not easily to be procured by people at large on account
of its bulk. . . ."[2]

Paul succeeded well in achieving his purpose. Because of the completeness
of his work, the conciseness and lucidity of his descriptions, and the systematic
organization of his books, large portions of his writings were incorporated
into the texts of the principal Arabic authors. In surgery, particularly, he
literally transmitted the entire body of Greek and Roman knowledge to Islam
whence it ultimately returned to medieval and pre-Renaissance Europe. He,
alone of the encyclopedists, separated the surgical sections into a compact
single volume (Book VI). This material is repeated, largely verbatim, by the
Arabic writers, particularly by Albucasis who wrote the only book in that
language which deals with surgery alone. From this source, large segments
were taken over bodily by the early Latin authors and formed the basis of
early European surgery.

Compared with earlier Greek writers, the surgery of Paul reveals certain
regressive trends which dominated therapy throughout the Middle Ages.
Bleeding and cupping, the senseless and barbaric use of the cautery, and the
"open" treatment, particularly in operative wounds, had already become
firmly established. Thoracotomy for empyema, which had been recommended
by Hippocrates, was abandoned in favor of cauterization of the chest wall.
Operations for hernia, although much more lucidly described than those of
Celsus, always included sacrifice of the testicle, a multilation not deemed
necessary by the earlier writer. On the other hand, the sections on tracheotomy, aneurism, neck dissections, and goiter (bronchocele) command our
admiration. It is from these latter chapters that the following excerpts have
been taken.

ON LARYNGOTOMY[3]

The most famous surgeons have also described this operation·
Antyllus, therefore, says, "In cases of cynanche [quinsy] we
entirely disapprove of this operation, because the incision is
utterly unavailing when all the arteries (the whole of the tra-

2. *Ibid.*, *loc. cit.*
3. *Ibid.*, Vol. II, Sec. 33, pp. 301–302.

chea?) and the lungs are affected; but in inflammations about
the mouth and palate, and in cases of indurated tonsils which
obstruct the mouth of the windpipe as the trachea is unaffected,
it will be proper to have recourse to pharyngotomy, in order to
avoid the risk of suffocation. When, therefore, we engage in the
operation we slit open a part of the arteria aspera [trachea] (for
it is dangerous to divide the whole) below the top of the windpipe, about the third or fourth ring. For this is a convenient situation, as being free of flesh, and because the vessels are placed at
a distance from the part which is divided. Wherefore, bending
the patient's head backwards, so as to bring the windpipe better
into view, we are to make a transverse incision between two of
the rings, so as that it may not be the cartilage which is divided,
but the membrane connecting the cartilages. If one be more
timid in operating, one may first stretch the skin with a hook and
divide it, and then, removing the vessels aside, if they come in
the way, make the incision." These are the words of Antyllus.
We judge that the windpipe has been opened from the air
rushing through it with a whizzing noise, and from the voice
being lost. After the urgency of the suffocation has passed over,
we pare the lips of the incision so as to make them raw surfaces
again, and then have recourse to sutures, but sew the skin only,
without the cartilage. Then we use the applications proper for
bloody or fresh wounds, but if it does not unite we must treat it
with incarnants. We must follow the same plan of treatment if
we should meet with the case of a person who had cut his own
throat from a wish to commit suicide.

ON STRUMAE, OR SCROFULOUS GLANDS[4]

The choeras, or scrofula, is an indurated gland, mostly forming in the neck, armpits, and groins, deriving its name either
from a Greek word, signifying a species of rock, or from swine,
because they are fruitful animals, or because swine have swellings of the neck. The strumae are formed either on the anterior
part of the neck, or on either side of it, or on both, and they
consist of one, two, or more, all contained in their proper membranes, like the steatoma, atheroma, and meliceris. Those,
therefore, which are painful to the touch, and on the application of medicine, are of a malignant nature, are to be considered
as carcinomatous and it is obvious that they do not readily
yield to a surgical operation. But such as are mild to the touch

4. *Ibid.*, Sec. 35, pp. 307–308.

and the seasonable application of medicines, may be operated upon in this manner. To such as are superficial and incline towards the skin we use a simple section, and free them from the surrounding bodies, and stretching the skin with hooks we flay the lips of the incision, as we said in describing the operation of angiology, and by degrees remove them entirely. But such as are larger, having transfixed them with hooks, we raise up, and dissecting away the skin from them in like manner, we must free them entirely from the surrounding bodies, avoiding in particular the carotid arteries and recurrent nerves. If any divided vessel obscure the operation, we may include it in a ligature, or cut it asunder, if not large. And when the base of the scrofulous tumour runs out into a narrow point, we may cut it away readily, and introducing the index finger search if there be any other strumae lying there, and remove them in the same manner. But if we suspect that a large vessel or vessels are situated at the bottom of the scrofulous tumour, we need not cut it out from the base, but include it in a ligature, so that it may fall off spontaneously in pieces without danger, when we may effect the cure by the application of lint; but if cut away at once we may unite the lips of the incisions. The incisions are to be made direct, and if there be nothing redundant we may immediately sew them up. But, if owing to the size of the scrofulous swelling there be a redundancy of skin, having cut away a part of it like a myrtle-leaf, we may have recourse to sutures, and use the applications for recent wounds.

ON ANEURISM[5]

Aneurism is a tumour soft to the touch and yielding to the fingers, having its origin from blood and spirits. Galen says "an artery having become anastomosed (i.e., dilated) the affection is called an aneurism; it arises also from a wound of the same, when the skin that lies over it is cicatrized, but the wound in the artery remains, and neither unites nor is blocked up by flesh. Such affections are recognised by the pulsation of arteries; but, if compressed, the tumour disappears in so far, the substance which forms it returning back into the arteries." Thus Galen.—But we distinguish them from one another in this way: That formed from anastomosis of an artery appears longer, is deep seated, and when pressed upon by the fingers, a sort of sound is heard; whereas no noise is heard in the cases arising

5. *Ibid.*, Sec. 37, pp. 310–311.

from rupture, and these, moreover, are more rounded, and feel superficial. Those therefore which form in the armpits, groin, and neck, and those in other parts of the body, which are very large, we must decline operating upon, on account of the large-ness of the vessels. But those which occur in the extremities, the limbs, or the head, we operate upon thus. We make a straight longitudinal incision in the skin, and then having separated the lips with hooks, as we mentioned in the operation of angiology, and having dissected away the skin, and separated it with the instruments used for operations on membranes, we lay bare the artery, and passing a needle under it, and tying it with two ligatures, and having first divided the intermediate part of the artery with a lancet used for bleeding, and evacu-ated its contents, we have recourse to the suppurative treat-ment until the falling off of the ligatures. If the aneurism be occasioned by rupture of the artery, we must seize in the fingers along with the skin as much as possible of the aneurism, and then below what we hold in our hand we push a needle having a double thread, and after it has passed through we cut the double, and thus with the two threads we bind the tumour on this side and on that, as we mentioned for staphyloma. If any apprehension be entertained from the falling off of the liga-tures, we must push another needle entirely through, in the course of the first, having in like manner a double thread, and, cutting the noose into four pieces, we may bind the tumour. Or, having opened the tumour in the middle, after the evacuation of its contents, we cut away what is redundant of the skin, leav-ing what is secured with the ligatures, and applying an oblong compress soaked in wine and oil, we have recourse to the treat-ment by lint.

ON BRONCHOCELE[6] [GOITER]

A large round tumour forms on the neck from the inner parts, whence it obtains the appellation of bronchocele, of which there are two varieties, the steatomatous and the aneurismatical. The aneurismatical we judge of from the symptoms of aneurism, and abandon as hopeless, like all other aneurisms which it is dangerous to meddle with, as is the case most especially with those of the neck, owing to the size of the arteries.

The steatomatous we operate upon like steatomes in general, distinguishing and avoiding the vessels, in the same manner as we described for strumae.

6. *Ibid.*, Sec. 38, p. 314.

PART II

ALBUCASIS AND THE SURGERY OF
THE ARABIC PERIOD

CHAPTER 8

Albucasis (Eleventh Century)
and the Surgery of the Arabic Period

"Whatever I know, I owe solely to my assiduous reading of the books of the Ancients, to my desire to understand them and to appropriate this science; then I have added the observation and experience of my whole life. . . ."[1]

With the crumbling of the Roman Empire, Islam became the military and political power of the world, and the Mohammedan Empire assumed its cultural leadership, which it held until the Renaissance. In medicine, it became the repository of Greek and Roman knowledge. Many of the classic texts were translated into Syriac and thence into Arabic and so escaped total perdition. They were later translated into Latin, often in a corrupted and multilated state, to provide the basis for the reawakening of European medicine.

Arabic medicine contributed little to the treasure it inherited from antiquity; and surgery, in particular, stagnated. The passivity and fatalism of the Orient, together with the religious proscriptions against the touching of the dead body, and a timidity in the face of hemorrhage, combined to reduce surgery to an inferior status. Guy de Chauliac wrote some centuries later, "And one finds that until him [Avicenna] all were physicians and surgeons combined, but since then, whether because of delicacy or the too great a preoccupation in cures, surgery has been separated and relegated to the hands of mechanics."

Of the many books on medicine written in Arabic, only one, emanating from the Western Caliphate, treats surgery separately. It is the *Altasrif* (or "Collection") of Albucasis. This author was born in Moslem Spain in El-Zahra, a little village near Cordova, in the year 1013.[2] He became an important member of the Cordovan center of Islam and was highly esteemed as a physician and as a very able surgeon. He died in 1106.

The Surgery of Albucasis, which forms part of the encyclopedic *Altasrif,*

1. *La Chirurgie D'Abulcasis*, translated by Lucien Leclerc, Paris, J. B. Baillière, 1861, Book III, Introduction, p. 270.
2. There seems to be great variance over the dates given for the birth and death of Albucasis. An alternate date for his birth is 936 A.D., supported by Dr. Donald Campbell.

was published separately. Like most other books of the period, it is literally a "Collection" and taken almost bodily from the texts of the late Alexandrians, particularly from Paul of Aegina, although no mention is made of these authors. However, occasionally, Albucasis introduces case histories from his own wide practice. He is revealed, from these interpolations, as being cautious, judicious, and critical. His chapter on the removal of arrows contains an interesting series of unusually severe injuries which he successfully treated, often with imaginative and original methods. One other feature of this book is the large number of illustrations of surgical instruments which, together with the descriptive text, serve to clarify the operative techniques he described.

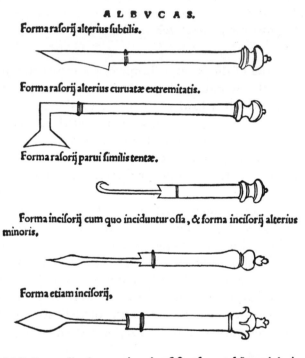

FIG. 9. Surgical instruments pictured by Albucasis. From: *Methodus medendi certa, clara et brevis . . . cum instrumentis . . . depictis. Autore ALBUCASE praestanti, ob excellentia artis opera medico.* Aesile ae per Henri cum Petrum [n.d.], p. 154.

According to Leclerc, who translated this book into French, Albucasis had little influence in the Moslem world. In Western Europe, however, he was very widely quoted. His book was translated into Latin by Gerard of Cremona within a century of his death, and it served as a basis for the early Italian and French surgical writings. Guy de Chauliac cites Albucasis close to two hundred times, and as late as the sixteenth century, William Harvey's teacher, Fabricius of Aquapendente, acknowledged his obligations to three earlier writers, Albucasis, Celsus, and Paul of Aegina.

In the Introduction to his book Albucasis gives a vivid picture of surgery in the Arabic period. He writes as follows:

"Surgery is no longer in honor in our country. In its actual decadence, it has disappeared, almost without leaving any traces. There remain some vestiges in the writings of the Ancients, but the transcriptions have corrupted them; error and confusion have overrun them, in a manner to render them unintelligible and useless.

"I have resolved to restore this science to life, and to consecrate this treatise to that purpose. I will proceed by way of explanation and demonstration, in curtailing that which is superfluous. I will give drawings of surgical instruments and cauteries; I will describe them and indicate the use of each of them.

"The reason one does not find skillful operators today is this: The art of medicine requires time; those who wish to practice it should first study anatomy, as Galen has written, to know the role of the organs, their form, their temperament, their relations and their divisions; to know the bones, the tendons and muscles, their number and their motion; the veins and arteries, and the regions through which they run. À propos of this, Hippocrates said: 'There are many physicians in name, but few in fact, particularly in the field of surgery.'

"If one disregards the knowledge of anatomy of which we have spoken, he necessarily falls into error and kills the patients. I have seen them boast of possessing this art, and having neither knowledge nor experience. I have seen an ignorant physician incise over a scrofulous tumor of the neck of a woman, open the cervical arteries and provoke such hemorrhage that the patient died in his hands. I have seen another doctor undertake the extraction of a stone in a very old man: the stone was huge; in performing the extraction, he removed a portion of the bladder wall,—the patient died in three days. I myself had been called to remove that stone, but its size and the condition of the patient made me decide not to attempt it. I have seen another, attached to the person of a ruler of the country and accredited as a physician, to whom they brought a young Negro with a fracture and laceration of the leg near the malleoli. In his ignorance he [the physician] hastened to apply a very tight bandage to the wound with compresses and splints, without permitting drainage from the wound. He left the patient so to himself for several days, forbidding him to remove the bandage. Finally, the foot and leg became swollen, and he was in danger of death. I was called; I hastened to remove the apparatus; he improved and the pain stopped. However, I was unable to control the corruption which had taken hold of the limb; it progressed and the patient died. I have also seen a physician open a cancerous tumor. The part ulcerated after several days, and the disease became aggravated. In effect, cancer, which is a special product of the atrabiliary humor (black bile) should not be attacked with a sharp instrument, at least not when it is so fixed in an organ that it cannot be radically excised.

"You know, my children, that surgical operations are divided into two classes: those that benefit the patient, and those that more often kill. Throughout wherever it is necessary, I will indicate in this book, those operations where there is danger and fear. It is necessary to be prudent and to abstain, not to give the ignorant a cause for malevolent comment. Conduct yourselves with reserve and caution: have gentleness and perseverance for the patients; follow the good road which leads to favorable and happy outcomes. Abstain from undertaking dangerous and difficult treatments. Avoid that which might injure your honor or your welfare: it is the better part for your reputation and more consistent with your interests in this world and the other. Galen has said in part: do not treat bad illnesses lest you pass for a bad doctor."[3]

The Surgery of Albucasis is divided into three books, the first of which is devoted to cauterization, a commentary on the premium placed by the Arabians on this form of therapy. The indications for the use of the cautery include all manner of diseases affecting all parts of the body. From the vantage point of modern knowledge, the whole strikes us as useless, senseless, and barbaric.

The second book covers all conditions amenable to surgical management other than fractures and dislocations. As was customary in early surgeries this includes a discussion of numerous ophthalmic conditions which assume a particular importance because of the frequency of eye disease in the Middle East. There is also a brief section on obstetrics, including normal and abnormal deliveries. In the introduction to this section, he writes:

"Before beginning, my children, know that the subject of this book

3. Ibid., loc. cit., pp. 5–7. Excerpts translated from the French by the authors.

is more serious than that of the first, which dealt with cauterization. It is necessary, therefore, to pay the closest attention. In effect, the operations which are presented in this chapter are often accompanied by an effusion of blood, of blood which is the supporter of life; that it includes the division of vessels, opening of tumors, puncture of abscesses, dressing of wounds, extraction of arrows, incisions for the removal of calculi and other operations of this type, all things in which the outcome may perhaps be uncertain, dangerous and frequently the cause of death.

"I recommend, therefore, that you do not undertake doubtful cures. In effect, in these operations you attack patients already tormented by the disease; they have suffered to the point where death is a matter of indifference to them, or even a relief since their suffering is intense and prolonged.

"In those serious illnesses in which the prognosis is fatal, you will find patients who will offer their fortunes for a hope of salvation, since their disease is mortal. Abstain completely from consenting to those who come to you with these conditions. Lest your prudence be overcome by cupidity, never embark on any such course until after you are assured that it will result in nothing but good.

"Before treating any of your patients, be sure to understand your subject and the methods of restoring his health.

"It is thus that you will attain consideration, glory, celebrity and honors. May God, my children, inspire you to a healthy direction and not deprive you of uprightness and of His graces. These favors are in His hands; there is no God but He!"[4]

The text of this book is taken largely from Paul of Aegina, and little of value is added. Needless to say, surgery is avoided wherever possible, and the cautery preferred to the knife if at all feasible. Bleeding, cupping, and leeching are important therapeutic measures. Wounds are treated, in general, by the application of ointments and the encouragement of suppuration. Speaking of hernia, he writes, "The treatment of these affections with sharp instruments is perilous; it is to be avoided as far as possible."

The third book deals with fractures and dislocations. The status of this branch of therapy is revealed in the Introduction to this section, which is appended below. One may assume, therefore, that it was intended to serve as a primer or compend of the Greek texts, and that nothing of significant value has been added. The zeal of Albucasis in his efforts to improve the quality of surgical care and, particularly, to teach the younger practitioners stands forth clearly, as do also his high ethical and moral standards.

4. *Ibid.*, *loc. cit.*, Book II, Introduction, pp. 58–59.

ʕ   ʕ   ʕ   OF THE REDUCTION (OF FRACTURES)[5]

ʕ   ʕ   ʕ   The third book is often indispensable in the practice of medicine: it is devoted to the treatment of fractures and dislocations
of the bones.

Know, my children, that this part of medical science is
claimed by ignorant physicians, by laymen who have never
cast an eye on the books of the Ancients and have never read
a word from them. Also this branch of science has fallen, among
us, to the point where I have not been able to meet anyone
who excels in it. Whatever I know, I owe solely to my assiduous reading of the books of the Ancients, to my desire to understand them and to appropriate the science; then I have added
the observation and experience of my whole life; finally, I have
composed for you this book which contains all my knowledge
and all my experience. I have adapted it to your intelligence,
I have disencumbered it of all superfluous digression, and have
made it as concise and as clear as possible. I have frequently
given drawings of the instruments used, to make it still clearer,
as I have done in the two previous books.

There is no strength but in God, most exalted, most powerful.

ON THE EXTRACTION OF ARROWS[6]

I will bring you several of my observations relative to arrows
to guide you in your practice.

For then, a man was wounded by an arrow at the angle of
the eye and close to the root of the nose. I extracted it from the
opposite side below the lobule of the ear. The man recovered
without sustaining any complication on the part of the eye!

I extracted another from a Jew, which had penetrated into
the orbital cavity from below the lower lid: it had imbedded
itself to the point that I was unable to take hold of it except
for the little end by which it was attached to the shaft. It was
a large arrow, shot by a Turkish bow, of iron, blunt and smooth,
and having no barbs. The Jew recovered and had no complications in the eye.

I extracted another from the throat of a Christian. It was an
Arabian arrow with barbs. I incised over it, between the jugular
veins: it had penetrated deeply into the throat; I operated with
precaution and I succeeded in extracting it. The Christian was
saved and recovered.

5. *Ibid.*, *loc. cit.*, Book III, Introduction, p. 270.
6. *Ibid.*, *loc. cit.*, Chapter 96, pp. 238–241.

I removed another arrow which had had penetrated into the abdomen of a man whom I believed to be lost. However, after some thirty days his condition had not changed; I incised over the arrow, and I did so well that I withdrew it without the patient feeling any effects since.

I have seen someone who received an arrow in the back. The wound scarred over, and seven years later the arrow came out through the buttock.

I have seen a woman who had received an arrow in the abdomen. The arrow remained there and the wound cicatrized. Nevertheless, she experienced no discomfort or pain, and missed no time whatever from her usual occupation.

I have seen a man into whose face an arrow had penetrated. The wound cicatrized and the arrow remained without the subject suffering much. I have seen several cases of this sort.

I have also extracted an arrow from one of the officers of the Sultan. It had entered through the middle of the nose and inclined a little to the right: It had so deeply embedded itself that it had completely disappeared. I was called to care for him three days after the accident. I found the wound very narrow; I explored it with a fine stylet, but felt nothing. However, the patient experienced distress and pain to the right, below the ear. I thought that was the arrow. I therefore applied cataplasms made of digestive and attractive substances, hoping to myself that the region would swell, so that I would have signs of the arrow, and would be able to incise over it. But nothing happened to indicate where it had lodged. I continued to apply the cataplasms for several days, and nothing new occurred. In the meantime, the wound cicatrized and the patient continued to despair of its extraction for some time, when, one day, the arrow could be felt in the nose. I took part and applied, for several days, an irritant and caustic medicament, of a sort that the wound opened.

I explored it and felt the small end where it had been attached to the shaft. I continued to enlarge the opening by the application of caustic until I could see the end of the arrow. It was about four months that I had been treating the patient. Finally, when the wound was large enough so that I was able to introduce a forceps and I pulled and was able to move it, but did not succeed in withdrawing it. I did not stop, however, using all the means, all the artifices, and all the instruments until, one day, having taken hold of it with an excellent pincer which I have described at the end of this chapter, I removed it and dressed the wound. Several physicians claimed that the cartilage would not reunite: nevertheless, it reunited and the wound cicatrized, the subject recovered perfectly without experiencing any discomfort.

CAUTERIZATION IN ARTERIAL HEMORRHAGE[7]

One frequently sees arterial hemorrhage supervene following rupture of an artery in injuries produced by external causes, in the opening of a tumor, in the cauterization of an organ, and finally in other similar circumstances, and it is difficult to arrest the flow.

If you should find yourself in such a case, promptly apply the hand to the opening in the vessel, press with the index finger until the bleeding stops under your finger, and there is no further flow. Put an assortment of olivary cauteries on the fire, large and small, and blow on them until they are well heated. Take one, large or small, depending upon the condition of the part in which the artery is ruptured: apply the cautery to the artery itself, after having quickly removed the finger, and keep it there until the bleeding is arrested. If, on lifting the finger, the blood spurts and your cautery has cooled, take another one promptly from those you have put on the fire. Continue thus in applying them successively until the blood no longer escapes.

Be careful in cauterizing, not to injure the nerves in the region, for this would be an additional malady for the patient.

Know that arterial hemorrhage, particularly if the artery is large, cannot be stopped except by one of the four following methods:

By cauterization, as we have said.

By division of the artery when it is not completely severed. In effect, when an artery is divided, its ends retract and the bleeding stops.

By a firm ligature.

By the application of remedies that have the property of arresting bleeding, aided by a compressive bandage.

Those who attempt to arrest hemorrhage by the application of bandages, compresses, caustics or any other method, will not stop it at all, or only very rarely.

In case of hemorrhage in the absence of a doctor and medica-

7. *Ibid., loc. cit.*, Book I, Chapter 56, pp. 56–57.

ments, one should hasten to apply the index finger to the opening of the wound, as we have said: he should press firmly until the hemorrhage stops; without ever removing the finger; cold water, as cold as possible, should be poured on the wound and on the artery, and this continued until the blood thickens, coagulates, and ceases to flow.

PART III

EARLY STIRRINGS

CHAPTER 9

Salernitan Surgery

"Use three Physicions still; first Doctor Quiet, *next Doctor* Merry-man, *and Doctor* Diet."[1]

The first stirring in the reawakening of medicine in Western Europe took place in Salerno, in southern Italy. Beautifully situated on the Gulf of Salerno and blessed with a pleasant climate, Salerno had long been famed as a health resort. It is reported that as early as the ninth century physicians practicing there had so wide a reputation that they drew students from great distances. Ailing royalty came for medical care, and crusaders, ill, worn, and wounded, stopped there for rest and healing and rehabilitation. When private instruction was replaced by organized teaching is not known and the origins of the "School" of Salerno are lost in legend. It is certain, however, that from its very beginning the School was a lay organization in contrast to the contemporary and subsequent universities, almost all of which were under ecclesiastic control. After the Norman conquest of southern Italy, in the twelfth century, the School of Salerno expanded rapidly and a significant medical literature flowed from it.

This flowering of the *civitas Hippocratica*, as Salerno came to be known, was due in considerable part to the wisdom of its rulers. Roger II of Sicily introduced in Salerno the first system of examination for doctors (1140); furthermore both he and his grandson, Emperor Frederic II (of the Holy Roman Empire), bestowed on this School the sole right to approve for practice all physicians and surgeons in their domains. The latter ruler, moreover, in 1240, established the first regulations concerning medical education which not only defined the length and content of the medical curriculum and the nature of the examinations but also made a postgraduate practical year mandatory before the conferring of a medical license.

The inclusion of surgery in this medical legislation was of special importance because it tended to counteract, to some extent, the separation which had

1. *The School of Salernum, Regimen Sanitatis Salernitanum*, the English version by Sir John Harrington, New York, Paul B. Hoeber, Inc., 1920, p. 75.

taken place between the two branches of healing. It will be recalled that in the classical period medicine and surgery were one. Arabic medicine, for reasons stated, shunned surgery; and the practitioner of the latter art became a person of lesser esteem. This breach was gradually widened during the later medieval period to reach its maximum in the twelfth century. A number of factors combined to bring about this development. One which Diepgen[2] considers of paramount importance was the prohibition of the practice of surgery by the clergy. According to this distinguished historian, the root of this interdict was that, by canon law, anyone who had caused the death of a person was forever barred from the priesthood, and this included the fatal outcome of a surgical operation.

The strictures against the practice of surgery by the clergy were extended to the lay physicians who took over the teaching and practice of medicine; and the vacuum created became filled with surgical practitioners who had no formal scholastic education. Thus, a deepening cleavage resulted which affected the social and economic standing of the physicians and surgeons, as well as their training and duties. The inferior position of the surgeons is indicated in the medical legislation of Frederic II in that the course of study required of them was considerably shorter than that required of the physicians. However, the surgeon definitely came within the framework of medicine and a number of Salernitan surgeons chose to take the physician's full training before seeking instruction in the practice of surgery.

Several streams of medical knowledge converged to form the source of Salernitan surgery. In one small part of Southern Europe the tradition of Greek surgery persisted without interruption. This small enclave of Greek surgery, as it was called by Sudhoff,[3] flourished in Calabria, at the very heel of the Italian boot, close enough for awareness of its surgical achievements to reach Salerno. In this region, it seems, operation for cataract, urethrotomy for stricture, radical hernia operations, and lithotomy continued to be practiced with increasing skill for many generations. It is probable that from its very beginning the Salernitan School maintained contact with the Calabrian surgeons and absorbed in its own practice the techniques that had been handed down by oral transmission. Another, and most important pathway, was the translation from the Arabic writers into Latin. The first of the great translators was the Carthagenian, Constantinus Africanus (1020–1087), whose *Pantegni* formed the chief source of Salernitan surgical knowledge. This was a translation of the *al-Maleki* or "Royal Book" of Ali Abbas, a Moslem physician and encyclopedist of the eleventh century. After Constantine, a number of other translators made the works of Greek and Arabic writers available in Latin.

2. Paul Diepgen: *Geschichte der Medizin*, Berlin, Walter de Gruyter & Co., 1949, Vol. 1, p. 227.
3. J. L. Pagel: *Einführung in die Geschichte der Medizin*, second edition by Karl Sudhoff, Berlin, S. Karger, 1915, pp. 169–170.

Soon after the stimulus afforded by these sources, the Salernitan physicians brought out, in rapid succession, a number of books, covering all aspects of medical knowledge. The most familiar of these is the famed *Regimen,* which was a popular guide for healthful living. Far more important, however, were the early surgical works because they represented the fruits of personal observations to a far greater extent than did the tradition-bound books on medicine. An important element in this development was the study of anatomy which had languished in both Western and Eastern Europe for more than a millenium. Although the earlier Salernitan anatomists lacked the courage and the materials to perform human dissection, their animal anatomies, especially that of the pig, reveal the first revival of the ancient desire for a personal observation of nature. Here it is also worthy of note that the medical legislation of Frederic II expressly sanctioned the use of anatomical dissection as an essential part of the medical and especially the surgical, training.

The earliest surgical book to emanate from Salerno is known as the "Bamberg Surgery." This work was never printed, but was perpetuated in manuscript form, the first copies of which to be discovered were found in the Royal Library in Bamberg, from which its name was taken. The oldest of the manuscripts as yet found dates back to the middle of the twelfth century. It is believed that this work represents a compilation of gradually accumulated notes and passages, by a number of authors, and over a considerable period of time.

From this apparent mode of development it must be expected that the "Bamberg Surgery" is not a well-ordered, systematic work. The individual passages readily reveal the sources from which they were taken and, among these, Paul of Aegina and Albucasis predominate. The work is eminently practical as a guide to treatment, including operative technique, and these sections contain shrewd observations based on personal experience. A wide range of subject matter is covered. Of particular interest is the formula of the "soporific sponge," mention of which has been found in earlier pharmacological tracts, but never before in a book on surgery. In the treatment of head wounds the use of oily substances in compound fractures of the skull was avoided because of the danger of inducing meningeal inflammations. This was contrary to usual practice and, again, probably reflects personal experience. Suture of the intestine over a hollow tube, and the manufacture of an apparently effective truss to retain inguinal hernia for the patient who refused to be operated upon, and the administration of burnt seaweed and sponge in the treatment of goiter are among the amazingly astute contributions.

After the "Bamberg Surgery," three significant surgical texts subsequently came from Salerno. The "Surgery of Roger" (Ruggiero Frugardi) appeared in 1170, about twenty years after the completion of the compilation of the Bamberg manuscript. This is a much more sophisticated and well-organized text, dealing systematically with the entire subject of surgery, logically arranged in order from head to foot. It is an independent work , which borrows little that is recognizable form the earlier Bamberg text. Castiglioni called it "the outstanding surgical work of Western Europe for more than two centuries." Its sources go back principally to the Byzantine compilations of Greek knowledge, but it is enriched greatly be newer, local empirical observations.

A few examples will suffice to illustrate the quality of these contributions. In wounds of the abdomen with protrusion of the viscera, the surfaces of which have become cold and dry from exposure to the air, Roger advised that the abdomen of an animal be opened and its contents placed over the exposed structures. What more physiologically correct application could be devised than the fresh, normal peritoneal surfaces of a living animal?

In the diagnosis of bladder stone Roger recommends a bimanual examination even at that early date. "If there is stone in the bladder, this certain method is to be used: . . . two fingers of the right hand are introduced into the anus, and with a thrust of the left hand compressing above the pecten [pubis], the bladder is elevated with the fingers which have been introduced, and manipulated throughout: and if something round, hard and heavy is encountered it proves that a stone is in the bladder; if it is softy and fleshy that is felt, then it is a fleshy mass that obstructs the urine." Such a fleshy structure occluding the bladder neck would in all probability, be a prostatic enlargement. This observation antedates by centuries the demonstration of the role played by prostatic hypertrophy in urinary obstructions.

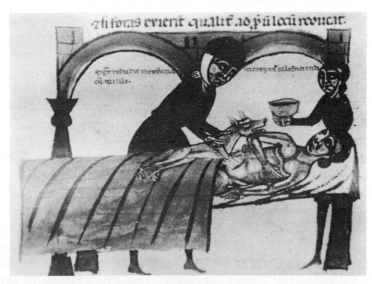

Fig. 10. The master reduces prolapsed abdominal viscera by applying a freshly opened abdomen of an animal. Reproduced from: *Magistri Salernitani nondum editi*, Atlante, by Piero Giacosa. Torino, Fratelli Bocca, 1901. Tavola 27.

FIG. 11. *Left*, the master cuts for stone. Reproduced from: *Magistri Salernitani nondum editi*, Atlante, by Piero Giacosa, Torino, Fratelli Bocca, 1901, Tavola 27. *Right*, the master operates for hernia (in deep head-down position). Reproduced from: *Magistri Salernitani nondum editi*, Atlante, by Piero Giacosa. Torino, Fratelli Bocca, 1901. Tavola 27.

The other two important surgical texts are largely commentaries and additions to the Surgery of Roger. These are the works of Roland of Parma (Rolando Capelluti), who was one of Roger's most distinguished pupils, and a later "Surgery of the Four Masters," which was the work of four Salernitan physicians. Through these commentators the teachings of Roger became widely disseminated and provided the basis for the tremendous growth of surgery throughout Italy, France, and even England.

ၜ ၜ ၜ   ON MANIFEST FRACTURE OF THE SKULL WITH SMALL
ၜ ၜ ၜ   EXTERNAL WOUND[4]

If the fracture of the skull is large but the superficial wound small so that you cannot be completely certain of the extent of the fracture, a finger is to be inserted in the wound and a diligent investigation made, because there is no better method for recognizing a fracture of the skull than digital palpation.

4. Passage from Sudhoff's text of Roger, *Stud. Gesch. Med.*, Part 2, p. 160, as translated by George W. Corner in "The Rise of Medicine at Salerno in the Twelfth Century," *Annals of Medical History*, Vol. 3, (N.S.) No. 1, January 1931, p. 12.

After you have made out the extent of the fracture in this way you should incise the small scalp wound with a razor in the form of a cross and separate the scalp from the cranium with a raspatory, and if there is not too much blood in the field of operation you should remove any fragments of bone with the small forceps. If, however, the hemorrhage is sufficient to prevent this, you may change your method until you have controlled it, after which you will be able to remove the fragments successfully. With a probe thoroughly and carefully insert a cloth between the dura mater and the cranium and proceed as we said in the previous section. Outside the cranium the wounded scalp is pressed together and the whole wound bound up with a linen cloth previously soaked in white of egg. A pad of cloth filled with feathers is laid over it and bound on according to the region of the head involved, and changed every morning or evening. If, when you dress the wound, you find the flaps swollen, it is a good sign; if, however, they are shrunken and mortified, it is a bad sign. In the course of healing when you find that the skull is entirely healed the dressing is to be reduced in size and the skin flaps are forced back to their proper situation.

ON THE CURE OF GOITER BY INCISION[5]

If the goiter is single, with the aid of a hot iron we put in one seton lengthwise and another from side to side and apply over them a cloth soaked in egg or in lard. Every day, morning and evening, the setons are drawn toward the outside until finally the flesh is cut through. When this is done if any part of the goiter remains, powder it with powder of asphodel and purified in this way the wound will heal like other wounds. If the tumor is not provided with too many arteries it may be removed by grasping it firmly in the hands and cutting the skin carefully lengthwise. The tumor is grasped with a hook and the skin is dissected away. A finger is then inserted through the wound and the goiter removed entirely with its capsule. The wound is lightly dressed with a linen cloth. If the hemorrhage is excessive we apply those remedies which have been described above for this purpose in the chapter on arrow wounds in the neck. These remedies are continued for three days. (Styptic drugs.) Afterward if any of the tumor remains, apply powder of asphodel,

5. Passage from Sudhoff's text of Roger, *Stud. Gesch. Med.*, Part 2, p. 198, as translated by George W. Corner, *loc. cit.*, pp. 12–13.

following it by egg, and then proceed as in other wounds. The greatest care should be taken to avulse the capsule of the goiter completely so that nothing is left, for if the slightest part remains the patient relapses. When the wound is entirely clean, it may be dusted with red powder and sutured as we have described elsewhere, and it will be cured. If however, the goiter is very large and the patient weak or elderly, in our judgment it is best to refrain from this treatment. These large goiters usually have several lobes which make them difficult to dissect away, and we avoid treating them with a hot iron for fear of injuring the arteries or nerves. When, however, it becomes necessary to treat these patients by surgery we tie them to a table and have them held firmly in order that we may see exactly what we are doing.

CHAPTER 10

Theodoric (1205–1296?)

"Indeed, above all else, a wound must be made clean."[1]

The influence of the School of Salerno spread northward in Italy. Bologna, with its great university which had been founded in the twelfth century, assumed the dominant position as Salerno declined. The founder of the Bologna School was Hugh of Lucca (ca. 1160–1257), a bold and creative surgeon and teacher who left no written record of his life and work. His achievements are known to us from the writings of his disciple, Theodoric (1205–1296?), who was thought by some to have been his son.

Theodoric was one of the small group of clerical surgeons who were university-trained in medicine as well as in surgery. This combination could be found in a few places only and at rare intervals in the medieval world. Small in numbers, they added mightily to the stature and luster of surgery, and their ranks include most of the important figures in early European surgery— Hugh of Lucca, Bruno, Theodoric, Arnold of Villanova, William of Salicet, Lanfranc, Pitard, and the two founders of French surgery, Henri de Mondeville and Guy de Chauliac.

Theodoric was a Dominican Friar who studied in Bologna, traveled widely, and visited many famous physicians. As the student and disciple of Hugh of Lucca he expounded the theories and practices of his illustrious master. Although a surgeon he became Bishop of Bitonto in 1262, Bishop of Cervia in 1266, and was confessor of Pope Innocent VI. He continued to live in Bologna, where he attained renown as a surgeon and amassed a considerable fortune.

The *Chirurgia* of Theodoric, which was completed in 1267, is built about the teachings of Hugh. The great contribution of this master was the "dry" treatment of wounds. Growing out of comments by Galen, which were distorted in the translations of the Arabs, had come the doctrine that suppuration was necessary to the healing of wounds. If this failed to occur spontaneously, it was promoted by medieval surgeons through probing, packing and dressing

---

1. *The Surgery of Theodoric*, translated from the Latin by Eldridge Campbell and James Colton, Appleton-Century-Crofts, Inc., New York, 1955, Vol. I, Chapter 11, p. 137.

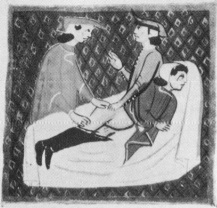

Fig. 12. Reproduced from the Frontispiece of *The Surgery of Theodoric*, translated from the Latin by Eldridge Campbell and James Colton, New York, Appleton-Century-Crofts, Inc., Vol. I.

with greasy ointments. This concept, later characterized by the phrase "laudable pus," held sway until the time of Lister, except for the convictions of a few independent thinkers, notably Hugh, Theordoric, and Henri de Mondeville. "For it is not necessary," wrote Theodoric, "as Roger and Roland have written, as many of their disciples teach, and as all modern surgeons profess, that pus should be generated in wounds. No error can be greater than this. Such a practice is indeed to hinder nature, to prolong the disease and to prevent the conglutination and consolidation of the wound."

Hugh is revealed to us as a bold and imaginative surgeon. Although he follows the dictates of Galen, he is not slavish in his adherence and at times has the temerity to disagree with the Galenic doctrine. Among other things, he used the "soporific sponge" to induce narcosis before operations, recognized ptyalism as a symptom of overtreatment with mercury, and improved the management of certain fractures. His great contribution, however, was the insistence on primary union of wounds. Unfortunately, and to the detriment of wound surgery, this teaching was not accepted for many centuries.

The "Surgery" of Theodoric gives evidence of the decline in medicine from the heights it had achieved in the Graeco-Roman period. The doctrine of the humors had become so all-embracing that all changes, even those occurring in wounds, were interpreted in terms of humoral dyscrasia, and treatment was correspondingly oriented. Instead of the clear and lucid analysis of the Greeks, the surgical precepts are buried in unintelligible jargon. Moreover, under the influence of the Arab writers cautery is used wherever possible, and the scalpel only as a last resort. Even Theodoric's management of wounds, so revolutionary for its time, shows this influence. Wound coaptation is achieved by bandaging, and sutures are used only when approximation is not otherwise possible. The polypharmacy is confusing, often irrational, and sometimes nauseating. Even texts of prayers and exorcisms are included to accompany the extraction of missiles and as part of the management of cranial injuries. Despite all these shortcomings, however, the book has considerable merit for it contains the first faint suggestions of recovery from the depths of medieval stagnation. Independence of thought and observation are evident. Although it still leans heavily on the authoritarian doctrines of Galen and the Arabs, it is the first step in the long upward path that surgery was destined to follow. As such, it must be counted among the significant landmarks in surgical progress.

WOUNDS ANYWHERE IN THE BODY[2]

In whatever part of the body a cut may have occurred, let everything be done in order, according to the rules laid down for wounds in the scalp and face. Indeed, above all else a wound must be made clean. Secondly, having brought the lips of the wound together, they should be replaced accurately in the position which they had in their natural state; if necessary, they should be held there by stitches taken in accordance with the size of the wound. Let the size and depth of the wound determine the closeness and depth of the stitches. For let the physician make no mistake; as has already been said many times, he should be prudent and attentive to every detail. After the suturing has been properly done and the dressings have been carefully arranged, let the wound be bound up skillfully as the position and condition of the part require, that is to say, so that neither the stitches nor the dressings can be disturbed at all. And, just as we have often said before, do not undo the dressing until the third, or fourth, or fifth day if no pain occurs. Afterwards let the dressings be changed every third day unless too much putridity should occur in the wound, in which case it should be changed every day, observing the aforementioned directions. And always, whenever the dressing is changed, by pressing gently upon the wound with a little wine-soaked tow you may express any retained bloody matter. Afterwards let it be bound up according to the aforesaid method and let it be kept thus until the patient has completely recovered. And if proud flesh should become excessive on a wound, as has been said before, put on the green ointment or something similar, for as long as you see that it is necessary.

2. *Ibid.*, pp. 137–138.

THE SOPORIFIC SPONGE AND SUBLIMATES[3]

The composition of a savour to be made by surgeons, according to Master Hugo, is as follows: Take of opium, and the juice of unripe mulberry, hyoscyamus, the juice of spurge flax, the juice of leaves of mandragora, juice of ivy, juice of climbing ivy, of lettuce seed, and of the seed of the lapathum which was hard, round berries, and of the shrub hemlock, one ounce of each. Mix these all together in a brazen vessel, and then put into it a new sponge. Boil all together out under the sun during the dog days, until all is consumed and cooked down into the sponge. As often as there is need, you may put this sponge into hot water for an hour, and apply it to the nostrils until the subject for operation falls asleep. Then the surgery may be performed and when it is completed, in order to wake him up, soak another sponge in vinegar and pass it frequently under his nostrils.

Likewise the juice of the roots of hay may be put under the nostrils, and the patient will soon be aroused.

3. *The Surgery of Theodoric*, translated from the Latin by Eldridge Campbell and James Colton, Appleton-Century-Crofts, Inc., New York, 1960, Vol. II, Chapter 8, pp. 212–213.

CHAPTER 11

William of Salicet
(ca. 1210–1277)

". . . For the wise physician does not commit any wickedness, he does not sow or excite discord among the relatives of the patient, he does not give any advice that is not asked for, he does not employ people who have a bad reputation or a vice which is displeasing to honest persons."[1]

The Middle Ages merged gradually into the Renaissance. The time of this transition has been associated with the intervention of the printing press and the fall of Constantinople with the resulting migration of scholars to the West, with the discovery of new parts of the world and the concomitant broadening of the physical and intellectual horizons. All these and numerous other events cover a period of many years but largely they occurred in the fifteenth and sixteenth centuries. It was at this period also that medicine experienced its Renaissance. In a few fields of human thought and endeavor, however, the awakening came much earlier than in others. Surgery experienced its rebirth at the time of the building of the great cathedrals and the founding of the universities, at least two centuries before that of medicine. After the first stirrings in Salerno which have been described earlier, there appeared in rapid succession in the thirteenth and fourteenth centuries a number of remarkable Italian, and later French, writers who revivified surgery, and who also made significant contributions to the medical sciences.

The men of the surgical Renaissance had much in common with one another, as will become evident in the following biographical sketches. They were, in the main, university-educated in both medicine and surgery, because the Italian institutions of higher learning, unlike those of other countries at that period, included surgery in their curricula. Although they practiced and wrote in both fields, their greater interest and most important contributions were in the domain of surgery. The movement began in southern Italy, swept up the

1. *Chirurgie de Guillaume de Salicet* par Paul Pifteau, Imprimerie Saint-Cyprien, Toulouse, 1898, *Prologue*, pp. 1–6.

peninsula and into France, and extended its influences to England and the Low Countries.

William of Salicet was among the earliest of this group, after those transitional figures, Bruno, Hugh of Lucca, and Theodoric, and probably the most influential. Little is known of his origins other than that he was born in the early years of the thirteenth century in the village of Saliceto, in Piacenza, a province in Lombardy. He had obviously had a good education, which included university training in medicine and surgery, and he was a cleric as were all those who attended the universities at that time. In his writings he speaks of an extensive experience, both in military and hospital practice. He taught surgery at the famed University of Bologna, and later was city physician at Verona. He was the author of a book on internal medicine and, toward the end of a long and rewarding career, he composed his own work on surgery, which bears the date 1275. This latter work stands as his greatest monument. His death followed shortly after the completion of this work.

GUILLAUME DE SALICET
D'après le bas-relief de Ferrarini, à Plaisance
Et la photographie de Giuseppe Caldi.

FIG. 13. From: *Chirurgie de Guillaume de Salicet* by Paul Pifteau, Toulouse, 1898

William of Salicet's "Surgery" is the first complete book on the subject to have emerged after the Middle Ages. It is a systematic treatise on all phases of surgery then known, and is the first to include a book on anatomy to serve the needs of the surgeon. William initiated the practice of reporting cases observed and treated by himself and indulged only infrequently in the common practice of quoting from the classics. Because of his familiarity with the entire field of healing he deplored the separation of surgery from medicine, and was instrumental in bringing back the scalpel into surgery in place of the ubiquitous cautery iron. He was a careful observer, describing dropsy as a sequel to contracted kidneys, and ascribing lesions of the penis to venereal contagion, for which he advised prophylactic cleansing of the penis after coitus and repeated ablutions if with an infected woman. His most distinguished pupil was Lanfranc, the man who brought the fruits of the Italian surgical Renaissance to France.

In the Introduction to his *Cyrurgia* he gives a detailed description of the approved conduct of the surgeon, as well as of the assistants and the patients, which was reiterated more or less unchanged by many of the subsequent authors. Speaking with equal authority as a physician and surgeon, he is keenly aware of the role played by psychic influences in the recovery from disease or operation. "Those who practice this art should . . . acquiesce to the wishes of the patients and conform to them, if they do not in any way result in disadvantage to his operations, and to comfort the patient by gentle actions, soft words, agreeable and proper, and promise him cure in all cases even though they are hopeless; and the operating physician himself remains convinced that there is no chance for health in such an infirmity . . . . For the mind of the patient derives, from such discourse and promises, a secret influence and a great disposition by which nature acquires vigor and resistance against the disease. That is why there will result an action more powerful than that which can be produced by all the efforts of the physician with his instruments and even his medicines, an action such that it routs the illness."[2]

William, like Hippocrates, had great faith in the healing powers of nature, and considered the physician to be her assistant or agent. Speaking of the role of immoral conduct on the part of the surgeon, he writes," . . . For the lack in the success of the operation might stem from that: the confidence of the patient is weakened by the bad opinion which he might conceive, and the physician finds himself diminished in his estimation. The action of the effort of nature which usefully supports the action of the physician is equally diminished by this deed, and the effort of the physician can but end in frustration. For it is this effort of nature which heals the disease and not at all the doctor, if this virtue does not intervene. It is nature, indeed, which effects all things, but the physician is her minister."[3]

2. *Ibid.* Excerpts translated from the French by the authors.
3. *Ibid.*

The text of the "Surgery" is divided into five books, the contents of which were announced by the author as follows: "The first treatise will contain all the illnesses manifestly of internal causes, from head to feet. The second will comprise all wounds and contusions which are inflicted on all parts, from head to feet. The third will comprise the "algebra,"[4] that is to say, the restoration which is proper to effect for fractured bones and dislocations. The fourth will have for its object the general anatomy of the parts and their forms, considerations with which one must preoccupy oneself in incisions and cauterizations. The fifth encompasses the cauteries which are employed on the parts, the forms of the instruments and those of all the parts. Finally, the medicaments necessary and useful to this art according to each operation."[5]

Of the very many observations in the first book which are of interest to the surgeon are William of Salicet's comments on cancer of the breast, which are quoted below. Then, regarding hernia, he writes: ". . . And if you were to be assured of this manner of opening, then permit the testicle to redescend to its place, and do not dream in any fashion of extirpating it, as do some stupid and ignorant doctors who know nothing; but take the nerve [the spermatic cord] itself and the conduit through which the intestines descend to the place which the testicle occupies [the sac], which canal is called didymus or oscheum [scrotum], and tie completely this conduit and nerve with a fine, four-fold thread of wool or linen, at the two ends of this nerve and conduit, both at the inferior and superior parts and in a manner that a distance of one finger remains between the two ligatures, and that this space and distance are incised in their middle, transversely, in their totality. . . ."[6]

Salicet is thus the first author since Celsus to reject removal of the testicle as an essential part of the operation for hernia. Similar shrewd observations are to be gleaned from the remainder of this remarkable work which must be read in its entirety to be fully appreciated. Standing as he does at the transition from medieval to Renaissance surgery, the author merits a high place among those who have contributed to the evolution of surgery.

ꙮ ꙮ ꙮ   SURGERY OF WILLIAM OF SALICET[7]

ꙮ ꙮ ꙮ   Good Reader, I propose to publish for you a book on manual surgical operation, for the purpose of giving full satisfaction to your needs and to those of your colleagues. You must know that suitable rectification of this art cannot be made except

4. William of Salicet uses the word "algebra" in the literal sense of the Arabic root *al-jabr*: reduction of parts to a whole, reunion of parts, bonesetting. This is derived from *jabara*, to bind together.

5. *Chirurgie de Guillaume, loc. cit.*

6. *Ibid.*, pp. 130–131.

7. *Ibid. Prologue*, pp. 1–6.

by the practice and performance; for the rectification of all operative art can only be made in this manner and by this means. Because of that, it appears right to me to proceed in this part of my teaching according to what the operative experience and practice have taught me over a long time, and to give you, in my lessons, of numerous examples taken from my personal practice. I will divide the work into five parts, and will dedicate first the particular chapters to each subject, so that it will be easier to find that which one seeks. But before arriving at the object itself, I will write a chapter in which I will establish the definition of surgery, and will specify several opinions useful and necessary for the operations, for the assistants, and for the patients, to the end that the outcome that we anticipate shall be attained in a better and more worthy fashion. But in order that I myself shall be able to achieve this suitably, and be able to satisfy your needs effectively, I ceaselessly implore Divine Grace.

Thus, the first treatise will contain all the illnesses manifestly of internal causes, from head to feet. The second will comprise all wounds and contusions which are inflicted on all parts, from head to feet. The third will comprise the "algebra," that is to say, the restoration which is proper to effect for fractured bones and dislocations. The fourth will have for its object the general anatomy of the parts and their forms, considerations with which one must preoccupy oneself in incisions and cauterizations. The fifth encompasses the cauteries which are employed on the parts, the forms of the instruments and those of all the parts. Finally, the medicaments necessary and useful to this art according to each operation.

WHAT SURGERY IS, AND THE CONDUCT OF THE PHYSICIAN IN THE PRESENCE OF THE PATIENT

Surgery is a science which teaches the rules and procedures for manual operations on the flesh, nerves and bone of man. One should not believe that such an operation in itself, which is done manually constitutes surgery, in view of the fact that it is one of the special sciences which does not exist but by the action of intelligence, the object of which is well indicated and determined, and which one cannot divide without changing it. Now, such a given operation, taken alone, is a part of the whole and the divisible, and thus any single operation does not constitute surgery, which is one of the various sciences included in medicine. But the particular operation is subject to surgery, which is a science, as any particular is subject to the general. For otherwise one would know nothing of the method, of the reason or the manner of operating; the method being not at all established, if a particular operation is independent of the general operative rules established by science which is the same as intelligence. So that it would seem (and it is true) that one could possess this science without ever having operated in it. This science conforms to the others which are bound to the operative principles and the particular operation in a particular case; thus many practice the operative art who work contrary to all reason and without motive and even in a defective fashion, as the ignorant men who have only learned to work from other ignorant persons and never from learned masters; who have never studied anything in the world of the forms, the proportions and the disposition of the parts, nor the signs of their diseases, and who are unable to perceive, and do not even suspect anything beyond the particular fact that strikes their senses, and they thus end a useless life because of their ignorance of the principles necessary to this art. It is with good reason that he is reputed to be a better doctor, who best learns to adapt or not, or to combine the general principles in a particular case. From this it is not necessary to conclude, however, that science is not in the observation of the isolated case, and that all of operative science receives its confirmation outside of practice and of the operation.

Three things are principally necessary for those who, in this science, operate according to art. The first is that the surgeon should be entirely [attentive] to the patient in the examination and disposition of the condition of the injured part, thereby to the cause of the ailment, and not commit the least error; for, otherwise, this science is turned to derision, and the surgeon does not at all pursue, by his operation, a result worthy of praise. Those who practice this art should, in addition, acquiesce to the wishes of the patients and conform to them, if they do not in any way result in disadvantage to his operations, and to comfort the patient by gentle actions, soft words, agreeable and proper, and promise him cure in all cases even though they are hopeless; and that the operating physician himself remains convinced that there is no chance for health for such an infirmity and in such cases. For the mind of the patient feels, from such discourse and promises, a secret in-

fluence and a great disposition by which nature acquires vigor
and resistance against the disease. That is why there will result
an action more powerful than that which can be produced by
all the efforts of the physician with his instruments and even his
medicines, an action such that it routs the illness. But it is
necessary that the doctor discuss the condition of the illness
with the friends or the relatives of the patient, as it appears to
him correct lest, by default of a good and frank explanation,
the friends might not find themselves prepared against all
cruel disillusion, and so that if the patient should die, one could
not say that the doctor has caused the death, but speak well of
his recovery if the patient is cured.

It is not seemly if the physician or surgeon speak in private
with a woman who acts as mistress or servant, or of such condition, be it what it may, at least if this conversation is not
necessary for the present or future operation, or for any matter
which concerns it. He must not in any way speak to them im-
modestly nor rest his gaze upon her, especially in the presence
of the patient: for the lack of success of the operation might
stem from that, the confidence of the patient is weakened by
the bad opinion which he might conceive, and the physician
finds himself lowered in his estimation. The action of the effort of nature which usefully supports the action of the physician is equally diminished by this fact, and the effort of the
physician can but end in frustration. For it is this effort of
nature which heals the disease and not at all the doctor, if
this virtue does not intervene. It is nature, indeed, which effects
all things, but the physician is her minister.

The wise physician does not commit any wickedness, he
does not sow or excite discord among the relatives of the patient, he does not give any advice that is not asked for, he does
not employ people who have a bad reputation or a vice which
is displeasing to respectable persons. He should not have any
quarrel with the inhabitants of the house, for all this spoils
the operation and degrades the physician. Finally, he should
have no familiarity with laymen. For lay people are always
wont to malign physicians, and too great a familiarity engenders slander and brings about, that one cannot, with assurance
and certainty, decently demand fees for the operation. Know
just this; a remuneration worthy of your labors, that is to say,
a very good fee, makes for the authority of the physician and
increases the confidence which the patient has in him, even
if the physician be of great ignorance. It is for this reason that

the patient believes his treatment can and should be better than that of others bring about his recovery.

If all these matters are suitably observed by the physician, they will aggrandize him if he is small, while the contrary will degrade profoundly him who is in an exalted position For the physician should also observe the laws of those among whom he finds himself or with whom he lives, and he should observe with them their customs and habits so far as he can; and he should actually visit the poor in person, whenever possible. This reputation of charity augments his renown before the public, and the estimation in which he is held, and the Divine Power will shed its Grace over him because of this; and his work, among those from whom he receives an honorarium, appears more grand and more efficacious.

Secondly, the patient should neither contradict the physician by his remarks, nor delay the operations by his objections. In this manner of action, the patient makes the physician suspect, makes him doubt his knowledge, enfeebles him, and the physicians become fearful, trembling, hesitant in all matters, their operation is defective and their efforts cannot result in anything but failure, of a sort that a disease which was curable becomes incurable or aggravated into prolonging its course. It is suitable, therefore, that the patient accept the words and the actions of the surgeon, at the time that he chooses him to treat his malady. For the cure and the operation which follow come about in this manner in the best conditions, and the result of the cure is most profitable for the one and the other.

Thirdly, the assistants should bear themselves with kindness toward the patient, they should be agreeable, and they should obey the physicians in everything that seems to relate to the operation. It is improper for them to dispute with the patient; and they should be heard to speak chiefly with the physician, so long as it deals with things which are agreeable and useful. The physicians should have no discussions between themselves or with the patient. They should abstain from talking among each other secretly; for, by so doing they provoke in the patient, all manner of suspicions concerning the subject of the conversation, and from this there arises in him fears and doubts about all that concerns him, the disease becomes worse and the operation of the doctor has been done in vain, or, for very little. The extrinsic matters rest upon the judgement of the physician who orders them according to the nature of the disease.

ON SCROFULA, INDURATION AND CANCER OF THE
BREAST[8]

But the treatment of cancer is of two sorts: firstly that the
affected part be radically and totally cut away with the entire
disease by means of a very sharp knife, that the part be subsequently cauterized with the hot iron, and that one proceeds
consequently with substances which soothe the irritation that
has been caused by the cautery, and then favor the separation
of the eschar. . . . But if this incision is poorly made it would
not please me.

[The second type of treatment is palliative consisting of
diet, regimen and local applications. He continues:] Therefore,
be aware that this disease cannot be truly cured except by the
amputation of the part, as I have said above, for its roots are
imbedded in the veins which course about it, and which are
full of melancholy blood [containing black bile]; and that it
is necessary for the perfect cure that the veins be cut and the
roots extracted in some fashion. This cannot be done except
by removing the part in its entirety, and the disease cannot be
cured by any other means. It appears to me that it is neither
good, nor useful, nor honest for the physician to interfere with
this cure. It would be better, to be sure, and I advise you, my
friend, to decline.

8. *Ibid., Chirurgie*, pp. 108–109.

CHAPTER 12

The Surgeon–Anatomists:
Mundinus (1275–1326) and Vesalius (1514–1564)

". . . Man hath a most perfect form which he shareth with the Angels and Intelligences that rule the Universe."[1]

The growth of medicine, which had been interrupted when the Roman Empire collapsed, and which began its slow revival at Salerno, first became manifest in the field of surgery. Of this period, Garrison writes, "The principal interest of the medieval period, therefore, lies not in its internal medicine, for there was precious little of it, but in the gradual development of surgery from the ground up by faithful, sometimes obscure followers of the craft. . . ." It is perhaps surprising to note that revival of interest in anatomy, which in all periods had been generally conceded to be the foundation stone of surgery, came somewhat later than did that in surgery. It is true, as was indicated in the chapter on Salernitan surgery, that some interest had been manifested in animal dissection as is demonstrated in Copho's *Anatomia Porci* (eleventh century) and similar works, but human dissection was shunned because of the prevailing religious and popular awe of violating the corpse of man. Yet, cautious though they were, these first beginnings to study from nature rather than from books helped to infuse new life into the stagnant practice of surgery, and these faltering initial steps were soon followed by the next one, the dissection of the human body.

The man who accomplished this task was Mundinus (Mondino de Luzzi, 1275–1326), who is universally credited with the revival of the study and teaching of anatomy. Indeed, he was the first to reintroduce systematic human dissection since the time of the great Alexandrians, Erasistratus and Herophilus, 1500 years before. Mundinus' reasons for his interest in the structure of the human body went beyond a scientific desire of inspection and instruction of medical students. To him the study of anatomy must have served an

1. "Introduction" of the "Anathomia of Mondino da Luzzi," from the *Fasciculo di Medicina*, Venice, 1493, with an introduction, etc. by Charles Singer, Florence, R. Lier & Co., 1925, p. 59.

Fig. 14. Title page of Mundinus' *Anathomia*, Leipzig, 1493

intensely practical purpose for he was primarily a surgeon. In the Introduction to his book, the *Anathomia*, he wrote, "I therefore purpose to give, among other topics, some of that knowledge of the human body and of the parts thereof which doth come of anatomy. In doing this I shall not look to style but shall merely seek to convey such knowledge as the chirurgical usage of the subject doth demand."

Little is known of the early life of Mundinus other than that he was born in Bologna in the latter part of the thirteenth century, and that he received his degree in medicine from the university of that city in 1290. He became professor at his alma mater, and practiced the healing art in his native city until his death in 1326. His professorship included both anatomy and surgery, a combination that persisted for 250 years after his time at the University of Bologna, until separate chairs were established toward the end of the sixteenth century. Similar conjoint chairs of anatomy and surgery were cus-

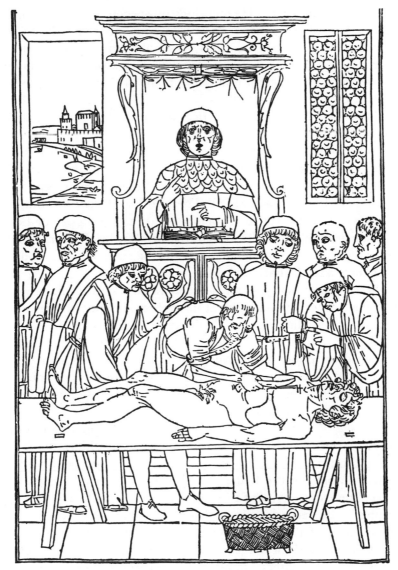

Fig. 15. From: Mundinus' *Anathomia*, Venice, 1495

tomary in the other Italian universities. Vesalius held such a dual professorship at Padua two centuries after the time of Mundinus, and he was succeeded
by a line of famous surgeon-anatomists such as Fallopius, Colombo, and
Fabricius ab Aquapendente who was the teacher of William Harvey.

Mundinus revolutionized the study of anatomy by personally and publicly
performing human dissections. In writing of the uterus he says, "For these
reasons a woman I anatomized last year, that is in the year of Christ 1315,
in the month of January, had a womb double as big as her that I anatomized

in March of the same year." He mentions no specific number of male bodies dissected but does describe the similarities and the differences in the reproductive structures in the two sexes. It is reasonable to suppose that the usual preponderance of male over female subjects prevailed in his material, and that he dissected a much larger number of men. The subjects apparently were the bodies of executed criminals, as he states, "Having placed the body of one that hath died from beheading or hanging in the supine position. . . " and proceeds with his discussion.

Mundinus took up the three "venters" or cavities of the body successively. The lower venter, or abdomen, containing the "natural members" was dissected first because, lacking preservatives, "the organs there, being most corruptible, may be first cast aside." There followed next the middle venter or chest cavity with its "spiritual members," then the upper or head cavity and its "animal members" The extremities are but briefly considered, Mundinus believing that the muscles could better be studied in "a body dried in the sun for three years" than in a fresh dissection.

Despite the revolutionary significance of his work, Mundinus was himself far from being a revolutionary. He approached his undertaking with a firm conviction of the infallability of Galen's writings and, rather than search for new truths, he attempted to prove the veracity of the traditional authors. The medieval descriptions of the liver, based on Galen's dissections of animals, always presented it as a five-lobed organ. Mundinus does not deny this fact from his own observations, but he does say, "The intrinsic and integral parts are five lobes. Yet in man these lobes are not always distinct."

The *Anathomia* of Mundinus served not only as a compendium of anatomy for the student, but as a dissection manual as well. Consideration is also given to physiology and pathology, as well as to diagnosis and operative technique. "As for the anatomy of the living, two points need to be considered which are also to some extent evident in dead anatomy. The first is as to purposes and workings. The second is as to distempers that may befall thereto and the showing forth of the proper cure, if such there be." The physiology is essentially Galenic, and the surgery reflects the accepted methods of the time. Among the clinical matters discussed are the management of penetrating wounds of the abdomen and intestines, and the recognition and treatment of ascites, lithotomy, hernia, cataract, jaundice, and colic.

Many manuscript copies of the *Anathomia* were made and a fair number still survive. The book was first printed in 1478 and went through very many subsequent editions. It served as the standard textbook of anatomy for two hundred years, until displaced by the *Fabrica* of Vesalius. The slender volume is one of the classics of medicine, even though its contents contain no strikingly new material; its author ranks among those who fundamentally influenced the growth of the medical sciences. He is one of a large group of men, surgeons by training and vocation, who made important contributions to the basic sciences as part of their specific professional interests, experiences, and capabilities.

Andreas Vesalius (1514–1564), of all the surgeon-anatomists, most significantly affected the evolution of the medical sciences. Living almost 250 years after Mundinus, Vesalius, more than any other single person, initiated

FIG. 16

the modern era in medicine. Alone, he transformed anatomy from a primitive to a highly developed science. Careful in his observations, and confident in what he saw, he dared to challenge the dogma of Galenism, and so helped liberate medicine from the bonds that held it chained for 1500 years. Himself a surgeon and a teacher of surgery, Vesalius' great contribution to this branch of medicine lay in the advancement of anatomy, so essential a part of surgery.

Vesalius was born in Brussels in 1514. For four generations his forbears were physicians or apothecaries, and he was early destined for a career in medicine. After preliminary education at the University of Louvain, he journeyed to Paris for the study of medicine. There he studied anatomy under Jacobus Sylvius, an ardent Galenist, who taught from the book in the medieval tradition, rather than from actual dissection. By this time, Vesalius, deeply devoted to the study of the human body, had by his own efforts become thoroughly proficient in dissection.

After three years in Paris, Vesalius was compelled to return to Belgium because of the outbreak of war between France and the Holy Roman Empire, of which he was a subject. He resumed his studies at Louvain, where it is assumed that he received his baccalaureate degree (1537). In the same year he traveled to Padua, attracted by the luster of the famous university of that city; before the year was over he was granted the degree of Doctor of Medicine "with highest distinction." On the day after graduation, at the age of twenty-three, he was appointed Professor of Surgery at that University. The duties assigned him included the teaching of anatomy and the holding of public dissections. Like Mundinus, and in contrast to his immediate predecessors, he performed the dissections himself. This innovation, in addition to the brilliance and boldness of his demonstrations, attracted students from all countries in Europe. As visual aids to supplement his lectures, he had prepared a series of six anatomical drawings, the "Tabulae Sex," which portrayed the individual systems of the human body. These were so popular that they were widely pirated and so intensively used by the medical students that extremely few copies survived.

At this time, Vesalius began the monumental task of preparing an entirely new book of the complete human anatomy. Very fortunately for the success of his enterprise, and for all posterity, he enlisted the aid of an excellent artist, Jan Stefan van Kalkar, who, like himself, was a native of Flanders. It is questionable which provided the greater contribution, the dissections of Vesalius or the drawings of Kalkar. Together, they achieved one of the greatest books of all time, and also created one of the most beautifully illustrated works in the history of book publication. This great treatise, *De humani corporis fabrica*, was publised in 1543, when its author was but twenty-eight years of age. Its impact was instantaneous. Widely hailed as a magnificent achievement, it also aroused bitter envy and resentment. Vesalius was subjected to

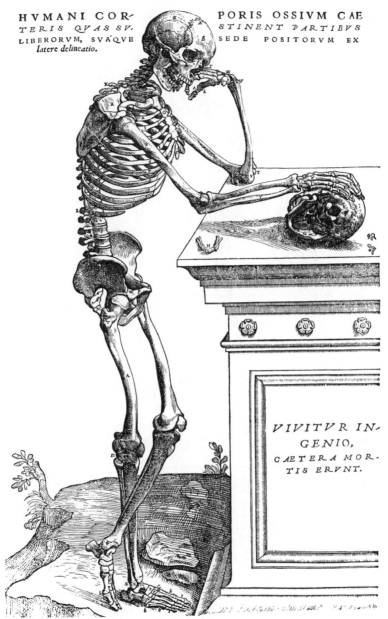

HVMANI COR-
TERIS QVAS SV.
LIBERORVM, SVÁQVE
latere delineatio.

PORIS OSSIVM CAE
STINENT PARTIBVS
SEDE POSITORVM EX

*VIVITVR IN-
GENIO,
CAETERA MOR-
TIS ERVNT.*

FIG. 17. Skeletal figure from Vesalius' *Fabrica,* 1543

vitriolic attack and contumely for his youthful arrogance in defying Galen.
To these criticisms, he replied with intemperate and immodest attacks.
Strangely, the deepest enmities arose between him and his erstwhile friends,
teachers, and assistants, including Sylvius and his successor, Realdo Colombo.

Disillusioned and embittered by these attacks, Vesalius retired from aca-

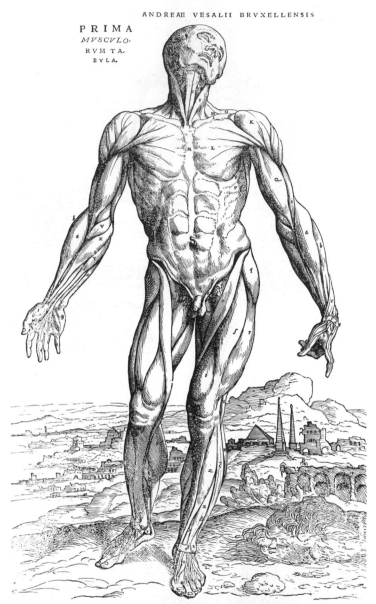

FIG. 18. Superficial muscle dissection from Vesalius' *Fabrica*, 1543

demic and largely from scientific life after the publication of the *Fabrica*, and devoted himself to the practice of medicine and surgery. He entered the service of Emperor Charles V, took part in several military campaigns, and served as Imperial Physician until the emperor abdicated his reign in 1555. After this, he served Philip II of Spain who succeeded Charles as emperor. For various reasons, he found himself discontent in this position, and planned to return to scholarly pursuits. However, as he was returning from a pilgrimage to the Holy Land, his ship was wrecked and he died on the tiny Peloponnesian island of Zante, in 1564.

Vesalius' monumental contributions were in the field of anatomy. Incidental observations in physiology, pathology, medicine, and surgery are seen in the *Fabrica* and in some of his lesser publications. A *Chirurgia Magna* was published under his name four years after his death by Prospero Borgarucci, who succeeded Vesalius as professor at the University of Padua. It is generally believed that this work was not written by Vesalius, but it has been suggested that it may have been based on students' notes of Vesalius' lectures on surgery.

Mundinus and Vesalius display in their achievements a strange phenomenon which is to be found throughout the evolution of surgery. Their great ideas in the basic sciences or allied fields have so overshadowed their contributions to surgery itself that their identity as surgeons has largely been lost or forgotten. This was also true of the British school of a later period with names such as Monro, Hunter, and Bell, and even of the great Edward Jenner whose benefactions to mankind have never been surpassed. Until the development of these sciences as separate disciplines, there could be found among the leaders in the fields of anatomy, physiology, and pathology the names of men whose training and original interest have been in surgery.

ᔇ   ᔇ   ᔇ   [A few surgical passages from the *Anathomia of* Mundinus are
ᔇ   ᔇ   ᔇ   quoted below as indications of his real activity as a practicing
surgeon.]

OF DISEASES OF THE MIRACH [ABDOMINAL WALL] AND SIPHAC [PERITONEUM] AND OF THEIR CURE[2]

In the cure of ascitic hydropsy proceed thus, following the authorities. This method, which greatly hangeth on anatomy, is the extraction of the watery matter by incision. The manner is to bring back over the guts the part of the *mirach* [abdominal wall] which thou hast not incised, that it standeth as before. After having placed the patient on his back draw the skin upward. Then take a knife and pierce as far as siphac [peritoneum] so as to make an incision in siphac also. Have to hand a canula and place it in the puncture and draw away as much of the watery matter as the patient may endure. But bear ever in mind that it were better to take too little than to empty wholly, for the loss of strength that cometh thereby.

2. *Ibid.*, pp. 63–64.

Then release the skin for it will return to its own place and cover the wound that no more water escape. When thou wouldst draw more, pull back the skin as at first. Do not make this incision save at the sides; first for that a wound made in the middle doth not unite speedily since there siphac is thicker and more solid; second for that, owing to the cords, the wound is apt to induce convulsions; and third for that water, being heavy, ever cometh forth more freely an [if] it hath a downward leading.

If the venter [abdomen] doth suffer interruption of continuity, then this interruption either goeth deeply or no. If it be not deep the cure is by no means hard. But if it go deep then some of the contents may come forth from the wound. If they do so, that which doth come forth is either *zirbus* [omentum] or some other part of the contents. If zirbus, sew with silk or tie as near the skin as may be, then cut off, since all that the air doth touch is infect, and, if put back, raiseth corruption of the other parts. After cutting off it must be returned and the thread brought outward. The lip of the wound is to be left open, for Nature will unite the zirbus and expel the thread. Afterward heal the wound.

If, however, what hath come forth be bowel, then it is either hurt or no. An [if] it be not hurt nor no other substance be involved, put back as speedily as may be. Yet should any substance such as dust or even blood cleave thereto, wash in warm water ere thou return it. If owing to lapse of time there be wind therein and it be distended that it may not be returned, lay thereon a solvent cataplasm or a sponge moistened in a solvent decoction. The swelling will thereby decrease that it may be returned. The wound of the mirach can be enlarged at need for the gut to be put back.

But it may be that the gut itself hath been cut. Then if it be one of the larger bowels the edges must be sewed with silk as are the edges of the other organs. But if one of the small bowels it will not bear sewing save the stitches be deep, and that would hinder his action. Therefore 'tis better to join together the edges of the wound in the bowel with heads of large ants. Unite the edges of the intestine and have large ants ready and cause them to bite the joined edges of the wound. Then cut off the head at once. Do this until the edges be united. Then return the gut as before.

I now return to the cure of wounds of the wall of the venter. Such wound must be cured by the union of the edges. These, when brought together by the fingers, must be held by silk stitches as thus followeth. In the first stitch take the whole of the mirach with the siphac on one side and on the opposite only the mirach. In the second stitch, on the side on which the siphac was omitted take both siphac and mirach, and on the side on which the siphac and mirach were first taken, take of mirach and omit siphac. Continue thus till the edge of the siphac be joined and brought again to the edge of the fleshy member that the junction of the wound may be made firm and sure. The same method is followed with the wound if nothing hath come forth.

CHAPTER 13

Lanfranc
(d. 1315)

"Oh Lord, why is there so great difference between a surgeon and a physician? But the philosophers have taken the craft into laymen's hands. Or as many men have disdain for to work with their hands. And yet many men ween that it is impossible for one man to know both the crafts. But thou shallt know well this, that he is no good physician that knows nothing of surgery. And the contrary thereof, a man may be no good surgeon if he knows no physic."[1]

The end of the thirteenth century saw the decline of surgery in Italy and the emergence of France in the position of leadership. Lanfranc of Milan bridges this transition, both in time and space. Driven from the land of his birth by the exigencies of the civil wars, he personally brought to France the attainments of Italian surgery, and helped to establish the French school which subsequently led the world for several centuries.

The early years of the life of Lanfranc are obscure. He is believed to have been born in Milan; and he studied under William of Salicet, whom he revered as his master. Like Theodoric and Salicet, Lanfranc was a cleric who had taken a university degree in medicine, but whose life was devoted primarily to the practice and teaching of surgery. Again, in the path of his master, he apparently took lightly the strictures of celibacy of both church and School. He had several children whom he publicly recognized, and one of his sons practiced medicine with distinction.

In Milan Lanfranc successfully engaged in surgical practice. Later, however, he became involved in the civil wars between the Guelphs and the Ghibellines, taking sides against the latter, who emerged victorious. In 1290 he was banished from his homeland by the Visconti. Fleeing to France, he took refuge in Lyon, where he resumed his studies and practice, and where

1. *Lanfrank's "Science of Cirurgie,"* edited from the Bodleian Ashmole MS. 1396 and the British Museum Additional MS. 12,056 by Robert v. Fleischhacker, Dr. Phil., Part I. Text, London, published for the Early English Text Society by Kegan Paul, Trench, Trübner & Co., 1894, III, 3, 16, p. 298.

he wrote his *Chirurgia Parva* ("Little Surgery"). Ambition drove him to Paris, and in 1295 he arrived in that city which was becoming the intellectual center of Europe. His reputation had preceded him, and he brought to France the full flowering of Italian surgery. On the recommendation of Jean de Passavant, Dean of the Faculty of Medicine, he was invited to give a course of

FIG. 19

lectures on surgery at the University of Paris, which were very well received. The following year, 1296, he completed his *Chirurgia Magna* which he dedicated to King Philip the Fair of France. His invitation to his colleagues to witness his operations and to hear him lecture as he worked was an innovation unprecedented for his time. He is thought to have died in 1315.

Lanfranc was a man of great erudition and of noble moral stature. As the first renowned surgeon in France, and the founder of French surgery, he fought valiantly to establish surgery as a learned and scientific profession, equal in dignity with and an essential part of medicine. He was bitterly critical of the unlettered and nonclerical practitioners of surgery. Disqualified from teaching at the university because of his lack of celibacy, he affiliated himself with the surgical guild of the Collège de Saint Côme, which had been founded in 1260, and which was destined to play an important role in the history of French surgery. The general tendency of surgeons to abandon bloodletting to barbers and women he lamented deeply. "Oh, Lord," he wrote, "why is there such great difference between surgeons and physicians? The philosophers have placed the craft in the hands of laymen, for many disdain to work with their hands; and many think it is impossible for one person to know both medicine and surgery. But know this well, that no man can be a good physician who knows no surgery; and conversely, no one can be a good surgeon without knowledge of medicine."

The surgery of Lanfranc is essentially conservative. His wound treatment was predicated upon suppuration being essential to healing, although in wounds of the face he strove for primary union and delicate scars. Cancer was not to be interfered with unless it was brought to the doctor's attention early enough so that it could be extirpated in its entirety. Lanfranc castigated those who would operate for hernia, and devised trusses and bandages which he used instead. Lithotomy, he believed, should be used only as a last resort after other measures had failed. In spite of these precautions and reservations he brought education and intelligence to the empiricism of the surgery of his day. Confronted with unfamiliar crises, he cleverly improvised and, like his master, he illustrated his writings with case reports of patients from his own practice.

Three excerpts from the *Chirurgia Magna* are quoted below. The first deals with the desirable characteristics and the conduct of a surgeon. The second, "On Wounds of the Head," gives remarkably astute and original methods for the diagnosis of skull fracture. In addition to the nature of the accident and the symptoms and signs, Lanfranc uses direct percussion of the skull. If the bone is intact the sound is comparable to that of an unbroken bell. Furthermore, he uses a waxed string held by the teeth of the patient which is drawn taut and then plucked as a harp string. Again the resonance, or lack of it, would indicate whether or not the skull is fractured.

The third passage quoted describes graphically a Ludwig's angina in which the patient was rescued by a timely incision. The wound, however, communicated with the pharynx, making it impossible for the patient to take liquid nourishment. As an expedient, Lanfranc had a silver tube fashioned by which food could be introduced beyond the fistula, and the patient recovered. These are but a few of the brilliant ideas found in this very interesting work.

THE QUALITIES, MANNERS AND CUNNING OF A SURGEON[2]

Needful it is that a surgeon be of a complexion well proportioned, and that his complexion be tempered. . . . A surgeon must have hands well shaped, long small fingers, and his body not quaking, and all must be of subtle wit, for all things that belong to surgery may not with letters be written. He must study in all the parts of philosophy and in logic, that he may understand scriptures; in grammer, that he speak agreeably; in art that teaches him to prove his propositions with good reason; in rhetoric that teaches him to speak seemly. Be he no glutton, nor envious, nor a niggard; be he true, humbly and pleasingly bear he himself to his patients; speak he no ribaldry in the sick man's house. Give he no counsel unless he be asked; speak he not with any woman in folly in the sick man's house; nor chide not with the sick man nor with any of his servants, but courteously speak to the sick man, and in all manner of sickness promise him cure, though thou be despaired of him; but never say the latter to his friends (but) tell them how it stands.

He should shun difficult cures and not intervene in desperate cases. Poor men help he by his might, and of the rich men ask he good reward. Praise he not himself with his own mouth, nor blame he sharply other leeches; love he all leeches and clerics, and by his might make he no leech his enemy. So clothe he himself with virtue that of him may arise good fame and name; and this teaches ethics. So learn he physic, that he may with good name; and this teaches ethics. So learn he physic, that he may with good rules defend his surgery, and that physic teaches.

WOUND OF THE HEAD[3]

Injuries of the head either that been made without wound or with wound. And whether that they been without wound or with wound, either they been with breaking of the brain pan

2. *Ibid.*, I, 1, 2, p. 8.
3. *Ibid.*, II, 1, pp. 116–119.

or without breaking of the brain pan, or whether that it be made with breach of the brain pan or without breach of the brain pan, some been with hurting of the brain, and some been without hurting of the brain, and right as such hurts have difference in tokens, so they have difference in perils and prognostications and manners in which they must be helped. . . .

And if that the brain pan were broken without wound of the head the which may be known by disposition of the cause and also of the sick man, in beholding, if that that smitest were strong, or else that the patient has fallen from his place, or else that he was smitten with strong smiting, and also if that he fell and might not hastily arise, and if that he had scotomia, that is to say a manner sickness when there seemeth as flies or other small gnats fly before his eyes, or else he spewith his meat, or he feelith too great ache in his head, and if he may not break a knot of straw with his teeth, and if the head be smitten with a light dry staff as of salow or else of pine—and then lay thine ear to his head, and that if the bone be whole thou shallt hear a whole sound after the comparison of the sound of a whole bell; also if thou makest the sick man to hold between his teeth thread twined and waxed and then begin to harp with thy nails upon the thread fast by the sick man's mouth, and so harp with thy nails upon the thread always stretched and making sound to the end of the thread, and this thread shall be on length from the mouth of a cubit, and so thou shallt harp oft times, and if that the patient may sustain the sound, he hath not his brain pan broke, for if his brain pan were broke the sick man might not sustain the sound of the thread. All these signs or else many of them betoken that the brain pan is broken and twain of the last signs be more certain than any of the others. And understand that the brain pan may oft times be broken, and nevertheless the brain feelith no harm in the beginning. But afterwards oft times of hurting of the brain pan, the brain is hurt.

APOSTEME OF THE THROAT[4]

I will set in this place a cure that befell a lady in the city of Midiolanensis [Milan] of a lady that was fifty winters old, and had a quinsy of phlegm that occupied all her neck in front within and without, except that most of the swelling

4. *Ibid.*, III, 2, 5, pp. 220–221. For explanation of "Aposteme" see footnote 7, Chapter 16.

was outward, and the woman could not speak nor swallow. And this woman was under the cure of a young man that was my scholar, and he could not well fare therewith and so he was in despair of her life. I was sent after and found her in a wicked state, for she ate no meat for many days before, and she dared not sleep, lest she should be choked. Then I felt her pulse and it was remarkably feeble, and I felt the place of the enpostym, [abscess], and I knew well that she would choke before the abscess broke externally or internally, for the matter was so great. And then I took a razor, and looked where the matter was most collected to accomplish drainage, and it was most able under the chin, and I felt the place with my hand and palpated it about that I might beware of nerves and arteries, and there I made a wound and drew out matter that was corrupt, and all and it was foul stinking matter and all might I not avoid anon. And so the patient had bettered breathing, and her pulse was comforted, for the lungs might take in air and herewith the heart was comforted, and then I gave her broth, and that escaped for the most part, through the wound. So I studied how I might best do, and I had made a pipe of silver, and put it in her mouth and passed it beyond the wound, that it might fullfill the place of the throat. And then I laid about her neck *Mundificatives* and *Maturatives* for to drain the remainder of the matter, and so I kept it till there came from the wound a great gobbet of viscous matter and stinking, shaped as if it were large bowel. And therein the first matter was engendered, and when this was out, the stinking went away therewith, and the woman began to be stronger, and when the wound was made clean I dried it up and sewed it; and it this manner the patient was made well.

CHAPTER 14

Jean Yperman
(1260?–1310?)

"The surgeon should have a perceptive eye, ideas that are always lucid, of the nature that will enable him always to act with promptness and assurance."[1]

The vigor imparted to surgery by the Italian masters of the Thirteenth century was brought to France by Lanfranc, and through him was disseminated to the nearby countries. Among the many foreign students who were drawn to Paris by the luster of its university was Jean Yperman, a native of Flanders. It was his good fortune to have studied medicine in Paris during the brief period when Lanfranc, at the invitation of the dean and regents, lectured on surgery at the university. So it was that Jean was one of the very few surgeons, outside of Italy, who had the privilige of a university education The teachings of Lanfranc impressed him strongly, and he not only became that master's most influential disciple, but also attained the greatest renown of any Belgian medical man before Vesalius.

Jean Yperman was born in the latter half of the thirteenth century in Ypres, then said to have been an important Flemish city numbering 200,000 inhabitants. Jean apparently had sufficient preliminary schooling to make him proficient in his native Flemish and French, and even probably in Latin. He was a cleric, as were all university students, but he never took holy orders.

His education finished, Jean returned to his native Ypres where he became a salaried surgeon to the city, and served on the staff of one of the principal hospitals, then called the *"l'ospital del Belle."* At first he lived outside the city, in the populous suburbs. But soon his continued presence within the gates, which were locked at night, was found necessary and he was provided with lodgings within the city proper. Although he practiced both

---

1. *La Chirurgie de Maître Jehan Yperman* (1260?–1310?), Livres I et II, Traduits du vieux flamand d'après les manuscrits de Cambridge et de Bruxelles et précédés d'une introduction par le Dr. A. De Mets, Paris, Éditions Hippocrate, 1936, Chapter IV, p. 30.

medicine and surgery, like his master Lanfranc, his greater attention was devoted to surgery.

During the thirty years of his professional life in Ypres, Jean's civilian practice was interrupted periodically by service in the army during the then frequent military campaigns. He wrote on both medical and surgical subjects, but his renown rests largely on his surgical treatises. Although he was presumably familiar with Latin, he chose to write in his native Flemish language. His prologue reads, "Here begins the Surgery of Master Jean called Ypermans, which he compiled in Ypres and there wrote in Flemish for his son, in order that he may profit from his art and his instruction, just as from the teaching drawn from the books of several great surgeons and good authors, as will be seen later."[2] There is no record, however, that his son did, in fact, succeed his illustrious father.

La Chirurgie of Jean Yperman possesses a charm and elegance of style not common in the scientific books of his time. The first chapter, as an example, dealing simply with the structure of the head, begins as follows: "Observe first, that the head is round, in order to be able to contain more with a smaller volume and also because the round form is the most beautiful; furthermore, so that blows, falls and projectiles have less hold and are more easily diverted." De Mets, biographer and translator of Yperman, characterizes his contributions in these words: "He knew the authorities and possessed their works. He always clung to the teachings of Lanfranc, whom he cited frequently. . . . He practiced ligature of arteries, studied torsion of the arteries which was known to the ancients, and described it minutely." Nevertheless, as De Mets pointed out somewhat ironically, "Two centuries later, the invention of the ligature was attributed to Ambroise Paré! As again in the nineteenth century, it was Amusat who deluded himself as having invented torsion!"[3]

Despite the fact that Yperman left no school of disciples and that his influence did not spread beyond the limited borders of his own country, nevertheless he holds a unique place in Belgian medicine. Indeed, De Mets characterizes him as the *"Father of Flemish Surgery."*

ᔐ ᔐ ᔐ   ON THE MEANS OF ARRESTING HEMORRHAGE IN INJURIES.
ᔐ ᔐ ᔐ   THE LIGATURE OF THE VESSELS AND TORSION[4]

When the surgeon finds himself in the presence of a wound, from which a great deal of blood is flowing, he should examine from which part it comes. If it flows from the wound by fits

2. *Ibid.*, Introduction. Excerpts translated from the French by the authors.
3. *Ibid.*, p. 14.
4. *Ibid.*, Chapter VI, pp. 33–37.

and spurts, then it is evident that it comes from an artery, and in that case it is limpid and of a lighter color. If the blood flows slowly, and is of a deeper color, it comes from the common veins which nourish the body.

The arteries proceed from the heart and have two coats, one of which is cartilaginous and never cicatrizes, because of the thinness, and of the heat of the fast flowing arterial blood.

The veins come from the liver and contain a slow, brown and thick blood: for this reason they need but one coat, which is loose. However this kind of coat is tendinous.

It often happens that hemorrhage comes from the veins and arteries at the same time, but rarely from the arteries alone, for they are more deeply placed than are the veins.

Be well aware that a hemorrhage from an artery is much more dangerous than that of a vein and that such a hemorrhage is formidable if it is too large. For this reason, I would advise you immediately to stop this flow of blood if it is in your power, for it results in serious accidents and threat of death, because of the spasms which may result from it. We will teach you later that this spasm, which, if it follows such a hemorrhage, must be considered as a fatal symptom, similar to the loss of strength, the cessation of digestive functions and delirium.

Here is how one should arrest hemorrhage from veins and arteries.

Those of the small veins are easily controlled by a wad of gauze applied and fixed, either dry or soaked in the blood itself, or in egg-white.

Hemorrhage from a large vein is combatted in the same manner and if one does not succeed in arresting it, one may stop it in the following manner: first the finger is applied to the wad to keep it from falling and so that the blood will not flow out so easily, then water is dropped on it to cool it; the coolness counters part of the heat and thereby the blood becomes less fluid; the coolness also contracts the skin, flesh and the vessels, and so diminishes the caliber of the veins. But be careful that no water enters the veins for that will cause accidents. If someone were to fall into the water while blood flows from a wound, the cold water would be very injurious to the coats of the vessels, for they are tendinous. If the wounds of the person who had thus fallen into the water were to be sutured, then it is necessary to wipe the wound and to let it bleed before proceeding to suture it.

If the hemorrhage is still not arrested one should have recourse to medicaments which have hemostatic properties of various degrees, one more effective than the other, which I will indicate at the designated point.

I would like to add here that if you do not succeed in arresting the hemorrhage with hemostatic powders or by the means indicated earlier, it is necessary to take resort to the ligature which is done in the following manner: Thread your needle with a strong waxed thread, and pass it under the artery, then tie well the two ends; but it is necessary to take care not to injure the vessels with the needle.

One can also resort to the following method: take a flat piece of iron with a hole in it and place it on the wound so that the hole corresponds to the injured vein; then take another piece of iron which can go through the hole, bring it to red heat and cauterize the vein through the hole. In these operations it is necessary to avoid burning to the point where it becomes wrinkled, also not to touch the nerves.

The arteries must be cauterized so that an eschar forms, and the cauterization should also be stronger in proportion to the size of the vein or the artery. Meanwhile care must be taken that the eschar does not fall off and that the hemorrhage does not recur. For this purpose the surest method is perhaps to seize the vein, twist it and then ligate it.

Résumé: Hemorrhage can be stopped in four ways. 1. by pressure exerted upon the vessel until the blood coagulates in the mouth of the opening; 2. by cooling of the part in which the wound is located; 3. by actual or potential cautery; 4. by ligature and torsion of the vein and artery.

THE FIRST DRESSINGS AND THE SUTURE OF WOUNDS OF DIFFERENT PARTS OF THE BODY[5]

If you are called for recent wounds, you should first examine if they were produced by blows, projectiles, falls, etc. If it is necessary, after having sponged the wound, put on it a wad of tow soaked in beaten white of egg. (In beating egg-white, one removes from it much of its humidity so that, by its viscosity it closes the pores of the skin in this region.)

If you do not have egg-white at hand, you soak the gauze in the blood of the wound itself, which works very well in such cases, since in becoming dessicated, it hardens. Others soak

5. *Ibid.*, Chapter V, pp, 31–32.

the gauze in water or in vinegar. As for me, I always use the blood of the wound for the dressing and have always found myself well served.

If there is a large wound made by a sword or similar instrument, suture it, beginning in the middle if the wound requires three stitches, and put the stitches at equal distance when only two sutures are needed, and then apply a mesh to the sloping part to favor the flow of pus. It is necessary to prick the suture points deeply enough so that the edges of the wound are approximated in the depths as well as the exterior, so that pus cannot accumulate in the depth, which occurs if only superficial edges of the wound are sutured and approximated, while the deeper parts are not. Then a deep suppuration sometimes forms which is called fistula, which we will speak of later.

The needle which one uses for the suture of wounds should be triangular and the eye should be grooved so that the thread can lie in it and the eye is not too thick when armed with its thread.

It is well to wax the twisted thread so that it does not cut the flesh. One can also use red or white silk thread.

Take note also, whether there is a splinter of bone or other foreign body in the wound; it is always necessary to remove these before proceeding with the suture.

If you are not called immediately, i.e., if you find the edges of the wound already dried, then it is necessary to freshen them, either by scraping or cutting with a knife until they bleed freely, then proceed with the suture.

If the two lips of the wound are widely separated from one another, bring them together by a third person with the aid of his two hands and twist the thread two or more times about the first suture and then make the knot and tie it so that it holds more firmly.

CHAPTER 15

Henri de Mondeville
(1260–1320)

"The moderns are, in relation to the ancients, as a dwarf placed on the shoulders of a giant; he sees all that the giant perceives plus a little more."[1]

The first great French master of surgery was Henri de Mondeville (1260–1320). Like the illustrious Italians who immediately preceded him, he was a cleric, university-trained in medicine, and passionately devoted to surgery. He was born in Normandy, studied at the universities of Montpellier and Paris, and learned surgery from Theodoric in Bologna. From Theodoric he took the doctrine of the primary union of wounds, which he expanded by his own observations in military and civilian surgery, and which he promulgated with an almost fanatical enthusiasm. He taught anatomy and surgery at Montpellier, then returned to Paris where he continued his public lectures. As a royal body surgeon he served King Philip the Fair, and his successor, Louis X (the Quarrelsome). His writings reveal him to be intelligent, literate, and independent of mind, a bold and resourceful operator, and an ardent campaigner for the dignity of surgery as an honorable and scientific profession worthy of consideration as an integral part of medicine.

The *Chirurgie* of de Mondeville, the first book on surgery from the pen of a native Frenchman, was written between 1306 and 1320. It is one of the great monuments of pre-Renaissance surgery but neither his contemporaries nor his immediate successors gave it the recognition it merited. Beyond advancing the author's professional views, the book gives a lucid insight as to the status of medicine and surgery in the fourteenth century. Henri is outspoken in his criticisms, not only of his colleagues and contemporaries, but of the patients as well, including the rich, the powerful, the high churchmen, and even the king. The work was never completed. Because of failing health—he suffered from chronic asthma and tuberculosis—and the demands

1. *Chirurgie de Maître Henri de Mondeville*, composée de 1306 à 1320, Traduction Francaise avec des notes, une introduction et une biographie par E. Nicaise, Paris, Ancienne Librairie Germer Baillière, 1893, Book V, Chapter 1, p. 745.

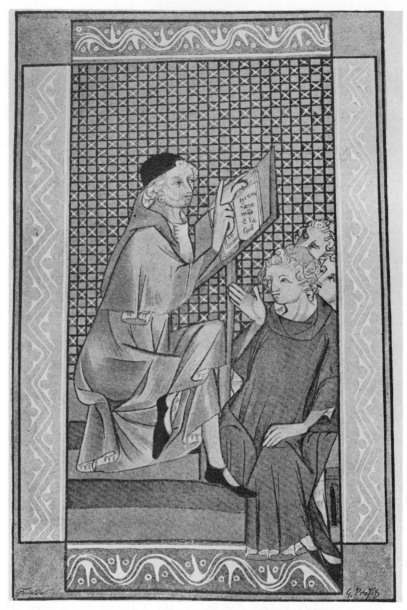

FIG. 20. Henri de Mondeville lecturing to his students. After a miniature in a French manuscript of 1314. Reproduced from the frontispiece of *Chirurgie de Maître Henri de Mondeville* by E. Nicaise, Paris, 1893.

on his time by service with the army, his lectures, and his extensive practice, part of the third book and all of the fourth, which was to have dealt with fractures and dislocations, remained forever unwritten. Whether because of his defiance of authority, or the truncation of his book, the *Chirurgie* re-

FIG. 21. Miniature illustration of the works of Henri de Mondeville, from the edition of E. Nicaise, Paris, 1893.

mained in manuscript form; and since it did not appear in print until late in the nineteenth century, it exerted but little influence on succeeding generations of surgeons.

As originally projected, the book was to have consisted of five "Treatises." Of those that were completed, the first deals with anatomy, adapted to the needs of the surgeon. Fourteen illustrations in miniature adorn the manuscript. Although the entire work is filled with citations and references from earlier sources, Henri tells us that he has drawn principally on three: on Avicenna for anatomy, on Theodoric for wounds, and on Lanfranc for the treatment of ulcers and other diseases. He also acknowledges his indebtedness to "my very able teacher, Master Jean Pitard," who like himself was surgeon to the king, and founder of the earliest surgical guild, the Collège de St. Côme.

Book II of the *Chirurgie*, dealing with the treatment of wounds and ulcers, is by far the longest and most important in the entire work. It begins with an introduction and a series of *Notables*, twenty-six in number, which deal in general with all aspects of surgery and its relation to medicine and to society. *Notable* XIV is divided further into fifty-two *Contingents* which discuss all of the factors that contribute to the success or failure of treatment. This entire lengthy preamble is unique in surgical texts, and offers delightful reading. The excerpts which follow are largely taken from this section of the book. They create for us an image of the author, his erudition, his high moral stature, his reverence for learning, and his contempt for the ignorant and dishonest. A curious and amusing preoccupation with the matter of surgical fees throws interesting light on the practice of surgery of his day.

Henri's most significant teaching, of course, has to do with the treatment of wounds. Nicaise writes, "According to the ancients, suppuration is useful, and if it is not produced of itself, it must be provoked by the use of suppurative medicaments. This established, when the ancient surgeons found themselves faced by a wound, first they allowed the escape of a certain amount of blood to prevent inflammatory complications, then they probed the wound, enlarged it, and inserted tents and *plumasseux* (compresses) soaked in egg-white and suppuratives, the whole held in place by a bandage. At the same time, the patient was submitted to a rigid regimen which excluded meat and wine; he was given a surgical potion, a *vulneraire*, the tradition of which still exists among laymen. This treatment always produced suppuration and often lead to inflammation and phlegmon."[2]

This was the method in vogue in de Mondeville's time, and to it he took violent objection. He insisted that suppuration was not only unnecessary to the healing of a wound, but was harmful and dangerous, that it increased the suffering and disability, resulted in disfiguring scars, and led to complications and death. In its place he championed the method of Theodoric, claiming, "In this entire book one supposes that *every simple wound can be cured without the production of a notable quantity of pus*, on condition that, without omitting any of the *contingents*, one treats them according to the teachings of Theodoric and ourselves." This treatment entailed the immediate removal of foreign bodies, the prompt control of hemorrhage by whichever means was required, and the closure of the wound as quickly as possible, by bandaging alone if that sufficed, otherwise by suture. Dressings consisted of compresses wrung out in hot wine and held in place by adequate bandages. Supportive treatment included rest, nourishing foods, and wine.

The violence of the opposition to these innovations is graphically expressed by de Mondeville. He states, "It is rather dangerous for a surgeon to operate differently than is the custom of the other surgeons. We have experienced this in the treatment of wounds according to the method of Theodoric, Master Jean Pitard and myself who have first brought it to France, and have employed it in Paris and in several wars, against the wishes and opinions of all, in particular of the physicians. We have suffered the disdain and shameful words on the parts of laymen and of our colleagues, the surgeons; and even threats and dangers. From certain laymen and physicians, every day and at each change of dressing, we have endured disputes and words so violent that half-vanquished and fatigued with all the opposition, we would have been close to renouncing this treatment and abandoning it entirely, had it not been

2. *Ibid.*, Introduction, p. XVII. Translated from the French by the authors.

for the support of the most serene Count of Valois. But this Prince has come to our aid, as have several other personages who have seen wounds cared for in the camps by this method. We were further sustained by truth; but if we had not been firm in our faith, known to be close to the King, royal physicians and somewhat lettered, it would have been necessary for us to abandon this treatment."[3]

The third book of the *Chirurgie*, dealing with surgical conditions other than wounds and ulcers, was begun in 1316, ten years after completion of Books I and II. In the introduction to this section, de Mondeville laments the ingratitude and perfidy of his regal patrons, "to the shame of his Royal Majesty," and complains bitterly of the demands on his time. Having completed the first and second treatises of his book, he writes, "I have read them immediately after having achieved them, in Paris, in the year of our Lord, 1312, publicly in the schools without reward, before the largest and most noble assembly of students of medicine and other distinguished persons. . . . On the order of our Lord the King, I have uselessly lost a great deal of time, to my great despair, in Arras, in England [probably Flanders], in other parts of his realm, in several of his armies and at his Court, hoping that he would pay me what was due me, —after which, on further order of the King, renouncing all profit, I have returned to Paris and have lived there, at least for short intervals; I have wished again to take up little by little the work which I have abandoned. . . . Greatly occupied, however, in Paris, by virtue of the great reputation which I enjoy among the students, the citizens, the personages at Court and the stranger in passage, I am often hard put to write a line a day, without counting that I must go to the schools and run all day here and there to earn a living, until with the sole grace of God who is not generous I have provided by the work of my hands, all that is necessary for me and my household. . . . Thus, not being either selfish, nor ambitious, nor avaricious, and not wishing avidly to embrace the whole world, but being content with that which is necessary for me to make a living; as I see our surgery, so indispensable to the human race, being insufficiently transmitted, and since I am able to arrange it a little better, not being obligated to any person as one will see later, not married out of fear that the perversity of a woman and the necessity of paying her expenses and furnishing her a home would divert my spirit from the composition of this book, and from the execution of other useful works of the same nature,— fearing for all these reasons the divine judgment and dreading to be held responsible for the ignorance of my colleagues I have decided to resume the present work.[4]

Far better than any other narrative, Henri de Mondeville's autobiograph-

3. *Ibid.*, Introduction, pp. XVI–XVII.
4. *Ibid.*, Introduction to Vol. III, pp. 492–493.

ical remarks continue to reveal his personality as well as his dedication to the task of reforming the field of surgery.

> "As to the reason why I have so long deferred to achieve or complete this *Chirurgie*, it was, in addition to the preceding reasons, in order to do better—God knows—in order to be able first to experience, reflect and see more, so that my work would be better ordered. But as I fear that death may prevent me, for there is nothing more certain than death, and nothing more uncertain than the hour of death, and that I do not see among my contemporaries a single surgeon who is disposed to study, that there is a great scarcity of lettered ones, and if there are a few, either they are inadequate, or entirely devoted to gain and not willing to cut as much as five cents (*sous*) from their usual earnings to compose a work useful to all,—for me then, who as I have said, am neither married, nor prebended, nor attached to anyone nor in the service of anyone, who receive no subsidy for my expenses, I no longer wish to defer the task which I have undertaken. Pushed by the fear of death, and the fear that if I die, this *Chirurgie* will remain unfinished, which would be unpleasing to God, I propose to write what remains to be written, after having first invoked the aid of Christ. May He clarify, enlarge and direct my spirit, obscure, insufficient, and poorly disposed, that it may sustain the weight and the labor of such a work, to the end that this work may happily achieve grace from His light and His power, that it may be faultless and perfect as possible, to His praise and glory, to that of all the citizens of the Heavens and in the interest of men of this time and of centuries to come."[5]

The preoccupation with illness and fear that death would prevent the completion of his task became more insistent as the years of toil and struggle passed. In the Introduction to the third section of Book III, which was never written, he says, ". . . although languishing, I have already lived for three years, so to speak, miraculously and by special grace; I have lived for these three years, contrary to the unanimous judgement of the physicians, asking of the Creator and begging that just as He prolonged the life of King Hezekiah, He prolong mine, if it pleases Him, for the common good, until I am able to finish this work, and that to complete it, my doctrine condense itself like rain, and that my words pour out like the dew."[6]

Despite these prayers, he apparently sensed that death would overtake him before his self-appointed task was done. Believing an "Antidotary" (Materia Medica) to be of the greatest urgency, he omitted the entire fourth book, on "Fractures and Dislocations," and devoted his wasting energies toward

5. *Ibid.*, pp. 492–494.
6. *Ibid.*, p. 739.

completing the fifth Book. In the Introduction to this section, de Mondeville reveals his intellectual courage in daring to differ with Galen, whom he nonetheless revered as master. The excerpt quoted *in extenso* below denies that God had expended all his genius on Galen, with none left to bestow on those who came later. In another passage, expressing his opposition to the so-called Galenic polypharmacy of the day, he says ". . . It is thus that contrary to the opinion of all the authors of medicine, it has been shown by experience that *all curable injuries are promptly, easily and certainly cured by means of a single medicament.*"[7]

He goes on to say "I am not destined to live long unless by special grace God will prolong my existence. I am asthmatic, *toussailleux*, phthisic and in consumption, and in consequence, it is preferable for me and also more useful for me to hasten my work."[8] His dire predictions were fulfilled. His fifth book was completed in 1320, and death claimed him soon after.

ॐ ॐ ॐ   ON WHAT IS REQUIRED OF THE SURGEON[9]

ॐ ॐ ॐ   The surgeon who wishes to operate according to the rules should first frequent the places where able surgeons often operate; follow with care their operations; fix them in his memory; and then practice by operating with these surgeons. . . . The surgeon should be, in addition, moderately audacious, not dispute before laymen, operate with prudence and wisdom, and not undertake a perilous operation without having foreseen what is necessary to avoid the danger. He should have well-formed limbs, especially the hands, the fingers long and slender, agile and not trembling; all the other limbs strong, in order to be able to execute in manly fashion, all the good operations of the mind. He should be complaisant, give himself entirely to the patient in a manner not to forget any accessory thing. He should promise a cure to all his patients, but not conceal the danger of the case, if there is any, from the family and friends. He should refuse, as much as possible, difficult cures. He should never meddle with desperate cases. He should give advice to the poor for the sake of God. He should make the rich pay well if he can. He should work to attain a good reputation. He should comfort the patient with good words, condescend or obey his just demands, if they do not interfere with the treatment of the disease.

7. *Ibid.*, p. 744.
8. *Ibid.*, Vol. V, Chapter 1, pp. 745–746.
9. *Ibid.*, Introduction to Book II, pp. 90–91.

It follows necessarily, from what has been said, that the perfect surgeon is more than the perfect physician, and that he is
required in addition, to know manual operation.

ON THE SUPERIORITY OF THE SURGEON[10]

It would be in vain for a surgeon today to know all the art,
science and operations of surgery if he does not have the art
and science of making it pay, since that is his principal intention
and a thing is useless if, being intended to arrive at a certain
end it does not reach it. Also, it is necessary for the surgeon who
wishes to operate, that he has by precaution several valid
arguments to accomplish this end. There are, in effect, patients,
even rich, who are so miserable, avaricious and stupid as to
give nothing, or if they pay, it is a little thing. They believe it
satisfactory to the surgeon if they give 12 *deniers* or 2 *sous* a day,
as if to a mason, a furrier or a cobbler, and do not realize that
wealth has no value without health, that there is no poverty
that can be compared with sickness.

Also, the law says that the human body should be preferred
to all other things; as a consequence, the surgeon should not
tolerate that, for having saved an arm or a hand, one should
offer him a modest fee or nothing. It is in this intention that
Cato said: when a work is a pure loss, human misery increases.
That is, in effect, that pure loss is prejudicial when the surgeon
works to his own detriment and to the advantage of the patient. . . .

What advantage has a surgeon, reputed and honest, if every
day, from morning to evening without respite he runs to right
and left, and visits the patients; if all his nights there passes
through his mind all that he has seen during the day at each of
his patients, he forsees and arranges all he will do on the morrow,
if he expends all his energies in the affairs of others, and if it is
said of him that he performs great marvels, and that with this
he is not given retribution worthy of his effort, and for the great
benefit of having restored health, a great reward and honor. . . ?

You then, surgeons, if you have operated conscientiously on
the rich for a suitable fee, and on the poor for charity, you need
not fear fire, rain or wind, you have no need to go into religion,
to make pilgrimages, or other acts of the sort, because by your
science you have been able to save your souls, live without
poverty and die in your homes, live in peace and joy, and exult

10. *Ibid.*, Book II, *Notable* XXV, pp. 196–202.

because your reward is great in the Heavens, so that it necessarily follows the words of the Savior, who said in the Psalm, by
the mouth of the prophet, "Happy is he who has pity on the
needy and the poor for on the day of evil, the Lord will deliver
him."

FINAL EXHORTATION[11]

The surgeon desiring to practice his art with sagacity and skill
should refer to the 26 *Notables* preliminary to all surgery, to the
52 *Contingents* relative to the treatment of surgical diseases and
to the 15 preliminary *Notables* specially consecrated to the treatment of wounds. He will find there a large number of useful
generalities which furthermore have never been formulated in
the other Practices of Surgery. He will also find there information as to the cautious, subtle and malicious procedures which
surgeons employ to put themselves on guard against the deceit
of other surgeons and of physicians, and against the patients,
as to the means of extracting from them an adequate and honorable remuneration. Finally, he will find there an explanation
of the preliminary general considerations which should guide
the surgeons in the canons and the general principles of surgery
and in the manner of operating manually. Certainly, it would
be sovereignly unjust that the surgeon who possesses all the art
of surgery and of manual operation, who each day, from morning to evening, trudges incessantly across the streets and squares,
going to visit the patients; who each night sits up and studies
that which on the morrow he will have to do for the patients he
has seen the previous day, who orders, disposes and employs all
his time, and uses his body for the service of others,—it would be
unjust that this man, in recompense for the admirable benefits
that he alone has lavished upon his kind in restoring their
health, did not receive a legitimate remuneration for his labor.
Does not the law say that no one is forced to serve in the army
at his own expense? One knows the maxim of the peasants:
Every worker deserves wages and recompense; and that of
Cato: Whenever one works without salary, human misery is
increased.

[Henri de Mondeville was well aware of the importance of
psychic factors in surgery, as the following two quotations indicate.]

11. *Ibid.*, Vol. V, Chapter 1, p. 760.

ON THE RELATION OF BODY AND SOUL[12, 13]

As Galen said, the bodies of animals are the instruments of the souls which are in them; by them, and by their diverse members, that is executed of which the soul has need. The soul is thus the principal agent; the body and the limbs are its organs or its organic instruments; it is like the hand and the axe when it comes to chopping down a tree: Just as the hand without the axe or the axe without the hand are not able to cut the tree, so neither the soul without the limbs nor the limbs without the soul are able to execute any outward action. The body and the soul are so closely united, one to the other, that when one is sick, whichever it may be, the other is unable to act outwardly. It is thus evident that whoever is overtaken by an illness, whether it be of a limb or of the body, or whether of the spirit, he is, like a raving maniac, unable to recognize the truth in any faculty, nor accomplish any legitimate action, work, study or teaching. Also Galen said: That whoever wishes to cure the soul, must first cure the body and Constantine proved the reciprocal, to know that whoever wishes to cure the body must first cure the soul.

OF ACCIDENTS OF THE SOUL[14]

Another *Contingent* results from accidents of the soul. . . . It is subdivided into five constituent parts of which the first results from *pleasure and joy*. Thus, the surgeon should regulate the entire regimen of the patient with a view to pleasure and joy, promising him, for example, a rapid recovery, surrounding him by those who are dear to him, his friends, a jester who will distract him by playing the viol or ten-stringed psaltery. The patient is led to believe that once cured, he will perform single-handedly, great wonders; if he is a canon of the church, he is told whether true or false, even if he is to be imprisoned or hanged after his recovery, that the bishop or prelate is dead, and that he has been elected; that he should be thinking of arranging his residence and his personnel; that he is even to hope of later becoming Pope. He might be given, without compunction, false letters announcing the death or disgrace of his enemies, or of persons whose death will mean a promotion

12. *l'ame, i.e., anima* are here translated as "Soul."
13. *Chirurgie de Maître Henri de Mondeville, loc. cit.,* Vol. III, 3rd Doctrine, *Introduction Particu-lière,* pp. 738–739.
14. *Ibid., Contingent* XXIII, pp. 144–145.

for him. His visions and dreams should be favorably interpreted, such as that he will succeed to a certain canonry of four prebends, who dreams that he will be brought two batons. On the following day he is promised a horse, he tells it to his companions, one of whom explaining it, says "Master, you are a canon here and there; your prelates are dead; it is not possible that you will not receive at least the staves of two prelatures." Then, full of joy, our canon rides so briskly, and neglecting the reins, he and his horse fall to the ground, he breaks both thighs in such a way that he is never cured. He does not walk for the rest of his life except with the two sticks of which he had dreamed.

Further, the surgeon should prevent in the patient anger, hate, sadness or the memory of an old quarrel, of a wrong, or of actual damages from which he is suffering; [the surgeon should see to it] that he should not be uneasy about any affair . . . that his confession, his will, and other similar matters are placed in order; all the things that must be aranged according to the prescriptions of the Catholic faith.

. . . It is necessary to be in fear of anger, anguish, sadness and similar things. Besides, it is known, even to the most ignorant, that joy and sorrow are accidents of the soul, and that the body is fattened by joy and thinned by sorrow.

[Although de Mondeville greatly esteemed Galen and the other authorities, and quoted them freely, he nevertheless had the courage and intellectual independence to differ with them when so convinced by his own experience.]

PLEA FOR OPENMINDNESS[15]

It would be an absurdity and almost a heresy to believe that God, glorious and sublime, had accorded to Galen a divine genius on condition that no mortal being after him never discovered anything new. What! Has the Lord thus abandoned part of His power! Has not God given to each of us, as to Galen, a natural genius? Miserable indeed would be our spirit if we should not know what had been discovered before us. The moderns are, compared to the ancients, as a dwarf placed on the shoulders of a giant; he sees all that the giant perceives, and a little more. Therefore if we know things unknown at the time of Galen, it is our duty to tell of them in our writings.

15. *Ibid.*, Introduction to Vol. III, p. 745.

We see in the mechanical arts, in architecture, for example, that if those who excelled in the time of Galen in the construction of temples and palaces returned to life, they would not even be worthy to assist an architect adequate for our times. Furthermore, we see that they have demolished the ancient temples and palaces in order to rebuild them in a better manner. In the same way, and with greater right, the ancient notions of liberal sciences should be improved; it is necessary to add to some and to describe the new.

PART IV

SURGERY BECOMES RESPECTABLE

CHAPTER 16

Guy de Chauliac
(d. 1368)

"The conditions required of a surgeon are four: the first is that he should be lettered; the second, that he should be expert; the third, that he should be ingenious; the fourth, that he should be agreeable. It is thus required in the first place, that the surgeon should be lettered, not only in the principles of surgery, but also of medicine, in theory as much as in practice.
"He should be agreeable; bold in safe things, fearful of dangers; that he avoid bad cures or practices. That he be gracious to the patients, kind to his companions, wise in his predictions. He should be chaste, sober, charitable and merciful; not covetous, not an extorsioner of money; he should accept a modest fee according to the work involved, the means of the patient, the outcome and his own dignity."[1]

Guy de Chauliac, the second great French surgeon of the pre-Renaissance, became the dominant figure in this field. Unlike Henri de Mondeville, who preceded him by half-a-century and who exerted little influence on succeeding generations of surgeons, Guy's book became the unchallenged doctrine for all of Europe for several centuries to come. Nicaise awards him the title of "Founder of Didactic Surgery", and Malgaigne wrote, "I do not hesitate to say that, Hippocrates excepted, there has not been a single treatise on surgery, Greek, Latin or Arabic, that I would put above, or even on the level of that magnificent work, the *Chirurgie* of Guy de Chauliac."

Guy was born in the closing years of the thirteenth century in Chauliac, a tiny village from which his name is taken, which he locates on the "frontiers of Auvergne, in the diocese of Mende." He took holy orders and received an excellent education in medicine and surgery in Toulouse, Montpellier, and Paris, and in addition studied anatomy with the successor of Mundinus in Bologna. Thus, like the famed predecessors of whom we have spoken, he was both cleric and physician, but his life's work was essentially that of a surgeon. He lived and practiced in Avignon during its years of splendor when it was

1. Guy de Chauliac, *La Grande Chirurgie*, edited by E. Nicaise, Paris, F. Alcan, 1890, *Chapitre Singulier*, pp. 17–19. Epigram and excerpts translated from the French by the authors.

GUY DE CHAULIAC

Fig. 22

the residence of the Papacy, and achieved the distinction of being appointed commensal chaplain successively to Popes Clement VI, Innocent VI, and Urban V. Guy de Chauliac's great book *L'Inventaire* or *Collectaire* (*Grande Chirurgie*), written toward the end of his career in 1363, was immediately successful. This work reveals Guy to have been the most widely read of any previous surgical author. It was his good fortune, not only to have lived during the time when translations of the Greek texts were being made in rapidly increasing numbers from the Arabic, but also when they were beginning to come directly from the original Greek sources. All this vast literary treasure was available to him in Avignon. Combined with this erudition was a keen and analytic mind, a sober yet critical judgment, a pithy, lucid style, and a genius for orderly, systematic organization which combined to make his book the dominant surgical text for centuries.

Guy de Chauliac emerges from this treatise as a less colorful and arresting personality than Henri de Mondeville. His comments are less intemperate, his crusading less passionate. In surgical matters, he is essentially conservative, and contributes little of his own. He states in the Prologue, "I have added nothing of my own, except perchance some little of that which the smallness of my mind has judged profitable." Nevertheless, his sober and weighty opinions formed the basis of surgical thought for so long a time.

The first chapter, bearing the provocative title *Chapitre Singulier*, contains many interesting generalities pertaining to surgery. His definition of surgery broadened its scope beyond that of being the third instrumentality of medicine (the other two being regimen and drugs). He states, "Surgery is the science which teaches the manner and quality of working, principally in consolidating, incising, and performing other manual operations, curing man to the extent that is possible." In this chapter, too, he reviews the history of surgery, the first to do so since Celsus. Speaking of Avicenna, the most honored author of Arabian medicine, he writes, "And one finds that until his time all were physicians and surgeons combined, but since then, whether because of delicacy or because of too great a preoccupation with cures [medicines], surgery has become separated and abandoned to the hands of mechanics." And, caustically, "After him (Bruno)[2] immediately came Theodoric, who ravishing all that Bruno had said and adding several fables of Hugh of Lucca, his Master, he made a book."

The first book of the *Grande Chirurgie* is on anatomy, which Guy considered indispensable to the surgeon, quoting Henri de Mondeville in support of his view on this subject. However, he considered Henri's method of teaching anatomy from drawings inferior to actual human dissection. "Anatomy is acquired," he writes, " by two means: one is by the teaching from books, which method, though useful, is not always sufficient to explain the things which are not known. . . . The other method is by experience on the dead body. For we practice on the bodies recently dead, that have been decapitated or hanged, at least on the internal organs, the flesh of the muscles, the skin, and of many veins and nerves, especially as to their origin, according to the treatise of Mundinus of Bologna, who has written of this.

"My master Bertrucius has done several [dissections] in this manner: Having laid the dead body on a bench, he does it in four lessons. In the first, the digestive organs are dealt with, because they decompose rapidly. In the second, the spiritual [thoracic] organs. In the third, the animal organs. In the fourth, one treats of the extremities. . . ." He goes on to state, "We also make anatomy on bodies dried by the sun or consumed in the earth, or immersed in running or boiling water; we see, at least, the anatomy of the bones, cartilages, joints, large nerves, tendons and ligaments. By these two means, one acquires knowledge of the anatomy of the bodies of men, apes, pigs and

2. Bruno of Longoburg, author of *Chirurgia Magna*, Padua, 1252.

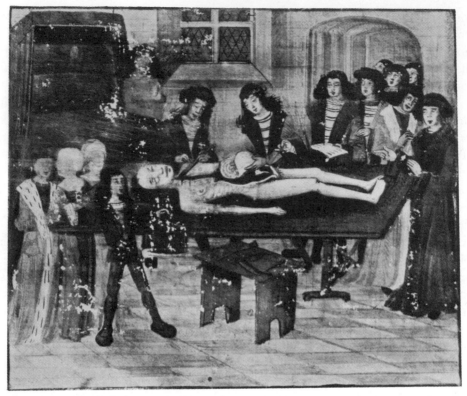

FIG. 23. A postmortem examination from a manuscript of the *Grande Chirurgie* of Guy de Chauliac at the Bibliothèque de la Faculté de Médecine at Montpellier of about 1450. Reproduced from: the *Fasciculo di Medicine* by Charles Singer, Florence, R. Lier & Co., 1925.

several other animals, and not by paintings, as was done by Henri, who, with thirteen pictures tried to demonstrate anatomy."[3]

The Black Death struck Avignon in two epidemics during Guy de Chauliac's residence in that city. It is to his everlasting credit, and to that of other surgeons, that they stayed and cared for the victims of the plague when most of the physicians fled. Guy's graphic description of the epidemics which appears below under his title, "The Great Mortality of 1348 and 1360," is one of the earliest contemporary records of the ravages of bubonic plague. Guy, himself, contracted the disease, as he describes, and his associates despaired of his life. He recovered, however, after an illness of six weeks. His acceptance of astrologic influences in causing the epidemics is symptomatic of the era in which he lived.

In the matter of the treatment of wounds, Guy de Chauliac has been harshly dealt with by historians. Such eminent authorities as Garrison and Sir Clifford Albutt have charged him with retarding the management of wounds for

3. Guy de Chauliac, *La Grande Chirurgie*, First Treatise, Doctrine 1, Chapter 1, pp. 30–31.

FIG. 24. The Physician, the Surgeon and the Apothecary. After a miniature of a manuscript of Guy de Chauliac. Reproduced from: *Chirurgie de Maître Henri de Mondeville* by E. Nicaise, Paris, 1893.

centuries by his rejection of the nonsuppurative methods. Curiously, his definitive biographer, Nicaise, does not share this view—nor do we draw the same impression from a critical reading of his chapters on wounds. Thus, he says of the treatment of wounds: "The common purpose in every solution of continuity, is union. . . . This general and primary intention is accomplished by two [ways]: by Nature, as the principal operator, which works with its own powers, and with suitable nourishment; and by the physician as servants working with five intentions, which are subalternate, one to the other.

"The first requires the removal of foreign bodies if there are any between the divided parts.

The second, to re-approximate the separated parts, one to the other.

The third, to maintain the re-apposed parts in their proper form, and to unite them together as one.

The fourth is to conserve and preserve the substance of the member.

The fifth teaches the correction of complications."[4]

He then describes, in detail, the methods of removing foreign bodies, the types of bandaging to approximate the separated portions, the various kinds of sutures, and the ways of dressing the wound. Of the "Methods and Qualities of Tents (drains) and Meshes (packs)," he lists the following indications for their use, to none of which can we take serious objection: "Primarily in wounds we wish to enlarge, cleanse, or remove something from its depth, such as deep wounds which require counteropening because of fluid or liquid discharge

4. *Ibid.*, Third Treatise, Doctrine 1, Chapter 1, p. 206.

FIG. 25. Miniature illustration of a fifteenth century manuscript of Guy de Chauliac's *Traité des Fractures et Dislocations*. Reproduced from: *Chirurgie de Maître Henry de Mondeville* by E. Nicaise, Paris, 1893.

which has collected in its depth or in its hollows. Secondly, in hollow wounds in which we must engender flesh. Thirdly, in wounds altered by air (contaminated) which must be purified. Fourthly, in contused wounds. Fifthly, in abscessed wounds. Sixthly, in bites. Seventhly, in wounds in which it is necessary to operate on bone. Eighthly, in ulcerated wounds. *In all other wounds we intend to consolidate without tents or meshes.*"[5] (Italics ours)

The *Grande Chirurgie* of Guy de Chauliac completely covers the field of surgery. In addition to the books mentioned, others deal with ulcers and fistulae, fractures and dislocations, surgical diseases other than those included in specific treatises, and an antidotary, or Materia Medica, in which are described in detail the methods of bleeding, cupping, and leeching, as well as drugs and medicaments, comprising a total of eight books. This work went through many editions and translations, was enormously popular and influential, and served as the principal text book for 200 years, until finally superseded by the works of Ambroise Paré in the middle of the sixteenth century.

5. *Ibid.*, p. 213.

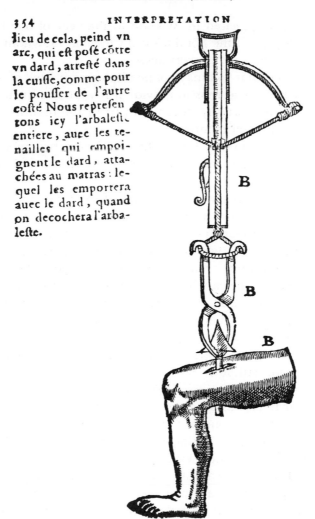

lieu de cela, peind vn
arc, qui eft pofé côtre
vn dard, arrefté dans
la cuiffe, comme pour
le pouffer de l'autre
cofté Nous reprefen
tons icy l'arbalefte
entiere, auec les te-
nailles qui empoi-
gnent le dard, atta-
chées au matras : le-
quel les emportera
auec le dard, quand
on decochera l'arba-
lefte.

B

B

B

BBB. Sont la figure que nous reprefentons.

Fig. 26. Extraction of an arrow by means of a crossbow. From: *La Grande Chirurgie de M. Guy de Chauliac ... 1363.* Restituée par M. Lavrens Joubert. Tournon, Clavde Michel, 1598, p. 354.

$\mathfrak{se}$ $\mathfrak{se}$ $\mathfrak{se}$ THE GREAT MORTALITY OF 1348 AND 1360[6]

$\mathfrak{se}$ $\mathfrak{se}$ $\mathfrak{se}$ We clearly saw that internal apostemes[7] are dangerous in the
great mortality, and that nothing like it had been described: that

6. *Ibid.*, Second Treatise, Doctrine 2, Chapter 5, pp. 167–173.
7. The word "aposteme" is frequently used in the older literature. It has many spellings and numerous meanings. It is often used synonymously with abscess. Actually, the word covers all swellings "against nature," which are due to accumulations of humors, either singly or admixed, and in normal or altered form.

which appeared in Avignon in the year of our Lord 1348, the 6th year of the Pontificate of Clement VI, whom I served by his grace and my unworthiness.

And that you may not be displeased if I tell of it because of its marvels, and thus to provide if it were to return.

This mortality began with us in the month of January and lasted seven months.

It was of two kinds: the first lasted two months, with continuous fever and bloody expectoration; and death in three days.

The second was for the rest of the time, also with continued fever and also with abscesses and carbuncles of the external parts, principally of the axillae and groins, and death in five days. There was so great contagion (especially with bloody expectoration) that not only by living together, but simply by looking, one caught it from the other: and people died without attendants and were buried without priests. The father did not visit the son, nor the son his father: charity was dead and hope was destroyed.

I called it the great mortality beacuse it occupied the entire world, with little exception. For it began in the Orient and cast its bark against the world, passing our region on its way westward. It was so great that barely a fourth of the people escaped. . . . None of the earlier epidemics were as severe, since they occupied a single region, while this involved the entire world; the others were curable in some manner, this by none.

Because it was futile and shameful for the physicians; in that they did not dare visit their patients for fear of infection, and when they did visit them, they cured none and they gained nothing: for all the patients died, except a few toward the end who escaped with burned out buboes.

Many were uncertain about the cause of this great mortality. In some parts it was believed that the Jews had poisoned the earth, and so they killed them. In others, that it was the mutilated poor [the lepers?] and they were driven away. And others, that it was the nobles, and therefore they were afraid to go out of doors. Finally, it came about, that guards were placed about the towns and villages, and no one was permitted to enter who was not well known. And if they found on them powders or ointments, fearing that they were poisons, they were made to swallow them.

But whatever the people said, the truth is that the cause of this mortality was double, one was a universal agent, and the other a particular culprit. The universal agent was the conjunction of three superior bodies [astrology], Saturn, Jupiter and Mars . . . which presage marvellous and terrible things on earth, such as changes in reigns, the advent of the Prophets, and great mortalities.

The particular cause was the disposition of the body of the patient, such as cachochymie [disturbed chemistry], debility and obstruction, because of which the populace, the heavy laborers, and the evil-livers died.

One strove for prevention before the attack, and for cure during the illness. For prevention there was nothing better than to flee the infected region, and to purge oneself with aloe pills, to diminish the blood by phlebotomy, to purify the air by fire, to comfort the heart with theriac and fruits, and things of pleasant odor; to console the humors with Armenian bole, and to resist decay by sharp-tasting things.

For curative treatment one used cups and evacuations, electuaries and syrup cordials. External abscesses (swellings) were ripened with figs and cooked onions, crushed with yeast and butter: they were then opened and treated as ulcers.

The carbuncles were cupped, scarified and cauterized. And I, to avoid infamy, did not dare to absent myself; but with continual fear, preserved myself as best I could by means of these remedies. Nevertheless, toward the end of the epidemic, I fell ill with a continued fever and an abscess of the groin. I was sick for six weeks, in such grave danger that my companions thought I would die. My abscess ripened, and was treated as I have said, and I survived, by grace of God.

Later, in the 60th year, and the 8th of the papacy of Pope Innocent VI, after recrossing Germany and the Northern Countries, the mortality returned to us. Beginning toward the feast of Saint Michael, with swellings, fever, carbuncles and anthrax, it became augmented little by little: and at times it remitted, until the middle of the 61st year. Then it remained so furious for the next three months, that it left in many places but half of the people. It differed from the preceding, in that in the first, most of the populace died: and in this one, mostly the rich and the noble and innumerable children, and few women.

During this, I assembled and compiled one of those theriacal electuaries according to Master Arnold of Villanova and the Masters of Montpellier and Paris. I took it like a theriac, and I was protected, with the aid of God whose name shall be blessed from century to century. Amen.

CHAPTER 17

John of Arderne
(1306–1390?)

"But the leech shall beware that he give no certain answer in any case, but that he first see the sickness and the manner of it. . . ."[1]

John of Arderne was the first English surgeon of note. D'Arcy Power wrote that he was "the earliest example" of a sequence of British surgeons who possessed "the qualities which make an English gentleman as well as a fine surgeon. They were all men of good education, wide experience, and sound judgement." The nature and source of Arderne's training is not known, except that he gained his surgical experience during the Hundred Years War, serving first under the Duke of Lancaster and later with John of Gaunt. He was present at the Siege of Algeciras against the Moors, where gunpowder was used for the first time. These early experiences profoundly impressed themselves upon his mind, and he mentions them frequently in his writings thirty years later.

On the termination of his military service, in 1349, John engaged in the civilian practice of surgery in Newark in Nottinghamshire. Although he encompassed the whole of surgery in his practice, he seems to have been particularly interested in diseases of the rectum, thus representing the first proctologist. He is best known for his operation for fistula-in-ano, but he also wrote on hemorrhoids, gave an excellent description of rectal cancer, devised an apparatus for clysters, and wrote a book on the subject.

It is apparent, from the persons he mentions by name as having been "cured" of anal fistula, that his patients included the nobility, high ecclesiastics, and wealthy landowners. Nor was he timid in the matter of fees.

> "And if he see the patient pursue busily the cure, then after that
> the state of the patient asketh [according to the condition of the pa-
> tient] ask he boldly more or less; but ever be he ware of scarce asking,
> for over scarce asking setteth at naught both the market and the

1. *Treatises of Fistula in Ano, Haemorrhoids and Clysters* by John Arderne, edited by D'Arcy Power, London, Kegan Paul, Trench, Trübner & Co., 1910, p. 5.

thing. Therefore for the cure of fistula in ano, when it is curable, ask he competently, of a worthy man and a great, an hundred mark or forty pound, with robes and fees of an hundred shilling term of life by year. Of lesser men forty pound or forty mark ask he without fees; and take he naught less than an hundred shillings. For never in my life took I less than an hundred shilling for cure of that sickness."[2]

After some twenty years of provincial practice, Arderne moved to London. His reputation must have preceded him for he was admitted to the Surgeons' Guild as a Master Surgeon. It was here in the metropolis that he composed his several treatises. He wrote on many subjects, but his best known is the book on anal fistula. This disease was apparently prevalent at the time and was considered to be incurable by the contemporary medical authorities. The techniques then in use were timid and inadequate. John of Arderne devised an operation not dissimilar from the one employed today. He threaded a ligature through the fistulous opening into the rectum, which he tied tightly to prevent hemorrhage. Then boldly incising the mass of tissue in the grasp of the ligature, he laid open the entire tract. If multiple sinuses were present, he recognized the necessity of opening them all in turn, although he did note that if the principal channel was divided, the lesser ones might heal spontaneously. A notable feature of his method was the aftercare, which consisted of simple cleansing, without the use of the irritating or suppurative medicaments which were so universally employed at that time. The instruments for this procedure were devised by him, and are shown in the illustration accompanying the text. It is to his credit that he reported his failures as well as his successes.

John of Arderne was well educated and familiar with the literature of surgery. His manuscripts were written in Latin, and in his own hand. He had the temerity to operate boldly and the courage to break with tradition. A man of high moral fiber, his description of the qualities required of the surgeon equalled in strictness that of the most demanding. He was truly the first great British surgeon.

First it behooves him that will profit in this craft that he set God before evermore in all his works, and evermore call meekly with heart and mouth [for] his help; and sometimes visit of his evenings poor men according to his ability, that they by their prayers may get him grace of the Holy Ghost; and that he be not found forward or boastful in his sayings or in his deeds; and abstain from much speech and mostly among great men. And answer wisely to things asked, that he be not caught in his

2. *Ibid.*, pp. 5–6.

FIG. 27. A section of John of Arderne's "Art of Medicine and Surgery." The figures from above downward show a servant bringing a urine specimen to the physician, two patients with abdominal pain, and a man with hematuria. From: *De Arte Phisicali et Cirurgia* of Master John Arderne . . . . Tr. by Sir D'Arcy Power, William Wood & Company, 1922.

words. Forsooth, if his works be ofttime known to disagree with his words and his behests, he shall be held more unworthy, and he shall blemish his own good fame. . . .

Also a leech should not laugh too much nor play too much. And as much as he can, without harm, he should flee the fellowship of knaves and dishonest persons. And he should evermore be occupied in things that serve his craft; either to read or study or write or pray; for a leech worships the exercise of books.

For this, he shall be both beholden and wise. And above all this it profits him that he be found evermore sober; for drunkenness destroys all virtue and brings it to nought. . . .

He should be satisfied in strange place with the meat and drink here found, using moderation in all things. . . . Scorn he no man, for "he that scorns other men shall not go away unscorned." If anyone speaks to him of another leech, he should neither set him at nought nor praise him too much, or commend him, but thus may he courteously answer: "I have no true knowledge of him, but I have learned nothing, nor have I heard anything of him but goodness and honesty." And by this shall honor and gratefulness of each party increase and multiply for him. After this honor is in the honorant and not in the honored.

He shall not look too openly at the lady or the daughters or other fair women in great men's houses, nor proffer to kiss them, nor touch either secretly or openly their breasts, nor their hands nor their pubes. So that he does not run into the indignation of the lord, nor of none of his [men]. Inasmuch as he can, he should offend no servant, but get their love and their good will. He should abstain from harlotry in words as well as in deeds in every place, for if he practices harlotry in private places, sometime in an open place there may fall to him onus of evil practice. [He goes on to warn the leech against being too rough or too familiar in his address; also to consider carefully before accepting a case for treatment, with suggestions for ways of declining or refusing patients without giving offense.] But the leech shall beware that he give no certain anwser in any case, but that he first see the sickness and the manner of it; and when he has seen, and assayed it, although it may seem to him that the sickness can be healed, nevertheless, he shall warn the patient of the danger to come, if the treatment be deferred.[3]

[John of Arderne recognized the role of ischiorectal abscess as the cause of anal fistula. He writes:] Although the principal intent was to treat of fistula-in-ano, nevertheless it helps first to touch somewhat of abscess in or near the rectum, since often abscesses breeding there are the cause of fistula or cancer. For, according to the authors, an abscess bred in any places of the body, if it be not healed by three or four months, it turns into a fistula or a cancer. Therefore, when there occurs an abscess in or near the anus thou shalt know it by these signs; that is by swelling, aching, burning, itching and pricking. And the pa-

3. *Ibid.*, pp. 4–5.

Fig. 28. Frontispiece from: *Treatises of Fistula in Ano, Hemorrhoids and Clysters.* By John Arderne. Ed. . . . by D'Arcy Power. London, Kegan Paul, Trench, Trübner & Co., 1910.

tient for aching and anguish may neither sit nor lie nor sleep. . . . And he be ever more wary of paining on *egestion*. And if his low bowel be constipated, it should be softened so that the hardness of the stool not bring anguish in doing *egestion*.[4]

But wit thou, according to all the authors—and I have proved if for certain experience—that an abscess breeding near the anus should not be left to burst by itself, but the leech should busily for to feel with his finger the place of the abscess, and where so is found any softness, there, the patient not knowing, carefully, be it boldly opened with a very sharp lancette, so that the pus and the corrupt blood may go out. Or else, forsooth, the gut or bowel that is called rectum, that leads to the anus will burst within the anus. . . . Which case befalling, if it only bursts within it is hard to cure, and then there will be *raggedies*, forsooth, if it bursts both within and without, then it can never be cured except by a surgeon fully expert in his craft. For then may it from the first day be called a fistula.

4. *Ibid.*, p. 11.

Some times it befalleth some men to have only one hole appearing outward piercing through the rectum within the anus by space of one inch or two. . . . And I have seen some who have seven or nine holes on one side of the buttocks, and six or five on the other side, none of which except one pierce the rectum.[5]

OF BUBO [CANCER] WITHIN THE RECTUM AND THE IMPOSSIBILITY OR GREAT DIFFICULTY OF THE CURE OF IT.

Bubo is an apostem breeding within the anus in the rectum with great hardness but little aching. This I say, before it ulcerates, is nothing else than a hidden cancer, that may not in the beginning of it be known by the sight of the eye, for it is all hidden within the rectum; and therefore it is called bubo, for as bubo, i.e., an owl, is always dwelling in hiding so that this sickness lurkes within the rectum in the beginning, but after passage of time it ulcerates and, eroding the anus, comes out. And often it erodes and wastes all of the circumference of it so that the feces of egestions go out continuously until death, that it may never be cured with man's cure. But if it pleases God, that made man out of nothing, to help with his unspeakable virtue; which, forsooth, is known thus: the leech put his finger into the anus of the patient, and if he finds within the anus a thing hard as a stone, sometimes on one side only, sometime on both, so that it permits the patient to have egestion it is bubo [cancer] for certain. Signs, forsooth, of ulceration are these: the patient cannot abstain from going to the privy because of aching and pricking and that twice or thrice within one hour; and he passes a stinking discharge mixed with watery blood.

Ignorant leeches will assure the patient, that he has dysentery, that is, the bloody flux, when truly it is not. Dysentery is always with flux of the intestines, but out of bubo [cancer] goes hard excretions and sometime they may not pass, because of the constriction caused by the bubo, and they are retained firmly within the rectum, so that they may be felt with the finger and drawn out. . . . [Here he advises enemas with various medicaments to soften the stool][6]

I never saw nor heard of any man that was cured of cancer of the rectum but I have known many that died of the foresaid sickness.[7]

5. *Ibid.*, pp. 11–12.
6. *Ibid.*, pp. 37–38.
7. *Ibid.*, p. 39.

CHAPTER 18

Antonio Benivieni
(1443–1502)

"On his death I was eager to prove this theory by examination and sought to cut open the body, but his relations refused through some superstition or other, and I was unable to gratify my wish."[1]

The role played by surgeons in the early evolution of anatomy has already been alluded to in this book. That they played a similar part in the development of pathology is perhaps less well known. The "Father" of this science is usually held to be Morgagni, whose masterwork was published in 1761. Yet, fully a century-and-a-half earlier, a Florentine surgeon, Antonio Benivieni, quite routinely performed autopsies to discover the "hidden causes of disease," and carefully recorded these findings as well as those in his clinical cases. Sir Clifford Allbutt says of him, "Benivieni's chief fame for us is far more than all this; it is that he was the founder of pathological anatomy. So far as I know he was the first to make the custom and to declare the need of necropsy to reveal what he had called not exactly 'the secret causes' but the hidden causes of diseases. Before Vesalius, before Eustachius, he opened the bodies of the dead as deliberately and clear-sightedly as any pathologist in the spacious times of Baillie, Bright and Addison."

Antonio Benivieni was born in 1443, in Florence, of a noble and well-to-do family. His education was as liberal as the times afforded, and he retained an interest in literature and philosophy throughout his life. After attending the universities of Pisa and Sienna, he practiced medicine and surgery in his native city until his death in 1502. The records indicate that he was esteemed in his profession, that he amassed a considerable fortune, and that he was elected to important public office.

Throughout his years of practice, Benivieni kept methodical records of his cases with an eye, apparently, to eventual publication. From these reports it is

1. *De Abditis Nonnullis ac Mirandis Morborum et Sanationum Causis* (The Hidden Causes of Disease) by Antonio Benivieni of Florence, translation by Charles Singer with a biographical appreciation by Esmond R. Long, Springfield, Charles C Thomas, 1954, p. 81.

Antonio Benivieni (1443–1502).

Fig. 29. Antonio Benivieni (1443–1502), Frontispiece of *De Abditis Morborum Causis*, Springfield, Charles C Thomas, 1954.

evident that his primary interest was in surgery. Indeed, after his death, his brother Geronimo went through his papers, seeking unsuccessfully for the unpublished manuscript of a book on surgery. During this search, he came upon the collection of case reports upon which Antonio's enduring place in medicine rests. Convinced of the importance of these observations, he turned them over to a physician friend, Rosati, who confirmed this opinion and prepared the material for publication. The book *De Abditis . . . Morborum . . . Causis* or "The Hidden Causes of Disease" appeared in 1507, five years after the author's death. This small but significant volume has recently been reprinted with an English translation by Charles Singer and a biographical appreciation by Esmond R. Long.

The text of the book consists of a random series of case reports, comprising a wide variety of diseases. Of the 160 cases in the original manuscript, unfortunately Rosati arbitrarily omitted about fifty. The most striking feature of the book is the frequency with which postmortem examination was done. Permission for autopsy was apparently quite easily obtained. In case **XXXII**, captioned "Death following Stoppage of the Small Intestine," Benivieni concludes plaintively and with quite a modern touch: "On his death I was eager to prove this theory by examination and sought to cut open the body, but his relations refused through some superstition or other, and I was unable to gratify my wish." Among the cases briefly described which are of particular interest to the surgeon are two of gallstones, a carcinoma of the pylorus, one of the colon with death from bowel obstruction, herniae of many varieties with diverse complications, two instances of destructive hip-joint disease (probably tuberculous), and the usual distribution of ulcers, wounds, and fistulae.

The autopsy protocols are brief and somewhat vague, as would be expected in the light of the contemporary status of anatomy, pathology, and knowledge of the causation of disease. The findings are sometimes obviously misinterpreted and often difficult to explain in terms of current knowledge. Evident anatomical abnormalities are accepted without question as the basis of the illness and the cause of death. Nonetheless, the scientific curiosity that prompted the search for the nature and location of disease, and the courage to seek these out in the bodies of the dead are truly remarkable for their period, and earn for Benivieni a lasting place among the pioneers of medical science. Esmond Long writes, in describing the work of Benivieni and others who followed him: "It was the beginning of the end of the old humoral traditions."

[CASE] III.   STONES FOUND IN THE COAT OF THE LIVER[2]

A woman of noble birth had been for long greatly tormented by pain in the region of the liver. She had consulted many physicians, but could not drive out the evil by any remedy. She therefore decided to try my help in conjunction with some others.

Thus several of us met and discussed at great length from different aspects the hidden causes of this disease. As often happens in doubtful cases, we were divided. Some thought there was an abscess on the liver, others that it was itself diseased, but I personally believed that the fault lay in the covering membrane. A few days afterward the disease took stronger hold and she departed this life, even as we had foretold by common consent from unmistakable symptoms.

I then had her dead body cut open. There were found in the lower part of the membrane round the liver, a collection of small stones varying in shape and colour. Some were round, some pointed, some square, according as position and chance

2. *Ibid.*, p. 25.

had determined, and they were also marked with reddish, blue and white spots. These stones by their weight had caused the membrane to hang down in a bag a palm's length and two fingers wide. This we judged the cause of her death and decided that discussions upon what was hidden were vain and futile.

VI. PROMINENCE OF THE NAVEL[3]

A moderately prominent navel is common. It is abnormal if it projects too far. Giovanni Bini had an eight months son whose navel had grown out four inches long. The end appeared to be joined to the tegument of the testicles and from this wind sometimes broke. Many physicians examined him. Some said it was an intestinal, others that it was an omental hernia and others that it contained only humour. I personally said it was a fleshy growth. As the father adhered to this opinion, I undertook the child's treatment. But, influenced by the authority of those who said it was intestinal on account of the wind which sometimes broke out from it, I was extremely doubtful whether I ought to cut away the flesh, and further whether this ought to be done with knife or cautery. At last, supported by a definite train of reasoning, I decided to ligate the flesh. I bound it every day more tightly, until it was thoroughly mortified and fell off of itself. The child thereupon regained perfect health.

XXXIV. A NUN WHO DIED THROUGH PAIN IN THE INTESTINES[4]

In the convent of San Donato in Pulverosa, there was a devout woman, a member of the convent, who had suffered for many months with pains in the intestines. Her bowels, moreover, passed nothing without pain and difficulty and that only every tenth day. No remedies availed. She was burdened long and grievously by this disorder till at last she died.

I had the body cut open and found the intestines contracted by a thick callus so that only a narrow channel was left and the excrement could scarcely pass through. This however I had suspected even in her lifetime, seeing that she had struggled against something hard that pressed on her bowel.

XXXVI. HARDENING OF THE STOMACH[5]

My kinsman, Antonio Bruno, retained the food he had eaten for too short a time, and then threw it up undigested.

3. *Ibid.*, p. 31.
4. *Ibid.*, p. 83
5. *Ibid.*, pp. 85–87.

He was most carefully treated with every kind of remedy for the cure of stomach trouble, but as none was of any use at all, his body wasted away through lack of nourishment till little more than skin and bone remained. At last he was brought to his death.

The body was cut open for reasons of public welfare. It was found that the opening of his stomach had closed up and it had hardened down to the lowest part with the result that nothing could pass through to the organs beyond, and death inevitably followed.

LXXIX.   FEMUR ERODED[6]

The daughter of Rogerio Corbinelli had almost continual pain in her right flank. Many practitioners were called in at diverse times, and though each treated the girl according to his individual judgment (for opinions differed) the remedies availed not at all. At last she died.

It was decided to open the body. The femur was found to be eaten away and most of it reduced to powder. Moreover around the os matricis were four yellowish lumps, like balls, three filled with watery fluid, and the fourth raised a little above the others, and tuberculated (dentatus), rough, and hard as to the surface, seeing that it was gendered of flesh and black bile.

It is not therefore surprising if the opinions and pronouncements of physicians differ in a disease of this kind whose causes are hidden and uncertain.

I.   OF THE DISEASE COMMONLY NAMED MORBUS GALLICUS[7]

In the year 1496 from the Christian salvation, a new kind of disease crept over Italy and nearly all Europe. It began in Spain, and spreading thence far and wide, first over Italy and then through France and the other countries of Europe, attacked most of the inhabitants.

Pustules of various kinds broke out first on the genitals (sometimes it might be on the head, but this rarely) and thence extended over the whole body. On some they stood out more or less plainly, but had a scabrous surface and were whitish in colour. Scales broke off from these and the flesh appeared corroded beneath. In other cases there were pimples, circular

6. *Ibid.*, pp. 157–159.
7. *Ibid.*, pp. 9–15.

in shape, and when these too had shed rather thinner scales, the flesh stood out redder in hue, and there came away a fetid and foul discharge. Some had larger pustules which were not raised above the skin and had thicker scales. From these came a more copious discharge and, when the scales fell off, the eroded flesh appeared of darker hue and slightly bluish. There was a fourth variety which, when the whitish scales had fallen off, remained like a scar, from which sometimes a flow of blood would indicate that the case would be obstinate. This would resemble a dry scurf and was in every way worse than the other varieties, and although less erosive would creep on and settle in various parts of the body, hitherto unaffected. This type affected mostly the common folk and serfs, but very few in the upper classes.

Such pustules were followed and sometimes even preceded by pains in the joints which racked the body with no less torment, and reached their maximum as the pustules abated. If an attempt were made to evacuate the humours by drugs, the pustules continued to break out on the throat and mouth with grave consequences to the patients. Thus some perished through the physician's carelessness or, what was nearly as bad, were with difficulty saved with their jaws and throat eroded.

In my opinion the substance of these pustules varies even as the kinds of pustules. For sometimes a sharp humour, erosive and mixed with blood, predominates. Sometimes the thicker is separated from the thinner part of the fluid and turns to black bile. Sometimes too the black bile itself rises up and without separating itself from the sharper humour, pierces and eats away the flesh. Dried up discharges, inclining to resemble black bile in composition, act similarly. If these occur on denser parts of the body which they cannot pierce, they fasten there and excite yet more violent pains until dispersed, or finally they break out in pustules, which though in other ways loathsome and difficult to treat, yet (as is the nature of black bile) inflict no pain upon their victims. Those attacked by this type of pustule should not rely on unskilled doctors who, in complete ignorance of the causes of this disorder, hasten with their mixtures of ointments to cure it in its first stages. Thus they often bring their patients to their death or to a worse or even completely incurable state. For, as the causes at work in this malady are difficult to eradicate, it cannot be treated save by industry and time; so those who look for a quick recovery usually meet with death, or at any rate with a prolonged disability. If the sufferer would safeguard himself and be assured of recovery, let him use the drugs and counsels set down below. The most skilled physicians claim to undertake a cure with these very drugs (which also cure lepra) if a disease of this type has spread over the whole body.

CHAPTER 19

Paracelsus
(1493–1541)

". . . I have labored incessantly to understand the essence of medicine and whether one might call it an art. . . ."[1]

"Internal medicine and surgery are based on philosophy and must not be separated except in practice; every physician must be a doctor of both medicines."[2]

Aureolus Philip Theophrastus Bombastus von Hohenheim (1493–1541), commonly called Paracelsus, is unquestionably the most controversial figure in the history of medicine. Variously considered a genius and a charlatan, hailed as a reformer of medicine and denounced as an ignorant quack, idolized by few but despised and persecuted by many, his true role is difficult to assess. The judgements of time are rather in his favor. Garrison characterizes him as "the most original medical thinker of the Sixteenth century," and Sigerist speaks of him as "one of the most forceful personalities of the Renaissance." His short but tempestuous life was filled with strife and wandering, despite which he wrote voluminously on chemistry, natural philosophy-theology, medicine, and, very importantly, on surgery.

Paracelsus spent most of his life in the cultural sphere of Germany. He was born at Einsiedeln, in Switzerland, and early in his youth moved with his family to Villach, one of the mining centers of Carinthia. His father was a physician from whom, presumably, he received his early education and his introduction into medicine. As a young man he worked in the mines of Villach and in the Tyrolean metallurgical laboratories, where his life long interest in chemistry was born. After this experience he embarked on a long course of travel, during which he visited many countries, mixed with all classes of

1. Theophrast von Hohenheim, gen. Paracelsus: *Die Grosse Wundarznei*, edited by Karl Sudhoff, München, R. Oldenburg, 1928, Vol. 10, p. 19, "Vorred doctor Paracelsi in den ersten tractat."
2. Paracelsus. From: Michael L. Mason: "Basel–1527." *Quarterly Bulletin*, Northwestern University Medical School, Chicago, Vol. 30, 1956, p. 279.

ALTERIVS NON SIT QVI SVVS ESSE POTEST

AVREOLVS PHILIPPVS   THEOPHRASTVS BOMBAST,
AB HOHENHELM,   DICTVS PARACELSVS

Stemmate nobilium genius PARACELSVS   *Lustra nouem et medium vixit: lustro ante*
auorum.   *Lutherum.*
Qua vetus Heluetia claret Eremus humo,   *Postque tuos lustro functus. Erasme, rogos.*
Sic oculos Sic ora tulit, cum plurima longum   *Astra quater Jena Septembris luce subiuit:*
Discendi studio per loca fecit iter   *Ossa Salisburgæ nunc cineresque jacent*

I. Tintoret ad viuum pinxit.   *F Chauueau sculpsit.*

FIG. 30

people, listened avidly to all, and retained a vast fund of medical fact and folklore. Whether he had formal university training is not definitely known. He claimed the title of Doctor of Medicine, although his right to it was questioned by his detractors. If a degree was conferred on him, its source has not come to light.

His practice of medicine began in 1526, at the age of 30, and from the start his unconventional methods earned for him the suspicion and hostility of the regular physicians. In that same year, he purchased citizenship in Strassbourg, and became a member of the guild to which surgeons belonged, as did also millers and grain dealers. But before he could settle in Strassbourg he received the appointment of City Physician (*Stadtarzt*) of Basel (1527), which carried with it professorship in medicine in the university of that city.

Paracelsus was deeply concerned with the stagnation that characterized medical thought and education. The challenge of the Renaissance was in him, and he launched himself into a war against sterile dogma and opposition to change which was to continue throughout his life. He denounced the current medical and surgical practices, burned the book of Avicenna in a public bonfire, and, worst crime of all, lectured in German instead of the conventional Latin. The ire of the profession as well as of the rest of the faculty was quickly aroused, and, after a stormy eighteen months, he was driven from the city.

The remainder of his life was spent wandering from place to place, preaching "heretical" doctrines, and pursuing his medical practice with varying success. At times he was reduced to abject poverty. Throughout these years he wrote frenetically, on many subjects, winning a small number of ardent adherents, but many more enemies. These adversaries often prevailed in preventing the publication of his books, many of which remained in manuscript until after his death.

The writing of Paracelsus, as has been stated, covered an exceedingly wide range. As an expression of his opposition to the static and dogmatic status of medicine, he violently attacked the Galenic-Arabic concepts and the natural philosophy upon which they were based. The system he offered as a substitute was largely rooted in chemistry with a liberal admixture of cosmology and astrology. Although no less irrational and incomprehensible than its predecessors, it served to loosen the iron grasp of medieval dogma, and so helped to liberate thinking in medicine. He wrote of chemistry, and is certainly to be credited with the introduction of that branch of science into pharmacology and medicine.

Paracelsus bitterly deplored the separation of surgery from medicine, and strove constantly to weld the two disciplines together. He personally practiced, as well as wrote, on both subjects and signed himself "beyder Artzney Doctorn" (Doctor of Both Medicines). He belonged to the craft of wound surgeons, and did not concern himself with elective operative surgery. In his wound management, he strongly believed, as did Hippocrates, that healing was solely the property of nature, and that the doctor could only assist the natural forces, primarily by supplying nutrition and in preventing complications. The integument was likened to the shell of the egg, the bark of the tree, or the skin of the apple. When breached, it permitted the noxious contact of the internal tissues with the outside air, whence arose all complications. The early closure of the wound with bland and nutritive substances was thus clearly indicated. The use of sutures for this purpose was deplored. The similarity of this concept with that of *asepsis* is obvious, differing only in attributing injurious influences to air rather than to microorganisms, knowledge which he could not possibly have possessed at that period.

The personality of Paracelsus has been as moot a subject as his doctrines. To his detractors he was a crude, debauched boor, devoid of ethics, principles, or character. That he was coarse-fibered, boastful, and arrogant (bombastic, as his name implied), and given to violent and intemperate conflict cannot be doubted. Beyond this, however, his writings indicate that he was a dedicated man, true to his own principles, tireless in his pursuit of knowledge, independent and original in his thinking, courageous beyond compare, and deeply religious according to his beliefs. Although his specific contributions to medicine and surgery may not have been of tremendous significance, his role as a reformer and liberator of medicine is certainly assured.

 relax relax relax   PARACELSIAN SURGERY[3]

relax relax relax   Students, I greet you. Medicine alone, of all the intellectual disciplines, is a necessity and since few doctors today practice it with success and to the advantage of their patients, it seems necessary to reinstate it in its original exalted position. It is my desire to rid medicine of its most glaring errors and to teach, not according to the rules of the ancients, but on those principles which derive from the nature of things and which I have reached through my own reflections and have found valuable in long use and experience. I am permitted by the generous honor of the Council of Basel to teach according to my own methods and to lecture daily on practical and theoretical medicine, both internal medicine as well as surgery. I shall read with diligence from text books of which I am the author, those things of greatest value to you. You may judge me only after you have heard me.

I should like to lecture to you on surgery, but first, you must understand certain things concerning medicine as a whole and the practice of surgery in particular. I have repeatedly attempted by constant observation and diligent work to determine the basis of medicine. Many things have compelled me to this. Firstly, the uncertainty of the practice, because so

3. This quotation from the writings of Paracelsus is part of a condensed version of the first tractate of the first volume of Paracelsus' *Grosse Wundartznei*. The translation was made by Dr. Michael L. Mason, and is used with his permission. It was published in the *Quarterly Bulletin,* Northwestern University Medical School, Vol. 30, 1956, p. 278ff. In the interest of continuity the deletions are not indicated in the text.

little honor and praise is attached to it, so many sick are made
worse, killed, maimed, and entirely forsaken, not just in one
disease but in almost all diseases. So uncertain is treatment
that even in my times scarcely a physician can cure even a tooth-
ache. Internal medicine and surgery are based on philosophy
and must not be separated except in practice; every physician
must be a doctor of both medicines. Secondly, you should
know that medicine is not based on science alone, but on science
and experience, and experience is what has been proved true
and right. Thirdly, medicine is changing and growing daily
and the physician must know not just one disease or know how
to care for one wound, but he must know all diseases and how
to cleanse and treat all wounds. You must use your eyes and
observe, look about, travel and ask questions. Do not be ashamed
to ask questions even if you are a doctor. You will not find
everything written in the books of Galen and Avicenna, all of
surgery has not been written, for new times bring new diseases
and new books will outmode the old.

The basis of medicine is love, and not everyone can be a
physician. Every surgeon should have three qualities, first
as regards his own *person*; second, as regards the *patient*, and,
third, as regards his *art*. As regards his own person, the surgeon
should not think he knows everything or is competent to handle
all things. Not the outlay of money, nor the attendance at
school, nor the reading of books will make a surgeon. The
surgeon should not run a house of ill-fame, he should not be
a hangman, or apostate, nor belong to the priesthood, or be
an actor or poet. The barbers, bathers and others of their ilk
think they have learned it all by the menial work of their
trade. But you must learn daily from your own experience and
from the experiences of others, for no matter how experienced
or wise you may be, the time comes when your knowledge fails
you and the patient suffers. Be modest and mild; do not praise
yourself but give credit to others where credit is due. Think
more of the patient than the money you may gain from him.

You should know the make-up of man, where the bones and
other structures lie and their relation to each other. If you do
not know these things how can you diagnose injuries or know
how to put them right? It is not enough that you know the
externals, you must know the internals better than the externals;
you must know all the veins and arteries, nerves and bones,
their length, number, form, location in every limb; also, where

the emunctoria are and how they are to be turned aside and what lies in each and where the intestines lie. The surgeon should know all this just as the carpenter knows the construction of a house. The surgeon must know anatomy and not be like the barber or bather who knows no more than the butcher who cuts, trims and separates his meat.

Finally, the surgeon should know and recognize all plants and in what way they may be used, which cure, which cleanse, which act rapidly and which act slowly. He must recognize all complications of wounds, of which you will find little written in the books of the ancients, but I shall give them to you. He should know what to order and what to forbid the patient. He should know the true remedies and not try new ones without understanding them. He should neglect no science but learn from all. He should know many remedies and not play on a fiddle with one string.

What are the things which characterize a surgeon and what are the things he must know? The surgeon must know as soon as he looks at a wound, what lies under his eyes; what he may accomplish with it and to what end he may bring it. He must not promise to do more, or less, for the wound than nature permits. For if he promises more than nature will permit, he will delay and thresh about and stall for time, all the while getting nowhere—and the longer the delay, the greater the harm to the patient and also to his reputation and to his shame. If he promises less than he can accomplish and he accomplishes more, he will be ridiculed for not understanding his tools and his art, or if he might have accomplished more than he did, how much greater is the shame.

The surgeon must also know that nature cannot be contraverted or changed, but that he must follow nature, not nature him. If he uses remedies contrary to nature, he will ruin everything. Now you cannot replace a limb that has been cut off and it is ridiculous to attempt it. In Veriul I saw a barber surgeon replace an ear that had been cut off and stick it back with mason's cement. He was given great praise and a loud cry of "miracle." However, the next day the ear fell off since it was undermined with pus. The same thing happens with limbs if one tries to stick them back on again, but what glory is there in such chicanery?

You should be instructed to recognize the good and bad signs in wounds, and by daily observation know what is to be expected and what the wound is building up to so that you may forestall evil complications. For a healthy body is not a matter of chance, how much less so one that has been injured. See to it likewise that you do not bring your patient into difficulties and that your treatment does not cause more trouble than the wound itself.

Learning and experience are the basis of surgical knowledge, so do not try to fly until you have learned how. Haughtiness, arrogance and feigned knowledge are of no avail; only real knowledge and skill. A serious fault with learning today is that it is not followed to completion but that each student wishes to become a master before the pupil has grown up.

You must work hard, much better too much work and study than too little. Man is subject to many accidents and any wound is more likely to be fatal than not. Time and the hour, nature and the patient's make-up seem more inclined to make things worse than better.

You should know what it is which heals a wound because without this knowledge you cannot use any medicine correctly. You should know that it is the nature of flesh, of the body, of the blood vessels, of the limbs to have within themselves an inborn balsam that heals all wounds, stab wounds or any other sort. It is the balsam in the limb that heals a fracture, the balsam that resides naturally in the flesh that heals flesh. So with every limb it should be understood that it carries its own healing in itself which heals it when it is wounded. Every surgeon therefore should know that it is not he who heals the wound but the balsam in the part that heals it. If he thinks he heals it, he fools himself, and does not know his art. To be a good surgeon, you should protect and shield the natural balsam from ever-present, external enemies, so that they do not destroy the balsam nor poison or damage it but permit it to work and act under your protection. If a wound is open and unprotected, it is evident that it cannot heal. The good surgeon affords this protection by suitable dressings under which in peace and quiet, nature heals the wound, makes grow the flesh, veins and all that has been injured. For what makes flesh, fat, grease, blood and bone marrow grow? Not man, not food, only nature has the growing and developmental powers which make the body whole. Through food and drink this strength is preserved. Rain and the earth do not make wood, only the tree can make wood, but without rain and earth, the tree dies.

The surgeon should know when he sees a wound what wounds are fatal, what may cause paralysis, what ones he may cure and what ones he cannot heal. For this, very much experience is necessary, and I have collected such experience, not alone from doctors, but from barbers, bathers, learned doctors, old wives and black magicians, from the alchemists, in the Klosters [monasteries], from the nobility and the peasant, the educated and the uneducated. The boob cannot learn it in a year or two and take a wife in one night and become a master.

There are many learned men in Germany who could further medical knowledge but they are so taken up with their useless labors and with poring over old books that they cannot be made to know that the real basis of medicine is, "love thy neighbor." Would I could make learned, pious, brave doctors out of them, that they might drive out the unscrupulous barbers, bathers and quacks. But they hold their learning higher than all the treasures of man, although their learning is no more than a wind which is neither hot nor cold, salt nor flesh, but passes like the ringing of a bell or the notes of a bag-pipe. Their learning seems great but because of it medicine has come into great disrepute and those who practice it work against God. They refute not only God but the evangelists who proclaim that the sick need the physician. What the wind has borne the wind will carry away. These men have been called to the monastery, not to medicine.

Medicine has become a field for the dishonest to plow, the nobleman and the merchant have much money, therefore they are cultivated. Not just the apostates, but other light-fingered folk have taken to medicine, the hangmen, poachers and others without honor. But just as there are true prophets and fake prophets, and true apostles and false ones, so there are true physicians and false ones, and the false patients seek the fake physician and the true ones the true physician.

CHAPTER 20

Ambroise Paré
(1510–1590)

"*What Chyrurgery is.*
Chyrurgery is an Art, which teacheth the way by reason, how by the operation of the
hand we may cure, prevent, and mitigate diseases, which accidentally happen unto
us."[1]
"*Of Chirurgicall operations.*
Thou shalt far more easily and happily attain to the knowledg of these things by long
use and much exercise, than by much reading of Books, or daily hearing of Teachers.
For speech how perspicuous and elegant soever it be, cannot so vively express any thing,
as that which is subjected to the faithfull eyes and hands."[2]

Ambroise Paré is the most celebrated surgeon of the Renaissance. The name
immediately conjures up the image of the genial figure who rose from obscurity to become the companion of kings. Anecdotes about him are legion.
Best known among them is the story of the wounded soldiers and the dearth
of boiling oil. Equally familiar is his expression of piety and humility found
in the recurring statement: "I dressed him, and God healed him." Of his
many surgical innovations three have most frequently been mentioned; these
are his rejection of boiling oil in the treatment of gunshot wounds, his introduction of the ligature in amputations, and the use of podalic version in
difficult deliveries.

Significant though these new ideas were, they do not, by themselves,
warrant the position of supreme importance which Paré has held in the history
of surgery throughout the ages. Further analysis is necessary to explain this
phenomenon. That Paré was a superb surgeon is beyond question. But how
can anyone compare the skill of any surgeon with that of others in various
lands and different times? More subtle evaluation must be sought to determine

1. *The Workes of that Famous Chirurgion Ambrose Parey*, translated out of Latine and Compared
   with the French by Tho. Johnson, London, Richard Cotes and Willi Du-gard, 1649, Chapter 1, p. 1.
2. *Ibid.*, Chapter 2, p. 1.

ET DES ARTS. Lɪv. II.   ɪoɪ

AMBROSIVS PAREVS.

AMBROISE PARÉ.

Fɪɢ. 31

why, according to Geoffrey Keynes, "He was in fact by virtue of his personality and independent mind the emancipator of surgery from the dead hand of dogma."

Little is known of Paré's early life. He was born in 1510 in a village near Laval (province of Maine) in the north of France. His parents were humble people, and his education meager. Apprenticed to a barber-surgeon, he served part of his indenture in the provinces and went to Paris to complete his training. Soon thereafter he was appointed house surgeon in the famous Hôtel Dieu. This training must have been invaluable, since he refers to it with pride, even after many years. At the age of seventy-five he recalled, "I was resident the space of three yeares in the Hospitall of Paris, where I had the meanes to see and learne divers workes of Chirurgery, upon divers diseases together with the Anatomy, upon a great number of dead bodies. . . ." Shortly after completing this period of service he entered the army as a surgeon.

Battle fields have always offered intensive opportunities for the training of surgeons. In the sixteenth century, when surgery consisted predominantly of the care of wounds, the vast number and variety of war injuries furnished an incomparable source of experience, particularly for one as resourceful and observant as Paré. During the remainder of his long and fruitful life, Paré alternated between successive military campaigns and periods of relatively quiet civilian practice in Paris, where he availed himself of the leisure to study anatomy and to write his many books. Each call to the service in turn was attended with growth of his stature and confidence, and likewise of his reputation. Beginning with Henry II, he served as body surgeon to four successive kings of France, attaining eventually the position of *Premier Chirurgien* and *Conseiller du Roi*.

When Paré entered military service at the age of twenty-six, he had completed the requisite training for admission to the Company of Barber-Surgeons, but he postponed his application for membership, presumably because he lacked the funds for examination and licensure fees. It was during his eventful first campaign that he learned from his own experience that gunshot wounds were not poisoned and then determined, in spite of his youth and in defiance of authority, to abandon the barbaric cauterization with boiling oil and to substitute soothing applications instead. That he was not without naiveté, however, he tells of himself. "Being at Turin [where this battle had taken place] I found a chirurgion, who had the fame above all others, for the curing of wounds of gunshot, into whose favour I found meanes to insinuate my selfe, to have the receipt of his balme, as he called it wherewith he dressed wounds of that kind, and hee held me off the space of two yeeres, before I could possible draw the receipt from him. In the end by gifts and presents he gave it to me, which was this, to boil young whelpes new pupped, in oyle of Lillies, [with] earthwormes prepared with Turpentine of *Venice*. Then I was joyfull and my heart made glad, that I had understood his remedy, which was like to that which I had obtained by great chance."[3] Many years later he abandoned this favored remedy for a mixture of honey and alum, and later of turpentine and brandy.

Paré was apparently already marked for greatness at that early period. Again to quote from his narrative, ". . . and if there were foure hurt, I had always three of them, and if there was question of cutting off an arm or legge, or to trepan, or to reduce a fracture or dislocation, I brought it well to passe. . . ."

3. From: "An Apologie or Treatis concerning divers Voiages," in *The Workes of that Famous Chirurgion Ambrose Parey, loc. cit.*, pp. 767–768.

A physician of high repute who had witnessed Paré's work and the results he obtained, counselled the commanding officer, "Thou hast a young chirurgion of age, but he is old in knowledge and experience, preserve him well; for he will do thee service, and honour." When this commander died of "hepatical fluxe," in 1538, Paré declined further military service for the time being and returned to Paris. Here he devoted himself to the study of anatomy, took his examination and license as a barber-surgeon, married, and settled down to civilian practice.

The recognition won through his initial campaign and those that followed endowed Paré with a position in the French surgical world that could not be ignored. The august and pretentious surgical guild, the Collège de St. Côme, conferred fellowship on him (1554) despite his lack of formal education and his barber-surgeon status, and without requiring the traditional examination or the payment of the usual fee. His intimacy with the officers in the army, who ranked among the highest nobility, and his eventual appointment as surgeon and counselor of successive kings brought honor and respect not only to his person but also to the profession he so ardently pursued. With such powerful support, and his own courage and intellectual conviction, he was able to challenge the authority of the Faculty of Medicine that had kept surgery in so humble a state of submission.

Ambroise Paré is revealed to us, from his writings, as having been extremely intelligent, upright, and conscientious; and even his less attractive traits such as his unconcealed ambition, vanity, and impetuosity were disarming and were balanced by his great kindliness and compassion. He had no formal education and did little, if any, systematic teaching. But he wrote voluminously and eventually so extremely well, that some of his later works became classics in form as well as in content. Although he was predominantly a surgeon his writings ranged over a large part of medicine. Unlike traditional medical authors, Paré wrote in the vernacular as did Paracelsus. Not only was he wanting in a knowledge of Latin, but he consciously addressed his works to fellow surgeons who were equally ignorant of the learned tongue.

His first book, *La Méthode de Traicter les Playes Faictes par Harquebutes et Aultres Baston de Feu. . . .* ("The Method of Treating Wounds made by Arquebuses and other Firearms"), which was published in 1545, records for the first time the observations made during his initial military campaign nine years earlier. Not only does he here recount the experience which led to his permanently rejecting the use of boiling oil in gunshot wounds, but he also describes the method of tracing the course of a projectile in the body by having the patient assume the position he was in when the injury occurred. This small and practical volume, written largely for his fellow barber-surgeons, was later followed by much more ambitious surgical works. In addition to the above, he wrote on anatomy, gout, plague, poisons, obstetrics, monsters, natural

FIG. 32. Rhinoceros. From: Ambroise Paré's Book, "Of Monsters and Prodigies"

history, and coroners' reports and composed a fascinating account of his travels and military experiences.

Paré was strongly convinced of the importance of anatomy as a prerequisite of surgery, and prepared several books on the subject. The relation between him and his contemporary, Vesalius, has been the source of a great deal of speculation. His first treatise on the subject, *Briefve collection de l'administration Anatomique: avec la maniere de conjoindre les os*, was published in 1539, some four years before the *Fabrica* of Vesalius was put into print. In his definitive text, however, the *Anatomie Universelle du Corps Humain* (1561), the influence of Vesalius is apparent despite Paré's alleged ignorance of Latin. References are made to the Vesalius text, and the illustrations are unquestionably influenced by those of the *Fabrica*. It may be assumed, therefore, that some cross fertilization of ideas did occur, and that Paré was, to a measure, a factor in making the work of Vesalius available in the vernacular to his less learned surgical colleagues.

Other achievements of Paré included the invention of new surgical instruments and artificial limbs and eyes, and the use of the truss in hernia. He suspected syphilis as a cause of aneurysm and described carbon monoxide poisoning. He had the courage to induce artificial labor in cases of uterine bleeding and even turned to dentistry, advocating reimplantation of teeth.

Of Paré's nonsurgical writings, one small book of directions for the composition of autopsy reports is of special importance because it constitutes one of the first works on medical jurisprudence. All of his writings are extremely interesting and hold a great deal of fascination for the modern reader.

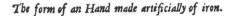

The form of an Hand made artificially of iron.

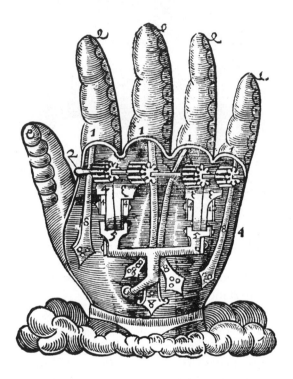

This figure following sheweth the back-side of an Hand artificially made, and so that it may bee tied to the arm or sleev.

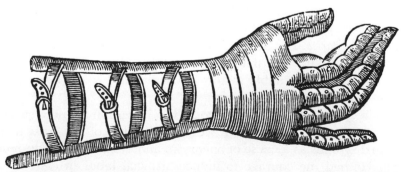

FIG. 33*A*. From: Paré's artificial articulated hand. Ambroise Paré's Book, "Of the Means and Manner to repair or supply the natural or accidental defects or wants in Man's bodie."

*The form of a nofe artificially made, both alone by it felf, and alfo with the up-
per-lip covered as it were with the hair of the beard,*

FIG. 33B. Nasal prosthesis; outer and inner aspects. From: Ambroise Paré's Book, "Of the
Means and Manner to repair or supply the natural or accidental defects or wants in Man's
bodie."

When the Collected Works of Paré were published in 1575, the Faculty
of Medicine, represented by its dean, vituperatively attacked the surgeon
because of his use of French instead of Latin,[4] and invoked an old statute that
no medical works could be published without the approval of the Faculty.
Characteristically, Paré rose to the attack and in challenging, boldly and
sarcastically, the entrenched authority of the Faculty, declared the independence of surgery. His reply, the *Apologie and Treatise, containing the Voyages
made into divers places*, which was first published in 1585 when he was seventy-five
years of age, is engrossing beyond all of his previous publications.

In the words of his bibliographer, Janet Doe, "His last piece of writing—
controversial, critical, historical— his 'Apologie et voyages,' is his supreme
literary achievement and is, besides, a unique historical document. His
realistic story of the siege of Metz can fearlessly be compared with the greatest
narratives of history. The golden thread running through it all is the personality of the author. In this *apologie pro vita sua* he paints vividly the arguments,
the history and judgment of his own methods, and the criticism of those of

4. Indeed, in order to gain for them wide acceptance among the learned circles of medicine
and surgery, Paré's *Opera* were eventually (1582) translated from the French into Latin.
Except for a Dutch edition all subsequent translations into other languages are based not
on Paré's original text but on the Latin version.

Fig. 34. Trusses for inguinal hernia. From: Ambroise Paré's Book, "Of Tumors against Nature in generall."

his enemies; he tells the story of his life shrewdly, with insight and kindliness and simplicity, a self-portrait by the hand of a master." Admiration for Paré's courage, ingenuity, intelligence, and humanity grows with the record of his adventures and achievements. His books, the exalted position he attained, his character and personality, and possibly something of that imponderable we call luck or fortune—perhaps these explain the position Paré holds among the great names of surgery.

ℰ ℰ ℰ [A FATAL CHEST WOUND WITH POSTMORTEM CONFIRMA-
ℰ ℰ ℰ TION OF THE CLINICAL FINDINGS.][5]

Now to return to my purpose being lead from the Castle to the Citty with Monsieur de Martigues, there was a Gentleman of the Duke of Savoyes, who asked mee if Monsieur de Martigues wound was curable, I answered, not; who presently

5. *Ibid.*, "An Apologie or Treatis," pp. 777–779.

went and told the Duke of Savoy; now I thought he would
send Physitions and Chirurgions to visit and dresse my said
Monsieur de Martigues; in the meane time I thought with
my self whether I ought to make it nice and not to acknowledge
my selfe a Chirurgion for feare least they should retaine mee
to dresse their wounded, and in the end they would know I
was the Kings Chirurgion, and that they would make me pay
a great ransome. On the other side I feared, if I should not
make my selfe knowne to bee a Chirurgion, and to have carefully dressed Monsieur de Martigues, they would cut my
throate, so that I tooke a resolution to make it appeare to them
he would not dye for want of good dressing and looking to.
Soone after, see, there arrives divers gentlemen accompanied
with the Physition and Chirurgion to the Emperour, and those
of the said Duke of Savoy, with sixe other Chirurgions following
the Army, to see the hurt of the said Lord of Martigues, and
to know of mee how I had dressed him and with what medicines. The Emperours Physition bid me declare the essence of
the wound, and how I had drest it. Now all the assistants had
a very attentive eare to know if the wound were mortall or
not: I begun to make a discourse that Monsieur de Martigues
looking over the wall to perceive them that did undermine it
received a shot from an Arquebuse quite through the body;
presently I was called to dresse him, I saw hee cast blood out
of his mouth, and his wounds. Moreover he had a great
difficultie of breathing, and cast out winde by the said wounds
with a whistling, in so much that it would blow out a Candle,
and he said he had a most sharpe pricking paine at the entrance
of the Bullet. I doe beleeve and thinke it might bee some little
peeces of bones which prickt the Lungs. When they made
their Systole and Diastole, I put my finger into him; where I
found the entrance of the Bullet to have broken the fourth Rib
in the middle and scales of bones which the said Bullet had
thrust in, and the outgoing of it had likewise broken the fift
Rib with peeces of bones which had beene driven from within
outward; I drew out some but not all, because they were very
deepe and adherent. I put in each wound a Tent, having the
head very large, tyed with a thread, least by the inspiration it
might bee drawne into the capacity of the Thorax, which hath
beene knowne by experience to the detriment of the poore
wounded; for being fallen in, it cannot be taken out, which is
the cause that engenders putrifaction, a thing contrary to

nature. The said Tents were annointed with a medicine com-
pos'd of yolks of Egges, Venice Turpentine, with a little oyle of
Roses; My intention for putting the Tents was to stay the flux
of blood, and to hinder that the outward ayre did not enter
into the breast, which might have cooled the Lungs and by
consequent the heart. The said Tents were also put, to the end
that issue might bee given for the blood that was spilt within
the Thorax. I put upon the wound great Emplasters of Dia-
calcitheos in which I had relented oyle of Roses and Vinigar
to the avoyding of inflammation, then I put great stupes of
Oxycrate, and bound him up, but not hard, to the end he
might have easie respiration; that done I drew from him five
porrengers of blood from the Basilicke veine of the right arme,
to the end to make revulsion of the blood which runs from the
wounds into the Thorax, having first taken indication from the
wounded part, and cheefely his forces, considering his youth
and his sanguine temper; Hee presently after went to stoole, and
by his urine and seege cast great quantity of blood. And as
for the paine which he said he felt at the entrance of the Bullet
which was as if he had been pricked with a bodkin, that was
because the Lungs by their motion beate against the splinters
of the broken Rib. Now the Lungs are covered with a coate
comming from the membrance called Pleura, interweaved
with nerves of the sixt conjugation from the braine, which was
cause of the extreame paine he felt; likewise he had a great
difficultie of breathing, which proceeded from the blood which
was spilt in the capacitie of the Thorax, and upon the Dia-
phragme, the principall instrument of respiration, and from
the dilaceration of the muscles which are betweene each Rib,
which helpe also to make the expiration and the inspiration;
and likewise because the Lungs were torne and wounded by
the Bullet, which hath caused him ever since to spit blacke and
putrid blood in coughing. The Feaver seazed him soone after
he was hurt, with faintings and swoonings. It seemed to mee
that the said feaver proceeded from the putredinous vapours
arising from the blood which is out of his proper vessells, which
hath fallen downe, and will yet flow downe. The wound of
the Lungs is growne great and will grow more great, because it
is in perpetuall motion, both sleeping and waking, and is
dilated and comprest to let in the aire to the heart, and cast
fuliginous vapours out: by the unnaturall heate is made
inflammation, then the expulsive vertue is constrained to cast

out by cough whatsoever is obnoxious unto it: for the Lungs cannot be purged but by coughing, & by coughing the wound is dilated, and growes greater, from whence the blood issues out in great abundance, which blood is drawne from the heart by the veine arteriall to give them nourishment, and to the heart by the vena cava; his meate was barly broth, stewed prunes, sometimes panada; his drinke was Ptisan: He could not lye but upon his backe which shewed he had a great quantity of blood spilt within the capacity of the Thorax, and being spread or spilled along the spondills, doth not so much presse the Lungs as it doth being laid on the sides or sitting.

What shall I say more, but that the said Lord Martigues since the time hee was hurt hath not reposed one houre onely, and hath alwayes cast out bloody urines and stooles. These things then Messieurs considered, one can make no other prognosticke but that he will dye in a few dayes, which is to my great greefe. Having ended my discourse I drest him as I was wont; having discovered his wounds, the Physitions and other assistants presently knew the truth of what I had said.

The said Physitions having felt his pulse and knowne his forces to be almost spent, and abolished, concluded with mee that in a few dayes he would dye; and at the same instant went all toward the Lord of Savoy, where they all said, that the said Lord Martigues would dye in a short time; he answered, it were possible if hee were well drest he might escape. Then they all with one voyce said, hee had beene very well drest, and sollicited with all things necessary for the curing of his wounds, and could not be better, and that it was impossible to cure him, and that his wound was mortall of necessity. The Monsieur de Savoy shewed himselfe to bee very much discontented and wept, and asked them againe if for certaine they all held him deplored and remedilesse, they all answered, yes. Then a certaine Spanish impostor offered himselfe who promised on his life that he would cure him, and if he failed to cure him, they should cut him in an hundred peeces; but he would not have any Physitions, Chirurgions or Apothecaries with him. And at the same instant the sayd Lord of Savoy told the Physitions and Chirurgions they should not in any wise goe any more to see the sayd Lord of Martiques. Also he sent a Gentleman to me to forbid me upon paine of life not to touch any more the said Lord of Martigues, which I promised not

to doe; wherefore I was very glad, seeing he should not dye in
my hands, and commanded the said impostor to dresse the
said Lord of Martigues.

And that he should have no other Physitions nor Chirurgions
but him; he came presently to the said Lord of Martigues, who
told him, Lord Cavalleere, Monsieur the Duke of Savoy hath
commanded me to come dresse thy wound; I sweare to thee by
God, that before eight dayes I will make thee mount on horse-
backe with thy Lance in thy hand, provided, that no man may
touch thee but my selfe; thou shalt eate and drinke any thing
thou hast a minde to, I will performe thy diet for thee, and of
this thou maist be assured upon my promise, I have cured
divers who have had greater wounds than thine: and the Lord
replyed, God give you the grace to doe it.

He demanded of the sayd Lord a shirt and tore it in little
ragges, which hee put a crosse, muttering, and murmuring
certaine words over the wound; and having drest him, permitted him to eate and drinke what he would, telling him hee
would observe a dyet for him, which he did, eating but six
prunes and sixe bits of bread at a meale, and drinking but beere.
Notwithstanding, two dayes after, the sayd Lord of Martigues
dyed; and my Spaniard, seeing of him in the agony, eclipst
himselfe and got away without bidding farewell to any body;
and I beleeve if he had beene taken he had bin hang'd for his
false promises, which he had made to Monsieur the Duke of
Savoy, and to divers other gentlemen.

He dyed about tenne of the clocke in the morning, and after
dinner, the sayd Lord of Savoy, sent Physitions and Chirurgions
and his Apothecary, with a great quantity of Drogues, to embalme him; they came accompanied with divers gentlemen and
Captaines of the Army.

The Emperors Chirurgion came neere to me, and prayed me
kindly to open the body; which I refused, telling him I was not
worthy to carry his plaster boxe after him: he prayed me againe,
which then I did for his sake, if it so liked him. I would yet
againe have excused my selfe, that seeing he was not willing to
embalme him, that he would give this charge to another
Chirurgion of the company; he made me yet answere, that he
would it should be I, and if I would not doe it, I might hereafter
repent it: knowing this his affection, for feare he should not doe
me any displeasure, I tooke the rasor and presented it to all in

particular, telling them I was not well practised to doe such operations which they all refused.

The body being placed upon a table, truely I purposed to shew them that I was an Anatomist, declaring to them diverse things, which should be heere too long to recite. I began to tell all the company that I was sure the bullet had broken two ribs, and that it had past through the Lungs, and that they should finde the wound much enlarged, because they are in perpetuall motion, sleeping or waking, and by this motion the wound was the more dilacerated. Also that there was great quantity of blood spilt in the capacity of the brest, and upon the midriffe, and splinters of the broken ribbes which were beaten in at the entrance of the bullet, and the issuing forth of it, had carried out. Indeed all which I had told them was found true in the dead body.

OF THE CURE OF RUPTURES.[6]

Because children are very subject to Ruptures, but those truely not fleshy or varicous, but watry, windy, and especially of the Guts, by reason of continuall and painefull crying and coughing: Therefore in the first place we will treate of their cure. Wherefore the Chirurgion, called to restore the Gut which is fallen downe, shall place the child, either on a table, or in a bed, so that his head shall be low, but his buttocks, and thighes higher; then shall he force with his hands by little and little, and gently, the Gut into its proper place; and shall foment the Groine with the astringent fomentation, described in the falling downe of the wombe. . . . Then let him apply Emplastrum contra Rupturam: but the chiefe of the cure consists in folded clothes, and Trusses, and ligatures artificially made, that the restored gut may be contained in its place, for which purpose he shall keepe the child seated in his cradle for 30 or 40 dayes, as we mentioned before; and keepe him from crying, shouting, and coughing. Aetius bids steepe paper 3 dayes in water, and apply it made into a ball to the groine, the gut being first put up; for that remedy by 3 dayes adhesion wil keep it from falling down. But it wil be, as I suppose more effectuall, if the paper be steeped not in common, but in the astringent water, described in the falling downe of the wombe. Truely I have healed many by the help of such remedies, and have delivered them from the hands

6. *The Workes*, Book 8, "Of particular Tumors against Nature," p. 239.

of Gelders, which are greedy of childrens testicles, by reason of the great gaine they receive from thence. They by a crafty cozenage, perswade the Parents, that the falling downe of the Gut into the Codde, is uncurable: which thing notwithstanding, experience convinceth to be false, if so be the cure be performed according to the forementioned manner when the Peritonaeum is onely relaxed, and not broken: for the processe thereof by which the Gut doth fall as in a steepe way, in progresse of time and age is straitned and knit together whilest also in the meane time the guts grow thicker.

> [ON ANEURYSM, IN WHICH THE RELATIONSHIP BETWEEN ANEURYSM OF THE AORTA AND SYPHILIS IS CLEARLY RECOGNIZED.][7]

Wherefore I diligently admonish the young Chirurgion that hee do not rashly open *Aneurismaes* unlesse they be smal in an ignoble part, but not indued with large vessells, but rather let him performe the cure after this manner. Cut the skinne which lyes over it untill the Artery appeare, and then separate it with your knife from the particles about it, then thrust a blunt and crooked needle with a thred in it under it, binde it, then cut it off and so expect the falling off, of the thred of it selfe whiles nature covers the orifices of the cut Artery with new flesh, then the residue of the cure may be performed after the manner of simple wounds. The *Aneurismaes* which happen in the internall parts are uncurable. Such as frequently happen to those who have often had the unction and sweat for the cure of the French disease, because the blood, being so attenuated and heated therewith that it cannot be contayned in the receptacles of the Artery, it distends it to that largenesse as to hold a mans Fist; Which I have observed in the dead body of a certaine Taylor, who by an *Aneurisma* of the Arterious veine suddenly whilest hee was playing at Tennis fell downe dead, the vessell being broken: his body being opened I found a great quantity of blood powred forth into the Capacity of the Chest, but the body of the Artery was dilated to that largenesse I formerly mentioned, and the inner coate thereof was bony. For which cause within a while after I shewed it to the great admiration of the beholders in the Physitions School whilest I publiquely dissected a body there; the whilst he lived said he felt a beating and a great heate over all his body by the force of the pulsation of all the Arteryes, by occasion whereof hee often swounded.

7. *Ibid.*, Book 7, "Of Tumors against Nature in generall," p. 225.

CHAPTER 21

Pierre Franco
(1500?–1561)

"Let us for this reason proceed with good method and good conscience in all our operations, which are of such great consequence, [and] not undertake them for our profit but to aid the poor patients, using charity toward them."[1]

The contemporary esteem and posthumous fame that came to Paré in such rich measure was withheld from others who were perhaps equally deserving but less gifted in the art of self-projection. Pierre Franco is one such person. A provincial surgeon of lowly origin and modest pretensions, he introduced innovations of far greater import than those of famed contemporaries whose names are familiar to all. Because of his accomplishments we can see in him a true figure of the Renaissance.

As the earlier chapters have shown, surgery of the Middle Ages and beyond concerned itself chiefly with the dressing of wounds and the cure of ulcers. Operative surgery, particularly for hernia, bladder stone, facial disfigurements, and cataract, was shunned by the leaders of the craft, probably because of the risks involved and the consequent dangers to their reputations and, perhaps, their persons—and progress suffered.

In the meantime, a new brand of surgical entrepreneur took over the initiative. Itinerant "cutters" appeared, often ignorant, brutal, mendacious, and unconscionable men, who wandered from place to place, promised even impossible cures, and undoubtedly left misery and death in their wake as they extracted their ill-earned fees and fled before the failures and disasters could overtake them. Some, however, attained remarkable proficiency in the performances of certain operations. Passing their "secrets" from generation to generation, certain families gained renown throughout Europe as specialists

1. Pierre Franco: *Traité des hernies*, Lyon, 1561 in E. Nicaise: *Chirurgie de Pierre Franco de Turriers en Provence composée en 1561.* Nouvelle édition avec une introduction historique, une biographie et l'histoire du Collège de Chirurgie, Paris, Ancienne Librairie Germer Baillière & Cie., 1895, p. 10. The epigram and the subsequent quotations are translated from the French by the authors.

in the cure of individual surgical diseases. Because their methods were closely held secrets, and perhaps because they were illiterate as well, few, if any, left written records of their achievements. Nevertheless, as we have already seen, other surgeons learned their techniques, and included them in their writings. Thus their crude efforts enriched the field of surgery.

Pierre Franco occupied a place somewhere between the barber-surgeons and the itinerant cutters. Little is known of his life beyond the few personal references in his own writings. He was born early in the sixteenth century (between 1500 and 1505) in Provence, of humble parents. He had no formal education, and was apprenticed either to a barber or a "cutter." Because of his Protestant religion, he was forced to flee his native France, and practiced his art for a number of years in Switzerland. During the time he was there, his first book, the "Little Treatise," was published in 1556. Subsequently, he returned to Orange, in France, and his major book, *Traité des hernies*, was published in Lyon in 1561. Death is assumed to have occurred shortly afterward.

From these writings, Franco stands out as an upright, courageous, and highly religious man. He is modest in his claims, having practiced his art over 30 years before committing his experiences to writing. He accepts the supervision of the physician and implores the approval of the master surgeons. Like Henri de Mondeville, he is bitter in his attack on the ignorance, dishonesty, and cupidity of those who debase the art of surgery. Above all, he is dedicated in his efforts to elevate the status of operative surgery.

Franco's greatest contribution is the recapture of operative surgery for the regular practitioner from the hands of the charlatans, the mountebanks, the itinerant quacks, "cutters," and bonesetters. He deplored the fact that the surgeons of his day rejected the performance of open operations because of lack of courage to face the hazards they entailed. He boldly ventured into the field, and performed, in large numbers, all known operations. "Considered especially from the point of view of the performance of operations," wrote Nicaise, "Franco is the premier surgeon of the 16th century."

Hernial surgery constituted his principal field of interest. He describes, in minute detail, the technique of radical operation for inguinal hernia. Like all who preceded him (except for William of Salicet) after the time of Celsus, he removed the testicle as part of his usual procedure. However, for patients who had but one testis he devised an operation, the description of which is quoted below, in which the organ was spared. Considering the usual incision at the level of the pubis to be unduly dangerous, he "invented" a low incision at the base of the scrotum which, he claims, was used in more than 200 persons by others and himself in the twelve or fifteen years since he first devised it. The clinical picture of strangulated hernia is clearly and vividly described, and methods for the surgical release of strangulation, both with and without

opening the sac, are presented. Thus, for the first time, this life-saving procedure became part of the surgical armamentarium.

In the surgery for bladder stone he was equally enterprising and inventive.
He described and pictured a number of instruments for catheterization and
lithotomy, and pioneered in the introduction of several incisions, including the
suprapubic approach.

Ophthalmic surgery and facial plastic operations also came within his
scope, and he developed a new technique for certain forms of harelip. Whatever subject he dealt with was enriched and advanced through his ingenuity.
It is with perfect justification that Nicaise said, "Where Franco appeared
with all his genius, it was in operative therapeutics; it suffices for us to recall
successively his operations to make evident the role that he has played, and to
show that no surgeon has attached his name to so many lasting discoveries."

꙳ ꙳ ꙳   [In the Preface to his Treatise, Franco paints a vivid picture of
꙳ ꙳ ꙳   the state of surgery of his time, reminiscent of the writings of
Henri de Mondeville.]

GREETINGS TO THE READER FROM PIERRE FRANCO[2]

Benign reader, I am sure that many will judge this work of
mine as superfluous, and me overly bold in having written a
separate book, especially since learned men have sufficiently
treated this material. But I hope that if it please them to understand the reason that impelled me to do so, that they will not
only find it not strange, but a work worthy of a Christian, and
laudable. Not that I am unaware that the wickedness of many
of our craft, accompanied by ignorance, is the reason that this
part of surgery is so held in contempt: for being ignorant and
knowing themselves so, they proceed nevertheless, without fear
of God or man, undertaking to heal all sorts of illnesses, curable
and incurable, just so that they can extort money from the poor,
simple people, whom they seduce and enchant by their lies and
fine words, to the great harm of the poor patients who are often
led to their death by such affronters: who commit infinite frauds
in putting forth their charms and their superstitions: who often
spend much time to charm, after which they begin by making
an incision but are unable to complete the operation, keeping
the poor patient in the meantime, in great languishment. Which
is the reason that I am constrained to recite here some of the

2. *Ibid.*, pp. 6–7.

frauds and plunderings which they commit. Thus for having
taken care of a hernia, extract, in addition to the fee agreed
upon, a shroud: and for a stone, a tablecloth, and for cataracts,
two napkins or two scarves: saying that they belong to them,
which is false. In addition, they are made to give money; to one,
thirteen farthings, or thirteen pieces of silver, or thirteen sous,
or more, according to the people they deal with. In addition, to
give color to their confusion, they make them give several
pieces of bread, and then prostrating themselves before the patient as if he were God, they repeat their charms, and say that
they charm the blood, but it is for the sake of the linen and
money.

Does this not subtly despoil the poor and simple people? I
might say further, if not for fear of being too prolix. Such people
no less deserve corporal punishment by the magistrate, than do
highwaymen. And it should be the duty of Physicians and
Surgeons to defend their art before the Courts, and not to permit further abuse of this art which is of so great importance.
Otherwise, not knowing how to do their duty as they are held
to do before God, they know the fault but do nothing to correct it, they allow their brother to perish. That is the reason in
part, that learned Physicians and Surgeons call such people
vagrants and abusers.

[RADICAL OPERATION FOR HERNIA][3]

[Although Franco usually practiced removal of the testicle as
part of the hernia operation, he devised and recommended a
method which spared the testis for those patients who had but
one organ. The description of this operation follows:]

*Otherwise, without Removal of the Testicle, the Invention of the
Author.*

After having shown the manner and procedure of the cure of
intestinal hernias by removing the sexual parts, we will now
teach the procedure and manner of curing them without the
waste of these parts. First, it is necessary that the patient be
prepared as has been said, whether by medicine or phlebotomy
or other necessary thing. One places the patient, as was said of
intestinal hernias, and one incises the scrotum in its highest part.
Then one passes the finger or some hook under the sac to include
all of it, and lifts it up; and having passed the finger under all of

3. *Ibid.*, Book 2, Part 2, Chapter XIII, pp. 41–43.

it, one dissects it by pulling it toward oneself as high as possible, toward the abdomen: in order to do the operation at the level of the hole through which the intestines emerge. And on the side of the scrotum toward the testicle, one does not dissect at all, or the least possible. And having done this, an assistant can take the testicle with the scrotum and draw it firmly [away] but not upward, so that the Master can do his operation with greater ease, and as high as it can be done, when the sac is held by this means, having separated the parts to which it adheres with its fibers. After these things are done, one puts, as far as is possible, the spermatic vessels to one side of the sac: this is done for the reason of the dilatation of the dartos and erythroides. Or else, take the sac there where there are no vessels, and take it doubled, that is if the sac has been pulled sufficiently, as has been described. One must take care not to dissect too vigorously, and rupture some of the spermatic vessels, for this is done to conserve them.

Having done these things, one applies the clamp shown in the illustration, so that it grasps and includes the entire sac, and one holds it partly closed: then one ligates the sac in this manner: after having mentally divided the width of the sac into four equal parts, he has a needle as described, threaded the same way. Which he passes at the beginning of the second part, and returning, passes at the end of the third part at the beginning of the fourth, in such a manner that the thread includes two of the parts of the width of the sac, the two that are in the middle, and then one ties the end of the thread together, as has been described above. Having done this it is necessary to cut across, close to the suture, the greater part of the sac, particularly that which is included between the two stitches of the needle which were made which is all that is in the grasp of the suture.

[Thus the operation consists in ligating and excising the sac itself, leaving unharmed the spermatic vessels and testis. The text continues with directions for providing drainage by incising the lowermost part of the scrotum.]

[OPERATION FOR STRANGULATED HERNIA][4]

Of Retention within the Scrotum.

When fecal matter is retained in the scrotum, sometimes a very dangerous complication occurs in intestinal hernias or

4. *Ibid.*, Book 1, Part 2, pp. 56–58.

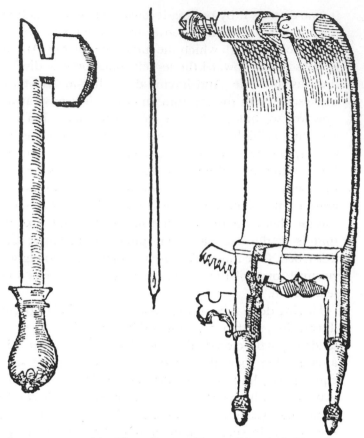

FIG. 35. Instruments used by Pierre Franco. From: *Chirurgie de Pierre Franco*, edited by E. Nicaise.

ruptures—even more dangerous than the preceding: which is to say, that: sometimes there is such an accumulation of fecal matter with some flatulence in the scrotum because of the great inflammation which occurs there, and neither the intestine nor the fecal matter can be reduced to their normal places, because the hole in the peritoneum is too small in comparison to the intestine; which causes also that the patient is unable to go to stool, for the retention of the matter and inflammation. It sometimes follows that they vomit, which is helpful in one way by diminishing the matter, but on the other hand bad, because the effort that it requires forces more substance into the part. They expel the gas by mouth, which may help; but equally often does not when the inflammation is too great. If this complication lasts for some little time, there is no doubt that it causes death.

Therefore it is necessary to remedy it in good time by the method we have described in the cure of hernias by medical means which we have briefly touched upon. If it happens that medical treatment is not sufficient, one must turn to surgery, to manual operation; except that, if the scrotum, and genitalia and surrounding parts change color to black, livid, or blue, or other bad color, and also that the hernia is *more round than long*, these all presage death. And I am of the opinion that one should not undertake such cures, not to incur blame, because hope is nil or very small.

It sometimes occurs that the mouth is livid or black, the nostrils pinched, and the eyes deeper sunk than before: all these things are presages of impending death. It is necessary to take care. If these things do not occur, and the scrotum retains its color, and the swelling is *more elongated than round:* after having tried all other means of medical cure, we turn to surgery.

Cure.

It is necessary to have a small probe of the thickness of a goose quill or a little larger, and round: and which is flat on one side, and semi-round. It should be round in front, so that it will enter more easily. Now it is necessary to make the incision in the highest part of the scrotum, extended toward the pubis, and making the opening at the beginning there, where the probe enters, guarding that nothing touches the intestine, as has been described in the preceding chapter. Having found the sac, one passes the probe between it and the flesh of the pubis, and pushes it upward and across. The flat side of the probe should be below, because if it were round, it would not be so easy to cut on it; for the scalpel or razor would slide to one side of the probe: in a manner not to injure the intestines, having made a good opening, for there is no danger in making it long enough, so that they may be reduced at their ease; because the sac and the peritoneum are better able to enlarge by this method, which is why the intestines are reduced to their proper place. It is necessary to try to replace them little by little.

If it occurs that it does not reduce easily and without much pressure, because of the great abundance of substance or inflammation, it is necessary to proceed by the following means: having taken the sac, and cutting it neatly on the finger nail as has been said, and elevating the membranes of the sac with hooks and cutting it down to the intestines: and having made

the opening where the probe could be passed, one pushes it between the intestines and the membranes of the sac and passing it
gently upward and across, holding it up, in order to better judge
if it takes any of the intestine with it; they are never easy to take
because they are smooth and slippery. Then one cuts the sac on
the probe up to the peritoneum, or the highest part, which is
toward the ring through which the intestines have descended
into the scrotum; but it is necessary to make a good opening in
the peritoneum, without fear or anything, and with greatest
assurance, as is done in such desperate cases. Then one must
take soft linen, and try to replace, little by little, the intestines,
beginning with those which are highest, toward the peritoneum
or abdomen. For when they have started, the rest follow easily.
Being reduced, it is necessary to begin (*repair of the hernia*) what
was described above, according to what the patient will tolerate,
and that which is *most expedient*.

PART V

GREAT IDEAS

APPENDIX A

CHAPTER 22

German Wound Surgeons:
Heinrich von Pfolspeundt, Hieronymus Brunschwig, and Hans von Gersdorff

Germany lagged far behind Italy and France in the awakening of medicine and surgery, and played no part in the early surgical renaissance of the twelfth, thirteenth, and fourteenth centuries. The position of German surgery is reflected in Guy de Chauliac's caustic commentary. Listing the sects of surgeons current in his time, he includes in the fourth group, "all the Teutonic gendarmes or chevaliers and other followers of war: who with conjurations and potions, oil, wool and cabbage leaves, dress all wounds, basing it upon that, that God has placed his power on words, on herbs and on stones."

This characterization is certainly unduly acrid. It is true that German surgery made no important contributions during this period when growth elsewhere was rapid. None could be logically expected. Surgeons there made no pretensions to belonging to a learned profession. They were simple crafts-men who joined together in guilds as did other artisans. Having no university training, they could read no Latin. Their subordinate position to the physi-cians was accepted, and conflict between the two groups was minimal. On the other hand, they profited from the advances made in the Latin countries, often by visiting these lands during their travels or military campaigns. Translations of the major works, contemporary as well as classic, gradually appeared in German, their familiar language. Moreover, they were diligent observers and widely experienced in the rich school of military surgery.

The earliest German surgical texts appeared in the latter part of the fifteenth and the first half of the sixteenth centuries, and were intended as guides or manuals for the use of fellow craftsmen. They were written in the vernacular, and dealt essentially with the treatment of wounds. The texts contained little that was original, yet, strangely, some of the early surgical innovations of other countries first appeared in print in the German surgeries. Three authors of this period wrote significant books and are here presented together—Heinrich von Pfolspeundt, Hieronymus Brunschwig, and Hans von Gersdorff.

HEINRICH VON PFOLSPEUNDT (FIFTEENTH CENTURY)

"He should bind with clean white cloths, for if they are not clean, harm results. He should also wash his hands before he treats anyone."

(Heinrich von Pfolspeundt)

Heinrich von Pfolspeundt is the earliest of the known German surgical writers, his *Buch der Bündth-Ertznei* having been composed in 1460. In this small volume he tells us he was a Brother of the German Order, and that he participated in a number of military campaigns between this order and the Polish kings. He is revealed as a totally uneducated person, unfamiliar with Latin, and but meagerly competent in his native tongue. He mentions "Masters" from whom he learned the craft, both Italian and German, none of whom are historically known; and he speaks of his own very wide experiences and observations. His text is largely limited to the management of wounds and other injuries, in which he seems to have acquired considerable empirical knowledge.

There is little original material in the book and it is poorly organized. The title, *Bündth-Ertznei*, has been interpreted to mean "Bandage Treatment" and, indeed, suture of fresh wounds is recommended in only selected cases. Oil of turpentine is poured in all recent wounds and suppuration is the usual result.

The soporific sponge known to the ancients is used. Gunshot wounds are not treated as such, but Pfolspeundt does tell how to remove gunpowder from the wounds. This is the earliest mention in surgical literature of war injuries from firearms, and, unlike later writers, Pfolspeundt does not refer to such wounds as being poisoned.

Actual operations are rarely discussed in the book, yet, strangely, rhinoplasty for the replacement of cut-off noses is described in considerable detail. The reconstruction of noses had been practiced in Italy by the Branca family for two generations. The father used the "Indian" method (described in the chapter on Indian surgery), by which skin from the cheek or forehead was used to fashion the new nose; the son, also used the pedicled-flap technique, utilizing skin from the arm. These operations were closely kept as family secrets, and therefore were not published. The description by Pfolspeundt is the earliest to be found in the Western surgical literature, and he too insists upon keeping it from others. In the description appended below, he mentions that he learned this operation from an Italian surgeon who had helped many people and earned a great deal of money from its use. Pfolspeundt also describes an operation for harelip.

The *Handbuch* remained long unknown to medical historians. Never having been printed, it remained in manuscript form, and apparently but few copies had been preserved. It was not until late in the nineteenth century that Haeser and Middeldorpf came into possession of one such copy, and published it in printed form with commentary and annotation. This edition has served to enrich our knowledge of early German surgery.

ﾐ ﾐ ﾐ   HERE THE MASTER TEACHES HOW A WOUND SURGEON
ﾐ ﾐ ﾐ   SHOULD CONDUCT HIMSELF TOWARD THE WOUNDED, AND
           WHAT HE SHOULD DO BEFORE HE APPROACHES THEM.[1]

Item, firstly I advise anyone who wishes to work in this art and to heal, that he should not go to a wounded or sick person in the early morning or treat him before he has heard Mass, so far as is possible, unless there is great need, but he shall pray to the good Lord to bless the wounds, to say a pater noster and an Ave Maria, and confess his faith, so that strength and wisdom be given him to heal the people whom he has under his hands.

And he should guard himself against drunkenness when he is to treat patients, for because of it they may easily be neglected, and the doctor would be guilty of that and be punished by God. And especially, he should guard himself, if he has eaten onions or peas, or slept the previous night with an unclean woman, in the morning, against breathing into anyone's wound. Also, he should bind with clean white cloths, for if they are not clean, harm results. He should also wash his hands before he treats anyone. Also he should love healing for the sake of God, if he is able: also if the doctor knows himself to be unclean, he should not look actively into the wounds, nor should any other unclean person, else mischief and harm arises, and may even cause death of the patient. And keep people protected, or you will have to do penance before God, if you are to blame.

HOW TO MAKE A NEW NOSE FOR SOMEONE: WHICH IS OFF
ENTIRELY: AND THE DOG HAS EATEN IT.[2]

Item, a master work is needed. If someone comes to you whose nose has been chopped off, and you wish to make him a new nose, let no one watch, and make him swear secrecy; as to how you will heal him. And after he has sworn, then give him your opinion. If he will chance it with you, and endure the pain, then proceed with logic, and tell him, how you must cut and

1. *Buch der Bündth-Ertznei* von Heinrich von Pfolspeundt . . . 1460. Herausgegeben von H. Haeser und A. Middledorpf. Berlin, Georg Reimer, 1868, pp. 1–2. The epigram and excerpts were translated by the authors from the contemporary German.
2. *Ibid.*, pp. 29–31.

bind, and how long he will have to lie. And therefore you do
not wish anyone to watch, so that he may not learn the art from
you. But if you or he knows a trustworthy person, who would
also swear to you, to keep the matter secret, then you may let
such a one watch, so that he assist you, and to assist him (the
patient), to eat and to drink and to supply other needs. And the
room in which he lies must also be locked, so that no one can
enter except you and the one who will assist you and the patient.

The Art

Take a [piece of] parchment or leather, and make it exactly
like the nose wound, and cut it as wide and as long as the former
nose was. And you must bend it a little over the nose, so that
the upper part of the nose will not be too broad. After that take
the same parchment or leather, and lay it a little behind the
elbow, on the arm, where it is thick; and mark it with ink or
other color, as wide and as long as the pattern is: and take a
good, sharp knife or razor, and cut through the skin, taking
with it a little of the flesh. Do not cut any farther than you have
marked with the ink or dye. And begin to cut from behind forward. And as you have followed the measurements in cutting,
continue to do so. That you do well with one cut as broad as two
fingers or more. And leave the flap that you have cut, hanging
on the arm, and do not cut it off. And raise his arm up to his
head, and sew the same flap right on to the nose, in the size that
it had been before. And therefore you must cut the flap longer,
so that you can better bring it to the nose. Then you must bind
his arm to his head, and behind the elbow, and must be sure
that the arm remains in place and does not become too tired.
Make the binding from cloths, better using more. Because he
must be bound so long till the flap is grown to the nose. That
will be from 8 to 10 days. Or until you see that it is united and
healed, then cut the flap off, but not too short, so that it pro-
trudes a little beyond the nose, so that the nose has a new opening. Then cut the flap in such length and breadth, that you can
sew it down below also. Therefore you must cut the skin away,
and leave raw flesh, and sew the same flap down to it, so the
nose appears doubled, but not inside. Then heal it with wound
potion and with oil and red salve. But before you cut him, raise
the arm to the head higher and lower, so you can see where
the cut should be made. And when you have so sewn it and want
to heal it, and all the while you heal him, so shape the nose and

bind it with such a bandage that will make it narrow, high or low. Should the nose be too broad, bind little sacs on each side of the nose. However, you must insert quills wrapped in flax and stuff the tip of the nose well. Thus the nostrils will not be too narrow and remain of the same width. If he tires of lying you must help him in time with pillows and cloths which you must bind and arrange to help him get rest. And at times he must be raised in bed on pillows, at others, he walks about in the room where he is confined. Help him with whatever will give him the best rest. If the flap has been properly cut, and is long enough, then you may treat him in this way without harm.

When someone has no nose, I now advise him. An Italian has taught me this, who has helped many people with it, and has earned much money. If someone comes to you whose nose has been hacked off, and his wound healed, so cut the skin away widely enough down to raw flesh, and proceed as before, after which heal it also. It undoubtedly works. It has been proved.

HIERONYMUS BRUNSCHWIG (BORN ca. 1450)

"But especially I say to all surgeons if there are two or several of them that they should never quarrel before the patient for that would frighten the patient very much."

(Hieronymus Brunschwig)

Hieronymus Brunschwig, who lived a generation later than Pfolspeundt, was a man of greater stature and wider erudition. He was born about 1450 in Strassburg, and spent his life in the practice of wound surgery in that city. He had not formal scholastic education but received his training through apprenticeship and travel. There is no record of military service, but he speaks of his wide experience in civil life over a forty-year period. He was widely read—according to him he had studied 3000 books—of the ancients and of his Latin contemporaries.

His book, *Cirurgia, ein Handbuch der Wundarznei*, published in 1497, toward the end of his life, is based on his many years of personal experience, plus his extensive reading. The book is adorned by a large number of beautifully executed drawings of doctors and patients. These illustrations are not used to clarify the text, but rather as simple decoration. They do serve to portray for us the costumes, furnishings, and medical customs of the period.

Strassburg was for a time the home of Gutenberg, the inventor of printing with movable type, and the *Handbuch* was written shortly after the beginning of

Fig. 36. Surgeons visiting a patient suffering from a facial wound. From: Hieronymous Brunschwig: *The Book of Cirurgia* with a study . . . by Henry E. Sigerist, Milano, Lier & Co., 1923, p. 105.

book publishing. It was one of the first books on surgery to appear in print, and the first to be illustrated. By virtue of its overwhelming superiority over anything previously printed in Germany, the elegance of its type and format, and the beauty of its illustrations, it had a great vogue and went through several editions, some of which were pirated.

Like Pfolzpeundt's book, the *Cirurgia* dealt essentially with wound and ulcer management, and introduces little that was original. However, here for the first time, the treatment of gunshot wounds is described. The concept that such injuries were "poisoned" had already become accepted, but their cauterization with boiling oil, later to be decried by Paré, was not yet in vogue. Instead of the soporific sponge, Brunschwig used a narcotic potion consisting essentially of scopolamine which Gersdorff later declared to be dangerous.

ᔌ ᔌ ᔌ   THE DUTIES OF THE SURGEON[1]
ᔌ ᔌ ᔌ

It is the office of the surgeon to unite with his hand that of man's body which has been separated or which is open and make it into a whole as it had been before, wherever possible. And, therefore, it is necessary that the surgeon be skillful, of a moral nature, and neither too slow nor too fast in his work.

He should be faithful and careful towards the wounded and the sick so that he will neither neglect nor forget anything through which the patients could suffer or be damaged, and so that he himself will not incur shame or blame. He himself should also not sin nor curse so that he will not merit the hatred of the wounded or the sick. He should not say too much except to promise health to the patients and he should talk with them pleasantly and suitably and cite good examples and gestures, but so that his words are understandable, clear and sincere.

He should not quarrel or swear at the wounded or the sick and should never talk to anyone else about that which he has heard in the house of the patient. Instead he should speak to the sick and the wounded chastely and gently and always promise them recovery. But, to their good friends he should tell the truth and hide nothing but he should not tell them that which he has to hold in confidence, for all things are open to God alone and not to men.

He should help the poor according to whatever they are able to pay but should ask good reward from the rich. In this manner you will achieve happiness and salvation. You should not praise yourself but also not belittle the others. You should honor all men but particularly the priests and the physicians so that you will have a good name.

You should also wear good clothes but you should not be vain so that the patients trust you all the more and derive hope from you, for hope is what the patients desire.

You should be tireless in your work and filled with special love for your fellowmen, exactly as you love yourself. For this

1. *The Book of Cirurgia* by Hieronymus Brunschwig, . . . 1497. With a study on Hieronymous Brunschwig and his work by Henry E. Sigerist. Milano, R. Lier & Co., 1923, pp. 14–15. Translated from the German by the authors.

reason the patient should obey the doctor in all his orders and
prohibitions.

The surgeon should also know anatomy and be aware that
there is a connection and a separation of the members of the
body so that he knows where he should cut or cauterize, so that
he will not incur fatal injury through cutting and cauterization,
and so that he will not tear or wrench a member of the body.
He should also understand how he can repair something of that
nature. He should know whether someone was shot with an
arrow or a gunshot or whether the iron is still in the body, or a
part of the bullet or a stone, whether he should cut this out or
draw it out with plasters or whether he should soften the spot
with softening poultices or how you can bring every member
back into its correct form and appearance.

You young beginning surgeons, open your ears and remember
with diligence this short word. When you are called to a patient
if the matter appears to you too difficult or not entirely familiar
do not be ashamed to send after one or two other surgeons so
that they can help you and give you good advice from which
you and the patient can derive great benefit.

Firstly, that you become aware that previously you have
accomplished nothing or very little.

Secondly, whether you have neglected anything that is corrected by the others.

Thirdly, that you be aware if you left the wounded in a
worsened condition.

Fourthly, if everything goes well, you will participate in the
success. If things go wrong they will share the burden.

Fifthly, you will be praised by the sages who will then say
"He desires to learn and neglects no one" and you will be
honored. . . . Thus you will learn that you can do it in this
manner and still not be deprived of honor and reward. Also if
two persons rather than one are involved in a work one can see
who of the two was mistaken. For this reason too you will derive
happiness and reward from the patient.

But especially I say to all surgeons if there are two or several
of them that they should never quarrel before the patient for
that would frighten the patient very much. Similarly, if one of
the surgeons is not present one should not talk badly or deroga-
torily about him but whatever they have to say to each other
should be said in the absence of the patient and they should all

obey each other and hide nothing from each other so that neither the surgeon nor the patient will be harmed.

HANS VON GERSDORFF
(SIXTEENTH CENTURY)

"Also guard yourself, if an injury comes to you which you do not understand how to heal it, you should willingly direct him away to another, experienced Master, so that you may not ruin the person, as often happens with lesser Masters who through their neglect bring people from life to death."

(Hans von Gersdorff)

Hans von Gersdorff, the third of this group of early German surgeons, was also from Strassburg. The dates of his birth and death are unknown, but his period was somewhat later than that of Brunschwig, because his book appeared twenty years later. His training, like that of his predecessors, was by apprenticeship, travel, and military service. A rich experience over a period of forty years in army and civil practice provided the knowledge which he transmitted to his contemporaries and successors in the form of a handbook of wound surgery entitled *Das Feldbuch der Wundarzney*, which was published in 1517. Of this book, Malgaigne wrote that its author "appeared at least to merit the distinction of having written in vulgar language the first book that one can cite with honor."

An important and valuable feature of the book is the large number of illustrations, some in color and many of full-page size. These illustrate the operative techniques, the instruments used, the costumes, interiors, and even a battle scene containing a cannon guarded by a trio of soldiers armed with muskets. The earliest reproduction of an amputation shows the use of animal bladders as the mode of dressing the stump.

Gersdorff wrote of gunshot wounds and, although he did not specifically speak of them as poisoned by the powder, he was concerned with its removal and inducing suppuration. Warm oil was poured into the wounds. He was apparently widely experienced in the management of injured limbs, parts of which had been shot off, as well as with amputations for gangrene; and recovery seems to have been the rule rather than the exception. He was given to mechanical devices, such as the tripod screw-elevators for raising depressed skull fragments shown here, as well as numerous machines for the reduction of fractures and dislocations, and for the correction of crooked limbs and stiff

Arm/bayn abſchneyden hat ſein kunſt/   Gehört auch nicht eim yeden zů/
Vertreyben ſant Anthonien prunſt.   Erſchick ſich dann wie ich/yhm thů.

FIG. 37. Amputation scene. Standing figure wears bladder over amputation stump on left forearm. From Gersdorff: *Feldbuch der Wundarztney* [Strassburg, J. Schott, 15-?].

Der pfeyl hat troffen mir mein hertz/
O brüder Veitt hab fleyß on schertz

Manns müt wil hin zü diser stund/
Ach Got wie tieff bin ich verwundt.

FIG. 38. Removal of an arrow on the battlefield. From Gersdorff: *Feldbuch der Wundarztney* [Strassburg, J. Schott, 15–?].

joints. Many of these instruments are of his own invention, or are improvements on older ones. There is no question that he furthered the management of skeletal injuries, and it is not surprising that his book went through at least a dozen editions and translations.

ON THE ORDER AND SKILL OF THE SURGEON AND HOW HE CONDUCTS HIMSELF IN THE CRAFT OF WOUND SURGERY[1]

He [the surgeon] distinguishes himself from the physician in that the physician does no manual work. Therefore, it is the office of the surgeon to work manually on the human body wherever it is open, cut or broken and, insofar as is possible, to bring it together again, or to make whole, as it was before. Therefore, it is necessary that the surgeon have good intelligence and understanding. Not too rash in his actions, but always well aware of the harm that might come to him or to the patient because of his lack of skill.

Galen said that every wound surgeon or barber should be of humble disposition and of a chaster nature than other manual workers, because this art and practice touches on human life, and therefore it is fitting that he be more industrious and skillful than any other artisan, and that he not promise the wounded more than he can accomplish. He shall also not for the sake of money, undertake the impossible that may do him harm or give him a bad reputation. Lanfranc, Guido and Albucasis have said that the wound surgeon should not seek difficult cures and should not undertake that which promises neither comfort nor hope. He should not praise himself nor criticize others. He should be tireless in his work. He should have a special love for the wounded persons as for his own body. He should always give industrious attention to the parts of the body and their action, and to the blood vessels, so that he may cut, cauterize with corrosives, or burn with iron or gold instruments, without doing injury to the limb. And last, but not least, so long as before all else, he is a Christian, standing in the fear of God, he shall hear Mass every day, so that no failures may befall him. If the wound surgeon is not successful in his practice or experiences because of his youth or inadequate understanding, he should not be ashamed to call on an experienced older surgeon,

1. Hans von Gersdorff: *Feldbuch der Wundarztney* [Strassburg, J. Schott, 15–?], p. 17. Epigram and excerpts translated from the contemporary German by the authors.

or one who has more knowledge than he, so that he passes before God and the patient, for I have seen much anxiety and distress arising from ignorance.

ON HEAD WOUNDS[2]

With this instrument you may elevate the skull when it is depressed, and one fragment can be seen beneath the other. The instrument may be applied above, at the side or in the back. The other flaps shall be made level so that it [the instrument] may be placed wherever you wish. The little screw with which you drill into the bone, should be very pointed as is shown here.

This is another instrument which serves better on the top of the head or on the sides or back, because is is not of the same width as the former instrument. And it serves also when the skull has been crushed in, so that one can draw it up.

THE SKILL WITH WHICH THE LIMB SHOULD BE AMPUTATED[3]

If the limb must be cut off, and nothing else will help, or if it has helped but the limb cannot be preserved, you should advise the patient above all to go to confession and receive the Holy Sacrament on the day before you amputate. And if the surgeon hears Mass before the operation, God will favor his work.

Before you operate you should have all your instruments and preparations in order, such as razor, saw, tourniquet, bandages, lint, eggs, and whatever else is needed, and arrange them in the order you will need them after the incision is made.

When you are about to cut have someone draw the skin firmly back, and tightly bind the skin with a constricting band, and then tie a cord near the constricting band, leaving a space about a finger's breadth between the two, in which the incision can be made, so that the cut will be correct and even and makes a good stump. When you have made the incision, take a saw and cut the bone. Afterwards, remove the constriction, and have someone draw the skin and flesh down over the bone and pull it firmly forward. And then have a bandage ready, two finger breadths wide, which has been moistened until it is thoroughly wet, and bind it about the limb down to the incision, to keep the flesh over the wound and bind it so. And afterwards, apply the hemostyptic over it. Do not be frightened by the

2. *Ibid.*, p. 21.
3. *Ibid.*, p. 63ff.

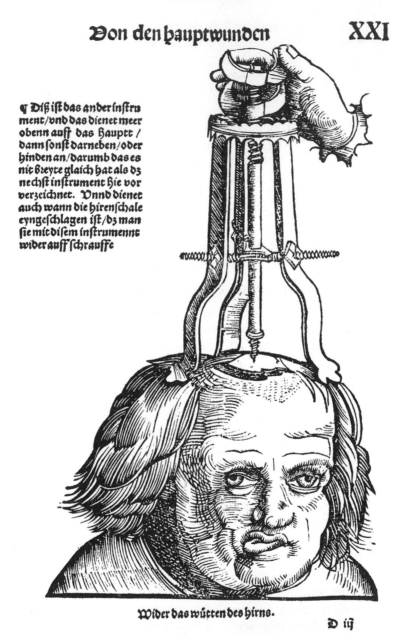

Von den hauptwunden XXI

Diß ist das ander inſtru
ment/vnd das dienet meer
obenn auff das Haupt /
dann ſonſt darneben/oder
hinden an/darumb das es
nit breyte glaich hat als dz
nechſt inſtrument hie vor
verzeichnet. Vnnd dienet
auch wann die hirenſchale
eyngeſchlagen iſt/dz man
ſie mit diſem inſtrumennt
wider auff ſchrauffe

Wider das wütten des hirns.

D iij

Fig. 39. Elevation of depressed skull fragment with instrument described in text. From Gersdorff: *Feldbuch der Wundarztney* [Strassburg, J. Schott, 15–?].

bleeding if it occurs, as was described before. And over the hemostyptic bind a good, thick compress.

And afterwards, take a bladder of a bull or ox or hog, which should be strong, and cut off the top widely enough so that it will go over the stump and the dressing. The bladder should be moistened, but not too soft, and draw it over and bind it firmly with a cord, then you need not worry that it will bleed.

I have never sewn a stump, but have always healed them with medicaments, as many good apprentices know who have served with me, many of whom are still alive.

CHAPTER 23

Caspar Stromayr
(Sixteenth Century)

"When you are certain of your knowledge/ you need neither letter nor seal/ for the work praises the master/"[1]

Caspar Stromayr was a little-known German surgeon of the sixteenth century, who belonged to the "incisor" class. Although he made no significant impact on the surgery of his time, he is included in this gallery of great surgeons because, from his own wide experience, he developed a concept of the essence of hernia which was in advance of his period. Moreover, he left as his legacy a remarkable book, the *Practica copiosa*, which has but recently come to light after a lapse of centuries.

Nothing is known of the life of Stromayr, other than that he was a "cutter" of hernia and a coucher of cataract (*Schnidt- und Augenartzt*) in Lindau im Bodensee, during the time of Vesalius, Franco, and Paré. Unlike many of his ilk, he was not itinerant, but maintained permanent residence in his native city. From the text of his book, he appears to have had some degree of academic education. He emerges as an upright, honorable, and God-fearing man who deplored the ignorance and mendacity of many of his colleagues. These he castigates in vitriolic terms that are reminiscent of Henri de Mondeville. A practical man, he teaches the manner of approach to patients, the words to use in advising radical surgery for hernia, and, emphatically, the importance of arranging all the details concerning the fee immediately before embarking on the operation.

The *Practica copiosa* of Stromayr was left as a meticulously worded, beautifully written manuscript, which bears the date, July 4, 1559. The language used is German, in the dialect of the region in which he lived. After the death of its author, the manuscript reposed in oblivion in the city library of Lindau

1. *Die Handschrift des Schmitt-und Augenarztes Caspar Stromayr*, [*Practica copiosa*] with an introduction by Walter von Brunn, Berlin, Idra-Verlagsanstalt, 1925, "Vorred an den Leser," p. 10. Epigram and excerpts are translated from the contemporary German by the authors.

for 350 years. It was finally resurrected by the librarian in 1909, and eventually was published in 1925 through the efforts of the surgical historian, Walter von Brunn. Thus, belatedly, has it come to attention.

A most unusual feature of the book is its illustrations. These, 186 in number, are, for the most part, full-page in size and beautifully colored. They appear to be actual portraits of patients, in lifelike poses, and with realistic facial expressions. Despite the age of these drawings, even in reproduction, the colors are vivid and bright. Although decorative, they are used to illustrate and clarify the text, and are frequently referred to in the discussion. Every detail of the author's concept of pathology, and each step in the operations are thus clearly represented. The insight they furnish into surgical mores, as well as costumes and interiors, adds unique qualities to the book. The artist who created these drawings is unknown, but it is suggested that probably they were done by the author himself. A couplet, in doggerel, on each plate adds further charm to this unusual volume.

The text of the *Practica copiosa* deals chiefly with hernia, with a lesser section on surgery of the eye. Stromayr sharply differentiates herniae which follow the cord from those which do not, thus for the first time distinguishing indirect inguinal herniae from other forms. The latter, in the male, are clearly direct; in the female, the position of the sac rather suggests a femoral hernia. The not infrequent simultaneous presence of both forms is recognized, as is also the necessity of repairing both. Stromayr further goes beyond all earlier writers on hernia in emphasizing the importance of the point of exit of indirect inguinal herniae, *i.e.*, the abdominal (internal) inguinal ring, and the necessity of removing the sac to that level.

The operation for radical cure of hernia consisted, as might have been expected, of the removal of the sac together with cord and testicle, in the indirect variety. In some respects, Stromayr's technique was an improvement over that of Franco in that his incision was placed in the groin rather than at the bottom of the scrotum, so that the entire canal could be visualized and the amputation made directly at the abdominal ring. In the direct herniae he spared the testes, recognizing the futility of sacrificing this organ, the cord of which bore no relation to the course of the sac. The operation consisted of excising the sac flush with the defect in the abdominal wall.

There is much more of interest in this refreshing and readable book. The other forms of "hernia," including hydrocele, sarcocele (all fleshy masses in the groin and scrotum), and "gaseous hernia" are discussed. Each step in the postoperative care is presented in detail, as are also the complications. In addition to the operative management of hernia, the author invented trusses which closely resemble those in use today, and are much less cumbersome than those pictured by Paré.

Jch bin ain fraw fchem mich gar fer /
hab ain Bruch / von der fcham nit feer /

FIG. 40. Woman with a femoral hernia. From: *Die Handschrift des Schmitt-und Augenarztes Caspar Stromayr*, with an introduction by Walter von Brunn, Berlin, Idra-Verlagsanstalt, 1925.

Thus, we see an obscure provincial surgeon, without formal medical education, who not only rose above his colleagues, but attained a knowledge in specialized fields of surgery, on the basis of his own empirical observations, which was greatly in advance of his time. The care and effort expended in the production of his manuscript attest his dedication to his self-imposed task. His writings had little contemporary influence, but they survive as a lasting monument to a surgeon of exceptional stature.

ᔒᔒ ᔒᔒ ᔒᔒ   [FROM THE PREAMBLE][2]
ᔒᔒ ᔒᔒ ᔒᔒ

    I cannot omit/ but must show you how such vagrants and destroyers of people acquire their masterships/ obtain diplomas and seals/ namely/ when an unsuccessful bather/ barber/ cobbler or tailor or whatever tradesman he may be/ when he does not know what to do/ to provide for himself in sloth/ and have a full belly every day/ and something left over besides/ and become rich/ if he has perhaps watched a surgeon once, twice, three or even four times/ then he dares/ to move away one, three or four miles away/ from those who know him/ to a place where he is not known/ then he injures the inhabitants of the new location/ he pretends to be a surgeon/ whom one would not trust at home with a sow/ and who could not open a vein/

    He dares and does not ask afterward how it turned out/ Now someone comes to him with a plea for help/ with an aqueous rupture [hydrocele]/ He talks him into believing it to be a rupture/ he wishes and knows how to help him but the patient must submit to an operation/ then the patient says "Dear Master I don't understand it/ I came to you for that reason/ so as to get advice and help from you"/

    He [the surgeon] cuts into it undaunted/ the water runs out/ he either shells out or removes the testicle/ assuming and saying/ that he had helped/ And after recovery he says to the patient/ I will reduce my fee by one guilder and give it to you as a present/ Give me a letter and your seal [testimonial] that I am a good surgeon/ and that I have helped you well/ The patient is happy/ does it gladly/ He would rather give him a letter than a guilder/

    Now, what does the surgeon do with it?

    He takes the letter and shows it to everyone/ hangs or nails it on all church towers or courthouses/ Preens himself as one who has cured a large rupture/ He knows this skill and is a Master/ as is the custom among such tramps/ and he as knows full well/ that an empty keg gives out a louder sound/ than a full one/ If he knows half as much as he pretends/ and claims/ he would

2. *Ibid., loc. cit.*

not have to wander around the country/ as a parasite/ to
defraud people of their money/ He could well be found at
home/ and then the simple minded common people would
believe and run to him/. . . .

Again he cuts for a rupture/ The patient recovers to the extent that he does not die/ However, what does he do for him?
Namely that/ he has him lie on his back for three or four
weeks/ and does not permit him to get up at all/ The patient
believes that things are going well/ and that he has been cured/
For as long as he is lying on his back/ his rupture lies within/
and does not protrude/ [whereupon the surgeon asks for his
testimonial and payment of his fee, and assures the patient that
all is well, and that he need never see the doctor again; that he
be careful of food, drink, etc.] He forbids him things which are
impossible to keep/ takes his money and departs/ When then
the patient gets up and believes himself cured/ his rupture
comes out as large as before/

Or he operates on a young child for a water bag or hy-
drocele/ which could have been corrected by himself by medicine or other means/ the child recovers/ and not without rea-
son/ for the operation was never needed/ Had one but pricked
it with a lancet it would also have emptied/. . . .

[SPIRITUAL PREPARATION FOR THE OPERATION][3]

Although any understanding person can judge for himself/
that I would rather see and it would be more useful and honorable to me/ if the patient were to recover completely/ than if he
were to die/ Yet I am not the good Lord/ that I could give
such assurance and promise to him or anyone else/ with God's
assistance I've helped many/ and if it is the will of God/ I will
also help this one/ yet as mentioned before I cannot promise
anything/ I haven't given him his life/ and if God wills I will
not take it/ Everything that I will undertake on behalf of the
patient/ will with God's help not contribute to his death/
It might be that God Almighty has seen fit to decree that his
time is up and that he is to be called to his Maker/ which
neither I nor anyone else can know/ for we like all others are in
the power of God/ and no one knows when and how God will
call him from this earth/ Nevertheless I'm not worried in the
least/ and if it should happen that God claims him from this
world/ and he dies/ . . . I will still expect my well-earned fee/

3. *Ibid.*, pp. 57–58.

for I have used and demonstrated my skill/ effort/ and labor exactly in the same manner/ as if he had survived and recovered/. . . . In the meantime exhort those who stand about/ and kneel down together with them all and say/ Now we shall call upon God Almighty and pray that He will grant us a fortunate hour/ that He may guide my hand according to His holy and best will/ that He should not judge us according to our merits/ but with His manifold grace and mercy/ Amen, and now all recite with devoutness the Paternoster/ (Fig. 41).

[DIFFERENTIATION BETWEEN INDIRECT AND DIRECT HERNIAE][4]

[Stromayr was the first to recognize that some inguinal herniae follow the course of the spermatic cord (indirect variety) whereas others do not (direct). As a corollary to this, he sanctioned the ablation of the testicle in the former but considered it a wanton sacrifice in the latter. He curiously employs the term *vena didymi* to refer to the spermatic cord as a whole, and also uses it as a designation for the hernial sac. To Stromayr also belongs the distinction of first recognizing the importance of removing the sac of a hernia to its point of emergence from the abdominal cavity. These two observations are described in the following excerpts from his book.]

You should also know/ that in all intestinal ruptures (enteroceles)/ be they inguinal or scrotal/ called bubonocele/ enterocele/ and epiploenterocele by the learned/ the vena didymi from which the testicle hangs dilates or relaxes to the extent/ that the bowel within the dilated vena didymi sinks down and descends into the scrotal sac/ As it sometimes happens/ that a rupture allows the bowel to extrude in which the vena didymi is not dilated or relaxed/ but such ruptures come out near the vena didymi/ and have a cyst or sac of their own into which the intestines fall/ (Fig. 42)

The above-mentioned figure shows you the form of a rupture/ which runs to one side and does not follow the vena didymi/—

Thus when you correctly recognize such a rupture which comes out on the side near the vena didymi/ you can help him by operation/ in which you leave him his testicle and do not remove it/ if however you do not recognize such ruptures/

4. *Ibid.*, pp. 22–23.

Kniend nider vnd rieffent an /
Gott das er euch wel bey stand thon /

FIG. 41. Prayer before operation. From: Stromayr, *op. cit.*

you would cut out his testicle/ and leave the rupture/ although
such ruptures are quite rare/ and occur hardly more often
than one in a hundred/ Nevertheless they do occur/ I've seen
them and operated upon them myself/ [The infrequency of
direct hernia is probably explained by the fact that operation was usually done in children or young adults]

Zue der prob er dir da Hie stat /
Sein bruch der Aber nit nach gatt /

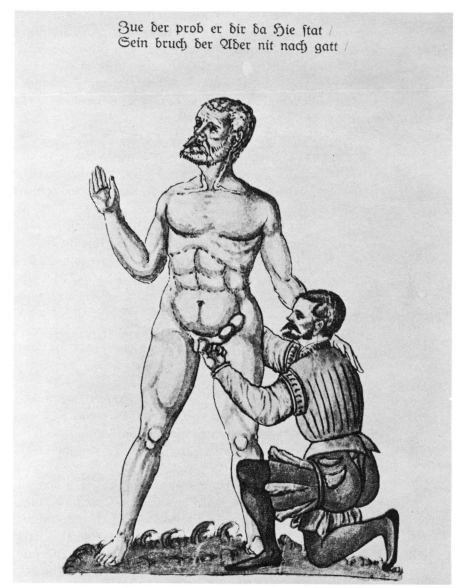

FIG. 42. Demonstration by examination of a direct inguinal hernia. From: Stromayr, *op. cit.*

Thus in order to recognize correctly such a rupture which does not follow the vena didymi/ do as you will hear/ and as the following figure shows/ stand the patient upright in front of you with the rupture out/ push the testicle on the side of the rupture upward between the skin and the thigh to the groin/ as high as you can/ then you will see that the testicle

makes a separate swelling from that of the rupture/ which
otherwise does not occur/ For whenever a rupture accompanies
the vena didymi/ when it is out/ and you push the testis up-
ward/ as described/ there would be no special swelling next
to the rupture/ for it would go into the same swelling/ so
that the testicle and rupture are contained in the same swelling/
which otherwise would not be the case—

HOW YOU PREPARE YOURSELF AND THE PATIENT/ AND EVERYTHING ELSE THAT IS NECESSARY FOR THE OPERATION/[5]

Firstly and above all before you undertake the operation/
you should cause the patient to have a bowel movement/
then have him prepare a bath in a tub in which he shall sit
and bathe about two or three hours according to his constitution and condition/ as to how long he can tolerate it considering his age and strength/ While he is in such a bath you
may give him light soup and a glass of wine/ and while he
thus sits in the tub and bathes you prepare all your instruments and materials which you think you may need. . . .

When you have all your instruments together and at
hand. . . . [place the patient in a head-down position on a
slanting board.]

Now when everything is ready and prepared/ approach the
patient at the tub and tell the patient that you will have to
shave the hair from the pubic region . . . and shave him
cleanly/ otherwise you might err in placing the incision/ and
the plaster will stick to it/—(Fig. 43) . . .

When you have shall have shaved his pubic region cleanly/
tell him to sit in the tub again and wash off the hair/ then roll
up both your sleeves so they don't disturb you/ then put
leather finger cots on your two little fingers/ so that you can
knit firmly enough/ for otherwise the threads would cut and
burn you/ and you perhaps would not be able to pull them
hard enough/ Then talk to his friends/ father or mother/
sisters/ or brothers/ also to all those who stand around and
care for the patient/ in the following manner: "Now my dear,
good N/ also my good neighbors and friends/ since now it
will next be/ that with the help of God we will proceed/ it is
necessary that I announce to you my opinion/ and we agree/
so that I and you know where we stand/—"

5. *Ibid.*, pp. 54–57.

So du auff dem Land dauſſen biſt /
Magſt machen alſo dein geriſt /

Fig. 43. Preparatory bath and shave. From: Stromayr, *op. cit.*

First and foremost as to my fee/ what it will be/ how/ when/ and from whom I am to receive it/ Also you may reach an agreement with him or them/ However I wish emphatically to warn you earnestly about one matter/ that you do not agree to trust anyone or have later to ask for it/ but always

Schell dapffer hinauff bis an Grund /
So machst In wider frisch vnnd gsund /

Fɪɢ. 44. The dissection of the sac and cord in indirect hernia is carried to the level of the internal ring. From: Stromayr, *op. cit.*

see to it and arrange/ that when you have finished your operation/ you will receive your money/ unless you have sufficient security/ So that no matter how things turn out you will still be sure of your fee/—

When you have reached an agreement about your fee/ say to the patient/ and all those who stand around/ "I will now use all the possible industry and effort/ given me by God the Almighty/ and not spare any skill/ effort/ and toil/ as much as God has endowed His poor instrument with grace and skill/ more I cannot promise you/"

[OPERATION FOR INDIRECT HERNIA][6]

When then you draw the testicle out of the wound as described above/ begin and shell the testicle and the empty bag or sac of the rupture in which the bowel had been/ called the vena didymi/ upward or outward as far as is possible to the hole from which the rupture takes its origin/ from which the bowel escapes/ and the vena didymi enters the abdomen/ Then it is necessary that you are careful/ that you are not too lazy/ cautious/ or timid in shelling or separating the rupture/ that you do not stop or discontinue/ when you come to the hole or the bottom/ for if you neglect it/ if you are timid or cautious in shelling it out/ and you do not remove it to the place where the bowel begins to escape/ then you will not help him/ Then you would still leave behind a little sac or small rupture/ and when he stands up believing himself cured/ the bowel again pops out into the same little sac/ down to the place where it had been ligated/ which would give him another rupture/ as big as the egg of a hen/ or pigeon/ and at times even of a goose/ However if you have removed it [the sac] diligently or high up to the hole and the very beginning of the rupture/ then such small lumps or ruptures remain forever/ in the groin/ in one place/. . . . For this reason I earnestly urge you/ that you remove it cleanly, systematically and diligently as far as you possibly can to the hole [internal ring]/ and that you leave no part of it behind/ (Fig. 44).

6. *Ibid.*, p. 64.

CHAPTER 24

Hieronymus Fabricius
ab Aquapendente (1537–1619)

"This being true, surgery should with good reason be preferred to pharmacy, since chance and circumstance contribute much to that part of medicine which deals with drugs; and by contrast, the effects of operations are clearly evident, obvious and certain."[1]

Hieronymus Fabricius ab Aquapendente (1537–1619), the most prominent Italian surgeon of the Renaissance, was one of the series of distinguished successors of Vesalius to the professorship of anatomy at Padua. Like those who preceded him, his influence extended widely beyond surgery, importantly enriching the fields of comparative and human anatomy, embryology, physiology, and medicine. His fame as a teacher attracted hundreds of students from all the countries of Europe who disseminated his doctrines throughout the continent. The most famous among the many influenced by him was William Harvey, whose two great projects, the discovery of the circulation of the blood and the study of generation, grew out of stimulation derived from his master during the time he was a student at the University of Padua.

Fabricius was born in Aquapendente, a village near Orvieto, about midway between Rome and Sienna, of a respected but not particularly wealthy family. His early education was good, and at the age of seventeen he was sent to the famed University of Padua for advanced study. He is described as an exemplary student, both as to character and personality, and regarding his application and native capabilities. Electing to study medicine, he was fortunate to have come in contact with Gabriele Fallopio (Fallopius) who had succeeded to the chairs of surgery and anatomy formerly held by Vesalius. Fallopius not only stood out brilliantly in both these fields, but was also a genial, modest, and amiable person. Between the famous master and the promising student a warm friendship and mutual helpfulness developed which cer-

1. Hieronymus Fabricius ab Aquapendente: *Oeuvres Chirurgicales de Hierosme Fabrice d'Aquapendente*, Lyon, Jean Antoine Huguetan, 1670, Part 2, p. 500. Epigram and excerpt translated from the contemporary French by the authors.

HIERONYMVS FABRICIVS ABAQVAPENDENTE EQVES
MEDICVS ET ANATOMICVS.

AUCULA ME GENUIT, TENET URBS PATAVINA. THEATRO
SUM, TABULIS, FOETU, CLARUS ET OSTIOLIS.

FIG. 45

tainly shaped the subsequent career of Fabricius. He received his doctorate in medicine and philosophy in 1559, and began the practice of medicine and surgery, without ever ceasing his anatomical activities.

After the death of his beloved master in 1562, Fabricius gave private demon-

FIG. 46. The Anatomical Theatre of Fabricius ab Aquapendente (1594)

strations in anatomy until, three years later, he was appointed to the professorships formerly held by Fallopius. His academic career, which continued for fifty years, was marked by brilliant achievement and recognition. Although he was a superb teacher and inspiring lecturer—when the spirit moved him—he was predominantly interested in anatomical research. So keen was his desire to further the study of his favorite science that he had an anatomical amphitheatre built at his own expense. The Senate of the Republic of Venice, which then included the city of Padua, followed his generous example and, in 1594, erected a larger and more solidly constructed amphitheatre and arranged that the name of Fabricius be affixed to its entrance.

Of his many contributions which enriched the sciences of human and comparative anatomy, perhaps the most important were his demonstrations of the valves in the veins. True, these structures had been observed by others, but Fabricius made the most complete study of them, describing their location, form, and structure. There is no doubt that Harvey's discovery of the circulation grew out directly from the observations of Fabricius which suggested to Harvey that, because the valves faced *toward* the heart and prevented the flow of blood away from it, the arteries must carry the blood in one direction and the veins in the other.

In addition to his academic and scientific endeavors, Fabricius was also a most influential and successful practitioner and teacher of medicine and, particularly, of surgery. His patients came from far and wide, and included the elite and the wealthy. A man of great modesty, however, he persistently refused to accept honoraria and his patients could only express their gratitude by sending him presents of valuable treasures. The Republic of Venice, however, cognizant of his great merits bestowed upon him a generous revenue and conferred upon him the title of Knight of Saint Mark. When Fabricius died, at the age of eighty-two, he was deeply mourned by the great many to whom he had been a doctor, a teacher, and a friend.

The writings of Fabricius covered a very wide range of subjects. His monograph on the valves of the veins, *De venarum ostiolis* (1603), and his embryological treatises are probably the most significant of his purely scientific works. His "Surgical Works," the *Opera chirurgica in duos partes divisa* (Padua, 1617), are of particular interest to us. Part I is the "Surgical Pentateuch," first published separately in 1592, which contains descriptions of tumors, wounds, ulcers, and fistulae and their treatment. Part II is entitled "Surgical Operations," and deals, in the order from head to foot (*a capite ad calcem*), with all afflictions which require surgical intervention. The great many editions and translations of this work, numbering eighteen altogether and spanning a century, indicate the great importance of Fabricius' writings for the actual practice of surgery. Indeed, as late as 1821, a French author stated that "even today one could read it with profit; it [*Opera chirurgica*] is the most important of all of Fabricius' works."[2]

The text of the *Opera* reveals him to be a cautious surgeon who advised operation only where all other methods failed. His classical education endowed him with a fluent Latin style; his material leaned heavily on Celsus and Paulus of Aegina. Nevertheless, he injected observations of his own on occasion and supplied improvements in the techniques of tracheostomy and thoracentesis, and in the treatment of urethral stricture. Among the numerous surgical instruments invented by Fabricius, there were also orthopedic appliances for the correction of contractures and deformities.

HOW ONE MUST PIERCE THE TRACHEA IN QUINSY[3]

Of all the operations that the doctor performs on man for his cure, I have always held *that* for the principal one, which gives prompt relief to those who are at the point of death;

2. *Dictionaire des Sciences Médicales. Biographie Medicale*, Vol. 4, Paris, C. L. F. Panckouke, 1821, p. 102.
3. Hieronymus Fabricius ab Aquapendente, *op. cit.*, Part 2, Chapter 44, pp. 623–632. This very lengthy chapter has been shortened appreciably by omitting sections dealing chiefly with reference to ancient authors. In the interest of readability the parts retained have been joined together without indicating the deletions.

that which makes the doctor entirely comparable to Aesculapius. Now one of this type is the opening of the trachea, whereby
the patients almost suffocated from the inability to breathe are
instantly relieved, and are again able to draw air into the
lungs and heart, so necessary to life, and so seem to regain the
life which they had almost lost.

Although this operation is placed in the forefront by almost
all Greek and Arabian authors, there are always, at first, two
difficulties. *The first* is that I see that these authors are not in
agreement as to in which illness, nor when it is necessary to
make an incision in the trachea; of what one can expect, in
which diseases, and when one should do it, and when to abstain.
In one word, in every instance of difficulty of respiration laryngotomy should be done, when there is eminent danger of suffocation, and where the other remedies are useless, providing the
trachea and the lungs are not filled with matter [pus], because
of which the patient would inevitably suffocate. It is necessary,
therefore, to abstain from making this incision in empyema,
pleurisy, peripneumonia, and in quinsy in which all the parts
below which serve in respiration, are filled. On the other hand,
it is necessary to do a laryngotomy when there is inflammation,
whether in the mouth, or beneath the chin, or in the tonsils, or
the uvula, or throat, or larynx, which are so great as to close entirely the tracheal tube, provided nonetheless that all of its
branches are not filled with matter. . . . In summary, when the
disease or the matter is only above the level of the larynx, it is
necessary to make the incision; but if it extends below the
larynx, it is necessary to abstain.

The surgeons of our time, frightened by all these authorities,
do not dare to undertake this operation, and I, myself, in
imitation of them, had never done it. But that which further
augments the fear of our surgeons, is that they fear to injure
the jugular veins or arteries, or the nerves, or the muscles,
or even that the wound may not be able to close itself afterward; or, finally, they fear that the breath will escape with
rumbling or something similar, so that they do not risk the
incision. But over all, the disgrace and dishonor is capable of
frightening them; because further, if the operation should be
executed happily, and with all the safety that one could wish,
nevertheless, if some time later the patient should die, being
suffocated because the trachea becomes obstructed, the blame

would be cast on the incision and not on the true cause of death. . . .

When, then, an inflammation suddenly attackes the larynx and the parts which are below, with great difficulty of respiration and danger of suffocation, and when this inflammation is severe, without as yet suppurating, we are able to assume that it is obstructed; then it is imperative that we make the incision: Even further, if he has some indications that it is entirely obstructed, I would do it nevertheless, since it is very safe, as you will see, because by means of the incision, it is possible to obtain great relief: having, however, first announced to those to whom the patient belongs, of the slight hope that he has of escaping, *so that if the art is vanquished by the illness, it would not appear that one had been an ignorant person, or a fraud,* as Celsus said. If those who make the incision are well acquainted with the anatomy, all will be done with assurance and very happy success. For primarily, he will not injure the jugular veins and arteries, which are far from the site where the incision should be made, neither will he damage the nerves, since this is part of the front of the neck is without nerves; nor the muscles, since at the location of the incision, there is a distance between the muscles, and since that this region is least fleshy: he should, therefore, not injure any other important part.

For, before coming to the incision, the surgeons have tried many things, among which (without speaking here of drugs but only of that which is surgical) are instruments which one introduces through the mouth and into the trachea and larynx: such as is done to rupture an aposteme of the larynx, or of the tonsils, or the gullet.

But when, having done all this, there is still great danger of suffocation, it is finally necessary to come to the operation, which is done in this manner. Having bent the patient's head backward, so that the trachea is most prominent (I add, for the purpose of extending and elongating the trachea, and to make the membranes and rings more visible) we cut the skin of the neck transversely between two of the rings, then we cut the membrane between the cartilages, and not the cartilages themselves: which incision should be made three or four rings below the larynx, which forms the head of the trachea. If the surgeon fears inadequacy in this operation, he should first cut the skin, elevate it with hooks and then cut the trachea, which lies just below.

Having then first placed the patient as has been described, one should mark with pen and ink, a straight line, along its length, and on the middle of the anterior part of the neck, almost to the fossa of the sternum; then touch the fingers along its anterior part to the lower end of the larynx: and finally have them descend until they pass over three or four rings of the trachea, three (as well as one can judge) if the neck is short, and four if it is long. For we reconnoiter the limit, either by touch or by reason: by touch, in a thin and emaciated neck; by reason, or imagination, and establish by conjecture the length of three rings: for which it is well to have before the eyes another trachea.

If one asks why it is advised to make the incision below the third or fourth cartilagenous circle, and not immediately below the larynx; the answer is, that it is intended that the incision should be as far as possible from the diseased part, or rather the site of derivation: for if one should make the incision close to the larynx, the inflammation resulting from that incision, would easily impart itself to the larynx.

Having found the membranous place between two cartilagenous rings, we mark it with ink, according to the thickness of the skin: then having one of the assistants first take hold of the skin here and there, with his fingers, and not with a hook, we cut along the line previously marked: for thus there is no danger of injury to the vessels, the nerves, or the muscles: at the place where they would have arrived otherwise, if we had made the incision crosswise; the wound is thus easily sewn together afterwards, and reunites. Now the measure of size of the incision should be about the width of the thumb, for example. Furthermore, the incision should be such that at the middle of its course, it meets the line drawn transversely and it should be so long, that having separated its margins, the scalpel which we use for drawing blood, should enter at its broadest point. And afterwards we retract and separate the skin to either side with the fingers, or with the large end of the measuring bar, or with a blunt hook, firmly enough so that the muscle which is over the trachea appears completely exposed: which would serve very well, if we avoid the veins, or cover them immediately with burnt cotton, and the white of an egg, and if we hurry, so that the blood does not flow.

After this has been done, it is necessary to be careful of the two muscles which lie on the trachea, and one must note, a certain white line, which separates them in the middle, one from the other. It is necessary thereupon to separate one muscle from the other by means of a lengthwise incision, and to create a large space on either side, through which the above mentioned muscles may be retracted, by means of a blunt hook: for thus the body of the trachea is immediately in sight: and when it is exposed, one should make an incision transversely between two rings, and to press firmly just deeply enough to reach the cavity of the trachea, which is much closer than one would imagine, for the breath leaves through the wound with a sound.

Having done this, it is necessary to introduce a small cannula, the size of the opening, and having two wings to prevent its being pulled out, or drawn into the interior by breathing; and it must be short so as not to touch the inner wall of the trachea; otherwise it will excite coughing, and cause pain. But some will perhaps believe that such a small cannula is not sufficient for natural respiration; for in order to be so, it should be of the same caliber as the trachea itself. I always reply, that although the cannula is small, it cannot fail to suffice for the following reason; since the air from the incision made below reaches the lungs and heart directly, without any alterations in its qualities; it is therefore, much colder than if it had passed through the nostrils, the throat, the larynx and the trachea; by passing through such a roundabout way and over a long course, it changes and is so separated from its coldness. Moreover, it [cannula] must be of such length that it does not touch the walls or the opposite part of the trachea. Beyond that, it is evident that a straight shape is much more suitable than a curved one; for the curved one can be shaken loose by the movement of the air which passes through. For this reason, a small fistula [tube] which does not go beyond the interior of the trachea; that is, its internal surface, which has wings, is the most suitable: It must be kept in place until the danger of suffocation is passed, which ordinarily occurs after three or four days. Thereupon, after having refreshed the skin wound by scarification, if it is necessary, the skin edges should be accurately rejoined, by suture, closely applied, and so held in place. And perhaps, if one were to make two sutures, one in the muscles, and the other in the skin above, the union would be made much more exactly, and hoarseness would not ensue.

In one word, there are only three parts which present themselves in this operation, the skin, the muscles, and the trachea.
It is easy to cut the skin; one does not cut the muscles, but
separates them, by pushing them back away from each other,
with the handle of the scalpel, in order to expose the trachea;
upon its appearance, one makes an incision into it without
much trouble. In this operation, bleeding cannot cause any
embarrassment, because in cutting the skin, there is very, very
little blood, and in cutting the trachea, none whatever comes
forth.

CHAPTER 25

Guilhelmus Fabricius Hildanus
(Wilhelm Fabry von Hilden) (1560–1624)

"Drinking, whoring, and gambling should not be indulged in by the surgeon, for because of them he may well forget or omit something today concerning the patient which cannot be corrected tomorrow."[1]

Wilhelm Fabricius von Hilden was the leading German surgeon at the time that his distinguished namesake, Fabricius ab Aquapendente, was the dominant surgeon of Italy. These two contemporary masters present an interesting study in contrasting conceptions of surgery and of surgical pathology, which reflect the differences in their educational experiences. The Italian Fabricius, as we have seen, was an eminent scholar, a graduate of the University of Padua, which was the center of higher learning of that period. Fabry von Hilden was initiated into the art of surgery by a thorough apprenticeship under a succession of skilled and experienced wound and barber surgeons, who made up for their lack of institutional training by diligent and penetrating observation upon the patients themselves. Thus, the Italian Fabricius was so thoroughly imbued with the doctrines of Galen, and their embellishments by Avicenna, Haly Abbas, and Avenzoar, he was forever unable to free himself from their fetters; whereas the German, Fabry, with a mind untrameled, could see what he looked at, and believe what he saw. Both enriched the art they professed, each after his own fashion.

Fabry von Hilden was born not far from Düsseldorf, in western Germany, in 1560. His father was a clerk in a court of justice, necessarily a man of some education. Fabry was given excellent preliminary schooling, and was early destined for a career in medicine. A succession of misfortunes supervened, however, which precluded a university education. His father died when he was but ten years of age, as did his stepfather some three years later. Shortly

---

1. *Wund-Artzney, gantzes Werck, und aller Bücher, so viel deren vorhanden.* . . . Ausz dem Lateinischen in das Teutsche übersetzt durch Friedrich Greiffen. . . . Franckfurth am Mayn, Joh. Aubry, 1652, p. 942. Epigram and excerpts are translated from the contemporary German by the authors.

FIG. 47. Guilhelmus Fabricius Hildanus. From: *De Gangraena et Sphacelo*, In nobili Oppenheimio, Hieronymus Gallerus, 1617.

afterwards, Fabry himself suffered from a severe attack of bubonic plague
which left him bedridden for months. Lacking, then, the means for a formal
study of medicine, he became an apprentice in the lowlier craft of surgery
instead. But his training was thorough. For twelve years, with a succession
of masters, an intensive grounding in anatomy, and considerable travel, he
was able to prepare himself for a truly distinguished career.

In his marriage, Fabry was indeed fortunate. Marie Colinet proved to be
a faithful and self-sacrificing wife and a devoted mother of his children. Be-

yond this, however, she was also highly esteemed as a surgeon and obstetrician in her own right and she skillfully assisted him in his work. She is credited with having suggested to her husband that he use a magnet for the extraction of a metallic foreign body from a patient's eye. It was a shattering blow to Fabry when she, together with their two daughters, succumbed to the ravages of the plague. His grief is poignantly expressed in the letters written at the time.

Fabry von Hilden was eminently successful in the practice of surgery. Although he was not itinerant in the usual sense, he nevertheless displayed a certain restlessness, changing his abode many times, from Hilden to southern Germany to Switzerland repeatedly, and frequently back to his birthplace. In addition, his renown was such that he was constantly being called for consultations, operations, or prolonged care of house-bound patients, over great distances. Throughout the busy years, he observed carefully, and kept detailed records of his observations. In addition, he carried on a wide exchange of lengthy letters with many prominent physicians and other surgeons, in which case histories were reported and discussed in detail.

From this wealth of clinical material, Fabry published several monographs, followed by collections of case reports in series of 100 each, entitled "Observations or Perceptions in Wound Surgery" (*Observationen, oder Wahrnehmungen in der Wundartzney*), to a voluminous total of 600. All these works subsequently appeared in a single, huge folio edition. Included with the clinical descriptions are many reports of postmortem examinations made to determine the seat of disease and the cause of death. A large number of excellent illustrations, possibly prepared by Fabry himself and definitely under his supervision, contribute greatly to the interest and the clarity of the text. Many of the "Observations" are contained in the exchange of correspondence with medical and surgical colleagues, which served in place of the medical journals of today as avenues for the dissemination of scientific information.

Despite Fabry von Hilden's lack of formal university education, he was very well read in the classics and in the works of contemporary writers. He wrote in Latin, from which language his books were subsequently translated into German. His "Observations" cover the entire field of surgery, and reveal him to be a bold and skillful surgeon, ingenious in meeting unfamiliar problems, and inventive in designing effective instruments for special needs. Early in his career he became interested in gangrene, and he wrote a monograph on the subject. When amputation was necessary, he emphasized the importance of doing so through healthy tissues above the level of necrosis. He devised a tourniquet for the control of bleeding, and is said to have first performed amputation through the thigh. He operated for selected carcinomas of the breast, and described the removal of axillary metastases.

In his concepts of surgical pathology, Fabry shows his independence of

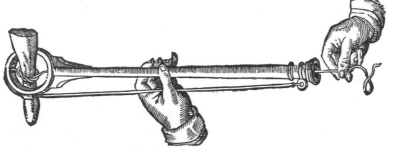

FIG. 48. Instrument for placing deep ligatures in removing polyps, etc. From: *Wund-Arztney, op. cit.*

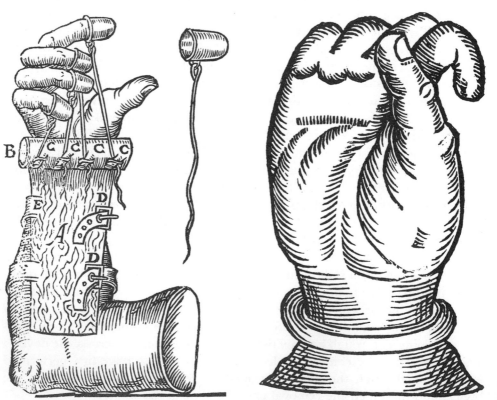

FIG. 49. Deformity of the hand (*right*) and method of correcting it (*left*). From: *Wund-Arztney, op. cit.*

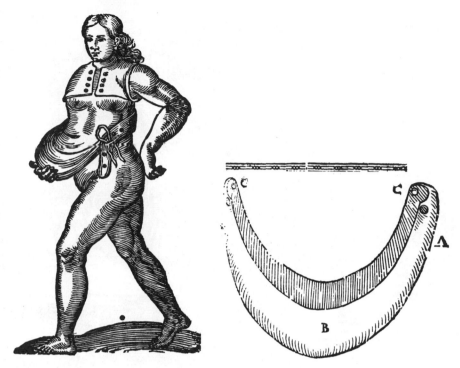

FIG. 50. Device for retaining huge umbilical hernia. From: *Wund-Arztney, op. cit.*

mind most clearly, and therein breaks sharply from all who preceded him. It is to be expected that ideas of local pathology should reflect the prevailing opinions of the nature of disease in general. During the many centuries in which the humoral doctrine was universally accepted, localized tissue changes were also attributed to accumulations of one or several of the humors, in their "natural" or "non-natural" state. Whether occurring spontaneously, or as complications of injuries, all swellings were thus explained, and their treatment was directed toward correcting their presumed cause. Henri de Mondeville, Guy de Chauliac, Paré, Fabricius ab Aquapendente, and many subsequent authorities subscribed to this doctrine.

In the writings of Fabry von Hilden, little mention is made of humors, and the effort instead is to explain disease on localized physical causes. Thus, trauma, foreign bodies, parasites, and thermal influences are usually found to be the source of the disturbance. The term "inflammation" is used quite as it is today, and irritation of sensitive structures is held responsible for the clinical manifestations. Even the remote sequelae of injuries are accounted for as influences transmitted along anatomical routes, rather than as aggregations of the various fluids. This does not imply that Fabry was unfamiliar

FIG. 51. Amputation for gangrene of the leg. From: *De Gangraena, op. cit.*

with the classical concepts, nor that he rejected them. He does relegate them, however, to a far less important role.

The books of Fabricius von Hilden are replete with testimony to his highly moral and conscientious character, as well as to his pride in the profession of surgery, and his concern with its reputation. Nevertheless, he was moderate in his criticisms of the less worthy practitioners of the craft. Toward his masters he retained a lifelong esteem and reverence, never failing to express his admiration whenever their names were mentioned. Toward the many prominent physicians with whom he corresponded so profusely, as well as with his surgical colleagues, his relations were always those of reciprocal high regard and friendship. He is among the best of the surgical empiricists, and not only advanced the surgery of his native country, but also imbued it with the spirit of science.

How a Hard Cancer [of the Breast] and Other Complications Were Caused by Curdled Milk.

(From a letter directed to Dr. Andreas Weickius)

A few days ago I visited again that woman at Solothurn whom you once saw with me who was afflicted with a very severe condition, namely, with a hidden cancer which had arisen from curdled and hardened milk. I prescribed for her several internal as well as external remedies, from which she experiences benefit and help. But I again indicated to the bystanders that the disease is incurable. Another Doctor had advised that one should apply corrosive or blistering medicaments so that the contained matter could be expelled. What senseless and dangerous advice this is, I showed them by thorough proofs and many examples. I particularly brought before them the tragic story of a noblewoman in the neighborhood to whom I was called in the year 1606 (and who was also well known to our patient). This lady, after she had been afflicted for several years with a hidden cancer of the right breast, had her nipple opened by a wound surgeon, from which arose a stinking malignant ulcer which terminated her life with great pain.

An honorable woman in the region of Berne who had nursed her baby, developed an inflammation in the right breast which caused the milk to coagulate and turn to curds. When the inflammation subsided, a curd or piece of curdled milk remained in the part of the breast which faced toward the axilla. A hard swelling gradually developed which finally turned into a malignant cancer. And although it had not reached the stage of final gravity, the pains were so severe, especially at night, that she, herself, often talked as if glowing coals were lying on her breast.

After five years (if I remember correctly) of such suffering, when the hard cancerous swelling had approached its gravest point, I was approached. I found in the right breast a hidden cancer, far larger than a fist, hard and pale. In the axilla there

2. *Ibid.*, pp. 192–193.

were also hidden three hard swellings, one of which was as big as an egg; the others, however, not yet malignant and not yet cancerous. After her body was sufficiently prepared, by a suitable regimen of food and drink, and also by purging and bleeding, . . . I cut out all these hard swellings, and she became well again.

That the excision of axillary tumors is difficult and dangerous, especially when they are large, I have observed in others as well as, particularly, in the woman spoken of above. It is dangerous because the breast veins come together in that spot, bleeding from which must be controlled. Furthermore, also through the contraction of such tumors, the breast muscles which aid in breathing might be injured, and for this reason there is danger of suffocation. Therefore it is necessary to proceed slowly, humbly and gently with such parts.

It is difficult because when the arm hangs down, the tumor lies hidden, and the entire axilla is covered by the inner side of the arm. But when the arm is elevated, the muscles, skin, and vessels, and also the tumor, are under such tension that it is difficult to tell one from the others, particularly if the tumor is deeply attached to the membranes. For this reason one must be very careful in this matter. Above all things, one must inform himself carefully whether the tumor weaves about or moves from one place to another, or whether it can be removed from the base, including its roots. For all would be for naught if a part of the tumor, be it ever so small, even a bit of membrane with which such tumors are generally surrounded, were to remain behind. For then it flares up again and becomes worse than ever before. There is also no hope that what has been left behind can be destroyed by cautery, for by these same cauterizing agents, cancers become incited so that they become highly malignant and of an evil nature. . . .

THE 61st OBSERVATION OR PERCEPTION (FIRST HUNDRED)[3]

How an Intestinal Disease Arose from a Hardened Swelling and Cancerous Ulcer in the Region of the Appendix.

I have several times visited the son of Theodor on the Koulen in Hilden, who for several years suffered from a persistent and progressive pain in the liver region. When he died

3. *Ibid.,* p. 61.

of severe intestinal disease, I was called to determine the cause of the preceding pain. When I opened the abdomen, I found that the appendix was shrunken and drawn into the small bowel, and so completely filled it, that no contents of the upper bowels could be forced into the colon; therefore such pain. When I finally cut the small bowel open and removed the appendix from it, I found the same to be inflamed and swollen throughout. In addition, there was ulcerated hardness present, or more likely a severe cancer in the base of the appendix itself to be seen.

Commentary and Explanation. Various causes are mentioned for the abdominal pain, such as *iliac passion* called by some "*Miserere mei*" or "Have compassion on me." The primary one is the drawing together and occlusion of the small intestine. And then, to find the cause of this condition, I have opened and examined various corpses, and as the stench was usually most revolting, that one could hardly inspect everything minutely, still I have observed in all, that the beginning and cause of this illness is situated about the appendix, that is in the little pouch which we see at the end of the small intestine and at the beginning of the colon.

For this reason, I believe that the little forward-falling door or valve (which the outstanding anatomist and excellent botanist Caspar Bauhin found in the beginning part of the colon), first, as a result of inflammation of the appendix is so contracted, that no feces or excrement can pass through; that then the inflammation so increases, that finally the entire small bowel, and indeed the surrounding parts become gangrenous and

FIG. 52

finally are attacked by cold gangrene. I have observed this in all that I have yet examined after death and not only in the above mentioned boy.

36TH OBSERVATION OR PERCEPTION. (FIRST HUNDRED)[4]

Which Teaches of the Manner How One Can Remove Bones and Other Things that are Stuck in the Throat.

It is a small silver or copper tube, bent, as thick as a swan quill, about a foot long, and perforated throughout. At its lower tip, a small, new sponge, of the size of a hazelnut is firmly tied. With this tube, when it is pushed into the throat, and turned around within as described above, and then withdrawn, bones and other similar things can be extracted. Then, if it so happens that one of the perforations of the tube takes hold of the bone or fishbone, this will be withdrawn together with the tube. If this does not happen, then the roughness or sharpness of the bone will become attached to the little sponge and be dislodged, which I have learned from experience, even before I had this instrument.

And if upon insertion of the instrument the bone or fishbone cannot be withdrawn on the first attempt, one should not let up or desist. For I have often had to repeat such attempts five or six times until finally the bone could be dislodged and withdrawn; or (if it could not in any other way) be pushed completely down into the stomach, which can be done without danger. Nevertheless, it is better if it can be extracted by way of the mouth.

4. *Ibid.,* pp. 38–39.

CHAPTER 26

Johannes Scultetus (1595–1645) and Matthäus Gottfried Purmann (1648–1721)

"The Ancients discovered much, and yet left much more still to be discovered."
(Scultetus)

"I would have nobody pin their Faith upon my Sleeve, but let them try and consider the Reasons that support this practice, and you will find, that the Ancients, in this Case are too erroneous to be imitated. . . . "
(Purmann)

Before leaving the German surgeons of the seventeenth century, mention should be made of two others who left important literary landmarks. Johannes Schultes (1595–1645), commonly called Scultetus, was a contemporary of Fabry von Hilden. Unlike the others of his countrymen so far considered, Scultetus was well educated in the Italian tradition and in a manner somewhat reminiscent of Vesalius. Born at Ulm on the Danube, on October 12, 1595, he went, at the very young age of fifteen, to Padua for the study of medicine. Here he came under the influence of Fabricius ab Aquapendente, and of Adriaan van den Spieghel, prominent Belgian surgeon and anatomist, for whom he served as prosector. The doctorate in medicine, surgery, and philosophy was conferred upon him in 1621, after which he practiced for a short time in Padua and, later, in Vienna. At the age of thirty he returned to Ulm in the capacity of city physician. This post he filled with distinction until his death in 1645 which occurred in Stuttgart whence he had been called to see a patient.

His famous book, *Armamentarium Chirurgicum* (Ulm, 1653), was published posthumously by his nephew who was also his namesake, called Scultetus the Younger, as well as his disciple and literary executor. The dedication to this book not only draws a picture of the elder Scultetus, but, also, in a charming manner, gives us some information as to his works and character.[1]

1. Johannes Scultetus: *The Chyrurgeons Store-House*, Englished by E. B., London, John Starkey, 1674.

"Whosoever doth behold clearly with the eye of his Understanding the wonderful works of the Eternal Moderatour, and Governour of all things, he is immediately delighted with the sweetness of that Contemplation; and the more he is delighted, the farther he searcheth into them. By searching daily he learns the more, and is the more ready and willing to consecrate his knowledge to the publick good; and by the help of drawing and engraving to transmit his experience to all posterity. The Antients discovered much, and yet left much more still to be discovered. My Uncle, of Pious Memory, first led by the admirable direction of God, devoted his mind to the study of physick from his youth, and without vanity, I may affirm, that he attained no small glory, in the happy performance of Chyrurgical Operations: and whilst he chose that stupendious Miracle of Nature, the Fabrick of Mans Body to be his subject, and did contemplate it with great delight; he collected every day new Observations, which he committed to writing intending one day, after having revised them, to make them Publick; and I wish to God a milder Fate had spared his Life for some years, that those Productions of his might by himself in their due time have been brought forth into the world; but God disposing it otherwise, upon his untimely departure out of this Life; and dying intestate, I came to be one of his Heirs; and having been ever observant to him, and of the Same Profession, I thought it would be a high offence, to involve, as it were, in Cimmerian darkness the works of him, to whom I owe my education; and as his Heir I hold my self obliged to perform the desires of the deceased, which I hope in this work, I have in some measure satisfied; as also the desires of friends, who, by Letters, have earnestly requested the Publication of it, but the chief motion which hath induced me to set it forth is, that I might Dedicate it to you my most honored [benefactor]. . . . without which liberality of yours, I could not have been at the University; especially the Venetian [Padua], nor have lived three years there, and followed my studies. You have since received me into the Counsell of Physitians, and have commanded me to be a fellow of their college; These and many other benefits heaped upon us, my Uncle while he was alive. . . . [and]

Your most obedient

JOHANNES SCULTETUS."

The *Armamentarium chirurgicum*, upon which the fame of Scultetus rests, is a remarkable book for its time. It contains a complete catalogue of all known surgical instruments, of the methods of bandaging and splinting, and of a vast number of operative procedures, all of which are illustrated in graphic detail by means of numerous plates. In addition, it contains a large number of case reports which give evidence of his surgical daring and skill. The original edition, published in 1653, contained 43 full-page illustrations. Numerous subsequent editions were published, to many of which additional

FIG. 53. Title page of Johannes Scultetus' *Armamentarium Chirurgicum*, Amsterdam, 1741

FIG. 54. Operations on the mouth and ears. From: Scultetus' *Armamentarium Chirurgicum*

illustrations and textual material were added by their respective editors. Moreover, translations into German, French, and English made the work accessible to those surgeons throughout Europe who lacked the ability to read the original Latin. The importance of this book may be judged by the reappearance of its illustrations in the surgical literature over the succeeding centuries.

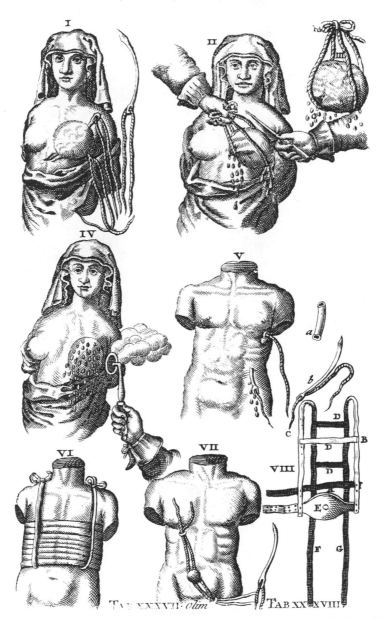

FIG. 55. Breast amputation for cancer; umbilical supports. From: Scultetus' *Armamentarium Chirurgicum*.

MATTHÄUS GOTTFRIED PURMANN is justly famed as a military surgeon of exceptional ability, a courageous operative entrepreneur, and a prolific author with a flair for the bizarre and the curious. Born very shortly after the death of Scultetus, whom he succeeded as the most prominent of the German wound surgeons of the seventeenth and early eighteenth centuries, he

FIG. 56. Cesarean section. From: Scultetus' *Armamentarium Chirurgicum*

is credited with having brought the current advances from France to his fatherland. Unlike the earlier important surgeons of Germany who came from its southern regions, Purmann was born in the North, at Lüben in Silesia, in the year 1648. He was trained under a wound surgeon in Gross-Glogau and served the Great Elector, Frederick William, in the Bradenburg army for twelve years (1667–1679). It was this ruler who established a standing army in Prussia and also assigned a wound surgeon to each company and regiment. The military campaigns carried Purmann to Western Germany, and again to the North against Sweden. His very extensive experience with war wounds as *Feldscheer* included the treatment of men seriously injured by glass grenades, and was interspersed with intervals of civil practice which also brought him distinction.

The termination of hostilities with the Peace of St. Germain in 1679 brought his army service to a close and he settled in Halberstadt as City Wound Surgeon. Plague epidemics during the next two years furnished him with

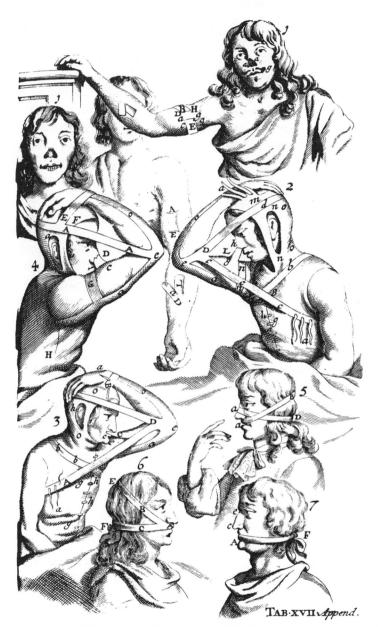

FIG. 57. Rhino- and chiloplasty in the manner of Tagliacozzi. From: Scultetus' *Armamentarium Chirurgicum.*

ample opportunities for service and experience with this disease as a patient as well as doctor. A decade later (1690) he became City Physician in Breslau where again he attained eminence as a surgeon and where he published his most important books. His death is assumed to have occurred in 1721.

That Purmann was a prolific writer has already been stated. His works include "The Proper Army Surgeon" (*Der recht und wahrhaftige Feldscheerer oder die Feldscheerkunst*), Halberstadt, 1680; two books on the plague; "Surgical Laurel Crown" (*Chirurgischer Lorbeerkranz, oder Wundarzney, etc.*), Halberstadt, 1684; "Twenty-five Remarkable Gunshot Wounds," Breslau, 1687; "Fifty Unusual and Wonderful Cures of Gunshot Wounds," 1693; "*Chirurgia Curiosa*," 1694; "*Curiosae Observationes Chirurgicae*," 1694; a book on "salivation cure;" and his *opus magnum*, "Great Wound Surgery" (*Grosse Wundartzney* h.e. *Chirurgia Magna*), Frankfort, 1692. Inasmuch as most of these works appeared in multiple editions, and many in translations, his output was indeed prodigious.

From these writings it appears that, despite his lack of formal schooling, Purmann had gained sufficient education to enable him to compose his books in Latin. He displays a keen intelligence and a gift for logical reasoning. When his own experience warranted it, he had the courage to break with traditional methods. In the brief excerpt on the management of gunshot wounds quoted below, he very ably establishes the superiority of simple protective dressings to the use of oily and greasy substances as well as to the customary enlargement of the wounds.

This rational approach stands in curious contrast to his professed advocacy of treatment by weapon salve which had first been described by Paracelsus. This latter method consisted of anointing the weapon that had inflicted the wound, or, in its absence, a wood shaving that had been smeared with blood or discharge from the wound, and leaving the wound itself strictly alone except for a protective dressing. It would seem that his apparent turning toward superstition in the light of his rational and empirical observations might have been a conscious subterfuge to dissuade wound surgeons from meddlesome therapy, or to satisfy the demands of the patients for more active treatment. Purmann's own comments on this subject are quoted in one of the following extracts.

Among the innovations introduced by Purmann may be mentioned the use of blood transfusion, the first reported case in the general literature. This and his experiments with the infusion of drugs into his own veins are of considerable interest and importance.

ꙅ ꙅ ꙅ   ON THE TREATMENT OF WOUNDS WITHOUT SUPPURA-
ꙅ ꙅ ꙅ   TION][2]

Whether in Curing Wounds, there is a Necessity to bring
them to Suppuration, by Emplasters, Oyls, Cataplasms, etc.,

2. *Chirurgia Curiosa:* or *The Newest and Most Curious Observations and Operations in the Whole Art of Chirurgery.* Written Originally in *High-Dutch*, by the Learned Matthaeus Gothofredus

according to Antient Custom? Or, whether they may not be Cured easier and sooner, by other Medicines without Suppuration?

The Antients were of Opinion, that no Wounds could be cured without *Suppuration*; and directed their Medicines accordingly. This Method I follow'd very strictly in several Campaigns, and thought there was no other Way, as many others do, that follow the Antient Method to this Day; but considering better of it, and observing the practice, and reading the Works of [others] . . . I saw Reason enough to leave off this Method, and adhere to a better, by the Invitation and Example of others; wherein I soon found it true, that wounds might be constantly and perfectly cured without *Suppuration*, or the Application of *Plaisters*, *Balsams*, *Oyls*, *Ointments*, and such like nasty greasie Medicines, which under Pretence of *suppurating*, *Mundifying* and keeping the Wound *Open* for some time; the Lips, Edges, and the Flesh were corrupted, by imbibing those greasie Drugs, and made more painful, by keeping it *Open*; not to mention other ill Accidents, that too often happen while you are waiting for a *suppuration*. I would have no body pin their Faith upon my Sleeve, but let them try and consider the Reasons that support this Practice, and you will find, that the Antients in this Case are too erroneous to be imitated; and that the latter Method is better. Who knows not, that *Nature* abhors Wounds or Divisions in any Part of the admirable Fabrick of our tender Bodies? And therefore proposes and takes the readiest Way of conjoining and consolidating them; Nature knows that Wounds cannot endure being exposed to the *Air* because it irritates the *Nervous Fibers*, and so occasions *Inflammations* and *Putrefactions*, and therefore contributes to the closing them up from that Enemy; and a Chirurgion being but *Natures Servant*, ought to do the like, with all possible Expedition; before any *Unctuous* and *Oily* Matter gives a check to it. I know some think we ought not to use the Word *Nature*; and I will comply with them, when they have found another *Word*, which better expresses the *Excretions*, *Nutritions* and *Secretions* of humane Bodies; but not to insist upon Words; take care in all your Endeavours to assist *Nature* in all her Operations, and take the

Purmannus, Chief Chirurgion of the City of *Breslau* in *Germany*, and of the Hospitals of *St. Job* and *All-Saints*. Translated by Joachim Sprengell, London, D. Browne . . . 1706, Book II, Chapter 1, pp. 109–112.

speediest Way to *Consolidation*, after you have removed every thing that may obstruct her Progress. . . .

[He gives prescriptions for a lotion to be used to cleanse deep wounds and a powder to be dusted into superficial ones. The edges of the wound are approximated and held in place by bandages.] . . . especially if you are sent for time enough, while the Wound is fresh; for then if you observe these Directions, you will admire the good effects of such Medicines, which cure sooner and safer than the nasty greasie ones of the *Antients*;. . . .

REMARKS UPON CURES BY SYMPATHY, AND THOSE PERFORM'D BY TRANSPLANTATION[3]

It's very well known to the Learned World, that upon the Invitation of Paracelsus, who was the first Inventer of the *Sympathetical* Ointment, *Petrus Servius*, Professor at *Rome*, and the great *English Digby*, with several Physicians and Chirurgions, set themselves on work to find out the true Preparation of it; that cured Wounds, only by applying it to the Weapon or Instrument that made it, or to some of the Blood or matter taken out of the Sore; and since their Eyes were witnesses that it did perform these things, their next Enquiry was how this Medicine came to operate after so strange a Manner? Which being a Nice Speculation, many have troubled their Brains to find out the reason of this peculiar Magnetical Quality, but to little purpose, having left it more intricate and perplexed than they found it, for among them all *Sir Kenelm Digby* has only given tolerable reason to render its operation intelligible. . . . .

OF CHIRURGICAL INFUSION AND TRANSFUSION, AND WHY THEY ARE IN NO GREATER REPUTATION IN THE WORLD.[4]

Chirurgical *Transfusion* was also for some time in great vogue and reputation; but since it could not be always practiced, and that Patients were unwilling to submit to it, it soon grew out of use; but I am of the opinion if Dr. Major, Etmuller, Eltzholtz, Dr. Wren and Clark had lived somewhat longer, it might have been further advanced in the World; but they dying the Operation began to be neglected and dyed soon after them.

I tried it on a Merchant's Son at Berlin who for severall years was afflicted with a Leprosie; I gradually drew out a great quantity of his Blood, and put into his Veins the Blood

3. *Ibid.*, Chapter V, p. 220.
4. *Ibid.*, Chapter XVI, p. 302 ff.

FIG. 58. Blood transfusion. From: Purmann's *Wundarzney*, 1722

of a Lamb; by which means the patient was happily cured, to the admiration of several ingenious Persons.

Transfusion is performed in this manner. Generally the Legs or Arms are chosen for this Purpose; in the Arm the *Vena Mediana,* and in the Leg the *Vena Cruralis;* from which you must take as much Blood as the Strength of the Patient will permit. The Arm or the Leg, where the Vein is to be opened, must be tyed fast below the opening with a strong Fillet. Then you

must have in readiness an Instrument which is a kind of a
Tube, surrounded with a Linen Cover, in which Cover you
must put some warm Water to hinder the blood from coagulat-
ing or congealing, which passes through the *Tube*. This *Tube*
must have on each side a fine *Silver Pipe*, one of which must be
put into the Vein of the Man and the other into the Vein of the
Beast, from whom Blood must be transfused, the Hair or Wool
of whose Neck must be cut away and a Fillet bound about its
Neck, and the Creature tyed so fast that it cannot move one
way or other; then the Vein being opened both in the Man
and the Beast, the Blood of the Beast will rise into the *Tube*
and empty it self into the Vein of the *Arm*; and so much for
this Operation.

CHAPTER 27

Gaspare Tagliacozzi
(1545–1599)

"Furthermore, I wished to show that material is not lacking—particularly in this vast field of Medicine—in which to prove one's ability, that is, by perfecting things which have been left incomplete and untouched by the ancients or others and by making new contributions to knowledge, not without glory to one's name."[1]

It is seldom given to one man to create, single-handed, a field of medicine. Gaspare Tagliacozzi was one such man. He created the specialty of plastic surgery.

During the late medieval period and in the centuries that followed, reputable surgeons tended to shun major elective operations. As has been mentioned before, the vacuum thus left became filled by irregular operators or incisors, who were often base and brutal men without learning or scruple. They were usually itinerants in search of wider opportunities as well as freedom from the penalties of their failures. There were exceptions, however. As indicated briefly in the discussion on Heinrich von Pfolspeundt (Chapter 22), certain families, particularly in Italy, developed great skill in the performance of individual operations, and passed these methods down from father to son for generations as closely held secrets. For the plastic restoration of nose and ears, the Brancas, father and son, of Catania in Sicily, developed an operative technique early in the fifteenth century. The elder Branca used the "Indian" method, which is well described by Sushruta, of taking skin from the cheek or forehead, with which to build the new nose. Antonio, the son, advanced the art by extending it to the restoration of lips and ears, and apparently invented the procedure of taking skin from the arm by the pedicled-flap technique which has since been designated as the "Italian" operation.

A second Italian family gained recognition a century later as facial plastic

1. From the dedication of the *De curtorum chirurgia*, translated by Virginia Burrell. In: *The Life and Times of Gaspare Tagliacozzi, Surgeon of Bologna 1545–1599*, with a documented study of the scientific and cultural life of Bologna in the sixteenth century. By Martha Teach Gnudi and Jerome Pierce Webster, New York, Herbert Reichner [1950], p. 453.

experts. The Vianeos lived in Calabria, in the southwestern part of the Italian peninsula, and at least four of its members practiced the art. Several eyewitness accounts of their work were published by laymen who had traveled in that part of the country. It was probably from some such source that the possibilities of nasal reconstruction came to the sixteenth century Bolognese surgeon, Gaspare Tagliacozzi, who wrote, "I had heard that there were certain men in Calabria who practiced this art rather by irregular and haphazard methods than methods based upon reason. . . ."

Tagliacozzi was born in Bologna in 1545, into an affluent and respected family. He was educated at the university of that city where he was granted a degree in medicine in 1570, and in philosophy in 1576. Immediately after receiving his first degree, Tagliacozzi was appointed Professor of Surgery at the university, which office he continued to occupy as he studied for the doctorate in philosophy. This achieved, he was admitted to the Doctoral College of Medicine and Philosophy. From this time on he engaged in practice with a definite predilection toward surgery. Existing records indicate that he gained renown and prestige in his profession, gave public demonstrations of anatomy, was elected to public office, and accumulated considerable property.

Life in the Italy of Tagliacozzi was filled with violence. Facial mutilations were frequent. Duels, street and tavern brawls, and retaliatory attacks, to say nothing of the penal cutting off of noses and ears and the widespread cosmetic ravages of syphilis, all combined to create a need for reconstructive plastic procedures. Tagliacozzi early became interested in the surgical correction of these facial deformities, made it the core of his life's work, and attained lasting fame from these efforts.

Tagliacozzi's teacher and friend, Aranzio, in all probability first took up this problem and transmitted it to his pupil, even though he left no record of it in his writings, nor is it mentioned by Tagliacozzi. Be that as it may, Tagliacozzi threw himself energetically into this field. By careful observation and minute attention to all steps in the operation, and making modifications as experience dictated, he perfected the operations of nasoplasty and of reconstruction of the ears and lips. He became the outstanding surgeon of his time in Bologna, and his esteem spread widely over Italy. His death occurred in Bologna in 1599, and the most celebrated figures in political and cultural life, as well as in medicine, vied with one another in paying tribute to him.

Tagliacozzi's book, *De curtorum chirurgia per insitionem* ("On the Surgery of Mutilations by Grafting"), was published two years before his death. In this volume, he describes, in most intimate detail, the operative methods which he had evolved over many years of tireless and dedicated effort. The text is illustrated with numerous, beautifully executed drawings, which show each individual step of the various operations and the postoperative results.

As a record of one man's achievement which marks the creation of a new field in surgery, this book endures as one of the great literary landmarks in the growth of the profession. The *De curtorum chirurgia* was translated into English in the seventeenth century.[2] This translation is included in a magnificent recent publication which contains much enlightening commentary on the life of Tagliacozzi, of his times, and on the history of facial reconstructive surgery.[3]

〜 〜 〜   [This excerpt is taken from a letter written by Tagliacozzi
〜 〜 〜   to a distinguished physician and anatomist, Girolamo Mercuriale of Padua. It succinctly presents what appears at much greater length in the *De curtorum chirurgia*.]

To Hieronymus Mercurialis from Gaspar Tagliacotius Greeting.

The method of restoring noses by the art [of surgery], which you recently requested of me in a letter, illustrious Sir, I take pleasure in indicating to you now, but briefly and offhand. For I cannot spend long on this because I am kept extremely busy in town with my medical duties, and furthermore there is the possibility that now I may have to lecture even abroad. Therefore I shall just outline the main points of the method— it will only be an imperfect sketch to give you an idea of it— for I have set forth everything pertaining to the subject in a special treatise. This is a lengthy work which, unless our muse encounters some difficulty, will soon be handed over to be printed so that this ability may be shared with all mankind. . . .

But now let us begin. First consider the body of the patient and examine carefully the temperament of the body and the brain. For toward it, as at a target, all therapeutic measures must be directed; and if in the patient the humors deviate in quantity or quality from balance, they must be brought into proper proportion: briefly, any cacochymia [dyscrasia] must be removed with suitable medication, and by the proper regimen we must guard against a disturbance in the humors being provoked during the course of the surgical operation. Therefore, anything unnatural must [if used] be used with deliberation and skill. And some things must be completely

2. Alexander Read: *Chirurgorum comes: Or the whole practice of chirurgery*. . . . London, Jones, 1687.
3. M. T. Gnudi and J. P. Webster: *The Life and Times of Gaspare Tagliacozzi*. . . . (see footnote 1). We are indebted to this work for biographical information on Tagliacozzi.

rejected. Thus, venery must be ruled out absolutely, and all anger, grief, and worry barred. The food given should be easily digestible, with little residue, and euchymous. The bowels should move daily or be stimulated appropriately. Night air is bad as well as rainy atmosphere or that in which the south wind prevails. In the case of passive individuals a temperate climate is best; in the case of active individuals, one somewhat on the warm side is best because if the exterior of the body is agreeably warmed, it enjoys a more suitable mixture of blood. Sleep likewise ought to be moderate, for a great deal of it fills the head with moisture. Hence the closing of the wound is protracted by the excess flow of moisture into the cutaneous region, and the conjoined parts are irritated by the flow of liquids. This disturbs and impedes the formation of a perfect cicatrix.

After these preliminary measures for the preparation and care of the body, an incision is made in the skin of either arm, left or right, down to the flesh, that is, only as far as the surface of the muscles; in other words, simple and solid skin is taken from the anterior brachial region, where the triceps muscle ends and the biceps begins. Furthermore, the extent of the mutilation of the nose will indicate the length and breadth of the skin which must be taken. Next, that same skin, having been separated, must be made to suppurate by medication, then dried out, so that it may be suitable for the grafting which is to be done on the nose. The time of drying and suppuration is not the same for all patients but varies according to their favorable temperament and nutrition. But when the skin is recognized as fit for the grafting, its margins, as well as those of the nose, are lightly scarified so that the arm skin may be joined to the nose with sutures by the art. However, in order that in the various motions of the body those parts joined in this way may not be torn apart and injured, the arm should be kept bound to the head with proper bandages, while the wound and the suture are being healed with cicatrizing agents. [The time for] release of the bandaging will be indicated by the union and satisfactory nourishment of the skin; this varies considerably according to the various temperaments of patients. But when excellent union of the wound and nourishment of the skin is observed, sever the arm from the face, and care for the wound as you do for other wounds for a period of several days; but the remaining skin,

FIG. 59. Nasoplasty showing the deformity and the flap which has been raised on the arm. From: Gasparis Tagliacotii Bononiensis, *De curtorum chirurgia per insitionem*, Libri duo, Venetiis, Apud Robertum Meiettum, 1597.

that is, the result of the grafting, which, of course, is attached to the nose, has to be made into the shape of a nose and fashioned with reamers, that is, at its lower end, so that the myxae or nares or foramina, as well as the columella, the tip and

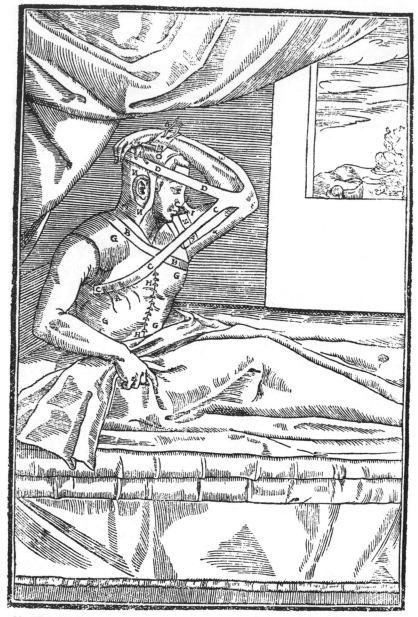

Fig. 60. The flap has been sutured in place, showing the method of immobilization. From: Gasparis Tagliacotii Bononiensis, *De curtorum chirurgia per insitionem*, Libri duo, Venetiis. Apud Robertum Meiettum, 1597.

the alae may be simulated by the skin which has been attached.

Now this procedure, as well as the rest of the operation, does not prove as difficult as practically everyone until now has seemed to believe, even the most illustrious men. For it is generally thought that the severity of the pain and the endless anguish involved in this operation are so great that it is better to keep the mutilated nose. But this is an absolutely mistaken idea. On the contrary, the patients find the procedure so bearable that even apart from the work itself [*i.e.*, the result], it wins universal admiration. Moreover there are other operations in surgery much more painful and difficult.

But let us proceed with our discussion, of which we are now in the midst. If the columella, which has been obtained with the reamers, needs to be joined to the opposing part, open a place by scarification slightly interiorly in the upper border of the philtrum, and also the base of the columella must be scarified, and when the sutures have been put in place, follow the usual treatment for healing wounds. Meanwhile, place tents [packing] in the hollow of the nostrils according to the size and shape of these—ultimately tubules of lead or silver should be inserted; and the outside should be provided with a covering of silver or lead in nature's mold, which firmly fits the nose, so that the exterior surface is able to acquire a nice shape.[4]

4. *Ibid.*, pp. 136–138.

PART VI

GREAT BRITAIN LEADS

CHAPTER 28

William Clowes
(1540–1604)

" . . . *idleness yieldeth as much profit, as a barren and dry tree good fruit. . . .* "

(William Clowes)

British surgery, like the German, lagged behind that of Italy and France. During the sixteenth century, however, there were feeble stirrings of that movement which was to carry, some two centuries later, English surgery to a prolonged and fruitful world domination. The Barber-Surgeons' Company of London was incorporated in 1540, with Thomas Vicary its first Master; and regulations were initiated governing the education, conduct, and licensure of surgeons. For the first time in that city anatomical dissections were legalized, and bodies of executed malefactors were provided for these demonstrations. Shortly afterward, books on surgery began to appear by Vicary, Hall, Thomas Gale, and William Clowes.

The ablest of the Elizabethan surgeons, according to general opinion, was William Clowes. Born in 1540 of Warwickshire gentry, he received his surgical training by apprenticeship. Later, he served in both the army and navy, and gained wide experience in the management of gunshot wounds. Subsequently, he engaged in practice in London, where he soon became a member of the Barber-Surgeons' Company and, later, staff surgeon to St. Bartholomew's Hospital. Success and fame attended his labors, and culminated in his appointment as surgeon to Her Majesty, Queen Elizabeth. At the time of his death in 1604, he was living in retirement in Essex.

Clowes' most important publication, *Profitable and Necessarie Booke of Observations*, appeared in 1596. It represents an expanded version of an earlier treatise (1588), *A Prooved Practise for all Young Chirurgions, concerning Burnings with Gunpowder and Wounds made with Gunshot, etc.*, and also contains *A Briefe and Necessary Treatise, Touching the Cure of the Disease now usually called Lues Venera*. He indicates in these writings an earnest desire to pass on the benefits of his observations to younger surgeons "for the good of my countrimen and countrey wherein I was borne and bred." In keeping with this purpose, he

271

wrote in English rather than in Latin, and, despite the precedents established by Paré, Franco, Pfolzpeundt, and Brunschwig, felt impelled to explain and justify his reasons for doing so.

Like his German contemporaries, Clowes was a *wound surgeon,* and he makes no mention of elective operative surgery. His *Observations* consist of a series of case reports, dealing chiefly with gunshot wounds or burning with gunpowder. Contrary to widely held early opinion, he did not believe gunshot wounds to be poisoned, although in the case reported below he became convinced that it was possible for a bullet to be intentionally smeared with poison before firing. He also describes the experiments he conducted by which he learned that the bullet was not sufficiently exposed to heat, as it was being discharged, to neutralize the poison applied. His account of this investigation is quoted below. This early application of scientific investigation of a clinical problem is of great interest and merits special attention.

Clowes' place in history is not dependent on important contributions to surgical knowledge. Like other wound surgeons of his day, his armamentarium of drugs, ointments, and plasters was voluminous, and great store was placed in the efficacy of these remedial agents (Fig. 61).[1] He was cautious, conservative, and conscientious, yet displayed an open mind and the courage to make independent observations and to profit from them. His references to other authors reveal a wide acquaintance with the writings of his contemporaries in other lands, and of the ancients. Thus, he represents an example of the best type of practical wound surgeon of his time.

꒜ ꒜ ꒜   THE CURE OF A LIEUTENANT WHO WAS SHOT IN THE RIGHT
꒜ ꒜ ꒜   BUTTOCK WITH A POISONED BULLET. CAP. 13.[2]

Friendly Reader, amongst sundry other special cures which I have noted, not onely in mine own works and proceedings, but also in other mens of greater yeeres, antiquitie, and experience in the art of Chirurgery, this one cure following in my simple opinion and judgement, is not to be passed slightly over and buried in forgetfulnes, if it were but in respect of the strangenesse and rarenes of such a cure, and of the good and happy successe that followed.

To proceede to my purpose, the said Lieutenant was a man

---

1. On the basis of his own wide experiences, he devised a surgical chest for the use of military and naval surgeons with a carefully compiled list of the drugs and supplies it should contain.
2. *A Profitable and Necessarie Booke of Observations, for all those that are burned with the flame of Gun powder. . . .* by William Clowes, London, Edw. Bollifant for Thomas Dawson, 1596. (With Introduction general and medical by DeWitt T. Starnes and Chauncey D. Leake, New York, Scholar's Facsimilies and Reprints, 1945), pp. 44–51.

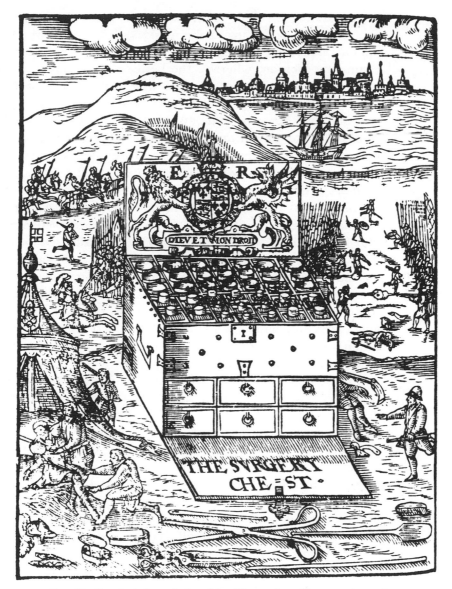

FIG. 61. Surgical chest designed by Clowes for military and naval use.

about the age of five and thirty yeeres, having a strong and
able body answerable to his valor and corage, which appeered
in his service against the enimie: he received a wound in his
right buttocke by a bullet, being then (as he said) somewhat
far off from the enimies fort when he was shot and wounded,
which bullet was so secretly lodged, that by no convenient
meanes possible at the first dressing, I could get knowledge or

understanding certainly where the shot would lie, by reason
of the turning or folding of the muskles, and sensibilitie of the
patients body, yet I would then very faine have enlarged the
wound by incision, whereby the better to have come to the
bullet, but the patient would in no wise suffer to have it done:
then I perceived he was partly over wearied by the probaba-
tion and searching, for that cause I thought it vaine to molest
or disquiet the patient any longer at that time, but so let him
rest, sith it was his mind and desire till the next day, supposing no evil accidents would have hapned, at the leastwise in
so short a time and space: and my reason that led me thus
to thinke, was for that I did read how Lead has a certaine
singularitie agreeing to nature, for which I preserved him at
that instant time, with the oile of Whelpes, called *Oleum cotu-
lorum*, with defensatives and comfortable oiles and plaisters fit
for that purpose, as I have used to many others which were
wounded with gunshot, especially in such fleshie places, where
the oile is best to be used, and have alwaies had therewith
good luck and happie successe, howbeit (contrary to expectation) within six houres after he was dressed, he did begin
to have a troubled minde, full of sorowes and disquietnes:
and complained much of his wound, how it did greatly molest
him, and that with a strong kinde of pricking and biting, as
if his wound had been laid in a bed of pricking or sharpe
stinging nettles, and for that cause he would very willingly
have been opened and new dressed againe: then I considered
it was but two of the clock in the afternoone when I preserved
him first, therefore I told him, I hoped that his paines would
cease without further trouble extraordinary, by reason of the
benefit of those remedies which I had applied to him, and so
I perswaded him to be quiet till the next day in the morning,
nevertheles in the night season he was extremely handled and
very sore vexed with a sharp and perilous feaver, and shiver-
ings without intermission or ceasing, his pulse great, swift
and fast, so that oftentimes he fell into soundings, by reason
of the anguish and paine, and did speake very idlely, coveting
to lie groveling on his face, with other perilous signes and
accidents.

The morning approaching, when the watch was discharged,
and the ports opened, there was sent in haste a messenger,
that imparted unto me as you have heard, what a lamentable
and miserable case he was in that night, as though the whole

member had been torne with dogs, the which to heare did not a little trouble me, for I considered with myself that the captaines and other brave servitors. . . who had been my patients, reposed a great trust and confidence in me, for which cause I did thinke it stood me upon to be circumspect and wary, least I might get but little credit thereby. And because I would be loth to be overtaken with unskilfull rashnes. I desired the messenger to returne backe againe with speede, and to intreat the patients friends that they would call some Physition or skilfull Surgeon, whom they thought good of, to be at his dressing, for I told him I suspected a *Grangraena*, and that was the cause of my long tarrying, till I had prepared all things in readines for that purpose: in which time and space, they had brought unto the patient a stranger, borne (as they said) in the east Countries, and being as it seemed of their acquaintance, which had many yeeres practised Physicke and Surgerie, sometimes in the enimies camp, and somtimes with the States, a man doubtles learned, and also of no lesse judgement and practise in the Art of Surgery: he was given to understand before I did come to the patient, how he was shot, and what evill accidents had hapned since his first dressing: in which time (as I have said) I did ordaine such remedies which I supposed to be the best and most meetest for the cure of a *Grangraena*. But after speeches had with him, he desired me before I did prepare any of my remedies for the dressing of the patient, that without staying I would take off all things from the wound, the which presently I did: and so all being laid open, the wound was found marvellously altered and changed, for it did looke in colour much like unto ashes, or rather more wanner like unto Lead, and the whole member very unweldy and heavy, which were to me very strange, and extraordinary signes, such as I never did see happen in other common wounds made with gun shot: then he conferred with me and others that were present, and said by all signes and tokens, the bullet is poisoned by some venemous mixture, and assure yourselfe that the danger is greater, and neerer at hand than you are aware of, and therefore, said he, if you should follow that course you have begun, and neglect the time, and so pretermit such knowne helpes, which I shall acquaint you withall, or the like in effect, the patient will hardly escape, for truly (said he) that which you have done, sith they are no apt remedies for extraction and drawing out venom and poison,

it is all ministred and done in vaine: then I remembred that
to use unapt and contrary remedies, was dangerous, specially
in such causes, and therefore without delay in due time, I
determined with myselfe to follow his counsell and direction,
and to deale plainly.

I suspecting mine owne knowledge in the cure of a poisoned wound made with gun shot, I thought it not best to
attribute unto my skill herein greater sufficiencie than was in
me to performe: and sith it stood upon the patients life, I did
with all curtesie of speech and great thankfulnes towards him,
so deale herein, that thereby I might become the more learned
and expert in the cure of a poisoned wound made with gun
shot, and so craved his further counsell in this cure: in which
doing I did not think it any discredit or disgrace unto me,
seeing Guido [Guy de Chauliac] a man of great knowledge and
understanding in Physicke and Chirurgery, as experience daily
doth teach us, "faith, it is not possible for one man to have all
knowledge in himselfe, for one may know that, which another
knoweth not": To proceede, I must confesse he was as willing
to show me anything he could pleasure me in, as I was desirous to crave it at his hands: . . . who without further detracting of time, counselled me to make deepe incision, and
then with a paire of Tenacles, crowes bills, and ravens bills,
to take hold of the bullet, and to bring it out so easily as may
be, then to scarifie well the lips or sides of the wound, which
done, yee shall presently set on a strong cupping glass on a
flame of fire, that yee may the better evacuate and draw out
the venomous and poisoned blood, which lurketh deepely in
the bottome of the wound, whereby his paines may be the
sooner asswaged. So understanding herein all his whole meaning, neverthelesse I did not take everie word he spake for a
gospell, till I had seene farther triall, but followed him as far
as reason and experience did lead me: and I told him, though
I had never seene a poisoned wound made with gun shot, and
so had not cured any, yet I did read in the writings of famous
men of our time, that hardly or not at all, can a bullet of Lead
receive any venomous or poisoned mixture, but that the flame
of the fire out of that piece doth extinguish and kill the force
and strength of any poisoned shot:. . . .

[EXPERIMENTAL INVESTIGATION]

Onely friendly Reader I must crave pardon for a little digression, but I will be short and so come againe to my pur-

posed matter. As I have said, I will not heere meddle with
the state and condition of this controversie as a controller of
learned men, lest I should greatly wrong them and unawares
defraud you of the truth: But this I must tell you, in seeking
after the experience and proofe of this matter according to
that gift which by Gods goodnes I attained unto, I have herein
confirmed my selfe: for not long since I being sent for to Portsmouth unto the right honorable the Earle of Suffer, about
the cure of master Muns, Lieutenant of the towne, who by
misfortune received a great wound in his head. In the time of
my abode there, I desired the master gunner of the towne,
that he would show me the favour, as to let me see an arrow
shot out of a Musquet: for I thought I could no way so wel
come to the true knowledge of my desire, but by such martiall
men, as were expert and well practised in such fiery engins so
very courteously he granted my request, and I asked his opinion, if it were possible by his art and skill to poison a bullet of
Lead: He answered that he did know that a bullet of Lead
might be poisoned, and moreover he said it is against the law
of arms to shoot a poisoned shot: againe, it is present death if
shot be taken or found about any enimy. And I have since
heard it confirmed by divers Captaines and old soldiers, who
also have said unto me, that they did know them that were
executed for the same. Now I come to the charging of his
peece which I did see himselfe do, and he delivered it to one
of the soldiers of the towne, who presently did take his rest,
and discharged the said peece against a gate, being distant
from the place where he stood, about two hundred or eight
score paces, and the arrow did stick very deepe in the post of
the gate, where by force it was taken out, but we found not so
much as one feather of the arrow touched with flame or fire
out of the peece. And although so manifest a truth needeth no
witnes, yet because there was at that present time in the towne
with the Earle of Suffer a learned Physition called M. Trip of
Winchester, which can witnes with me that speak the truth
heerin, who saw the arrow that was shot out of the peece, and
I have seene the like done in a Caliver with our common sheafe
arrowes. All this (me thinke) as I have said prooveth that
much lesse doth the fires burne out the impression of a poisoned bullet if it be not able to burn the feathers of the arrow:
for being charged, as I have seen it, to my judgement the
arrow is gone out of the peece afore the flame of fire doth

appeere in sight, or the report of the peece can be heard: And
if it were so that the flame of fire should burne the feathers, I
see no reason why the arrow should be feathered at all: but
I suppose every man cannot shoot off an arrow and save the
feathers, yet I am perswaded, he that hath learned to poison
a shot, hath also learned so to shoot it off, that it shall worke
the mischiefe he purposeth.

And now for that I woulde be loth to make a long and
tedious discourse of that, wherein I have had so small experience: I will therefore proceed unto the order of the cure, that
was this: I did presently as I was directed, make reasonable
large and deep incision, which don, I did take out the bullet
that lay somwhat deep, but by the way, it was (we thought)
strange to see the bullet flat and ragged on the one side, as if
it had been battered against a rough wall, and very round on
the other side: and also manifestly seene certaine stabs in
many places, as if it had been the pricking of a dagger, neither
carried it the color of other bullets: for it seemed as though
the powder of rustie iron, greene Copperas, or some glassie
color had been sprinckled or stained in the Lead. Then it was
put into the fire, and being melted, these colors vanished away,
but what manner of poison it should be, I could not learn.

After the bullet was taken out, and the edges of the wound
scarified, I did set on a large cupping glasse, such as compre-
hended all the wound, and did mightily draw a good quantity
of blood; then I would willingly have used a bright cauterizing iron, because it was in a place it might be safely done
without danger to the patient, for that the fire, is to tame
the malice and fury of venome and poison, all this he con-
fessed may well be used, and it is allowed of many excellent
men: But (said he) I have found out by diligence a more safe
and familiar remedie, which doth also make an eschar, but
not like an actuall cauterie with so much paine, and moreover
it doth stay the venome from creeping upwards, neither will
it suffer the poisoned vapors to spread abroad, or enter into
the noble or unnoble parts, as to the hart by the arteries, or
into the liver by the vaines, or into the braine by the sinews,
and so consequently into all the rest of the parts and members of
the bodie: then still heedily I followed his direction, and thought
myselfe happy of such a conductor or leader, so I applied this his
foresaid remedy, which truly wrought marvellous strangely

and to great effect, and I filled the wound with pledgets dipped into the same very hot: and this is the composition and receit thereof now following, [He then describes the various mixtures, plasters and dressings which were continued until the wound was healed]

And thus friendly Reader yee shall understand, I write not this observation in mine own praise, but chiefly (as may appear) for the good of my countrimen and the countrey wherein I was borne and bred, so that they which will be carefull and diligent in spending their time in labor and studie, not onely in reading good authors, but also to endevor themselves (as I have before said) to be conversant with learned Physitions, and well experienced Surgeons, for the better attaining unto learning and knowledge, may in the end enjoy the fruits of their labors and diligence: for idleness yeeldeth as much profit, as a barren and dry tree good fruit. . . .

CHAPTER 29

Peter Lowe
(1550–1612)

" . . . *that intemperancy and gluttony feebleth the body, dulleth the minde, and bringeth soon old age, whereof proceedeth this saying,*
> *Many more persons by gluttony are slain,*
> *Then is by warr, famine, or other pain.*"[1]

Glasgow, Scotland, holds a unique place in medical history. In this city alone, in all of Great Britain, there never existed a separation of medicine and surgery. The earliest organization of doctors, the Faculty of Physicians and Surgeons, was chartered in 1599, and to this day it is the joint organization of the entire healing profession. The creation of this Faculty was the achievement of one man, the Scottish surgeon, Peter Lowe.

Little is known of the early life of Lowe, but it is inferred that he left his native Scotland about the time of the Reformation in that country, some time after the middle of the sixteenth century. From the titles attached to his name in his writings, it is probable that he studied medicine in Orleans, in France, and that he became a surgeon of the Collège de St. Côme of Paris. He states, "But I impart to you my labours, hidden secrets, and experiments by me practised, and daily put in use, to the great comfort, ease, and delight of you, and such as have had occasion to use my help in France, Flaunders, and elsehwere, the space of 22 yeers: thereafter being Chyrurgion-Major to the Spanish Regiments at Paris 2 yeers: next following the French King my Master in the Warrs 6 yeers, where I took commoditie to practise all points and operations of Chyrurgery." Thus, he practiced on the Continent, with distinction, for thirty years and then, in 1598, returned to Scotland.

The state of medicine in Glasgow and the West of Scotland was chaotic. There were no schools for the training of doctors, nor were there any provisions for the supervision or licensing of medical practitioners. Healers of

---

1. *A Discourse of the Whole Art of Chyrurgery* by Peter Lowe, London, R. Hodgkinsonne, 1654, p. 47.

Photogravure by T. & R. Annan & Sons, from a Painting in the possession of the Faculty of Physicians & Surgeons, Glasgow.

DOCTOR PETER LOWE.

Fig. 62

varying degrees of incompetence, ignorance, and charlatanry abounded. The lack of adequate medical personnel became glaringly obvious by the outbreak of a most devastating epidemic of plague in the last years of the sixteenth century, which was followed soon after by an equally alarming spread of syphilis. Such was the state of affairs when Lowe reached the city.

After his long tour of duty abroad, Peter Lowe settled first in London in 1596, and in that year his book on the "Spanish Sickness," one of the many euphemisms for syphilis, appeared. The following year his *Chirurgerie* was

published, and in 1598 he arrived in Glasgow where he was engaged by the
city as a salaried surgeon.

Shortly after taking office, Lowe brought pressure to bear on the civil
and church authorities, and a board was set up to examine the qualifications
of those who professed to be healers. In the same year, he brought the matter
before King James VI of Scotland, who issued a charter authorizing Peter
Lowe, "our Chirurgiane and Chief Chirurgiane to our dearest son the
Prince, with the assistance of Mr. Robert Hamiltone, Profesoure of medicine"
and their successors to examine and license all practitioners of medicine and
surgery in Glasgow and the surrounding countryside embracing the entire
western portion of Scotland. This corporation later took the name of the
Faculty of Physicians and Surgeons of Glasgow.

The *Chirurgerie* of Peter Lowe is his most important book and is the earliest
systematic work on the whole subject of surgery to be published in England.
It is written in English, and in part is in the form of a dialogue in which the
teacher, Peter Lowe, interrogates his son, John, largely on the precepts of
the Ancients. Other parts are written in narrative form, and contain references to his own observations and experiences. The treatise went through
four editions, thus attesting a considerable vogue.

Because of his superior attainments, Peter Lowe held a high place in the
medicine and surgery of the Glasgow of his time. Confident in the "nobility
of surgery" as a profession, he labored to elevate its position, to purge it of
the unworthy who professed to practice it, and to give the earnest and dedicated students of the craft the benefits of his studies and experiences. Because of his personal reputation and esteem he could influence the king,
himself, in bringing about greatly needed reforms and erecting the founda-
tions of an important medical center of the future.

ᔐ ᔐ ᔐ   OF THE TUMOR CALLED *ANEURISMA*.[2]

ᔐ ᔐ ᔐ   *Aneurisma* is a tumor soft to touch, the which is engendered
                 of blood and spirit under the skin and muscles, which hap-
                 peneth in divers parts of the body, chiefly in the sides of the
                 crag. The Cause is either dilatation, incision, or ruption of
                 the artery, which often chaunceth to Women in the time of
                 their birth, to Trumpetters, Criers, Waterman, and others,
                 who use violent labour, and great crying, or other violence, by
                 the which some of the artery doth dilate. The Signes, are tumor,
                 impressing on with the finger, great pulsation. The tumor is
                 of the same colour, as the rest of the skinn, soft to touch, yield-

2. *Ibid.*, pp. 216–218.

ing to the finger, by reason the blood and spirit retyreth unto the arteries and parts adjacent, and having removed the finger, it presently returneth with a noise or bruite, by reason of the blood and spirit that returneth.

This happeneth when the *Aneurisme* is done by anastomies, that is, the artery be opened and cut: When the artery is riven, as happeneth to women, and those of greater exercise, there issueth forth more aboundance of blood then spirit, and is more hard than the other, and maketh lesse noise in the retyring.

Those which are superficiall in the exterior parts, as the head, legs, and armes, may be knit, and are curable: those which are profound and interior, in the breast, as often happeneth to those who sweat excessively of the venerian sicknesse, and otherwise: also those in the neck under the armes and roots of the thighes, and when there is great dilatation of the arteries, are not curable, but death ensueth within few dayes, or at the least are very perilous, as saith Paulus: and if the tumor be opened, the patient dyeth presently.

This happeneth oftentimes by the unskilfulnes of ignorant Barbors and other abusers, who meddle with this art, who ruyne a number of People through their ignorance, as I have often seen: such ignorants doe esteem all tumors that are soft, should be opened as common Apostumes.

I remember in Paris in Anno 1590, there happened such a disease to a valiant Captain (my great friend Captain Jayle, who was one of the chiefest Captaines amongst the Spaniards at Paris) on the right side of his cragg, for the which, I a Chyrurgion Major to the regiment, was sent for, and found it to be an *Aneurisme*, so not to be touched; of the which opinion was my good friend Andrew Scot, who was a great Practitioner at Paris for the time and well exercised in the art of Chyrurgery, we did ordain remedies to let the increase of it, which receipt being sent to the Apothecary, who before had seen the sayd Captain, did think it no meet medicine for an Apostume (as he termed it:) so presently he sent for an ignorant Barbor like unto himself, who did swear unto the Captain that they had sawes and charmes for all sores, so without further tryall did open it with a Launcet to avoyd the matter (as they thought) which being done, the spirit and blood came forth with such violence, that the Captain dyed in few hours after. I doubt not but in these Countries divers such errors are committed by ignorants. I doe use alwayes in such, chiefly in the neck, under the armes, and in the papps, those remedies which I have prescribed to the Spaniard. . . . These things doe let the growing for a time, although it be neer the noble parts. If it happen in the extremities of the legs or armes, they may live a long time by the usage of the foresaid remedies. I knew a woman in Paris, who had a very great one in her thigh, and did live ten years. If it be little and superficial, I finde nothing better than Cataplasmes made of Claret wine, with cropps and leaves of Cyprus. When the artery had been opened in the place of the vain, as sometime happeneth, I doe knit it after this form: first makes incision in the skin long-wayes, then discovers the artery, then passeth a Curbit needle with a double thread under the sayd artery, two inches above the incision or ruption thereat, then knits it with a double knot, voyds away the blood contained, so cures the wound.

[APPEAL TO SURGEONS TO USE THEIR INFLUENCE IN ESTAB-LISHING LICENSING AND CONTROL OF THE PRACTITIONERS OF THE ART.[3]]

. . . yet I hope all honest men, especially you, who are towards his Majestie, will be earnest in purchasing of priviledges and lawes, for restraining of all ignorant abusers in this Kingdome, like as is granted to Men of our Art, in other civill Countries to the great ayd and comfort of all Kings of those parts. It pleased his Sacred Majestie to hear my complaint about some fourteen yeers agoe, upon certain abusers of our Art, of divers sorts and ranks of people, whereof wee have good store, and all things failing, unthrifts, and idle people doe commonly meddle themselves with our Art, who ordinarily doe passe without either tryall or punishment. The matter being con-sidered, and the abuse weighed by his Majestie and Honoura-ble Councell, thought not to be tolerated, for the which I got a priviledge under his Highnesse privie seal, to try and exam-ine all Men upon the Art of Chyrurgerie, to discharge, and allow in the West parts of Scotland, who were worthy, or un-worthy, to professe the same. The which I observed as I might, although there be Men of greater authoritie and sufficiency to punish, and correct such if they would. But such is the iniq-uitie of time, that abusers are commonly over-seen by such as ought to punish them: in such sort that one blinde guides

3. *Ibid.*, "Dedication," pp. A$_2$–A$_3$.

another, and most commonly fall both into the ditch. In the
mean time these cheaters are permitted to use charms, lies,
excreable oaths, mortiferous poyson, fallacious and uncertain
experiments, whereby they destroy both friend and foe, ever
detracting the true professors of the Art. Now worshipfull
Brethren, in respect of those enormities with divers moe [more],
which were long to repeat, I doubt not but all yee who are
learned and true professors, having accesse, and credit with
his Majestie, will seek and obtain such priviledges, and lawes,
as well to correct and punish abusers, as also to withstand the
frivolous or fantasticall opinions of such as use them, and
neither for request nor lucre, to admit any such ignorant
abusers to professe our Art, ...

[Lowe was interested in the problems of the aged. He inter-
prets the biblical allegory of *Ecclesiastes 12* as a description of
senility and paraphrases it with anatomical and physiological
ideas as he understood them.]

THE ALLEGORY OF OLD AGE[4]

This last age is set down in *Eccle. 12*. Be thou wise Salomon.
With such a brave Allegorie, that nothing in the world can
be found so excellent, for the which I shall set it down at
large in this place.

Have minde (saith hee) of thy Creator in the dayes
of thy Youth, or in the dayes of adversity: Come,
while the Sunne is not darkened; nor the Moon; nor
the Starres; nor the Clouds returne after the raine:
When the keepers of the house shall tremble, and the
strong men shall bow themselves; and the Grinders
shall cease, because they bee few in number; and they
shall waxe darke which look out by the windowes;
and the dores shall bee shut without, because of the
base sound of the grinding. And all the daughters of
Singing shall bee abashed, also they shall be affraid of
the high things: And fear shall bee in the way: And the
Almond Tree shall flourish: And the Grashopper shall
bee a burthen: and concupiscence shall bee driven
away: while the Silver cord is not lengthened, nor the
Golden Ewer broken; nor the Pitcher broken at the

4. *Ibid.*, pp. 30–32.

Well: nor the Wheele broken at the Cesterne, and
Dust returne to the Earth as it was, and the Spirit to
God that gave it.

This is the true description of the last age, which is admirable, and required a good Anatomist to expound the same;
the Allegory followeth. Have mind (saith he) of thy Creator
in the dayes of thy Youth, while the Sunn is not darkened:
that is to say, while the eyes have not lost their sight nor the
Clouds return after the raine, which is, when the eyes hath
long wept, there passeth before them grosse thick Vapours
like Clouds. When the Keepers of the house shall tremble:
which is when the Armes and Hands which are given for the
defence of man, are failed. And the strong men shall bow
themselves: which is, the leggs whereupon the whole body
stands, doth bow and becommeth weak. The Grinders shall
cease: that is, the Teeth which breaketh and grindeth the
meat, shall be decayed. And they shall wax dark which look
out by the Windowes: that is, when the Eyes are overwhelmed
with some cataract or taye which covereth the prunall, called
the window of the Eye. The Door shall bee shut without, by
the base sound of the grinding: that is, the Chapps and Lips
which cannot well open, and the Chanells whereby the meat
doth passe, groweth narrow. And he shall rise at the voice of
the Bird, that is, old people cannot sleep, but doe rise at the
crow or calling of the Cock. And all the daughters of Singing
shall bee abased: which is, when the voice doth decay. The
Almond Tree shall flourish: that is, the head and Beard of all
people becommeth all white. The Grashopper shall be a
burthen: which is, when the legges groweth great, swelling,
and tumified with aboundance of cold watery humors. Concupiscence shall be driven away: which is to say, old people
shall have little or no appetite to meat. When the Silver cord
is lengthened: that is, when the marrow that goeth along the
back groweth supple, and boweth the back forward. When the
Golden Ewer is broken: that is, the heart which containeth
the arteriall blood and vitall spirits shall be weakened. The
Pitcher broken at the fountain: that is, the great vaine Cave,
that may no more shoot blood from the liver, which is, the
Spring that humecteth the whole body in such sort, that it
serveth no more than a broken vessell. The wheel broken at
the Cestern, that is, the Nerves and bladder doth grow so
weak, that they can no more retaine the water. When all these

things do arrive, the dust returneth to the earth as it was, which is, when the materiall body returneth to the earth: and the Spirit shall turn to God that gave it. These be the best descriptions that can be given of old age, with their times and yeers, according to the opinion of our ancients.

CHAPTER 30

Richard Wiseman
(1621?–1676)

"Thou wilt also learn one necessary piece of Humility, viz. not to trust too much on thy own Judgment, especially in difficult cases; but to think fit to seek the Advice of other Physicians or Chirurgeons. . . ."[1]

The middle years of the seventeenth century found England torn by civil war. Both sides, of course, had their medical adherents. Richard Wiseman was devoted to the Royalist cause. He shared the tribulations and the eventual triumph of the monarchy, and was rewarded by being appointed Sergeant-Surgeon to King Charles II. His was an eventful life, much of it spent in naval and military service with foreign nations as well as his own. He accompanied the Prince of Wales into exile on the Continent, was twice a prisoner, and narrowly escaped execution for participation in a Royalist plot during the Republic. Despite these activities, he became the leading British surgeon of his time, greatly enriched the surgical literature with books based largely on his own wide experiences, and exerted effective influence in elevating the status of his profession.

Richard Wiseman was born between 1621 and 1623, about the time the Pilgrims were struggling to establish their colony in the New World. Nothing is known of his early education, but his facile use of words and many quotations in Latin bespeak good schooling for the time in which he lived. He was bound as an apprentice surgeon at about the age of fifteen, and shortly afterward joined the Dutch Navy. It is assumed that he served his apprenticeship at sea under the flag of Holland, and he remained in this service for a total of almost twenty years. He wrote many years later that his experience in surgery had been gained by practice on board ship no less than on shore. Conditions on board fighting ships of that period were primitive, indeed, for the handling of the severely wounded and Wiseman's treatises contain many references to such circumstances.

1. Richard Wiseman: *Eight Surgical Treatises*, London, 1734, 2 Vols., sixth edition, "The Epistle to the Readers" (May 24, 1676), Vol. I, p. vi.

Richard Wiseman, A.D. 1660.
from a miniature in the possession of
His Grace the Duke of Rutland.

Fig. 63

Wiseman's service as surgeon in the Dutch Navy continued until after the outbreak of England's Civil War, at which time he returned to his homeland and joined the Royalist forces; here he was assigned to the troops in the West of England which were under the command of the Prince of Wales. The campaign was one of successive defeats and withdrawals, and eventual flight, first to the Scilly Islands, thence to Jersey, and finally to France. Throughout these misfortunes the prince was accompanied by the faithful Wiseman who not only became his personal surgeon, but a confidential friend as well. After the execution of King Charles I, in 1649, the prince, now Charles II, made his way to Scotland, with Wiseman still in attendance. At the battle of Worcester, Wiseman was taken prisoner and marched to Chester where he was held for two years. "At last," he wrote, "having procured a Passe to come to London, I hastened away."

He arrived in the capital, then the seat of the Cromwell government, early in 1652 at the age of thirty, and took up his "freedom of the Barber-Surgeons' Company." This gave him the right to practice, which he exercised initially by accepting an assistantship with an established surgeon. Soon afterward, however, he engaged in practice by himself and rapidly established an excellent following. But his was a perilous state. Immediately after reaching London he was arrested as were other Royalist prisoners and released on bail, which made him liable to peremptory apprehension at any time and to imprisonment without further trial. The danger was real. Royalist supporters were under constant suspicion, and on the slightest pretexts were tried before a military tribunal and summarily executed. Under these circumstances it would have been expected that Wiseman would conduct himself with the utmost discretion. Yet, he was soon arrested again for complicity in a Royalist plot—the degree of his participation remains obscure—and he was again thrown into prison.

How long he was kept there, and by what means his release was effected, is not known. But conditions in London must have been uncongenial to him, for again he left England and took service with a foreign fleet, this time in the navy of Spain. His return to London after an absence of three years coincided with the restoration of the monarchy and the entry of Charles II as King of England in 1660. From this point on, Wiseman's fortunes took a more favorable turn. He was appointed Surgeon to the King, and subsequently promoted to Principal Surgeon and Sergeant-Surgeon.

As his material welfare improved, however, his health began to fail. From the time of his return to England after serving in the Spanish Navy, he apparently suffered from tuberculosis and experienced periodic pulmonary hemorrhages. His professional activities had to be curtailed but, taking advantage of the enforced leisure, he turned to writing. "I have made a virtue of necessity," he wrote, "and have employed those hours for the public service which a frequently repeated sickness hath for this last twenty years past denied me the use of in my private occasions. It hath pleased God, by casting me into such a condition, to give me opportunity of reading and thinking, as well as practising; both of which are necessary to the accomplishment not only of an author, but indeed of a chirurgeon. I cannot be so uncharitable to my brethren as to wish them the like sickness, to oblige them to the like retirements for comtemplation and study."[2]

The *Chirurgical Treatises* which grew out of these efforts are a fitting monument to a great surgeon. They constitute a record of wide surgical experience afloat and ashore, in military and civilian practice. "I do pretend to have spent my time in armies, navies, and cities, not in universities; nor to have been much conversant in books, through my constant employment in,

2. *Ibid.*, p. ii.

and the little leisure I had from my profession." In the *Treatises* he cites no less than 600 cases from his personal experience, admitting his failures as well as his successes. He wrote, "For my part, I have thought it no disgrace to let the world see where I failed of success, that those that come after me may learn what to avoid: there being more instructiveness often in an unfortunate case than in a fortunate one; and more ingenuity in confessing such misfortunes which are incident to mankind, and which have attended all my Brethren as well as my self, and will attend thee, also, Reader, if thou undertake the employment."[3]

The *Chirurgical Treatises* of Wiseman represent a distinct advance in maturity, both as to content and style of presentation, when compared to the works of Clowes and those who preceded him. The book is inclusive, logically arranged, and definitely modern in sentence structure and spelling. The progress in surgical knowledge during the elapsed seventy-five to 100 years is also notable. As might be expected from his long years of military experience, Wiseman is at his best in the sections devoted to injuries, and his treatment is daring, imaginative, and logical. He strove to preserve limbs if they offered reasonable hope of salvage. On the other hand, he emphasized that the decision as to amputation should be made promptly, because, in the excitement from the heat of battle, the patients were less sensitive to the pain of operation. In abdominal wounds he would have elected to operate in the hope of saving some of these desperate cases, had he not been deterred by the prevailing feeling against such radical procedure, and the censure that violation of these beliefs would invite.

The book on *The King's Evil* is particularly intriguing. Here he correctly includes tuberculous infections of the various structures—other than the lungs—and introduces the term "spina ventosa," a word still applied to tuberculous bony swellings. A dedicated Royalist, he pays extravagant tribute to the efficacy of the "Royal touch," adding, ". . . yet I must needs profess that what I write, will do little more than show the weakness of our [the surgeons'] ability, when compared with his Majesty's, who cureth more in any one year, than all the Chirurgeons of *London* have done in any age." Curiously, however, he goes on to say, "Withal, as feeble as our Art is, this Treatise will shew you that it is not altogether ineffectua ; and though the difficulty of cure will sufficiently appear, yet the possibility will also be made out in many remarkable instances."[4] And in the long discussion that follows, there is no single mention of a case referred by him for the king to "touch" despite his closeness to His Majesty. Instead, he gives detailed treatment by regimen, medicaments, and, in well-selected instances, by surgical extirpation. Because of the unique-

3. *Ibid.*, p. vi.
4. Wiseman, *op. cit.*, "A Treatise of the King's Evil," Chapter I, pp. 396–397.

ness of the treatise on the King's Evil, the excerpts of Wiseman's writings selected for quotation in this book concern themselves solely with this subject.

The esteem in which Wiseman was held, the outstanding physicians who used him in consultation, his insistence on better education for surgeons, and his own personal example of probity and diligence served to enhance the dignity and standing of the profession. He paved the way for the illustrious men who came after him.

ɕ   ɕ   ɕ   A TREATISE OF THE KING'S-EVIL
ɕ   ɕ   ɕ
                    Chap. II.

OF THE DEFINITION OF THE DISEASE, AND ITS CAUSES. Those who are born of Strumous Parents are usually subject to these Diseases, and derive it from them; so they will from a Nurse so diseased whose Milk they suck'd.[5]

Chap. III.

THE HISTORY OF THE DISEASE, WITH THE DIAGNOSTICKS AND PROGNOSTICKS. The *King's-Evil* is already described in short, but that will not serve the uses of a young Practitioner, unless he may have the History of it more fully delivered; which cannot be well done, unless we give an account of the Parts themselves which are concern'd in it. Now the Parts usually affected are either Glandules, Muscles, *Viscera*, Membranes, Tendons or Bones. I do not remember ever to have seen the Nerves or Brain affected immediately with any Humour of this kind: Or if they have, the Juices of those Parts are rather dissolved, and the Fibres corroded by this Acidity after the likeness of Marrow and Bones, than coagulated into a Tumour; which Corrosion when it happens, the Disease gets another name, and being indeed mortal, needs not be insisted upon in this Treatise, it admitting of no other Doctrine but that of a Prognostick.[6]

Bones are as frequently affected as any part of the Body, Glandules only excepted; but there the manner of the Tumour differs: for though the Bone swell, and the outward shell thereof appear hard, yet the inward Juices are all putrid and rotten. This sort of Tumour is sometimes called *Spina ventosa*, how properly let others judge; but it is certain that not only the Bones of the Fingers, carpus, metacarpus, tarsus, metatarsus,

5. *Ibid.*, p. 399.
6. *Ibid.*, p. 401.

and Toes, are liable to this Evil, but also the Skull itself and the Jaw-bones, and all the other Bones of the Body; the venomous nature of which will be seen by those who upon opening some of these Tumours have found the Bone when laid bare at the first appearance sound, but when pierced into, to be in the Heart wholly rotten.[7]

When it affects a conglobate Glandule, the Tumour is usually round, moderately hard, and moveable without Pain. Those of an oval Figure, which are hard, and accompanied with Pain without Inflammation, are of an ill quality; and if they grow unequal, they threaten a *Cancer*. When a Conglomerate is the Seat of it, it usually observes the shape of that Glandule, especially if the whole Gland be diseased: But it is not unfrequent to see those Glandules (which are indeed but Compositions of lesser Glandules clustered up together like a Bunch of Grapes) particularly affected; so that some of those lesser *Glandulae*, or Kernels, shall swell into oval, round or flat, or other Figures, leaving the remainder sound enough; as indeed having no other Communication with them, but only by that small pedunculus which tieth them to, and dischargeth them by, the common great duct of the Glandule.[8]

Chap. IV.

OF THE METHOD OF CURE. In the Cure of the *King's-Evil* you must consider the Habit of Body, Strength and Age of the Patient, the Affection of the *Viscera*, and particularly whether the *Struma* be simple or complicated.

If all Things appear benign, according to the Diagnostick or Prognostick before delivered, you may hope well; if otherwise, then you are to defend your self with a Prediction, and work warily.

In order to the Cure, three Intentions are required. The First consists in the regiment of Diet and the other Non-naturals; the Second, in Pharmacy or internal Prescriptions; the Third, in the application of Externals, either to discuss, suppurate or extirpate the Glands.[9]

The common way of taking out all the *Species* of *Strumae*, *Atheromata & Meliceris*, by Incision, is in cutting the Skin the

7. *Ibid.*, p. 404.
8. *Ibid.*, p. 406.
9. *Ibid.*, p. 408.

length of the Tumour: in these latter you must make the Incision more warily, lest you divide the *Cystis*, and the matter
flow forth. After you have separated them around to the *Basis*,
it may be sometimes necessary to make a Ligature upon the
Vessels before you cut them off. Those which are of a great
bulk, generally called *Wens*, are sometimes taken out by making
a cross Incision, other-while by an oval, one taking off so much
of the Skin as may be judged superfluous; then separate it,
proceed calmly in the Work, for in these the Skin commonly
adheres so close to the *Cystis*, that it will not part from it without the help of your Knife: having separated it, turn it out, and
make a Ligature underneath upon the Vessels, and cut it off;
then bring the Lips of the Wound together with two or three
stitches, and dress it up as you see cause. Some Empiricks cut
them off without more ado, scarce making a Ligature on them;
but this way being always attended with a flux of Blood, others
chuse rather to pass a Seton-needle with a strong Ligature close
under the *Basis*, or as near it as may be, and that way make a
Ligature strictly about it. Sometimes we make the like Ligature
without Incision, and are content to eat off the Tumour by
streightening it. Thus it falls off without effusion of Blood; but
hereby there is a hazard in mortifying the sound parts underneath, or of causing such Disturbance as prolongeth the Cure:
upon which consideration, I do propose in great *Steatoma's* and
complicated Tumours, which are inclosed in *Cystis's* rather to
cut into the *Cystis*, and with your hands to pull out that preter-
natural Body, and leave the *Cystis* behind. So shall you be
secured from a flux of Blood; and for the *Cystis*, you need not
doubt but by Digestion it will separate and cast off; the Wound
will also heal smooth by Agglutination afterward, if you cut off
the superflous Skin, and bring the remaining Lips together, as
in such Operations is usual. An Instance of this I shall give you,
amongst the following Observations.

   After the same manner I usually treat all those Tubercles in the
Eye brows and Face, where the *Cystis* separates difficultly from
the circumjacent parts, or where a great Scar may be unsightly.[10]

   The other sort of Abscesses which take their beginning from an
Ulcer in the Bone, I have already mentioned in the general

10. *Ibid.*, pp. 416–417.

Description of the Disease under the name of *Spina ventosa:* It hath been taken notice of by very few Authors, and I my self succeeded happily in the curing those in the lesser Bones, many years before I knew what to call the Disease. And in truth I do not now greatly approve of the Name, but shall acquiesce in it, and represent it to you as I have frequently seen it in my Practice in the *King's-Evil*, it being a certain *Species* of that Disease, and of no other that ever I saw.[11]

In the time of the last great Sickness, whilst I was in the Country, a young Woman was brought to me who had a large unequal Tumour near her Neck moveable, and without Inflammation. I designing to take it out by Incision, prepared Dressings ready, and had two Women, and a Boy that I had taken to attend me that Journey, present to assist me. During the separation of the Skin from the Wound, it bleeding, my two Women left me, and the Boy dropt down in a Swoon: the Patient also growing froward, and the work of Separation being not very easy, I was put upon a necessity of cutting into the *Cystis* the whole length: in the doing of which, there discharged about half a large Porringer full of *materia polenta:* after which, putting in my Hand, I pulled out a hard Body of Suet.[12]

11. *Ibid.*, p. 423.
12. *Ibid.*, p. 439.

CHAPTER 31

William Cheselden
(1688–1752)

"What is most worth knowing, is soonest learned and least the subject of disputes."[1]

William Cheselden ushered a new era into British surgery. He was remarkable as a man for the many-sidedness of his interests, and his professional career was no less remarkable for the multiplicity of his significant achievements. The most prominent surgeon of England in the first half of the eighteenth century, and probably of the world, he perfected the operation for bladder stone and wrote importantly on surgery of the eye. He was the first to introduce the formal and regular teaching of anatomy in London as a prerequisite to surgery, and his example was followed by the later surgeon-anatomists of the city. A literateur, artist and architect, bon vivant and pugilist, he was the intimate friend and companion of the leading writers, artists, physicians, and scientists of his day. Because of his intellectual and professional standing, including his appointment as surgeon to Queen Caroline, he elevated the status of surgery in the eyes of the rest of the world. Largely through his influence, the surgeons were liberated from their link with the barbers, and so could rise to their destined place as professional equals of the physicians. But perhaps more telling than all was the outstanding succession of pupils, disciples, and successors, including Percivall Pott, the Hunters, and Astley Cooper, to name a few, who came under his influence and who, in turn, made Great Britain the surgical center of the world for almost a century.

William Cheselden was born in 1688, in Leicestershire of an ancient and landed family. He learned surgery through apprenticeship with James Ferne, a surgeon on the staff of St. Thomas's Hospital, in London. He also studied anatomy with William Cowper (of Cowper's glands eponym), a "bonesetter," who introduced the private teaching of anatomy in England. On completion of his training, Cheselden "took upon him the cloathing of the

---

1. William Cheselden: *The Anatomy of the Humane Body*, London, C. Hitch and R. Dodsley, 1756, Preface, p. iii.

[Barber-Surgeons'] Company," passed the requisite examination, and was qualified to practice.

Hospital appointments were difficult to come by, and practice slow to develop, so the young Cheselden began giving courses in anatomy. According to Sir Zachary Cope, he was the first regular and established teacher of anatomy in London. He drew up a syllabus to accompany the thirty-five lectures, which were given four times a year. Three years later (1713), he published his *The Anatomy of the Humane Body*, which subsequently went through thirteen editions, and was the standard students' textbook of anatomy for a hundred years. He illustrated the book with his own drawings, and included surgical applications and even some physiology in the text, making it truly a surgical anatomy. His election to Fellowship of the Royal Society even preceded the publication of his first book and was the result of his first lecture before that august body. The subject of this lecture further indicates the breadth of his interests since it was based on his archeological studies of an ancient skeleton.

Sir Zachary Cope also relates the following story, which he uncovered in his biographical research: Like so many of his modern counterparts, as he was still struggling to establish himself, Cheselden invested the very large sum of £1000 in the ill-fated South Sea Stock (along with Sir Isaac Newton and many other prominent figures). It is probable that he ventured into this speculation because his wife was the niece of the cashier of the company who subsequently fled the country because of alleged misappropriation of its monies.

The success of Cheselden's anatomical lectures is indicated by an episode in which action was brought against him by the Barber-Surgeons' Company, charging that his dissections made procurement of bodies difficult and that his demonstrations drew members away from the "publick dissections and lectures at the Hall." He was severely reprimanded and made to promise that he would give no more lectures at a time that would conflict with those being given at the Hall, nor without permission of the Governors of the Company. It was this action on the part of the Company that probably provoked him ultimately to free the surgeons from the barbers.

After having been passed over several times, Cheselden was finally appointed to the staff of St. Thomas's Hospital, and he soon demonstrated his unusual abilities. His interest turned to the problem of lithotomy, in which field he earned his greatest renown. The operation long in vogue used the mid-line perineal approach, which was fraught with frequent and serious complications, and a formidable mortality. John Douglas, lithotomist to Westminster Hospital, and a brother of James Douglas, physician and anatomist ("pouch," "fold," and "line" of Douglas), revived the suprapubic or

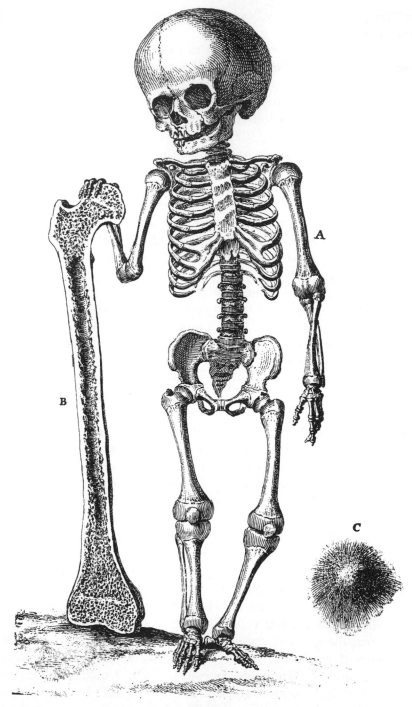

Fig. 64

"high" operation. He was initially successful, and published a book on this method. Cheselden was impressed and soon had a larger series with a lower mortality. In his book, *Treatise on the High Operation for Stone* (1723), full credit was given to Douglas, but the latter took bitter umbrage and became Cheselden's lifelong enemy. Fuel was added to this hatred when Cheselden was chosen over Douglas as lithotomist at Westminster Hospital. During the years of embitterment, the brother, James Douglas, remained a close friend and supporter of Cheselden.

The hazards, however, of the high operation led Cheselden to abandon the method shortly afterward. The French itinerant "cutter," Frère Jacques, had developed the lateral perineal incision, which obviated certain dangers of the median operation. His ignorance of anatomy, however, and the crudeness of his technique, led to frequent disasters. Cheselden chose to adopt this method, and to improve upon it. This he did, after considerable cadaver dissection, and his operation became standard for the next century-and-a-half.

Cheselden's reputation became worldwide, and important personages from distant places came to him for relief from stone. His operative dexterity was amazing; the elapsed time from incision to delivery of the stone was measured in seconds. Because of his great reputation, he was appointed lithotomist to St. George's Hospital, in addition to the former two institutions. Moreover, he became a member of the French Academy of Sciences, and the first foreign member of the Royal Academy of Surgery of France. It was at this time, too, that he was appointed surgeon to Queen Caroline. His friendship with the great men of the arts, letters, and sciences has been mentioned; a further indication of his social position was his daughter's marriage to Dr. Charles Cotes, a member of parliament and a prominent physician.

Surgery of the eye was also one of Cheselden's important interests. In his *Anatomy* he discourses on the structure of the lens and describes some operative experiences. He is credited with being the first ever to have made an artificial pupil. Among his other publications was his *Osteographia*, or the *Anatomy of the*

FIG. 64. "A. The sceleton of a child twenty months old, in which all the bones differ in shape from those of an adult. The scull is much larger in proportion, and the bones of the limbs without those roughnesses and unevennesses which afterwards appear; their texture is every where more loose and spongy, and their outlines what the painters call tame and insipid; their extremities are separate and formed cartilaginous, which is accurately distinguished in the plates by the manner of graving. B. The thigh bone of a man, sawed through, in the middle of which is seen the cavity which contains the oily marrow, and at the extremities the lesser cells, which contain the bloody marrow. The white line across the head of this bone, beginning at the fingers of the sceleton, is the place where the epiphysis and the bone are united. A like line, across the lower end of this bone, shews there the same thing. C. The os bregmatis of a foetus six months old, which shews the fibres ossifying from the center to the circumference." Cheselden, *op. cit., Fig. 1.*

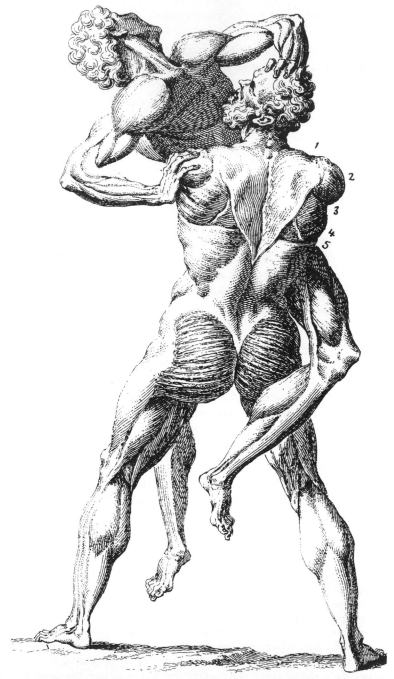

FIG. 65. Dissection of the superficial muscles. "This table is done after the famous statue of Hercules and Antaeus. The muscles here exhibited being all explained in the other plates, the figures are omitted to preserve the beauty of the plate." Cheselden, *op. cit., Fig. 20.*

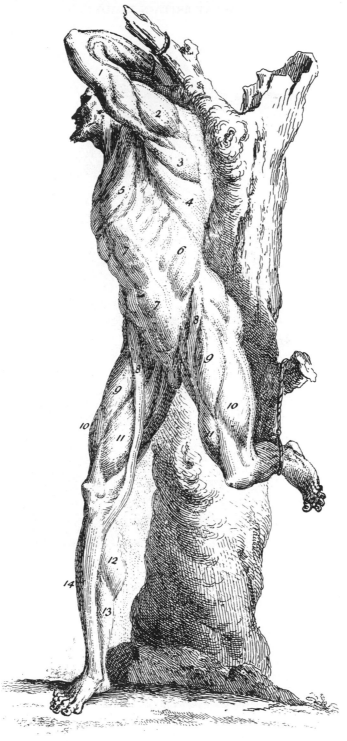

Fig. 66. Topographical anatomy of the human muscles. Cheselden, *op cit.*, *Fig. 59.*

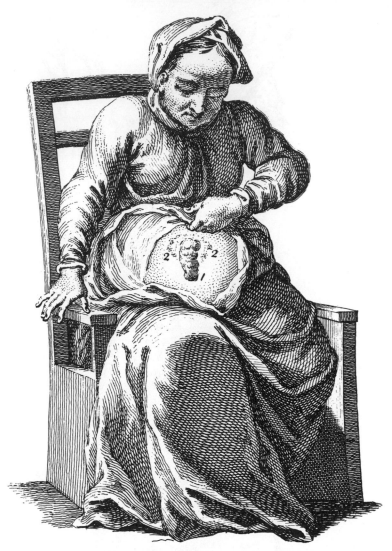

FIG. 67. "The case of Margaret White, the wife of John White, a pensioner in the fish-mongers alms-houses at Newington in Surry. In the fiftieth year of her age, she had a rupture at her navel, which continued till her seventy-third year, when, after a fit of the cholic, it mortified, and she being presently after taken with a vomiting, it burst. I went to her, and found her in this condition, with about six and twenty inches and an half of the gut hanging out, mortified. I took away what was mortified, and left the end of the sound gut hanging out at the navel, to which it afterwards adhered; she recovered, and lived many years after, voiding the excrements through the intestine at the navel; and though the ulcer was so large, after the mortification separated, that the breadth of two guts was seen; yet, they never at any time protruded out at the wound, tho' she was taken out of her bed, and sat up every day.

"1. The gut.

"2. The cicatrix of the wound." From: Cheselden, *op. cit., Fig. 40.*

Bones, which was published in 1733. This was a labor of love, a beautiful folio edition, illustrated with striking and imaginative drawings. Financially it was a failure because of its costly format. Nevertheless it gratified his pride as an artist and anatomist.

While thus at the height of his professional career, and a man of great distinction, Cheselden retired from the staffs of the three hospitals in which he had been so active, and accepted the post of resident surgeon to the Chelsea Hospital. Here he lived and worked in semiretirement for fifteen years, from 1737 until his death in 1752. It was during this time that he took an active part in the affairs of the Barber-Surgeons' Company which led to the separation of the surgeons from the barbers. Cheselden was elected one of the wardens of the Company. During his tenure in this office the surgeons petitioned the House of Commons for a separation. A counter petition from the barbers requested that the *status quo* be maintained. The matter was referred to a committee of the House, with Dr. Cotes, Cheselden's son-in-law, as chairman. After due hearings and deliberations, the committee reported in favor of the surgeons, and the house concurred with the recommendation. A new Corporation of Surgeons was formed in 1745; Mr. Ranby was elected president, and Cheselden Senior Warden. The following year Cheselden succeeded to the presidency, an office which he held until his death. "There can be little doubt, however, that the motive power for the separation of the Surgeons from the Barbers came from Cheselden. It was probably because he was the prime mover that the House of Commons made his son-in-law, Dr. Cotes, the chairman of the special committee to consider the question and to bring in a Bill. Medical education had begun its upward progress and Cheselden was one of those who had a vision of what it was to become in the future. The first step had been taken." [2]

[ANATOMY AND EXPERIMENTAL STUDIES ON THE PHYSIOLOGY OF RESPIRATION][3]

Diaphragma arises on the right side by a process from three lumbal vertebrae, and one of the thorax; and on the left, from the one superior of the loins, and inferior of the thorax; this last part being less to give way to the great artery, and is inserted into the lower part of the sternum and the five inferior ribs. The middle of this muscle is a flat tendon, from whence the fleshy fibres begin and are distributed, like radii, from a centre to a circumference. When this muscle acts alone, it con-

2. Sir Zachary Cope: *William Cheselden,* London, E. & S. Livingstone, Ltd., 1953, p. 53.
3. William Cheselden, *op. cit.,* pp. 103–106.

stricts the thorax, and pulls the ribs downward, and approaches toward a plane; which action is generally performed to promote the ejection of the faeces. In large inspirations, when the intercostals lift up the ribs to widen the thorax, this muscle acts enough to bring itself toward a plane, without overcoming the force of the intercostals, by which means the breast is at once widened and lengthened: when it acts with the abdominal muscles, it draws the ribs nearer together, and constricts the thorax, and the superior force of the abdominal muscles thrusting the parts of the lower belly against it, it becomes at the same time convex upward, and shortens the thorax, which occasions the largest exspirations; or acting alternately with the abdominal muscles only, a more moderate inspiration and exspiration is made by shortening and lengthening the thorax only, which is what we chiefly do when lying down; or acting alternately with the intercostals only, a moderate exspiration and inspiration is caused, by the widening and narrowing of the breast, which is what we are most prone to do in an erect position, the muscles of the abdomen at such times being employed in supporting the parts contained in the abdomen. And though these motions of the ribs require at any one time but very little force, the air within the thorax balancing that without; yet that these muscles, whose motions are essential to life, may be never weary, the inspirators in most men have force sufficient to raise mercury in a tube four or five and twenty inches in an erect posture, and the exspirators six or seven; the first of which will require about four thousand pound force in most men, and the other proportional. But I imagine, that lying down, these proportions will differ by the weight of the parts contained in the abdomen. In all the bodies I have dissected, I have found the diaphragm convex upward, which gave me occasion to think, that all animals died in exspiration; till the forementioned experiment discovered, that the muscles of inspiration were stronger than those of exspiration; which led me to make the following experiment. I cut the wind-pipe of a dog, and having a string ready fixed, I put a corke into it, and tied it fast instantly, after inspiration; upon which I observed, that the diaphragm, and the other muscles of inspiration and exspiration, were alternately contracted and distended for some time; but when he was dead, the abdominal muscles were in a state of contraction, the ribs were elevated to dilate the thorax, and the diaphragm was convex upward. This experiment also shews, that the diaphragm is not a muscle of equal force either to the depressors or elevators of the ribs, it neither hindering the elevators from raising the breast; nor the depressors from thrusting it upward, by compressing the parts contained in the abdomen, through the breast was full of air.

[THE MAXILLARY SINUSES' COMPARATIVE ANATOMY, AND SINUSITIS AND ITS TREATMENT BY OPENING THE SINUS INTO THE MOUTH][4]

Between the posterior grinding-teeth and the orbits of the eyes are two great sinuses, called *antra maxillae superioris,* which open in the upper part of the nose. And in the lower edge of this jaw are the alveoli, or sockets for the teeth. Part of the sides of these cavities, that lie next the nose, are only membranes which makes the cavities like drums, perhaps to give a grave sound to the voice when we let part of it through the nose; but brutes not needing such variety of sounds, have these cavities open to the nose, and filled with lamellae, which are covered with membranes, in which the olfactory nerves terminate, for a more exquisite sense of smelling than is necessary for men. Imposthumations sometimes happen in these cavities: The signs of this disease are, great pain about the part, matter in the nose on the side diseased, stinking breath, and rotten teeth. Mr. Cowper first described this case, and the cure; which is performed by drawing out the last tooth but one, or two, or more if rotten; and through their sockets making a perforation into the antrum; or if drawing a tooth makes a perforation, which sometimes happens, and perhaps gave the first hint of this cure, then that opening must be enlarged, if it is not sufficient to discharge the matter.

[A GRAPHIC DESCRIPTION OF THE PATHOLOGY AND CLINI-CAL COURSE OF OSTEOMYELITIS][5]

Sometimes matter is formed in the large medullary cavities of the cylindrical bones, which constantly increasing and wanting vent, partly by corroding and rendering the bone carious, and partly by pressure, tear asunder the strongest bone in an human body, of which I have known several instances. In one case where the matter had sufficient discharge by an external caries formed together with the internal one, all the internal hard part of the bone which contains the medulla was sepa-

4. *Ibid.,* pp. 18–19.
5. *Ibid.,* pp. 40–41.

rated from the rest; and being drawn out through the place where the external caries made a vent, the patient received a perfect cure. In another case of this kind, where the internal part which contains the medulla was also separated from the rest, and there being holes through which the matter was discharged, but none sufficient to take out the exfoliated bone; the matter continued to flow in great quantity till it destroyed the patient; and possibly, if this case had been rightly known, the internal exfoliated part might have been taken out, and the patient cured. In both these cases, it seems as if only so much of the internal part of the bone was become carious, as receives nourishment from the artery which enters the middle of the bone; and as a caries is a mortification of a bone, might not this disease arise from a hurt in the vessel which nourishes that particular part?

[OBSERVATIONS ON PATHOLOGICAL CHANGES CAUSED BY ABNORMAL CALCIUM DEPOSITION IN ARTERIES, SOFT TISSUES, AND OTHER STRUCTURES][6]

Sometimes the ossifying matter flows out of the bones, and forms bony excrescences; and frequently in very old men it fixes on the arteries, and makes them grow bony; and when this happens to a degree, the arteries lose their power to propel the blood, until the extreme parts mortify. And though the cartilages and arteries are most subject to these changes, yet no part is secure from them; for I have seen a large part of the muscular fibres of the heart itself perfectly ossified. I have known one instance of a deficiency of this ossifying matter, in the lower jaw of an adult body; where all that part on one side, which is beyond the teeth, was of a substance between that of a cartilage and a ligament. In children that have died of the rickets, I have found the nodes on the bones soft, spongy, and bloody, and in one subject several of them as limber as leather, and the periostaeum in some places many times its natural thickness; but the cartilages and cartilaginous epiphyses had no apparent alteration in their texture, though some were swelled to more than twice their natural diameters.

[THE DEFORMITY AND TREATMENT OF CONGENITAL CLUB-FOOT][7]

Children are sometimes born with their feet turned inwards, so that the bottom of the foot is upwards: in this case the bones

6. *Ibid.*, p. 5.
7. *Ibid.*, pp. 37–38.

of the tarsus, like the vertebrae of the back in crooked persons, are fashioned to the deformity. The first knowledge I had of a cure of this disease was from Mr. Presgrove, a professed bone-setter, then living in Westminster. I recommended the patient to him, not knowing how to cure him myself. His way was by holding the foot as near the natural posture as he could, and then rolling it up with straps of sticking plaster, which he re-peated from time to time, as he saw occasion, until the limb was restored to a natural position, but not without some imper-fection, the bandage wasting the leg, and making the top of the foot swell and grow larger. After this, having another case of this kind under my care, I thought of a much better bandage, which I had learnt from Mr. Cowper, a bone-setter at Leices-ter, who set and cured a fracture of my own cubit when I was a boy at school. His way was, after putting the limb in a proper posture, to wrap it up in rags dipped in the whites of eggs, and a little wheat flower mixed; this drying, grew stiff, and kept the limb in a good posture. And I think there is no way better than this in fractures, for it preserves the position of the limb without strict bandage, which is the common cause of mis-chief in fractures. When I used this method to the crooked foot, I wrapt up the limb almost from the knee to the toes, and caused the limb to be held in the best posture 'till the bandage grew stiff, and repeated the bandage once a fortnight.

A SHORT HISTORICAL ACCOUNT OF CUTTING FOR THE STONE.[8]

The most ancient way of cutting for the stone is that described by Celsus, which was indeed cutting upon the gripe, but in a very different manner from that operation in later ages, for he directs a lunated incision with the horns towards the coccyges, which was plainly that the gut might be pressed downwards to avoid wounding it, and then a transverse incision upon the stone might be made safely, but not in very young children, for want of room, nor after puberty, for then the prostatae are too large to allow of this operation; therefore they did not usually cut any younger than nine years, nor older than fourteen: After-wards, but when we know not, this operation was improved by cutting lower, and on one side, which is the operation now called cutting on the gripe, or with the lesser apparatus.

In the year 1524, Marianus published the method of cutting by the greater apparatus, now commonly called the old way,

8. *Ibid.*, pp. 325–334.

but he owns it was invented by his Master Johannes de Romanis.

In the year 1697, Frère Jacques came to Paris, full of reputation for the success of his new operation for the stone; he soon obtain'd leave to cut in the hospitals, where great numbers of his patients dying, and being dissected, they were found with their bladders cut through, guts wounded, etc. which brought the operation into disgrace, as Mery and Dionis have related, who saw these things. They say he performed the operation without any direction, and without any knowledge of the parts he was to cut; a thing not to be mentioned without horror! But of late his character has been set in a very different light; and though 'tis more than probable he himself knew not what he did, yet there are now, who pretend to tell us exactly; though, if their testimonies are to be regarded, who saw him operate, there is no place that he did not cut one time or other, and therefore he may have a sort of right to be called the inventor of any operation for the stone that can ever be performed in these parts. It is also own'd that he sometimes had great success, which was enough to put others of that nation upon trying of it in a more judicious manner; but if there were such, failing of success, they have conceal'd their experiments.

Mr. Rau of Amsterdam, who saw F. Jacques operate, profess'd to do his operation with the necessary improvement of a grooved staff, which, if Jacques ever used, he surely learned that of Rau. He succeeded wonderfully; and if he, who was an excellent anatomist, may be allow'd to understand his own operation, it was directly into the bladder, without wounding either the urethra or the prostates: besides this, other competent judges, who were witnesses to his operations, have bore the same testimony.

In the year 1717–18, Doctor James Douglass, in a paper presented to the Royal Society, demonstrated, from the anatomy of the parts, that the high operation for the stone might be practised; which had been once performed by Franco injudiciously, and by him disrecommended, though his patient recovered; and afterwards strongly recommended, but not practised by Rosset. Yet no one undertook it, till his brother Mr. John Douglass, about three years after, performed it, and with great applause, his two first patients recovering. Soon after, a surgeon of St. Thomas's hospital cut two, who both recovered; but the same gentleman afterwards cutting two, who miscarried by the cutting or bursting the peritonaeum, so that the guts appeared, this way immediately became as much decried as it was before commended; upon which the surgeons of St. Bartholomew's hospital, who had prepared to perform this operation, altered their resolution, and went on in the old way. The next season, it being my turn in St. Thomas's, I resumed the high way, and cutting nine with success, it came again in vogue; after that every lithotomist of both hospitals practised it; but the peritonaeum being often cut or burst, twice in my practice, though some of these recovered, and sometimes the bladder itself was burst, from injecting too much water, which generally proved fatal in a day or two. Another inconvenience attended every operation of this kind, which was, that the urine's lying continually in the wound retarded the cure, but then it was never followed with an incontinence of urine. What the success of the several operators was, I will not take the liberty to publish; but for my own, exclusive of the two before mentioned, I lost no more than one in seven, which is more than any one else that I know of could say; whereas in the old way, even at Paris, from a fair calculation of above 800 patients, it appears that near two in five died. And though this operation came into universal discredit, I must declare it my opinion, that it is much better than the old way, to which they all returned, except myself, who would not have left the high way but for the hopes I had of a better; being well assured, that it might hereafter be practised with greater success; these fatal accidents having pretty well shewn how much water might be injected, and how large the wound might safely be made. But hearing of the great success of Mr. Rau, professor of anatomy at Leyden, I determined to try, though not in his manner, to cut directly into the bladder; and as his operation was an improvement of Friar Jacques, I endeavoured to improve upon him, by filling the bladder, as Douglass had done in the high way, with water, leaving the catheter in, and then cutting on the outside of the catheter into the bladder, in the same place as upon the gripe, which I could do very readily, and take out a stone of any size with more ease than in any other way. My patients for some days after the operation seemed out of danger; but the urine which came out of the bladder continually lodging upon the cellular membrane on the outside of the rectum, made foetid ulcers, attended with a vast discharge of stinking matter; and from this cause I lost four patients out of ten. The case of one which escaped was very remarkable; a few days after he was cut, he was seized with a great pain in his back and legs, with very little power to move them; upon which he turned upon his face, and rested almost constantly upon his knees and elbows above a fortnight together, having no ease in any other posture all that while; at length his urine coming all the right way, his wound soon healed, and he recovered the use of his back and limbs.

I think all these severe symptoms could proceed from no other cause than the urine and matter somehow offending the great nerves; which come out of the os sacrum to go to the lower limbs. I then tried to cut into the bladder, in the same manner that Mr. Rau was commonly reported to do, but there had the same inconvenience from the urine's lodging upon the cellular membrane on the outside of the intestinum rectum.

Upon these disappointments, I contrived the manner of cutting, which is now called the lateral way. This operation I do in the following manner: I tie the patient as for the greater apparatus, but lay him upon a blanket several doubles upon an horizontal table three foot high, with his head only raised. I first make as long an incision as I can, beginning near the place where the old operation ends, and cutting down between the *musculus accelerator urinae*, and *erector penis*, and by the side of the *intestinum rectum*: I then feel for the staff, holding down the gut all the while with one or two fingers of my left hand, and cut upon it in that part of the urethra which lies beyond the corpora cavernosa urethrae, and in the prostate gland, cutting from below upwards, to avoid wounding the gut; and then passing the gorget very carefully in the groove of the staff into the bladder, bear the point of the gorget hard against the staff, observing all the while that they do not separate, and let the gorget slip to the outside of the bladder; then I pass the forceps into the right side of the bladder, the wound being on the left side of the perinaeum; and as they pass, carefully attend to their entering the bladder, which is known by their overcoming a straitness which there will be in the place of the wound; then taking care to push them no further, that the bladder may not be hurt, I first feel for the stone with the end of them, which having felt, I open the forceps and slide one blade underneath it, and the other at top; and if I apprehend the stone is not in the right place of the forceps, I shift it before I offer to extract, and then extract it very deliberately, that it may not slip suddenly out of the forceps, and that the parts of the wound may have time to stretch, taking great care not to gripe it so hard as to break it, and if I find the stone very large, I again cut upon it as it is held in the forceps. Here I must take notice, it is very convenient to have the bladder empty of urine before the operation, for if there is any quantity to flow out of the bladder at the passing in of the gorget, the bladder does not contract but collapse into folds, which makes it difficult to lay hold of the stone without hurting the bladder; but if the bladder is contracted, it is so easy to lay hold of it, that I have never been delayed one moment, unless the stone was very small.

Lastly, I tie the blood-vessels by the help of a crooked needle, and use no other dressing than a little bit of lint besmear'd with blood, that it may not stick too long in the wound, and all the dressings during the cure are very slight, almost superficial, and without any bandage to retain them; because that will be wetted with urine, and gall the skin. At first I keep the patient very cool to prevent bleeding, and sometimes apply a rag dipt in cold water, to the wound, and to the genital parts, which I have found very useful in hot weather particularly. In children it is often alone sufficient to stop the bleeding, and always helpful in men. The day before the operation I give a purge to empty the guts, and never neglect to give some laxative medicine or clyster a few days after, if the belly is at all tense, or if they have not a natural stool. What moved me to try this way, if I may be allowed to know my own thoughts, was the consideration of women scarce ever dying of this operation; from which I concluded, that if I could cut into the urethra, beyond the *corpora cavernosa urethae*, the operation would be nearly as safe in men as women.

What success I have had in my private practice I have kept no account of, because I had no intention to publish it, that not being sufficiently witnessed. Publickly in St. Thomas's hospital I have cut two hundred and thirteen; of the first fifty only three died; of the second fifty, three; of the third fifty, eight; and of the last sixty-three, six. Several of these patients had the small pox during their cure, some of which died, but I think not more in proportion than what usually die of that distemper; these are not reckon'd among those who died of the operation. The reason why so few died in the two first fifties was, at that time few very bad cases offered; in the third, the operation being in high request, even the most aged and most miserable cases expected to be sav'd by it; besides, at that time, I made the operation lower in hopes of improving it, but found I was mistaken. But what is of most consequence to be known is the ages of those who recovered, and those who died. Of these, under ten years of age one hundred and five were cut, three died; between ten and twenty, sixty-two cut, four died; twenty and thirty, twelve cut, three died; thirty and forty, ten cut, two died; forty and fifty, ten cut, two died; fifty and sixty, seven cut, four died; sixty and seventy, five cut, one died; between seventy and eighty, two cut, one died. Of those who recovered the three biggest stones were — xii, x¼, and viii [12, 10¼ and 8 ounces], and the greatest number of stones in any one person was thirty-three. One of the three that died out of the hundred and five, was very ill with a whooping cough; another bled to death by an artery into the bladder, it being very hot weather at that time: But this accident taught me afterwards, whenever a vessel bled that I could not find, to dilate the wound with a knife, till I could see it. Now if Jacques or others, who of late have been said to have performed this operation, whether by design or chance, did not take care to secure the blood-vessels, which as yet has not been supposed, whatever their dexterity in operating might be, their success at least can be no secret, for many of their children and most of their men patients must have bled to death. If I have any reputation in this way, I have earn'd it dearly, for no one ever endured more anxiety and sickness before an operation, yet from the time I began to operate, all uneasiness ceased; and if I have had better success than some others, I do not impute it to more knowledge, but to the happiness of a mind that was never ruffled or disconcerted, and a hand that never trembled during any operation.

CHAPTER 32

Lorenz Heister
(1683–1758)

"Some call Surgery *a* Science, *others an* Art; *but in my opinion, it may claim either appellation."* [1]

During the period of Great Britain's leadership in the surgical world, significant advances, of course, emanated from other lands. A German contemporary of merits comparable to those of the British masters was Lorenz Heister, with whom a new type of surgeon was introduced in Germany. In contrast to the unlettered, craft-trained, and often entirely ignorant practitioners who preceded him, Heister was a widely educated student of languages and humanities, a graduate in medicine of the leading university of the period, and a thoroughly trained anatomist and surgeon. He became the outstanding German surgeon of the first half of the seventeenth century and one of the most prominent in Europe. His book was the accepted text in his own country for many years, and was widely read throughout the medical world. One of the early professors of surgery in German univerisitcs, he was a powerful force in elevating the educational standards of European surgeons.

These achievements are particularly noteworthy when viewed against the prevailing conditions of German surgical practice. In a period when superstition flourished and charlatanism reigned, when not only the barber and the itinerant cutter and bonesetter, but even the public executioner were officially permitted to practice surgery, the example set by Heister was particularly striking and beneficial to the public welfare. He rendered eminent service, indeed, to all of the healing arts.

Born in Frankfurt-am-Main, he attended school in that city and excelled in the arts, music, poetry, and painting, as well as in the usual humanistic disciplines. So proficient was he in these scholastic pursuits that his father,

---

1. Lorenz Heister: *A General System of Surgery*, in three parts, containing the doctrine and management of wounds . . . by Laurence Heister, sixth edition, London, W. Innis & J. Richardson *et al.*, 1757, p. 2.

although a man of modest means, felt impelled to endow his gifted son with a university education. In spite of the excellent record achieved in his cultural studies, Heister wisely recognized that his strongest leanings were toward a career in medicine. After four years of distinguished scholarship at the University of Giessen, he went for further training to Leyden, in Holland, then the center of medical education of the world, and thence to Amsterdam to study with Ruysch and Rau, outstanding surgeons and anatomists. In a quotation from an introduction to one of his books which is given below, it will be noticed that he reversed somewhat the order of his places of study; nor does he mention the fact that he ultimately took the doctoral degree in medicine at the University of Hardewyk in Holland in 1708.[2] On the acquisition of this degree, and thanks to the sponsorship of Professor Ruysch, he was appointed chief surgeon of the army of the Netherlands. His personal account of his training and experiences is interesting:

"After having studied Physic with great Assiduity above four Years in our *German* Universities, my Affections, being strongest for *Anatomy* and *Surgery*, led me to the then celebrated Professors Ruysch and Raw [Rau], at *Amsterdam*, in the Year 1706; whose anatomical and chirurgical Demonstrations I diligently attended for about the Space of a Year. During which Time I was also employed in frequent Dissections, and in trying chirurgical Operations upon dead Subjects; in the mean time omitting no Opportunities of being present at the Performance of any considerable Operation by these Professors, or by the other eminent Surgeons of the same City, as Verduin, Bortel, Koenerding, etc. By which Means, joined with an attentive Reading of the best Writers, I acquired a considerable Knowledge in Surgery.

"But being desirous of all Helps to render myself still more expert and successful in the Practice of this Art, there being at that Time a sharp War in *Flanders*, betwixt the *French* and *Dutch*, in the Summer following, *viz.* in the Year 1707, I went from *Holland* to the *Dutch* Camp in *Brabant*, that I might inspect and observe the Practice of the *English*, *Dutch*, and *German* Surgeons, who there attended. Thus, through many Dangers and Hardships, I spent this whole Summer in the Hospitals of the Camp, for the Sake of Improvement. But in Autumn I went from *Brabant* to *Leyden*, and spent the whole Winter in attending the Lectures of the then celebrated Professors in that University, Bidloo, Albinus senior, and Boerhaave: And thus I continued till the Beginning of the Summer 1708. After which,

2. *Dictionaire des Sciences Médicales, Biographie médicale*, Paris, C. L. F. Panckouke, 1822, Vol. 5, pp. 131–138.

FIG. 68. Amputation techniques. From: Heister's *A General System of Surgery*, London, 1757

having taken my Degree of *Doctor*, I returned again to the Camp, where I found large Opportunities of learning and improving myself in Surgery, from the Multitude wounded, *etc.* in the several bloody Fights, particularly at the Siege of *Lisle*, and the Battles of *Audinarde* and *Wynnendale*. Upon the Approach of Winter again, I was determined to settle in the Practice of *Physic* and *Surgery* in *Holland*, at *Amsterdam*, partly from the Delight I had in the Country, and partly through the Sollicitations of the famous Ruysch, who respected me as a Son. Here therefore I stayed the Winter, and Part of the ensuing Spring, teaching *Anatomy* and *Surgery* to Students and Gentlemen, as Raw had done before me, who was now rejected for his ill Conduct or Misbehaviour.

"The following Summer, in 1709, I had still a strong Desire to follow the Camp, to become more and more perfect in the Practice of *Surgery*; and *Tournay* being at that Time invested by the confederate Army in *Flanders*, I was, by the Recommendations of my Friend Ruysch, appointed Physician to the Camp-Hospital for the *Hollanders*. I had now an Opportunity of performing all the chirurgical Operations which offered in the Camps and adjacent Cities, which I generally executed with Success. After the taking of *Tournay*, the confederate Army marched to besiege *Mons*, near which Place the *French* Army was also assembled. That, however, did not prevent us from investing and taking the City; before which the numerous

Army had such a bloody Battle, that the Wounded were brought in upon us in Crowds. Their Number continually increasing, from the uncommon Heat of the Combat, every Surgeon had now his Hands full of Business, and infinite Calls for the Practice of his Art: For the Wounded, on the Side of the *Hollanders* only, amounted to above Five thousand. I had here therefore an ample Occasion to extend

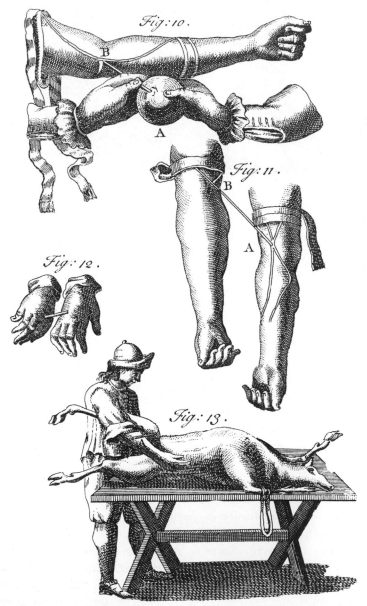

FIG. 69. Infusion and transfusions. From: Heister's *A General System of Surgery*, London, 1757

the Bounds of my Practice, and was obliged to put on that Intrepidity of Mind, which Celsus requires as an essential Qualification in a Surgeon; and for want of which, some, who are, in other respects, skillful Operators, do frequently miscarry.

"After the Army had entered into their Winter-Quarters, and the wounded Men recovered, I returned again to *Amsterdam*, where I continued my *Anatomical* and *Chirurgical* Demonstrations this Winter as before. In the mean time, I never refused my Assistance at the Operations of the other Surgeons there.

"But in the Beginning of the Spring following, 1710, I was, beyond Expectation, called by the Republic of *Norimberg* [Nürnberg] to teach *Anatomy* and *Surgery*, as public Professor in the University of *Altorf*. Being therefore unwilling to neglect this honourable Invitation, having obtained Leave from the Republic, I first made a Tour into *Great Britain*, where I was, from Spring to Autumn, collecting every thing new in the several Branches of Physic, and then, returning to *Norimberg* and *Altorf*, I assumed my new *Professorship*."

Heister remained in Altdorf for eleven years where he "was under a Necessity of teaching publicly, among the other parts of *Physic*, that most ancient, necessary, and useful Branch of it which we call *Surgery*, and which I had before taught privately during the two preceding winters in *Holland*." It was during this period that he brought out his great "Surgery," motivated by the conviction that there was no adequate textbook to supplement his lectures. "To our want of such a *Compendium* I also attributed the general Ignorance and Insufficiency of the young Surgeons and Students in this Branch of *Physic*, which at that Time universally prevailed, through *Germany* especially. And from the same Cause the generality of our Surgeons, being unequal to the more difficult Operations, were content with being able to cure a slight Wound, open a Vein or Abscess, or at most to set a Fracture, and reduce a Luxation; leaving those Disorders and Operations, which require the greatest Skill, to the Management of daring Quacks and itinerant Operators, with which *Germany* at the Time swarmed."

Shortly after the publication of his book, Heister was called in 1719 to the University of Helmstadt, in the Duchy of Brunswick, to fill the Chair of Anatomy and Surgery. Some time later the Professorship in Botany was added to his duties, in which capacity he established a famous botanical garden. Heister remained at Helmstadt for thirty-eight years, and he brought the school of surgery from obscurity to a position of first rank, an eminence which was short-lived, coinciding with his tenure and disappearing abruptly after his death in 1758.

Heister's *Chirurgie* was one of the early systematic treatises on the subject.

It reflects the author's wide reading and unusual command of languages in that it summarizes virtually all that had been written before, ancient and recent. The book is richly illustrated with folded copper plate engravings of instruments and operative techniques. It was written originally in German, although its author informs us he intended to publish it in Latin, but that students lacked sufficient command of this language. The importance of the book is apparent from the numerous editions issued, seven in German, three in Latin, and translations into English (ten editions), Spanish, French, Italian, and Dutch.

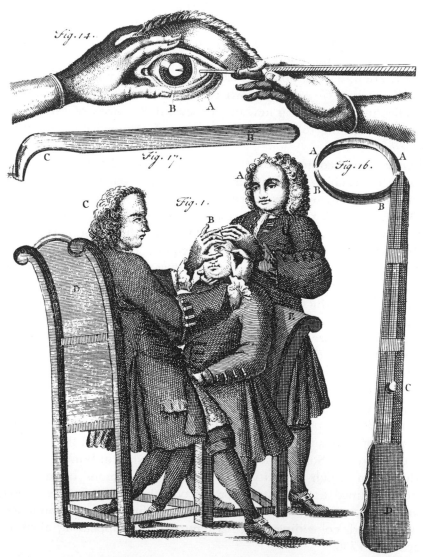

FIG. 70. Cataract operation. From: Heister's *A General System of Surgery*, London, 1757

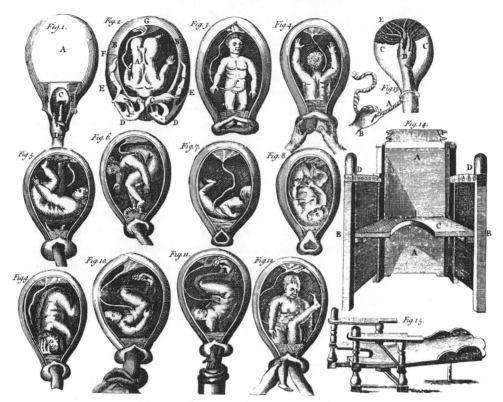

FIG. 71. Delivery chairs, presentations, and obstetrical manipulations. From: Heister's *A General System of Surgery*, London, 1757.

In addition to this major surgical work, Heister wrote a Compendium of Anatomy which went through some twenty-five editions in various languages, a Compendium of the Practice of Physic, numerous treatises on ophthalmology, botany, and other subjects, and collected case reports. He described the spiral valve of the cystic duct, which still bears his name. These many contributions and his long years of teaching have earned for him a lasting place among those who have advanced the science of surgery.

ᔆᕮ   ᔆᕮ   ᔆᕮ   [ON THE SPONTANEOUS OR OPERATIVE CREATION OF AN
ᔆᕮ   ᔆᕮ   ᔆᕮ   EXTERNAL INTESTINAL FISTULA IN INJURIES OR GANG-
                  RENE OF THE BOWEL.]

Of Loss of Substance in the Intestines.[3]

I. Where any Part of the Intestine is carried away, the Case seems to be plainly desperate. It was therefore wonderful that

3. Lorenz Heister: *A General System of Surgery*, London, 1757, Part I, pp. 74–75.

Persons thus wounded did not all die upon the Spot, or in the Operation of making the Sutures: til [various surgeons] observed, that the Lips of Intestines so wounded, would sometimes quite unexpectedly adhere to the Wound in the Abdomen; and therefore there seemed to be no Reason why we should not take this Hint from Nature. Whenever therefore a Surgeon is called to a Case of this Kind, after he has diligently examined the State of the Upper Part of the Intestine, which has suffered a Loss of Substance, he should stich it to the external Wound, either by the continued or interrupted Suture. For by this Means the Patient may not only be saved from instant Death, but there have been Instances where the wounded Intestine has been so far healed, that the Faeces which used to be voided *per Anum*, have been voided by the Wound in the Abdomen: Which, from the Necessity of wearing a Tin or Silver Pipe, or keeping Cloths constantly upon the Part to receive the Excrement, may seem to be very troublesome: But it is surely far better to part with one of the Conveniences of Life, than to part with Life itself. Besides, the Excrements that are voided by this Passage, are not altogether so offensive, as those that are voided *per Anum*.

II. The same Method of Cure may conveniently enough be put in practice, where any Part of the Intestine is mortified by being forced out of the Abdomen. For in this Case, if you tie up the mesenteric Arteries, the corrupted or mortified Part of the Intestine may be cut off, and the remaining sound Part made to adhere to the Wound of the Abdomen. For it is better to try this Method, though but few should be saved by it, than to suffer all to perish, as Celsus observes; It is wiser to attempt a doubtful Remedy, than absolutely to despair. I once published a Cure of this Kind in a Dissertation containing various Observations, printed at *Helmstadt*.

[Heister is credited with the introduction of the term *tracheotomy*. He expanded the indications and also divided the cartilagenous rings and inserted a tube much in the manner that that is used today.]

OF BRONCHOTOMY, LARYNGOTOMY, OR TRACHEOTOMY.[4]

I. By all these Names is intended an Opening or Incision made in the *Aspera Arteria* or Windpipe: which is necessary in

4. *Ibid.*, Part II, pp. 51–53.

many Cases, and especially in (1) a violent Quinsey, to prevent
Suffocation from the great Inflammation or Tumor of the
Parts. (2) When a Bean, Pea, Plum, or Cherry-stone, or some
such Bodies are slipt into the Trachea, and seem to threaten
Suffocation: (3) And lastly, this Operation may be practised
upon People that have been lately drowned, and are not yet
entirely suffocated: for by dividing the Trachea and inflating
Air into the Lungs of such Persons several have been recovered.
I am not altogether ignorant that many Physicians are averse to
this Operation, either esteeming it dangerous, deadly, or in-
humane. But those Gentlemen are greatly mistaken: for the
the small Wound made in the Trachea by this Operation, is
so far from killing, that even much larger, which are not
made with this intention, are not to be judged mortal, as we
intimated in treating of Wounds in this Part. So that we cannot
help thinking with Casserius, that those are both ignorant and
timorous, who rashly neglect this safe, easy, and often salutary
Operation in the forementioned Cases.

II. When this Operation is to be performed, the most
convenient Part of the *Trachea* to be opened, is between the
second and third of its annular Cartilages: though it may be
also opened much lower without Danger. The Method of
proceeding, especially when any Stone, Bean, Pea, or the like,
are to be extracted, take as follows. In the first Place, the
Patient is to be inclined backward upon a Bed or in a Chair,
and his Head held firm by an Assistant, who is to stand at his
Back: then the Skin, Fat, and Muscles, are to be divided by
making a longitudinal Incision with a Scalpel according to
the length of the *Trachea*, beginning about two Fingers breadth
below the Scutiform Cartilage, and continuing it for the Space
of two, three, and in tall People four Fingers breadth. Then
the Sides of the Wound are to be drawn asunder by an Assistant, either with proper Hooks or his Fingers, and after
wiping off the Blood with a Lint or a Sponge to render the
Trachea conspicuous, three or four of its annular Cartilages are
to be divided in a right Line: by which Means the Body lodged
in its Cavity may be found by searching with a Probe, and
afterwards extracted by a Hook or Pliars. When the Operation
is finished, the Wound is to be cleansed with a Sponge, and
dressed with some sticking Plaster, retained by Compress and
Bandage; and afterwards it may be treated with some vulnerary
Balsam, as mentioned in our treating of Wounds in this Part.

By these Means I happily extracted a Piece of a boiled Mush-
room, which slipped into the *Trachea* of a jocose Man at Helmstadt, with Danger of Suffocation by Laughing, while he was
eating Broth, in which Mushrooms were boiled. By the same
Method Ravius told me he happily extracted a Bean which
had fallen into the *Trachea* notwithstanding the rest of our
modern Surgeons are negligent on this Head. Some Surgeons
advise that kind of Suture which is used in the Hare lip for the
more speedy and uniform Cicatrisation of the Wound in this
Part. But in my Opinion that Apparatus may be properly
omitted, as it usually gives great Pain and Uneasiness to the
Patient, and as the Wound may be cured by a Treatment much
milder and equally safe.

III. When repeated Bleeding and the Use of proper Medicines
take no Effect in a Quinsey, this Operation may be necessary to
prevent the Patient from being suffocated. In this Disorder there
are three Ways of performing *Bronchotomy*, each of which we
shall describe in order. The first is by placing the Patient in a
supine Posture, his Head being held firm by an Assistant, as
before. The Surgeon then proceeds to make an Incision in the
Integuments to the *Trachea*; or the Skin may be elevated by
the Surgeon and an Assistant, and afterwards divided longi-
tudinally together with the Fat and Muscles which cover the
Trachea. Some advise these Muscles to be cautiously separated
from the *Trachea* or from each other: but that is not necessary,
and these Muscles may be safely incised without Danger. When
the integuments have been divided, the wound is to be cleansed,
and the Blood stopped with a Sponge which has been dipt in
warm Wine or its Spirit, while the Assistant draws one Side of
the Wound from the other, with Hooks or his Fingers. Then the
Surgeon makes an Incision with his Scalpel between two of
the annular Cartilages, or else, as I have sometimes seen, by
dividing one of the Cartilages in the Middle, at the same Time;
after which he may easily introduce a small round or flat
Tube of Silver or Lead. But before the Surgeon withdraws his
knife out of the Incision, it may be proper for him to insert a
Probe by the Side of it, by which Means he may afterwards
more easily introduce the Cannula. This Cannula or Tube is
to be fastened to the Neck with a Ligature passing through
Rings or small Holes in its Side, and held firm in its Place by
a Piece of perforated Emplaster, being careful that the End of
the Tube does not touch the back Part of the *Trachea*; and

occasion a troublesome Cough. But to prevent the external Cold and Dust from injuring the Lungs, it may be proper to let the Air pass through a Piece of Sponge in the Tube, which should be frequently dipt into, and expressed out of warm Wine; or, as Garengeot advises, through a Piece of fine Lint, having a Piece of perforated Emplaster behind it. This being performed, the Patient may be bled in the Arm, Foot, Neck, or under the Tongue: and Clysters, Gargles, with a Cataplasm under the Chin, cupping on the Sides of the Neck, with other Medicines proper in Quinseys, should be diligently applied, till the Patient either recovers his Respiration or wholly expires, one of which usually happens within four Days after the Operation When a free Respiration by the Mouth succeeds two or three Days after the Operation, which may be known by stopping the Orifice of the Tube with a Finger, it may be then taken out, and the Wound afterwards dressed and treated as we before directed. But if the Difficulty of Respiration still continues, it should be continued in its Place with the other Remedies, till Death or a free Respiration put a Period to the Experiment.

CHAPTER 33

Percivall Pott
(1714–1789)

". . . it never can be right to counteract nature, and oblige her to do that she is not inclined to, and which she would otherwise accomplish better." [1]

Cheselden's leadership of English surgery descended, like the mantle of Elijah, to his sometime pupil and younger contemporary, Percivall Pott. Of the two names, the latter is much the more familiar because of the several eponyms still in common use. From the association of his name with clinical phenomena one can draw inferences as to the man and to the nature of his contributions. For he was a penetrating observer who brought to his surgical practice a grounding in anatomy far deeper than the norm of his time. He was elegant in person, gave elegant lectures, and wrote his treatises in elegant English. Gentleness and simplicity characterized his surgery. He left the profession richer for his influence.

Percivall Pott was born in London of an old and respected family, but his early years were passed under straitened circumstances. When he was but three years old, his father died at the age of thirty-six, leaving the family poorly provided for. Percivall's mother had previously been married to the scion of a wealthy commercial family who was killed in military action shortly after their marriage. A distant relative of hers, Bishop Wilcox of Rochester, took over the responsibility of providing for Percivall's education, perhaps with the assistance of her former parents-in-law. The quality of the education is attested by the literary style of Pott's subsequent writings. Between mother and son a tender and devoted affection prevailed, the depth of which may be suggested by the fact that he did not marry until after her death, when he was thirty-two years old.

A career in the church was planned for him, but he would not hear of it. Surgery called him, even in his youth. He was apprenticed, accordingly, at the age of fifteen, to Mr. Nourse, one of the two surgeons at St. Bartholomew's

1. *The Chirurgical Works of Percivall Pott*, Vol. I, London, Johnson *et al.*, 1808, p. 14.

PERCIVALL POTT Efq.ʳ

Engraved by Heath, from a Picture
of Sir Joshua Reynolds.

Hospital. In addition to his practice of surgery, Nourse was giving lectures in anatomy in his home, and Pott was soon set to preparing the dissections for the demonstrations. So it was that he gained knowledge and experience in the two related fields of endeavor. To these he added the fruits of voracious reading, including contemporary and ancient, as well as nonprofessional, literature.

His apprenticeship completed in 1736, when he was twenty-two years old, he was admitted to the "freedom" of the Barber-Surgeons' Company. On

the same day he successfully passed the examination, and was awarded the
Great Diploma, and was prepared to practice.

Pott, like Cheselden, failed on his first application for hospital appointment,
but at the next election, in 1745, he became Assistant Surgeon at St. Bartholomew's, and four years later was elected full Surgeon. He was an intelligent
and engaging person who quickly made lasting friendships, and his practice
prospered. Except for an early article in the *Philosophical Transactions,* he had
not yet begun to write, but he was accumulating the observations that one
day would make him famous.

It was a mishap that brought this about. As he was riding to a hospital on
a frosty morning when he was forty-two years old, he was thrown from his
horse and suffered a compound fracture of the tibia. Recognizing the gravity
of the injury, and, indeed, in that day a compound fracture was serious, he
refused to let himself be moved. Instead, he sent to Westminster, across the
Thames, for two bearers, and continued to lie patiently on the frozen ground.
When they arrived whith their poles, he purchased a door which he had
nailed to the poles, then allowed himself to be laid on the improvised stretcher
and carried to his home. The surgeons who were called advised immediate
amputation, then the accepted treatment for the condition, and Pott assented.
As the instruments were being prepared, however, his old Master, Nourse,
arrived and decided that he might save the leg. The fracture was reduced and
"the wound healed, in some measure, by first intention."

Like Richard Wiseman, Pott, too, made a virtue of necessity, utilizing his
prolonged immobility for the purpose of writing, an activity which he pursued
energetically through the rest of his life. His treatise on *Ruptures* was finished
during the year after his accident, and the others followed in rapid succession,
*Congenital Hernia, Fistula Lachryimalis, Head Injuries, Hydrocele, Fractures and
Dislocations, Palsy of the Lower Limbs,* and several lesser works.

The reading of Pott's works is rewarding because of their uncommon
literary qualities as well as for the abundance of shrewd observations and
their logical conclusions. The older authors are recognized and appreciated,
but their limitations are pointed out. He writes, "Our ancestors deserve our
best thanks for the assistance which they have given us: where we find them
to be right, we are obliged to embrace their opinions as truths; but implicit
faith is not required from man to man; and our reverence for our predecessors
must not prevent us from using our own judgements." Most of the ideas he
expresses are his own judgements, based on perceptive observation, fortified
by his knowledge of anatomy, and confirmed often by postmortem examination.

The prevading theme in his therapy is gentleness. The cautery he rejects
almost entirely. Caustic and irritating medicaments and unnecessary manipulations are shunned. Simple methods are preferred. The instruments used are

reduced to the barest few (for trephining operation "we require only a tre-phine . . . and an elevator; or perhaps, now and then, a pair of forceps"), and these of the plainest design. Complicated apparatus, as for the reduction and dressing of fractures, are categorically abandoned.

The literary quality of his writings has been mentioned. The first para-graph of the Preface to the *Treatise on Ruptures*, 1756, may be quoted as an example: "The disease which makes the subject of the following tract, is one in which mankind are, on many accounts much interested. No age, sex, rank, or condition of life, is exempted from it; the rich, the poor, the lazy, and the laborious, are equally liable to it; it produces certain inconvenience to all who are afflicted by it; it sometimes puts the life of the patient in such hazard, as to require one of the most delicate operations in surgery; and it has in all times, from the most ancient down to the present, rendered those who labor under it subject to the most iniquitous frauds and impositions." The very many illustrative case reports not only emphasize the statements of the text, but they also reflect the enormous clinical experience that lies be-hind them. At the same time, they provide vivid insight into the customs, occupations, and pleasures of his day.

The collected works of Pott contain such a wealth of significant material that space does not permit mention of but a fraction. In the treatise on the *Injuries of the Head from External Violence*, Pott describes the signs by which extradural hematoma can be differentiated from abscess. Characteristic of the latter is the "puffy tumor" (Pott), a circumscribed swelling of the scalp over the involved area. He also recognized the lucid interval which precedes the coma of extradural hemorrhage, and adds that the initial con-cussion causes a loss of consciousness which may merge into that of cerebral compression without the period of lucidity. The far graver significance of subdural or intracranial hemorrhage was known to him, as was also the impossibility of positively differentiating between them and those of the extradural variety. He was partial to the use of the trephine and employed it much as modern neurosurgeons do their exploratory burr-holes when the presence of a fluid accumulation cannot otherwise be ruled out. If the hemor-rhage or abscess was beneath the dura, this membrane was incised. The description of the clinical manifestations of the various injuries is excellent.

In other books he correctly explains the physiology of the lachryimal apparatus and the pathology of fistula, and improved on its operative manage-ment. The use of the cautery, as advocated by Cheselden, he considered barbarous. In the management of fractures he showed the fallacy of attempt-ing reduction with the extremity extended and the muscles tense. Flexing the limb to relax the muscles and gently positioning it on pillows was sub-stituted. Splints, when used, should immobilize the joints above and below the fracture, and be well padded. Attempts to correct deformity by making

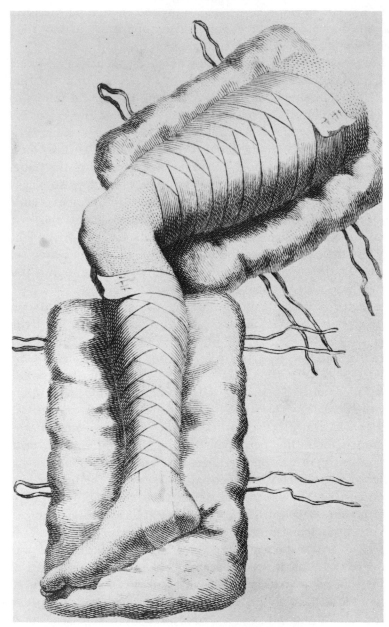

FIG. 73. Pott's method of positioning and bandaging for leg fracture. From: *The Chirurgical Works of Percivall Pott*, Vol. I, p. 309.

pressure on the projecting end of the proximal fragment could lead only to necrosis. Correct management brought the distal end in line with the proximal. The difficult decision as to amputation in compound fractures required weighing the chances of saving a limb against the hazard of death from infection. His classic description of "Pott's fracture" is quoted below.

Pott was first to describe "congenital hernia," which embroiled him in a controversy with William Hunter who charged that the observations had been taken from preparations made by his brother, John. The radical cure for hernia was denounced by Pott, but operation for strangulation was often done. Hydrocele and scrotal tumors are discussed in considerable detail.

"Chimney Sweeps' Cancer," one of the early-known occupational diseases, was first described by Pott, and often bears his name. This form of cutaneous cancer of the scrotum from prolonged exposure to the carcinogenic agents in the chimney soot was the first demonstration that such irritation could lead to malignant change. Speaking of the victims of the disease, he writes: "The fate of these people seems singularly hard: in their early infancy, they are most frequently treated brutally, and almost starved with cold and hunger; they are thrust up narrow and sometimes hot chimneys, where they are bruised, burned, and almost suffocated; and when they get to puberty, become peculiarly liable to a most noisome, painful, and fatal disease."[2]

Pott's name is probably most familiar from its association with tuberculous caries of the spine. He gave, indeed, a classic description of the clinical manifestations of the disease, together with the correlative anatomical findings. Curiously, Pott believed he had found a cure for this usually hopeless condition, by creating superficial abscesses in the back. He cites a large number of cases dramatically restored from complete invalidism to active life, by this simple means. The observations extend over a period of several years and were confirmed by many other doctors. It seems strange that so astute an observer as Percivall Pott should be so firmly convinced of the results of a therapeutic measure, which in the light of subsequent times could only be found to be a delusion. Despite this error, Pott amply merits the fame he has enjoyed for his presentation and interpretation of the pathology and clinical manifestations of "Pott's disease."

The clinical acumen of Percivall Pott demonstrated in these references to his published works was matched by an equally high ethical concept. In concluding this brief biographical sketch, his idealistic concept of the obligations of the surgeon may be summarized in the following brief excerpt from the *Treatise on Injuries of the Head from External Violence.* "It is to be presumed, that every practitioner wishes to cure his patients as soon as he can, by the least painful means, and in such manner as shall be productive of the least

2. *Ibid.*, Vol. III, p. 178.

possible deformity or defect; taking care at the same time, not to be inat-
tentive to any evil which may arise, nor to omit or neglect doing whatever
may be necessary during such cure."

ʕ●   ʕ●   ʕ●   [THE CLASSIC DESCRIPTION OF "POTT'S FRACTURE"][3]

ʕ●   ʕ●   ʕ●   I have already said, and it will obviously appear to every one
who examines it, that the support of the body, and the due and
proper use and execution of the office of the joint of the ancle,
depend almost entirely on the perpendicular bearing of the
tibia upon the astragalus, and on its firm connexion with the
fibula. If either of these be perverted or prevented, so that the
former bone is forced from its just and perpendicular position
on the astragalus; or if it be separated by violence from its
connexion with the latter, the joint of the ancle will suffer a
partial dislocation internally; which partial dislocation cannot
happen without not only a considerable extension, or perhaps
laceration of the bursal ligament of the joint, which is lax and
weak, but a laceration of those strong tendinous ligaments,
which connect the lower end of the tibia with the astragalus
and os calcis, and which constitute in great measure the ligamentous strength of the joint of the ancle.

This is the case, when, by leaping or jumping, the fibula
breaks in the weak part already mentioned; that is, within
two or three inches of its lower extremity. When this happens,
the inferior fractured end of the fibula falls inward toward the
tibia, that extremity of the bone which forms the outer ancle
is turned somewhat outward and upward, and the tibia having
lost its proper support, and not being of itself capable of steadily
preserving its true perpendicular bearing, is forced off from
the astragalus inwards, by which means the weak bursal, or
common ligament of the joint, is violently stretched, if not
torn, and the strong ones, which fasten the tibia to the astragalus
and os calcis, are always lacerated; thus producing at the
same time a perfect fracture and a partial dislocation, to which
is sometimes added a wound in the integuments, made by the
bone at the inner ancle. By this means and indeed as a necessary
consequence, all the tendons which pass behind or under, or
are attached to the extremities of the tibia and fibula, or os
calcis, have their natural direction and disposition so altered,

3. *Ibid.*, Vol. I, pp. 327–329.

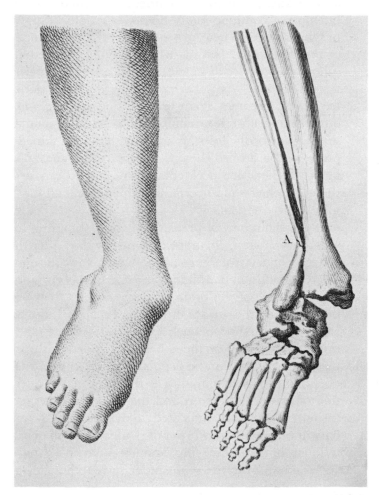

FIG. 74. Pott's fracture. From: *The Chirurgical Works of Percivall Pott*, Vol. I, p. 327

that instead of performing their appointed actions, they all
contribute to the distortion of the foot, and that by turning it
outward and upward.

[SOME COMPLICATIONS OF HEAD INJURIES INCLUDING
"POTT'S PUFFY TUMOR"][4]

It is no very uncommon thing for a smart blow on the head
to produce some immediate bad symptoms, which after a short
space of time disappear, and leave the patient perfectly well.
A slight pain in the head, a little acceleration of pulse, a vertigo

4. *Ibid.*, Vol. I, pp. 40–41.

and sickness, sometimes immediately follow such accident, but do not continue many hours, especially if any evacuation has been used. These are not improbably owing to a slight commotion of the brain, which having suffered no material injury thereby, soon cease. But if, after an interval of some time, the same symptoms are renewed; if the patient, having been well, becomes again feverish and restless, and that without any new cause; if he complains of being languid and uneasy, sleeps disturbedly, loses his appetite, has a hot skin, a hard quick pulse, and a flushed, heated countenance; and neither irregularity of diet, nor accidental cold, have been productive of these; mischief is most certainly impending, and that most probably under the scull.

If the symptoms of pressure, such as stupidity, loss of sense, voluntary motion, etc. appear some few days after the head has suffered injury from external mischief, they do most probably imply an effusion of a fluid somewhere: this effusion may be in the substance of the brain, in its ventricles, between its membranes, or on the surface of the dura mater; and which of these is the real situation of such extravasation, is a matter of great uncertainty, none of them being attended with any peculiar mark or sign that can be depended upon as pointing it out precisely; but the inflammation of the dura mater, and the formation of matter between it and the scull, in consequence of contusion, is generally indicated and preceded by one which I have hardly ever known to fail; I mean a puffy, circumscribed, indolent tumor of the scalp, and a spontaneous separation of the pericranium from the scull under such tumor.

[POTT'S SUMMARY OF THE DISEASE OF THE SPINE WHICH BEARS HIS NAME][5]

From an attentive examination of these morbid appearances, and of their effects in different subjects, and under different circumstances, the following observations, tending not only to illustrate and explain the true nature of the disease in question, but also to throw light on others of equal importance, may, I think, be made.

1. That the disease which produces these effects on the spine, and the parts in its vicinity, is what is in general called the scrophula; that is, that same kind of indisposition as occasions the thick upper lip, the tedius obstinate ophthalmy, the in-

5. *Ibid.*, Vol. III, pp. 287–293.

FIG. 75. Pott's disease. From: *The Chirurgical Works of Percivall Pott*, Vol. III, Plate II

durated glands under the chin and in the neck, the obstructed mesentery, the hard dry cough, the glairy swellings of the wrist and ancles, the thickened ligaments of the joints, the enlargement and caries of the bones, etc. etc. etc.

2. That this disease, by falling on the spine, and the parts connected with it, is the cause of a great variety of complaints, both general and local.

3. That when these complaints are not attended with an alteration of the figure of the back bone, neither the real seat, nor true nature of such distemper are pointed out by the general symptoms; and consequently, that they frequently are unknown, at least while the patient lives.

4. That when by means of this distemper an alteration is produced in the figure of the back bone, that alteration is different in different subjects, and according to different circumstances.

5. That when the ligaments and cartilages of the spine become the seat of the disorder, without any affection of the vertebrae, it sometimes happens that the whole spine, from the lowest vertebrae of the neck downwards, gives way laterally, forming sometimes one great curve to one side, and sometimes a more irregular figure, producing general crookedness and deformity of the whole trunk of the body, attended with many marks of ill health.

6. That these complaints, which are by almost every body supposed to be the effect of the deformity merely, are really occasioned by that distempered state of the parts within the thorax, which is at the same time the cause both of the deformity and of the want of health.

7. That the attack is sometimes on the bodies of some of the vertebrae; and that when this is the case, ulceration or erosion of the bone is the consequence, and not enlargement.

8. That when this erosion or caries seizes the body or bodies of one or more of the vertebrae, it sometimes happens that the particular kind of curvature which makes the subject of these sheets is the consequence.

9. That this curvature, which is always from within outward, is caused by the erosion or destruction of part of the body or bodies of one or more of the vertebrae; by which means that immediately above the distemper, and that immediately below it, are brought nearer to each other than they should be, the body of the patient bends forward, the spine is curved from within outward, and the tuberosity appears behind, occasioned by the protrusion of the spinal processes of the distempered vertebrae.

10. That according to the degree of carious erosion, and according to the number of vertebrae affected, the curve must be less or greater.

11. That when the attack is made upon the dorsal vertebrae, the sternum and ribs, for want of proper support, necessarily give way, and other deformity, additional to the curve, is thereby produced.

12. That this kind of caries is always confined to the bodies of the vertebrae, seldom or never affecting the articular processes.

13. That without this erosive destruction of the bodies of the vertebrae, there can be no curvature of the kind which I am speaking of; or, in other words, that erosion is the *sine qua non* of this disease; that although there can be no true curve without caries, yet there is, and that not infrequently, caries without curve.

14. That the caries with curvature and useless limbs, is most frequently of the cervical or dorsal vertebrae; the caries without curve, of the lumbal, though this is by no means constant or necessary.

15. That in the case of carious spine, without curvature, it most frequently happens, that internal abscesses and collections of matter are formed, which matter makes its way outward, and appears in the hip, groin, or thigh; or being detained within the body, destroys the patient; the real and immediate cause of whose death is seldom known, or even rightly guessed at, unless the dead body be examined.

16. That what are commonly called lumbal and psoas abscesses, are not infrequently produced in this manner, and therefore when we use these terms, we should be understood to mean only a description of the course which such matter has pursued in its way outward, or the place where it makes its appearance externally, the terms really meaning nothing more, nor conveying any precise idea of the nature, seat, or origin of a distemper subject to great variety, and from which variety its very different symptoms and events, in different subjects, can alone be accounted for.

17. That contrary to the general opinion, a caries of the spine is more frequently a cause than an effect of these abscesses.

18. That the true curvature of the spine, from within outward, of which the paralytic, or useless state of the lower limbs, is a too frequent consequence, is itself but *one* effect of a distempered spine; such case being always attended with a number of complaints which arise from the same cause: the generally-received opinion, therefore, that all the attending symptoms are

derived from the curvature, considered abstractedly, is by no means founded in truth, and may be productive of very erroneous conduct.

19. That in the case of true curvature, attended with useless limbs, there never is a *dislocation*, properly to be so called, but that the alteration in the figure of the back-bone is caused solely by the erosion, and destruction of a part of one or more of the corpora vertebrarum; and, that as there can be no true curvature without caries, it must be demonstrably clear, that there must have been a distempered state of parts previous to such erosion; from all which it follows, that this distemper, call it by what name you please, ought to be regarded as the original cause of the whole; that is, of the caries, of the curvature, and all the attendant mischiefs, be they what they may, general or particular; a consideration, as it appears to me, of infinite importance to all such infants and young children, as show either from their general complaints, or from their shape, a tendency to this kind of evil; and whose parents and friends generally content themselves with a swing, or piece of iron machinery, and look no further.

20. That whoever will consider the real state of the parts when a caries has taken place, and the parts surrounding it are in a state of ulceration, must see why none of the attempts, by means of swings, screws, etc., can possibly do any good, but on the contrary, if they act so as to produce any effect at all, it must be a bad one.

21. That the discharge, by means of the issues, produces in due time (more or less under different circumstances) a cessation of the erosion of the bones; that this is followed by an incarnation, by means of which the bodies of the vertebrae which had been the seat of the disease, coalesce, and unite with each other, forming a kind of anchylosis.

22. That the different degrees and extent of the caries, in different subjects, must render all attempts to cure uncertain, both as to the time required, and as to the ultimate event: the least and smallest degree will (every thing else being equal) be soonest relieved and cured: the larger and more extensive will require more time; and where the rottenness is to a great degree, and all the surrounding parts in a state of distempered ulceration, it must foil all attempts, and destroy the patient.

23. That when two or more vertebrae are affected, forming a large curve, however perfect the success may be with regard to

the restoration of health and limbs, yet the curvature will and must remain, in consequence of the union of the bones with each other.

24. That the useless state of the limbs is by no means a consequence of the altered figure of the spine, or of the disposition of the bones with regard to each other, but merely of the caries: of this truth there needs no other proof, than what may be drawn from the cure of a large and extensive curvature, in which three or more vertebrae were concerned: in this the deformity always remains unaltered and unalterable, notwithstanding the patient recovers both health and limbs.

CHAPTER 34

John Hunter
(1728–1793)

"I think your solution is just; but why think? Why not try the experiment?" [1]

Among all the figures in medicine, John Hunter is one of the truly great. A man of incredible breadth, he extended the horizons not only of surgery, but of medicine and of science as a whole. Yet no career had a less promising beginning. As a child he was incorrigible. Badly spoiled, lazy, indifferent to learning, given to tantrums, he reached maturity without vocation, training, or apparent inclination. His later writings reflect his lack of scholarship. Although a great teacher, he never attained fluency or ease as a lecturer. His crude exterior and irascible personality made enemies of his colleagues. Despite it all he became a great anatomist, a pioneer in the fields of physiology and pathology, and an outstanding surgeon. More than any other single figure, he brought science into surgery and medicine. Much has been written of Hunter; but so numerous are his individual contributions, so contradictory his personal traits, that an evaluation of the whole is difficult to achieve. But of this there can be no doubt, he belongs to the great.

John Hunter was born at Long Calderwood, a small farm in Scotland, not far from Glasgow, the youngest of ten children. His thrifty and God-fearing Scotch parents struggled to provide for this brood against illness and want. Despite their poverty, they imbued the children with high standards and aspirations. Tragedy as well as hardship dogged their years; three of the offspring died in childhood and four in early adulthood, chiefly from pulmonary disease. The two sons who survived were the famed brothers, William and John; and the sister became the mother of the great physician and pathologist, Mathew Baillie.

William Hunter was ten years older than John, and cast from a different mold. He was gentle, studious, and correct. Diligent in school, he was granted a scholarship at Glasgow College, which he attended for five years. Intended

1. From Hunter's letter to Jenner, August 2, 1775.

FIG. 76. Reproduction of Sir Joshua Reynolds' portrait of John Hunter. By courtesy of the President and Council of the Royal College of Surgeons of England.

at first for the ministry, he found himself, as a matter of conscience, unworthy of the calling, and turned to medicine instead. He worked with William Cullen, then a small town practitioner, who subsequently became a most influential physician and one of the founders of the Medical School of Glasgow. Cullen was greatly taken with Hunter and invited him to partnership with him, which offer, however, was not accepted. In describing Hunter, Cullen wrote: "His conversation was remarkably lively and agreeable, and his whole conduct was more strictly and steadily correct than that of any young person I have ever known," After attending the lectures of the first of the three Alexander Monros in Edinburgh for a year, William went to London where he worked with

Smellie, the famous obstetrician, who came from the same county in Scotland as did the Hunters. Later, he became assistant to the anatomist and obstetrician, James Douglas, and enrolled under this master as a student in St. George's Hospital. After Douglas' death, William Hunter began to lecture on surgery and anatomy. He introduced the "European" method in which the students did their own dissections. His school became famous, and he was renowned as surgeon and anatomist, but particularly as an obstetrician. He subsequently received a degree in physic from Glasgow College by which he was qualified as a physician. He then resigned from the Corporation of Surgeons, and became *Doctor* Hunter. He was a highly respected gentleman, and ater was appointed Physician Extraordinary to the Queen.

William Hunter, although eclipsed by his younger brother, made important scientific contributions. He was first to describe arteriovenous fistula, wrote numerous papers, and published a magnificent atlas of *The Anatomy of the Gravid Uterus* which has never since been surpassed. It was this work which led to the estrangement of the two brothers. William was embroiled in many acrimonious controversies with other surgeons and anatomists on the matter of priority of authorship. When his atlas was published he paid tribute to the excellence of the dissections made by John, which formed the material upon which the book was based. John apparently felt that he had been slighted, and five years later bitterly denounced his brother in a letter to the Royal Society. The coolness persisted until William died in 1783, although John ministered to him in his final illness, and was deeply grieved at his passing.

John Hunter's beginnings, as has been stated, were quite different. Of his childhood, the following two characterizations are revealing. His elder sister wrote of him, ". . . he was extremely indulged, and so humoursome that he would often, when a pretty big boy, sit for hours together crying when he could not get what he wanted; and could not be taught to read but with the greatest difficulty, and long after the age when other children read English fluently, and have even made some progress in Latin."[2] And later, his niece said, "He would do nothing but what he liked, and neither liked to be taught reading nor writing nor any kind of learning, but rambling amongst the woods, braes, etc., looking after Birds'-nests, comparing their eggs—number, size, marks, and other peculiarities; . . ."[3] Hunter, himself, said of his childhood, "When I was a boy, I wanted to know all about the clouds and the grasses, and why the leaves changed colour in the autumn; I watched the ants, bees, birds, tadpoles, and caddis-worms; I pestered people with questions about what nobody knew or cared anything about."[4]

At the age of twenty, after several false starts, he wrote to his brother Wil-

2. Stephen Paget: *John Hunter*, London, T. Fisher Unwin, 1897, p. 31.
3. *Ibid.*, p. 35.
4. *Ibid.*, p. 27.

liam, asking if he might come to join him in London. To this, William very cordially assented, and this marked the beginning of John's career. He was set to the task of preparing anatomical dissections, and proved to be amazingly proficient. He had found his *metier*. Throwing himself into anatomical studies with the enthusiasm and tireless energy that was to prove characteristic of him, he literally worked day and night, and was soon making original obser-

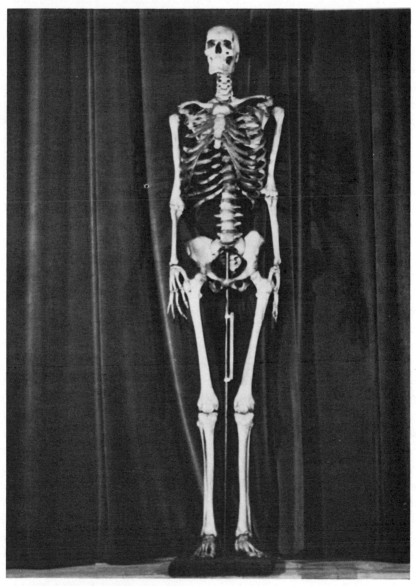

FIG. 77. The skeleton of Charles Byrne, the Irish Giant. By courtesy of the President and Council of the Royal College of Surgeons of England.

vations of primary importance. He listened to William's lectures and, in the summers when no teaching was done, followed Cheselden at Chelsea Hospital and, later, Pott at St. Bartholomew's. Determined now on a career in surgery, he enrolled as a pupil in St. George's Hospital in 1754. The following year William, wishing for his brother to gain some polish, had him enrolled at the Oxford University. But this effort was doomed to failure, and after two months he returned to London. "They wanted to make an old woman of me;" he said later, "or that I should stuff Latin and Greek at the University; but these schemes I cracked like so many vermin as they came before me."

By this time, Hunter's thirst for scientific knowledge became insatiable. Anatomy alone no longer satisfied him. He must probe in their entirety the secrets of life. Animals of every sort were dissected to find their similarities as well as their differences. Function must be understood, and he devised countless experiments on man, beasts, birds, fishes, and even plants—simple experiments, yet strikingly ingenious and imaginative. Nor was normal physiology sufficient. He had to know the derangements in form and action wrought by injury and disease. So he drove himself, endlessly and tirelessly, beyond the endurance of even his rugged constitution.

An attack of pneumonia in his thirty-second year led to the threat of that scourge of the Hunters, phthisis. Rest and escape from the putrid air of the dissecting rooms was needed, and again William rose to the occasion. The Seven Years' War was in progress, and through friendship in high places he secured a commission for John as an army surgeon. For two years he served at Belle Isle in France and in Portugal, and acquired the familiarity with war wounds and their sequelae that was to provide material for his last and greatest work. Between times he continued his studies of nature, every change of flora and fauna providing him with new objects for investigation.

When John returned to London—on half his army pay—he found his place in William's school occupied, so he branched out on his own, in the private practice of surgery. But a practice was hard to come by, and he opened his own school of anatomy. And his scientific investigations went on. He was convinced that two diseases could not exist in one part at the same time. He was equally certain that gonorrhea and syphilis were different manifestations of the same disease. To prove the point he inoculated himself with gonorrheal pus, not knowing that a chancre was also hidden within the urethra from whence the pus was taken. When syphilis developed it proved to him that his ideas were right. To what extent this infection contributed to the vascular disease from which he later suffered and eventually died, can only be speculated upon. On another occasion he ruptured an achilles tendon as he was dancing. Refusing to submit to the usual treatment by bed-rest and immobilization, he continued up and about with the knee extended and the heel elevated. This, of course, led to experiments on the healing of tendons during which he

Fig. 78. The spur of a cock transplanted into the comb. Hunter refers to this in his *Treatise on the Natural History of the Human Teeth*, and in his *Treatise on the Blood*. By courtesy of the President and Council of the Royal College of Surgeons of England.

divided tendons subcutaneously—a tenotomy technique to come into surgical vogue many years later.

Despite the slow growth of his practice, honors and recognition began to come to John Hunter. He was elected a Fellow of the Royal Society in 1767, ten years before William attained this distinction. The following year he was elected Surgeon to St. George's Hospital, which not only gave him a much needed connection, but also enabled him to take hospital pupils in surgery, then a recognized source of income for staff members. Shortly after his election he was made a member of the Corporation of Surgeons, thus fully qualified after twenty years of indefatigable preparation.

His first book, *Treatise on the Natural History of the Human Teeth* (1771), was published about this time, the profits from which, it is said, were used to pay the costs of his wedding. His bride was twenty-nine, he was forty-three, but the marriage was a happy one. Ann Home had charm, intelligence, and gaiety, and she made him an excellent wife. Few women could have put up with the biazrre surroundings and the drives and whims of her husband, but she maintained a life of serenity and intense social activity. Four children were born to them, but two died in infancy. Neither the son or daughter who survived had children of their own.

The remaining years of his life were full, indeed. Practice grew slowly but steadily until eventually it became as large as he could manage. "As to my business, it is very nearly what I want, because it very nearly gets me what I want; beyond which I have no ambition." Hospital work and teaching occupied considerable time. Still dissatisfied with the prevailing teaching of surgery in London, he began his courses of public lectures on the Principles of Surgery. His dissections and experiments went feverishly forward. He had already started building his famed collection of natural history which subsequently became the prized possession of the Royal College of Surgeons. For this and for his experiments, he expended huge sums of money and, even in the days when his income was large, it never sufficed for these purposes. Space was also required, and, in the difficult years of struggle for a livelihood, he bought a piece of land in the country outside of London called Earl's Court, and built a house which served as laboratory and museum. Here he kept his amazing variety of domesticated and wild beasts, birds, fish, bees, and other animal forms, to say nothing of his botanical specimens.

As Hunter's collection grew, more and more space was needed. He purchased a large house in Leicester Square, together with a neighboring house and the ground between. He built into this space, converting the whole into a huge, rambling structure to house laboratories, lecture rooms, museum and printing shops (he published most of his own books), as well as living quarters and the necessary stables, servant quarters, and work rooms. The menage included some fifty persons, and the upkeep was terrific. His practice grew with his reputation as did also his income, but, regardless of how much he earned, it never sufficed for the innumerable demands, and he was in constant debt. At his death, his widow was left unprovided for.

After Pott's death, Hunter became the leading surgeon of London, and his consultations were greatly in demand. He was appointed Deputy Surgeon General of the Army in 1786, and, three years later, Surgeon General of the

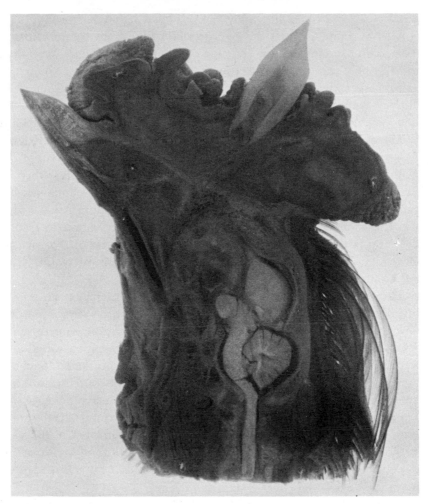

Fig. 79. Successful implantation of human tooth into the comb of a cock. From a specimen in the Hunterian Museum. By courtesy of the President and Council of the Royal College of Surgeons of England.

Army and Inspector General of Hospitals. Honors came to him from all parts of the Empire and the Continent. But the teaching, hospital work, scientific studies, and writing continued unabated.

The amazing achievements of this remarkable man become even more incredible with the story of his declining health. Shortly before the beginning of his first course of lectures, he had his first symptoms of angina pectoris, and from that time onward he suffered further attacks with constantly increasing severity and frequency. He did not know their cause but he recorded their subjective manifestations in detail. He recognized the role of emotional disturbances in initiating the anginal episodes and said, "My life is in the hands of any rascal who chooses to annoy me." The words were prophetic. In a quarrel with his colleagues at St. George's Hospital as to the teaching to be carried on in that institution, his veracity was challenged. Anger overwhelmed him, and in a few minutes he was dead.

His labors had indeed been prodigous. He dissected over 500 different varieties of living creatures, from insects to whales. His experiments covered almost every conceivable facet of normal and morbid function. He assembled a magnificent collection of biological specimens, now the property of the Royal College of Surgeons, that Professor F. Wood Jones called "John Hunter's Unwritten Book."[5] "It is the medium by which he sought to express those great principles of life, which he so profoundly understood, but which neither by speech nor by writing could he make clear to his contemporaries."[6] He pioneered in the sciences of geology and paleontology and, again to quote Dr. Jones: " . . . it is true to say that had he left no other record of his genius than his work on geology and his great collection of fossils, he would still rank among the founders of modern science."[7]

John Hunter's contributions toward the advancement of surgery have probably not been surpassed by any individual before or after his time. He made surgery scientific. His rejection of a formal education proved beneficial in that he approached the subject without preconceived ideas. His observations were objective, and references to the long-held humoral concepts are almost entirely absent from his writings. The individual contributions are too numerous to mention, ranging as they do over the extensive fields of hemorrhage, shock, blood coagulation, the treatment of wounds, inflammation, hernia, phlebitis, aneurysm, venereal diseases, transplantation of tissues, artificial respiration, and many others. It is hardly possible, indeed, to trace the development of any phase of surgery without meeting, as one of the pioneers, the name of John Hunter.

Hunter wrote three books in addition to the treatise on the teeth which already has been mentioned. *Venereal Diseases*, published in 1786, deals exhaustively with this subject. His *Observations on Certain Parts of the Animal Oeconomy* is a compilation of papers which had been published previously in the *Philosophical Transactions*. His last and most important work, *Treatise on Blood, Inflammation, and Gun-Shot Wounds*, appeared posthumously, and represents observations going back thirty years to his military experiences at Belle Isle. This is a remarkable work. It reveals the wide range of his knowledge and the observations and experiments on which it is based. Nowhere

5. F. Wood Jones: "John Hunter's Unwritten Book," *Lancet*, 261: 778–790, 1951.
6. *Ibid.*
7. F. Wood Jones: "John Hunter as a Geologist," *Annals of the Royal College of Surgeons of England*, 12: 219–245, 1953.

does he depend upon earlier authorities; countless prevalent ideas as to physiology and pathology he proved to be in error. Despite the tenacity of the humoral concepts even long after his time, he, significantly, scarcely gives mention to them. This gives the work a definitely modern approach. So vast is the wealth of material it contains that nothing less than its actual perusal can give any appreciation of its magnitude.

After Hunter's death in 1793, his brother-in-law, Sir Everard Home, became custodian of his unpublished notes and manuscripts, data which covered many thousands of pages. Some thirty years later this invaluable material was burned by Home. Various reasons are ascribed for this apparently shocking act of vandalism. It is implied by some that Home had published some of it under his own name, and took this means of destroying the evidence. Others have suggested that, despite his protestations of devotion to Hunter, he was jealous of his pre-eminence and took this means of reducing his stature. A more charitable view is that Home burned the papers to protect the memory of Hunter from the charge of heretical beliefs, which are certainly implied in his statements concerning genesis and creation.

Whatever the reasons, the loss was great, but there was some salvage. William Clift, faithful assistant to Hunter and subsequently first custodian of the Collection, had kept copies of some of the notes and preserved them for posterity. These were later published by Sir Richard Owen under the title *Essays and Observations on Natural History, Anatomy, Physiology, Psychology, and Geology* (1841).

John Hunter's writings, as were also probably his lectures, are difficult to comprehend because of his peculiarly obscure style. They reveal the glaring deficiencies in his early education. Furthermore, he applied connotations to otherwise familiar words which were without precedent or authority. It is for this reason, perhaps, that few of his contemporaries were aware of his great contributions to the body of scientific knowledge, and it was only through the paraphrasing by some dedicated disciples and students of his works that his ideas gained wider appreciation and acceptance. His involved style is exemplified in the quotation below on the management of gunshot wounds.

Hunter's influence did not cease with his death, nor was it limited to his publications. His many pupils carried his teachings far and wide. The succeeding generation of British surgeons, which brought world leadership to its country, were all pupils of Hunter. This included men like Clift, Cline, Abernethy, Blizard, and Astley Cooper. Edward Jenner, humanity's greatest single benefactor, who released mankind from the scourge of smallpox, was not only a "house pupil" of Hunter, and also a collaborator in the investigative work, but remained a lifelong friend and confidant. America, too, benefited from Hunter's teachings. John Morgan and William Shippen, Jr., the cofounders of the first medical school in North America, what is now the Medical Faculty of the University of Pennsylvania, both came under the Hunters' influence, as did also Philip Syng Physick, sometimes called the Father of American Surgery.

ᔥ ᔥ ᔥ
ᔥ ᔥ ᔥ
[Hunter's most familiar contribution of purely surgical import is his operation for popliteal aneurysm. The surgeons of his time either refused entirely to operate or, if of sufficient courage, ligated the artery immediately above the aneurysmal sac. This often entailed the necessity of tying through a diseased portion of the vessel with subsequent death from hemorrhage. Having convinced himself, from repeated animal experimentation, that the collateral circulation would support viability of the extremity after ligation of the femoral artery in the thigh, he raised the question, "Why not tie it up higher in the sound parts, where it is tied in amputation, and preserve the limb?" This he did, as was described in 1793 by Sir Everard Home from whose article the following brief excerpts are taken.]

AN ACCOUNT OF MR. HUNTER'S METHOD OF PERFORMING THE OPERATION FOR THE CURE OF THE POPLITEAL ANEU-RISM.[8]

Mr. Hunter, from having made these observations, was led to propose, that in this operation the artery should be taken up in the anterior part of the thigh, at some distance from the diseased part, so as to diminish the risk of haemorrhage, and admit of the artery being more readily secured, should any such accident happen. The force of the circulation being thus taken off from the aneurismal sac, the progress of the disease would be stopped; and he thought it probable, that if the parts were left to themselves, the sac, with its contents, might be absorbed, and the whole of the tumour removed, which would render any opening into the sac unnecessary.

Upon this principle Mr. Hunter performed the operation at St. George's Hospital.

8. From the *Transactions of a Society for the Improvement of Medical and Chirurgical Knowledge*, Vol. 1, 1793, pp. 138–181. Also in *The Works of John Hunter*, edited by James F. Palmer, London, Longmans, Rees, Orme, Brown, Green, and Longman, 1837, Vol. III, pp. 594–612.

The patient was a coachman, forty-five years of age; he was admitted into the hospital in December 1785, with a popliteal aneurism, which he had first perceived three years previous to his admission, and had observed it gradually to increase during the whole of that period. It was so large as to distend the two hamstrings laterally, and make a very considerable rising between them; the pulsation was very distinct, and to be felt on every side of the tumour. The leg and foot of that side were so swelled as to be much thicker than the other, and were of a mottled brown colour; the swelling was not of the oedematous kind, but felt firm and brawny, probably from the extravasation of coagulable lymph; the leg retained its natural shape, excepting that it was larger. Previous to performing the operation, a tourniquet was applied upon the upper part of the thigh, but not tightened, that the parts might be left as much in their natural situation as possible.

The operation was begun by making an incision on the anterior and inner part of the thigh, rather below its middle, which incision was continued obliquely across the inner edge of the sartorius muscle, and made large, to give room for the better performing of whatever might be thought necessary in the course of the operation. The fascia which covers the artery was then laid bare about three inches in length, after which the artery itself was plainly felt. A slight incision, about an inch long, was then made through this fascia, along the side of the vessel, and the fascia dissected off; by this means the artery was exposed. Having disengaged the artery from its lateral connections by the knife, and from the other adhering parts by the help of a thin spatula, a double ligature was passed behind it, by means of an eyed probe. The doubling of the ligature brought through by the probe, was cut so as to form two separate ligatures. The artery was now tied by both these ligatures, but so slightly as only to compress the sides together. A similar application of ligature was made a little lower. The reason for having four ligatures was to compress such a length of artery as might make up for the want of tightness, it being wished to avoid great pressure on the vessel at any one part. The ends of the ligatures were carried directly out at the wound, the sides of which were now brought together, and supported by sticking-plaster and a linen roller, that they might unite by the first intention.

After leaving the hospital the man returned to his usual occupation of driving a hackney coach, and being, from the nature of his employment, much exposed to cold, in March 1787 he was seized with a fever of the remittent kind, which carried him off. He had not made any complaint of the limb on which the operation had been performed from the time of his leaving the hospital.

He died on the 1st of April, 1787, fifteen months after the operation, and leave was procured, with some trouble and considerable expense, to examine the limb seven days after death, at which time it was entirely free from putrefaction.

[John Hunter's most important book, *A Treatise on the Blood, Inflammation, and Gun-Shot Wounds*, was written in 1793 and in it for the first time he published his observations on war injuries which he had made during his military service thirty-two years earlier. In his dedication to this book, addressed "To the King," he wrote:[9]]

May it please Your Majesty,

In the year 1761 I had the honour of being appointed by Your Majesty a Surgeon on the Staff in the expedition against Belleisle.

In the year 1790 Your Majesty honoured me with one of the most important appointments in the medical department of the army, in fulfilling the duties of which every exertion shall be called forth to render me deserving of the trust reposed in me, and not unworthy of Your Majesty's patronage.

The first of these appointments gave me extensive opportunities of attending to gun-shot wounds, of seeing the errors and defects in that branch of military surgery, and of studying to remove them. It drew my attention to inflammation in general, and enabled me to make observations which have formed the basis of the present Treatise. That office which I now hold has afforded me the means of extending my pursuits, and of laying this work before the public.

As the object of this book is the improvement of surgery in general, and particularly of the branch of it which is peculiarly directed to the service of the army, I am led by my situation, my duty, and my feelings, to address it, with all humility, to Your Majesty.

9. *The Works of John Hunter*, edited by James F. Palmer, London, Longmans, etc., 1837, Vol. III, pp. ix–x.

That Your Majesty may long live to enjoy the love and
esteem of a happy people, is the fervent wish of

Your Majesty's

Most faithful subject,

And most dutiful Servant,

JOHN HUNTER.

Leicester Square,
May 20, 1793.

[Hunter's essential innovation was his belief that war wounds
were essentially the same as wounds in general. He therefore
deplored the dilatation of missile wounds and the attempt to
remove the foreign bodies. The following excerpt on this subject acquaints us with his views.]

OF THE TREATMENT OF GUN-SHOT WOUNDS.[10]

It has been hitherto recommended, and universally practised by almost every surgeon, to enlarge immediately upon
their being received, or as soon as possible, the external orifice of all gun-shot wounds made by musket-balls. So much
has this practice been recommended, that they have made
no discrimination between one gun-shot wound and another.
This would appear to have arisen, and to be still continued,
from an opinion that gun-shot wounds have a something peculiar to them, and of course are different from all other
wounds, and that this peculiarity is removed by the opening.
I own that I do not see any peculiarity. The most probable
way of accounting for the first introduction of this practice is
from the wound in general being small, and nearly of a size
from one end to the other; also the frequency of extraneous
bodies being forced into these wounds by the ball, or the ball
itself remaining there; for the way in which these wounds are
made is by the introduction of extraneous body, which is left
there, if it has not made its way through, so that the immediate cause of the wound makes a lodgement for itself, often
carrying before it clothes, and even the parts of the body
wounded, such as the skin, &c. From hence it would naturally
appear at first view that there was an immediate necessity to
search after those extraneous bodies, which very probably led
the surgeon to do it; and in general the impossibility of finding them, and even of extracting them when found, without

10. *Ibid.*, pp. 541–542, 548–550.

dilatation, gave the first idea of opening the mouths of the wounds. But from experience they altered this practice in part, and became not so desirous of searching after these extraneous bodies; for they found that it was oftener impossible to find them than could at first have been imagined, and when found, that it was not possible to extract them, and that afterwards these bodies were brought to the skin by the parts themselves, and those that could not be brought to the external surface in this way were such as gave little or no trouble afterwards, such as balls. Yet they altered this practice only so far as respected the attempt to extract extraneous bodies; for when they found from experience that it was not necessary nor possible to extract these immediately, yet they did not see that it therefore was not necessary to take the previous or leading steps towards it.

The circumstance I have mentioned of gun-shot wounds being contused obliges most of them to suppurate, because in such cases there is more or less of a slough to be thrown off, especially at the orifice made by the entrance of the ball: there is therefore a freer passage for the matter, or any other extraneous substance, than the same-sized wound would have if made by a clean cutting instrument, even if not allowed to heal by the first intention.

From all which, if there is no pecularity in a gun-shot wound, I think this of dilating them, as a general practice, should be rejected at once; even if it were only for this reason, that few gun-shot wounds are alike, and therefore the same practice cannot apply to all.

This treatment of gun-shot wounds is diametrically opposite to a principle which is generally adopted in other cases, although not understood as a general rule, which is, that very few wounds of any kind require surgical treatment at their commencement, excepting with an opposite view from the above, viz. to heal them by the first intention. It is contrary to all the rules of surgery founded on our knowledge of the animal oeconomy to enlarge wounds simply as wounds. No wound, let it be ever so small, should be made larger, excepting when preparatory to something else, which will imply a complicated wound, and which is to be treated accordingly; it should not be opened because it is a wound, but because there is something necessary to be done which cannot be executed unless the wound is enlarged. This is common surgery, and ought also to be military surgery respecting gun-shot wounds.

As a proof of the inutility of opening gun-shot wounds as a general practice, I shall mention the cases of four Frenchmen and a British soldier, wounded on the day of the landing of our army on the island of Belleisle; and as this neglect rather arose from accident than design, there is no merit claimed from the mode of treatment.

A. B. was wounded in the thigh by two balls: one went quite through, the other lodged somewhere in the thigh, and was not found while he was under our care.

B. C. was shot through the chest: he spit blood for some little time.

C. D. was shot through the joint of the knee: the ball entered at the outer edge of the patella, crossed the joint under that bone, and came out through the inner condyle of the os femoris.

D. E. was shot in the arm: the ball entered at the inside of the insertion of the deltoid muscle, passed towards the head of the os humeris, then between the scapula and ribs, and lodged between the basis of the scapula and spinal processes, and was afterwards extracted. The man's arm was extended horizontally when the ball entered, which accounts for this direction.

These four men had not anything done to their wounds for four days after receiving them, as they had hid themselves in a farm house all that time after we had taken possession of the island; and when they were brought to the hospital their wounds were only dressed superficially, and they all got well.

A grenadier of the 30th regiment was shot through the arm; the ball seemed to pass between the biceps muscle and the bone; he was taken prisoner by the French. The arm swelled considerably, they fomented it freely, and a superficial dressing only was applied. About a fortnight after the accident he made his escape, and came to our hospital; but by that time the swelling had quite subsided, and the wounds healed; there only remained a stiffness in the joint of the elbow, which went off by moving it.

[The well-known experiments which Hunter conducted upon himself by inoculating himself with what he thought was gonorrheal pus and which led to an infection with syphilis are quoted in their entirety below. Although he does not use the first person, there can be no question that he speaks of himself. In the edition of Hunter's *Treatise on Venereal Disease*, published by Dr. Philip Ricord, the following annotation is found: "The author inoculated himself with the matter of gonorrhoea, and the consequence was the production of chancres, followed by bubo, and by secondary symptoms. The experiment is related, at length, in Part VI. Chap. II. Sect. 2, of the present work."[11]]

EXPERIMENTS MADE TO ASCERTAIN THE PROGRESS AND EFFECTS OF THE VENEREAL POISON.[12]

To ascertain several facts relative to the venereal disease, the following experiments were made. They were begun in May, 1767.

Two punctures were made on the penis with a lancet dipped in venereal matter from a gonorrhoea; one puncture was on the glans, the other on the prepuce.

This was on a Friday; on the Sunday following there was a teasing itching in those parts, which lasted till the Tuesday following. In the mean time, these parts being often examined, there seemed to be a greater redness and moisture than usual, which was imputed to the parts being rubbed. Upon the Tuesday morning the parts of the prepuce where the puncture had been made were redder, thickened, and had formed a speck; by the Tuesday following the speck had increased, and discharged some matter, and there seemed to be a little pouting of the lips of the urethra, also a sensation in it in making water, so that a discharge was expected from it. The speck was now touched with lunar caustic, and afterwards dressed with calomel ointment. On Saturday morning the slough came off, and it was again touched, and another slough came off on the Monday following. The preceding night the glans had itched a good deal, and on Tuesday a white speck was observed where the puncture had been made; this speck, when examined, was found to be a pimple full of yellowish matter. This was now touched with the caustic, and dressed as the former. On Wednesday the sore on the prepuce was yellow, and therefore was again touched with caustic. On Friday both sloughs came off, and the sore on the prepuce looked red, and its basis not so hard; but on the Saturday it did not look quite so well,

11. John Hunter: *A Treatise on the Venereal Disease*, with copious additions by Dr. Philip Ricord .... Philadelphia, Blanchard & Lea, 1853, p. 35.
12. *Ibid.*, p. 401 ff.

and was touched again, and when that went off it was allowed to heal, as also the other, which left a dent in the glans. This dent on the glans was filled up in some months, but for a considerable time it had a bluish cast.

Four months afterwards the chancre on the prepuce broke out again, and very stimulating applications were tried; but these seemed not to agree with it, and nothing being applied, it healed up. This it did several times afterwards, but always healed up without any application to it. That on the glans never did break out, and herein also it differed from the other.

While the sores remained on the prepuce and glans a swelling took place in one of the glands of the right groin. I had for some time conceived an idea that the most effectual way to put back a bubo was to rub in mercury on that leg and thigh; and thus a current of mercury would pass through the inflamed gland. Here was a good opportunity of making the experiment. I had often succeeded in this way, but now wanted to put it more critically to the test. The sores upon the penis were healed before the reduction of the bubo was attempted. A few days after beginning the mercury in this method the gland subsided considerably. It was then left off, for the intention was not to cure it completely at present. The gland some time after began to swell again, and as much mercury was rubbed in as appeared to be sufficient for the entire reduction of the gland; but it was meant to do no more than to cure the gland locally, without giving enough to prevent the constitution from being contaminated.

About two months after the last attack of the bubo, a little sharp pricking pain was felt in one of the tonsils in swallowing anything, and on inspection a small ulcer was found, which was allowed to go on till the nature of it was ascertained, and then recourse was had to mercury. The mercury was thrown in by the same leg and thigh as before, to secure the gland more effectually, although that was not now probably necessary.

As soon as the ulcer was skinned over the mercury was left off, it not being intended to destroy the poison, but to observe what parts it would next affect. About three months after, copper-colored blotches broke out on the skin, and the former ulcer returned in the tonsil. Mercury was now applied the second time for those effects of the poison upon the constitution, but still only with a view to palliate.

It was left off a second time, and the attention was given to mark where it would break out next; but it returned again in the same parts. It not appearing that any farther knowledge was to be procured by only palliating the disease a fourth time in the tonsil, and a third time in the skin, mercury was now taken in a sufficient quantity, and for a proper time, to complete the cure.

The time the experiments took up, from the first insertion to the complete cure, was about three years.

The above case is only uncommon in the mode of contracting the disease, and the particular views with which some parts of the treatment were directed; but as it was meant to prove many things which, though not uncommon, are yet not attended to, attention was paid to all the circumstances. It proves many things, and opens a field for farther conjecture.

It proves, first, that matter from a gonorrhoea will produce chancres.

It makes it probable that the glans does not admit the venereal irritation so quickly as the prepuce. The chancre on the prepuce inflamed and suppurated in somewhat more than three days, and that on the glans in about ten. This is probably the reason why the glans did not throw off its sloughs so soon.

It renders it highly probable that to apply mercury to the legs and thighs is the best method of resolving a bubo; and, therefore, also the best method of applying mercury to assist in the cure, even when the bubo suppurates.

It also shows that buboes may be resolved in this way, and yet the constitution not be safe; and therefore that more mercury should be thrown in, especially in cases of easy resolution, than what simply resolves the bubo.

It shows that parts may be contaminated, and may have the poison kept dormant in them while under a course of mercury for other symptoms, but break out afterwards.

It also shows, that the poison having originally only contaminated certain parts, when not completely cured, can break out again only in these parts.

PART VII

EMINENT PRE-LISTERIANS

CHAPTER 35

Pierre-Joseph Desault (1744–1795) and French Surgery of the Eighteenth Century

"Two things are necessary to make a great surgeon, genius and experience. One maps its route, the other rectifies it; the two lend one another mutual asisstance in forming him. Without experience, genius would be ineffectively fertile; without genius, experience would not offer him anything but a sterile benefit." [1]

Although England's leadership in surgery during the greater part of the eighteenth century has not been seriously challenged, important men and contributions also emanated from France. Pierre Dionis, one of those who did much to advance the teaching of surgery, even went so far as to say: "Paris shone in furnishing better means of instruction [in surgery] than in any other city of Europe: public demonstrations were made there in three different localities, in the Royal Garden, at the École de Médicine, and at St. Côme, all three of which were given by sworn masters of surgery (*Maîtres Chirurgiens Jurez de Paris*), where they demonstrated with exactitude."[2] Later in the century, courses of lectures were arranged in the hospitals, as further opportunities for teaching. It is not to be wondered, therefore, that students came in great numbers from all of Europe to avail themselves of these offerings. A decisive development at this time was the liberation of surgery from the repressive control of the Faculty of Medicine of the University of Paris. A three-way struggle had been waged for several centuries between the Faculty of the École de Médecine, the surgeons of the Collège de St. Côme (surgeons of the long robe), and the barbers (surgeons of the short robe). The physicians of the Faculty, jealous of their prerogatives and fearful of the pretensions of the master surgeons, had succeeded, in 1660, in obtaining a parliamentary decree which wiped out the distinctions between the surgeons and barbers, erased the word "Collège" from St. Côme, and placed the

1. Xavier Bichat's Introduction to *Oeuvres chirurgicales, ou exposé de la doctrine et la pratique de P. J. Desault* par Xav. Bichat, Paris, Mequignon, 1801, Vol. I, p. v.
2. *Cours d'opération de chirurgie démontrées au jardin royal* par M. Dionis, fourth edition, edited by G. de la Faye, Paris, chez d'Houry, 1746.

barbers and surgeons together under complete subservience to the Faculty of Medicine. The story of the "liberation" of surgery from this bondage is a thrilling chapter in the history of the profession.

The elevation of the status of surgery in France is owing largely to the influence of King Louis XIV and to his great-grandson and successor, Louis XV. As early as 1672, Louis XIV ordained that public demonstrations in anatomy and of the operations of surgery should be given annually in the Royal Garden with "open doors and gratuitously, in order to facilitate for students of surgery the means of perfecting themselves in an art which he had always regarded as one of the most necessary in a State." This task was entrusted to Pierre Dionis, who carried it out faithfully for many years. To supplement his demonstrations, he published a treatise on anatomy, and his famous *Cours d'opérations de chirurgie, démontrées au jardin royal*, which went through many editions, was widely translated, and retained its popularity for half-a-century.

The second forward stride was also effected by Louis XIV, in gratitude to his *premier chirurgien*, M. Félix the Younger, who cured His Majesty (in 1686) of a troublesome and intractable fistula-in-ano by a successful operation. The surgeon was given a fee of 300,00 francs and an estate, and was elevated to the nobility. This high honor did much for the dignity and social status of the surgeon.

The "liberator" of French surgery was Georges Mareschal, son of an Irish soldier of fortune who had been obliged to leave Britain and take refuge in France where he died in poverty, leaving his thirteen-year-old orphan son, Georges, almost penniless. This boy, apprenticed to a provincial surgeon, subsequently wandered to Paris. Here, despite his lack of funds or influence, he succeeded in becoming a maître-juré (sworn master) of surgery, surgeon-in-chief to the Charité Hospital, and, ultimately, at the death of Félix, the *premier chirurgien du Roi*.

As friend and confidant of the king, and of his successor, Louis XV, Mareschal dedicated himself for the next thirty years to the improvement of the training and position of surgeons. He extended his influences, and his reforms, far beyond Paris to include all of France. In letters patent, the king declared that "those who practise purely the art of surgery should be held to practise a liberal art and shall enjoy all the provisions attached to such arts." Arrangements were made to establish schools of surgery in the various communities, with a master surgeon designated to "demonstrate publicly the principal details of the said art."

The final liberation of surgery from the domination of the Faculty of Medicine was effected by act of *Parlement* in 1724. In the same year, at the request of Mareschal, teaching of surgery was re-established at St. Côme. Five master surgeons were appointed to give public demonstrations, creating, in effect, a

Faculty of Surgery. The opposition to this action by the physicians of the Faculty of Medicine, and their subsequent rout, is vividly related by Garrison:

"Decked out in their scholastic robes, the physicians, headed by the dean of that Faculty, preceded by a beadle and an usher, marched to St. Côme in solemn array, in spite of the bitter cold weather, the snow and sharp sleet, which made their red robes almost unrecognizable. Cheering one another on with cries and oaths and followed by a great crowd of people, they at length ranged themselves in a long line against the wall, while the dean presented himself at the door of the Collège accompanied by the only anatomist of the Faculty, who stood behind him holding a skeleton. Cries and imprecations, knocks and threats to break down the door were only greeted by the jeers of the students from within, and when an usher tried to make himself heard as to what the surgeons owed the physicians, the people suddenly turned against these formalities, which they had once respected like a religion, and drove the doctors away without regard for their furs and costly raiment."[3]

Mareschal was aided in these and subsequent activities leading to the total emancipation of surgery by his disciple and, later, his successor as First Surgeon to the King, François de la Peyronie (1678–1747). This eminent surgical scholar and philanthropist came to Paris from Montpellier. It was due to him, according to Garrison, "that Paris became the surgical center of the world in the 18th century." The king, at the suggestion of these two leaders, created, in 1731, the Royal Academy of Surgery. This organization, with all other learned societies, was suppressed during the French Revolution, but was later revived as the present National Society of Surgery. The final step in this evolutionary process was taken in 1743 when Louis XV, at the instigation of Peyronie, issued the ordinance which separated the surgeons from the barbers and wigmakers, and limited the practice of surgery to those who were so specifically trained.

In the congenial atmosphere created by these successive significant and forward-looking steps, the practice of surgery flourished. A large number of notable surgeons participated in the advancement of knowledge and technique, their cumulative observations and their literary contributions combining to build an impressive whole. Jean-Louis Petit (1674–1750) was the most distinguished surgeon in Paris during the first half of the eighteenth century. He was truly precocious and even as a child he preferred anatomical dissection to playing with toys. Under the guidance of Alexis Littre, anatomist

3. Fielding H. Garrison: *An Introduction to the History of Medicine*, fourth edition, Philadelphia, W. B. Saunders Co., 1929, p. 393.

and surgeon who lived in the Petit home, the boy began to assist in the teaching of anatomy at the age of seven, and at eighteen was on the surgical staff of the army. Between campaigns he gave public demonstrations in anatomy and surgery. Ultimately reaching Paris, he qualified as a master surgeon, and assumed a foremost position in the surgical life of the city, where he excelled as a teacher, practitioner, and author.

During the second half of the eighteenth century the political storms which eventuated in the Revolution slowed, but did not halt, the progress of science and medicine in France. The impetus of the earlier dynamism persisted and important contributions were made by numerous figures in all of the fields. In this period the most influential surgeon was Pierre-Joseph Desault (1744–1795), who was equally distinguished as an educator. Despite the poverty of the large family into which he was born, he received a good education in his native village of Lure in the Haute-Saône. In these early years he displayed a leaning toward science and a proficiency in mathematics. These interests made him oppose his father's wish that he become a priest, and he chose surgery.

The limitations of the village surgeon to whom he was apprenticed impelled Desault to seek better training elsewhere, and he entered the school at Béfort. The promise he showed there induced him, after three years of study, to migrate to Paris, the center of the French surgical world. While he studied anatomy, he also attended the lectures in surgery at the Collège and the surgical operations in the large hospitals. Two years later, at the age of twenty-two, he began giving private lectures in anatomy, and shortly afterward, in surgery. Although handicapped by a poor delivery, the clarity of his ideas and the precision of his knowledge brought such success as to evoke the resentment of his elders who were chagrined to see the benches at the Collège empty as the students flocked to the private school of a young upstart, no older than most of those who came to hear him. The old regulations that medical teaching could only be given at the École de Médecine or the Collège de St. Côme were invoked, and Desault was ordered to desist. However, these restrictions were circumvented when a prominent physician lent his name under which the lectures could be given. Moreover, two of the chiefs of surgery, to their everlasting credit, supported Desault even to the point of themselves attending the sessions.

Desault initiated profound changes in the methods of anatomical teaching, rejecting illustrations and models and emphatically returning to observation of the dissected cadaver. His biographer, Xavier Bichat, credits him with having created surgical anatomy in France and carrying it toward perfection. This discipline embraced a knowledge of function and, very importantly, the recognition of pathological variations in addition to normal structure. These activities quickly brought him international renown as an anatomist, but his surgical reputation grew more slowly, largely because he lacked a major hospital appointment. Although he made important innovations, the clinical experience necessary to establish them had to be delegated to others. This was true of his method of treatment of fractured clavicle which is still very much in vogue. He introduced further improvements in the technique of amputation, including the reintroduction of arterial ligation, and in the surgical management of aneurysm.

These and many other contributions eventually brought Desault recognition as an outstanding surgeon. Despite the envy of the less able and the rigidity of the rules concerning appointments, he was admitted to the *Collége de Chirurgie* and was appointed professor of the *École Pratique*; shortly afterward he was nominated to the Royal Academy. The post of Chief Surgeon to the *Charité* Hospital was opened to him and, some six years later, he attained the pinnacle when he became Chief of Surgery at the *Hôtel-Dieu*, with its vast numbers of patients in dire need of surgical care.

Desault introduced a new form of clinical teaching in France. Utilizing the wealth of patient material now available to him, he taught from the bedside, rather than from the lectern. His classes were extremely popular, drawing students from all of Europe, and most of the famous surgeons of the ensuing period had profited from his teaching.

At the peak of his career, when Desault was acclaimed the "first surgeon of Europe," the march of events was interrupted by the explosion of the French Revolution. Denounced by one of his personal rivals, Desault was arrested, but, after three days of imprisonment, the popular outcry against this detention compelled his being restored to freedom. He attempted to resume his teaching but the *École de Médecine* and the *Collège de Chirurgie*, together with all other institutions of higher learning, had been closed by the Revolutionary government. In their place, the *École de Santé* (School of Health) had been created, in which both medicine and surgery were to be taught, and Desault was made professor of clinical surgery. He was not happy with the changes that had been wrought because of his disaffection with the combined teaching of surgery and medicine in the same institution. At about this time, the *dauphin*, a prisoner at the *Temple*, became seriously ill. Desault was called to treat him, and lavished his attentions on the royal patient. As he was so engaged, Desault himself became violently ill with fever and toxemia, and died on June 1, 1795, when only fifty-one years of age.

As an anatomist, Desault was little concerned with research but intensely devoted to its teaching as an essential preparation for surgical practice. As a surgeon, on the contrary, he made very many additions to the knowledge

FIG. 80

of pathology, and to treatment. New techniques, and, particularly, new instruments were devised to meet special problems. He published a *Treatise on Surgical Diseases*, together with his friend Chopart, but this book gave him little pleasure because of the minor role he had played in its preparation and also because his knowledge and ideas had become greatly expanded with his subsequent enormous clinical experience. Desault also started a *Journal de Chirurgie* (1791–1794) which presented his views in articles written by his most distinguished pupils. This journal went through four volumes, the last of which appeared after his death under the editorship of his beloved disciple and biographer, Xavier Bichat (1771–1802). This young scientific genius issued in 1801 a posthumous edition of the *Oeuvres chirurgicales* of Desault which he wrote entirely by himself, but which expounded the doctrines of his master.

Bichat, whose name and whose life were so closely linked to those of Desault, spanned, in his brief but brilliant career, the gap between surgery and medicine. Although his training was exclusively that of a surgeon, his interests embraced an immeasurably wider field. He decided, therefore, to abandon surgery in favor of medicine, saying, ". . . liberated for some time to the study of medicine, then to hospital practice, I no longer consider surgery as an essential basis of all medical knowledge, but as an important means of analogy in a mass of difficult cases, and as a guide without which the physician would often walk into danger; it has ceased to be a special object of my researches." This decision, however, was not made until 1798, only four years before his death. Thus, the greater part of his professional life was spent in surgery. For this reason, he must be included in this account of the great French surgeons of the eighteenth century.

Bichat's father was a provincial physician who had received his degree from Montpellier. A career in surgery was chosen by Xavier Bichat and an apprenticehsip was begun, but this was interrupted by the outbreak of war with Austria, and the young student was drawn into the army where he completed his practical training. Then attracted to Paris, he elected to study with Desault, who was at that time surgeon at the *Hôtel-Dieu*. In a very short time he won the admiration and confidence of his teacher who appointed him to a position in the hospital and took him into his home to live. During the final year of Desault's life, Bichat not only acted as his surgical assistant, but was also entrusted with the preparation of lecture material. It was at this time that he was appointed to the editorship of the *Journal de Chirurgie* which had been founded by Desault, but which languished because its originator lacked time and vigor to carry out these duties. Bichat published the final volumes of this journal, the last of which he had written entirely by himself, although still but twenty-three years of age.

After the death of his chief, Bichat became Desault's literary executor. He established a private school and laboratory where he taught anatomy, physiology, and operative techniques, and also carried out animal experimentation and anatomical studies on the cadaver. It was while he was completely engrossed in these scientific endeavors that he decided to abandon surgery and turn to medicine as a career.

Bichat died at the extremely early age of thirty-one (of tuberculous meningitis consequent upon years of pulmonary disease); but the few years allotted him were filled with prodigious effort and crowned with enormous achievement. His studies embraced all of anatomy, physiology, and pathology, from which he developed general concepts of morbid structure and function. His books, *Traité des membranes* (1800), *Recherches physiologiques sur la vie et la mort* (1800), and *l'Anatomie générale* (1801), presented his gradually expanding ideas. His emphasis on *tissues* as the units of which organs were composed definitely contributed to the acceptance of solid pathology. At his death, the great French physician, Corvisart, wrote to Napoleon, "No one has in so short a time produced so much and so well." And the First Consul responded by ordering that a monument be erected at the *Hôtel-Dieu* in honor of Desault and Bichat.

FRACTURE OF THE CLAVICLE[4]

I. Man shares with certain classes of quadrupeds an advantage which nature has refused to the majority; that is, in every sense, the extension of the movements of the upper extremity. The clavicle, a type of flying buttress placed between the chest and shoulder, is the mobile but solid center of these movements, in which one part is unable to act the instant in which its interruption of continuity ceases to offer them a point of support; from which it follows that the fracture of that bone, considered in the light of its functions, places, so to speak, the individual so affected in the numerous divisions of animals without clavicles.

II. Few of the maladies of this type occur as frequently as this one. The natural curvature of the clavicle, its location immediately beneath the skin, the lack of support in its middle part, the large proportion of its spongy tissue compared to its compact tissue, the frequency with which the prominence of the shoulder exposes it to the impact of outside forces; all concur to multiply it [the fracture], especially in that class of persons exposed by their status to violent movements of the upper extremity.

Thus, more often than in most similar injuries, the progress of the art [of healing] should be of interest; limited until now to ineffective methods, there have not yet been but imperfect results. Hippocrates had observed that a deformity almost always accompanies the consolidation; all authors have mentioned it after him; experience has confirmed it, and this complication

4. *Oeuvres chirurgicales . . . de P. J. Desault*, Vol. I, p. 63ff. Translation of excerpts from the French made by the authors.

has given birth, perhaps, to as many hypotheses to explain it, as researches to prevent it, when Desault proved that to the inadequacy of the treatment alone was due the lack of success, and that more methodically, the art could be as fortunate as in other fractures. In order to present with precision this point of his practice, I will examine the causes, varieties and the signs of fractures of the clavicle; the accidents to which it is susceptible; the nature and causes of the constant displacement of its fragments; the indications which arise from these causes, and the manner of satisfying them, be it during or after the reduction.

Reduction

XXII. Desault became convinced in 1768, that in order to reduce methodically the fracture of the clavicle it was necessary not only to bring, as is ordinarily done, the shoulder backward and upward, but above all outward, and that the force exerted in this last direction, should act horizontally, following the direction of the clavicle; just as in an oblique fracture of the thigh, one pulls in the direction of the bone to bring the fragments into place.

XXIII. The junction of the humerus to the clavicle by means of the scapula, communicates to the one the movements of the other; it is easy, by placing the pad of Paul of Aegina under the axilla to use the arm as a lever of the first order, by which the lower end, approximated to the trunk, separates at will, the upper, which maneuver in regard to the clavicle is what to the foot of the patient are the efforts made by the assistant who exerts tension in fracture of the leg.

The mode of reduction having been found, it was necessary to develop the proper bandage to maintain contact of the fragments. Desault thought that one could in the same procedure combine the two stages of treatment; that is to say, reduce and at the same time, maintain the reduction of the fracture. Here the art [of surgery] is indebted to him for the combined progress, I dare call it, of perfection. . . . (Fig. 81).

REMARKS AND OBSERVATIONS ON THE EXTIRPATION OF THE THYROID GLAND[5]

Obs. I. (Reported by Giraud). Jacqueline Hyoms, in 1784, on violently extending her head, experienced a very acute pain

5. *Ibid.*, Vol. II, pp. 298–306.

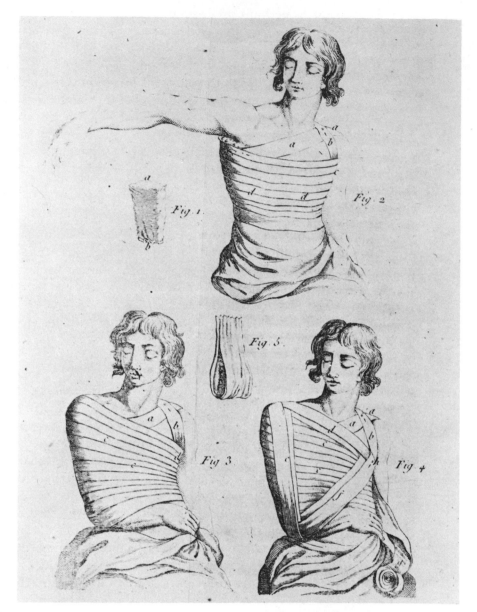

FIG. 81. Desault's bandage for fractured clavicle. From: *Oeuvres chirurgicales de P. J. Desault*

in the middle and anterior part of the neck, a pain which soon passed and left behind only a slight impairment in the movements. But three months later there was observed, presenting on the right side of the trachea, a small, firm, indolent tumor, without heat nor change of color of the skin, and exhibiting palpable pulsations indicating its position along the course of the common carotid artery.

Little inconvenienced by this tumor, the patient neglected it until June, 1788, at which time its growth became very rapid. It was treated without effect with internal and external emollients. In the center it soon showed a point of fluctuation, which on being opened with a knife, exuded a yellowish serous fluid. Three months later caustics were employed, but their action did nothing toward the cure, and finally tired of the inadequacy of the methods of treatment, the patient came to the *Hôtel-Dieu* on May 21, 1791.

At that time, the tumor was two inches in diameter, rounded, hard, fixed to the right side and to the middle part of the trachea; it displaced the sternomastoid muscle outward, pulsated palpably with each movement of the arteries, followed the movements of swallowing, and even slightly embarrassed the passage of solid foods. The patient eagerly wished to be relieved of this uncomfortable deformity, and decided immediately to submit to its extirpation, which had been presented to her as the only resort; neither the dangers nor the length [of the operation] nor the pain of which had been withheld from her. A few general remedies were administered to prepare her for the operation which was carried out in the following manner a few days after her admission to the *Hôtel-Dieu*.

1. The patient having been placed on her back, a little inclined to the left side, the head and neck elevated above the rest of the body, Desault made a longitudinal incision over the middle of the tumor, which began a finger's breadth above and ended the same distance below, in order to have enough room to extend the operation; included in the primary cut was the skin, platysma, some fibres of the sternohyoid andsternothyroid, and penetrating to the glands.

2. While an assistant drew the inner edge of the wound to the left in order to fix the tumor, he separated it from the sternocleidomastoid muscle, by cutting the cellular tissue uniting these structures, he divided at the same time two small arteries which he immediately ligated, while they were elevated with dissecting forceps.

3. After having thus disengaged the external side of the tumor, he separated, in the same manner, its internal side by having an assistant draw it outwards by means of an elevator, in order to be better able to isolate it from the anterior parts

and from the side of the trachea. During this part of the dissection several branches of the thyroid arteries were successively ligated as they were cut.

4. The assistant who held the elevator drew the gland back inwards and forwards, and at the same time the surgeon completed the dissection on the outside, above and below. This part of the dissection was the most painstaking and difficult; it was necessary constantly to sponge the small amount of blood which still oozed and interfered with the clear recognition of the parts. Because of this it was necessary to cut but very little at a time, and to probe with the finger before each cut with the bistoury, that which was to be incised. In dissecting with these precautions he was able to expose without injury, the superior and inferior thyroid arteries, and he ligated them by means of a curved, blunt needle. The same arteries were then divided transversely, and he completed the detachment of the tumor from the trachea to which it had firmly adhered.

5. The wound resulting from this operation was almost three inches in depth, was bounded on the outside by the sternomastoid muscle, on the inside by the trachea and esophagus, and behind by the common carotid artery and the eighth pair of nerves which were visible in the depth. After having irrigated this wound with luke-warm water, and sponged out all the blood it contained, it was filled with coarse gauze powdered with resin. Square compresses held in place with loose bandages formed the rest of the dressing.

The tumor which had been extirpated was nearly five inches in circumference, and did not differ from other cirrhous glands, except for a cartilagenous core which had developed in its center.

The patient, who had endured this long and painful operation with fortitude, tranquilly passed the rest of the day, and did not experience more than the ordinary discomfort: the following night she complained of a little heat in the neck and difficulty in breathing. The bandage was moistened with mallow juice. She was given couch grass moistened with oxymel to drink; the third day the difficulty in swallowing increased greatly, although the fever remained moderate. At that period, for the first time, the external gauze bandages were changed, and the dressings were moistened as had been done the previous days.

The fever ceased on the fourth day and swallowing became less painful; suppuration was already beginning to develop; in the morning she had taken off the gauze so that the entire dressing could be changed. The wound was in good condition; it was dressed only with soft gauze soaked in an emollient decoction; which was continued on the following days.

Nothing special happened in the course of the treatment. The wound followed its ordinary course, was cicatrized at the end of a month, and the patient left the hospital completely cured on the thirty-fourth day after the operation.

CHAPTER 36

Dominique-Jean Larrey
(1766–1842)

"By adverting to the various dangers to which army surgeons are exposed, while laboring to secure the wounded and sick to their country and families, [the readers] will afford us that tribute of respect which we value as one of the best recompenses of our labours." [1]

Surgery and warfare have been linked together as far back as military history is recorded. The relationship has been reciprocal; for those wounded in battle, medical care was desperately needed, and the question of life or death often depended on its availability. Conversely, the large numbers and serious degrees of the injuries constituted the historic training ground for surgeons; and many improvements in wound management grew out of military experience. It is to be emphasized, however, that the quality of medical care under the exigencies of warfare usually left much to be desired. The skill and training of many of the army surgeons were grossly inadequate, and the facilities often totally lacking. Even the master surgeons of the battlefield, those of the stature of Paré, Wiseman, and Gersdorff, limited their efforts almost entirely to the treatment of the wounded. Military medicine, as we now understand it, which encompasses the entire field of the physical and even the mental welfare of the personnel, was totally unknown until the time of the Napoleonic Wars, when a new dimension was added to its concept by Larrey, the Chief Surgeon of the French Army.

History has tended to immortalize the military genius, and to forget the doctors who strove to assuage the inevitable suffering which results from war. Napoleon is a name familiar to all, but how many are aware of Baron Larrey, his Chief Surgeon? And yet, the man who followed the armies, not to destroy but to comfort and heal, was as courageous, as indomitable, and as skillful in his endeavors as was the general he so loyally served. He created the new

1. Dominique-Jean Larrey: *Memoirs of Military Surgery and Campaigns of the French Armies,* from the French of D. J. Larrey by Richard Willmott Hall, Baltimore, Joseph Cushing 1814, Vol. I, p. vii.

FIG. 82. Baron Larrey (Portrait by Guérin, Musée de Versailles)

concept of military surgery which embodied sanitation, epidemiology, procurement of food and supplies for the sick and wounded, training of medical personnel, transport of the injured, and the provision for definitive care at the front which is so emphatically stressed today. Beyond this, he was a humanitarian in the midst of the savagery of warfare, tireless in his solicitude for his patients, heedless of personal danger, and steadfast in the direst adversity. His *Memoirs,*[2] which he modeled after those of Ambroise Paré, provide a fascinating record of the campaigns, the medical problems encountered, and the scenes and customs in the many lands traversed by the Grand Army. His

2. *Ibid.,* 2 Vols.

greatest monument was the affection he inspired in common soldier and officer alike, and even the respect of the enemy.

Larrey was born in the village of Baudéan in the Hautes Pyrénées. Orphaned at the age of thirteen, he was taken in charge by his uncle, Alexis Larrey, who was chief surgeon of the hospital in Toulouse. Under his supervision, the boy studied for six years to become a surgeon. At the age of twenty he went to Paris with the intention of completing his studies under Desault. When he arrived in the Capital, however, he learned that a competitive examination was being held for the posts of assistant surgeons for the navy. He applied and won one of the coveted appointments. Further examination found him so well prepared that he was given an unprecedented commission at the age of twenty-one as chief surgeon on a ship sailing to North America.

The narrative account of this initial journey begins with a description of his preparations, and is indicative of all that followed.

> "Soon after, I embarked as first surgeon on board the frigate *Vigilante*. . . . While waiting for the period of our departure, I passed the winter in giving lectures on anatomy and surgery to the young students. I visited the prison of the galley-slaves, the arsenals, the magazines and ship-yards; and I turned by attention to everything that related to navigation, and to the duties which would devolve on me while on ship-board.
>
> ". . . as surgeon, I directed the supply of medicines, dressings and surgical instruments. I also took care to examine the light articles of diet intended for the sick during the voyage, and to have them properly packed and stowed in a convenient place. . . .
>
> "Being aware that our vessel was ordered to North America, and in particular to Newfoundland to protect the cod-fishery, I obtained from Dr. Lapoterie, and other officers who had sailed to this country, all the information which they could afford, relative to the nature of its climate, its influence on the health of Europeans and also of the character of the inhabitants of Newfoundland and its productions. I took notes on the difficulties of the voyage, on the seas and climates which we should traverse to reach our destination. I supplied myself with such books as were best calculated to direct me while on board, and after we should arrive in Newfoundland."[3]

Violent storms soon rose and the young surgeon was "much distressed" by seasickness. He wrote an excellent description of this disease, including the familiar observation: "The faculties of the mind suffer in common with the organs of animal life, and this change takes place to such a degree, that

3. *Ibid.*, Vol. I, pp. 2–4.

instead of dreading death, as in the commencement of the disease, their suffering is so intolerable that they desire it; and as I have seen, attempt to commit suicide." During the rest of the voyage he vividly describes the countries, their climate, and their inhabitants, together with their manners and customs. Returned to France after an absence of six months, Larrey resigned his commission despite the pressures made to keep him in the service, and again journeyed to Paris to resume his education.

True to his earlier intention, he studied with Desault for a period of three years. He witnessed the outbreak of the Revolution, and later worked with his Chief at the *Hôtel-Dieu* and at the *Hôtel Royal des Invalides*, caring for the victims and acquiring experience for his subsequent life as an army surgeon.

When war broke out in 1792, Larrey was assigned to the Army of the Rhine with the rank *aide-major* (surgeon major). In the very first engagements he recognized the need for better transport of the wounded, which led to one of his most important contributions to military surgery.

> "I now discovered the inconveniences to which we were subjected in moving our *ambulances*, or military hospitals. The military regulations required that they should always be one league distant from the army. The wounded were left on the field, until after the engagement, and were collected at a convenient spot, to which the *ambulances*[4] repaired as speedily as possible; but the number of wagons interposed between them and the army, and many other difficulties so retarded their progress, that they never arrived in less than twenty-four or thirty-six hours, so that most of the wounded died for want of assistance. . . . This suggested to me the idea of constructing an *ambulance* in such a manner that it might afford a ready conveyance for the wounded during the battle. I was unable to carry my plan into execution until some time after."[5]

After the conquest of Mayence, Larrey, now Chief Surgeon, proposed the plan of constructing an ambulance sufficiently mobile to follow the advance guard into action.

> "My proposition was accepted, and I was authorized to construct a carriage, which I called the *flying-ambulance*. I first thought of having the wounded conveyed on horses, furnished with panniers; but experience soon convinced me of the insufficiency of this plan. I next thought of a carriage, so suspended, as to unite swiftness to solidity and ease."[6]

4. The term *ambulances* is used to denote mobile hospitals as well as the conveyances for the transport of the sick and wounded, much as we use it today. This makes for some confusion in the reading.
5. *Ibid.*, pp. 23–24.
6. *Ibid.*, p. 28.

The efficacy of these conveyances was soon demonstrated. A citation reads, "Among those who so brilliantly served the republick on this day, were, adjutant-generals Bailly, Abbatouchi, of the light artillery, and the surgeon-major Larrey, with his companions of the *flying ambulance*, whose indefatigable attentions to the wounded have contributed essentially to the cause of humanity, and of their country." Shortly afterward, during the misfortunes encountered by the army, Larrey reported, ". . . I was in jeopardy, and escaped from the arms of the enemy by miracle, after receiving a slight wound in the left leg." He was sent to Paris to provide ambulances for use in all the armies of the Republic, so useful had they proved on the Rhine.

Immediately upon reaching Paris, however, before having opportunity to achieve this mission, he was ordered to Toulon in the capacity of Chief Surgeon of the Army of Corsica. As he waited to embark he made some experiments on the resuscitation of drowned or asphyxiated persons which included artificial respiration by the blowing of air into the nose with bellows. His gratification, when life was saved by these measures, is vividly expressed in the following lines:

> "How is the surgeon transported, to discover motion returning to the lips and eyelids of a man apparently dead, and when he perceives that the heart palpitates, and respiration is restored! It is the rapture of a Pygmalion, when he perceives the marble becoming animated under his fingers! In proportion as the torch of life is relumed, I redouble my exertions, and the patient is at length placed in a warm bed, where he usually remains some days."[7]

There followed a brief campaign in Spain, civilian practice, a term as Professor of Surgery at the military school at Val-de-Grace, and orders to the Army of Italy to organize, establish, and take charge of flying ambulances with that force. This he accomplished together with important services which he rendered in controlling both human and cattle epidemics. His efforts met with flattering recognition by the local Italian government.

Then came the adventurous campaigns under the direct command of Napoleon, with Larrey in the capacity of Chief Surgeon. The Mediterranean expedition, with its conquest of Egypt, Palestine, and Syria, filled with new experiences and unprecedented problems, makes an exciting chapter in the *Memoirs*. The obverse aspect of the glowing victories of the brilliant young general is depicted in terms of the hardships and privations of the troops and the succession of epidemic diseases to which they were exposed.

> "The main body of the army, without provisions and water, entered the arid deserts on the borders of Lybia, and after a painful march of five days, reached Damanhour, the first place in the interi-

7. *Ibid.*, p. 39.

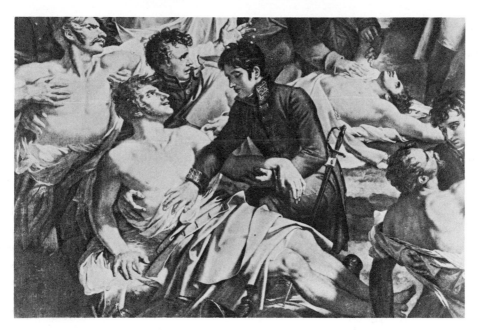

Fɪɢ. 83. Painting of Larrey caring for the wounded after the battle of Wagram, 1809. (Musée de Versailles)

our of Egypt, which afforded a supply. Never did an army experience such great vicissitudes and such painful privations. Tortured with the rays of a scorching sun during the day, marching on foot over a still more scorching sand, traversing an immense extent of dreary wastes, in which with difficulty, we procured a little muddy water, the most vigorous soldiers, parched with thirst and overcome by heat, sunk under the weight of their arms."[8]

On this voyage, as in all the others, Larrey wrote individual "Memoirs" describing the various epidemic and endemic diseases encountered, largely intended for the instruction of the medical officers. These treatises covered, separately, anthrax, bubonic plague, typhus, yellow fever, Egyptian ophthalmia, leprosy, and tetanus. The "Memoir" on tetanus gives superb descriptions of the clinical forms and manifestations of this disease, including the recommendation for early amputation of the wounded limb, and it contains case histories of the lives saved thereby. In the light of present knowledge of the endotoxin produced while the infection is still localized, it is completely credible that such timely intervention might have accomplished its purpose.

Throughout these adventurous marches, the ingenuity exhibited by Larrey

8. *Ibid.*, p. 103.

in his solicitude for his sick and wounded adds immeasurably to his stature. When suitable food was lacking, he ordered the preparation of a nutritious broth of horse meat, seasonsed with gunpowder. When horses were no longer available, he ordered cooked camel meat, and found it acceptable. For the transport of patients in the desert, he had panniers constructed to fit on either side of the camels' humps, each of which would carry a wounded man. (Unfortunately, the quartermasters commandeered the camels for other purposes.) Thus, endlessly matching his wits against the vicissitudes of climate and disease, he won the undying gratitude of the soldiers, and of the government they served. When the campaign ended, Napoleon was made Consul, and Larrey Surgeon-in-Chief of the elite Consular Guards, as well as an Officer of the Legion of Honor and Inspector General of the Service of Health of the Armies.

The incredible numbers of wounded which passed through Larrey's hands afforded him a wealth of clinical material never before equalled. He was a bold and brilliant operator, and his memoirs are interspersed with descriptions of wounds of every conceivable type and all degrees of severity. Profiting by these experiences, he wrote many treatises on the management of war injuries, which embody numerous ideas of his own. Having performed as many amputations as two hundred in a single day, he could indeed speak authoritatively on the subject. Always an ardent advocate of *early* amputation if a limb were to be lost, he established this principle beyond dispute. His surgical skill is revealed in the large numbers of disarticulations he performed at

PL.VII

Fig. 84. Panniers devised by Larrey for the transportation of patients in the desert. From: Larrey's *Memoirs of Military Surgery*, Baltimore, 1814, Vol. II.

the shoulder joint, and even at the hip joint, with a high incidence of recovery. When one remembers that these were done at the front, or on the battlefield itself, without benefit of anesthesia or any of the aids considered so essential today, the magnitude of the achievement is enormously enhanced. Other major operative procedures, including trephining, thoracotomy, and the management of penetrating wounds of the abdomen, are described in profuse numbers. The lessons learned from these experiences are preserved for his colleagues and for surgeons generally in the famous "Memoirs." In all, he participated in twenty-five campaigns, sixty battles, and more than 400 skirmishes. At the battle of Eylau (Prussia) he writes:

"I then attended to the imperial guard, but according to a rule which I had established, dressing those first who were most grievously wounded, without regard to rank or distinction. The cold was so intense that the instruments frequently fell from the hands of the pupils, who held them for me during the operations. Fortunately I enjoyed an unusual vigour, doubtless produced by the great interest which I felt for so many brave fellows.

"The desire which we all felt to save the lives of the wounded, enabled us to persevere in the discharge of our difficult duties. Night came on, and we had not been able to satisfy the cravings of nature. In the midst of such heart-rending scenes, how could we attend to anything but the performance of our sad but humane task?" [9]

Then came the disaster of the retreat from Moscow. The chronicle of this catastrophe is filled with evidences of Larrey's fortitude and selflessness. It tells of the miseries of that calamitous withdrawal, in which the freezing cold, the parched-earth policy of the defenders, the endless wastes of barren earth to traverse, and the onslaughts of the Cossacks at their heels, reduced the once proud Grand Army of 400,000 men to a battered, disorganized, ragged, and motley few who managed to reach France. It is a heartbreaking recital by one who endured every trial and danger. Throughout, it bears testimony of his dedication to the care of his charges, and of the esteem in which he was held by officers and men alike. And when the urgency of flight and the absence of any means of transport made it necessary to leave the patients behind, he was often able to entrust them to officers of the enemy force who themselves had been rescued by Larrey's conscientious care some time before.

The remainder of the story is not entirely happy. Larrey followed Napoleon through his declining fortunes, even to the field of Waterloo. There, wounded and left for dead, he was captured by the Prussians and sentenced to be shot. At the final quarter hour, however, he was recognized by a German doctor who had attended his lectures, and who interceded for him. He was brought before Field Marshal Blücher, whose son had been badly wounded and taken

9. *Ibid.*, Vol. II, p. 142.

captive by the French on a previous occasion. At that time, Larrey had exerted his efforts and saved the life of the young officer. It is not surprising, therefore, that the sentence of death was cancelled, and Larrey was given an escort to Belgium.

The restoration of the monarchy found Larrey lonely and dispirited, but his reputation for valor and humanity had not dimmed. His baronetcy, which had been bestowed upon him after the battle of Wagram (1809), was soon restored as well as his pensions and he was given important missions. These duties permitted him to complete his writings. He died at the age of seventy-six, an honored and beloved man. His former chief, Napoleon, who predeceased him by twenty years, had written in his will, "I bequeath to the Surgeon-in-Chief of the French army, Larrey, 100,000 francs. He is the most virtuous man I have ever known." No man had a better-earned epitaph.

ᔐ ᔐ ᔐ   MEMOIR ON TRAUMATICK TETANUS.[10]
ᔐ ᔐ ᔐ   Tetanus, as defined by all authours, is a contraction of the muscles of greater or less violence and extent, with tension and rigidity of the parts affected, and is presented to us under four different varieties:

It is called trismus or trismos, when it confines its effects to the muscles of the jaw and throat;

Tetanus, when the whole body is affected, and becomes rigid, preserving its ordinary rectitude;

Emprosthotonos, when the body is bent forward;

Opisthotonos, when it is bent backward.

Each of these varieties presents remarkable differences; the two first frequently appear at the same time, and form what is called complete tetanus.

Tetanus may be distinguished, according to its severity, into acute or chronick.

The first is very dangerous, and generally mortal.

The chronick tetanus is less dangerous, by reason of its gradual progress, and affords time for the employment of more numerous remedies.

I shall mention the principal phenomena presented by tetanus from wounds, in its different stages, as I observed it in Egypt.

I remarked that wounds from fire-arms on the course of the nerves, or on the articulations often produced it, in this climate, particularly during the seasons in which the temperature

10. *Ibid.*, Vol. I, pp. 130–149.

changes from one extreme to the other, in moist places or those bordering on the Nile or on the sea.

Men of a dry and irritable temperament were most subject it, and its termination was generally fatal.

This disorder commences by general indisposition, and a sort of restlessness; the suppuration of the wound quickly diminishes, and is finally suppressed. The flesh becomes dry and bloated; first of a red colour and then marbled. This symptom is accompanied by acute pains, which are increased by contact with the air, or the lightest substances. These pains gradually extend along the course of the nerves and vessels; the whole limb becomes painful; the wounded parts inflame; the muscles experience convulsive contractions, accompanied or preceded by violent cramps, and twitching and subsaltus tendinum.

Muscular irritation extends rapidly from those muscles nearest to the wound, to those farthest removed from it, which contract violently, and become rigid: or it is suddenly translated to the muscles of the jaw and throat, and is concentrated there; the jaws approach together gradually, and almost close. Deglutition soon becomes difficult and impracticable, from the forcible contraction of the pharynx and oesophagus.

When tetanus is general, all the muscles are affected at the same time. The eyes have little motion; they sink in their orbits, and become watery; the face is suffused, the mouth distorted, and the head inclined variously, according to the species of tetanus. The parietes of the abdomen approach the columna vertebralis, and act on the viscera of this cavity, which appear to be hidden in the hypochondria, in the pelvis, and in the lumbar fossa, where the muscles contract upon and compress them.—The excretions are diminished or suppressed, and especially the stools. The ribs, to which the abdominal muscles are attached, are drawn down. The chest is contracted; the diaphragm is confined; respiration is short and laborious, the heart is bound and becomes rigid, in the same manner as the muscles; its contractions are frequent and imperfect, which must enfeeble the circulation of the blood; yet the functions of the brain remain unimpaired, to the last moment of existence, so that the unfortunate subject of this disease is sensible of the approach of death.

I shall not venture to say why the morbid principle of the affected nerves is not communicated to the brain.—This fact proves that the nervous cords are not elongations of this organ, as Dr. Gall supposes.

In complete tetanus, the limbs become so rigid, and the whole body so stiff, that it may be lifted by one of the extremities without bending. The patient falls into a state of insomnia: if he dozes, he is troubled with perplexing dreams, he is agitated, tormented, and disquieted; and endeavours to free himself from the constraint in which he is held by the rigidity of his muscles.

All these symptoms increase so rapidly, that frequently, in the course of twenty-four hours, the patient is unable to swallow, or swallows with the greatest pain. Sometimes he is seized with delirium; his pulse is small and quick; fever, followed by partial and copious sweats generally appears at night. He becomes emaciated, and experiences acute pains; the rigidity increases, the muscles cease to act, and the skin adheres to their circumference, the salivary glands emit a white frothy substance, which is discharged from the mouth; deglutition is interrupted. It is then that the unhappy patient is sensible of his danger, and while he retains his mental faculties, he expires on the third, fourth, fifth or seventh day: an instance rarely occurs of a patient reaching the seventeenth day.

Here the immediate causes of death, are the strong compression of the viscera of the abdomen, constraint of the organs of respiration, stricture of the heart, and subsequently injection of the brain. Dissections which I have made after death from tetanus, confirm what I advance.

In emprosthotonos, the flexor overpower the extensor muscles, so as to throw the head forward on the trunk, and the pelvis on the thorax; the body then takes the form of a bow.

In opisthotonos, on the contrary, the extensors overpower the flexors; the head is thrown back, and the columna vertebralis is curved backwards; the limbs generally remain extended. This species of tetanus is more rare than emprosthotonos: I have remarked that it more speedily ends in death. It appears that the forcible retraction of the vertebrae of the neck and head causes a strong pressure on the spinal marrow, and produces a permanent contraction of the larynx and pharynx.

[The treatment of tetanus is discussed in detail. Of particular interest is Larrey's recommendation of early amputation. In addition to the brief quotation given below he cites numerous cases reports of patients salvaged by this operation.]

The unexpected and complete success that followed the amputation of a wounded limb of an officer, attacked by chronick tetanus, induces me to propose a quere, whether, in this disease, which arises from a wound in some part of the extremities,

"Is it not better to amputate the wounded limb as soon as the symptoms of tetanus appear, than to rely on the uncertain resources of nature and art to effect a cure."

When tetanus is chronick, as it sometimes is, amputation may be resorted to in any stage of the disease, provided the operator choose a period when the symptoms intermit. It will not succeed as well in acute tetanus, if it be advanced, and the muscles of the limb to be amputated, be strongly contracted and rigid, as I had occasion to observe at the siege of Saint-Jean d'Acre, in the case of a soldier who was attacked by it, in consequence of a gun-shot wound at the joint of the left elbow.

Although I saw that the disease in this case was already far advanced, I thought proper to attempt the amputation of the arm: this was followed by a calm, which promised success; but being unable to defend the patient from the coolness of the nights, and the disease being far advanced and very acute, the symptoms returned, and the patient died in three days after the operation.

May I now be permitted, without attempting to resolve the above important quere, to give some reasons that appear to me to corroborate my opinion in favour of amputation.

When it is well known that tetanus is caused by a wound, we ought not to have any hesitation in amputating immediately on the appearance of the symptoms. We may be assured that it is *traumatick*, by the nature of the wound, the progress of the first symptoms, and by considering the time of their appearance, which is from the fifth to fifteenth day, or later.

Amputation of the limb being made on the first appearance of the symptoms, all communication with the origin of the evil is cut off. This operation unloads the vessels, removes the twitchings of the nerves, and convulsive motions of the muscles. These first effects are followed by a general collapse, which promotes the excretions and repose, and re-establishes the equilibrium of the body.

FLYING AMBULANCE[11]

[This chapter begins with a description of the table of organization, uniforms, etc. The total personnel of each ambulance consisted of 113 persons. Then follows the structure and
operation of the ambulances.]

Each division of *ambulance* consisted of twelve light carriages
on springs for the transportation of the wounded: they were of
two sorts, some with two wheels, others with four. The former
kind were calculated for flat level countries, the others to carry
the wounded across the mountains. The frame of the former
resembled an elongated cube, curved on the top: it had two
small windows on each side, a folding door opened before and
behind. The floor of the body was moveable; and on it were
placed a hair mattress, and a bolster of the same, covered with
leather. This floor moved easily on the two sides of the body,
by means of four small rollers; on the sides were four iron
handles through which the sashes of the soldiers were passed,
while putting the wounded on the sliding floor. These sashes
served instead of litters for carrying the wounded; they were
dressed on these floors, when the weather did not permit them
to be dressed on the ground.

When the army was engaged in rugged mountains, it was
indispensably necessary to have mules, or pack-horses, with panniers to carry the materials for dressings, with the surgical instruments, medicines, etc.

The small carriages, were thirty-two inches wide, and were
drawn by two horses. Two patients could conveniently lie at
full length in them; to the sides were attached several pockets,
to receive bottles or other articles necessary for the sick. These
carriages united solidity with lightness and elegance.

The second kind of light carriages, on springs, was a chariot
with four wheels; the body of which was larger and longer than
those with two wheels, but of a similar form; it was also hung
on four springs, and furnished with an immoveable mattress,
and the pannels were stuffed a foot in height, like the bodies of
the small carriages. The left side of the body opens almost its
whole length, by means of two sliding doors, so as to permit
the wounded to be laid in a horizontal position. Small windows
disposed at proper distances have a good effect in ventilating

11. *Ibid.*, pp. 81–83.

the carriage. A hand-barrow may be fixed under these carriages for various useful purposes.

The large carriages also have pockets, and behind, a place to carry forage; they were drawn by four horses, and had two drivers. In these carriages four men might lie with their legs slightly contracted.

We had a board of consultation for the three divisions, which was composed of the officers of the medical and surgical departments. The order and march of these *ambulances*, and the duties of every one attached to them were laid down by special rules.

They were designed to convey the wounded from the field of battle to the hospitals of the first line.

The legion of *ambulances* was under the immediate command of the chief surgeon of the army and each division under the command of a surgeon-major of the first class.

They were also introduced to carry off the dead for burial. The overseers who marched on foot were especially charged with this duty under the direction of the inspector of police, who was authorised to require from the inhabitants the labours necessary for this service.

With these *ambulances*, the most rapid movements of the advanced guard of an army can be followed up, and when necessary, they can separate into a great many divisions, every officer of the medical staff being mounted, and having at command a carriage, a mounted overseer, and every thing necessary for affording the earliest assistance on the field of battle.

CHAPTER 37

Antonio Scarpa
(1752–1832)

"In Surgery, as in all the other sciences and arts which have for their basis observation and experience, there remains for a long time a degree of obscurity on some points, to dissipate which it is necessary to have recourse repeatedly to the same kind of observations and experiments, varying them in many different ways." [1]

Italian leadership in the medical sciences which had endured for nearly a millennium waned as the eighteenth century advanced toward its close, and from this period few names stand out in the fields of surgery and anatomy. The sole exception of universal repute was Antonio Scarpa (1752–1832). He was a strange character in whom superb scientific capabilities were combined with unfortunate personal traits. His talents were multiple: an unsurpassed anatomist, an excellent surgeon who was as proficient in ophthalmology and orthopedics as in the general field, a polished writer, effective teacher, superb medical illustrator, and what Garrison euphemistically calls "a master of sarcasm." He was endowed with a brilliant and calculating intellect, prodigious energy, unlimited ambition, a passion for accuracy and exactitude in his researches, and a wide range of cultural and artistic interests. His name is familiar because of many eponyms, but the true significance of his achievements has not generally been recognized. Deplorable traits of personality earned for him hatred and antagonism which were kept in check during his life by fear of his power and ruthlessness. These were unleashed after his death and served to dim the luster of his scientific accomplishments. Only with the passage of time have these influences faded to the degree that permits the greatness of this remarkable man again to emerge.

Antonio Scarpa was born in 1752 in the village of Motta in northern Italy, just south of the Tyrol. He was a precocious child who achieved a good education despite the poverty of his parents. Taught by an uncle who was a priest, he became an excellent Latinist and, at the early age of fifteen, he easily

1. Antonio Scarpa: *A Treatise on Hernia*, translated by John Henry Wishart, Edinburgh, Longman, Hurst, Rees *et al.*, 1814, p. 6.

Scarpa

FIG. 85

passed the entrance examinations to the famed University of Padua where he
was admitted as a student of medicine. Here he came under the influence of
Giovanni Battista Morgagni, and won that famous pathologist's lasting paternal friendship. He became Morgagni's assistant and, later, his personal
secretary. From his illustrious mentor he gained his passionate interest in the
medical sciences, particularly in pathological anatomy, and developed the
meticulousness of his investigative methods. At the age of twenty he received
his degree and only two years later, in recognition of his diligence and natural
aptitude together with Morgagni's recommendation, he received the appoint-

ment as Professor of Anatomy and Clinical Surgery at the University of Modena.

The brilliance of Scarpa's lectures brought him early acclaim, and his surgical skill soon resulted in his appointment as chief surgeon to the military hospital at Modena. Shortly afterward he was also put in charge of the teaching of obstetrics at the university. In the meantime he engaged energetically in his researches in anatomy and physiology. In the course of these investigations he found himself embroiled in a vicious quarrel with the famous clinician and anatomist, Luigi Galvani, on a matter of priority and a suspicion of plagiarism. At the height of this unpleasantness he managed to have himself sent on a tour of other medical centers to study newer teaching methods.

The two years of travel proved of enormous value to Scarpa. He visited Paris and London, and made very valuable friendships. From Pott and the Hunters he took ideas which are discernible in his later work, including his study of comparative anatomy and the building of an imposing anatomical and pathological collection.

A more immediate benefit from one of the friendships was the invitation to assume the Chair of Anatomy at the University of Pavia, with enticing salary and perquisites. Scarpa entered upon his new duties with vigor and enthusiasm. New teaching methods, modeled after those observed abroad, replaced the traditional professorial lectures by demonstrations which correlated structure with function, and emphasized the application of these sciences in surgery. Handsome new buildings were erected for him, an anatomical theatre, laboratories, and museum. A second extensive lecture tour of the universities of Germany was arranged for him, together with the renowned physicist, Alessandro Volta, at lavish government expense. This journey not only enriched his own experience, but greatly expanded his reputation and influence.

Scarpa's long tenure at Pavia coincided with, and largely contributed to, that university's pre-eminence among the centers of learning and science of all Europe. By his contemporaries he was considered the leading anatomist of the world of his time; and he was an equally able and prominent surgeon. His researches and publications covered a great variety of subjects, and certain of his works have become classics. The magnificent drawings with which he illustrated his books are among the finest ever made. Among his many important contributions are his studies on the nerves of hearing and smell; his treatise on the inner ear in which he first described the round window and the labyrinthine fluid, both of which bear his name; his work on the nerves of the heart with its excellent plates; his publications on the structure of bone, on aneurysm, and on the ligation of arteries; and his well-known books on hernia and on diseases of the eye. He experimented with blood transfusion, was the first to describe perineal hernia, and he devised an orthopedic shoe for club-foot that is the pattern for those in use today.

Scarpa became very wealthy and lived in a grand manner. He remained a bachelor, but his life was not devoid of romantic attachments and several sons born from these liaisons were furthered in their careers by their father. Scarpa's artistic leanings and gift for acquisition enabled him to accumulate an invaluable collection of great paintings by the leading Italian masters. His knowledge of art and its history, together with his broad cultural attainments and literary talents, was sufficient for him to write learned essays on painting and sculpture. As an accomplished linguist, a lucid thinker, and a commanding speaker, he won universal admiration as a lecturer and orator.

Scarpa was a power at Pavia, and he exercised his position in a ruthless and tyrannical manner. After retirement from active teaching in 1813 he had himself appointed Director of the Medical Faculty, in order to retain his dictatorial control. His enemies he destroyed without compunction, and his favorites he pushed far beyond their merits. "He was as cold as death," wrote

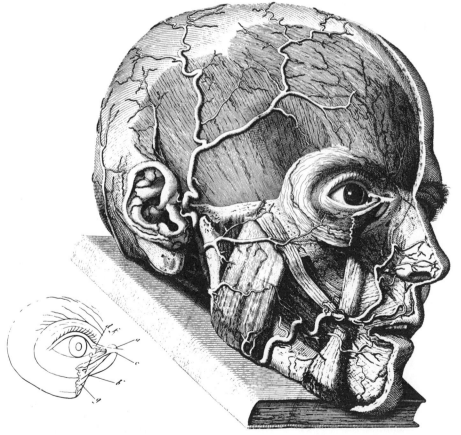

FIG. 86. Dissection of the head with special emphasis on the eye. Drawing made by Scarpa. From: *Saggio di osservazioni e d'esperienze sulle principali mallattie degli occhi* di Antonio Scarpa. Venezia, Giannantonio Pizzana, 1802.

a recent biographer, "and as inexorable as destiny itself. Accordingly, he was feared very much like some dreadful god of antiquity who had gone on much beyond his allotted time. He was implacably revengeful, and usually without mercy. One gets the impression that he was feared even after his death."[2]

Immediately after this death which came to him at the age of eighty, there was a violent release of the bitterness and hatred that had been held pent up by fear for many years. His reputation was attacked, his achievements derogated. Even the inscriptions on the marble tablets erected to his memory were defaced. The greatness of the man was obscured for many decades. Now that time has blunted the memory of his failings, the importance of his scientific contributions is regaining its merited place in history.

[SLIDING HERNIA][3]

[Scarpa described sliding hernia in a remarkably full and accurate manner. Parts of this lengthy description are here quoted.]

In dissecting several of these herniae, I have found, that the caecum, with the appendix vermiformis, and the beginning of the colon descending through the inguinal ring into the scrotum, not only relax the natural bridles which connect these intestines to the os ilium, and to the psoas muscle, but likewise that these intestines, in descending, draw after them into the scrotum that part of the great sac of the peritoneum, to which they are naturally united opposite to the right side. Consequently the hernial sac, within which these intestines are contained in the scrotum, is formed by the same identical portion of the great sac of the peritoneum, which in the sound state lined the right ileo-lumbar region, and formed the duplicatures and ligaments connecting the caecum with the appendix vermiformis, and the beginning of the colon to the right os ilium and to the psoas muscle; from whence it happens, that on opening the hernia, these intestines are found adhering to the hernial sac in the same manner as they were united to the great sac of the peritoneum within the abdomen in the right ileo-lumbar region. And it is precisely on this account, that I call this species of adhesion of the viscera to the hernial sac *natural fleshy*, because it is formed by the same *natural* connections which the caecum

2. Achille Monti: *Antonio Scarpa in Scientific History and His Role in the Fortunes of the University of Pavia*, translated by Frank L. Loria, New York, The Vigo Press, 1957, p. 25.
3. Antonio Scarpa, *op. cit.*, pp. 205–221.

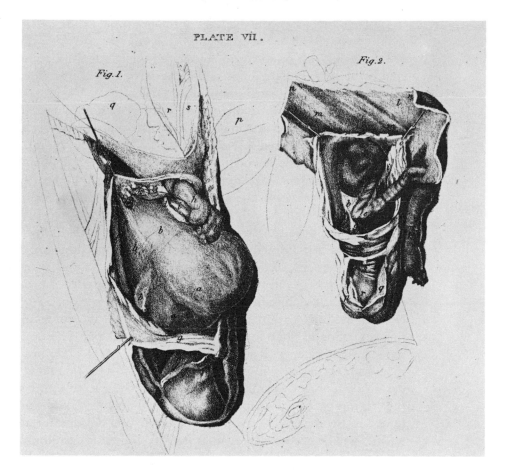

FIG. 87. (*left*) Sliding hernia of the cecum, appendix, and ascending colon; (*right*) lesser degree, sliding hernia of the cecum and the appendix. From: *A Treatise on Hernia* by Antonio Scarpa, transalted by John Henry Wishart, Edinburgh, 1814.

and the appendix vermiformis have, in common, in the abdomen with the great sac of the peritoneum. However strange, and perhaps incredible, this phenomenon may seem to beginners in surgery, it will not surpass the belief of those who are acquainted with the great extensibility of the peritoneum, and of the cellular substance which unites it loosely to the muscular parietes of the abdomen, and who are not ignorant, that there are similar facts well authenticated, even more wonderful than this, of which I have already made mention in the preceding Memoir, viz. of viscera firmly connected to the great sac of the peritoneum, which have been found in the dead body at a considerable distance from their natural situation, and removed to

that place, together with the part of the great sac of the peritoneum to which they were naturally firmly united.

I have had an opportunity of examining, and of following
step by step, to use the expression, the formation of this complicated hernia of the groin and of the scrotum.

[He then details a series of autopsy findings with progressively
larger sliding hernias of the colon in which the true nature of
this lesion is recognized.]

The scrotal hernia formed by the caecum with the appendix
vermiformis, and the beginning of the colon, being always large,
presents appearances in the act of operating which may lead to
error, and especially it might be thought, that these intestines
were on the outside of the hernial sac, or unprovided with a
membranous sac formed by the descent of the peritoneum. If
anyone skilled in anatomy will reflect a little on this transposition of parts, and recollect, that the caecum with the beginning of the colon in the right ileo-lumbar region, is not
entirely inclosed within the great sac of the peritoneum, and
that a portion of these intestines, sunk in the cellular substance
on the right side, is absolutely without the great abdominal
membranous sac, he will immediately discover, that in a scrotal
hernia of such a description, a portion of the caecum and of
the beginning of the colon, will be found included and contained in the hernial sac, while another portion of the same intestines will be necessarily without the sac, and lying denuded in
the cellular substance which accompanies the descent of the
peritoneum in the hernia. Now, if any one, not sufficiently
skilled in anatomy, and unaccustomed to the examination of
this disease in the dead body, shall cut into this species of hernia, carrying the incision too much towards the outer side of
the tumor, after opening the sheath of the cremaster, he will
meet with the caecum and the beginning of the colon denuded,
and will think that these intestines have descended into the
scrotum, without the usual hernial sac formed by the peritoneum. But he will very soon discover the error into which he
has fallen, if he make the incision precisely in the middle, and
a little towards the inner side of the tumor. Then under the
sheath of the cremaster and the subjacent cellular substance, he
will without doubt find the true hernial sac formed by the peritoneum, and within this sac he will see the greater portion of
the caecum with the appendix vermiformis, and likewise the

membranous folds and bridles which seem to be detached from the hernial sac, to be inserted into these intestines, the smaller portion of which will be without the sac, in the same manner as when these viscera occupied the ileo-lumbar region. . . . And it ought not to excite surprise, that a young surgeon should be deceived with regard to the nature of this disease, since we now know, that the same mistake was committed by two celebrated masters of the profession, Desault and Chopart, who said openly, that they had seen *the caecum denuded under the integuments of the scrotum*, without at all suspecting, that the greater portion of this intestine was included in the hernial sac formed by the descent of the peritoneum, as in hernia in general.

[In the management of sliding hernia he sagely recommends release of strangulation without opening the sac.]

But supposing, that a large and inveterate hernia formed by the caecum is actually affected by strangulation, so that the operation is absolutely necessary for freeing the patient from so dangerous an accident, the surgeon will prepare for it, guided by the reflection that the protruded viscera, on account of their particular connexion with the hernial sac, are not susceptible of being completely returned into the abdomen. On which account, there not being the smallest suspicion of gangrene, and knowing likewise that in this case, as in all those of large and old scrotal hernia, the neck of the hernial sac is never the immediate cause of strangulation, the surgeon having divided the common integuments, will lay bare the inguinal ring, and will divide it from without with his hand unsupported, taking care not to wound the subjacent neck of the hernial sac, in such a manner as to set the protruded viscera at liberty, without exposing them to the contact of the air, and by gentle pressure on the tumor he will make the accumulated feces and flatus resume their course, and will, at the same time, endeavour as much as possible to return the protruded viscera.

CHAPTER 38

Astley Cooper
(1768–1843)

"In the collecting of evidence upon any medical subject, there are but three sources from which we can hope to obtain it: viz. from observation on the living subject: from examination of the dead; and from experiment upon living animals." [1]

Astley Paston Cooper, next to Edward Jenner, was John Hunter's most influential pupil. In the lives of master and student there were many similarities, and as many, and perhaps more striking, differences. Both came from large families, and of families scourged by tuberculosis. As boys neither of them submitted to the discipline of early education, Hunter because of his waywardness and intractability, Cooper because of his high spirit and adventurous disregard for danger which made him the leader of his boyhood fellows—and he was too engrossed in games and escapades to be bothered with schooling and study. A career in surgery eventually was chosen for both rather unpromising young men, and they were sent from their homes to London to be placed under the guardianship of older relatives already well established in the profession. On reaching the metroplis, a period of dissipation and wild living earned for each the displeasure of their elders, although the company sought by Cooper was more genteel and respectable than that of Hunter. Traffic with "resurrectionists" and "body snatchers" came to both in their need for anatomical material; and when introduced to the study of anatomy, both sobered quickly and became tireless workers in their search for knowledge.

In contrast to Hunter's crude external appearance and truculent manner, Cooper was distinguished by his good looks, personal charm, and winsome personality. Hunter led a solitary life, often ridiculed and misunderstood. Cooper was everywhere surrounded by warmth and esteem and popularity. Hunter was unable to communicate the priceless treasure of knowledge and wisdom which he had amassed, because of his limitations as a writer or

1. Astley Cooper and Benjamin Travers: *Surgical Essays*, Philadelphia, James Webster, 1821, Vol. I, p. 84.

SIR ASTLEY PASTON COOPER, BART

From the Original Picture by Sir Thomas Lawrence, P.R.I.

Fig. 88

speaker. Cooper was a facile and fluent lecturer who drew students in such unprecedented numbers that the halls could scarcely accommodate them. Struggle and penury marked much of Hunter's life. Cooper married well, and quickly built the most lucrative practice ever known. Only in their domestic lives was Hunter the more fortunate. Mrs. Cooper fell into a long depression after the death of her only child, and a later tragedy, the death at childbirth of an adopted daughter, resulted in an almost complete withdrawal for the balance of her life. Hunter probed the secrets of life to a depth far beyond Cooper's capabilities. Cooper interpreted and popularized, and extended, somewhat, Hunter's investigations. He was a careful observer, and made his greatest contributions in the advancement of clinical surgery.

Astley Cooper was born in 1768, at Brooke in Norfolk, the son of a clergyman whose family had considerable intellectual distinction. The home provided a background of breeding and respectability, and so shaped the character of the high-spirited boy. Astley's uncle, William Cooper, was Senior Surgeon to Guy's Hospital, and it was under his care that the future young surgeon was placed. When young Cooper reached London, at the age of sixteen, he was sent to live in the home of Henry Cline, another of Hunter's important pupils, who was Surgeon at St. Thomas's Hospital. At that time the two hospitals, Guy's and St. Thomas's, were close together geographically and also in their operation and teaching programs, and together they were known as the United Hospitals.

Astley soon found himself drawn to Cline because of his genial manner, his liberal views, and his stimulating personality, and requested that he be apprenticed to him rather than to his uncle. The matter was so arranged, and it proved to be most fortunate for young Astley. Cline was an ardent admirer of John Hunter, and soon transmitted this appreciation to his apprentice. Cooper attended the lectures of Hunter for several years, pondered over them to extract their somewhat obscure meaning, and made them part of himself. The impact of Hunter on the shaping of his life and work was great, as will be shown later.

The zeal with which Cooper threw himself into his studies, particularly of anatomy, brought him early recognition. By the end of his second year of study he had become an unofficial demonstrator in the dissecting room, and, three years, later, although still an apprentice, was formally appointed Demonstrator in Anatomy at St. Thomas's Hospital. Just before completion of his apprenticeship in 1791, he was invited by Cline to share the lectureship in anatomy and surgery with him. Two years later he was also chosen to give the lectures on anatomy for the Surgeon's Company.

During all of his student years Astley Cooper carried out independent animal experiments in physiology. After finishing his training, for all of his life to its very end, he labored ceaselessly in human dissection, comparative anatomy, physiology, and pathology, a pattern of life modeled on that of John Hunter. Many years later he said, "If I laid my head upon my pillow at night without having dissected something in the day, I should think that I had lost that day."

With the security provided by his wife's dowry, Cooper decided to defer his entrance into private practice and to use the time solely for further preparation. "For three years after my apprenticeship expired," he wrote, "I did not seek business, but devoted myself to the study of my profession, and to teaching the students entirely. My industry at this time may be gathered from the following circumstances.

"I went to the hospital before breakfast to dissect for lecture. I demonstrated to the students before lecture. I injected their subjects. I lectured from two o'clock till half-past three. In the evening, three times per week, I lectured on surgery. I attended to the interesting cases in the hospital, making notes of them, and in this latter practice I always persevered."[2]

This was indeed an arduous schedule. Although he kept his resolution to accept no private patients during the first three years, he did, from the first, encourage the indigent persons of the neighborhood to come to his house every morning for treatment without charge. This practice, also continued for many years, added to his clinical experience and made him many friends. For the more serious illnesses and those that had teaching value for his students, he arranged admittance to the hospitals.

In addition to the formal lectures, which were in themselves a heavy burden, Astley Cooper made hospital rounds with both Cline and William Cooper, in the two hospitals. The large classes of students crowded around him, as he made use of the patients visited to teach on an informal basis, much as is done with our students and house staffs today in our "teaching rounds." The appreciative and grateful students from all these teaching endeavors maintained their affection and friendship for him, and in later years provided a wide basis for patient referrals and contributions to Cooper's "collection."

This museum, in further emulation of John Hunter, was another of Cooper's lifelong preoccupations. Although his "preparations" never approached in number and variety those of his predecessor, his accumulation of instructive and interesting pathological specimens was greater. Unlimited expenditure of effort and money went into the securing of parts that had been operated upon by himself even after the lapse of many years. He was able in this manner to follow his cases and to ascertain and demonstrate the end results of his treatment.

When his Uncle William relinquished his position as Surgeon to Guy's Hospital in 1800, Astley Cooper was among those considered to fill the vacancy. This greatly coveted position was almost lost to him because of his political views. His preceptor, Cline, was "radical" in his political thinking, and in his home Cooper was brought into contact with the advocates of democracy, which at that time was a suspect and unpopular movement. Astley embraced these leanings with his characteristic unequivocal enthusiasm, to the great dismay of his uncle and parents. The stirring revolutionary

2. Bransby B. Cooper: *The Life of Astley Cooper*, London, John W. Parker, 1843, Vol. I, pp. 227–228.

activities then current in France aroused his sympathies for the underprivileged masses in their struggle against the monarchy. On their wedding trip the Coopers journeyed to Paris, motivated in part by the desire to witness the conflict; and by coincidence they were in that city when the first blows were struck. The excesses of the terror, the brutality exercised on the monarchist victims, and the dangers and difficulties to which the Coopers were exposed dampened his ardor for a time only. On his return to England he continued to voice his support of the revolutionaries.

Fortunately, as time went on, both Cooper and his friend Coleman, who shared his beliefs, independently and simultaneously came to a realization of the actual physical danger they were courting, and resolved completely to abandon all political interest and activity. It was shortly after this decision was made that the appointment to Guy's Hospital became available. Although undeniably the superior candidate of the three under consideration in all professional respects, Cooper was about to be rejected as unfit for the post. He was able, however, to convince the authorities of his withdrawal from all politics and received the appointment, to his own great advantage, as well as to that of the hospital, and certainly to the profit of many hundred students. His resolve never again to mix politics and surgery was faithfully adhered to for the rest of his days.

Secure in his position as Surgeon to Guy's Hospital, Astley Cooper moved quickly forward to become the world's most prominent surgeon. His winning personality, his ability to make and hold friends, his acknowledged mastery of his profession, and his courage to undertake the unprecedented brought to his practice and earnings a volume never before enjoyed. His patients included the most influential social groups, even to the royal family. For successfully removing an infected sebaceous cyst from the scalp of King George IV, a baronetcy was conferred upon him. He was later made Sergeant-Surgeon to this monarch and subsequently to William IV and Queen Victoria. Honors of all variety were showered upon him, including twice the presidency of the Royal College of Surgeons.

Astley Cooper's contributions to surgery and anatomy were varied and numerous. His greatest interests were in the field of arterial surgery, hernia, and the breast. In the management of aneurysm, he pioneered in the ligation of the common carotid and external iliac arteries and attained the ultimate of ligating the abdominal aorta. His book on hernia, his first published treatise, is a truly classic work on the subject. Here Cooper described for the first time the transversalis fascia, with full appreciation of its importance in hernia, as well as the superior pubic ligament which bears his name, and is importantly mentioned in current hernial surgery. Other works concern the breast, testis, fractures and dislocations, and numerous case reports. The following passing mention of free, full-thickness skin graft is of interest.

Singular case of a Successfull Operation of Amputating at the Hip Joint performed January 17th 1824 on William Jones Aged 47 at Guys Hospital by Sir Astley Cooper Bart Surgeon to the King &c &c &c.

London Published May 1 1824 by W for Medical Bookseller to the London Hospitals.

FIG. 89. Amputation at the hip joint. From: R. C. Brock: *The Life and Work of Astley Cooper*, Edinburgh, E. & S. Livingstone, Ltd., 1952.

"*Copy of a curious and valuable paper.*

Hartfield, a young man admitted into Guy's Hospital (Cornelius ward) April 9th, 1817, with a diseased thumb which Mr. Cooper, now Sir Astley, amputated between the phalanges on the 18th July.

He then cut off a healthy piece of integument from the ampu-

tated part and applied it to the piece of the stump where he secured
it by means of adhesive slips.

1st week to July 25. Union seems to have taken place.

2nd week to August 1. Mr. Cooper proved the vascularity of the
newly attached portion by pricking it very slightly with the point
of a lancet which produced blood as readily as from any other
part of the limb. Sensibility has not yet returned.

3rd week from operation. In the course of this week sensation was
restored in the end of the stump.

September 23rd. The stump appears quite well."[3]

Astley Cooper never published his lectures. However, they were printed
serially in the Lancet from notes taken at the lectures. This was an unprecedented venture in medical journalism, and evoked a storm of protests from
other lecturers, who characterized it as unethical advertising. Although
Cooper had not been consulted concerning the matter, he gave his permission, provided his name were omitted, and this arrangement prevailed. The
lecture notes were subsequently published as a book and in this form became
the standard text of the period, a position retained for many years after the
author's death.

≶ ≶ ≶   [COOPER'S LIGAMENTS OF THE BREAST]

≶ ≶ ≶   *Of the Internal Parts of the Breast, or Mammary Gland.*

First, of the *fascia mammae.* This is divided into two layers;
the superficial, and the deeper layer of the breast, between
which the gland of the breast is included.

If I begin to trace this fascia from the sternum, I find both
layers adhering to the ligamentous substance which covers
that bone. From thence they proceed towards the breast, when
one layer separates from the other, to include the breast between them.

The anterior or superficial layer passes upon the anterior
or cutaneous surface of the breast: here it forms a fibrous
covering, but not a true capsule, spread upon the surface of
the gland, and passing between the gland and the skin; but it
also enters the interior of the secretory structure.

Here it sends out two sets of processes of a fibrous nature
from its two surfaces.

Anteriorly, large, strong, and numerous fibrous or fascial
processes, to the posterior surface of the skin which covers the

3. R. C. Brock: *The Life and Work of Astley Cooper*, Edinburgh, E. & S. Livingstone, Ltd., 1952,
   pp. 47–48.

breast, and to the substance of which it is received, and with which it is incorporated.

It is by these processes that the breast is suspended in its situation, and I shall therefore call them the *ligamenta suspesoria*.

By these processes, the breast is slung upon the forepart of the chest, for they form a moveable but very firm connexion with the skin, so that the breast has sufficient motion to elude violence; yet by this fibrous tissue it is, excepting under age, lactation, or relaxation, prevented from much change of place.

The ends of these ligaments are spread out and incorporated with the posterior surface of the skin, and give it its whiteness and firmness.

When raised and dried, the preparations of these ligamentous processes form a curious, irregular surface of folds, between the skin and the mammary gland. They are seen in a section of the breast, spread out and lost upon the inner surface of the skin at their anterior extremities. *See Plate* [Fig. 90]. When the breast is placed in its natural position, the posterior extremities of the ligamenta suspensoria are spread over the fore-part of the gland, support numerous folds of the glandular structure, penetrate the substance of the organ, and every where connect the portions of glands to each other.[4]

[DESCRIPTION OF THE TRANSVERSALIS FASCIA]

When the lower portions of the internal oblique and transversalis muscles are raised from their subjacent attachments, a layer of fascia is found to be interposed between them and the peritoneum, through which the spermatic vessels emerge from the abdomen. This fascia, which I have ventured to name *fascia transversalis*, varies in density, being strong and unyielding towards the ilium, but weak and more cellular towards the pubes. Midway between the spine of the ilium and pubes, the opening will be seen, which is now generally known as the internal abdominal ring; the edges of it are indistinct on account of its cellular connexions with the cord; when these are separated, the fascia in which it is formed will be found to consist of two portions; the outer strong layer, connected to Poupart's ligament, winds in a semi-lunar form around the outer side of the cord, and bounds the aperture by a distinct

4. Sir Astley Cooper: *The Anatomy and Diseases of the Breast, with Surgical Papers*, Philadelphia, Lea & Blanchard, 1845, pp. 45–46.

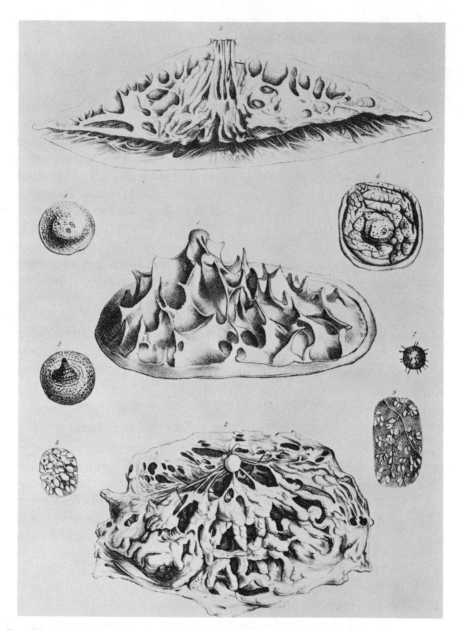

FIG. 90. Suspensory ligaments of the breast. From: *Anatomy and Diseases of the Breast* by Sir Astley Cooper, Philadelphia, Lea & Blanchard, 1845.

margin, from which a thin process may be traced passing down upon the cord. The inner portion, which is found behind the cord, is attached to, but less strongly connected with the inner half of the crural arch, and may be readily separated from it by passing the handle of a knife between it and the arch.

It ascends behind the tendon of the transversalis, with which it is intimately blended, passes around the inner side of the cord, and joins with the outer portion of the fascia above the cord, being at length firmly fixed in the pubes; the inner margin of the ring is less defined than the outer, the fascia transversalis being doubled inwards towards the peritoneum, to which it is firmly attached. Thus, then, it appears, that the *internal ring* is not a circumscribed aperture like the external abdominal ring, but is formed by the separation of two portions of fasciae, which have different attachments and distributions at the crural arch; the outer portion terminating in Poupart's ligament while the inner portion will be found to descend behind it, to form the anterior part of the sheath that envelopes the femoral vessels. The strength of this fascia varies in different subjects; but in all cases of inguinal hernia it acquires considerable strength and thickness, especially at its inner edge; and if these parts had been formed without such a provision, the bowels would, in the erect posture, be always capable of passing under the edge of the transversalis muscle, and no person would be free from inguinal hernia.[5]

[Arterial surgery was one of Cooper's greatest interests. He experimented extensively on the collateral circulation after ligation of arterial trunks and, fortified by the evidence so secured, pioneered in the ligation for the control of aneurysm of the carotid and external iliac arteries and of the abdominal aorta. His first case of carotid artery ligation died of infection, but his second case survived for thirteen years, at the end of which time Cooper was able to do a postmortem examination. In a similar fashion he ligated the external iliac artery for a large femoral aneurysm. The patient died eighteen and one-half years later and Cooper, "at considerable expense," secured the body and had preparations made of the parts involved.]

CASE OF LIGATURE ON THE AORTA

I fear that the title of this paper may impress the reader with an idea that nothing could justify me in performing the operation which I am about to describe; for that a ligature made upon the aorta must necessarily prove fatal. But I trust, that it will be seen in the sequel, that the operation was not attended with the immediate danger which might have been

5. Sir Astley Cooper: *The Anatomy and Surgical Treatment of Abdominal Hernia*, Philadelphia, Lea & Blanchard, 1844, pp. 26–28.

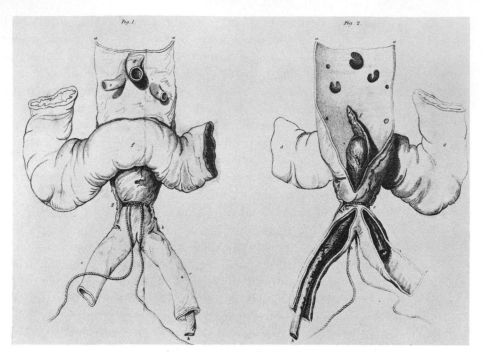

FIG. 91. Postmortem drawing of ligated aorta. From: Cooper and Travers: *Surgical Essays*, Philadelphia, 1821.

apprehended; that the patient complained of but little pain during its performance; that it afforded the only hope of safety, and that we had to lament, not that the operation was performed, but that it had not been sooner done.

Sorry indeed should I be, to sport with the life of a fellow-creature who might repose a confidence either in my surgical knowledge or in my humanity; and I should be equally disposed to consider myself culpable, if I did not make every possible effort to save a person, whose death was rendered inevitable, if a disease were suffered to continue which it was possible for surgery to relieve, as in the case which forms the subject of this essay. In the performance of our duty one feeling should direct us; the case we should consider as our own, and we should ask ourselves, whether, placed under similar circumstances, we should choose to submit to the pain and danger we are about to inflict. Guided by this principle, and having collected all the evidence which applies to the case, we perform our duty without the reproaches of conscience which must await those who unnecessarily subject their patients to pain and danger.

Those who feel disposed to condemn the attempt which I have here described, will have the kindness to recollect, that although my first operation for carotid aneurism proved equally unfortunate with this, yet in the second operation, I was gratified by the successful issue of the case.[6]

[Cooper then discusses the question of collateral circulation, in the course of which he describes two cases of coarctation of the aorta. The actual ligation of the abdominal aorta for a bleeding aneurysm of the common iliac artery is given as follows:]

As I was quitting the patient's bed-side, I felt a great regret, in which all the students by whom I was surrounded joined me, that the patient should be left to perish without giving him the only chance which remained of preventing his immediate dissolution from haemorrhage, by tying the aorta; and I therefore said, "Gentlemen, this only hope of safety I am determined to give him."

The operation was performed as follows: The patient's shoulders were slightly elevated by pillows, in order to relax, as much as possible, the abdominal muscles; for I expected that a protrusion of the intestines would produce embarrassment in the operation, and was greatly gratified to find that this was prevented by their empty state, in consequence of the involuntary evacuation of the faeces; and here let me remark that I should, in a similar operation, consider it absolutely necessary, previously to empty the bowels by active aperient medicines.

I then made an incision three inches long into the linea alba, giving it a slight curve to avoid the umbilicus: one inch and a half was above, and the remainder below the navel, and the inclination of the incision was to the left side of the umbilicus in this form (b). Having divided the linea alba, I made a small aperture into the peritoneum, and introduced my finger into the abdomen; and then, with a probe-pointed bistoury, enlarged the opening into the peritoneum to nearly the same extent as that of the external wound. Neither the omentum nor intestines protruded; and during the progress of the operation, only one small convolution projected beyond the wound.

Having made a sufficient opening to admit my finger into the abdomen, I then passed it between the intestines to the spine, and felt the aorta greatly enlarged, and beating with excessive force. By means of my finger nail, I scratched through

6. Cooper and Travers: *op. cit.*, pp. 83–84.

the peritoneum on the left side of the aorta, and then gently moving my finger from side to side, gradually passed it between the aorta and spine, and again penetrated the peritoneum on the right side of the aorta.

I had now my finger under the artery, and by its side, I conveyed the blunt aneurismal needle armed with a single ligature behind it; and my apprentice, Mr. Key, drew the ligature from the eye of the needle to the external wound; after which the needle was immediately withdrawn.

The next circumstance, which required considerable care, was the exclusion of the intestine from the ligature, the ends of which were brought together at the wound, and the finger was carried down between them, so as to remove every portion of the intestine from between the threads: the ligature was then tied, and its ends were left hanging from the wound. The omentum was drawn behind the opening as far as the ligature would admit, so as to facilitate adhesion; and the edges of the wound were brought together by means of a quilled suter and adhesive plaster.

During the time of the operation, the faeces passed off involuntarily, and the patient's pulse, both immediately, and for an hour after the operation, was 144 in a minute; he was ordered thirty drops of tincture of opium and camphorated mixture, and the involuntary discharge of faeces soon after ceased. I applied my hand to his right thigh immediately after the operation, and he said that I touched his foot; so that the sensibility of that leg was very imperfect.[7]

[Although this patient died forty hours after the operation, it was a heroic intervention which showed the way for subsequent surgery of the great vessels.]

[The following brief excerpt from Cooper's introductory lecture has a strikingly modern ring.]

CASE OF MALPRACTICE

Some years since, one of the profession, whom I had long known, but had not seen for many years, called on me; I naturally inquired respecting his success. He replied, that his life had been like April, sometimes sunshine, sometimes rain. I rejoined, "How so? you have brought up a family genteelly, and have, I understand, a respectable practice." "True," said he, "but a circumstance occurred some time ago which has

7. *Ibid.*, pp. 96–97.

given me much uneasiness; I was called to attend a case of
dislocation of the shoulder joint, but it so happened that I
could not discover it; after attending the patient for a considerable time, another surgeon was requested to see him, who
at once pronounced the bone to be out, which in reality was
the case, for in a very short time he reduced it. When the man
recovered, he brought an action against me; I had to pay two
hundred pounds damages, and the law expenses were two
hundred pounds more. The loss of the money I did not feel,
but I have severely felt being pointed at as an ignorant man."[8]

8. Sir Astley Cooper: *The Principles and Practice of Surgery*, edited by Alexander Lee, London, E. Cox, 1837, Vol. I, p. 4.

CHAPTER 39

The Bells of Scotland

"If it be a great operation, and especially if the assistants and nurses are not habitu-ated, be careful to appoint them their places and their duties; for nothing tends more to the right performance of an operation of magnitude, than that composure and quietness which result from arrangement." [1]

"When you come to be an operator, you would do well to catechise yourself:—Does the operation bid fair to give relief? Is it to be of advantage, as promoting the im-provement of the profession? Has self *any thing to do in the matter—vanity of dis-play, or personal distinction and consequent emolument?"* [2]

The name Bell is intimately associated with the history of Scottish surgery. Because two unrelated families and several generations of Bells are involved in this history, confusion of the individuals, their relationship to one another, and the roles they played generally prevails. In the interest of clarity, there-fore, the surgical members of the two Bell families will be listed first, after which the lives of those who made the most significant contributions will be briefly sketched. Finally, excerpts of the writings of the greatest Bell, Sir Charles, will be given because they have most importantly influenced the growth of medical science.

Benjamin Bell (1749–1806) was the leading Scotch surgeon of his time and the founder of a surgical dynasty which extended into the twentieth century. His two sons, George and Joseph, were surgeons in Edinburgh, as were also Joseph's son, the second Benjamin, and the latter's son, the second Joseph, who died in 1911. The other Bells, of a different family, were the brothers John (1763–1820), the elder, and the younger, Charles (1774–1842).

BENJAMIN BELL, born in Dumfries in 1749, served as an apprentice in his native town, then went to Edinburgh at the age of seventeen to attend the university there. He apparently thought very little of the education offered, for he left after two years to study in Paris and with William Hunter in Lon-

1. Charles Bell: *Illustrations of the Great Operations of Surgery*, London, A. and R. Spottiswoode, 1821, p. 3.
2. *Sir* Charles Bell: *Institutes of Surgery*, Edinburgh, Adam and Charles Black, 1838, Vol. 1, p. xxii.

don, explaining in a letter to his father, "Had I been now entering to the world as a physician, I should never have thought of going farther than where I have been; but for a *surgeon*, I assure you, Edinburgh comes greatly short of either Paris or London, (and for that reason, Dr. Monro and any others I have spoken to upon the subject, approve of the scheme very much.)"

On his return to Edinburgh, he engaged in practice, and became the most successful surgeon in Scotland for that period. He experimented with various means of allaying the pain of surgical operations, and wrote a treatise on *Gonorrhea Virulenta* and *Lues Venerea* (1793) in which he proved these to be two different diseases, thereby correcting the earlier error made by John Hunter. His most ambitious work, a *System of Surgery* (1783–1787) in six volumes, was written in an attempt to displace Heister's *Surgery* as the standard textbook, an aim that was not entirely achieved. Nevertheless, it was the first comprehensive publication by a British surgeon covering the entire subject; it went through seven editions, and was translated into French and German.

The brothers John and Charles Bell were born in an Edinburgh suburb into the family of an impoverished clergyman. Their father was an Episcopalian and Jacobite whose livelihood was precarious because he lived in a society that was overwhelmingly Protestant and conservative. Their mother was a remarkable woman, intelligent, artistic, and affectionate, who instilled into her four sons high ideals, ambition, cultural interests, and a devotion that bordered on reverence. Despite their meager financial status, she saw to it that they were well educated, and she lived to see all of them attain a high place in their various pursuits.

JOHN BELL (*1763–1830*), the older of the two who chose surgery as their profession, studied at the University of Edinburgh, under such noted teachers as Cullen, Alexander Monro II, and Alexander Wood. He qualified as a surgeon at the age of twenty-three, and became a Fellow of the Royal College of Surgeons of the city of Edinburgh. His studies had left him a dissatisfaction with the teaching of anatomy at the University of Edinburgh, and he wrote:

"In Dr. Monro's class, unless there be a fortunate succession of bloody murders, not three subjects are dissected in the year. On the remains of a subject fished up from the bottom of a tub of spirits, are demonstrated those delicate nerves which are to be avoided or divided in our operations: and these are demonstrated once at a distance of 100 feet!—nerves and arteries which the surgeon has to dissect, at the peril of his patient's life."[3] After entering into practice, he sought to improve this teaching for the benefit of surgeons and began to give private lectures. These proved very popular and

3. From: John Bell: *Letters on the Education of a Surgeon*, quoted in *History of Scottish Medicine* by John D. Comrie, London, The Welcome Historical Medical Museum, 1932, Vol. I, p. 324.

attracted students in great numbers, for whose accommodation John built an anatomical school adjoining Surgeons' Hall. In addition to great proficiency in anatomy, he was a scholar, artist, fluent speaker, and lucid author. Comrie, the historian of Scottish medicine says of him, "It is no exaggeration to say that he founded the subject of Surgical Anatomy."

After thirteen years of successful teaching—and perhaps because of the success he enjoyed—Bell became the object of a most vicious and bitter and, apparently, unwarranted attack by members of the faculty of the university, which was led by Dr. James Gregory, Professor of the Practice of Medicine. Reciprocal recriminations of unbounded acerbity were exchanged, and all Edinburgh was torn by the feud. Bell was forced out of the hospital and discontinued his lectures. He devoted himself to his surgical practice, and for twenty years he enjoyed great success and popularity as a surgeon and consultant.

In 1794, John Bell published his *Engravings of the Bones, Muscles and Joints*, for which he supplied his own illustrations. Somewhat later he wrote a three-volume work on the *Anatomy of the Human Body* (1794–1800), some of the drawings for which were made by himself and some by his brother Charles.

CHARLES BELL (*1774–1842*) was eleven years younger than John and, at the time of his birth, his father was aging and in declining health. Four years later, the father died, leaving the responsibilities of the sons in the capable hands of their mother. To Charles, as to John, she imparted a talent for drawing, and, in addition, an esthetic and sensitive personality. The early misfortunes left the younger son somewhat moody and timid, with alternating periods of discouragement and exalted aspiration, traits that determined his actions in later years.

Charles was sent to the local high school, where he was an indifferent and unhappy pupil. He later wrote, "I received no education but from my mother; neither reading, writing, ciphering, nor anything else. My education was the example set me by my brothers; there was in all the members of my family a reliance on self—a true independence—and by imitation I obtained it. People prate about education, and put out of sight example, which is all in all."

When Charles was eighteen he was indentured to John as an apprentice and began assisting him in his anatomy school. At the same time he attended lectures at the University of Edinburgh. Of delicate sensibility, he reacted with revulsion against the unsavory aspects of human dissection; however, he fought this repugnance and quickly overcame it to become an eager and skillful anatomist. His scruples against animal experimentation remained with him during his many years as an outstanding physiologist, and his flinching from the infliction of pain on the patients upon whom he operated was a perpetual trial during all of his surgical career.

While still a student, Charles published *A System of Dissection* (1798) with

Fɪɢ. 92. Sir Charles Bell, K. H., F. R. S. Portrait by Dorofield Hardy from the miniature by Ballantyne. From: *Sir* Gordon Gordon-Taylor and E. W. Walls: *Sir Charles Bell: His Life and Times*, Edinburgh, E. & S. Livingstone, Ltd., 1958.

illustrations engraved from his own drawings. He wrote, in addition, the description of the nervous system for John's *Anatomy of the Human Body*, the three volumes of which were published serially from 1794 to 1800. Further exercise of his artistic talents went into the modelling in colored wax of pathological specimens, creating pieces of great teaching value as well as objects of remarkable beauty.

His period of training completed, Charles Bell was admitted to the College of Surgeons of Edinburgh, which gave him not only the right to engage in practice, but also to operate, in rotation with other surgeons, on patients in the Royal Infirmary. His future might have been assured had it not been for the feud between John and the Faculty of the University, the outcome of which was the exclusion of both brothers from the hospital service. Convinced that his outlook was bleak in his native city, he acquiesced to John's urging that he seek a less prejudiced environment in London. Consequently, in 1804 at the age of thirty, he migrated to the British capital where he remained for thirty-two years.

The early years in London were filled with loneliness, frustration, and discouragement, but they also had their triumphs. Shortly after his arrival (1806), he published his "Anatomy of Expression." This beautiful work combined his skill in anatomy with his artistic capabilities, and won him quick recognition in art circles, although not in surgery. To achieve the latter, and to provide an income, Charles opened a private school of anatomy in an old, dilapidated "haunted" house, which again, however, at first attracted more

In rage the features are unsteady, the eyeballs are seen largely; they roll and are inflated. The front is alternately knit and raised in furrows by the motion of the eyebrows; the nostrils are inflated to the utmost; the lips are swelled, and being drawn, open the corners of the mouth.

Fig. 93. From: *The Anatomy and Philosophy of Expression* by Charles Bell, London, 1806

students of art than of surgery. In addition to these lectures on anatomy and surgery, he published the first volume of his *System of Operative Surgery* (1807), thus gradually establishing for himself a place in the surgical life of the city. It was at this time, also, that he conceived the idea which was to be his greatest contribution of "a new anatomy of the brain." He was immensely excited with his discovery because he was convinced ". . . it really is *the only thing that has appeared in anatomy since the days of Hunter.*"

These activities were interrupted for a time in January 1809, when Bell volunteered his services to care for wounded British soldiers who were being returned from Corunna (Spain) to Portsmouth. This was his first experience with a massive influx of seriously ill and wounded patients, and he threw himself into the task with total disregard of himself. His descriptions of this episode vividly reveal his emotional involvement; and his surgical observations formed the basis of a *Dissertation on Gunshot Wounds* which he published some years later. He also made numerous drawings of the patients and their wounds which provide a record more striking than a written description.

Following his marriage (1811) Bell used part of his wife's modest dowry to purchase the Old Windmill Street School of Anatomy originally started by William Hunter. From this time onward things were better for him, his classes larger, his reputation rapidly growing. Two years later he was elected Surgeon to the Middlesex Hospital. After this his days were filled, as were those of Pott, Hunter, and Cooper, with private practice, hospital work,

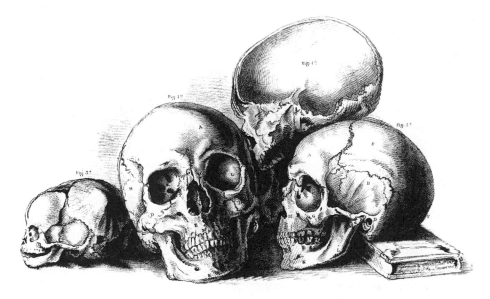

Fig. 94. From: *The Anatomy and Philosophy of Expression* by Charles Bell, London, 1806

teaching, writing, and research. Patients came from afar as did distinguished guests from the Continent to visit him. He had attained eminence but his greatest contribution was yet to be made.

A second episode of military surgical experience created an unforgettable impression. Word came of the victory at Waterloo with reports of the vast numbers of wounded who needed attention. Bell and his brother-in-law John Shaw, who was his favored pupil and assistant, left at once for Belgium. The impressions on a sensitive mind left by visiting the scenes of the glorious victory as well as the horrible aftermath of battle are eloquently described in a letter written to a friend shortly after his return to England.

"I write this to you, after being some days at home engaged in my usual occupations, and consequently disenchanted of the horrors of the battle of Waterloo. I feel relief in this, for certainly if I had written to you from Brussels, I should have appeared very extravagant. An absolute revolution took place in my economy, body and soul; so that I, who was known to require eight hours' sleep, found three hours, and then one hour and a half, sufficient, after days of the most painful excitement and bodily exertion.

"After I had been five days engaged with the prosecution of my object, I found that the best cases, that is, the most horrid wounds left totally without assistance, were to be found in the hospital of the French wounded. This hospital was only forming; they were even then bringing these poor creatures in from the woods. It is impossible to convey to you the picture of human misery continually before my eyes. What was heart-rending in the day, was intolerable at night; and I rose and wrote, at four o'clock in the morning, to the chief-surgeon, Gunning, offering to perform the necessary operations upon the French. At six o'clock I took the knife in my hand, and continued incessantly at work till seven in the evening; and so the second day, and again on the third.

"All the decencies of performing surgical operations were soon neglected; while I amputated one man's thigh, there lay at one time thirteen, all beseeching to be taken next: one full of entreaty, one calling upon me to remember my promise to take him, another execrating. It was a strange thing to feel my clothes stiff with blood, and my arms powerless with the exertion of using the knife; and more extraordinary still, to find my mind calm amidst such a variety of suffering. But to give one of these objects access to your feelings was to allow yourself to be unmanned for the performance of a duty. It was less painful to look upon the whole, than to contemplate one.

"When I first went round the wards of the wounded prisoners, my sensations were very extraordinary. We had everywhere heard of the manner in which these men had fought—nothing could surpass their devotedness. In a ward containing fifty, there was no expression of suffering; no one spoke to his neighbour; there was a resentful, sullen rigidness of face, a fierceness in their dark eyes, as they lay half covered in the sheets.

"Sunday.—I was interrupted, and now I feel I was falling into the mistake of attempting to convey to you the feelings which took possession of me amidst the miseries of Brussels. After being eight days amongst the wounded, I visited the field of battle. The view of the field, the gallant stories, the charges, the individual instances of enterprise and valour, recalled me to the sense which the world has of victory and Waterloo. But this was transient. A gloomy, uncomfortable view of human nature is the inevitable consequence of looking upon the whole as I did—as I am forced to do.

"It is a misfortune to have our sentiments at variance with the universal sentiment. But there must ever be associated with the honours of Waterloo, in my eyes, the shocking signs of woe: to my ear, accents of intensity, outcry from the manly breast, interrupted, forcible expressions from the dying—and noisome smells. I must show you my note book, for as I took my notes of cases generally by sketching the object of our remarks, it may convey an excuse for this excess of sentiment."[4]

It will be remembered that, during the time that he was still a student, Charles wrote the section on the nervous system for John Bell's *Anatomy of the Human Body*. As so frequently happens, this earliest interest became the enduring preoccupation of his life, to which he returned time after time, and the contributions he made in this field were his greatest achievements. The great advances that had been made in the science of physiology in the 200 years that followed Harvey's discovery of the circulation had not extended to the knowledge of the functions of the nervous system, which had remained essentially that of Galen. Charles wrote that, in the period immediately preceding his first publications on the subject, ". . . there was a singular indifference to the study of the nerves; and an opinion very generally prevailed that as the notion of the ancients had descended to us uncontroverted and unimproved, the subject was entirely exhausted. The hypothesis that a nervous fluid was derived from the brain, and transmitted by nervous tubes, was deemed consistent with anatomical demonstration, and there was no hope of improvement."

Bell's contributions regarding the nervous system cover a very wide range. He established the facts that the nerves of the special senses could be traced

---

4. Amédée Pichot: *The Life and Labors of Sir Charles Bell*, London, Richard Bentley, 1860, pp. 80–82.

from specific areas of the cerebrum to their end-organs, that the spinal nerves carry both sensory and motor functions, and that the sensory fibers traverse the posterior roots whereas the motor fibers run through the anterior roots (Bell's Law). He described muscle sense or proprioceptive sensation. He demonstrated that the fifth cranial nerve was sensory to the face, and motor to mastication, whereas the seventh controlled the muscles of expression. The long thoracic nerve is still called the respiratory nerve of Bell, and facial paralysis, Bell's palsy.

It is the more remarkable that most of Bell's observations were made from anatomical dissection. Although he did some animal experimentation, this was limited by his repugnance to inflict pain. He wrote:

> "I should be writing a third paper on the Nerves, but I cannot proceed without making some experiments, which are so unpleasant to make that I defer them. You may think me silly, but I cannot perfectly convince myself that I am authorized in nature, or religion, to do these cruelties—for what?—for anything else than a little egotism or self-aggrandizement; and yet, what are my experiments in comparison with those which are daily done? and are done daily for nothing."[5]

A fruitless and acrimonious dispute as to priority arose between Bell and the brilliant French physiologist, François Magendie, who later, but much more definitively, established the functions of the spinal nerve roots by animal experimentation. In other respects, the discoveries of Charles Bell were received with approbation. His own evaluation, expressed in confidence in letters to one of his brothers, may be ascertained from the following quotations. As early as 1810, he wrote: "I write to tell you that I really think I am going to establish my Anatomy of the Brain on facts the most important that have been discovered in the history of science." Some time later (1821) he said, "Joking apart, I stand alone in anatomy! This business of the nerves may be long of coming forward exactly as it should; but my ambition has a rest in this—*I have made a greater discovery than ever was made by one man in anatomy*, and I have not yet done."

His conception of the importance of his discovery is confirmed by the honors conferred upon Bell. He was knighted (1829) in recognition of his achievements, was appointed to the Chair of Anatomy of the Royal College of Surgeons, and, together with Astley Cooper, received an honorary degree from the University of Göttingen. On a later trip to the Continent he was received with further honors. When visiting Paris, the eminent surgeon Roux dismissed his class, saying, "You have seen Charles Bell, that is enough."

As a medical author Bell had few equals. He wrote numerous books and

5. *Sir* Gordon Gordon-Taylor and E. W. Walls: *Sir Charles Bell: His Life and Times*, Edinburgh, E. & S. Livingstone, Ltd., 1958, p. 111.

FIG. 95. Opisthotonos. From: *The Anatomy and Philosophy of Expression*, by Sir Charles Bell, London, 1806.

articles, in addition to those already mentioned. Among the former may be listed his *System of Operative Surgery, founded on the Basis of Anatomy* (1807–1809); *A Dissertation on Gunshot Wounds* (1814); *Surgical Observations: being a quarterly report of cases in surgery, treated in the Middlesex Hospital, the Cancer Establishment and in Private Practice* (1816–1818); *Illustrations of the Great Operations of Surgery* (1821); and an engaging and highly informative monograph, *The Hand: its mechanism and vital endowments, as evincing design, and illustrating the power, wisdom, and goodness of God* (1833). This monograph is charmingly written, beautifully illustrated by the author, and contains many philosophical as well as comparative anatomical facts concerning the hand and its adaptation to function. His many journal publications cover an enormously wide range and actually embrace the entire domain of surgery.

As an educator, Charles Bell played an important part in the establishment of the Middlesex Hospital Medical School in 1835. Shortly afterward he was invited to return to Edinburgh to the Chair of Surgery. This he decided to do, although with considerable reluctance. The remaining six years of his life were rather quietly spent, teaching and writing and indulging his hobbies. His life had been full, and his rewards great. Because of his many achievements, his extraordinary gifts of communication, and his personal qualities, he is the one of the Scottish Bells who has been dealt with *in extenso* in this book.

꧁ ꧁ ꧁   [The essential humanity of Charles Bell and his faculty for
꧁ ꧁ ꧁   succinct expression are clearly revealed in his introduction to
his *Great Operations of Surgery*:]

TO THE READER

The reader will forgive me, if I now address him with the same freedom I would a pupil who had sat beside me for successive winters.

Before entering on the subject of this work, in which there will be few opportunities of discussion, and in which the demonstration only is to be made, I take the occasion to impress upon him the necessity of his prescribing strict rules for himself, in the performance of operations.

The Public, who are so ready to determine on the merits of our Profession, and even the patients who are to suffer, are surprisingly ignorant both of the Surgeon's motives for what he does, and the propriety of the methods he puts in practice. He is continually operating in secret as a matter of necessity; the most sensible give the decision up to him; so that he is answerable to his own conscience, and to that alone. Nor is the Public aware of the temptations which men of our Profession withstand. Credit for great abilities, gratitude for services performed, and high emoluments, are ready to be bestowed for a little deception, and that obliquity of conduct, which does not amount to actual crime. This is precisely the situation in which a man requires a thorough devotion to the principles of honour and right conduct, to preserve him from the commission of error. These are the considerations which should make it the interest of Society to hold the Profession in respect, and which make it the duty of every member of it to keep it pure.

I shall place the matter before you in another light. If we go into a court of law, we see the bench occupied by the learned judges; before them are counsel, skilled in the law, and a jury of twelve honest men, to hold the balance betwixt the severity of the law and the weakness of human nature. What are they met to decide? Perhaps a matter of money or of succession. Even if it should be a criminal court, what a contrast have we with the situation of the Surgeon, on whose single decision the life of a fellow-creature depends; one, perhaps, bearing all the relationships of society; having all the ties which bind a man to existence, and the virtues which make his life dear. The Surgeon cannot lean upon the judgment of others, nor say, for this the wisdom of the legislature has provided. He has to examine an evidence, often strangely perverted; he must judge, unaided by friendly counsel; and, to determine upon what is right to be done, when the life of a friend hangs on the issue, and where the execution depends on his own dexterity, is a thing of the greatest difficulty.

When we thus consider the weight of responsibility, it is not surprising, that so many shrink from the performance of the duties which belong to our Profession; the more especially that success in it draws no sympathy. If there be some eminent men who esteem our Art, and express themselves differently, yet it must be acknowledged, that the Public consider him, who deserves the first honors of the Profession, as only more eminently divested of common feeling.

That the Surgeon, in order to do his duty, must be divested of the common feelings of Humanity, is a vulgar error. Let my lady's maid still suppose, that he must be a brute whose occupation soils his hands with blood. It is not supposed that she can have very accurate notions of the difference of his service who inflicts the wound, and of his who closes it; but for a reasonable man, and most of all, for one educated to Surgery, it is very ridiculous to assign as a reason for not doing his duty, that his feelings prevent him. These feelings are not for his patient! Instead of having a true compassion for the wounded or for the diseased, instead of neglecting his first painful impressions, and being happy to render assistance, he stands, like the foolish maid, who holds her apron betwixt her pretty eyes and the object of her horror. Let no man boast of feelings, until they are of that genuine kind, and amount to that degree, that he can forget himself, in the desire to give aid to another.

In performing the operations of Surgery, this neglect of yourself is very necessary. Why simplicity should be so rare a virtue in Operators, is very remarkable; since it requires but this one rule—think only of your patient. Any thing like a flourish on such an occasion, does not merely betray vanity, but a lamentable want of just feeling. It is as if a man said—Look at me now—see how unconcerned I am, while the patient is suffering under my hand! Simplicity is always becoming; often a great excellence; but, in regard to operations performed on a fellow-creature, it is a moral obligation.

In truth, the anxiety of a Surgeon, before an important operation, is the greatest any man can suffer, where there is not a consciousness of crime; and do not suppose that this belongs to a Surgeon in his early practice only, or to such feeble spirits as cannot summon resolution to do their duty. The greatest Surgeon this country has produced, the celebrated Cheselden, was,

even in his later days, anxious to sickness, before the performance of a severe operation.

These are the considerations which incline me to believe, that
our Profession has not been sufficiently honored; and that men
are esteemed, only in proportion to the emoluments they have
drawn from it. It depends on the conduct of those who are now
entering their Profession, whether Surgery will continue to be
confounded with meaner arts, or rise to be the very first in estimation; as requiring great abilities and long study to attain the
knowledge of it, and purity and the strictest honor in the
practice of it.[6]

[ON THE ANATOMY OF THE BRAIN.]

[Bell's concepts of the nervous system were first expressed in a
very brief monograph entitled *Idea of a New Anatomy of the Brain*,
which he published in 1811 in an edition of only 100 copies.
These were circulated chiefly to his friends in order to obtain
their opinion. The following excerpt is characteristic of this
important medical document.]

The prevailing doctrine of the anatomical schools is, that the
whole brain is a common sensorium; that the extremities of the
nerves are organized, so that each is fitted to receive a peculiar
impression; or that they are distinguished from each other only
by delicacy of structure, and by a corresponding delicacy of
sensation; that the nerve of the eye, for example, differs from
the nerves of touch only in the degree of its sensibility.

It is imagined that impressions, thus differing in kind, are
carried along the nerves to the sensorium, and presented to the
mind; and that the mind, by the same nerves which receive
sensation, sends out the mandate of the will to the moving parts
of the body.

It is further imagined, that there is a set of nerves, called
vital nerves, which are less strictly connected with the sensorium, or which have upon them knots, cutting off the course
of sensation, and thereby excluding the vital motions from the
government of the will.

This appears sufficiently simple and consistent, until we begin
to examine anatomically the structure of the brain, and the
course of the nerves,—then all is confusion: the divisions and
subdivisions of the brain, the circuitous course of nerves, their

---

6. Charles Bell: *Illustrations of the Great Operations of Surgery*, London, A. and R. Spottiswoode,
   1821, pp. v–viii.

intricate connections, the separation and re-union, are puzzling in the last degree, and are indeed considered as things inscrutable. Thus it is, that he who knows the parts the best, is most in a maze, and he who knows least of anatomy, sees least inconsistency in the commonly received opinion.

In opposition to these opinions, I have to offer reasons for believing, That the cerebrum and cerebellum are different in function as in form; That the parts of the cerebrum have different functions; and that the nerves which we trace in the body are not single nerves possessing various powers, but bundles of different nerves, whose filaments are united for the convenience of distribution, but which are distinct in office, as they are in origin from the brain:

That the external organs of the senses have the matter of the nerves adapted to receive certain impressions, while the corresponding organs of the brain are put in activity by the external excitement: That the idea or perception is according to the part of the brain to which the nerve is attached, and that each organ has a certain limited number of changes to be wrought upon it by the external impression:

That the nerves of sense, the nerves of motion, and the vital nerves, are distinct through their whole course, though they seem sometimes united in one bundle; and that they depend for their attributes on the organs of the brain to which they are severally attached.

The view which I have to present, will serve to shew why there are divisions, and many distinct parts in the brain: why some nerves are simple in their origin and distribution, and others intricate beyond description. It will explain the apparently accidental connection between the twigs of nerves. It will do away the difficulty of conceiving how sensation and volition should be the operation of the same nerve at the same moment. It will shew how a nerve may lose one property, and retain another; and it will give an interest to the labours of the anatomist in tracing the nerves.[7]

[Bell described many case of paralysis of the face of different causes, and correctly interpreted the source of the disturbance. Included are a number of seventh nerve paralyses which are now known as "Bell's palsy."]

7. *Sir* Gordon Gordon-Taylor and E. W. Walls: *Sir Charles Bell: His Life and Times*, Edinburgh, E. & S. Livingstone, Ltd., 1958, Appendix XII, pp. 219–220.

NO. XXVII.—PARALYSIS OF THE FACE.

A housemaid, Jane Smith by name, twenty-eight years old, presented herself here as an out-patient, with the following symptoms. She had lost all power of moving the right side of her face. When she endeavoured to raise her eye-brows, the right side of the forehead remained smooth, and the left was wrinkled. When she attempted to raise her eyes, the right eye was but partially covered, the eye-ball rolling upwards, and carrying the cornea within the curtain of the upper lid, which descended a little to meet it. When she smiled, the right side of the face remained immovable, and it wore at all times a blank and expressionless character. When she was told to perform the action of blowing, the right cheek was puffed out like a loose bag, and the breath issued, whether she would or no, at the right angle of her mouth. The same thing happened with her food and drink: she could not prevent their escaping at the right corner of her mouth, nor could she convey morsels of food from the right to the left cheek without the aid of her hand applied externally in support of the paralysed cheek. The masseter and temporal muscles acted, however, as strongly on the one side as on the other; and the sensation of the palsied parts remained perfect. There was no paralysis on any other part of the body. [8]

NO. XXIX.—PARALYSIS OF THE FACE.

Some of you will recollect one of my patients (Richard Hills) who was in Pepy's Ward about this time last year: in him the same kind of paralysis (of the face) seemed to have been occasioned by a mere shock or jar. He was a coachman; and one day, when he was off his box, his horses started away, and he ran to their heads to stop them, but was thrown down in the attempt, striking his right hip and elbow. He received no blow on the head at all. Three hours afterwards he found that he could not spit properly—that he could not avoid spitting on his clothes on one side, and that he could not whistle. Another circumstance worthy of notice took place in this man, which often, though not always, happens in these cases, and which I did not mention before. He remained for about two months in the hospital, and regained during that time, in some degree, the power of exercising the affected muscles; but he still was unable to close the right eye-lids. The eye itself was unharmed.

8. *Sir* Charles Bell: *The Nervous System of the Human Body*, Edinburgh, Adam and Charles Black, 1836, p. 301.

After he was made out-patient, he resumed his functions on the coach-box, and his eye, permanently half open, was more exposed to colds and currents of wind than it had been while he was here. Moreover, he got drunk; and he soon presented himself again, with universal redness and inflammation of the conjunctiva.

That the greater number of cases of this kind are free from serious peril, is a fact of great practical importance. It enables us to quiet the alarm of the patient and his friends, and regulates, in many instances, the treatment, rendering it less rigorous than it might and should be if the palsy were really the harbinger of apoplexy. At the same time, you ought to know that a similar limitation of paralysis to the particular muscles supplied by the portio dura, is sometimes (though rarely) observed, when the disease has a more inward origin—when it affects and involves the brain itself. [9]

NO. XXIV.

When we see a person alarmed without cause, and there is no danger in the case, there is something approaching to the ludicrous in the scene. A physician paid me a visit who had come up from the country in the mail, and had fallen asleep in the night-time, with his cheek exposed at the open window to the east wind. On the morning of his arrival, when preparing to go abroad, he found, upon looking into his glass, that his face was all twisted. His alarm gave more expression to one side of his face, and produced more horrible distortion. Both laughing and crying, you know, depend on the function of the portio dura, but when he came to me he considered it no laughing matter: I never saw distortion more complete. It was difficult to comfort him; but I am happy to add, that the paralysis gradually left him, as I told him it would. I have at present a young lady under my care who has paralysis of the face, and who has received great benefit from galvanism. And I have lately seen an instance of the same kind; the more remarkable only as shewing how the want of expression will injure the finest countenance. I mention these things to remind you of the frequency of the occurrence, and of the necessity of your distinguishing the slighter cases, where the exterior branches of the nerve are affected, from those wherein the cause is deeper seated, and more formidable. [10]

9. *Ibid.*, p. 302.
10. *Ibid.*, p. 283.

CHAPTER 40

Baron Guillaume Dupuytren
(1777–1835)

"All that I will bequeath is the fruit of my labors which has never been tainted by any culpable act which might have given birth to ideas other than those of power of order and of labor without stint."

(From Dupuytren's Will)

The years that followed the French Revolution were contentious years, and Dupuytren was a man of his time. He was a contentious man. To reach the heights of success and recognition as a scientist and a surgeon, as indeed he did, he exercised an irresistible ambition, tireless energy, and a total disregard for the opinions of his colleagues. Stimulated, perhaps, by the penury and bleakness of his student days, he fought his way upward with a ruthless indifference to the welfare of teachers or friends. He was characterized as "the first of surgeons and the least of men."

Born in the village of Pierre-Bouffière in 1777, the son of a parliamentary attorney, Dupuytren experienced in his early childhood exciting episodes which foreshadowed the dramatic character of his later years. When but three years of age, he was abducted by a strange woman who had been captivated by his animation and carried him off in a stagecoach. Fortunately, the father learned of the abduction in time and, giving chase, overtook the abductress and reclaimed his child. Once as a schoolboy the young Guillaume submitted poorly to discipline and ran away to escape punishment, only to be returned after due chastisement. Shortly afterward the boy so amused a group of hussars stationed in the village that the captain requested that he be allowed to take the youngster to Paris, and, strangely, the parents acceded.

In Paris he was again enrolled in a boarding school where for a period of four years his performance was undistinguished indeed. Afoot and penniless, he made his long way back to the paternal home imbued with the revolutionary excitement, so rampant in 1793, and announced his intention to become a soldier. But his father, less emotional and more practical, enrolled him in the medico-surgical school of the Saint-Alexis Hospital at Limoges, with the

Lith. de Delpech à Paris

DUPUYTREN.

Bon Dupuytren.

FIG. 96

authoritarian injunction "You will be a surgeon!" After several weeks, however, Dupuytren returned to Paris for his surgical training.

The beginning was not auspicious. His first exposure to the dissecting room
evoked a revulsion to the point of illness, but he quickly overcame this weakness and developed a passionate love for anatomical dissection. At the *Charité*

FIG. 97. Dupuytren performing a cataract operation on a woman in the presence of Charles X. (Musée Carnavalet)

in Paris, where his studies began, he won a prosectorship in anatomy in an open competition when but eighteen years of age. To his anatomical studies he added physiology, surgical pathology, and chemistry; and he engaged seriously in his own researches, beginning with the ligation of the thoracic duct, the chemistry of chyle, nerve section, and structure of the inguinal canal. He also initiated his private series of lectures in anatomy.

In the midst of all these activities, Dupuytren obtained the position of second-surgeon at the *Hôtel-Dieu* by competitive examination (1802). Six years later he became joint-chief and, finally, in 1815, Chief Surgeon. In the meantime he had won the professorship of surgery at the Faculty of Medicine. With remarkable singleness of purpose, he threw himself into the performance of his duties with zeal and devotion. The patients were the recipients of his most meticulous care. Through his careful observation and minute inquiry, he developed an almost uncanny diagnostic skill. His operative technique and his judgment as to the timing of his interventions, both carefully developed by constant attention, made him a superb surgeon. A perfectionist in everything he did, he spared no effort in his lectures and bedside teaching. His commanding voice, excellent diction, and complete knowledge of his subject drew crowds of students to his classes and built the reputation of the Faculty to unprecedented heights.

Every facet of surgery was enriched by the labors of Dupuytren. He resected the lower jaw for the first time, invented the crushing enterotome for closing spontaneous colostomies, pioneered in ligation of arterial trunks, improved the handling of fractures, described the contracture of the fingers which bears his name, and invented new devices and new techniques. It was characteristic of the man thoroughly to test his innovations in the laboratory. In discussing the development of the crushing clamp for the closure of enterostomies he writes, "experiments performed on living animals also proved to me, very satisfactorily, that in the proposed operation the patient would run no greater risk than in those frequently performed on the abdomen." And again, "Before using the instrument on man, I made some experiments on living animals; the effects surpassed my hopes." Dupuytren wrote little, but what he wrote was good. His various *memoires* have been collected, published, and translated, as were also his "oral lectures."

Honors and emoluments were showered upon him. He was made a baron by King Louis XVIII, became surgeon to this monarch and to his successor, Charles X, and was elected to the Academy of Medicine and to the Academy of Sciences. He had an enormous practice beyond his hospital work and is reputed to have amassed a great fortune.

Throughout all these achievements and the recognition they brought him, he remained austere, arrogant, cold, and calculating. Never deigning to court favors, he met each obstacle head on, shunning friendships, alienating colleagues, mercilessly attacking those who stood in his way. The conflicts which characterized his professional life extended into his domestic sphere. He attained his ambitions, he had power, wealth, and fame, but his life was devoid of friendship and love. At his death at the early age of fifty-seven he was honored by many for his achievements, but as a man he was mourned by few. But the large mass of his patients, many of them indigent, who had benefited from his tireless care and from the advances in treatment which he developed, expressed their gratitude by joining the colleagues and dignitaries who followed his coffin.

ᔒ   ᔒ   ᔒ   [DUPUYTREN'S CONTRACTURE]
ᔒ   ᔒ   ᔒ
On Permanent Contraction of the Fingers, and its Causes.[1]

The cause of contraction of the fingers, and especially of the ring finger, was almost unknown until the present time. It is not

1. *On Lesions of the Vascular System, Diseases of the Rectum, and other Surgical Complaints,* selections from the Collected Edition of the Clinical Lectures of Baron Dupuytren, translated and edited by F. Le Gros Clark, printed for the Sydenham Society, London, 1854, pp. 220–228.

a matter of surprise that it should have been regarded as incurable, when we consider the numberless causes to which it was attributed, the endless remedies that were tried, and the theories that were framed as to its origin. The authors who have treated of the subject, have done so in a very incomplete manner.

Probably, if search were made, something more might be found in books; but my life has been so entirely passed in practice, that I have not had time to go through the various works; and I shall be glad to learn that they who have preceded me, and have written on this subject, have discovered the cause and the means of cure.

These contractions have at different times been supposed to proceed from rheumatism, gout, external violence, fracture, or from the infection of some poisonous matter in the system. We shall soon see what little foundation there is for these assumed causes.

Most of those who are thus affected, have been in the habit of using force with the palm of the hand, and of handling hard bodies, such as a hammer, an oar, or a plough. Thus the wine-dealer and the coachman, whose cases I shall cite, were in the habit, the one of boring his casks with a gimlet, or piling up his casks; and the other of continually using his whip on the backs of his horses. I could also give, as an example, the case of a clerk, who used to stamp his letters with a seal, the handle of which pressed forcibly against the palm of his hand. It is found also in masons, who lay hold of stones with the ends of their fingers, also in gardeners, etc. It, however, generally attacks those who are compelled to use the palm of the hand.

The affection usually commences in the ring-finger, whence it extends to the others, especially to the little finger, and increases by almost insensible degrees. The patient at first feels a little stiffness in the palm of the hand, and a difficulty in extending the fingers, which soon become a quarter, a third, or half bent. The flexure is sometimes carried much farther, and the ungual extremities of the fingers are bent into the palm of the hand. From the very beginning a cord is felt on the palmar surface of the fingers and hand, which is drawn tighter when an effort is made to straighten the fingers, and disappears entirely when they are quite bent. It is of roundish form, and its most salient part is at the articulation of the finger with the corresponding metacarpal bone, where it forms a sort of bridge.

Its extremities are lost insensibly at the second phalanx of the finger, and about the middle of the palm of the hand, or perhaps short of this point.

The skin covering the finger is thrown into arched folds, the concavity of which is below, and the convexity above. This condition is for a time limited to the finger primarily affected; but at a later period the other fingers are, though in a less degree, involved in the deformity.

Notwithstanding all these appearances of deep-seated mischief, the joints of the affected fingers show no trace of anchylosis, and, without excepting even the first phalanx, they may be easily bent; but, beyond a certain point, they cannot be straightened with any amount of effort; and I have seen one hundred to one hundred and fifty pounds weight suspended by the hook which the finger forms, without changing its position a line. It would seem as if the finger were prevented from being straightened by an inflexible barrier placed along its dorsal aspect; but there is really no other obstacle than the cord on the palmar surface of the fingers and hand, the bold prominence of which is proportioned to the efforts made to straighten the finger. The affection begins, proceeds, and reaches its climax without any pain. Even the efforts I have mentioned cause scarcely any; and it would seem to consist in some mechanical obstacle, in tissues having very few of the properties which render other parts sensible to external violence.

But how are these inconveniences to be accounted for? The ring-finger is incapable of extension, and the others will not admit of it completely; the patient, consequently, cannot lay hold of large objects; if he presses anything tightly, he experiences a sharp pain; the act of grasping is obstructed, and causes a painful sensation. When at rest there is no pain; and none is felt till he endeavours to straighten his fingers too suddenly.

I have seen thirty or forty such cases, and could cite numberless opinions on the cause of contraction of the ring-finger. Some have regarded it as due to a thickened or horny texture of the skin, not considering it as arising from any specific cause; others have thought that it depends on spasmodic affection of the muscles; but this explanation is purely hypothetical, for all the movements, excepting that of extension, are executed with perfect freedom. Many have considered that the contraction is connected with a disease of the flexor tendons, and I was of this opinion for a length of time. But I was anxious to ascertain the nature of the disease; whether it was the result of inflammation, or of abnormal adhesion of the cellular tissue, or a chronic affection of these parts. By repeated dissections I found that none of the supposed alterations existed. Some have ascribed it to a disease of the thecae of the tendons; others to some peculiarity in the articular extremities of the phalanges and the lateral ligaments. If the articulation be examined, it will be seen that the surfaces are very extended, and that they are united in such a manner as to render the motion of flexion much easier than that of extension. The lateral ligaments on both sides of the joint present a peculiarity which is worth noticing. They are nearer to the anterior than to the posterior surface, the result of which is that the fingers have a greater tendency to bend than to straighten. But, admitting that this hypothesis is of some value, it cannot be applicable to men in the prime of life; besides, it will not stand against facts. Lastly, there are some who fancy that the contraction is owing to a disease of the articulating surfaces, which may deprive them of their polish, and lead to wear or anchylosis of the joints.

I will not dilate any further on these various opinions, and I have merely alluded to them because they are connected with the history of the disease. The important point is that an obstacle exists, and we should endeavour to discover the true cause. A very few years ago, it was thought that contraction of the ring-finger arose from an alteration in the flexor tendons; and, on looking at the projection at the anterior part of the finger, this opinion seemed plausible.

Such was the state of the question, when a man suffering from the affection died. I had watched him for some time, and I availed myself of the opportunity to seek further information.

Case I.—*Permanent contraction of the fingers. Death. Dissection.*— An old man, who had suffered for a length of time from contraction of the fingers, having died, I determined on having a careful anatomical examination of the parts; as soon as I obtained possession of the arm, I had a drawing made of it, and then proceeded to the dissection. Having removed the skin from the palm of the hand and from the palmar surface of the fingers, the folds and wrinkles which it presented previously entirely disappeared; so that it was evident that this appearance, which it assumed during the affection, did not appertain to the skin itself, but was imparted to it secondarily. Continuing the dissection, I laid bare the palmar fascia, and observed with surprise that it was in a state of tension, contracted and diminished in length; from its lower part something like cords proceeded to the sides of the affected finger. On endeavouring to extend the fingers, I clearly perceived that the fascia became still more tense; here was a ray of light, and I suspected that this tissue had something to do with the disease. But it remained to discover the affected point; I cut through the prolongations which it gave off to the sides of the fingers, and the contraction ceased instantly; the fingers became nearly straight, and a very slight effort extended the phalanges completely. The tendons remained entire, and the thecae were not opened; all that had been done was the removal of the skin, and the section of the prolongations of the fascia which proceeded to the base of the phalanges. With the view of leaving nothing in doubt, and resolving all objections, I laid bare the tendons; they were of the natural size, and were as supple as usual, the surfaces being smooth. I then proceeded further; the articulations were in their normal state, the bones were neither enlarged nor uneven, nor did they show the least sign of alteration either externally or internally; I could perceive no change in the inclination of the articulating surfaces, no alteration in the external ligaments, no anchylosis, neither had the synovial sheaths, the cartilages, nor the synovia experienced any change. It was, therefore, natural to conclude, that the origin of the affection was in the extreme tension of the palmar fascia, and that the contraction itself resulted from injury of the fascia by the forcible and continued action of some hard body against the palm of the hand. It only remained, therefore, to apply this new theory to cases as they might occur.

The various opinions which have been given to the world as to the cause of this affection, have necessarily involved great uncertainty of treatment. Many practitioners have considered it incurable. Dr. Bennati, on consulting Astley Cooper about an Italian pianoforte player named Ferrari, who suffered from the deformity, was told by this celebrated English surgeon that it is incurable; from which it is clear that the nature of the disease was not then known to him. Others, whilst admitting the possibility of curing it, have lauded various methods, which have generally proved ineffectual. Having had many such cases under my care, I have at different times tried poultices and

various emollient applications, leeches, and friction with ointments, especially mercurial; I have also tried alkaline and sul-
phurous douches, etc., at every temperature, but without
success. I then attempted permanent extension, with the aid of
an instrument made by Lacroix; but this led to no improvement, on the contrary, it gave rise to severe pain in the palm of
the hand, after continuing it for some time, and it was abandoned. Some surgeons proposed section of the flexor tendons,
which operation was performed twice. The first time the tendon
was cut through the middle, which gave rise to inflammation
and contraction along the sheath; the patient's life was endangered and the finger continued contracted. In the other case
the section was made much lower; no accident followed, but
the finger remained almost as much bent as before. Some time
after these operations, which were performed by very good
surgeons, I was consulted in a similar case.

Case II.—*Contraction of the ring and little fingers, completely cured
by simple division of the palmar fascia.*—

The patient's hand being firmly fixed, I began by making a
transverse incision, six lines in extent, opposite the metacarpo-
phalangeal articulation of the ring finger; the bistoury first
divided the skin, and afterwards the palmar fascia with a
cracking noise which was distinctly heard. When the incision
was completed, the ring finger was immediately liberated, and
could be extended almost as easily as in a natural state. Wishing to spare the patient the pain of another incision, I endeavoured to extend the section of the fascia, by slipping the bistoury transversely and deeply beneath the skin towards the
ulnar edge of the hand, so as to disengage the little finger, but
I did not succeed. I determined, in consequence, on making a
fresh transverse incision opposite the articulation of the first and
second phalanges of the little finger, and thus detached its extremity from the palm of the hand; but the remainder of the
finger continued as before. Another incision then divided the
skin and the fascia opposite the corresponding metacarpo-
phalangeal articulation, which disengaged the finger in a slight
degree, but the effect was incomplete. At last I made a third
transverse incision opposite the middle of the first phalanx, and
the finger was immediately set free; showing clearly that this
last incision had included the point of insertion of the digital
process of the fascia. Very little blood was lost. The wounds
were dressed with dry lint, and the two fingers were kept ex-

tended by an appropriate instrument fixed on the back of the hand.

. . . .

This contraction, especially of the ring finger, is therefore an affection, of which the cause is now ascertained, as well as the the method of treatment.

[A second typical case is described in which the operation devised by Dupuytren was performed.]

[THE ENTEROTOME FOR CLOSING FECAL FISTULAE]

On Artificial Anus: Its Anatomical Characters, Effects, Seat' Prognosis, Diagnosis, and Treatment.[2]

Of all the diseases to which man is liable, there is no one so inconvenient and disgusting as the artificial anus. How wretched is the patient from whom, despite of his will, the alimentary, bilious, and fecal matter contained in his intestines are constantly escaping. He endeavors in vain to palliate his horrible disease, by pockets, reservoirs, boxes, etc.; he must forego society, and be condemned to lead a solitary and miserable life.

But before giving an account of the manner in which I have generally succeeded in curing this disease, always disgusting, often dangerous, and in some cases inevitably fatal, it will be indispensable to explain the morbid anatomy of the intestine, and review the causes, prognosis, diagnosis, and remedies of other surgeons. . . .

Founding my opinion on the adhesive property of serous membranes, when in contact and in a state of inflammation, I thought that an instrument which would seize a large extent of both ends of the intestine, approximate, compress, and inflame it, and lastly divide the whole of the double septum behind the spur, would completely answer the end proposed. The adhesion must precede the division of the parts, and this division effected by pressure, could never extend beyond the adhesions previously established. It was to be feared indeed, that the inflammation, instead of being confined to the narrow limits of the instruments, might extend to the rest of the peritoneum; but we know, from

2. *Lectures on Clinical Surgery* delivered in the *Hôtel-Dieu* of Paris, by Baron Dupuytren, collected and published by an association of physicians, translated from the French for the Register and Library of Medical and Chirurgical Science, stereotyped and published by Duff Green, Washington, 1835, Chapter LIII, pp. 453–474.

the history of foreign bodies, such as needles, pins, etc. which perforate slowly the intestinal canal, and make their appearance outwardly, after having caused the adhesion and division by pressure of the parts included in their passage, that this extension of inflammation does not take place. Experiments performed on living animals also proved to me, very satisfactorily, that in the proposed operation the patient would run no greater risk than in those frequently performed on the abdomen. . . .

At last, after many attempts, the *enterotome*, or instrument intended to divide the approximated ends of the gut, was constructed. It is composed of three pieces, or two lateral branches and a screw with several threads. The branches are about seven inches in length; one of them, which may be called the male branch, is formed of a blade about four inches long, three lines wide, and half a line thick on its cutting edge. This edge is undulating, and terminates in a spheroidal enlargement. At the junction of the blade with the handle there is a mortice of some lines in extent, behind which is the handle itself, two or three inches in length and divided throughout nearly its whole length by another mortice of four lines in width.

The female branch of the enterotome is slightly shorter than the male. It has on one edge a groove intended to receive the male blade. The bottom of this groove is furnished with undulations alternating with those of the male blade, and having at its extremity a cavity destined to receive the button-like termination of the latter. At the union of this blade with the handle, there is a pivot which is received into the mortice of the male branch; lastly comes the handle, having at its extremity a perforation to receive the screw.

The latter, or the third part of the enterotome is about one inch and a half in length, terminating in an oval head; it is passed through the long mortice of the male, and received into the perforation in the female branch; its action consists in approximating at will the blades of the instrument.

The mechanism of this instrument may be readily understood. Two branches which may be separated at pleasure, having blades with very blunt and undulating edges, are put in motion by a screw through their handles; and thus they seize and retain all substances which may be between them. The first effect of their pressure is to bring the parts in contact; this pressure may be carried as far as to deprive the parts of life, but yet not to immediately divide them, on account of the thickness of the edges.

Before using the instrument on man, I made some experiments on living animals; its effects surpassed my hopes. The parts were always divided in six or eight days, and whenever serous membranes were included between the branches of the enterotome, they were found to adhere on the second or third day, consequently, long before the division which happened only on the seventh or eighth.

This highly important adhesive inflammation extends on each side, along the whole length of the branches of the enterotome, as well as around its point, which it exactly circumscribes. It is accompanied by the signs of moderate inflammation, at first weak and easily destroyed; at the end of five or six days, this adhesion is pretty strong. It afterwards becomes cellular, and is as solid as a natural union.

The action of the enterotome and the division of the parts are never attended by acute pain; the inflammation is always limited to the vicinity of the parts, around which it forms a small areola, but never extends to the tissue of the organs. It operates by causing mortification of the included parts, and the solution of continuity resulting proceeds from the fall of a slough which is always found between the blades of the instrument. . . .

The cure has not been equally perfect in all these cases. In nine there have remained fistulas of various extent, obliging the patient to wear constantly a bandage in order to prevent the escape of flatus, mucous, bilious or faecal matter. The other other twenty-nine were radically cured in from two to six months. The fatality has therefore been one in fourteen; and taking away the one who perished accidentally from indigestion, it is reduced to one twentieth of the cases operated upon; a result much more favorable than generally obtained in great surgical operations. Lastly, it is to be remarked, that the last fourth of the patients, although less fortunate and obliged to wear a bandage with a pad, were in a situation incomparably preferable to that in which they had previously existed.

CHAPTER 41

Marion Sims and Early American Surgery

"Let man learn to be honest and do the right thing or do nothing."

(Marion Sims)

The evolution of medical practice and training in the New World followed a pattern which was imposed by the conditions of colonial and frontier life, and hence differed strikingly from those of older countries. In the early Colonial period there were virtually no trained physicians to aid the settlers in their constant struggle against the privations and dangers of a strange and hostile environment. As the population grew, some doctors who had been educated in Europe settled on this continent, but their numbers were totally inadequate, particularly in view of the widely dispersed settlements. Those young men who later entered the medical profession were taught the rudiments of healing by preceptorships with physicians who were already in practice. A few rounded out this type of practical preparation by attending the schools and hospitals of Great Britain and the Continent. At the time of the founding of the earliest schools of medicine in America in the closing years of the eighteenth century, the separation of medicine and surgery, which had been traditional throughout the rest of the world, was everywhere beginning to break down. On this continent the cleavage had never come into being because the scarcity of doctors in a scattered population did not permit specialization. From the beginning, therefore, surgery and medicine were indivisible.

The rigors of pioneer life and the meagerness of educational opportunity would hardly appear propitious for the making of important medical contributions. And yet, a number of discoveries of prime significance emerged from some of the least promising regions. Perhaps the very conditioning for frontier life, the courage to undertake the unprecedented, and the absence of restraint by established schools and authorities explain these pioneer achievements.

Thus it was that Ephraim McDowell (1771–1830) made surgical history when, in 1809, he performed the first ovariotomy and proved to a skeptical world that not only was massive ovarian cyst amenable to operative extirpation, but also that elective invasion of the peritoneal cavity was feasible and practical for the cure of abdominal disease. A backwoods physician and able surgeon, he had supplemented his apprentice training by attending the University of Edinburgh and by studying with John Bell. On his return to the States, he settled in the frontier town of Danville, Kentucky, which then had a population of less than 1000 inhabitants. There, without benefit of hospital, anesthesia, asepsis, or consultation, he undertook what was generally believed to be impossible. His patient, Mrs. Jane Todd Crawford, no less heroic than himself, made the sixty-mile trip through the wilderness to Danville on horseback, with the pendulous abdomen resting on the pommel of the saddle. She was fully informed as to the hazards of the "experiment," and accepted the dangers as well as the agonies of the operation with admirable fortitude. Her confidence was rewarded. She was restored to health and survived the experience for thirty-one years.

McDowell waited until he had two additional cases before making a report of his achievements. The scientific world scoffed, and even considered his claims to be fabrications. But as his series grew and those of others were reported, his detractors were compelled to accept the truth. Although the exact number is unknown, according to his contemporaries, McDowell performed the operation of ovariotomy a total of thirteen times, only eight of which were reported during his lifetime.

William Beaumont (1785–1853) was another of the pioneer surgeons of America to win a lasting place in the history of medical science. An army surgeon stationed at the remote outpost of Fort Mackinac, on an island between Lake Huron and the northernmost tip of Lake Michigan, he was summoned during the summer of 1822 to attend a French-Canadian trapper named Alexis St. Martin who had been shot at close range with a shotgun. The victim miraculously survived the wound of the lower chest and abdomen, to be left with a large gastrocutaneous fistula. Beaumont recognized the possibilities of using his patient as a subject for the study of the physiology of digestion. Despite his lack of background in investigative methods, he carried out a long series of well-planned experiments which continued intermittently for twenty years. The results of some of these studies were published at his own expense in 1833 in a booklet entitled *Experiments and Observations on the Gastric Juice and the Physiology of Digestion*.[1] This book created a great deal of excitement in scientific circles, was translated into German (1834), and was frequently mentioned in the writings of the prominent European physiologists, including Claude Bernard. It survives as one of the classics of medicine.

The greatest gift of the new nation to suffering humanity, important beyond

1. It is true, as Dr. Bruno Kisch has reported, that similar studies were made by Jacob Helm in Germany thirty years earlier in a case of spontaneous fistula after infection. However, his little book escaped the attention of his contemporaries and therefore did not contribute to the science of gastric physiology. "Jacob Helm's Observations and Experiments on Human Digestion" by Bruno Kisch, *Journ. Hist. Med. and Allied Sciences*, 1954, Vol. 9, p. 311.

all others in the development of surgery, was anesthesia. Although the question of priority raged furiously and has never been resolved, it is a curious fact that all those participating in the discovery were Americans. The first of these successfully to use ether inhalation for surgical anesthesia was Crawford W. Long, a young physician in Jefferson, Georgia, who, however, failed to report his experiences until 1849. In the meantime, Horace Wells, a dentist of Hartford, Connecticut, employed nitrous oxide for the painless extraction of teeth in 1844. When, however, he attempted to demonstrate his great discovery in the surgical amphitheater of Massachusetts General Hospital, the patient cried out as the tooth was drawn and Wells was discredited. Two years later (1846) William Morton, also a dentist, a pupil of Wells, and subsequently a student of medicine, successfully demonstrated the employment of ether inhalation in an operation performed by Dr. J. C. Warren at Massachusetts General Hospital. The publication of this achievement quickly led to the adoption of anesthesia throughout the surgical world. With this, the horror of operative ordeals was eliminated and the way opened to the development of modern surgery.

Formal medical education became readily available in America with the founding of its earliest medical schools. The first institution of this type was established in 1765, as part of the College of Philadelphia, which subsequently became the present University of Pennsylvania. The guiding spirit in the formation of this medical school was John Morgan (1735–1789), a native of that city. After an apprenticeship with the prominent Philadelphia physician, Dr. John Redman, and a four-year term of duty as an army surgeon, he went to London where he is said to have studied not only with William but also with John Hunter; and subsequently to the University of Edinburgh from which institution he received his degree in medicine in 1763. Two further years were spent in the clinics of France and Italy and completed the course of his long training. He brought back with him to Philadelphia fellowships in the Royal Academy of Surgery of Paris and the Royal Society of London, as well as the Royal College of Physicians of England. More important, however, was his plan to establish an American school of medicine comparable to those of the Old World. In this infant institution he held the first Chair of the Theory and Practice of Medicine. Morgan was aided in these efforts by William Shippen (1712–1781), a fellow Philadelphian, who had likewise studied in London with the Hunters. On his return to the city of his birth in 1762, he began giving private lectures in anatomy which attracted large classes of students, to which later were added lectures in obstetrics. He joined Morgan in the founding of the medical school, where he held the Professorship of Anatomy and Surgery. Benjamin Rush (1745–1813) joined as the third member of this faculty in 1769 in the position of Professor of Chemistry. The college merged into the University of Pennsylvania in 1791, since which time it has continued to play an important part in American medical education. Other schools of medicine rapidly developed, chiefly on the eastern seaboard, and later spread over the entire country.

The first American surgeon to stand out prominently was Philip Syng Physick (1768–1837). A Philadelphian, as were so many of the medical pioneers, he took his A.B. degree, and later his M.A., at the University of Pennsylvania, and then spent three and one-half years under the preceptorship of Dr. Adam Kuhn, Professor of Materia Medica and Botany at Philadelphia College of Medicine. During these years Physick attended lectures at the college, but did not take his medical degree. To complete his training he went to Great Britain, where he served as house pupil of John Hunter, a relationship which proved to be of mutual benefit to teacher and student. The latter absorbed the ideas of his master and made them the core of his subsequent teaching and practice. For the remainder of his life he cherished the recollection of his association with a man for whom he always maintained a profound veneration. Hunter, on the other hand, was closely drawn to his American pupil and made him assistant in his experiments; he even procured for him an appointment as house surgeon at St. George's Hospital and, at its termination, offered him a partnership in practice. The inducement was flattering, and must have tempted him, strongly, but Physick was determined to return to America.

After receiving his license from the Royal College of Surgeons (1791), Physick went to Edinburgh where finally he took his degree in medicine. He then returned to his native Philadelphia to engage in practice. After a slow and discouraging start, his natural aptitudes and extraordinary preparation commanded recognition, and he soon became an important medical figure in the city. His participation in the care of the victims of the successive epidemics of yellow fever (which disease he himself contracted on two occasions) brought him added stature.

Physick began giving private lectures on surgery in 1800, and quickly established himself in the role of an effective teacher. Five years later he was appointed to the Chair of Surgery at the university. The duties required by this position were added to those of surgeon to the Pennsylvania Hospital and to the Almshouse Dispensary. Superimposed on all were the demands of an extremely large and lucrative practice. For a quarter of a century Physick was indeed the best-known surgeon in Philadelphia, and probably in the nation.

With all the success and recognition he earned, he was neither happy nor popular. Except for a few brief reports in the medical journals, he wrote nothing, nor did he permit the publication of his lectures. He introduced a number of innovations, none of which were of revolutionary import, which were either described in the journal articles mentioned, or were presented in the book *Elements of Surgery* published in 1813 by his nephew and pupil, John Syng Dorsey. This book constitutes his principal literary monument.

A large number of very able surgeons attained prominence during the nine-teenth century, men like Valentine Mott, Samuel D. Gross, and Daniel Brainard, to mention just a few, who are credited with many "firsts," particu-larly in the fields of arterial ligations, joint excisions, and gynecological opera-tions. The pioneer spirit, with its characteristic boldness to undertake the un-precedented, was undoubtedly a factor in these enterprising undertakings. The one man, however, who was most effective in bringing the achievements of American surgery to the attention and admiration of Europe was James Marion Sims (1813–1883).

The early life of Sims in his native South Carolina as related in his charm-ing and informal *The Story of My Life* (1884) provides a vivid picture of the

FIG. 98

harshness and intellectual poverty of the frontier. His early education, as well as his medical training at the North Carolina Medical School and later at Jefferson Medical College in Philadelphia, left him woefully unprepared for the practice of medicine. Coupled with the lack of confidence in his knowledge was an absence of enthusiasm for the profession which he had reluctantly entered. The worst of his doubts and fears were soon realized. Established in practice in his native town of Lancaster, South Carolina, his first two patients were infants with "summer complaint." Completely at a loss as to the management of infantile diarrheas, he copied random prescriptions from a textbook. Both of his young charges died, and he felt constrained, from shame and discouragement, to migrate to Alabama which was then an even more primitive settlement.

The opportunity to buy an established practice in Mount Meigs induced him to stay in that town. Shortly afterward he was called to see a man who had been sick for weeks and the many doctors who had examined the patient had failed to make a diagnosis. Sims, of course, was unable to offer anything more. Sometime later, however, when the disease had progressed to a pre-terminal state, Sims again had the opportunity to see the patient and found a huge, fluctuant swelling in the right side of the abdomen. Convinced that there was pus (he thought it was an abscess of the liver but in all probability it was of appendiceal origin), he advised incision and, despite the protests of the consulting physician, quickly did so and evacuated several quarts of purulent material. The patient quickly recovered. The story of the remarkable cure spread swiftly in the little communities, and contributed toward building the reputation of Sims as a surgeon. Moreover, he had an intuitive sense of capability in the manipulative field and a confidence which was lacking when faced with problems of internal disease.

Sickness has played an important part in determining the migration of settlers in America. Rural Alabama was a hotbed of malaria, and the young Dr. Sims soon found himself overwhelmed by its prevalence. Quinine bark was not then available in the rural South, and the death rate was high. Not only the physician himself, but his entire family fell victims to the disease, and were debilitated by its violence. Simple survival demanded a change of location and, after several moves, the family settled in the city of Montgomery, where Marion's practice had to be built over again.

Sims's reputation as a surgeon had preceded him, however, and his services soon were in demand not only by patients, but by other practitioners as well. He read of operations for cross-eyes and club-feet, and was soon correcting these congenital defects with notable success and in large numbers. A heavily veiled young woman came to him from an adjacent county, drawn by his reputation as a plastic surgeon. Otherwise attractive and charming, her life was made intolerable by a severe degree of harelip, which was so deforming that she kept her face hidden from sight. If Dr. Sims could not correct nature's horrible mistake, her life was not worth living. Sims boldly accepted the challenge and succeeded in making this miserable person happy, to say nothing of enormously augmenting his own surgical status.

The great triumph of Marion Sims, and the one which brought him worldwide renown, was in a totally different field. Ironically enough, he had always had an aversion toward gynecological problems, and avoided handling them whenever he could. When a young negro slave was brought to him with a large vesicovaginal fistula consequent upon a difficult delivery, he firmly insisted he could do nothing for her. And no wonder. The most experienced surgeons of Europe had never succeeded in repairing this defect, and its sufferers were doomed to lifetimes of incapacity, misery, and exclusion from society. Two additional cases were brought to him, also in young slaves, within a short span of time, and these, too, he refused to treat. At about this time he was urgently summoned to a woman who had fallen from a horse and was in excruciating pain from an acutely retroflexed uterus. Scraps of a lecture he had heard during his college days came to his mind. He placed the woman in the knee-chest position, and, by vaginal manipulation, corrected the malposition. To his amazement, he found that if air were allowed to distend the vaginal cavity, its walls could be clearly visualized. In great excitement, he fashioned a speculum from a pewter spoon—the forerunner of the still popular Sims's speculum—and with its aid examined the patients who had been waiting for treatment of their fistulae. He easily "saw everything as no man had ever seen before. The fistula was as plain as the nose on a man's face. The edges were clear and well defined, and the opening could be measured as accurately as if it had been cut out of a piece of paper."

To see meant to be able to cure, and he felt assured that this could be

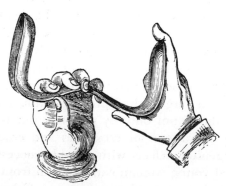

Fig. 99. Sims's speculum. From: *Clinical Notes on Uterine Surgery* by J. Marion Sims, New York, 1869.

easily accomplished. In his enthusiasm, he invited the other physicians of the city to witness the operation. To his dismay, however, when the sutures were removed, smaller openings persisted. He altered his suture techniques, devised an effective indwelling catheter, and re-operated over and over again on the three longsuffering women, and always with the same results. The doctors, friends, family, all urged that he give up the impossible. He was impoverishing himself by supporting these patients and ruining his health by overwork, but he could not abandon his dream. And when success came, it was due to so tiny a change. He decided to try silver wire as a suture material instead of silk, and that proved to be the answer. After having been operated upon more than thirty times before, these women eagerly agreed to another try, and all were cured. This was a superb and well-merited triumph.

Sims had but a few short months to enjoy his victory when again his health broke down, this time with a severe, chronic, debilitating diarrhea that, for the next four years kept him an invalid, incapable of work, and several times at the point of death. He traveled from place to place, to the North and back to the South seeking to stay alive. Finally, he became convinced that the northern climate—and perhaps its water supply—was his only hope. So, with resources exhausted, his strength depleted, with a sizable growing family to provide for, he departed from friends and relatives, abandoned his flourishing practice, and moved to New York.

His welcome in the northern metropolis was discouraging indeed. The established surgeons, centered about the medical schools and larger hospitals, were not inclined to make place for the stranger from the South. True, they did watch his operation for fistula, not for the purpose of referring their patients to him, but so that they might perform the operation themselves. It was a period to crush a less resolute spirit. But from the depths of his failure Marion Sims conceived his second big dream, which was to construct, for the first time in this country, a hospital designed exclusively for the care of diseases of women. Some scoffed, many denied the need for such an institution, but Sims marshaled the same enthusiasm and dedication that brought success to his fistula operations. Enlisting the aid of influential friends and supporters, and availing himself of the efforts and contributions of the leading society women, this dream, too, became a reality, and in May, 1855, The New York Woman's Hospital was opened with Sims as its surgeon. The hospital has since occupied several successively larger buildings, has served as a center for patient care, research, and training, and has been the model for similar institutions throughout the country.

Although many successful operations for fistula were performed in the hospital, Sims's interests went far beyond this condition. All "female troubles," until then largely ignored by the male doctors, became his sphere. Sterility, in particular, claimed his attention because failure of conception

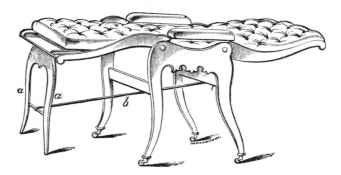

FIG. 100. Sims's operating chair. From: *Clinical Notes*

was considered such a tragedy. Such patients were carefully studied, and all
existing anatomical abnormalities were corrected by surgical operation, with
a gratifying frequency of success. Even artificial insemination was used and
not without the expected jibes and criticisms. With increasing experience
surgical intervention was also applied to other diseases of the female genera-
tive tract. Thus Marion Sims and the Woman's Hospital were potent factors
in the development of the field of operative gynecology.

The outbreak of the Civil War found Sims in a quandary. He had been
born and reared in the South, its ways and customs were his own. His family
and closest friends were still there. All his interests and background made
him sympathize with its causes. Later, his father was to fight on its side and
his eldest son, whose future as his assistant and successor was his most cherished hope, was to die of yellow fever while serving in the Confederate Army.
Yet, the North had provided him a haven when his life was threatened by

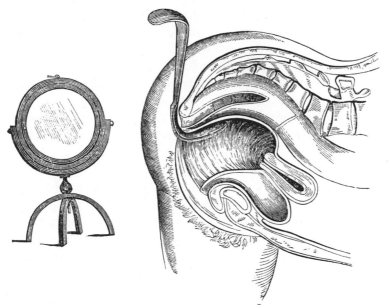

Fɪɢ. 101. Method of visualizing vaginal vault. From: "On the Treatment of Vesico-Vaginal Fistula" by J. Marion Sims in the *American Journal of the Medical Sciences*, New Series, Vol. 23, Philadelphia, 1852.

illness, and it had become his home. He could not be disloyal. In rebellions there can be no neutrals; the individual must choose one side or the other. His was a dilemma without solution. Feeling ran high. He took the only course open to him. He left for Europe.

His avowed purpose, when he sailed in 1861, was to have a much-needed vacation and the opportunity to study hospital construction and gynecological methods in the old, established centers. His journey turned out to be a triumphal tour. Wherever he went, in Ireland, Scotland, and England, and particularly in France, he was most warmly greeted and most hospitably entertained. He was repeatedly urged to demonstrate his operation for vesicovaginal fistula in the leading clinics and before large audiences composed of the foremost medical and surgical figures; and everywhere his success was enthusiastically applauded. He described his recognition in Paris by its famous surgeons as a *furore.* To his great surprise, too, private patients from among the nobility and the wealthy sought his care and paid fees far higher than he had ever heard of in the States. An affluent practice was awaiting him. He returned to New York, arranged his affairs, and, with his family, went back to France for the duration of the war.

Europe took the Sims family to its heart and the five years spent there were little less than fantastic. The Duchess of Hamilton and Empress Eugenie herself were patients of the American doctor, both noble ladies insisting that he reside with them during the months required for their treatment. Other wealthy and aristocratic patients in massive numbers clamored for his assistance, and the fee scale was beyond the imaginings of the former country practitioner. Socially, too, the Sims family was drawn into the gayest whirl that nineteenth century Paris could provide. The older daughters, now of marriageable age, were surrounded by suitors, and life was a continuous round of gaiety. Concern with the misfortunes of the Confederacy, and the death of their son threw deep shadows, however, on the otherwise pleasant life of the expatriates.

The temptation to reside abroad permanently was indeed strong, but Sims felt himself irresistibly drawn by the call of home. His first tentative return to New York in 1867 exposed him to a mixed reception of extreme adulation and of bitter disappointments. Nevertheless, he moved his family back and made America his permanent residence. For the rest of his life, however, he shuttled back and forth across the Atlantic, with progressively longer intervals spent abroad. From the point of view of practice and income, life was infinitely easier in Europe, but this could not weigh against his unwavering loyalty to the land of his birth.

As a child, Marion Sims had convinced himself that he was unable to write, and he came within a hairsbreadth of failing to graduate from college because he flatly refused to write the required five compositions. Only because the indulgent professor reduced the number to two, and these were composed by an admiring lower classman who appended Sims's name, was the diploma granted. In a similar way, Sims had declared himself incapable of public speaking. As time went on, however, he became both a facile writer and an eloquent and convincing orator. His handsome bearing and engaging personality together with his deep sincerity and the youthful enthusiasm which remained permanently with him made him a most effective and popular lecturer and teacher.

Most of Sims's contributions to the literature of gynecology and surgery appeared in the form of articles in American and foreign journals. His major opus, a comprehensive treatise covering the entire field of gynecology and including his work on vesicovaginal fistula, remained unwritten. He did publish his *Clinical Notes on Uterine Surgery, with Special Reference to the Management of the Sterile Condition*, first serially in the London *Lancet* and later in book form (1866). It evoked considerable comment, and was translated into French and German. He also wrote his autobiography, *The Story of My Life*, but death prevented his completing or revising it, and it was edited and published posthumously by his son, a year later (1884).

Gynecology was the major interest of Marion Sims, but he made significant contributions in other surgical fields. Throughout his career, cleanliness was almost a fetish with him.

"The table being properly prepared, the patient is requested to loosen all the fastenings of the dress and corsets, so that there may be nothing to constrict the waist or to compress the abdomen. While this is being done, the physician should bathe his hands in warm water, and wash them well. It may seem odd to insist upon this, but I do most earnestly; 1st, because it softens and warms the hands; 2nd, because it insures their cleanness; and 3rd, because it assures our patient against any dread of contamination by the touch, a thing by no means to be despised."[2]

In addition to washing his hands thoroughly before each operation, he also scrubbed the parts as well. To these precautions are ascribed his reputedly low incidence of septic complications and deaths. Between him and Lord Lister there developed a warm reciprocal regard and friendship. Lister adopted Sims's use of silver wire sutures and confirmed their superiority to more absorbent materials. Only after he had introduced sterile catgut did he abandon the wire. Conversely, Sims was an early disciple of the antiseptic methods of Lister, and he even suggested simplifications in management which their founder adopted.

During the Franco-Prussian War of 1870, Sims was instrumental in organizing a hospital unit to work behind the French lines, with himself as Chief Surgeon. The unit had its baptism of fire at the disastrous battle of Sedan. Here the care of overwhelming numbers of casualties under the inadequate conditions of military emergency made the application of antiseptic methods impossible, and the customary complications ensued. Abdominal wounds were almost inevitably fatal. Sims then became convinced that under more favorable circumstances many such lives could be saved by early laparotomy. He wrote, "The time will assuredly arrive when peritonitis . . . will not kill, because we will learn that the effusions in the peritoneal cavity may be as safely evacuated as those in the pleural cavity. . . . The time will also come when gunshot and other wounds of the abdomen . . . will be treated by opening the peritoneal cavity and washing out or draining off the septic fluids that would otherwise poison the blood."[3] The nature of his own practice did not provide the material for putting these revolutionary ideas into effect, but for the remainder of his professional career he continued to advocate them, and his last public lecture was devoted to this subject.

Another important field in which Sims pioneered was that of gallbladder surgery. He performed a cholecystostomy (1878) in a desperately ill and jaundiced patient, and, although she died eight days later, the feasibility of

2. J. Marion Sims: *Clinical Notes on Uterine Surgery*, New York, William Wood & Company, 1869, p. 6.
3. Seale Harris: *Woman's Surgeon*, New York, The Macmillan Company, 1950, p. 284.

the operation had been demonstrated. "The great lesson this case teaches is this: in dropsy of the gallbladder, in hydatid cysts of the liver, and in gallstones we should not wait 'til the patient's strength is exhausted, or 'til the blood becomes poisoned with bile, producing hemorrhages; we should make an early abdominal incision, ascertain the true nature of the disease, and then carry out the surgical treatment that the necessities of the case demand. If this should be done under antiseptic precautions, I am sure that much suffering will be relieved, and many lives saved that otherwise would be lost. Without Listerism the operation would be hazardous."[4] When Lawson Tait, three years later, reported the first series of successful gallbladder operations, he credited Sims with the first such procedure, adding, "His attempt emboldened me to perform the same operation in 1879, with a perfectly successful result. . . ."[5]

James Marion Sims had enjoyed the friendship of the great medical figures of two continents, had lived and worked with the nobility and royalty, as well as with the slave and the indigent. He had won international acclaim and had received many honors and decorations, including the presidency of the American Medical Association. He had pioneered in the fields of surgical gynecology and abdominal surgery, had been instrumental in creating a great institution, and he made American surgery known and respected in the medical capitals of the world. His career like his life stretched from the frontier to modern urban refinements and in the medical aspects of this evolution he played a significant role.

ℱ ℱ ℱ   TWO CASES OF VESICO-VAGINAL FISTULA, CURED.[6]
ℱ ℱ ℱ
By J. Marion Sims, M.D., of New York, (Late of Montgomery, Ala.)

When I began to investigate the subject of Vesico-Vaginal Fistula in 1845, the field was truly a barren one. What my predecessors had done was of but little more use than to show the almost absolute hopelessness of undertaking its treatment. I had therefore, to begin anew. The difficulties to be overcome, and the many disappointments that had to be borne, can scarcely be imagined by any one who has not had some experience in the management of this dreadful affection. Experiment, properly directed, could alone accomplish anything.

4. *Ibid.*, p. 346.
5. The first cholecystotomy was actually performed a year earlier than the Sims operation by Dr. John S. Bobbs of Indianapolis. This was published in 1878 in the *Trans. of the Indiana Medical Association*, but the report had not come to the attention of either Sims or Tait.
6. *New York Medical Gazette*, 1854, Vol. 5, No. 1, pp. 1–7.

For this purpose I was fortunate in having three young healthy colored girls given to me by their owners in Alabama, I agreeing to perform no operation without the full consent of the patients, and never to perform any that would, in my judgment, jeopard life, or produce greater mischief on the injured organs—the owners agreeing to let me keep them (at my own expense) till I was thoroughly convinced whether the affection could be cured or not. To the liberality of these gentlemen, but more to the heroic fortitude of my patients, is the profession indebted for an operation by which nine tenths of all cases of this hitherto intractable affection may now with certainty be cured. I worked diligently for three years before I cured a single case, operating on these three upwards of forty times during that period. One of them submitted to more than twenty operations, not only cheerfully but with thanks. The history of these three cases is truly interesting in many points, and particularly as exhibiting the slow degrees by which my originally clumsy mechanical apparatus was gradually improved and brought to its present state of simplicity. I shall, however, pass them by for the present, and relate a case or two, bearing on the question, "How long ought the suture apparatus to remain." I was nearly two years determining this point, a very important thing to know, as I have had repeated failures, in consequence of the too early removal of the clamps. In a favorable case, when the operation is well done, the parts unite by the "first intention," the line of union being so perfect and smooth, as scarcely to be visible on the third day. At first, not knowing how long I might safely allow the clamps to remain, I began my experiments by removing them in three days, when I found the cicatrix invariably gave way in the course of 24 hours, whereby the fistulous opening was reproduced exactly of its original size and shape. So I gradually extended the time, with the same results, till the following case occurred, in which the suture apparatus was removed on the seventh day.

Case I.—Amy McRee, black, aged but 16 years, very small, weighing not more than 90 pounds, gave birth to her first child about the middle of August, 1849. Was attended by an old negro woman, and in labor three days, when Dr. Cilley, of Lowndesboro, Ala., was called in, who succeeded in delivering her without instruments. To the doctor's kindness was I indebted for the case.

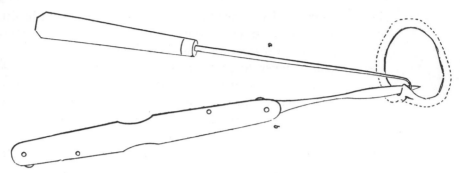

Fɪɢ. 102. Method of excising cicatrized edge of fistula. From: "Treatment of Vesico Vaginal Fistula," *loc. cit.*

The accompanying cut is intended to represent the relative size and position of the fistulous opening. It was altogether favorably located for an easy and successful operation—its edges smooth, rounded and healthy in appearance,—with no loss of vaginal surface, except the perforation, which was large enough to admit the passage of the index finger; while its anterior border was as elastic and yielding as the posterior.

The operation was performed on the 25th of Oct., 1849, a little more than two months after the injury. The dotted line around the fistula shows the extent of the scarification, which of course, made the opening considerably larger. It was closed by three silver sutures, secured by clamps in the usual way. The operation was completed in less than thirty minutes. The opening was closed accurately and firmly. To exhibit to some friends present, the great adaptation of the *clamp suture* to this particular sort of injury, while the patient was still on the table, in the position in which the operation was performed, I threw a syringe full of tepid water into the bladder with such force that it gave her excessive pain, distending the organ to its greatest extent, and regurgitating in a bold stream from the uretha by the side of the catheter attached to the syringe, without a single drop passing through the fistula. There could be no stronger evidence of the power and immobility of the *clamp suture.*

The patient was now put to bed, the self-retaining catheter introduced, and the usual regimen enjoined to insure a constipated state of the bowels. [*Vide*: *Am. Jour. Med. Sci.*, Jan. 1852.]

The catheter in this case had to be smaller than any heretofore used on any grown person. Her urethra was very small, considerably less than an inch long, while all other parts were in a like proportion undeveloped.

The day after the operation, she had a chill, followed by a high fever, lasting 36 hours, which was arrested by the use of Quinine. I now ascertained she had been for several weeks subject to intermittent fever, and that this was just the time for its regular bi-hebdomadal return. If I had been aware of this fact, of course I would not have hazarded the success of the operation by performing it at such an unfortunate juncture.

Oct. 29th, 4th day.—She is very weak and greatly prostrated by the fever—complains of her abdomen, which is somewhat tympanitic and tender to the touch. As the urethra is very much swollen and inflamed, the catheter producing great distress, I removed it this morning, allowing her to retain the urine and discharge it spontaneously. I was much surprised to find the fistula perfectly healed, notwithstanding the unlucky accident of the ague, with its attendant prostration. The clamps were entirely imbedded in the substance of the vaginal septum, nothing being visible but the projecting ends of the fine silver wires, and the leaden knots or mashed shot.

When the operation was performed, I had some slight apprehensions lest I had used a little too much force in bringing the clamps to bear on the fistulous borders, thereby producing unnecessary, and perhaps injurious pressure. On first seeing the extent to which they were imbedded, I now felt pretty sure of this fact, and was almost tempted to cut them loose, but, after a more minute examination, I concluded that all danger had passed, so they were allowed to remain a while longer.

9 P.M.—As stated above, the catheter was removed this morning. She urinated three or four times during the day—says not a drop has passed involuntarily. An examination of the vulva proves the truth of her assertion. Owing to her debilitated condition I had permitted her to sit up whenever she pleased, and even to walk about the room occasionally.

Oct. 30th, 9 P.M.—Doing well. Urine still retained and passed spontaneously.

31st.—The urethra and meatus urinarius having recovered from the excessive soreness, the catheter was reapplied, and patient put to bed again.

Nov. 1st., (7th day.)—The clamps still perfectly buried in the substance of the vesical septum. Cut off the leaden shot, and removed the anterior clamp, leaving the posterior one, and the wires in situ. Did not remove this last, because I feared the necessary traction might endanger the integrity of the cicatrix, preferring to leave it another day to loosen and rise gradually from its bed in the vaginal structure.

Nov. 2d.—Removed the remaining clamp with the wires attached to-day, which was much easier than it could have been yesterday.

Nov. 3d.—The cicatrix seems to be firm, presenting scarcely a vestige of its locale. To test the success of the operation, tepid water was thrown into the bladder till it regurgitated by the side of the catheter, the cicatrix remaining firm and unyielding. Supposing her cure now permanent, I turned her loose, and laid the catheter aside. Two days after this, (which was the 11th since the operation, and the 4th since the removal of the suture apparatus) I examined the cicatrix again, and was much surprised to find it greatly changed in appearance. The sulci on each side of it, made by the clamps, were filled up by granulations, while the cicatrix, which two days ago was so compact as scarcely to be visible, is now considerably *widened, thinned, and depressed below the vaginal surface,* and evidently seems to be on the point of giving way. Instead of presenting a mere line as represented by *a,* it had very much the shape and size of the diagram *b,* the philosophy of which is explained in my paper, "On the treatment of Vesico Vaginal Fistula" before alluded to. To prevent all further mischief from distention of the bladder, she was put to bed, and the catheter reapplied. The integrity of the cicatrix was endangered by the too early removal of the suture apparatus; but, by this timely attention, it continued to strengthen for the next six or seven days, when it appeared to be firm, smooth, and free from all depression and induration. She soon returned home well, having been with me but twenty days.

Two months afterwards her husband, visiting Montgomery, informed me that she was in fine health, and no longer followed the injunction of living absque marito. Three years after this I heard she was a mother—the cure remaining permanent.

This was the first case I had cured by a single operation, and I felt great satisfaction at the result, particularly as it was obtained under such unfavorable circumstances.

Case—II. Mrs. A. F., aged 40 years, very large, weighing nearly 200 pounds, the mother of seven children; labors always easy till the last one, in which delivery was not accomplished under four days. Dr. Wilson, now of Montgomery, Alabama, was called in consultation, and delivered her without the aid of instruments. Several days after delivery, she did not know how long, she discovered the urine dripping from her, and she lost all desire to make water. The fistula was considerably larger than the one just described, but occupied precisely the same relative position with regard to other parts. Per se, it was favorable for an operation; but Mrs. F. had been laboring under Intermittent Fever for the last two or three months, and was very weak, irritable, and quite hysterical. In consequence of a local determination of blood to the brain, she could not submit to the proper position long enough to bear the operation. Besides, she was not strong enough to support her own weight on her knees for any length of time. Ascertaining that she could not return to Montgomery again for several months, I determined to operate now, notwithstanding this unfavorable state of things.

Placed on the table on her left side, with the thighs well flexed on the abdomen, the nates forcibly pulled upwards and backwards, the lever speculum was introduced, and the parts brought into view, which was accomplished more easily than I anticipated, but did not show the fistula so well as when the proper position on the knees is resorted to. However, I managed to get through with the different stages of this operation with tolerable ease. It was done on the 12th November, 1849, two years after the injury was sustained. Three days after the operation, the catheter accidentally came away, and was not replaced for nearly four hours. There was no dripping of urine, showing that the fistula was perfectly closed. On the sixth day, the clamps were removed. They were buried in the substance of the bladder, and entirely hidden from view, the leaden knots alone being visible. The fistula seemed to be accurately and perfectly closed, the line of union being scarcely perceptible. On the seventh day she was allowed to lay aside the catheter, and to sit up; but it was reapplied at night, and on the following day given up entirely. It was not prudent to stop its use so soon, but her general health was very bad, and confinement to bed appeared to debilitate her system, and she became excessively irritable and uncontrolable; so I had no choice about the course to be pursued. I examined the cicatrix from day to day. It underwent precisely the same changes as noticed in the former case, only to a greater degree—viz., *a stretching,* *thinning and depression,* which gradually disappeared, the cicatrix then becoming smooth and regular. She went home cured, having remained in Montgomery but a fortnight. Her cure was permanent. She lived three years, dying of uterine hemorrhage, from undelivered placenta, as I was informed by her attending physician last winter.

Now, the point that I wish to call attention to in these two cases, is the peculiar change that occurred in the cicatrix, showing that the clamps were removed too soon, thereby endangering its integrity. Every point gained in the treatment of this affection has been the result of experiments cautiously conducted, and carefully watched. Previously to these cases, I had performed some five or six operations, in which the suture apparatus was allowed to remain three and four days, the line of union appearing as perfect as could be desired; and yet, after its removal, the parts gradually opened in every instance, reproducing the fistula in from twenty-four to forty-eight hours. In these two cases the cicatrices evidently yielded, being *widened,* *thinned and depressed,* but the clamps had remained long enough to give a certain degree of resistance, barely enough however to save them from a gradual disruption.

It follows, then, that three or four days is not long enough for the suture apparatus to remain, because the fistula has always been reproduced after its removal; and that seven or eight days is not sufficient, because there is great danger of the same accident. My large experience has demonstrated the fact, that about twelve days is the proper length of time for the *clamp suture* to remain in the tissues. It is evidently unsafe to remove it sooner, and it may remain till the fifteenth day with impunity; but a longer time is altogether unnecessary.

79 Madison Avenue, New York.

REMARKS ON CHOLECYSTOTOMY IN DROPSY OF THE GALL-BLADDER.[7]

By J. Marion Sims, M.D., Honorary Fellow of the Obstetrical Societies of London, Dublin, and Berlin; Ex-President of the American Medical Association; etc.

An American lady, aged 45, living in Paris, was married at twenty-three, and had one child, now nineteen years old. She

7. *The British Medical Journal,* edited by Ernest Hart, London, Francis Fowke, 1878, Vol. 1, January–June, pp. 811–812.

had change of life at forty-three, without any constitutional disturbance. A woman of fine intellect and fine appearance, weighing one hundred and sixty pounds, she had enjoyed un-interrupted good health all her life. Her family history was excellent, and her regular habits of living were such that she had not consulted a physician for the most trifling ailment in the last twenty-five years. Besides all this, she was most happily married and enjoyed every comfort and luxury of life that wealth, friends, and a loving husband could bestow. But at last a great sorrow fell upon her, and her husband wisely sug-gested change of scene, and she spent the months of August and September 1877 in Switzerland. While there, she com-plained of the cold, and occasionally of pain in the right lum-bar region, high up under the false ribs. For the last twelve months, she had now and then complained of pain in the right hypochondrium, when she stooped over to button her shoes, but not under any other circumstances. She returned home in October, not much improved in health; and, in the later part of November, she became suddenly jaundiced. In two or three days, the jaundice was of a *deep mahogany colour.* . . .

Operation.—April 18th, 10 A.M. There was great tenderness and pain in the region of the tumour, aggravated by pressure. For the last three or four days, there was marked tympanites. The pulse had risen from 75 up to 110 and the temperature to 100 deg. Her sufferings were altogether so much worse than they had ever been before, that she implored us to lose no time in giving her the relief she expected from the operation. Dr. Hayden gave ether, and Dr. Bremond and Dr. Pratt as-sisted me. The operation was performed under proper anti-septic precautions, with carbolic spray, and carbolic lotion for hands, sponges, and instruments. It took an unusually long time (twenty-four minutes) to get the patient under the influ-ence of the ether. An incision, three inches long, parallel with the linea alba, was made, over the most prominent part of the tumour, about three inches to the right of the umbilicus. It was begun an inch above the level of the umbilicus, and extended two inches below it. The peritoneal membrane was soon reached, but was not opened till all bleeding from di-vided vessels was controlled. As there was such a haemorrhagic tendency, this required six artery forceps on each side of the incision. When the peritoneum was opened, several ounces of pinkish serum (perhaps six or eight) were discharged. I am somewhat in doubt whether the pinkish colour of the serum was due to the rupture of recent adhesions between the cyst and the parietal peritoneum, or to osmosis from the peritoneum. But I think it was from the latter cause; for I did not, by sense of touch, discover the adhesions, if any existed. A Dieulafoy's trocar of the largest size was thrust into the tumour, and twenty-four ounces of a dark-brown fluid withdrawn, which I supposed to be bile. As soon as the cyst was emptied, it was hooked up with a tenaculum and pulled to the outer edge of the incision, where it was seized with forceps and drawn out for about two inches. It was there held while the finger was passed into the peritoneal cavity, along its under and upper surfaces, when it was ascertained, by its attachments to the liver, to be the gall-bladder. Dr. Bremond, Dr. Pratt, and myself each thoroughly explored the sac by touch, and satisfied ourselves that it was the gall-bladder. This multiple manual investigation would have been unjustifiable and hazardous without antisepticism. The gall-bladder was then incised with scissors, to the extent of about two inches, and was thoroughly cleaned out with sponge-probangs passed to the bottom of the sac, which, on measurement, was ·found to be eight inches deep. At first, there were removed about two ounces of a dark-brown fluid, much thicker (containing more mucus) than that already drawn off; and then there were drawn out with the probang a half-dozen or more gall-stones. One probang after another was then passed in, and swept around, till sixty gall-stones were removed.

Having emptied the gall-bladder, it now only remained to secure its open border to the upper angle of the abdominal incision to insure a fistulous outlet. As it was already drawn out through the incision to a considerable extent, I resolved to amputate the projecting portion, which was a mistake. Its walls were greatly thickened, and bled when cut, so as to require the use of several artery-forceps. The puckered mouth of the amputated cyst was then crowded into the upper angle of the abdominal incision, and there secured with eight fine carbolised silk sutures, taking good care to pass each suture through the whole thickness of the abdominal walls, including the peritoneum. After this process was finished, we waited several minutes with small carbolised sponges (on probangs) resting just within the cavity of the peritoneum, to be sure that there was no bleeding from the needle-punctures. When we were satisfied on this point, the lower portion of the abdominal incision was closed with fine carbolised silk sutures, including the peritoneum. The whole wound was then covered with some cotton-wool saturated with carbolised oil, over which was placed a large compress of fine cotton-wool secured with adhesive strips and a flannel binder. When the wound was closed, there still remained a considerable quantity of pinkish serum in the peritoneal cavity, such as I formerly thought to justify the use of a drainage-tube. But the experience of Bantock and Thornton at the Samaritan Hospital proves pretty conclusively that drainage is not always necessary under Listerism, because it prevents putrefaction, and the reddish serum is absorbed without producing septic symptoms.

The operation lasted one hour and sixteen minutes, exclusive of the time consumed in getting the patient etherised. The most tedious part of it was in securing the cyst in the incision and closing up the wound. This took up all of thirty-five minutes. The patient recovered from the anaesthesia half an hour after the operation, and vomited once from its effects, and then lay quiet and comfortable, sleeping a good deal during the afternoon; and she slept all night.

PART VIII

LORD LISTER

Lord Lister
$(1827-1912)$

"The medical student may be sometimes a rough diamond; but when he comes to
have personal charge of patients, and to have the life and health of a fellow creature
depending upon his individual care, he becomes a changed man, and from that day
forth his life becomes a constant exercise of beneficence."

(Lister)

Many have contributed to the development of modern surgery. Two of the steps in this long evolution that were most decisive in bringing the profession to its present stage of development were made in the nineteenth century. These, of course, are the introduction of anesthesia and the development of the antiseptic method. The anesthesia story, as mentioned in an earlier chapter, grew out of fortuitous observations made by several men on the actions of persons under the influence of certain intoxicating agents. The control of infection, on the contrary, came as a result of persistent and dedicated scientific effort which was specifically directed toward this purpose. This great idea was the contribution of Joseph Lister who devoted his life to the solution of the problem of wound infection, to the perfection of the methods for its achievement, and to securing their adoption by a skeptical profession. He succeeded in all these endeavors and, unlike many other innovators, lived to see their completion and to enjoy the honor and appreciation of a grateful world.

Lister came from a Quaker family and displayed the serenity of disposition, the modesty, and the seriousness of purpose that characterizes adherents of that creed. Although he "married out" of the sect, the early influences persisted for the rest of his life even to the use of the familiar pronouns, thee and thou. His father was a well-to-do wine merchant whose leanings were toward science, and whose hobby was optics. He taught himself the fundamentals of this branch of physics, ground his own lenses, and made important discoveries which led to the development of the achromatic lens and to the perfection of the compound microscope. A wide reputation and even Fellow-

FIG. 103

ship in the Royal Society attest to the significance of his contributions. He followed the career of his illustrious son with intense interest, and often gave counsel and encouragement.

Joseph Lister was born in 1827 at Upton, in Essex, then a suburb and now a part of Greater London. He had a happy childhood in a family where affection and harmony reigned, and an excellent education. Early drawn toward scientific pursuits, as is evidenced by his childhood preoccupation with dissecting, drawing, and preserving biological specimens, he determined when still very young to become a surgeon. At the age of seventeen he entered University College in London, took his A.B. degree in three years, and then began his study of medicine. He excelled particularly in his surgical subjects, served as house surgeon, then took his degree in medicine and, in 1852, became a Fellow of the Royal College of Surgeons.

During these years of preparation, Lister began his scientific career. Two papers appeared based on microscopic and physiological studies, one on the involuntary muscle fibers of the iris of the eye, the other on the muscular tissue (erector pili) of the skin. These were the first of the research projects which, in one field or another, continued throughout Lister's active professional life.

Before settling down to the practice of surgery in London, he planned a visit to the Continent, but he was advised by his professor of surgery to spend a month with James Syme in Edinburgh, who then was the leading surgeon of the British Isles. The month stretched to seven years and proved to be a decisive period in shaping his future. Greatly impressed with the surgical activity in the Scottish city, and the vastly greater opportunities for teaching and practical training, he stayed on and, when a house residency under Syme became available, he eagerly accepted it. One year later he applied and won an appointment as Lecturer at the Royal College of Surgeons of Edinburgh and an assistant surgeoncy at the Infirmary. He also married Agnes Syme, eldest daughter of his chief.

In addition to preparing his lectures, caring for the Infirmary patients, and establishing himself in private practice, Lister now began the important researches that were to lead to his great discovery. Interested in the earliest stages of inflammation, he studied this phenomenon in the web of the feet of frogs, observing the responses to irritation under the microscope. These studies led to further work on blood coagulation, which together with many other investigations brought him such recognition that when, in 1859, the Professorship of Surgery at the University of Glasgow became vacant, Lister was chosen for the post.

Here it was that Lister's great work was done. As Chief Surgeon to the Royal Infirmary he came face to face in a very personal way with the problems of hospital infections. Despite the great boon of anesthesia, elective surgery was limited in its scope and application because of the grave danger to life in even the simplest operation or the slightest wound. The four horsemen of infection were erysipelas, septicemia, pyemia, and hospital gangrene.

The first three are readily understood in the almost inevitable contamination and cross-infection inherent in the surgical practices of the day. The last mentioned, hospital gangrene, has completely disappeared from the roster of modern diseases, and its cause or identity can only be conjectured. Presumably as a result of a symbiotic mixed infection, spreading necrosis of the wound edges with severe toxemia and early death was a constant specter of the hospital wards. In a paper on resection of the wrist joint for tuberculosis (1865), Lister wrote, ". . . and also that they have been treated under the disadvantages of a hospital atmosphere, so that I have had to contend in no less than six instances with hospital gangrene and in one with pyemia . . ." in a series of fifteen reported cases.

Contemporary records are replete with statistics which tell the awful story of death following injury or operation. One fairly well-controlled aspect will suffice as an example. Amputations were much more frequent in those days during which conservative means of treatment were not available. The death rate following this rather limited procedure varied from 25 to 60 per cent in civilian hospitals and in military practice reached the appalling rate of 75 to 90 per cent (Godlee). For centuries, surgeons and patients alike had welcomed what was called "laudable pus," because such infections tended to be benign. Surgical invasion of the joint or body cavities was shunned in terror.

The evolution of the antiseptic method was a logical, well-thought-out progression from one fact to the next over a period of many years. With a mind prepared by his previous researches and the wealth of material available to him in the Infirmary, Lister attacked the problem as a mission. His first insight came in 1865 when his colleague, the Professor of Chemistry, called his attention to the work of Pasteur on fermentation and putrefaction. At that time Lister considered putrefaction an essential part of infection. (It was only later that he learned that nonodorous conditions such as erysipelas were also infections.) When he found out from the work of Pasteur that putrefaction was caused by minute organisms carried by the air, and that such living bodies could be destroyed by heat or other means, the solution to the problem suggested itself. If he could prevent these air-borne structures from gaining access to the wound, infection would be prevented. He wrote, "But when it had been shown by the researches of Pasteur that the septic property of the atmosphere depended, not upon the oxygen or any gaseous constituent, but on minute organisms suspended in it, which owed their energy to their vitality, it occurred to me that decomposition of the injured part might be avoided without excluding the air, by applying as a dressing some material capable of destroying the life of the floating particles."

Carbolic acid was known at that time, and had in fact been used to combat the odor of sewage. Lister decided to use this agent. He experimented with various means of maintaining dressings soaked in this substance in constant contact with the wound. He tried his method on a compound fracture and failed because of what he considered improper management. Still confident, he applied his dressing again to a compound fracture of the ankle in a boy eleven years of age. He wrote, in a letter to his father dated May 27, 1866:

> "There is one of my cases at the Infirmary which I am sure will interest thee. It is one of compound fracture of the leg: with a wound of considerable size and accompanied by great bruising, and great effusion of blood into the substance of the limb causing great swelling. Though hardly expecting success, I tried the application of carbolic acid to the wound, to prevent decomposition of the blood, and so avoid the fearful mischief of suppuration throughout the limb. Well, it is now 8 days since the accident, and the patient has been going on exactly as if there were no external wound, that is as if the fracture were a simple one. His appetite, sleep, etc., good, and the limb daily diminishing in size, while there is no appearance whatever of any matter forming. Thus a most dangerous accident seems to have been entirely deprived of its dangerous element."[1]

In addition to the use of carbolized dressings to prevent infection, Lister also treated established abscesses, particularly those of tuberculous origin, by the instillation of carbolic acid with considerable success. Many modifications were made in the technique of the dressings, in the manner of applying and retaining them, and in the choice of antiseptic solutions of various concentrations. The carbolic spray is the most frequently remembered detail, but one which he himself abandoned after a trial of sixteen years (1871–1887).

A second important contribution made by Lister was the development of sterile absorbable ligatures. Convinced that deep suppuration was caused by contaminated silk, he experimented with catgut that had been treated by prolonged sterilization in carbolic acid. Demonstrated first experimentally, then clinically, he proved that sterile ligatures could be safely cut short and left buried in the tissues. The quest for the perfect ligature, like that for the dressing, was a continuous one over a period of many years. As a result of these studies surgeons were able to employ absorbable ligatures with complete confidence.

Lister's first publication on the aseptic method appeared in the *Lancet* in the spring of 1867. Two years later, Syme was compelled to resign his professorship because of ill health and Lister was recalled to Edinburgh as Pro-

---

1. *Sir* Rickman John Godlee: *Lord Lister*, Oxford, Clarendon Press, 1924, third edition, revised, pp. 184–185.

fessor of Clinical Surgery. Here his labors continued. From accidental wounds, the antiseptic principle was carried over to elective operations, with gratifying success. Growing experience and confidence led to increasingly extensive operative procedures. Even as late as 1877, however, when Lister opened the knee joint to repair a fractured patella, a prominent London surgeon is reported to have said, "Now when this poor fellow dies, it is proper that some one should proceed against that man for malpraxis." Fortunately, the wound healed without infection, and the operation brought not death, but restoration of function.

Contrary to what might have been expected, Lister's discovery was not quickly accepted. In a paper published in 1870 entitled "On the Effects of the Antiseptic System of Treatment upon the Salubrity of a Surgical Hospital," he contrasted the mortality rate after amputation during the two-year period preceding the use of antisepsis and the three years after: "Comparing the aggregate results, we have—before tha antiseptic period, 16 deaths in 35 cases; or 1 death in every $2\frac{1}{5}$ cases. During the antiseptic period, 6 deaths in 40 cases; or 1 death in every $6\frac{2}{3}$ cases."[2] And then he adds: "The contrast under the antiseptic system has been most striking. For the first nine months, as before mentioned, we had not a single case of the disease [hospital gangrene]. Since that time it has shown itself now and then, but in a mild form, invariably yielding to treatment, never occurring in recent cases, but only in old sores weakened by the influence of surrounding cicatrix. But even this has been very rare, and I do not recollect more than one example of it during the last year. In short, hospital gangrene, like pyaemia and erysipelas, may be said to have been banished by the antiseptic system."[3]

Despite the statistical evidence presented, Lister's method met with indifference and even with violent opposition. This was particularly true in Great Britain. Continental surgeons, particularly those in Germany, quickly adopted the treatment and enthusiastically confirmed the excellent results reported by Lister. Fully twenty years of patient trial, improvement, demonstration, and education were required before the British surgeons were won over to the idea, and not before many of the senior members of the profession had been replaced by a younger and more malleable generation.

It was the very resistance of the London surgeons that impelled Lister to leave Edinburgh and accept a lesser position as Professor of Clinical Surgery at King's College Hospital. His motivation is revealed in a letter to a friend at that time (1877) in which he wrote that the new appointment would "enable me to carry out the two objects which I should in reality have in

2. *The Collected Papers of Joseph, Baron Lister*, in two volumes, Oxford, Clarendon Press, 1909, Vol. 2, p. 129.
3. *Ibid.*, p. 134.

view, *viz.*, the thorough working of the antiseptic system with a view to its diffusion in the metropolis and the introduction of a more efficient method of clinical surgical teaching than has hitherto prevailed in London."

Lister's reception in London would have disheartened a less modest and dedicated man. In contrast to the throngs of eager and devoted students to which he had been accustomed in Edinburgh, he lectured to a handful of apathetic and disinterested young men. His professional colleagues ignored his presence. Only the stream of important visitors from foreign lands, and the enthusiastic applause showered upon him at the international congresses where his papers were greatly in demand gave testimony of the esteem in which he was held abroad. By patient and persistent effort, however, he was able slowly to spread his doctrine and overcome the most obstinate resistance. He fulfilled his mission.

Much has been made in the years since Lister elaborated his method of the distinction between antiseptic and aseptic surgery. The latter term was introduced by Ernst von Bergmann, a renowned Berlin surgeon, who initiated methods of sterilization similar to those in use today. However, Sir Rickman Godlee, nephew and disciple and definitive biographer of Lister, makes it

Fig. 104. Accolade of Lister and Pasteur in the big amphitheatre of the Sorbonne, December 27, 1892 (painting by Rixens).

clear that there was no essential difference in the rationale behind the two techniques. Both sought to prevent access of bacteria to the wound, Lister by the use of occlusive dressings saturated with bactericidal chemicals, von Bergmann by heat.

It is important to mention that Lister was among the first to have recognized the capacity of normal tissues, and, in particular, of the peritoneum to cope with lesser degrees of bacterial contamination. As a corollary to this, he was also concerned with the potential deleterious effects of antiseptic chemicals upon this protective property and experimented ceaselessly, seeking the least injurious and yet effective concentration of such agents.

Lister's monumental preoccupation with the problems of wound infection also made of him a pioneer in the early science of bacteriology. Somewhat in the nature of an avocation he studied the lactic acid fermentation in milk. He isolated *Bacterium lactis*, gave it its name, and established its properties. During these investigations he developed pioneer methods of growing bacteria, including the first technique for obtaining organisms in pure culture.

An indication of Lister's courage and the strength of his convictions is revealed in his relationship with the queen. During the time that he was still her personal surgeon in Edinburgh, Victoria appealed to him for support in her opposition to animal experimentation for scientific purposes. Rather than comply with the royal request, which was contrary to his own beliefs, he took advantage of the occasion to write a letter to the Queen in which he warmly espoused the use of laboratory animals as a humane and essential requirement in man's conquest of disease.

Great achievement and personal gratification marked Lister's life. His domestic life was equally fortunate, for his marriage to Agnes Syme proved to be extraordinarily felicitous. They had no children and the full warmth of their mutual affection made for true companionship. She shared his labors, acted as his secretary, and accompanied him on his many travels. Together they shared gentle pleasures, of travel, of nature study, and of quiet meditation. In 1893, on one such holiday trip in Rapallo, on the Italian Riviera, Lady Lister was stricken with a fulminant pneumonia and died within four days. The light went out of Lister's life; he remained a lonely man for his final nineteen years. Shortly after his great loss he relinquished his duties at the King's College Hospital and retired from active practice. Fortunately, his stature was such that he was drafted into innumerable commissions and activities which made his life a busy one. Honors and decorations were conferred by many nations, including a baronetcy which was bestowed upon him in 1883 by Queen Victoria, upon whom he had operated some thirteen years earlier. At the age of seventy he was elevated to the peerage, the first medical man to have attained this honor.

ᔍ ᔍ ᔍ   [The following excerpt is taken from Lister's initial publica-
ᔍ ᔍ ᔍ   tion on the antiseptic method].

ON A NEW METHOD OF TREATING COMPOUND FRACTURE, ABSCESS, ETC. WITH OBSERVATIONS ON THE CONDITIONS OF SUPPURATION.

On Compound Fracture

Turning now to the question how the atmosphere produces decomposition of organic substances, we find that a flood of light has been thrown upon this most important subject by the philosophic researches of M. Pasteur, who has demonstrated by thoroughly convincing evidence that it is not to its oxygen or to any of its gaseous constituents that the air owes this property, but to minute particles suspended in it, which are the germs of various low forms of life, long since revealed by the microscope, and regarded as merely accidental concomitants of putresence, but now shown by Pasteur to be its essential cause, resolving the complex organic compounds into substances of simpler chemical constitution, just as the yeast plant converts sugar into alcohol and carbonic acid.

A beautiful illustration of this doctrine seems to me to be presented in surgery, by pneumothorax with emphysema, resulting from puncture of the lung by a fractured rib. Here, though atmospheric air is perpetually introduced into the pleura in great abundance, no inflammatory disturbance supervenes; whereas an external wound penetrating the chest, if it remains open, infallibly causes dangerous suppurative pleurisy. In the latter case the blood and serum poured out into the pleural cavity, as an immediate consequence of the injury, are decomposed by the germs that enter with the air, and then operate as a powerful irritant upon the serous membrane. But in case of puncture of the lung without external wound, the atmospheric gases are filtered of the causes of decomposition before they enter the pleura, by passing through the bronchial tubes, which, by their small size, their tortuous course, their mucous secretion, and ciliated epithelial lining, seem to be specially designed to arrest all solid particles in the air inhaled. Consequently the effused fluids retain their original characters unimpaired, and are speedily absorbed by the unirritated pleura.

Applying these principles to the treatment of compound

fracture, bearing in mind that it is from the vitality of the
atmospheric particles that all the mischief arises, it appears
that all that is requisite is to dress the wound with some mate-
trial capable of killing these septic germs, provided that any
substance can be found reliable for this purpose, yet not too
potent as a caustic.

In the course of the year 1864 I was much struck with an
account of the remarkable effects produced by carbolic acid
upon the sewage of the town of Carlisle, the admixture of a
very small proportion not only preventing all odour from the
lands irrigated with the refuse material, but, as it was stated,
destroying the entozoa which usually infest cattle fed upon such
pastures.

My attention having for several years been much directed to
the subject of suppuration, more especially in its relation to
decomposition, I saw that such a powerful antiseptic was
peculiarly adapted for experiments with a view to elucidating
that subject, and while I was engaged in the investigation the
applicability of carbolic acid for the treatment of compound
fracture naturally occurred to me.

My first attempt of this kind was made in the Glasgow Royal
Infirmary in March 1865, in a case of compound fracture of
the leg. It proved unsuccessful, in consequence, as I now believe, of improper management; but subsequent trials have
more than realized my most sanguine anticipations.

Carbolic acid proved in various ways well adapted for the
purpose. It exercises a local sedative influence upon the sensory
nerves; and hence is not only almost painless in its immediate
action on a raw surface, but speedily renders a wound previously painful entirely free from uneasiness. When employed
in compound fracture its caustic properties are mitigated so as
to be unobjectionable by admixture with the blood, with which
it forms a tenacious mass that hardens into a dense crust, which
long retains its antiseptic virtue, and has also other advantages,
as will appear from the following cases, which I will relate in
the order of their occurrence, premising that, as the treatment
has been gradually improved, the earlier ones are not to be
taken as patterns.

Case I.—James G-----, aged eleven years, was admitted into
the Glasgow Royal Infirmary on the 12th of August, 1865,
with compound fracture of the left leg, caused by the wheel of

an empty cart passing over the limb a little below its middle. The wound, which was about an inch and a half long, and three-quarters of an inch broad, was close to, but not exactly over, the line of fracture of the tibia. A probe, however, could be passed beneath the integument over the seat of fracture and for some inches beyond it. Very little blood had been extravasated into the tissues.

My house surgeon, Dr. Macfee, acting under my instructions, laid a piece of lint dipped in liquid carbolic acid upon the wound, and applied lateral pasteboard splints padded with cotton wool, the limb resting on its outer side, with the knee bent. It was left undisturbed for four days, when, the boy complaining of some uneasiness, I removed the inner splint and examined the wound. It showed no signs of suppuration, but the skin in its immediate vicinity had a slight blush of redness. I now dressed the sore with lint soaked with water having a small proportion of carbolic acid diffused through it; and this was continued for five days, during which the uneasiness and the redness of the skin disappeared, the sore meanwhile furnishing no pus, although some superficial sloughs caused by the acid were separating. But the epidermis being excoriated by this dressing, I substituted for it a solution of one part of carbolic acid in from ten to twenty parts of olive oil, which was used for four days, during which a small amount of imperfect pus was produced from the surface of the sore, but not a drop appeared from beneath the skin. It was now clear that there was no longer any danger of deep-seated suppuration, and simple water dressing was employed. Cicatrization proceeded just as in an ordinary granulating sore. At the expiration of six weeks I examined the condition of the bones, and, finding them firmly united, discarded the splints; and two days later the sore was entirely healed, so that the cure could not be said to have been at all retarded by the circumstance of the fracture being compound.

This, no doubt, was a favourable case, and might have done well under ordinary treatment. But the remarkable retardation of suppuration, and the immediate conversion of the compound fracture into a simple fracture with a superficial sore, were most encouraging facts.[4]

4. This article was originally published in *Lancet*, 1867, Vol. 1, pp. 326, 357, 387, 507; Vol. 2, p. 95. Also in *Collected Papers*, Vol. 2, pp. 2–5.

[The article then goes on to describe in detail ten additional cases of compound fracture, in which the successive modifications and improvements in the manner of applying and retaining, as well as in the concentrations of, the carbolic acid are described. In the total series of eleven cases there was but one death and one limb that came to amputation. These results stand in striking contrast to those which have been mentioned in the intoductory section of this chapter.]

[The dramatic effects of the antiseptic system on the healthfulness of the hospital environment is described in an early article which appeared in the *Lancet*.]

There is, however, one point more that I cannot but advert to—namely, the influence of this mode of treatment upon the general healthiness of a hospital. Previously to its introduction, the two large wards in which most of my cases of accident and of operation are treated were amongst the unhealthiest in the whole surgical division of the Glasgow Royal Infirmary, in consequence, apparently, of those wards being unfavourably placed with reference to the supply of fresh air; and I have felt ashamed, when recording the results of my practice, to have so often to allude to hospital gangrene or pyaemia. It was interesting, though melancholy, to observe that, whenever all, or nearly all, the beds contained cases with open sores, these grievous complications were pretty sure to show themselves; so that I came to welcome simple fractures, though in themselves of little interest either for myself or the students, because their presence diminished the proportion of open sores among the patients. But since the antiseptic treatment has been brought into full operation, and wounds and abscesses no longer poison the atmosphere with putrid exhalations, my wards, though in other respects under precisely the same circumstances as before, have completely changed their character; so that during the last nine months not a single instance of pyaemia, hospital gangrene, or erysipelas has occurred in them.

As there appears to be no doubt regarding the cause of this change, the importance of the fact can hardly be exaggerated.[5]

I have also made observations on the effects of exposure of uncontaminated blood to air in different localities, and I have found that even the introduction of considerable quantities of dust has not led to putrefactive change.

5. *The Collected Papers*, Vol. 2, p. 45; and *Lancet*, Vol. II, p. 668.

Applying this knowledge to the discussion of ovariotomy performed without antiseptic precautions, the question naturally suggests itself whether in many cases any septic organisms have really been introduced into the peritoneal cavity, either from air or from water, in a condition capable of developing in the effused serum. And thus we have suggested to us a further explanation of the success of such operations.

But the facts which have been elicited by the experiments referred to have a far wider range of application than to the special case of ovariotomy. They seem to indicate that the putrefaction so apt to occur in wounds not treated antiseptically is due rather to septic matter in a concentrated form than to the diffused condition in which it exists either in water or in air. They suggest the highly important question, is the spray really necessary? In other words, Is there sufficient chance of the air of an operating theatre or private room containing septic matter which can prove effective in blood serum to make it needful to regard the question of contamination from the atmosphere at all? If the answer must be given in the affirmative, and the choice must lie between the spray and antiseptic irrigation during the operation at intervals varying according to the discretion of the surgeon, with syringing of the cavity of the wound after stitching, and syringing also at every dressing, then I should give my voice decidedly in favour of the spray, as being more sure of attaining its object and involving less irritation of the wound, and also (if carbolic acid be the antiseptic used) much less risk of carbolic poisoning. At the same time it must be distinctly borne in mind that the spray is, beyond all question, the least important of our antiseptic means, and that the circumstance that a surgeon does not happen to have a spray-producer at hand is no excuse whatever for his abandoning the attempt to obtain aseptic results. But if the apparatus for the spray is at my disposal, I for my part do not as yet dare to abandon it. By the careful use of our present means, the spray included, we have arrived, I think I may venture to say, at absolute security of attaining the great object in view, provided that we have the two essential conditions complied with: an unbroken skin to start with and the seat of operation sufficiently distant from any source of putrefaction to admit of adequate overlapping of the surrounding integument by the requisite dressing. I leave it to those who have done me the honour to visit my wards to judge whether I am guilty of exaggeration in making this strong statement. Such being the case, I should not feel justified, except on perfectly established grounds, in omitting any part of the machinery by which results so important to our fellow creatures have been arrived at.

Nevertheless I am aware that, concomitantly with the perfecting of the spray, there has been an improvement in other parts of our antiseptic arrangements, and I am not prepared to say that our increased uniformity of good results may not be due to the latter rather than to the former. And it may be, for aught I know, that when the International Medical Congress next meets I shall be able to speak of results of a still higher order obtained without using the spray at all. For if further investigation should confirm the conclusion to which our recent facts seem to point, and it should indeed be proved that all idea of atmospheric contamination of our wounds during operations may be thrown to the winds, then no one will say with more joy than myself "Fort mit dem Spray."[6]

[Evidence of Lister's growth in his conception of the processes of infection, and of his greatness in not only changing his methods as experience warranted but also in retracting what he had formerly enthusiastically promulgated, is to be found in many of his writings such as the excerpts quoted below.]

AN ADDRESS ON THE PRESENT POSITION OF ANTISEPTIC SURGERY

And yet I must confess that I have for a long time doubted whether either the washing or the irrigation was really necessary. These doubts have been raised partly by experiments— some of which I mentioned at the London Congress—which had proved to me that normal blood and serum, and even pus, were by no means favourable soils for the growth of microbes in the form in which they are present in the air—and partly by reflection upon the experience we had when we used the carbolic spray.

As regards the spray, I feel ashamed that I should have ever recommended it for the purpose of destroying the microbes of the air.[7]

6. *Ibid.*, pp. 279–280; *Lancet*, 1881, Vol. 2, pp. 863, 901.
7. *The Collected Papers*, Vol. 2, p. 336; and *British Medical Journal*, 1899, Vol. II, p. 377.

ON THE INTERDEPENDENCE OF SCIENCE AND THE HEALING
ART

*Being the Presidential Address to the British Association for the
Advancement of Science, Liverpool 1896.*

And at the London Medical Congress in 1881, I hinted,
when describing the experiments I have alluded to, that it
might turn out possible to disregard altogether the atmospheric
dust. But greatly as I should have rejoiced at such a simplifica-
tion of our procedure, if justifiable, I did not then venture to
test it in practice. I knew that with the safeguards which we
then employed I could ensure the safety of my patients, and I
did not dare to imperil it by relaxing them. There is one golden
rule for all experiments upon our fellow men. Let the thing
tried be that which, according to our best judgement, is the
most likely to promote the welfare of the patient. In other
words, Do as you would be done by.

Nine years later, however, at the Berlin Congress in 1890, I
was able to bring forward what was, I believe, absolute demonstration of the harmlessness of the atmospheric dust in surgical operations. This conclusion has been justified by subsequent experience: the irritation of the wound by antiseptic
irrigation and washing may therefore now be avoided, and
Nature left quite undisturbed to carry out her best methods of
repair, while the surgeon may conduct his operations as simply
as in former days, provided always that deeply impressed with
the tremendous importance of his object, and inspiring the
same conviction in all his assistants, he vigilantly maintains
from first to last, with a care that, once learnt, becomes in-
stinctive, but for the want of which nothing else can compen-
sate, the use of the simple means which will suffice to exclude
from the wound the coarser forms of septic impurity. [8]

8. *Ibid.*, pp. 499–500.

MODERN SURGERY

Edoardo Bassini (1844–1924) and the Surgery for Hernia

"In order to achieve a radical cure [of inguinal hernia] it is absolutely essential to restore those conditions in the area of the hernial orifice which exist under normal circumstances." [1]

The problem of hernia has challenged surgeons throughout the ages, and has been a preoccupation of many of the authors quoted in this book. Repair of inguinal hernia, like all of elective operative surgery, necessarily had to await the advent of the twin blessings, anesthesia and antiseptic methods, for its solution. The status of herniology at the time when Lister was developing ways for circumventing the hazards of sepsis can be briefly summarized. The anatomy of the inguinal region had been thoroughly studied by surgeons whose names are intimately linked with the subject of hernia, including Camper, Scarpa, Hesselbach, and Astley Cooper. The various types and forms of herniae had been described and their complications were well known. Therapy, however, had made little progress. The leaders among surgeons abjured radical operation for reducible hernia, and only "irregulars" dared to provoke criticism and condemnation by violating this restriction. After the example of Pierre Franco, however, operation for relief of strangulation was approved and frequently performed.

With the adoption of antisepsis, radical repair of nonstrangulated herniae was immediately put to the test. The pioneers of post-Listerian herniology were Czerny, Lucas-Championière, Macewen, and Wood; their methods actually differed little from those of Celsus. It is true that the concept of the need for closing the aperture in the abdominal wall had been added to the classical ligation and excision of the sac, but the methods advocated fell far short of being adequate; and the results were most unsatisfactory. W. S. Halsted wrote (1890), "Just now, most of the so-called radical cure operations

1. Eduard Bassini: "Über die Behandlung des Leistenbruches," *Archiv für klinische Chirurgie,* Berlin, 1890, 40, p. 441.

are under a cloud. They have not withstood the test of time. Modern text-books refer to operations for the radical cure of hernia with more or less mis-giving." He quoted William T. Bull, one of New York's leading surgeons of the time, who reported recurrence rates of forty per cent in the first year, and practically 100 per cent failures within four years. Bull advised dropping the term "cure," and considered operation indicated merely for the temporary relief it afforded. Then came the work of Bassini.

Edoardo Bassini was born in Pavia, in Lombardy, on April 14, 1844. He received his doctorate from the University of Pavia in 1866, at the early age of twenty-two years. This was the year of the liberation and unification of Italy, and young Bassini fervently participated in the movement for national freedom. Although a graduate in medicine, he chose to fight as a private in the ranks, and engaged in two campaigns in that capacity. In the second of these he sustained a bayonet wound of the groin which festered and resulted in a fecal fistula. Taken prisoner, he remained in the hospital for a number of months. When eventually discharged, he returned to Pavia where he was successfully treated by Luigi Porta, Chief of the University Surgical Clinic, who subsequently became his teacher in surgery.

After he recovered, Bassini served as second assistant to Porta. He was particularly interested in anatomy and surgical pathology, and even in this early period made numerous dissections of the inguinal region. To complete his studies, he visited other famous clinics: Billroth's in Vienna, Langen-beck's in Berlin, and those of Lister and Spencer-Wells in London. He was invited, at the age of thirty (1874), to return to Pavia as first assistant to Porta, and to teach in the university. The following year his chief became ill, and Bassini carried on his work. When Porta died, however, the chair was awarded to someone else and, disappointed, Bassini resigned from the uni-versity and returned to London.

Six months later he was called to Parma to teach clinical surgery, and at the end of another two years he became head of the Department of Surgery at Spezia. In both institutions he introduced Listerian methods, being one of the first to bring antiseptic surgery to Italy. In 1882 he was appointed to the Chair of Surgical Pathology of the University of Padua, in which famous in-stitution he spent the following thirty-seven years of his life. He became Professor of Clinical Surgery in 1888, a position he held until his retirement at the age of seventy-five, in 1919. During this long and fruitful period, his epoch-making work on hernia appeared, as well as numerous other contributions to the surgical literature, for which he was widely honored. He was simple, almost austere in his tastes, of rigid moral fiber, a meticulous and cautious operator, and a kindly and interesting teacher. It is not surprising that he enjoyed the affection, as well as the admiration, of his associates and pupils. He died in Verona at the age of eighty, on July 19, 1924.

Bassini's interest in the problem of inguinal hernia dated back to his experiences in the Institute of Pathology in Pavia. As a clinician, he was impressed by the fact that all of the contemporary radical operations necessitated the subsequent wearing of a truss if recurrence were to be prevented This was also true of the first few patients upon whom he operated according to the most popular of the prevailing methods. He became convinced that the essential inadequacy of all the current operations was that the repair depended upon the occlusion of the hernial opening by a single layer of scar tissue which was further weakened by the necessity of leaving a passage for the spermatic cord. The solution of the problem, he thought, would lie in a physiological reconstruction of the inguinal canal, so that it again possessed an internal and an external opening and an anterior and a posterior wall. Applying his knowledge of anatomy, and experimenting on the cadaver, he evolved his renowned method which, he believed, fullfilled the requirements of a radical operation, namely, that it would cure the hernia without necessitating the subsequent wearing of a truss. His results confirmed the correctness of his idea. The first report of his operation was made before the Italian Surgical Society in 1887, and covered a series of forty-two cases. The following year, before the same body, he reported 102 cases successfully treated by his technique. His comprehensive treatise on "The Treatment of Inguinal Hernia," which appeared in the *Archiv für klinische Chirurgie* for 1890, made his discoveries available to the rest of the surgical world.

The technique described in this report not only differs somewhat from, but is actually better than that usually taught as the Bassini operation. The high ligation and excision of the sac are clearly and concisely described. Bassini then separated the internal oblique and transverse abdominal muscles and the *fascia verticalis Cooperi* (transversalis fascia) from the external oblique aponeurosis above and the subjacent preperitoneal tissue. The "triple layer" was then sutured to the shelving border of Poupart's ligament with interrupted silk stitches. The two lowermost sutures included the outer margin of the rectus abdominis muscle. Thus, the internal ring and the posterior wall of the canal were restored. The aponeurosis of the external oblique was then reunited over the cord, reconstructing the anterior wall and external ring.

Bassini recognized that large indirect herniae dilated the internal ring downward, depriving the canal of its obliquity. He emphasized the necessity of closing the floor from below upward, so that the newly narrowed internal ring lay above and lateral to the external ring, thus restoring obliquity to the canal. He recognized the valvelike closure of the canal by the approximation of the anterior and posterior walls when abdominal pressure is exerted. Beyond this, the differentiation between indirect and direct herniae, and their variations in location, structure, and treatment gave evidence of his complete mastery of the subject.

The report is based on a consecutive series of 262 cases, and there were no deaths among the patients with nonstrangulated herniae. All but four of the subjects were followed for periods ranging from one month to four-and-a-half years, truly a commendable achievement in clinical research. Only seven recurrences (two and seven-tenths per cent) were found in the total series, a record that would be gratifying today. A graphic demonstration of the superiority of the Bassini method is furnished by the contrast between his results and those reported from the famous Vienna Clinic of Billroth, which appeared in the same issue of Langenbeck's *Archiv für klinische Chirurgie* as did the definitive report of Bassini. The death rate in the Vienna material was about six per cent, and the incidence of recurrence high. On the basis of a very limited follow-up, it was found that over one-third of the operations were failures, and were marked by prompt reappearance of the hernia. The late results were admittedly much poorer.

The response to Bassini's work was instantaneous, and his methods were widely adopted. Overnight, hernial surgery of classical antiquity gave way to that of today, and little that is basic has since been added despite the myriads of alleged modifications and improvements. In the tradition of Vesalius, Harvey, Morgagni, and Scarpa, Bassini added his name to the list of those who made Padua a center of dissemination of knowledge to the medical world.

A number of other surgeons contemporary with Bassini, and motivated by the same discontent with the prevailing post-Listerian hernial methods, introduced techniques similar to those of Bassini and almost at the same time. Claims for priority have been made for some of these, notably for Henry O. Marcy of Boston and William S. Halsted of Baltimore. Careful analysis of the writings of these authors indicates that Marcy did, indeed, publish earlier than did Bassini, and that ultimately he did emphasize the importance of restoring the obliquity of the inguinal canal. However, his successive publications and also those of Halsted describe a series of gradually changing methods, and their ultimate operations, which could justly challenge the Bassini technique, actually appeared considerably later than did that of the Italian master. Furthermore, their operations had comparatively little influence on the trend of hernial surgery whereas that of Bassini was revolutionary. Of the myriad of improvements, modifications, and innovations which even yet continue to flood the literature, none have been decisive. The role of Bassini as the creator of modern hernial surgery stands unchallenged.

ON THE TREATMENT OF INGUINAL HERNIA

[The article begins with a discussion of the operations in vogue and their unsatisfactory results, including Bassini's own experience with these methods.]

The knowledge gained by the experiences of others and by my own observations convinced me of the need for another operative procedure to achieve and make certain the radical cure of inguinal hernia. I thought that this could be accomplished by restoring the inguinal canal to its physiological condition, i.e., a canal with two openings, an abdominal and a subcutaneous; and further, with two walls, one posterior and one anterior, through the center of which the spermatic cord would pass obliquely. By means of experiments on the cadaver, together with my knowledge of the anatomy of the inguinal canal and of inguinal hernia, it was not difficult for me to devise an operation which fulfills the above mentioned requirements, and yields a radical cure without necessitating the wearing of a truss. By this method, which I have employed exclusively since 1884, and which I now recommend, I have operated upon 262 hernias, of which 251 were either reducible or incarcerated, and 11 were strangulated.

Before reporting on the results of the operation I believe it necessary to describe the procedure. In external [oblique] acquired inguinal hernias I operate in the following manner:

The patient is deeply anesthetized, and of course strict antisepsis is maintained. I incise the skin over the inguino-scrotal hernia region, expose the aponeurosis of the external oblique over an area which corresponds to the inguinal canal (aperture of the hernia), thus exposing the crura of the subcutaneous inguinal ring, and control bleeding. This is the first step in the operation.

In the second step, I divide the aponeurosis of the external oblique muscle from the external ring to the level of the internal inguinal ring, and mobilize the upper and lower flaps of the aponeurosis, isolate and elevate in toto the spermatic cord and the neck of the hernial sac. Keeping the index finger beneath these structures, I dissect the neck of the sac from the elements of the cord to the opening of the hernia. This dissection proceeds with little difficulty with the aid of blunt instruments, regardless of whether it is an acquired or congenital hernia. The

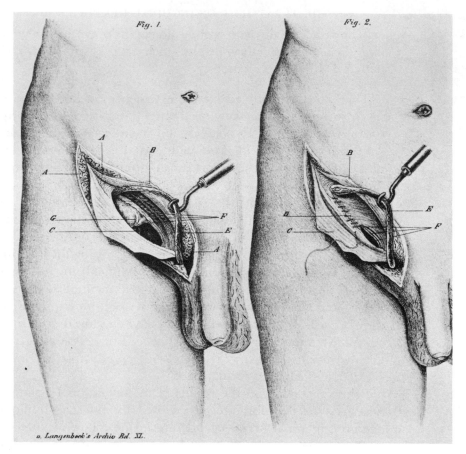

FIG. 105. Bassini's method of reconstruction of the inguinal canal. *Fig. 1*. The dissection has been carried down to the preperitoneal fatty layer. *Fig. 2*. The "triple layer" of internal oblique and transversus abdominis muscles and transversalis fascia is sutured to the inguinal ligament. (*See next figure.*)

isolation of the neck of the sac should extend to the iliac fossa, i.e., beyond the opening of the sac itself. Immediately afterward I dissect the body and fundus of the sac and draw it outwards, then open its fundus and inspect to see whether or not the viscera contained in the hernia show adhesions, and whether the omentum is thickened. If so, I separate the adhesions and remove the omentum as widely as is necessary. After reducing the contents I twist the sac (the neck), place a ligature proximal to it, and cut off the sac one-half centimeter beyond it. If the hernia is very large, and the neck and mouth of the sac are broad, I use, in addition to the single ligature, two suture-

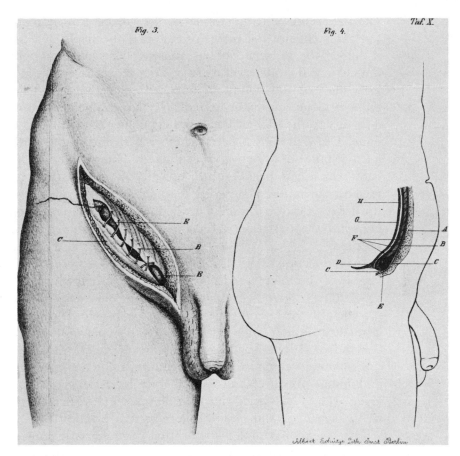

FIG. 105. (*Continued*). *Fig. 3*. The external oblique aponeurosis is sutured over the cord
Fig. 4. Sagittal section to show the restoration of obliquity of the inguinal canal. From: Bassini's:
"Über die Behandlung des Leistenbruches," *Archiv für klinische Chirurgie*, Vol. 40, Plate X.

ligatures placed distal to it, to assure closure and prevent the
slipping of the ligature. The peritoneum closed in this fashion
becomes retracted into the iliac fossa. With the extirpation of
the sac, and its ligation proximal to the opening, the second
step of the operation is concluded.

In the third step, I elevate the cord onto the abdominal wall
by gentle traction; and if necessary do the same to the testicle,
if it has been drawn out of the scrotum. With broad sharp re-
tractors I have an assistant pull the lower flap of the aponeurosis downward and the upper flap upwards, to expose the
groove formed by the inguinal ligament and its posterior wall
[shelf] to a level one centimeter above the point where the

spermatic cord emerges from the iliac fossa. I then mobilize the outer edge of the rectus muscle and the triple layer, consisting of the internal oblique muscle, transversus abdominis muscle and the fascia verticalis of Cooper [transversalis fascia], from the external oblique aponeurosis and the preperitoneal adipose tissue, until this united layer can be brought without difficulty to the shelf of Poupart's ligament. After this has been done, I sew these two parts together with interrupted sutures for a distance of 5–7 cms., from the pubic bone, laterally to the cord which has been pushed upwards approximately 1 cm. toward the anterior superior iliac spine. This concludes the third step of the operation, and the interior or abdominal opening, and the posterior wall of the inguinal canal have been restored.

In connection with the above-mentioned suture, it is advisable to use interrupted silk and to grasp the triple layer 2–3 cms. from its edge. The first two stitches placed on the pubis include also the lateral edge of the rectus muscle. If the patient is made to vomit after this phase of the operation has been concluded, (I have tried this in the first 50 cases) one sees that the inguinal region is able to withstand the strongest intra-abdominal pressure, and that the triple musculoaponeurotic layer which has been fixed to Poupart's ligament remains tightly stretched and immovable in its new position.

In the fourth step of the operation the spermatic cord is replaced, and the testis also if necessary; and the external oblique aponeurosis is reunited down to the pillars of the external ring. The skin is brought together, and finally a bandage is applied. I drain only in very voluminous old hernias in which the dissection and isolation of the sac is performed with difficulty. In this manner the inguinal canal is reconstructed with an inner opening and a posterior wall, both formed by the union of the triple musculoaponeurotic layer to the shelving edge of Poupart's ligament; and with an anterior wall and narrowed external or subcutaneous opening formed by reuniting the flaps of the external oblique aponeurosis. In indirect hernias, especially when they have a considerable circumference, the inguinal canal loses its obliquity and becomes straight or almost straight. By the operation here described it regains its normal course; the spermatic cord, displaced slightly outwards passes obliquely through the abdominal wall where the canal has been reconstituted. The deep suture lines are not superimposed on one another; the posterior remains below and the anterior above the spermatic cord.

[The article continues with a brief description of each of the 262 patients operated upon. This is followed by a statistical discussion of the various types of hernia, the complications, follow-up, recurrences, and observations on the strangulated hernias which were encountered in this series.]

2. *Ibid.*, pp. 429–476.

CHAPTER 44

Theodor Billroth (1829–1894) and the Rise of Abdominal Surgery

"There is only one way to train capable university teachers—one way that has been practically tested—and that is to secure for the universities the most distinguished men of science, and to furnish them with the necessary equipment for their teaching." [1]

The heights reached by French and British surgery described in the preceding chapters were not equalled by similar growth in the German-speaking countries. Here a backward status persisted well into the second half of the nineteenth century. Then, with a mighty upsurge, German surgeons (including those of Austria and Switzerland) not only closed the gap, but attained a dominant position which they held for almost half-a-century. The reasons for this rapid development are not easily pinpointed, but undoubtedly they are related to political and economic changes, as well as to the general cultural and scientific climate. The developments in physiology brought about by Johannes Müller and Carl Ludwig certainly played a significant role. The revolution in the concepts of pathology, in which Rokitansky and Virchow played so important a part in establishing the true nature of disease processes, were particularly contributory. The multiplication in the number of chairs of surgery in the universities, the unification of the disparate branches of the healing art, and the organization of learned societies with journals to publicize their proceedings were among the factors that gave impetus to this upward trend.

The only really significant German surgical figure in the century-and-a-half that separated Lorenz Heister from the new galaxy of German surgeons was August Gottlieb Richter (1742–1812). A graduate of the University of Göttingen, he subsequently became Professor of Surgery in the same institution, and there spent all of his active professional years. Before entering upon his university career he visited and observed the famous surgeons of England,

1. Theodor Billroth: *The Medical Sciences in the German Universities,* Translated from the German with an introduction by William H. Welch, New York, The Macmillan Company, 1924, p. 244.

France, and Holland. Percivall Pott, in particular, won his admiration and greatly influenced his subsequent activities. The regard was mutual and long-lasting.

Educated as a physician and trained in practical surgery, Richter commanded both disciplines to a superlative degree for the Germany of his time. The very high esteem in which he was held, coupled with his personal example and persistent urging, enabled him greatly to elevate the dignity of surgery and promote its rapprochement with medicine. To the practice of surgery, which had been dominated by men of the *Feldscher* or wound surgeon class who had imposed their stamp upon it, he personally brought the fruits of British and French achievements. He was, in addition, a most effective teacher and a lucid and gifted writer who provided books and periodicals in the German language, then so urgently needed. In these directions he made great contributions to the surgery of his country despite the fact that no important individual discoveries can be credited to him.

The great wave of surgical progesss of the late nineteenth century brought to the fore a large number of creative teachers, scientists, and practitioners, whose names are still familiar. The most influential of these was Theodor Billroth. This genial and cultured man was a talented musician and an intimate friend of the leading literary and musical personages of his day. A pathologist of note, an adventuresome surgeon who broadened widely the field of visceral surgery, an inspiring teacher whose pupils later filled many important chairs of surgery, and a medical educator, statesman, and historian, his was the greater accomplishment of standing forth, not against a background of mediocrity but by comparison with a generation of titans.

Theodor Billroth was born in 1829, on the Baltic island of Rügen, off the coast of Pomerania. His father was a Lutheran pastor, descendant of a long line of clergymen. Although he died when Theodor was but five years old, the education of his son was provided for by relatives. The family moved to Greifswald, where Theodor attended the *Gymnasium* (secondary school) and matriculated at the university. He was an indifferent pupil whose natural leaning was toward music. Left to his own choice, he would have pursued that art as a career, but his mother insisted that he study medicine and retain music as his avocation. After the first semester he transferred to the University of Göttingen, and here his scientific interests were aroused; the former indifference gave way to ardent application. The final year of his medical training was spent in Berlin, in which city he received his degree and his license to practice.

A year of travel to visit eminent professors in various fields was followed by the opening of an office for general practice in Berlin. Destiny took a strange course to alter the pattern of his life. In the first two months no single patient entered his office and the prospects appeared bleak. At this juncture he met

Th. Billroth, M.D.

Member of the Austrian House of Lords.
Imperial and Royal Aulic Councillor and Professor.
Director of the Surgical Institute of the University Vienna.
President of the Imperial and Royal Medical Association in Vienna
&c. &c. &c.

Fig. 106

an acquaintance who had just given up an assistantship in the eminent surgical clinic of Professor Bernhard von Langenbeck at the *Charité* in Berlin,
and urged that Billroth apply for the vacant position. This he did and, fortunately, was accepted.

Recognizing his need for vastly greater knowledge, Billroth turned toward
microscopic pathology, a science then in its developmental stage. The large
number of tumors that had been extirpated in the clinic provided the material

for study, and endless hours of intense and concentrated labor went into the examination and classification of these neoplasms. After three years as assistant, in 1856 he became *Privatdozent* in surgery and pathological histology.

After refusing several calls to other institutions, and failure to obtain one of several that he desired, he was appointed to the Chair of Surgery in Zürich, in 1860. A congenial environment and the opportunity for the assumption of responsibility and the exercise of his manifest and manifold capabilities brought him quickly to recognition. It was here, in 1863, that he brought out his excellent *General Surgical Pathology and Therapy in Fifty Lectures.* Here, also, he instituted the investigations that were to occupy him for the remaining years of his active life. Wound healing, and particularly the "accidents" due to infection which were then so pressing a problem that their solution was imperative for the development of surgery, particularly occupied his attention. He pioneered in the introduction of routine taking of temperatures in surgical patients, as an early indication of impending complication. The modest medical school with its tiny classes flourished under his influence and rapidly attained a position of distinction among German-speaking institutions.

Flattering offers from other schools failed to draw him from this pleasant and profitable situation. But when, in 1867, the chair in the famed University of Vienna, which was second in influence only to that of Berlin, was offered to him, he could not refuse. Here, a great man in a great institution combined to build worldwide prominence for both. The Billroth Clinic drew students and visiting surgeons from all quarters, and its chief became the outstanding surgeon of his time. For twenty-six years he reigned supreme in his profession and, at the same time, his home was a center of social activity which drew the intellectual and artistic leaders of the great Austrian capital. The intimate friendship between Billroth and the great musician and composer, Johannes Brahms, is popularly known. The many enjoyable evenings surrounded by men of genius, with whom Billroth could participate as an equal, gave warmth and color to his life. Under so favorable an environment, all latent potentialities expanded and flourished to the utmost of their capabilities.

As a surgeon Billroth took the lead in the expansion of the horizons of operative intervention made possible by anesthesia and antisepsis, particularly in the field of abdominal diseases. The experimental laboratory served as the testing ground for the exploits in the operating amphitheater, and his loyal and enthusiastic assistants worked together with their chief as a unit.

The interplay between the chief of the clinic and his assistants which made for such excellent teamwork has been well described by Billroth himself, in his report of the first successful gastric resection:

> "In 1871 I proved that one can extirpate pieces of the esophagus in large dogs. The esophagus healed well with a slight narrowing which could be dilated easily. Czerny was the first to perform this

operation successfully in man. Then followed Czerny's experiments on the extirpation of the larynx, a few years after which I successfully removed a carcinomatous larynx in a human being. There followed the experiments of Gussenbauer and Al. v. Winiwarter of resections of pieces of bowel and stomach, which in turn were proved and enlarged upon by Czerny and Kaiser. Martini's and Gussenbauer's success in resection of the sigmoid and my successful gastrorrhaphy (1877) proved that further advances in this realm would be feasible. The last-mentioned operation also eliminated the question of whether the gastric juices would dissolve the scar of the stomach thus formed. That is why I closed the report of that operation with these words, 'It is only a courageous step from this operation to the resection of a piece of carcinomatous degenerated stomach.' "

Billroth did indeed take this first courageous step, and in 1881 he performed the first successful removal of a portion of the stomach for carcinoma of the pylorus. (This operation had been done earlier by Péan in Paris (1879) and Rydigier in Kulm (1880) but the patients of both died.) Billroth united the ends of the stomach and duodenum, a procedure still known as the Billroth I operation which is currently enjoying a revival in the surgery of peptic ulcer.

In the same year, Billroth's assistant, Anton Wölfler, did the first gastroenterostomy for an inoperable carcinoma which obstructed the pylorus. Billroth subsequently found that his original method of restoring continuity between stomach and duodenum carried with it the danger of leakage at the site of anastomosis because of the disparity in size of the two lumens being brought together. He therefore closed both severed ends and performed a gastroenterostomy, the operation now designated as the Billroth II (1885). Thus, with the addition of numerous minor modifications, the entire repertoire of gastric operations had been ushered in, leaving only the recent introduction of vagus nerve resection by Lester Dragstedt.

Many further innovations flowed from the Billroth Clinic in all phases of surgery, but particularly in that of the gastrointestinal tract. Thus it was that its famous chief broadened greatly the field of visceral surgery and gave to it the impetus which has led to its present dimensions.

The first flush of success stimulated Billroth to an exaggerated optimism as to the feasibilities of the new operative methods. For a period he was carried away by enthusiasm, and he boldly undertook desperate measures in hopelessly advanced cases. The sobering realization of a mortality rate unwarranted by the limited successes achieved brought about a reversal in his attitude. Instead of the reckless application of operative measures without due regard to the risks involved, he adopted a policy of most careful weighing of the hazards against the hope of benefit to the patient, a theme that characterized his later writings.

A rigid honesty pervades the reports from the Billroth Clinic, the failures being presented as openly as the successes. This example has had a constructive effect upon the publications from other institutions and must be included among his greatest contributions. But of all his achievements, he personally was most gratified by the men he had trained. The "School" of Billroth supplied professors to numerous clinics, surgeons of the highest stature who, in turn, were the teachers and the inspiration of their younger men. So, by his own efforts, by his writing, and by the propagation of his stimulus to successive generations of surgeons, Billroth has indeed played a major role in the development of modern surgery and particularly in that of the abdomen.

It is obvious, of course, that the explosive expansion of abdominal surgery consequent to the impetus given to it by the work of Billroth was not due to technical advances alone. Many factors outside of the domain of surgery itself contributed to it, including better understanding of disease processes, new diagnostic methods, and significant improvements in pre- and postoperative care. Of the diagnostic aids, specific mention should be made of the advent of roentgenology. The initial publication of Wilhelm Conrad Röntgen's paper on "A New Kind of Ray" in 1895 was followed by the succession of improvements in equipment and the development of special techniques which have permitted an accuracy of diagnosis never before remotely anticipated.

The adjuvants to surgical care of greatest import are the correction of disturbances in fluid and electrolyte balance and the replacement of blood by transfusion. Biochemistry has joined the other sciences basic to surgery, and has taught the means of controlling the "internal environment" of the patient. The idea of replenishing the exhausted and depleted organism with fresh blood grew out quite naturally of Harvey's discovery of the circulation, and was first put into practice in the seventeenth century. (See Chapter 26 on Scultetus and Purmann.) In the earliest transfusions, beginning with those of Denis in Paris, in 1666, the blood of animals was used. The indications included both mental and corporeal illnesses; and because such abnormal states were based upon the prevailing humoral theories, the rationale was entirely different from that of present-day transfusions. It was the contribution of the English obstetrician, James Blundell (1825), to prove that only human blood was suitable for transfusion into man; to establish correct indications, namely exsanguinating hemorrhage, for the operation; and to devise the first of a long series of technical methods and apparatus for the transfer of the blood from donor to recipient.

There remained, however, the accidents which are now understandable in the light of the recognition of blood grouping. Not until Landsteiner (1900) demonstrated the presence of isoagglutinins and the division of human blood into specific groups was the road open to the avoidance of incompatibility reactions. Jansky and Moss independently worked out the classification of the blood groups and Ottenberg (1908) developed clinical methods for typing human blood, thus eliminating the final major hazard. This was followed by the introduction of numerous techniques to prevent coagulation during transfusion, including that of citration by Lewisohn, in 1915, which method has become standard. Blood banking of citrated blood has provided the surgeon with the indispensable weapon with which to cope with the conjoined menaces of hemorrhage and shock.

A better understanding of disease processes within the abdomen grew out of the manifold contributions of pathologists and physicians. Although surgery profited from these advances, it also made contributions which not only served its own needs but also added significantly to the general knowledge of clinical medicine. The recognition at operation that ulcers of the duodenum were very much more frequent than those of the stomach, and the enormous volume of experimental work on the production of pancreatitis are but two examples of this type of collaborative effort. The widely dispersed laboratories of experimental surgery which play so vital a role today are but a continuation of the tradition established by John Hunter, Charles Bell, Billroth, and their many successors throughout the modern world.

ʂ• ʂ• ʂ•   OPEN LETTER TO DR. L. WITTELSHÖFER, BY PROF.
ʂ• ʂ• ʂ•   TH. BILLROTH, VIENNA, FEB. 4, 1881[2]

Esteemed Colleague!

It is with pleasure that I comply with your wish and tell you about the resection of the stomach which I performed on Jan. 29, of this year, since it deals with the very important question as to whether the frequently occurring cancers of the stomach, which are resistant to all medical treatment can be cured by surgery.

It is now 70 years since a young physician, Karl Theodor Merrem, published a dissertation in which he showed by means of experiments performed on dogs, that it is possible to excise the pylorus and unite the stomach with the duodenum, and that of the three animals so operated upon, two survived the

2. *Wiener Medizinische Wochenschrift*, Vol. 31, No. 1, 1881, pp. 162–166. This excerpt was translated from the German by the authors. The style and sentence structure are maintained as in the original.

operation. He was so bold as to suggest that this operation might also be performed on human patients with hitherto inoperable carcinoma of the pylorus. However, at that time the conviction had not yet been accepted that the vital processes, their disturbances and recovery were essentially the same in animal and human bodies, and further, the operative techniques were not sufficiently advanced to enable one completely to understand the significance of these experiments and to apply their physiological results to man. The question as to the best way to close wounds in the stomach or the intestines had concerned surgeons repeatedly over a long period of time. The most prominent anatomists and surgeons of France, England and Germany have dealt with this question in the course of this century; but only since Lembert found the correct principle for this procedure (accurate approximation and union of the serous surfaces), has successful intestinal suture of accidental injuries become more frequent. But no one has yet dared to undertake the excision of diseased segments of bowel. Definite new advances have been made in this field only during the last decade. In 1871, I demonstrated that it is possible to remove portions of the esophagus in large dogs, and that the wounds heal well with but the formation of slight and easily dilatable stricture. Czerny was the first to perform this operation successfully in man. Then followed Czerny's experiments on the extirpation of the larynx, after which I succeeded, a few years ago, in removing a larynx that was affected with a cancerous growth. Then came the experiments of Gussenbauer and Al. v. Winiwarter on the resection of portions of the stomach and bowel, which were subsequently confirmed and expanded by Czerny and Kaiser. The success of Martini and Gussenbauer in resecting the sigmoid, and my successful gastrorrhaphy (1877), showed that further advances could be made in this field; the latter operation relieved us of the worry that the scar in the stomach would be digested away by the gastric juices. Thus I concluded the report of the last-mentioned operation with the words: "Only one courageous step is required from this operation to the resection of a portion of carcinomatous stomach."

To those who fear that my present operation is a foolhardy experiment on man I would give assurance that this is by no means the case. The groundwork for gastric resection has been as thoroughly laid both anatomico-physiologically and technically by my pupils and myself as has any other new operation. All surgeons who are experienced in animal experimentation and in similar operations on man must reach the conviction that gastric resection should also succeed!

The few cases which I encountered in the course of the past year did not appear to me particularly suited for an initial operation of this kind. But last week, my clinical assistant, Dr. Wölfler, brought a woman to me in whom the diagnosis of a movable carcinoma of the pylorus could be established without doubt. After several days of observation and repeated examination, I decided to undertake the operation, to which the patient agreed, since because of her increasing fatigability and inability to retain food, she felt that her end was near.

This 43-year-old, pale but previously healthy and well-nourished woman, mother of eight living children, apparently became suddenly ill with vomiting. Soon all symptoms of carcinoma of the stomach with stenosis of the pylorus developed (I shall omit the descriptions here because they are well-known). The vomiting of coffee-ground material occurred only a few times, and the severe pallor and emaciation, as well as the small, rapid pulse appeared only in the last six weeks as a result of the continued vomiting and the limited nutritional intake; the only thing which she could retain, at least for some time, and which kept her from starvation, was sour milk.

The preparation for the operation consisted in accustoming [the patient] to peptone enemas and gastric lavage by the customary injection and pumping method. . . . Because of the patient's severe weakness and the anticipated long duration of the operation . . . I requested one of my experienced private assistants, Dr. Barbieri, to administer the anesthetic. You will understand my need to be free from worry about the anesthetic in order that I might devote myself solely to the operation. The operating room which had been specially prepared for laparotomies had, for well-known reasons, been heated to the temperature of 24° R. All my assistants were deeply aware of the great significance of our undertaking; there was not the least disturbance nor a minute of interruption.

The movable tumor apparently as large as a medium-sized apple lay immediately above and slightly to the right [of the umbilicus]. A transverse incision was made over the mass through the thin abdominal wall, approximately 8 cms. long.

Because of its size the tumor was difficult to deliver; it was found to be a partly nodular and partly infiltrating carcinoma of the pylorus and involved more than the distal third of the stomach. Separation of the adhesions to the omentum and the transverse colon. Careful detachment of the greater and lesser omenta. Ligation of all vessels prior to their division; insignificant loss of blood. Complete delivery of the tumor into the abdominal wound. Incision through the posterior wall of the stomach 1 cm. beyond the infiltrated part, and then through the duodenum. An attempt to approximate the severed ends showed that union was possible. Six sutures through the wound margins; the sutures were not tied but were merely used to hold the margins in place. Further incision of the stomach, obliquely from above and inward to below and outward 1 cm. away from the infiltrated part.—First, then, the union of the oblique stomach wound from below upward until the opening was just large enough to fit the duodenal lumen. Then complete separation of the tumor from the duodenum 1 cm. beyond the infiltration by means of an incision parallel to the stomach incision. Accurate insertion of the duodenum into the remaining gastric opening. In all about fifty sutures of Czerny's carbolized silk. Irrigation with 2 per cent carbolic acid solution. Revision of the entire suture line; insertion of several auxiliary stitches at apparently weak places. Reposition into the abdomen. Closure of the abdominal wound. Dressing.

The operation, including the slowly administered anesthesia took 1½ hours. No weakness, no vomiting, no pain after the operation. During the first 24 hours only ice by mouth, and peptone enemas with wine. On the first day, at first every hour then every half-hour, a tablespoonful of sour milk. The patient, a very understanding woman, feels quite well, lies extraordinarily quietly, [and] sleeps through the greater part of the night with the help of a small morphine injection. No pain in the wound, moderate febrile reaction. The dressing remains untouched. Nourishment, after a few attempts with bouillon which were disagreeable to the patient, consisted entirely of sour milk of which she took one liter in the course of the day. The peptone and pancreas enemas are prone to produce flatulence and colic, and are therefore omitted; an injection of a little wine per anum two or three times daily is agreeable to the patient. Yellowish farinaceous stools like those of infants. The pulse much slower and fuller than before the operation. Thus it continues without the slightest disturbance. As proof of the well-being of the patient, I must also tell you that on the day before yesterday, in response to her urgent request, I had her transferred into a general ward because in the isolation room she found too little entertainment lying next to an equally bored ovariectomized woman who had been operated on the same day.

The excised portion measures 14 cms. (*horribile dictu*) on the greater curvature; a quill is passed through the pylorus with difficulty. The shape of the stomach has been little changed by the operation, it is only smaller than before. I am, myself, pleasantly surprised with this completely smooth course; I would have expected more local and general reaction, I might almost say misbehavior on the part of the stomach. I still hardly dare to believe that all will proceed so quietly. There could be a relapse into the former state of weakness: the most fatal complication, since little could be done about it. By the end of 6 days without reaction the wound and everything around it must be firmly united so that even with suppuration of one or another suture, a sudden generalized peritonitis can hardly be expected. However, circumscribed suppuration [and] abscess might still arise about the scar; I hope we can discover them early enough; in order to drain them exteriorly.

The course to date suffices to prove the feasibility of this operation. To establish the indications and contraindications and to develop a technique for the most varied cases must be the concern and the object of our further research. I hope we have taken another step forward to cure the illnesses of unfortunate patients, heretofore considered incurable, or in recurrent carcinomas to relieve them for a while. You will surely forgive me if I feel a certain pride in the work of my pupils that has made this possible.—*Nunquam retrorsum*! is the motto of my master Bernhard v. Langenbeck; it is also to be my motto and that of my pupils.

CHAPTER 45

Theodor Kocher (1841–1917) and the Surgery of the Endocrine System

"Surgeons who take unnecessary risks and operate by the clock are exciting from the onlookers' standpoint, but they are not necessarily those in whose hands you would by preference choose to place yourself." [1]

The art of surgery, in its long upward climb, has always been based on a substrate of science. In its earliest stages, anatomy was its foundation structure. Later, when the nature and causation of disease became known, pathology was added as providing the essential background. Today we have further progressed and are now in the era of physiological surgery. Not only is the knowledge and control of all phases of bodily function necessary to the care of the surgical patient, but operations may be done solely for derangements of physiology, and the structures so attacked may be morphologically normal.

Nowhere is this physiological basis more striking than in surgery of the endocrine system. Of all the organs of internal secretion, the thyroid gland was the first to come within the domain of the surgeon. It has been the object of by far the largest number of operations, and the experiences thereby gained introduced the entire concept of endocrine physiology. Mechanical disturbances from enlargement of the thyroid gland were recognized in the Graeco-Roman period and occasional operations for goiter found their way into the literature since that time. The proximity of large blood vessels, important nerves, and vital structures including the larynx and trachea made such operations too dangerous to undertake except by the most courageous.

The pioneer in modern thyroid surgery was Theodor Kocher, the greatest Swiss surgeon of all time. This scholar and scientist enriched virtually every field of surgery but his contributions to the knowledge and treatment of thyroid diseases in particular were of such overwhelming significance that they brought him the Nobel prize in 1909.

1. Theodor Kocher quoted by Harvey Cushing in J. F. Fulton: "Arnold Klebs and Harvey Cushing at the 1st International Neurological Congress at Berne in 1931," *Bull. Hist. Med.*, Vol. 8, No. 3, 1940, p. 345.

In contrast to the lives of many whose careers have formed the content of this book, that of Kocher was singularly devoid of drama and adventure, except for the excitement of discovery, the disappointment of unexpected failure, the gratification of fulfillment, and the esteem and devotion of those he taught and those he helped. In many respects his career is reminiscent of that of Lister. His father was prominent as an engineer; his mother, a descendant of the sect of Moravian Brethren, instilled within him a deeply religious feeling, and with it a sense of high ethical responsibility. Although he was quiet, withdrawn, and austere, he possessed a lively humor of which, however, none but his intimates were aware. Surgery was his whole life and, except for a talent for painting, he had no other interests. Both science and the welfare of his patients benefited from his whole-souled devotion to his work.

Theodor Kocher was born in Bern, and there spent his entire life. From early childhood he displayed an extraordinary aptitude for scholarship, and throughout his years of study he ranked high in his classes. Medicine was chosen as his vocation, and he matriculated at the University of Bern where he maintained the high standards of which he had earlier given promise. After his graduation he traveled for a year, visiting the famed clinics of the world, those of Langenbeck, Billroth, Lister, Spencer-Wells, Nélaton, and Verneuil. The predominance of surgical centers among those to which he was attracted indicates that he already had acquired an interest in surgery.

Returning then to Bern (1865), Kocher entered the Surgical Clinic of the university and, in the short space of seven years, at the early age of thirty-one, was awarded the Professorship when his chief was called to another post. Here he spent the remaining forty-five years of his life, and died while actively at work at the age of seventy-six. A long, unbroken career as an enterprising and inventive surgeon, tireless and productive investigator, esteemed and stimulating teacher, author of almost 150 significant articles and monographs and a popular and widely translated *Operative Surgery*, and the founder of a large school of able and distinguished disciples was crowned by the reverence of his countrymen, the respect of his colleagues throughout the world, and the ultimate honor of the Nobel prize.

Goiter had always been endemic in its severest form in Switzerland. Thyroid enlargements and their associated problems, cretinism, endemic deaf-mutism, had for centuries constituted the greatest medical and social problems. It is not surprising, therefore, that Kocher's greatest achievements were in the realm of these disorders. His successes made Bern the capital of goiter therapy and the haven for patients with thyroid diseases from all over the world.

Gigantic nodular goiters causing respiratory obstruction to the point of asphyxia, to say nothing of the cruel cosmetic disfigurements, constituted the

F<small>IG</small>. 107

initial challenge. Here his precise and detailed knowledge of anatomy and the meticulousness that was the keynote of his every action enabled him to invade with security a narrow operative field that abounds with a multiplicity of massively engorged blood vessels and important nerves. The pre-

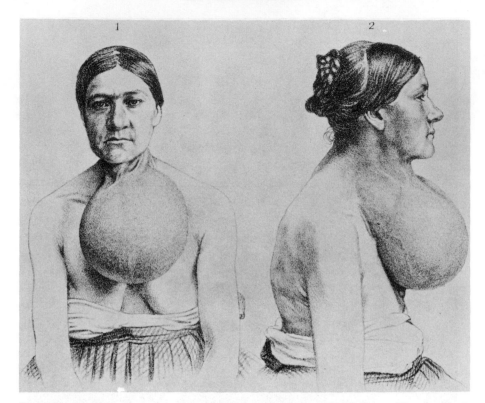

Fig. 108. Massive goiter of the type common in Kocher's material. From: Theodor Kocher: "Zur Pathologie und Therapie des Kropfes," *Deutsche Zeitschrift für Chirurgie*, 1874, Vol. 4, pp. 417–440.

liminary ligation of the four principal arteries which he introduced very materially reduced the volume and the danger of bleeding. Year after year during his long tenure at Bern, Kocher issued successive reports of his goiter material. These trace the refinements of his surgical methods and disclose a reduction in the mortality rate from very high initial figures to 12.8 per cent (1883) and an eventual level of less than 0.5 per cent. Indeed, in one series of 600 cases (1898) there was but one death and that was due to chloroform anesthesia.

Three pitfalls threaten in the radical extirpation of the thyroid gland, injury of the recurrent laryngeal nerves with subsequent loss of voice or even respiratory insufficiency, removal of the parathyroid glands with the consequent tetany, and absence of sufficient functioning thyroid tissue which results in myxedema. In the period of the beginning of Kocher's work, the hazard of laryngeal nerve injury was well recognized. Galen had demonstrated the effect of section of these nerves on phonation, and those of his surgical successors who were sufficiently anatomically aware had this danger in mind when major operations in the neck were contemplated. The precision and deliberateness of Kocher's technique enabled him to preserve these important structures with a degree of security at least equal to that of the surgeon today.

The function of the thyroid gland, however, was still wrapped in mystery, although several theories as to its physiological activity had been advanced. However, it had not been demonstrated that this gland was essential to life and well-being. It came as a disheartening shock to the conscientious Kocher when he suddenly discovered that those grateful patients he had so skillfully relieved of their suffocating goiters had been reduced to a cretinoid and almost imbecilic state. His attention had been called to this alarming possibility when he heard his countryman, Professor Jacques-Louis Reverdin of Geneva, report that those patients on whom he had done total thyroidectomies had degenerated into the condition to which Kocher subsequently gave the name *cachexia thyreo-* or *strumipriva*. The misfortune was spared those who had had removal of but one thyroid lobe. Reverdin's description recalled to the mind of Kocher that some such change had been described in a letter from a referring physician concerning one of his patients. An immediate follow-up investigation, by letter or personal examination, was instituted, and the sad facts were disclosed. Of the thirty-four patients upon whom total extirpation had been done, eighteen returned for examination and all but two of these revealed the evidences of myxedema. Those with partial resections had escaped. Kocher determined never again to remove the whole gland for benign disease, and to begin immediate animal experiments to elucidate the phenomenon. Thus surgery had established an important physiological fact, namely, that the thyroid gland is essential to normal life, and that the cretinoid or myxedematous state which had been observed in spontaneous form is a manifestation of thyroid insufficiency.

Tetany, the third potential major complication of thyroidectomy, was confused with myxedema, and in the minds of many was thought to be an acute form of cachexia thyreopriva. The tiny parathyroid bodies which lie so closely in apposition with the under-surface of the thyroid gland had but recently been discovered and their function was entirely unknown. It was only later learned that tetany was the result of the inadvertent removal of these glands, which control the metabolism of calcium and, through that mineral, the tonicity of the body's musculature. In the early period of Kocher's experience with the operation of thyroidectomy, when both of these mishaps—myxedema and tetany—were coming into prominent notice, Billroth had performed more operations for goiter than had any other surgeon. It is curious that he observed no patients with myxedema, but had a high incidence of tetany, whereas Kocher had the opposite experience. William S. Halsted, who was a friend of Kocher, in a beautifully complete historical review of "The Operative Story of Goitre," offered an enlightening explanation of this contrary occurrence. In this, as well as in almost all other fields of surgery, Halsted was an authority, having made noteworthy contributions to thyroid surgery, and even more important ones on hernia and breast, general operative technique, asepsis, and surgical teaching and training. He wrote, "I have pondered this question for many years and conclude that the explanation probably lies in the operative methods of the two illustrious surgeons. Kocher, neat and precise, operating in a relatively bloodless manner, scrupulously removed the entire thyroid gland, doing little damage outside its capsule. Billroth, operating more rapidly and, as I recall his manner, with less regard for the tissues and less concern for hemorrhage, might easily have removed the parathyroids or at least have interfered with their blood supply, and have left fragments of the thyroid."[2]

In addition to his surgical and physiological contributions to the thyroid problem, Kocher also made important investigations on the relationship between geological environment and the endemicity of goiter. He further studied and wrote authoritatively on such varied subjects as gunshot wounds, localization of spinal cord lesions, gynecology, diseases of the male genito-urinary tract, fractures, and many aspects of abdominal surgery. His operation for hernia, for carcinoma of the rectum, his method of mobilizing the duodenum to expose the retroperitoneal structures, and his maneuver for reducing dislocations of the shoulder are all well known and still bear his name. Numerous instruments which he devised, such as the Kocher hemostat, the Kocher dissector, and many others are still found on the instrument tables of the modern operating room.

Theodor Kocher was a master surgeon in the fullest sense of the word. Meticulousness and conscientiousness were his essential characteristics. A highly religious man, he carried the responsibility of his profession with all seriousness. His diagnostic study was complete, his indications for operation most scrupulously drawn. Gentleness, precision, and a sensitive respect for tissues marked his operative technique. Calm and order prevailed in his operating room. In the words of the simple people whom he served so well, he had "lucky hands."

Serenity marked Kocher's life, as it did his personality. He was spared struggle, turmoil, and strife. A happy childhood, a most rewarding career, a felicitous family life with a perfect companion in his wife, and five children, and a quick and painless death while still actively engaged in the work for which he lived; all these and an abiding faith that sustained him in times of doubt and trial made his, indeed, a good life.

Mention has been made of the fact that the presenting challenge of goiter

2. William S. Halsted: "The Operative Story of Goitre," *The Johns Hopkins Hospital Reports*, Vol. 19, 1919, Supplement, pp. 71–257.

to Kocher and his early contemporaries was the huge, suffocating thyroid enlargements, which were frequently associated with hypothyroidism and rarely with hyperthyroidism. Exophthalmic goiter had been described by Parry (1825), Graves (1835), and Basedow (1840), and the relationship between its manifestations and the thyroid gland was beginning to be recognized. In Kocher's successive series of thyroid operations, a very low incidence of such cases were included (five out of 250 cases reported in 1881). Other surgeons in Germany and elsewhere in Europe were struggling with hyperthyroidism as the second indication for thyroidectomy, one in which the nature of the disease itself made the operation very dangerous. Here, in fact, were alarming disturbances in physiology, a problem to be overcome by surgery.

The conquest of this phase of the thyroid problem was subsequently largely effected by American surgeons. In this country the concurrence of both the simple and the toxic forms of goiter in vast numbers brought the challenge of hyperthyroidism much more strongly to the fore. The work of George W. Crile is still remembered. Alert to the damaging effects of emotional factors in increasing the perils of thyroidectomy in severely toxic patients, he developed his elaborate ritual of "stealing" the thyroid, creeping up on the patient, as it were, and snatching the gland before fear and excitement could wreak their devastating effect. The introduction of iodine as a properative measure by Plummer of the Mayo Clinic (1922), a drug that had been considered literally a poison to goiter patients, led to a degree of safety at surgery almost comparable to that for simple goiter.[3] The later developments, the antithyroid drugs and finally the radioactive isotopes, have not only further increased the safety of operation, but have largely supplanted surgery for hypothyroidism entirely.

The other glands of internal secretion have also yielded many of their secrets, and disorders of function remote from the structures themselves are being successfully treated by surgery. As indicated earlier, postoperative tetany, the manifestation of parathyroid deficiency, was known before the function of these tiny glandules had been discovered. Although they were described by Ivar Sandström in 1880, little attention was paid to them until Gley (1891) and Vassale and Generali (1896) proved the relationship of their removal to tetany. Their role in the control of calcium metabolism grew out of the observation by MacCallum and Voegtlin (1909) that the blood calcium was low in hypoparathyroidism. This, in turn, led to the recognition of hyperfunctioning parathyroid tumors and their association with von Recklinghausen's disease of bone; and Felix Mandl, in 1925, removed an adenoma

3. Charles H. Mayo and Henry S. Plummer: *The Thyroid Gland*, Beaumont Foundation [Annual Lecture Course IV, 1925.], St. Louis, C. V. Mosby Company, 1926, p. 74.

of the parathyroid and thereby relieved a patient suffering from osteitis fibrosa cystica. The association of hyperparathyroidism with aberrant calcification and renal lithiasis is a recent addition to the recognition of systemic disorders arising from hyperfunction of these structures.

The rapid growth of knowledge of the other endocrine glands, the islands of Langerhans and their relation to carbohydrate metabolism, the several hormones of both medulla and cortex of the adrenals, and the many of the pituitary have extended the surgery of these organs. Of current interest is the concept of "hormonal environment" of certain cancers, first elaborated by Charles B. Huggins with relation to malignant growths of the prostate and breast. Modifying this environment by surgical means is now finding increasingly frequent application as a weapon in combating inoperable carcinomas.

ON THE EXTIRPATION OF GOITER AND ITS SEQUELAE[4]

Although it is my purpose to direct your primary attention to the effects of the removal of the thyroid gland, it seems desirable to orient you as to our indications for the extirpation of the diseased gland, our methods of its performance, and the results of the operation. I consider myself justified in discussing this subject with you because in the Canton of Bern goiter is so frequent that—so far as I know—only one surgeon, Billroth in Vienna, is performing goiter extirpations more frequently than we are.

I have, to the present time excised 101 goiters. Of these 101, 13 patients died, a mortality of 12.8 per cent.

In the past 17 months we have performed 43 goiter extirpations in the Bern Clinic, with a mortality of only 3 (6.9 per cent). The deaths occurred in very complicated cases: in one with sarcomatous goiter actual asphyxia occurred at the very moment when he presented himself for examination, and there was no other recourse but to make a rapid opening into the trachea through the struma. Sepsis developed. In a female patient who already had bilateral recurrent nerve paralysis with severe attacks of asphyxia before the operation, death occurred from supervening laryngobronchitis. Finally, in the third patient death resulted from asphyxia, and we found, in addition to the enormous goiter which had been extirpated, a totally independent retrosternal mediastinal goiter consisting

4. Theodor Kocher: "Über Kropfextirpation und ihre Folgen," *Archiv für klinische Chirurgie*, Vol. 29, 1883, pp. 254–337. Translated from the German by the authors.

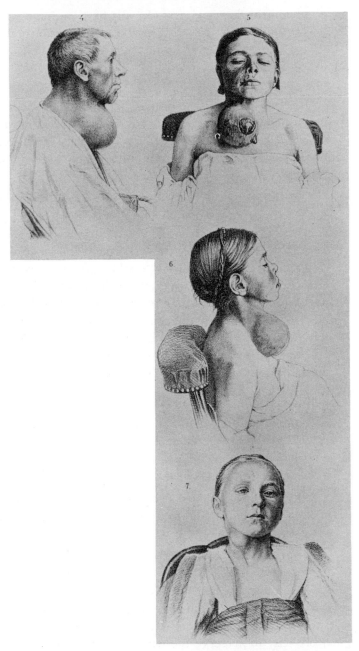

FIG. 109, No. 4. Cystic goiter with secondary inflammation. Nos 5–7, large inflamed goiter before and after operation. From: Theodor Kocher: "Zur Pathologie und Therapie des Kropfes," *loc. cit.*

of an almost fist-sized cyst. In all these patients who died following operation, tracheotomy had been performed.

If we consider the malignant goiters separately, we had one
death in four operated upon (25 per cent); and of 39 non-
malignant goiters the mortality then is 5.1 per cent.

[Kocher discusses the dangers of hemorrhage and recurrent
nerve paralysis, and the various operative techniques used by
other surgeons. He then presents his own operative method,
but in such minute detail that only selected passages are quoted
below.]

The blood inflow and outflow of the thyroid gland can be
studied in any anatomical handbook. First of all, it must be
emphasized that one should not be misled by the lack of uniformity of the thyroid blood vessels which has been emphasized
by Virchow who said that it "could scarcely be exceeded in any
other organ." In the large majority of cases the vessels can be reduced to a fixed pattern. The upper poles of both lobes are supplied by the superior thyroid arteries which come from the external carotids; the lower poles from the inferior thyroids which
arise from the subclavians. In addition, according to the anatomists, there is, in about one of ten cases, a thyroid ima artery,
usually coming directly from the arch of the aorta or the innomi-
nate artery or from branches of either. We have found this vessel
only in exceptional cases. It supplies the isthmus and the inner
aspects of the lower poles. A priori, one should think that preliminary ligation of the five arteries should suffice to guarantee
a relatively bloodless operation.

[There follows a most detailed description of the abundant
venous drainage of the thyroid, and the methods for securing
these vessels.]

What makes particular caution necessary after the veins
have been ligated in goiter operations is the preservation of the
recurrent laryngeal nerves. Wölfler was the first to emphasize
this danger in an exhaustive manner, and explain the reasons.
I must completely agree with him and Billroth, that it is relatively easy to preserve the trunk of the nerve when ligating the
inferior thyroid artery. Here it is necessary meticulously to
isolate this vessel before one puts a ligature around it, and not
to tie its trunk at the point of entrance into the goiter, but to
ligate it laterally. . . .

[The further cautious dissection to avoid nerve injury is minutely described, as are also the manifestations of unilateral and bilateral nerve damage.]

On the basis of the results of goiter extirpation here reported, we maintain that even in this difficult operation we have arrived at the point where we generally recommend the radical operation for goiter as the surest and simplest method of treatment. We are far from interpreting this to mean that all goiters should be removed surgically; we rather adhere to our previously expressed view that operative therapy should be restricted to cases with severe symptoms, or those with lesser difficulties but in which nonoperative therapy cannot prevent further enlargement of the goiter. . . . The second question of importance in regard to the generalized use of surgery for goiter has to do with the physiological importance of the thyroid gland. Unfortunately, the physiologists know almost nothing about it, and this has probably been the main reason why surgeons have simply assumed that the thyroid gland has no function whatever. As soon as it had been learned that from the standpoint of technique total extirpation could be carried out successfully there was no longer reason to hesitate to remove the entire organ when both lobes are diseased.

In a previous publication we collected 99 cases [from the literature] of total excision with a mortality of 14.1 per cent. To these we now add 16 further cases of our own with only one death (the patient had bilateral recurrent nerve paralysis before the operation). Thus we arrive at a mortality rate of 12.1 per cent in 115 cases of total extirpation. It is also statistically evident that the dangers of total excision are no greater than those of partial excision; on the contrary, in our experience the course is generally smoother because no ligated pedicle is left behind, as is done in partial thyroidectomy.

Wölfler . . . states, "We know now that the removal of the degenerated thyroid gland is well tolerated in man, so well indeed, that we cannot yet justifiably draw any certain conclusions as to the physiology of the normal gland on the basis of the effects of its removal." For a long time I shared this opinion. Only concerning one patient upon whom I had operated on Jan. 8, 1874, has the referring physician incidentally reported that the girl had undergone marked change in her personality; indeed, he finally informed me that she had be-

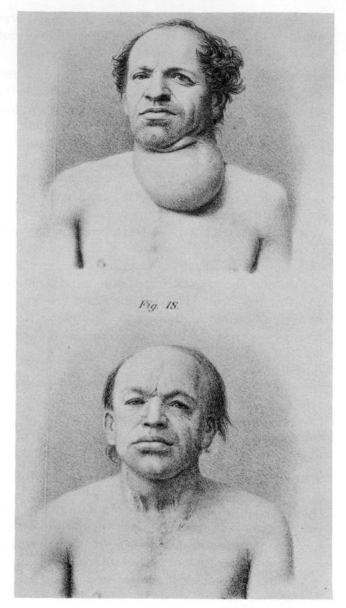

Fig. 18.

FIG. 110. Typical goiter patient in Kocher's series before and after operation. From: Theodor Kocher: "Über Kropfextirpation und ihre Folgen," *Archiv für klinische Chirurgie*, 29, 1883, p. 254ff.

come quite cretinoid. This seemed to me so important that I made every effort to examine the girl, which was not easy since this physician had died very shortly after making this report. We were all the more intent upon it since our colleague, Rever-

din of Geneva, had informed us that he had observed two patients who had suffered diminution of mental capacity following
goiter operations. I was highly astonished at the striking appearance of my patient. To crystallize somewhat your impression, I shall show photographs of the girl and her younger
sister, taken before and after the operation. At the time of the
operation, according to the mother, both girls looked so much
alike that they were frequently mistaken for one another.
Whereas in the ensuing nine years the younger sister blossomed
into a very pretty young woman, the one operated upon remained small, and has an ugly, almost idiotic appearance.

As soon as this was determined, . . . I immediately requested
all of my goiter patients to return for examination. Excluding
the 11 who were operated upon this year, and the 13 who had
died, there remained 77 out of our 101 individuals to whom
such invitations had been sent. Of these 77 postoperative patients, no information could be obtained concerning 17. Among
the remaining 60, there were 5 with malignant goiters who
had been discharged as cured after the operation. Of these,
one patient who had been enjoying good health for many years
was then lost to follow-up. (According to a recent letter she
died of meningitis, with no recurrence of the cancer.) Another
died a few months after the operation of sudden asphyxia.
One, in whom a carcinoma of the larynx complicated the picture, and a simultaneous laryngectomy had to be done, has
recurrent lymph-node involvement. The remaining two are
quite well after 5 and 8 months respectively.

Of the 55 non-malignant goiter patients, two who had had
total thyroidectomy have since died, one of pneumonia, the
other of unknown cause. Thirty-four of the remaining 53 patients came for examination and 19 reported in writing. Concerning those in whom partial excision had been done, i.e., one
lobe of the thyroid, with or without the isthmus, we can report
very briefly. One female patient became mentally deranged.
Until the advent of this condition she had a glowing appearance. In only one woman has there been a pigeon egg-sized
recurrent nodule on the same side. In general, all the rest, 28
in number, enjoy the best of health and are pleased and grateful with the success of the operation so far as it bears on their
previous complaints and state of well-being. As an indication
for partial excision it seems particularly important to emphasize
that with a single exception, there were no recurrences after the

Figs. 111 and 112. The dramatic case of Maria Richsel, the first patient to have come to Kocher's attention with postoperative myxedema. Fig. 111 shows the child and her younger sister before the operation. Fig. 112 reveals the changes nine years after the operation. The younger sister, now fully grown, contrasts vividly with the dwarfed and stunted patient. From: Theodor Kocher: "Über Kropfextirpation und ihre Folgen," *loc. cit.*

operation; and even those individuals who had more or less marked enlargement of the opposite lobe, as was often the case, have permanent relief. The operation, therefore, has actually achieved a radical cure. It should be mentioned incidentally, that if this experience should be further confirmed, it supports the theory of an early predisposition or origin of goiter.

It is entirely different in those patients in whom a total extirpation of the thyroid gland has been performed. Of 34 total excisions which we have done, three died of the sequelae of the operation, and two later from causes unknown to us after an

Fig. 112

initial good recovery, and one of malignant goiter. Of the remaining 28, we were unable to gather information in only four;
18 came in person and 6 reported in writing. The latter are of
lesser importance, of course, in evaluation: in four of the six
it is emphasized that the patients are quite well so far as the
neck and their general well-being is concerned, and that they
feel better than they did before the operation. These patients

were 22, 24, 44 and 51 years of age at the time of surgery. It is noteworthy that these patients had severe difficulties pre-operatively which were due to their goiters. One had whistling inspiration. Both lobes, each of goose egg-size, consisting of colloid-cystic tissue, had caused a severe sword sheath-shaped flattening of the trachea. She had a most pronounced anemia. After the operation there was an attack of tetany of several days duration, which was repeated later in milder form. Now she writes that "her anemia is greatly improved, her breathing is better, and walking is no longer hampered, as it formerly was, by dyspnea; and she has no other complaints."

Of a second of these patients her physician writes that "she feels entirely well, has a healthy appearance, and has no diffi-culties in breathing or swallowing." In her case the lateral flattening deformity of the trachea was so pronounced that for ten minutes during the operation it was necessary forcibly to compress the trachea from the front to combat the extreme dyspnea. The right lobe was significantly hyperplastic, the left, fist-sized, consisted primarily of a hemorrhagic cyst. It is noted that a hazelnut-sized, movable swelling had formed between the larynx and hyoid bone.

In the third of these cases the enlargement of the left lobe was considerable; there was a fist-sized nodule with marked dis-placement and significant stenosis of the trachea. The patient writes, "I have no complaints or pains whatever and enjoy the best of health."

[The fourth case follows a similar pattern with equally good result.]

In the two other patients whom I was unable to examine following total extirpation, the reports were not so favorable. The husband of one writes, "Her operation was successful and the difficulties in the throat are relieved. But otherwise, my wife has not since had one healthy hour. Her abdomen is con-stantly swollen, her limbs without sensation; she has no warmth, complains constantly of freezing, her periods are very irregu-lar." Her follicular-colloid goiter had caused moderate diffi-culty in breathing and swallowing, but had not been very large. No untoward accident happened during the operation.

Concerning the other patient the husband writes, "Since my dear wife has not been able to write for months because of ner-vous pains in her hands and feet [I am answering for her.] Since her successful operation she has no further trouble with her throat; but her hands and feet are as if paralyzed. Particularly since her confinement the year before last, her health has failed progressively." The colloid-cystic struma which had been excised was not large, and had caused only slight dyspnea and complaints, and had been removed primarily because of its continued growth and the ineffectiveness of previous therapy. Both of the last-mentioned women had been in good health before their operations, although there had been definite nervous symptoms; but no striking anemia.

Of the 18 patients with total excision who presented themselves for examination, only two show a state of health as good as or better than before the operation.

The remaining 16 patients with total excision of the diseased thyroid gland all show more or less severe disturbances in their general condition, the analysis of which has been drawn from precise records in each individual case. The time elapsed since the operation ranges from $3\frac{1}{2}$ months to 9 years and 2 months, and the severity of the symptoms is far graver in the oldest cases. They [symptoms] are obviously progressive. All younger patients who were operated upon more than two years ago show these manifestations to a pronounced degree. Furthermore, all 10 patients upon whom the operation was done during their growing period, i.e., before they were twenty years old, show the disease picture. . . . Of the older patients, only two show the abnormal condition in a highly developed form, a girl of 20 and a man of 45. The four others had only moderate signs, and are 26, 26, 28 and 29 years old. The only older patient who has severe difficulties had had a tracheotomy during the operation, and he is also the only one who has since had attacks of dyspnea. Two women of 36 and 38 years of age are among those who reported only in writing and whose significant change in general well-being was mentioned above.

So far as the disease picture itself is concerned, it consists of the following:

As a rule, soon after discharge from the hospital, but in occasional cases not before the lapse of 4 or 5 months, the patients begin to complain of fatigue, and especially of weakness and heaviness in the extremities. In many cases the sensation of weakness is preceded by pain and drawing in the arms and legs, but frequently only in the arms. There are also complaints of throat, shoulder and abdominal pain.

In addition there is a sensation of coldness in the extremities, not of their having "gone to sleep," but of freezing; and in the winter the hands and feet swell; they turn bluish-red and cold, and develop chillblains.

The mental alertness decreases. This is particularly striking in children of school age, inasmuch as they drop in class standing, and that the teachers note a progressive diminution of their intellectual capabilities. This manifests itself predominantly in slowness of thinking, so that they have to deliberate longer than usual before they give an answer. Children who were formerly among the brightest pupils suddenly fall back, so that the teachers are forced to discontinue exerting special efforts with them. Arithmetic proves particularly difficult for them.

Associated with the slowness of thinking, there is gradually increasing slowness of speech and of all other movements. The slow speech amazed us in all patients whom we saw again. The slowness and clumsiness in their work resulted in servants losing favor and being discharged, although formerly they had been particularly valued as diligent farm hands and skillful maids.

The awareness of their loss in skill and ability is not lacking in most patients, rather the contrary is true. Some who felt that they had been conspicuous because of their slow speech and thought, withdrew, became noticeably silent and introverted; others complained to their mothers of their frustration because of their inability to get along in school, that they were no longer like other children or as they had been before the operation. One girl frequently became angry at her slowness in answering or speaking.

With the onset of the clumsiness and tiredness in thought and movement swellings appear, sometimes intermittent, involving the face, hands and feet, lasting a few hours and then disappearing. It is frequently mentioned that these swellings are particularly striking in the morning. They are most noticeable in the eyelids, and the families often reported that sac-like swellings could be seen in the lower lids. In one case, edematous swellings of lids, hands and feet occurred at longer intervals only and at those times this patient had difficulty in breathing which was also noted between attacks.

In the majority of the cases, the swelling is a permanent puffiness of the face. Second only to the clumsiness, it is this which creates the impression among more distant acquaintances that the patient has become an idiot. The entire face becomes thicker, the lids are translucently [durchscheinend] swollen as is seen in some nephritics, the nose thickened, the lips are puffed; in the lower extremities there is, on rare occasions, edema of the legs and ankles.

The body also thickens; in girls this becomes particularly noticeable around the waistline. The circumference of the lower thorax appears expanded, the abdomen large. The distension of the abdomen is only in rare cases due to demonstrable ascites. We could diagnose this [ascites] in only two cases in which, at the same time, edema was clearly noticeable.

The skin shows changes which are associated with the puffiness of certain parts of the body. It is slightly infiltrated, its flexibility lost, and it can be picked up only in thick folds, just as in cases where edematous swellings have existed. The surface is dry which is often very noticeable in the face because of the scaling of the cheeks and ears. In addition to these changes in the skin, in two cases there was marked loss of hair, with only a few fringes along the part, where it was thinner and less flexible. This baldness adds to the cretin-like appearance of these individuals since the body resembles that of a child while the head is that of an old man.

Anemia is pronounced in advanced cases. The skin and mucous membranes, especially of the ears and lips, are pale; the pulse is small even to the point of threadiness, and easily suppressible. The heart sounds are clear but weak, the second aortic, and even more so, the pulmonic are loudly snapping. In 17 cases we examined the blood, counting the red and, in part, the white corpuscles. We have never observed any qualitative abnormality in these cases, except for a relative increase of the white cells, relative insofar that when there is a marked reduction of the red cells, the white cells appear more numerous. Where counts were made, the ratio was always one leucocyte to more than 300 red cells. On the other hand, the decrease in red cells could be clearly demonstrated. In general, the decrease in the red cell count was in direct relationship to the other abnormal manifestations. The lowest, however, was 2,168,000 and was found in a young girl eight months after the operation. [The degree and variations of the anemia in the respective cases is presented.]

Whenever the individuals were in the growing period at the time of operation, the longitudinal growth of the body remained markedly retarded. [See illustration above.]

If we are to give a name to this picture, we cannot fail to recognize its relation to idiocy and cretinism: the stunted growth, the large head, the swollen nose, thick lips, heavy body, the clumsiness of thought and speech, in the presence of a well-developed musculature undoubtedly point to a related evil. It is interesting that the individuals are not really stupid, which has often been emphasized by their families; they are fully conscious of the retardation of their mental capabilities and especially of the slowness of their comprehension, deliberation, and particularly, of their speech. They feel that they must exert much more effort to progress with their studies, and one of our patients attempted to keep pace with her schoolmates by redoubled industry.

We prefer, for the time being, to use an entirely innocuous name for this symptom-complex. For the nutritional disturbances which accompany the disappearance of goiters after iodine administration (Virchow), the name goiter cachexia or cachexia iodica has been used; we see no objection for the time being, to the use of the name *cachexia strumipriva*.

CHAPTER 46

Sir Victor Horsley
and Modern Neurosurgery

". . . Thus love, joy, ardour, courage, hate, fear, rage, passion, all seek expression which, unless directed by reason, may become a danger; love degenerating into passion, joy into orgy, ardour into impatience, and courage into recklessness." [1]

The earliest operations of which objective evidences have survived were neurosurgical. Trepanation of the skull was frequently done in prehistoric times, as far back as the neolithic period, and in widely dispersed areas throughout the world. Trephined skulls in large numbers have furnished evidence of the techniques used and of prolonged survival after the operation in not a few. The reasons for which so grave a procedure was undertaken are largely a matter of speculation, but it is highly doubtful that the operation was frequently done for medical indications that would be valid today.

In the centuries of recorded history, virtually all surgical writers have dealt with the problems of cranial injury and most accounts include commentary on the use of the trephine and other operative manipulations. This, however, continued to comprise essentially the totality of neurological surgery until shortly before the beginning of the present century. Even the freedom from pain during the operation and the hazards of infection after it were not sufficient to widen significantly the scope of intervention for cure of diseases of the nervous system. Although occasional intrepid individuals did succeed in draining an intracranial abscess or removing a tumor with external manifestations, the management of lesions of the central nervous system was as yet all but a closed book. Requisite for opening it was knowledge of the physiology of the brain and spinal cord, and specifically that of *localization of function* by which the site of the disease could be determined.

The first important step toward achieving this was taken by the French surgeon and anthropologist, Paul Broca (1824–1880), who, in 1861, discov-

1. Sir Victor Horsley and Mary D. Sturges: *Alcohol and the Human Body*, London, The Macmillan Company, 1911, p. 87.

519

ered the "speech area" in the third left frontal convolution, which is still named after him. Some time later (1864–1870) the English neurologist, Hughlings Jackson, established the fact that irritative foci in the cerebrum evoked convulsive movements in specific muscle groups (Jacksonian epilepsy), thus confirming the localized nature of brain function. The German investigators Fritsch and Hitzig further demonstarted (1870) this principle by the electrical stimulation of various areas of the cerebral cortex in laboratory animals. It remained for David Ferrier, in England, carefully to map out the motor centers, and even some sensory areas, by similar methods; and when Rickman Godlee, nephew, disciple, and biographer of Joseph Lister, found and removed the first brain tumor to have been localized by Bennett, with Ferrier's technique, the way was opened for the induction of the modern era in neurosurgery.

The pioneer figure who most significantly contributed toward developing this field was Sir Victor Horsley (1857–1916). Like many of the eminent surgeons dealt with in this book, he was, from childhood, an unusual person. He came from a family prominent on both sides as painters, writers, and musicians. With this background it is not surprising that he had artistic leanings and delicate perceptions. Of extremely high moral fiber, he shunned alcohol, tobacco, loose talk, and sexual digressions, and even disapproved of the theater. This does not imply, however, that he was at all lacking in virility. On the contrary, he loved all vigorous sports and excelled in them. Always interested in riding and shooting, he would have preferred a military career had his father not directed him toward medicine.

Horsley received his medical education at the University of London, where his diligence and application won for him a number of honors. There followed the sequence of posts as clerk, resident, and eventually as both Surgical Registrar at the University Hospital and Assistant Professor of Pathology (1882). In the meantime he had passed the successive examinations leading to an including a degree of Bachelor of Medicine and Surgery and Fellowship in the Royal College of Surgeons.

Neurology early claimed Horsley's primary interest. While still a clerk he came into contact with such eminent figures in this field as Hughlings Jackson, Charcot, Gowers, and Ferrier; and he made drawings for a book on the brain which was written by Bastian. In collaboration with this same author he published his first paper, which naturally was on a neurological subject. During his house-surgeoncy he studied his own subjective reactions to anesthesia, having himself anesthetized no less than fifty times, truly a heroic research project. "He used to come into our sitting-rooms, where having set us down at a table with pen and paper, he proceeded, whilst lying back in an armchair, to administer chloroform to himself. At his dictation we had to

Fɪɢ. 113. Sir Victor Horsley. From: Stephen Paget: *Sir Victor Horsley: A Study of His Life and Work*, London, 1919.

write down in what order his cerebral centres became inactive. It was found that the loss of brain function always took place in the same order, and that after he was able only to mumble a few words he could still move his arms. When quite unconscious, we had to remove the mask and allow him to sleep off the effects of the drug."[2]

When he was still a young man Horsley was appointed Professor-Superintendent of the Brown Institution, a quaint veterinary hospital and research laboratory. This provided him with greatly needed research facilities and with a staff of scientifically oriented younger colleagues. Here much of his investigative work was carried out, on the nature and treatment of myxedema,

2. Stephen Paget: *Sir Victor Horsley: A Study of His Life and Work*, London, Constable & Company, Ltd., 1919, p. 40.

the eradication of rabies in Great Britain, and, importantly, on further studies of neurological localization. This last-mentioned subject so vitally concerned him that he simultaneously engaged in additional studies in collaboration with the distinguished physiologist Schaefer at the University of London. Thus the pattern of his work was established, consisting of research, publication, and lectures. The localization studies, in particular, furnished the material for a large series of important articles.

It was not until 1885, when he was twenty-eight years old, that Horsley received his first appointment as Assistant Surgeon to the University College Hospital; and the following year he was made Surgeon to the National Hospital for the Paralysed and Epileptic, Queen Square, the principal hospital in England for the treatment of nervous diseases. At this time, also, his private practice began to grow, and his career as a surgeon, and particularly as a neurosurgeon, began. He was, in fact, the first surgeon whose principal, although not exclusive, work was in the field of neurosurgery. It is not to be wondered at that he soon dominated this newly developed subspecialty, and that his recognition became worldwide.

The scope of his investigations, the range and number of his discoveries, and the important "firsts" in operative achievements embrace the entire subject. His introduction of the use of bone-wax for the control of bleeding from the bone edges, which continues to be an important aid in cranial surgery, is but one of his many contributions. His writings and researches extended into the fields of pathology, physiology, bacteriology, chemistry, anthropology, and clinical neurology; and his operative material included lesions of the brain, spinal cord, pituitary gland, Gasserian ganglion, and peripheral nerves. Thus, certainly, he created a transition from a stage which had not significantly advanced beyond that of Paré and Fabry von Hilden to the present era in neurosurgery.

At the height of his professional career, Horsley quite abruptly relinquished much of his professional activity and devoted himself to political action. It is difficult to fathom the reason for this extraordinary change and even Stephen Paget, Horsley's eminent biographer, fails to speculate on it. He does state, however, that quite early in his career, Horsley had made up his mind that in his sixtieth year he would retire from practice and enter Parliament. There is no clue as to why he anticipated this decision by ten years, except for Paget's statement that "it is to be remembered first, that he never for one moment regarded politics as less important than science and practice. . . ."

Thus at the age of fifty, Horsley resigned his position as Surgeon to the University College Hospital, his Professorship of Surgery at the university (he had earlier given up his position at the Brown Institution and his university Professorship of Pathology), and gave himself largely to political matters.

He was, from the first, a zealous reformer. Mention was made earlier of his antipathy toward tobacco and alcohol, and this he never abandoned. As early as 1882, at the age of twenty-five, he wrote a paper for the Students' Medical Society "On the Evil Effects of Tobacco," and in his later years he took a leading part in the Temperance movement. Matters of public health, vital statistics, and social and economic reforms received his ardent support.

As part of his medico-political activities, Horsley assumed the presidency of the Medical Defence Union, which had been set up to protect the interests of the physicians. Elected to the General Medical Council, he energetically strove to increase the activities of this organization in advocating essential reforms within the profession. He further led the attacks for greater democracy within the national medical organizations; and when the National Insurance Bill, which subsequently introduced the panel system, was under consideration, he was effective in so modifying the act as to make it more acceptable to the physicians of Great Britain. On the broader platform of national politics he tried for election to Parliament but without success. Advocating unpopular movements such as Womens' Suffrage and Temperance, refusing to compromise with his convictions for political gain, and fearless in his attacks on those who opposed him without regard to person or station, he made many enemies and found himself involved in the personal acrimony that is the price of political struggle. Yet he continued his battles without loss of courage or personal dignity, or even confidence in the eventual triumph of right.

Although by conviction he was a pacifist, the outbreak of World War I found him completely in sympathy with the cause of the Allies and he insistently sought active service despite the fact that he was fifty-seven years old. Months dragged by as he chafed at the delays before he was assigned duties commensurate with his stature and abilities. Early in 1915, he was placed in charge of the Surgical Division of the 21st General Hospital which was to have served in France. The orders, however, were changed and the unit was sent to Egypt instead. Later, he was appointed Consultant to the Mediterranean Expeditionary Force with the rank of colonel. These duties carried him to India and subsequently to Mesopotamia where, on July 16, 1916, he died, presumably of heatstroke. In a prefatory note to Sir Victor's biography Lady Horsley wrote:

"When at the age of fifty-nine Victor Horsley died, struck down by the furnace heat, the mental misery, and the overwork of Mesopotamia, he was still in the fulness of his powers. These he had planned to use, on his return home, for the promotion of the social reforms in which he was most keenly interested, the health, housing, and land of the people. He intended again to offer himself for Parlia-

mentary election and, as the letter from Huddersfield quoted in the
Memoir shows, he would probably have been returned to Parliament
by a constituency choosing him as their representative for his personal qualities and his high ideals."[3]

Horsley's death, although tragic indeed, came after his work in building
the science and practice of neurosurgery had been completed. It remained
for others to carry on the effort so ably begun; and of the many who shared
in this enterprise, none played so important a role as did the well-known
American neurosurgeon, Harvey Cushing. The story of Cushing's life is too
familiar to warrant detailed review, thanks to the several biographies, particularly the masterful treatise by John F. Fulton. Cushing knew Sir Victor,
admired his achievements, and shared his vigorous opposition ot the restrictions on animal experimentation by the enactments secured by the British
antivivisectionists.

Cushing brought into neurosurgery the ultrarefinements of preoperative
preparation and operative technique. Himself a thorough perfectionist, he instilled in his assistants a degree of regard for the ritual of the brain operation
that amounted almost to reverence. His introduction of the silver clip method
of hemostasis in tissues that cannot be subjected to ligation or tamponade was
not the least of his innumerable technical improvements. By insistence, as
well as by example, he established neurosurgery as a full-time specialty. His
crowning achievement was the creation of a school of neurosurgeons, and
many of the leaders in this division of surgery bear the stamp of his teaching.

In addition to these contributions to the technical aspects of neurosurgery,
Cushing and his associates made highly important additions to the pathology
and classification of cranial neoplasms, as well as to the functions and dys-
functions of the pituitary gland and their treatment. The mere mention of the
Cushing syndrome brings to mind the now familiar and striking clinical picture. Beyond all his professional attainments, Cushing was a medical historian,
a bibliophile of note; and his matchless *Life of Osler* was a major literary
monument that won for him the Pulitzer prize in biography.

ᔒ ᔒ ᔒ   [The celebrated neurologist W. R. Gowers referred a patient
ᔒ ᔒ ᔒ   to Victor Horsley with the diagnosis of spinal cord tumor. The
                   lesion was removed with complete restoration of function. This
                   case was published conjointly by Gowers and Horsley, the
                   former presenting the medical history. Horsley's description
                   of the operation is given herewith.]

3. *Ibid.*, p. vii.

A CASE OF TUMOR OF THE SPINAL CORD. REMOVAL; RE-
COVERY.[4]

Surgical History of the Case, by Mr. Victor Horsley.

I saw Captain G——————— on the 9th of June, 1887, at
1 p.m. The patient was half sitting up, complaining of parox-
ysms of very great pain in the lower limbs and abdomen, the
former being completely paralysed and frequently flexed in
clonic spasm, the pain accompanying which was so severe as to
cause the patient to cry out. On careful examination of his
spine, there appeared no undue prominence of any vertebra,
and the only abnormality detected was tenderness on pressure
to the left side of the sixth dorsal spine. This was very constant
though slight; on movement the patient complained of a sensation of weakness (rather than pain) referred to the middle
of the dorsal region, but such movement did not seem to start
the spasm in the legs by interference with, or pressure upon,
the spinal cord. He was very loth to move because it necessitated voluntary change of position of his legs, movement of any
of the joints of which was liable to bring on a severe paroxysm
of painful flexion. In addition to the complete loss of motor
power just noted, there was loss of tactile sensibility as high as,
and involving the distribution of, the fifth dorsal nerve. There
was some doubtful diminution of sensibility in the left fourth
intercostal space, but this could not be satisfactorily demonstrated when I saw the patient. On the right side the insensibility was limited to the fifth interspace. The anaesthesia was
complete for all kinds of stimulus.

There was complete loss of power over the bladder and rectum, and catheterisation had been found difficult with a metal
instrument on account of the severity of the urethral spasm
thus excited. (After the operation, when the spasmodic condition was equally severe, the passage of a soft rubber catheter
was unattended by this trouble.)

The morning temperature during the week preceding the
operation varied from 97.4° to 99.2°, and the evening temperature between 99° and 99.4°.

For the history and present state see the foregoing description
by Dr. Gowers.

4. W. R. Gowers and Victor Horsley in *Medico-Chirurgical Transactions*, London, 1888, Vol. 71,
    p. 376 ff.

OPERATION.—June 9th, 3.30 p.m. Present: Drs. Gowers, Percy Kidd, and Edmunds. Mr. White anaesthetised the patient with ether while he was lying in the semi-prone position on the right side, and I was kindly assisted by Mr. Stedman and Mr. Ballance. The skin was shaved and thoroughly cleaned with ether and 5 per cent carbolic acid solution, the spray was used throughout the operation, and the instruments and sponges were kept in 5 per cent carbolic solution. Free incision was then made in the middle line through the skin and the subcutaneous tissues extending from the third dorsal spine to the seventh. The deep fascia and tendinous attachments of the muscles were then cut from the spines and a transverse cut was carried outwards from the spines over the spinous muscles through the vertebral aponeurosis, so as to prevent all tension on the sides of the wound. (See Remarks.) Vessels bled freely by the sides of, and between, the spinous processes, and were secured with Wells's forceps. The muscles were then completely detached from the spinous processes, from the laminae, and from the mesial aspect of the transverse processes. This was done in a way which I shall refer to later, namely, by free use of the knife, and subsequently blocking the wound with sponges, while the same procedure was carried out on the other side of the spinal column. The sides of the wound being now strongly retracted and most of the vessels ligatured, the spines and laminae could be seen perfectly.

The fourth, fifth, and sixth dorsal spines were then cut off close to their bases with powerful bone forceps, the laminal arch of the fifth vertebra was then trephined with a three quarters of an inch trephine, the pin being placed in the middle line. The bone was very hard and tough and one sixteenth of an inch thick. The rest of the laminae were then removed with a bone forceps and knife, the ligamenta subflava giving much trouble owing to their toughness. The laminal arches of the fourth, fifth, and sixth vertebrae being thus cleared away, the dura mater was easily exposed by an incision in the middle line through the fat covering it. This fat, being pressed aside, shrank and showed the dura mater of a normal appearance, colour, and tension. Nothing very abnormal was then observed, save that on the left side the dura mater was distinctly pressed nearer to the bony wall of the neural canal. This, of course, was due to the fact that the tumour lay on the left side of the cord, and consequently pressed the dura mater on that side closer to the vertebrae. The wound being practically bloodless, the dura mater was slit open in the middle line with a knife and dissecting forceps. The cerebro-spinal fluid escaped freely, but not with any undue pressure to signify pathological tension. The spinal cord was now exposed for about two inches and appeared to be perfectly natural in colour and density; moreover, the vessels coursing on its surface were in every respect normal.

It will now be readily understood that the upper part of the roots of the sixth nerve and the whole course of the fifth nerve on each side from the spinal cord to the intravertebral foramen was completely exposed. Examination of the spinal cord on all sides with the finger and cautiously with an aneurism needle failed to reveal anything abnormal. Another lamina was removed at each end of the wound, the dura mater as before slit, up, and the cord still further exposed, but still nothing pathological was discovered. At this juncture it appeared as if sufficient had been done, but I was very unwilling to leave the matter undecided, and my friend Mr. Ballance being strongly of the opinion that further exposure of the cord was indicated, I determined to go further if the state of the patient warranted me in so doing. Finding that his pulse was very strong, and that there would be no difficulty whatever in the anaesthetisation, I removed another lamina at the upper part of the incision. On opening the dura mater I saw on the left side of the subdural cavity a round, dark, bluish mass about three millimetres in diameter, resting upon the left lateral column and posterior root-zone of the spinal cord. I recognised it at once to be the lower end of a new growth, and therefore quickly cut away the major part of the lamina next above. This enabled me to see almost the whole extent of the tumour when the dura mater was divided. It was an oval or almond-shaped body of a dark, bluish-red colour, resting upon, and attached at its lower extremity to, the highest root of the left fourth dorsal nerve, just where the posterior nerve-roots were gathered together in one trunk. On palpation the tumour markedly fluctuated. Above, it extended as far as the third dorsal nerve to which it appeared to be loosely attached by connective tissue, evidently a fold of the arachnoid. The tumour occupied exactly the position of the point of the ligamentum denticulatum, being jammed between the dura mater and the left side of the spinal cord. The pia mater and the arachnoidal sheath of the spinal cord evidently passed continuously from the cord over the surface of the tu-

mour, forming a kind of capsule on its upper surface. At the
same time it seemed as if the tumour could be pressed away
from the spinal cord, so as to give the idea of its not actually
invading the substance of the cord. I therefore made an incision
through the pia matral sheath of the spinal cord, and then
found that I could easily dissect the tumour from the surface of
the cord, lifting it out of the deep bed which it had formed for
itself in the lateral column of the cord. It was easily detached
above by cutting through the loose tissue before described.
Below, as it was firmly adherent to the fourth dorsal nerve, and
as that nerve was of course of insignificant importance, I cut
away the portion of nerve adherent to the growth. The outer
border of the tumour was bathed in the cerebro-spinal fluid, and
so required no dissection, but in removing the growth its inner
surface, formerly of course in close contact with the cord, apparently gave way and some turbid serous fluid escaped, this
reducing the volume of the tumour to about three fifths of its
former size. (For description of the tumour *vide infra.*)

The cavity left by the removal of the growth was of course
for the most part simply the subdural space, but the spinal cord
was evidently greatly damaged by the pressure of the growth.
The lateral column was so depressed or notched, so to speak,
that the bottom of the groove in it nearly reached the middle
line of the cord. It seemed likely, therefore, that most of the
fibres in this column would be completely destroyed, moreover,
there was evidently no resiliency in the damaged cord, for
during the time that it was under observation the bottom of this
pit showed no tendency whatever to rise. The surrounding adhesions of loose connective tissue oozed rather freely, but gentle
pressure with a fragment of sponge for a few minutes soon
arrested this bleeding. The cord and subdural space were then
carefully sponged with 5 per cent carbolic acid solution and
freed from blood-clot. The edges of the long incision in the dura
mater were then approximated (incision fully four inches) and
laid in position but not sutured at all. The few remaining vessels
were ligatured, and the sides of the wound brought together
by strong silk sutures passed vertically with curved needles
through almost the whole thickness of the side of the wound,
and at a distance of about half an inch from the border. These
sutures were placed at distances of about one inch, and on
being tied firmly were found to readily approximate the two

sides of the cavity close to the dura mater. The edges of the skin were carefully approximated with numerous horsehair sutures, a small superficial drainage-tube was placed at the lower extremity of the wound, and a long drainage-tube was placed vertically to the dura mater and reaching so far as that membrane at the upper end of the wound. The whole was then covered with a strip of carbolic gauze dipped in 5 per cent carbolic solution, and a carbolic gauze dressing applied. The patient was put back to bed.

THE TUMOUR.—The growth, on microscopical examination, was found to be fibro-myxoma. It presents a nodular appearance, and the cavity referred to was found to be on the inferior and outer surface, being such a cystic space as might have resulted from a haemorrhage. The wall of the cavity was found to be a false capsule derived from the pia mater and arachnoid. Unfortunately its contents were lost in the operation. The mass of the growth on section was pale and homogeneous, but indications of separation into nodular masses could be seen here and there. The tumour was enveloped, as already described, in a thin capsule, and consequently the parts will first be described under the headings of capsule and substance. . . . .

REMARKS.—This being the first case in which a tumour involving the spinal cord has been exposed and removed, it is very advisable that a full explanation should be given of the reasons which led to the adoption of the surgical procedure above described, and I think at the same time it is worth while to look back over the literature on the subject of tumours of the membranes of the spinal cord, and to see what light may thereby be thrown on this subject.

[The histopathological findings of the tumor are described as well as the postoperative course and the follow-up record. The final notation dated one year after the operation reads as follows: "Letter received this day from patient states that he is in excellent health, of which the best evidence is that he recently did a sixteen hours day's work, including much standing and walking about."

It will be noted that Horsley believed that this was the first tumor of the spinal cord which had been removed. Actually, William Macewen, a Glasgow surgeon who had performed a considerable volume of neurosurgical operations before those of Horsley, had reported the removal of what he called a "fibrous neoplasm of the theca" in two patients with complete recovery.

Horsley's article further contains an exhaustive discussion of all phases of spinal cord tumors including a tabulation of all other reported cases that he had been able to find.]

REMARKS ON THE SURGERY OF THE CENTRAL NERVOUS SYSTEM.

Read in the Combined Sections of Surgery and Neurology at the International Medical Congress, held in Berlin, August, 1890. By Victor Horsley, B.S., F.R.C.S., F.R.S.[5]

GENTLEMEN,—In fulfilling the wish you have done me the honour to express that I should open the discussion on the Surgical Treatment of Diseases of the Nervous System, it appeared to me that the subject was one of such wide extent that it could only be treated profitably by the adoption of some definite plan, excluding details as far as possible, or leaving them to publication in tables. Such a plan I have endeavoured to form, and it is as follows:

I propose to enumerate and to place in tabular form the various conditions of the brain and spinal cord which it is at the present time considered reasonable and justifiable to attack by surgical interference, and to illustrate in some way the object of such treatment, its chance of success, and the reasons for or against it. Of course, I need hardly say that I do not intend to do more than touch upon some of the most debateable points among those described in the tables, and I hope you will permit me, in support of my observations, to allude to certain cases which have come under my own care.

Of diagnosis I shall not speak, as it does not come under the title of this discussion, but it is the subject of surpassing interest and importance in the present issues. Modern surgery provides for the *technique* of the therapeusis of these conditions: I am therefore very sorry that I have no time to enter upon the question of their correct detection. Taking the first of the conditions, indicated on the table as being in any way debateable, namely, that of depressed fracture of the skull, I wish to urge in the most emphatic manner the necessity of operating upon every such case, whether or not accompanied by an external wound of the soft parts or by immediate symptoms of gravity.

5. *The British Medical Journal*, 1890, Vol. II, pp. 1286–1291.

It is of course—in the latter contingency, and especially where the patients are children, who frequently, as we have all seen, are extremely tolerant of extensive injuries of the kind—easy to understand how the present practice finds favour of letting, as it is called, "well" alone, but I would submit that the adoption of such a course is not "well" but ill, for it is just in these cases, and particularly where the injury has been received early in life, that the future will almost certainly bring with it, not only epilepsy, but also mental defect, persistent loss of memory, and, in fact, general deterioration. From this lamentable condition it is now, through the discoveries of Sir Joseph Lister, possible for us, without undue risk—a point upon which I propose to touch in my concluding remarks—to restore the patient to health. As an example, I may mention that in one instance . . . I was able successfully to elevate into its normal position the whole fronto-temporal region of a child, and it seems to me that such should be our invariable practice in these cases, especially when we consider that it affords the only opportunity of clearing the subdural space of blood and clots.

The next condition to be considered is that of laceration of the brain, and, in compound cases, recent or of long standing, I do not imagine that any exception would be taken to the active treatment proposed in the table, but I should like to go further, and say that these measures should equally be applied to all simple cases of laceration, as by such means the remote or, even sometimes, immediate consequence of epileptic convulsions may be prevented or entirely relieved. I here show, in relation to this subject, two photographs. The first is one of extensive laceration of the brain in an elderly man, not under my care, who died at the end of a week in coma, after epileptiform convulsions, and upon whom no operation was performed. The second—illustrating what I believe to be a rare complication of such cases—is that of a medical gentleman suffering from extensive laceration of the brain, involving the frontal, parietal, and temporal lobes. He was hemiplegic and partly unconscious for ten days, at the end of which time he suddenly, after exertion, developed most dangerous symptoms, became absolutely comatose, the respiration periodic, that is, Cheyne Stokes, etc. On trephining him freely (the opening is represented by the white lines) and washing out the whole left dural sac, free of blood and clots, he completely recovered, and is now practising his profession. I have no doubt that this was a very rare instance of secondary haemorrhage, occurring from a torn vessel. We must now, in order to preserve the systematic classification of the table, pass from the more surgical conditions just mentioned to deal with other forms hitherto regarded as outside its province, of which the principal is simple apoplexy.

The treatment of ordinary cerebral haemorrhage, that is, from the lenticulostriate artery which I am now about to propose, and to bring to your notice, may seem at first sight not only chimerical but dangerous; I must nevertheless earnestly commend it to your consideration, and it is that in cases of simple apoplexy ligature of the common carotid should be performed. My reasons for urging it are as follows, and I trust they may appear to you to be cogent.

1. Present measures, for example, position, application of cold, bleeding, counter-irritation to the legs, etc. can in no wise be considered as in any way able to check the haemorrhage from the injured vessel. Indeed, in appreciation of this view, most modern writers advise leaving the patient alone to take his chance.

2. The remote consequences, namely, permanent hemiplegia, even if death itself does not ensue, vary directly with the number of fibres torn through by the haemorrhage, it is therefore absolutely incumbent upon us to, under all circumstances, stop the bleeding if possible.

3. This can be effected either by arrest of the carotid stream, or by ligature of, or pressure upon, the bleeding point.

4. To effect the latter a dissection would have to be performed which would certainly produce more destruction than concomitant benefit.

5. On the other hand, compression, or better, ligature of the common carotid, not only arrests the flow of blood from the lenticulostriate artery, but in a few seconds also even the flow from the middle cerebral artery. These facts were discovered by Mr. Spencer and myself by experiments on the monkey, and published in the *British Medical Journal*, March 2nd, 1889, page 457.

6. Aseptic ligature of the common carotid is a very simple procedure, and primary union can be ensured in a few days; the temporary paresis which has occasionally been noticed and which has been accounted for by the experiments alluded to I myself have never seen and the occurrence of permanent hemiplegia, cerebral softening, etc., is only to be met with, so far as

I am aware, in cases of septic operations. The dread of, and the importance ascribed to, ligature of the carotid are therefore quite fictitious and ought not to be allowed to stand in the way of the suggested procedure, and I believe myself that if a patient had had a slight haemorrhage it would be justifiable to tie the carotid as a prophylactic measure.

In the treatment of the next class of diseases which I shall review, namely, tumours, so many debateable points immediately suggest themselves to us that I can only attempt to touch upon a few of them, and putting in the first place the one of greatest urgency, I desire to remark upon the general routine or empirical treatment by drugs, and the inordinate length of time usually accorded to their "fair" trial before operation is resorted to. It is to my mind a most regrettable fact that there is no common consensus of opinion as to the proper limits of such a "fair" trial, and thus the operation is often only called for when the patient is quite unfit to undergo it, which certainly would appear to be unjust not only to the surgeon, but, what is of a great deal more importance, to the patient also. The two cases I have seen were both instances of this practice; in one I removed the skull freely, and gave much relief by simply releasing the tension, and in the other refused to operate, the wisdom of which course was evidenced by the patient dying six days later. The routine treatment I allude to is that by iodide and bromide of potassium, and the point in question is not merely how long are we to continue giving these drugs when they are manifestly inoperative, but it is further complicated by a fact which we must recognise, that in many cases of sarcoma there is often a temporary and delusive improvement on the free use of the iodide, as if it in some way reduced the activity of growth or the pressure effects of the tumour. To bring the matter to a head, I would urge that unless very notable, not merely temporary, improvement is obvious after large doses have been given for six weeks, treatment by drugs should be abandoned, and exploratory operation resorted to. The ordinary reliance on internal remedies in the treatment of tumours is so constantly shown to be futile, that further insistance on this point would be unnecessary, were it not even now so constantly a bitter disappointment to the surgeon to find that the growth has been allowed to become far too extensive to admit of removal. I therefore hope that this distinguished gathering will finally express a practical opinion of this (to the patient) most momentous question.

Passing over as unnecessary to discuss the obvious advantage of removing a simple tumour with the certainty of permanent relief, I now proceed to the more important question of the proper treatment of malignant and diffusedly-growing tumours. Even where the necessity of early operation has not been recognised, these growths can be excised with temporary and remarkable benefit to the sufferer, but with, of course, an increasing risk of death from shock in proportion to the extent of the disease and the age of the patient. I have myself operated in such a case, which was admitted hemiplegic and comatose, as you see in this photograph, and from which I removed this large sarcoma, with the result that the patient walked out of the hospital but died in the following year of recurrence.

The peaceful and painless end of this man suggested that in hopeless cases of malignant growth a good deal could be done in the way of palliation. I have therefore to propose that the growth should be thoroughly explored, and if deemed irremovable that the wound should be closed. The effects are much better than might be anticipated. Not only are the intense headache and vomiting relieved, but a most interesting arrest of the optic neuritis occurs, a phenomenon which I have now observed repeatedly during the last five years, and which, in many cases, is a source of much amelioration to the patient from the consequent recovery of sight. Further, I have observed that the operation has conferred the additional benefit of notable prolongation of life, one case in particular, on whom I operated nearly two years ago for gliosarcoma of the cortex is now enjoying very good health, and it seemed as if the effect of the interference was to check for a year the progress of the growth, for the symptoms steadily improved. A striking instance of the kind, which I shall publish shortly with all my cases, is that of a gentleman who presented the very rare condition of epileptic attacks in which the body rotated towards the left violently round the central axis, and, further, in whom the most distressing attacks of dyspnoea occurred. Having made the diagnosis of a tumour of the middle cerebellar peduncle I removed first one half of the occipital bone, and later, at the patient's own request, the other half, with the effect of abolishing the respiratory attacks, which were very painful, the severe headache, and finally the turning convulsions for a time. His life has been prolonged with much comfort nearly two years, the symptoms of pressure on the pyramidal tracts, which disappeared after the first operation, recently becoming marked again. As is seen from my necrological table I have operated in six such cases with no death.

To sum up, the inference is that we should operate in all cases of tumour for the sake of the relief it affords, even should it be found during the operation that cure by removal is impossible.

CHAPTER 47

Ferdinand Sauerbruch
and the Explosive Expansion of Thoracic Surgery

"I wonder what will happen when I am called before the final tribunal to join the countless legions. Maybe I shall be accused of having paid attention to the major facets of life to the neglect of the minor ones. Will the many bottles I have drunk be counted against me, or the many women I have loved? And then again, I hope I shall be able to bring forward the many whose lives I have made happier by my ministrations. But I shall be very polite, and, for once, meek." [1]

Surgery of the chest, like that of the cranial cavity, attained a remarkable level of maturity in early classical times as is evidenced in the Hippocratic writings, but failed to advance significantly beyond that stage until the beginning of the present century. The barrier to progress was the problem of maintaining respiratory function when the thoracic cavity was opened. Pneumothorax had long been recognized as a serious danger, but the mechanism of its deleterious effects has been only recently fully explained. On empirical grounds, the urgency of closing wounds of the chest was a lesson learned, and "closed" aspiration or drainage of pleural effusions to prevent the entrance of air had been advocated. But the appalling mortality from empyema during the influenza epidemic of World War I was not reduced until the Joint Empyema Commission, under the leadership of Evarts A. Graham, established its relation to pneumothorax; the clarification of the mechanics of respiration by animal experiments under the aegis of the Commission is now of historical import.

The breach of the barrier to the safe elective opening of the chest cavity for operations upon its contents was achieved by the German surgeon, Ferdinand Sauerbruch (1875–1951). This stormy personality came from humble beginnings to become one of the most celebrated surgeons of a generation ago.

1. Ferdinand Sauerbruch: *Master Surgeon: Ferdinand Sauerbruch*, translated by Fernand G. Renier and Anne Cliff, New York, Thomas Y. Crowell Company, 1954, p. 257. For a somewhat fuller version of Sauerbruch's autobiography see: *Das war mein Leben*, Bad Wörishofen, Kindler und Schiermeyer Verlag, 1951.

From his informal, distinctly sensational, and not infrequently "racy" auto-biography entitled *Master Surgeon*, we read of his early struggles. He speaks of the bitter recollections of his childhood, of the death of his father when he was but two years old, and of the menial labor of his elders as shoemakers, a voca-tion in which he, too, had some training. The desire "to belong" was strong in him, and this no doubt colored his later life, as did also his capacity to evoke either hate or love in those with whom he associated, with nothing be-tween the two extremes.

Despite the burden of poverty his family and, later, his friends urged and assisted in providing his education. Having discovered a leaning toward the natural sciences, he studied medicine, and was graduated from the University of Leipzig (1901) at the age of twenty-six. After several not particularly happy experiences in practice, Sauerbruch obtained an appointment in the Department of Surgery at the University of Breslau, under the highly esteemed Professor von Mikulicz-Radecki.

Strange coincidences apparently marked the career of Sauerbruch. On the basis of an earlier experience he had become interested in the problem of pneumothorax, and when von Mikulicz suggested this subject as a research project, he was prepared to accept the idea with enthusiasm. The essential difficulty occasioned by pneumothorax is interference with the normal re-spiratory function which is dependent on the maintenance of a lower pressure within the pleural space than in the surrounding air. When the thorax is opened, air rushes into the cavity, neutralizing the negative pressure and col-lapsing the lung. Sauerbruch conceived the idea of building a low-pressure chamber within which the chest might be opened; this was immediately put to test and found to be successful, although not without certain initial vicissi-tudes. His next chamber was large enough to accommodate the operator as well as the animal, the head of which protruded through a snugly fitting aper-ture. Numerous experiments proved that operations so performed could be carried out with complete safety and without respiratory difficulty. A great idea had again resolved a fundamental difficulty.

The public demonstration of the method by the twenty-eight-year-old ex-perimenter under the sponsorship of his respected chief, which took place in Berlin at the German Surgical Congress of 1904, was a triumphant success. Returning to Breslau, a room-sized chamber was quickly built by a profes-sional staff for the performance of human operations. The patient's head and the anesthetist were outside the enclosure, the surgeon and assistant within. A large crowd of spectators, doctors, and students came to watch the first operation with von Mikulicz handling the scalpel; and as might have been ex-pected, there was mechanical failure of the valvular apparatus and the patient died. Sauerbruch was crushed by the catastrophe, but the older surgeon, steeled in the unpredictable reverses of his profession, comforted him and the work went on. Subsequent operations within the opened chest were done without mishap, and the efficacy of the low-pressure chamber was proved.

The death of Professor Mikulicz the following year made it necessary for Sauerbruch to move elsewhere because the new incumbent brought his own chief assistant (*Oberarzt*), which forestalled Sauerbruch's hopes of promotion to that position. There followed a dreary period at Greifswald and one of restlessness and dissatisfaction at Marburg. The latter, however, was marked by a promotion to professorial rank and an invitation to address an American surgical society on his method of operating within the chest. A tour of the United States took him as far west as Minnesota and a stimulating visit of the Mayo Clinic.

In the meantime, the report of his successful exploits in the field of thoracic surgery had so broadened Sauerbruch's recognition that he was called to Switzerland in 1910, to fill the Chair of Surgery at the University of Zürich. The Swiss mountain regions had long been the haven for patients with pulmonary diseases, and they abounded with large, and often luxurious, sanatoria, to which came the ailing from all continents. The juxtaposition of this enormous concentration of patients with pulmonary affections, and a clinic headed by the leading thoracic surgeon was providential, if not entirely fortuitous. Sauerbruch here came into his own. He was frequently called in consultation, and many patients were sent to him for operative care. A private clinic was built by him to provide facilities for his extensive private practice. Now famous and highly respected, expanding the range of his operative interventions, frequently invited to address professional gatherings, preparing his book, *Thoracic Surgery*, his domestic life relatively tranquil, he was busy and happy. He finally belonged.

Mention has been made of the sensational features of his autobiography. Adventure seemed to be drawn to him as to a magnet. His book abounds in cloak-and-dagger tales, secret missions, conspiracies, narrow escapes, romantic intrigues, and bacchantic libations. Famous names dot its pages and dramatic cures follow one another in rapid succession. Two penniless young Russian students were given help. One whose face was swollen from an infected tooth was unable to afford a dentist. Sauerbruch personally extracted it and, of course, without charge. The recipient of this care gave his name as Ulyanov, later to be known to the world as Lenin. The other student, deeply obligated to Sauerbruch, miraculously appeared years later when his benefactor had been condemned to be shot, and literally effected a last-minute rescue. Matching rudeness and disrespect with the aged Baron Rothschild, he won an influential and generous patient. A wartime secret mission from King Constantine of Greece, who was his patient in Zürich, to Kaiser Wilhelm in Berlin was so well executed that the latter monarch later sent him on a dangerous journey to carry messages to the King of Bulgaria and the Sultan of Turkey, which is recounted with titillating sidelights on personal episodes within a Turkish harem. And, accused of complicity in the plot of the generals to assassinate Hitler (1944), he narrowly escaped the fate of the others, some of whom were his close friends.

Sauerbruch was called to service during the First World War. Distressed with the incapacity suffered by young soldiers who had lost arms or hands, he set himself to designing articulated artificial limbs that could be worked by the muscles of the stump. The satisfaction he drew from the "Sauerbruch Hand" was second, apparently, only to his achievements in surgery of the chest.

After the war (1918), Sauerbruch was called to the University of Munich and ten years later to Berlin, Germany's most important assignment. During World War II he attained the post of Surgeon-General of the Armed Forces, despite his professed opposition to the Hitler regime. At the close of the conflict, with the world he knew brought to chaos and desolation, he resigned all positions to live in retirement until his death in 1951.

In his book Sauerbruch admits without reservation those temperamental qualities which made for him many enemies and which frequently brought him into conflict with authorities. He was quick to anger, impatient, and abusive toward his assistants. He was charged at various times with arrogance, insubordination, and mistreatment of those who were under him. He was a perfectionist and a martinet. His only justification for the display of these traits was that surgery is a jealous mistress, and, during the stress of an operation, just as in the heat of battle, there is no time for niceties.

The low-pressure chamber method of Sauerbruch initiated the modern era in thoracic surgery, but it was soon superseded by the positive-pressure anesthetic techniques now so universally employed. Although this latter method had been used in animal experiments in the nineteenth century by way of tracheotomy, it did not become clinically practical until Meltzer and Auer (1909) introduced peroral intubation. This, together with the development of modern anesthesia apparatus, has overcome the age-old problem of maintaining respiration during open thoracotomy.

Thoracic surgery was the latest of the subspecialties to conquer the barriers to rapid expansion, but when this was achieved by Sauerbruch it became the most vigorously growing field of the twentieth century.[2] This burgeoning peroid coincided with the era of American leadership in medicine and much of the newer work was done by American surgeons, many of whom are still in active practice. Evarts Graham, whose role in the pneumothorax story has already been mentioned, retained an active interest in the surgery of the chest.

2. Rudolph Nissen and Roger Wilson: *Pages in the History of Chest Surgery*, Springfield, Charles C Thomas, 1960.

His well-known successful removal of an entire lung was the first operation of this kind to have been performed for cancer and also the first one-stage procedure. (The two earlier total pneumonectomies had been done in two stages and for nonmalignant disease.) Graham's patient was operated upon in 1933, led a normally active life as a physician, and is still alive at the age of seventy-seven.

John B. Murphy, famed Chicago surgeon, played an important role in furthering the treatment of pulmonary tuberculosis by artificial pneumothorax which was first put into use by Carlo Forlanini in Italy. Excisional surgery is now the favored method in this disease; its safety and success are enhanced by supplementary chemotherapy. The delineation of the segmental anatomy of the lung by Kramer and Glass, and by Herrnheiser, not only represents a significant addition to fundamental anatomical knowledge, but also furnishes the basis for the presently employed segmental resections which have been ably developed, primarily by Churchill, Overholt, and Chamberlain. Further reduction in the incidence of tuberculosis which has already been so strikingly effected, largely as the result of public health measures, would give reason to hope that this indication for lung surgery may eventually cease to exist.

Surgery of the heart and great vessels constitutes the most recent and most dramatic aspect of operations within the chest. Here, as in the other fields mentioned, the exciting achievements of the present were anticipated in the nineteenth century. Thus, Daniel Hale Williams, a Chicago surgeon, performed the first successful operation for stab wound of the heart in 1893.[3] He found a rent in the pericardium and "a small puncture wound of the heart, about one-tenth of an inch in length and about one-half inch to the right of the right coronary artery, between two of its lateral branches. . . ." Bleeding from both the heart and the pericardium had ceased. The pericardial sac was sutured and the patient made a complete recovery. Ludwig Rehn of Frankfurt am Main is generally credited with having first successfully repaired a wound of the heart itself in 1896, and several other such repairs were reported in the same year. The feasibility of applying surgical manipulation to this organ, which so long had been considered with almost suspicious awe, became a demonstrated fact. Pericardial aspiration and surgical drainage had also been done in the nineteenth century, and, in 1895, Weill suggested operative intervention for adhesive pericarditis. Similarly, Brentano and Samways, independently in 1898, suggested commissurotomy for mitral stenosis, a procedure that was actually carried out by Souttar in London, in 1925. Also, Niehans (1899) proposed transthoracic resuscitation for cardiac arrest.

The anticipations of the nineteenth century gave way to actual performance

3. Lew A. Hochberg: *Thoracic Surgery before the 20th Century*, New York, Vantage Press, 1960, and Helen Buckler: *Doctor Dan, Pioneer in American Surgery*, Boston, Little, Brown & Company, 1954.

in the twentieth. Trendelenburg's operation (1908) for pulmonary embolism has been followed by highly successful interventions for patent ductus arteriosus, coarctation of the aorta, and the excision of intrathoracic aneurysms. The first ductus operation was done by Robert E. Gross of Boston in 1938, the initial resection of the stenotic segment in coarctation of the aorta by Crafoord in Sweden (1945); and no discussion of aortic resections for aneurysm can justly omit the name of the energetic and resourceful Michael De Bakey and his group.

Congenital malformations of the heart stimulated the efforts to correct disturbances of this vital organ which for millenia was considered far beyond the surgeon's realm. The diagnostic and medical studies of Helen Taussig, teamed with the surgical genius of Alfred Blalock, both of The Johns Hopkins Hospital, led to the first attempts to relieve the cyanosis of pulmonary stenosis and atresia by creating an artificial ductus arteriosus, and later by anastomosis between the pulmonary artery and the aorta. The latter operation was improved by Potts, and subsequently the complex derangement of the transposition of the great vessels was corrected by Baffes of the Potts' group at Chicago's Children's Memorial Hospital.

The story of surgical therapy for acquired cardiac defects begins with the mitral commissurotomy of Souttar already mentioned. It was taken up again by Sir Russel Brock who was led from his experiences with pulmonary valvulotomy in congenital malformations to mitral commissurotomy in acquired stenosis. The latter procedure was carried to further development by Harken of Boston and Bailey and Glover of Philadelphia.

The range of operative interventions upon the heart has been vastly widened by the development of open heart surgery. Cardiopulmonary bypass by means of extracorporeal circulation utilizing artificial oxygenating devices and pumps, begun by Gibbon and improved by many others including the Minnesota group in the Wangensteen Clinic, is making it possible to correct more and more crippling abnormalities with increasing safety. The employment of hypothermia and of controlled cardiac arrest constitute but a few of the dramatic and effective adjuvants to surgery of the heart.

The greatest challenge of all, because of its vast numerical preponderance, is posed by coronary artery occlusions. Claude Beck has devoted most of his surgical life in experimental and human operative methods to find practical ways of revascularizing the ischemic heart, with some measure of success. This tireless worker also merits recognition for his energetic furtherance of transthoracic resuscitation of cardiac arrest, whether in asystole or ventricular fibrillation. The everyday salvage of persons already dead, according to conventional definition, by these methods is a recurring modern miracle wrought by cardiac surgery. The replacement of the open chest manual systole and defibrillation will apparently give way to external resuscitation if the recent methods worked out so carefully, over so long a period of time by W. B. Kouwenhoven and his Johns Hopkins group, live up to their expectations.

Cardiac surgery is still so young, despite its many very real and significant attainments, that further advances can be anticipated with the fullest justification. However, the pattern of events which offers the greatest hope for the future lies in the field of prevention. Great strides have already been taken in the reduction of rheumatic heart disease with its crippling valvular sequelae by antibiotic prophylaxis. Dissemination of knowledge and earlier and more thorough application of effective means should reduce the incidence further. Similar concerted programs toward prevention of atherosclerotic vascular damage by dietetic and metabolic regimens offers hope for the reduction of the appalling mortality from coronary—and also from cerebral, visceral, and peripheral—arterial disease. In these efforts, the surgeons are working side by side with their colleagues in all of the medical sciences and specialties, striving for a success that will make surgery no longer necessary.

ॐ   ॐ   ॐ   THE PREVENTION OF THE DELETERIOUS EFFECTS OF PNEU-
ॐ   ॐ   ॐ   MOTHORAX IN INTRATHORACIC OPERATIONS[4]

In October of last year, Prof. [Geheimrat] von Mikulicz suggested that I undertake an experimental attempt to find some possible means of avoiding the injurious effects of pneumothorax during intrathoracic operations. Here, he had in mind, primarily, transpleural resection of the esophagus which hitherto, in man as well as in experimental animals, had yielded only the saddest results. One of the chief causes of failure was the pneumothorax incidental to the operation, and the functional exclusion of the lung which was collapsed by atmospheric pressure. Since in dogs resection of the lower segment of the esophagus almost always leads to the opening of the opposite pleural cavity, a large percentage of the animals so operated upon died while still on the operating table. In intrathoracic operations such as vagotomy the physiologists have, for a long time, maintained activity in the collapsed lung by artificial rhythmical pumping of air (through an airtight tracheal cannula). Prof. v. Mikulicz attempted an esophageal resection in the dog by this method last year; the results, however, were not satisfactory, and he was forced to regard this technique as of little promise. It occurred to me that the deleterious effect of

4. Ferdinand Sauerbruch: "Über die Auschaltung der schädlichen Wirkung des Pneumothorax bei intrathorakalen Operationen." *Zentralblatt für Chirurgie*, 31, 1904, pp. 146–149. Translated from the German by the authors.

the atmospheric pressure might be avoided in another manner, namely, by providing an appropriate negative pressure in that part of the operating room with which the open pleural cavity would communicate.

Whether this would prove practical and lead to the desired result was, at the outset, rather questionable. It was my task to study the physiological prerequisites and to determine how this problem could best be solved technically.

By way of physiological preparation, I first conducted experiments on rabbits and dogs, studying blood pressure levels and the nature and depth of respiration with and without artificial respiration (*i.e.*, pumping of air into the lungs by the method of the physiologists).

The publications to date on this question do not give sufficient attention, so far as I can see, to all factors which are harmful in pneumothorax with and without artificial respiration.

I emphasize the following:

1.) The deviations in the form of respiration (variations of the lung volume between complete collapse and maximal distension).

2.) Interstitial emphysema of the lung as a consequence of the artificial insufflation of air into the lungs.

3.) The enormous loss of heat in pneumothorax, especially with artificial respiration (as much as 3° C in a half-hour).

4.) Its influence on the circulation.

5.) The persistence of a pneumothorax after cessation of artificial respiration.

6.) The need for tracheotomy in artificial respiration, and the possible pneumonia resulting from it.

7.) The difficulties in anesthesia, which in the animal, however, can be avoided by use of Kionka's apparatus.

8.) The increased hazard of pleural infection because of the extensive exchange of air in the pleural cavity.

The main problems in thoracic operations by the methods heretofore used are, without doubt, the prevention or overcoming of pneumothorax and the harmful effects of artificial respiration. In entrusting me with this project, Prof. v. Mikulicz gave special emphasis to these factors and assigned me the specific task of finding a method which would obviate these hazards.

Pneumothorax occurs because the pleural surface of the lung which is normally under negative pressure, is suddenly

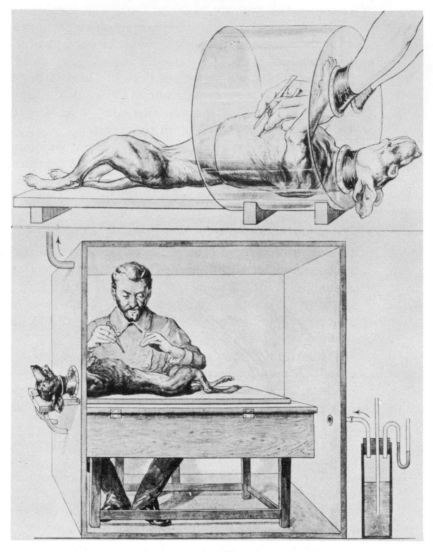

Fig. 114. *(upper)* Original low-pressure cylinder in use; *(lower)* animal experiment in the larger chamber. From: Ferdinand Sauerbruch: "Zur Pathologie des offenen Pneumothorax and die Grundlagen meines Verfahrens zu seiner Ausschaltung, *Mitteilungen aus den Grenzgebieten der Medizin und Chirurgie*, Vol. 14, Jena, 1904.

exposed to atmospheric pressure. In order to exclude atmospheric pressure from the open thorax, I first constructed a very primitive apparatus: a glass cylinder was closed on both sides by means of sheets of gutta-percha. On one side, three holes were made in the gutta-percha (two smaller ones and one larger), in the other side, only one larger opening. The experimental animal was pulled through the two larger openings, so that the head protruded from one and the hind legs and lower abdomen from the other, while the thorax and upper abdomen remained in the cylinder. After inserting the necessary instruments, I introduced both hands through the smaller holes. After all openings were hermetically closed by means of rubber bands and adhesive material, an assistant sucked air from the cylinder through a tube which was also airtight, so that there was a negative pressure within the cylinder equal to a column of mercury of approximately 10 mm. Both sides of the chest were then opened; the lungs did not collapse and the animal's respiration continued without disturbance. After about three minutes one of the closing membranes [of the cylinder] tore and the animal died after violent respiratory efforts and collapse of the lungs.

The success of this experiment encouraged me to have an apparatus constructed on the same principle by a mechanic, in which the closure was effected with rubber sheets.

Within this chamber I made numerous experiments on the feasibility of opening the thorax. They showed that it is possible to open both sides of the chest widely, and that the sternum and ribs can be resected down to small stumps attached to the vertebral column with no essential interference with the respiration of the animal.

From the construction of this apparatus which permitted only physiological experiments but not the performance of actual operations, it was only one step to the building of a room which would permit operations according to the rules of surgery without hindrance. I had such a chamber constructed 1.5 m. in length, 1.0 m. in width, and 1.3 m. high. The chamber was built of sound boards 2 cm. thick, lined with tin-plate which was soldered at the junctions, and closed above with a heavy glass plate. The door approximately 1.15 m. high and 0.60 m. wide can be closed hermetically by means of rubber flaps. In the wall opposite to the door, at sitting level, there is a circular window, 55 cm. in diameter, closed by a rubber cap with an opening in its center. Through this opening the head of the animal passes; a rubber cuff closes the opening hermetically about its (previously shaved) neck.

The room provides a comfortable space for an operating table on which the body of the animal is firmly tied, and seats on either side for the operator and his assistant. Two coin-sized

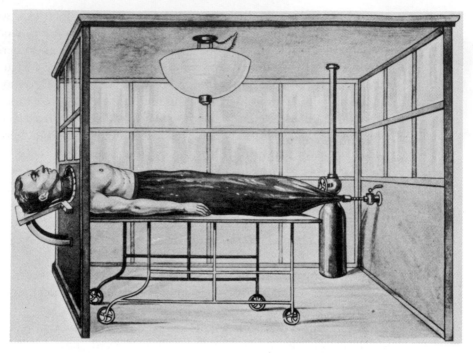

Fig. 115. Patient in position in the low-pressure operating room. From: Sauerbruch: "Zur Pathologie des offenen Pneumothorax," *loc. cit.*

openings lead into the chamber, one of which is connected to a suction pump, the other to a valve. When suction is applied this valve permits as much outside air to flow into the chamber as is needed to maintain a constant controllable negative pressure.

During the experiments which I was able to conduct in our Pharmacological Institute through the courtesy of Prof. Filehne, the air in the chamber was totally renewed every four minutes. I found that for middle-sized dogs the optimum of negative pressure is 12–16 mm. hg. The stay in the chamber is perfectly well tolerated by the two persons working therein—we have spent more than two hours without interruption there. Prof. v. Mikulicz has also performed, with my assistance, an operation which lasted more than an hour without experiencing the least discomfort.

The temperature always rises, to be sure, several degrees (to 22–23° C); once a temperature of 29° C was reached. The humidity also naturally increases. These disadvantages will be avoided by the construction of larger apparatus for human operations.

The operations so far performed on animals in my chamber (resections of esophagus and lungs, opening of the pericardium and of the mediastinum) give reason to hope, I believe, that it will also be possible to perform these operations in man and to avoid the above-mentioned deleterious factors in intrathoracic operations.

Just to mention one example of how far one can go in surgical operations: in a chloroformed dog I performed a bilateral large pulmonary resection, opened both pleural cavities, did an esophagotomy, and opened the pericardium and mediastinum. After closing the wounds, the animal awoke from the anesthesia and ran about for a few minutes. That the animal died on the second postoperative day is understandable since the operation was done without antiseptic precaution or rib suture. At autopsy, the lungs collapsed when the pleurae were opened as under normal conditions, and showed no atelectases.

One can extrude up to two-thirds of both lungs of an animal; they do not collapse but retain their normal circumference, and respiration remains adequate.

BIBLIOGRAPHY

GENERAL REFERENCES

T. Clifford Allbutt: *The Historical Relations of Medicine and Surgery to the End of the 16th Century*. London, Macmillan & Company, 1905.

John Shaw Billings: *The History and Literature of Surgery*. Philadelphia, Lea Bros. & Company, 1895. (From: F. S. Dennis: *System of Surgery*, Vol. 1.)

Biographishes Lexikon der hervorragenden Ärzte aller Zeiten und Völker, herausgegeben von A. Hirsch, 2 Aufl., 6 vols. 1929–1935.

W. von Brunn: *Kurze Geschichte der Chirurgie*. Berlin, Julius Springer, 1928.

Albert H. Buck: *The Growth of Medicine from the Earliest Times to about 1800*. New Haven, Yale University Press, 1917.

Adolphe Pierre Burggraeve: *Histoire de l'anatomie; physiologique, pathologique et philosophique*. Paris, C. Chanteaud, 1880.

Arturo Castiglioni: *A History of Medicine*. New York, Alfred A. Knopf, 1947.

Charles Daremberg: *La Médecine: histoire et doctrines*. Paris, Librairie Académique, 1865.

Charles Daremberg: *Histoire des sciences médicales, contenant l'anatomie, la physiologie, la médicine, la chirurgie, et les doctrines de pathologie générales*. Paris, Baillière, 1870.

Dictionaire des Sciences Médicales. Biographie médicale, 7 Vols. Paris, C. L. F. Panckouke, 1820–1825.

Paul Diepgen: *Geschichte der Medizin*, Die historische Entwicklung der Heilkunde und des ärztlichen Lebens, 2 Vols. Berlin, Walter de Gruyter & Company, 1949, 1951, 1959.

[Sir John Eric Erichsen]: *Observations on Aneurism Selected from the Works of the Principal Writers on that Disease from the Earliest Periods to the Close of the Last Century*, translated and edited by John E. Erichsen. London, Sydenham Society, 1844.

Fielding H. Garrison: *An Introduction to the History of Medicine*, 4th edition. Philadelphia, W. B. Saunders Company, 1929.

Harvey Graham: *The Story of Surgery*. New York, Doubleday, Doran & Company, 1939.

Samuel D. Gross: *Lives of Eminent American Physicians and Surgeons of the Nineteenth Century*. Philadelphia, Lindsay and Blakiston, 1861.

E. Gurlt: *Geschichte der Chirurgie und ihrer Ausübung*, 3 Vols. Berlin, August Hirschwald, 1898.

Guy's Hospital, 1725–1948, edited by Hujohn A. Ripman for Guy's Hospital Gazette Committee. London, Guy's Hospital Gazette Committee, 1951.

Heinrich Haeser: *Lehrbuch der Geschichte der Medizin und der Volkskrankheiten*. Jena, F. Manke, 1845.

Heinrich Haeser: *Übersicht der Geschichte der Chirurgie*. Stuttgart, Verlag von Ferdinand Enke, 1879.

Samuel Clark Harvey: *The History of Hemostasis*. New York, Paul Hoeber, Inc., 1929.

Justus F. K. Hecker: *Geschichte der Heilkunde*, 2 Vols. Berlin, Euslin, 1822–29.

A. Hurwitz and G. A. Degenshein: *Milestones in Modern Surgery*. New York, Paul B. Hoeber, Inc., 1958.

548

A. Jentzer: *La chirurgie ancienne et moderne*, deux conférences faites à l'Aula de l'Université de Genève en janvier 1924. Genève, Imprimerie Atar, 1925.

Howard A. Kelly and Walter Burrage: *American Medical Biographies*. Baltimore, The Norman Remington Company, 1920.

Richard A. Leonardo: *History of Surgery*. New York, Froben Press, 1943.

Cecelia Mettler: *History of Medicine*, edited by Fred A. Mettler. Philadelphia, Blakiston Company, 1947.

Th. Meyer-Steineg und Karl Sudhoff: *Geschichte der Medizin*, 2nd edition. Jena, Verlag von Gustav Fischer, 1922.

Max Neuburger: *History of Medicine*, translated by Ernest Playfair, Vol. I. London, Oxford University Press, 1910.

J. L. Pagel: *Einführung in die Geschichte der Medizin*, Zweite Auflage, Durchgesehen, teilweise umgearbeitet und auf den heutigen Stand gebracht von Karl Sudhoff. Berlin, S. Karger, 1915.

Sir D'Arcy Power: *British Masters of Medicine*. London, The Medical Press and Circular, 1936,

Sir D'Arcy Power: *A Short History of Surgery*. London, John Bole, Sons and Danielsson, Ltd., 1938.

Puschmann's Handbuch der Geschichte der Medizin, Begr. von Puschmann, herausgegeben von. M Neuburger und J. Pagel, 3 Bände. 1902–1905.

le Chevalier Richerand: *Histoire des progrès recens de la chirurgie*. Paris, Béchet Jeune, 1825.

David Riesman: *The Story of Medicine in the Middle Ages*. New York, Paul B. Hoeber, Inc., 1936.

K. E. Rothschuh: *Geschichte der Physiologie*. Berlin, Göttingen, Heidelberg, Springer-Verlag, 1953.

Henry E. Sigerist: *The Great Doctors, A Biographical History of Medicine*, translated by Eden and Cedar Paul. Garden City, N. Y., Doubleday Anchor Books, Doubleday & Company, 1958.

Henry E. Sigerist: *Grosse Ärzte*, 4th edition. München, Lehmanns Verlag, 1959.

Charles Singer: *A Short History of Medicine*. Oxford, at the Clarendon Press, 1944.

John Flint South: *Memorials of the Craft of Surgery in England*. London, Cassell and Company, 1886.

Kurt Polykarp Joachim Sprengel: K. *Sprengel's Geschichte der Chirurgie*, Erster-zweyter Teil.... Halle, K. A. Kümmel, 1805–1819.

Leo M. Zimmerman: "Cosmas and Damian, Patron Saints of Surgery," *The American Journal of Surgery*, Vol. 33, pp. 160–168, 1936.

Leo M. Zimmerman: "The Evolution of Blood Transfusion," *The American Journal of Surgery* Vol. 55, pp. 613–620, 1942.

Leo M. Zimmerman and Katherine M. Howell: "History of Blood Transfusion," *Annals of Medical History*, Vol. 4, pp. 415–433, 1932.

I. THE BEGINNINGS

Sir T. Clifford Allbutt: *Greek Medicine in Rome*. London, Macmillan & Company, Ltd., 1921.

Appolonius of Kitium: *Illustrierter Kommentar zu der hippokratischen Schrift* ΠΕΡΙ ΑΡΘΡΩΝ [*Peri Arthron*], herausgegeben von Herman Schöne. Leipzig, B. G. Teubner, 1896.

René Brian: *Chirurgie de Paul D'Egine*, Paris. Victor Masson, 1840.

Arthur J. Brock: *Greek Medicine*, being extracts of medical writers from Hippocrates to Galen. London and Toronto, J. M. Dent & Sons, Ltd., 1929.

Celsus: *De Medicina*, with an English translation by W. G. Spencer, 3 Vols. Cambridge, Harvard University Press, 1938 (The Loeb Classical Library).

CHANDRA CHAKRABERTY: *An Interpretation of Ancient Hindu Medicine*. Calcutta, Ramchandra Chakraberty, 1923.

A. CHAMFRAULT: *Traité de Médecine Chinoise*. Angoulême, Éditions Coquemard, 1954.

GALEN: *Galeni pergameni omnia quae extant, in Latinum Sermonem Conversa*. Basel, Froben, 1562.

GALEN: *On the Natural Faculties*, with an English translation by Arthur John Brock. London, William Heinemann, 1916.

GALENOS: *Über die Krankhaften Geschwülste* (zwischen 169 und 180 n. Chr.), übersetzt und eingeleitet von Dr. Paul Richter (*Klassiker der Medizin*, herausgegeben von Karl Sudhoff). Leipzig, J. A. Barth, 1913.

WILLIAM ARTHUR HEIDEL: *Hippocratic Medicine*. New York, Columbia University Press, 1941.

Hippocrates, with an English translation by W. H. S. Jones. London, William Heinemann, Vols. I and II, 1923; Vol. IV, 1953 (The Loeb Classical Library).

Hippocrates, with an English translation by E. T. Withington. London, William Heinemann, Vol. III, 1948 (The Loeb Classical Library).

HIPPOCRATES: *The Genuine Works of Hippocrates*, translated from the Greek with a preliminary discourse and annotations by Francis Adams. New York, William Wood and Company, 1929.

A. F. RUDOLPH HOERNLE: *Studies in the Medicine of Ancient India*, Part 1, Osteology or the Bones of the Human Body. Oxford, at the Clarendon Press, 1907.

PIERRE HUARD ET MING WONG: *La Médecine Chinoise au cours des Siècles*. Paris, Les Éditions Roger Dacosta, 1959.

JULIUS JOLLY: *Indian Medicine*, translated from the German and supplemented with notes by C. G. Kashikar, with a foreword by Dr. J. Filliozat. Poona, Kashikar, 1951.

W. H. S. JONES: *Philosophy and Medicine in Ancient Greece*. Baltimore, The Johns Hopkins Press, 1946.

FRED B. LUND: "Hippocratic Surgery," *Annals of Surgery*, Vol. 102, No. 4, 1935.

K. F. H. MARX: *Herophilus, Ein Beitrag zur Geschichte der Medicin*. Karlsruhe, Baden, 1838.

PAUL OF AEGINA: *The Seven Books of Paulus Aeginata*, translated from the Greek by Francis Adams. London, printed for the Sydenham Society, 1844.

GEORGE SARTON: *Galen of Pergamon*. Lawrence, Kansas, University of Kansas Press, 1954.

HENRY E. SIGERIST: *A History of Medicine*, Vol. I, Primitive and Archaic Medicine. New York, Oxford University Press, 1951.

The Edwin Smith Surgical Papyrus, published in facsimile and hieroglyphic transliteration with translation and commentary by James Henry Breasted, 2 Vols. Chicago, University of Chicago Press, 1930.

SUSHRUTA: *An English translation of the Sushruta Samhita*, based on the original Sanskrit text, edited and published by Kaviraj Kunja Lal Bhishagratna ... 3 Vols. Calcutta, Wilkins Press, 1907.

ILZA VEITH: *Huang Ti Nei Ching Su Wen, The Yellow Emperor's Classic of Internal Medicine*. Baltimore, Williams & Wilkins Company, 1949.

ILZA VEITH: "Medicine in Japan," *Ciba Symposia*, Vol. II, No. 4, 1950.

ILZA VEITH: "The Surgical Achievements of Ancient India: Sushruta," *Surgery*, Vol. 49, No. 4, pp. 564–568, 1961.

ILZA VEITH: *Medizin in Tibet*. Leverkusen, Bayer: Pharm. Wiss., Abteilung, 1961.

HENRY R. ZIMMER: *Hindu Medicine*, edited with a foreword and preface by Ludwig Edelstein. Baltimore, The Johns Hopkins Press, 1948.

J. P. KLEIWEG DE ZWAAN: *Völkerkundliches und Geschichtliches über die Heilkunde der Chinesen und Japaner*. Haarlem, De Erven Loosjes, 1917.

II. ALBUCASIS AND THE SURGERY OF THE ARABIC PERIOD

ALBUCASIS: *De Chirurgia*, french translation by L. Leclerc, *Gazette Médicale de l'Algérie*, Nos. 3–6, 1858–60.

ALBUCASIS: *La Chirurgie D'Albucasis*, translated by Lucien Leclerc. Paris, J.-B. Baillière, 1861.

ALBUCASIS: *Methodus medendi certa, clara et brevis . . . cum instrumentis . . . depictis. Autore ALBUCASE praestanti, ob excellentia artis opera medico.* Aesile ae per Henri cum Petrum [n.d.].

EDWARD G. BROWNE: *Arabian Medicine*, being the Fitzpatrick Lectures delivered at the College of Physicians in November 1919 and November 1920. Cambridge, at the University Press, 1921.

DONALD CAMPBELL: *Arabian Medicine and Its Influence on the Middle Ages*, 2 Vols. London, Kegan Paul, Trench, Trübner & Company, Ltd., 1926.

III. EARLY STIRRINGS

ADOLPHE PIERRE BURGGRAEVE: *Études sur André Vésale, précedées d'une notice historique sur sa vie et ses écrits;* ouvrage publié sous le patronage des médecins belges. Gand, C. Anoot-Braeckman, 1841.

ARTURO CASTIGLIONI: "The School of Salerno," *Bulletin of the History of Medicine*, Vol. VI, pp. 883–898, 1938.

ARTURO CASTIGLIONI: "Fallopius and Vesalius," in HARVEY CUSHING: *A Bio-Bibliography of Vesalius.* New York, Schuman's, 1943.

GEORGE W. CORNER: *Anatomical Texts of the Earlier Middle Ages . . .* with translation of four texts. Washington, Carnegie Institution of Washington, 1927.

GEORGE W. CORNER: "The Rise of Medicine at Salerno in the Twelfth Century," *Annals of Medical History*, Vol. 3 (N.S.), No. 1, 1931.

GEORGE W. CORNER: "On early Salernitan Surgery and especially the 'Bamberg Surgery,'" *Bulletin of the History of Medicine*, Vol. V, pp. 1–32, 1937.

L'école de Salerne, traduction en vers français par M. Ch. Meaux Saint-Marc, précédée d'une introduction par M. le Docteur Ch. Daremberg. Paris, J. B. Baillière & Fils, 1861.

PIERO GIACOSA: *Magistri Salernitani nundam editi*, 2 Vols. Torino, Fratelli Bocca, 1901.

JOHN HARRINGTON: *The School of Salernum, Regimen Sanitatis Salernitanum*, the English version by Sir John Harrington, . . . New York, Paul B. Hoeber, Inc., 1920.

PAUL OSKAR KRISTELLER: "The School of Salerno; its development and its contribution to the History of Learning," *Bulletin of the History of Medicine*, Vol. XVII, pp. 138–194, 1945.

SAMUEL W. LAMBERT, WILLY WIEGAND, AND WILLIAM M. IVINS, JR.: *Three Vesalian Essays to accompany the Icones Anatomicae of 1934.* New York, The Macmillan Company, 1952.

LANFRANC: *Chirurgia Magna.* London, T. Marshe, 1565.

Lanfrank's "Science of Cirurgie," edited from the Bodleian Ashmole MS. 1396 and the British Museum Additional MS. 12,056 by Robert V. Fleischhacker, Dr. Phil., Part I, Text. London, published for the Early English Text Society by Kegan Paul, Trench, Trübner & Company, Ltd., 1894.

LOREN CAREY MACKINNEY: *Early Medieval Medicine with Special Reference to France and Chartres*, The Hideyo Noguchi Lectures. Baltimore, The Johns Hopkins Press, 1937.

HENRI DE MONDEVILLE: *Die Chirurgie des Heinrich de Mondeville*, herausgegeben von Julius Pagel. Berlin, A. Hirschwald, 1892.

HENRI DE MONDEVILLE: *Chirurgie de Maître Henri de Mondeville*, composée de 1306 à 1320, traduction Française avec des notes, une introduction et une biographie par E. Nicaise. Paris, Ancienne Librairie Germer Baillière, 1893.

"Anathomia of Mondino da Luzzi," in *Fasciculo di Medicina*, Venice, 1493. With an introduction, etc. by Charles Singer. Florence, R. Lier & Company, 1925.

WILLIAM OF SALICET: *Chirurgie de Guillaume de Salicet, achevée en 1275*, traduction et commentaire par Paul Pifteau. Toulouse, Imprimerie Saint-Cyprien, 1898.

C. B. DE C. M. SAUNDERS AND CHARLES D. O'MALLEY: *The Illustrations from the Works of Andreas Vesalius of Brussels*. Cleveland and New York, The World Publishing Company, 1950.

CHARLES AND DOROTHY SINGER: "The Origin of the Medical School of Salerno, the First University, an Attempted Reconstruction," in *Essays on the History of Medicine Presented to Karl Sudhoff*, pp. 121–138. Zürich, 1924.

KARL SUDHOFF: "Beiträge zur Geschichte der Medizin im Mittelalter," Part 2, *Studien zur Geschichte der Medizin*, Nos. 11–12, Leipzig, 1918.

KARL SUDHOFF: "Salerno eine mittelalterliche Heil-und Lehrstelle am Tyrrhenischen Meere," *Archiv für Geschichte der Medizin*, Vol. XXI, pp. 43–62, 1929.

THEODORIC: *The Surgery of Theodoric*, translated from the Latin by Eldridge Campbell and James Colton. New York, Appleton-Century-Crofts, Vol. 1, 1955; Vol. 2, 1960.

ANDREAS VESALIUS: *De humani corporis fabrica*. Basileae, *ex off.* Ioannis Oporini, 1543.

ERNEST WICKERSHEIMER: *Anatomies de Mondino dei Luzzi et de Guido de Vigevano*. Paris, E. Droz, 1926.

JAN YPERMAN: *La chirurgie de maître Jean Yperman* . . . Mise au jour et annotée par J. M. F. Carolus. Gand, F. & E. Gyselynck, 1854.

JEAN YPERMAN: *La Chirurgie de Maître Jehan Yperman* (1260?–1310?), Livres I et II, traduits du view flamand d'après les manuscrits de Cambridge et de Bruxelles et précédés d'une introduction par le Dr. A. de Mets. Paris, Éditions Hippocrate, 1936.

IV. SURGERY BECOMES RESPECTABLE

JOHN OF ARDERNE: *Treatises of Fistula in Ano, Hemorrhoids and Clysters*, edited by D'Arcy Power. London, Kegan Paul, Trench, Trübner & Company, Ltd., 1910.

JOHN OF ARDERNE: *De Arte Phisicali et Cirurgia* of Master John Arderne. . . . translated by *Sir* D'Arcy Power. New York, William Wood and Company, 1922.

ANTONIO BENIVIENI: *De abditis nonnullis ac mirandis morborum et sanationum causis*, translated by Charles Singer with a biographical appreciation by Esmond R. Long. Springfield, Illinois, Charles C Thomas, 1954.

GUY DE CHAULIAC: *La pratique en chirurgie du maistre Guidon de Chauliac*. Lyon, Barthelmy Buyer, 1478.

GUY DE CHAULIAC: *La Grande Chirurgie de M. Guy de Chauliac* . . . 1363, restituée par M. Lavrens Joubert. Tournon, Clavde Michel, 1598.

GUY DE CHAULIAC: *La Grande Chirurgie*, edited by E. Nicaise. Paris, F. Alcan, 1890.

GUY DE CHAULIAC: *On Wounds and Fractures*, translated by W. A. Brennan. Chicago, published by translator, 1923.

JANET DOE: *A Biobibliography of the Works of Ambroise Paré*. Chicago, University of Chicago Press, 1937.

PIERRE FRANCO: *Chirurgie de Pierre Franco de Turriers en Provence composée en 1561*, nouvelle édition avec une introduction historique, une biographie et l'histoire du Collège de Chirurgie, par E. Nicaise. Paris, Ancienne Librairie Germer Baillière & Cie., 1895.

JOSEPH FRANÇOIS MALGAIGNE: *Histoire de la chirurgie* en occident dépuis le VIe jusquau XVIe siècle et histoire de la vie et des travaux d'Ambroise Paré. Paris, J.-B. Baillière et fils, 1870.

MICHAEL L. MASON: "Basel–1527 [Paracelsian Surgery]," *Quarterly Bulletin*, Northwestern University Medical School, Vol. 30, No. 3, 1956.

Francis R. Packard: *Life and Times of Ambroise Paré*, with a new translation of his *Apology* and an *Account of his Journeys in Divers Places.* New York, Paul B. Hoeber, Inc., 1921.

Walter Pagel: *Paracelsus, An Introduction to Philosophical Medicine in the Era of the Renaissance.* Basel and New York, S. Karger, 1958.

Paracelsus (Theophrast von Hohenheim): *Sämtliche Werke*, herausgegeben von Karl Sudhoff, 14 Vols. München, Berlin, R. Oldenburg, 1922–1933.

Ambroise Paré: *The Workes of that Famous Chirurgion Ambrose Parey*, translated out of Latine and compared with the French by Tho. Johnson. London, printed by Richard Cotes and Willi Du-jard, 1649.

Ambroise Paré: *Oeuvres complètes D'Ambroise Paré*, précédées d'une introduction sur l'origine et les progrès de la chirurgie en occident du seizième siècle, et sur la vie et les ouvrages d'Ambroise Paré, par J.-F. Malgaigne, 3 Vols. Paris, J.-B. Baillière, 1840.

Ambroise Paré: *The Apologie and Treatise of Ambroise Paré*, edited and with an introduction by Geoffrey Keynes. Chicago, University of Chicago Press, 1952.

V. GREAT IDEAS

Hieronymus Brunschwig: *Dies ist das Buch der Cirurgia Hantwirkung der Wundartzny von Hieronimo Brunschwig.* Strassburg [J. Grüninger], 1497.

Hieronymous Brunschwig: *The Book of Cirurgia* with a study . . . by Henry E. Sigerist. Milano, Lier & Company, 1923.

Hieronymus Fabricius ab Aquapendente: *Oeuvres chirurgicales de Hierosme Fabrice de Aquapendente.* Lyon, Jean Antoine Huguetan, 1670.

Hieronymus Fabricius of Aquapendente: *De venarum ostiolis 1603* of Hieronimus Fabricius of Aquapendente (1533?–1619). Facsimile edition with introduction, translation, and notes by K. J. Franklin. Springfield, Illinois, Charles C Thomas, 1933.

Hieronymus Fabricius ab Aquapendente: *The Embryological Treatises of Hieronymus Fabricius of Aquapendente*, a facsimile edition, with an introduction, a translation, and a commentary by Howard B. Adelmann. Ithaca, New York, Cornell University Press, 1942.

Guilhelmus Fabricius Hildanus: *De gangrena et sphacelo.* In nobili Oppenheimio, Hieronymus Gallerus, 1617.

Guilhelmus Fabricius Hildanus: *Wund-Artzney, Ganzes Werk, und aller Bücher, so viel deren vorhanden. . . .* ausz dem Lateinischen in das Teutsche übersetzt durch Friedrich Greiffen. . . . Franckfurth am Mayn, Joh. Aubry, 1652.

Wilhelm Fabry von Hilden: *Von der Fürtrefflichkeit und Nutz der Anatomie*, herausgegeben von Prof. F. de Quervain, Dr. Hans Bloesch und Dr. phil. Th. de Quervain Aaran. Leipzig, H. R. Sauerländer & Companie, 1936.

Hans von Gersdorff: *Feldbuch der Wundarztnev* [Strassburg, J. Schott, 15–?].

M. T. Gnudi and J. P. Webster: *The Life and Times of Gaspare Tagliacozzi: Surgeon of Bologna 1545–1599*, with a documented study of the scientific and cultural life of Bologna in the 16th Century. New York, Herbert Reichner [n.d.].

Ellis W. P. Jones: "The Life and Works of Guilhelmus Fabricius Hildanus (1560–1634)," Parts I and II, *Medical History*, Vol. IV, No. 2, pp. 112–134; Vol. IV, No. 3, pp. 196–209, 1960.

Giovanni Maria Lancisi: *De Aneurysmatibus, Opus posthumum* (1654–1720), revised and translated by Wilmer Cave Wright. New York, The Macmillan Company, 1952.

Heinrich von Pfolspeundt: *Buch der Bündth-Ertzney . . .* 1460, herausgegeben von H. Haeser und A. Middeldorpf. Berlin, George Reimer, 1868.

Matthäus Gottfried Purmann: *Chirurgia Curiosa* or *the newest and most curious Observations and Operations in the Whole Art of Chirurgery*, written originally in *High-Dutch*, by the learned

Matthaeus Gothofredus Purmannus, Chief Chirurgion of the City of *Breslau* in *Germany*
. . . translated by Joachim Sprengell. London, D. Browne . . . , 1706.

ALEXANDER READ: *Chirurgorum comes:* or the whole *practice of chirurgery.* . . . London, Jones,
1687. [Earliest English translation of the work of Tagliacozzi.]

R. J. SCHAEFER: "Wilhelm Fabricius von Hilden," in *Abhandlungen zur Geschichte der Medicin*,
edited by H. Magnus, M. Neuburger, and K. Sudhoff, Heft XIII. Breslau, 1904.

ROM. JOH. SCHAEFER: *Wilhelm Fabricius von Hilden, Sein Leben und seine Verdienste um die Chirurgie*,
Studie aus der Geschichte der Chirurgie, Heft 13. Breslau, J. U. Kerns Verlag, 1904.

JOHANNES SCULTETUS: *The Chyrurgeons Store-House*, englished by E. B. London, John Starkey,
1674.

JOHANNES SCULTETUS: *Armamentarium Chirurgicum*. Amsterdam, 1741.

CASPAR STROMAYR: *Die Handschrift des Schnitt- und Augenarztes Caspar Stromayr*, mit einer his-
torischen Einführung und Wertung von Walter von Brunn. Berlin, Idra-Verlagsanstalt,
1925.

GASPARE TAGLIACOZZI: *Gasparis Tagliacotii Bononiensis De curtorum chirurgia per insitionem*, Libri
duo. Venetiis, Apud Robertum Meiettum, 1597.

VI. GREAT BRITAIN LEADS

JOHN ABERNETHY: *Surgical Observations*. London, Longmans, 1809.

JOHN BARON: *The Life of Edward Jenner, M.D.*, 2 Vols. London, Henry Colburn, 1838.

F. BEEKMAN: "Rise of British Surgery in the 18th Century," *Annals of Medical History*, Vol. 9,
pp. 549–566, 1937.

F. BEEKMAN: "William Hunter's Education at Glasgow," *Bulletin of the History of Medicine*, Vol,
15, pp. 284–297, 1944.

British Masters of Medicine, edited by *Sir* D'Arcy Power. London, The Medical Press and
Circular, 1936.

WILLIAM CHESELDEN: *The Anatomy of the Human Body*. London, C. Hitch and R. Dodsley, 1756.

WILLIAM CLOWES: *A Profitable and Necessarie Booke of Observations*, for all those that are burned
with *the flame of Gun powder.* . . . London, Edw. Bollifant for Thomas Dawson, 1596. With
introduction general and medical by De Witt T. Starnes and Chauncey D. Leake, New
York, Scholar's Facsimiles and Reprints, 1945.

JOHN DIXON COMRIE: *History of Scottish Medicine*. London, Wellcome Historical Medical Museum, Baillière, Tindall & Cox, 1932.

Sir ZACHARY COPE: *William Cheselden*. London, E. & S. Livingstone, Ltd., 1953.

Sir ZACHARY COPE: "William Cheselden and the Separation of the Barbers from the Surgeons,"
Annals of the Royal College of Surgeons of England, Vol. 12, pp. 1–13, 1953.

Sir ZACHARY COPE: *The Royal College of Surgeons of England*, A History. [London] Anthony
Blond, 1959.

ALEXANDER DUNCAN: *Memorials of the Faculty of Physicians and Surgeons 1599–1850*. Glasgow,
James Maclehose and Sons, 1896.

Sir E. FINCH: "The Influence of the Hunters on Medical Education," Hunterian Lecture, 1957;
Annals of the Royal College of Surgeons of England, Vol. 20, pp. 205–247, 1957.

ARPAD A. GERSTER: "Laurentius H. Heister, A Sketch," *Proceedings of the Charaka Club*, Vol. 2,
pp. 131–141, 1906.

LORENZ HEISTER: *D. Lavrentii Heisters Chirurgie*. Nürnberg, Johann Hoffmann, 1731.

LAURENCE HEISTER: *A Compendium of Anatomy*, translated from the Latin, with notes by M.
Henault and the editor. London, W. Innys and J. Richardson *et al.*, 1752.

LORENZ HEISTER: *A General System of Surgery*, in three parts, containing the doctrine and management of wounds . . . by Laurence Heister, 6th edition. London, W. Innis & J. Richardson
et al., 1757.

JOHN HUNTER: *A Treatise on the Blood, Inflammations, and Gun-Shot Wounds*, by the late John Hunter, to which is prefixed "A Short Account of the Author's Life" by his brother-in-law Everard Home. London, George Nichol, 1794.

JOHN HUNTER: *The Works of John Hunter*, with notes, edited by James F. Palmer, 4 Vols. London, Longman, Rees, Orme, Brown, Green and Longman, 1837.

JOHN HUNTER: *A Treatise on the Venereal Disease*, with copious additions by Dr. Philip Ricord. . . . Philadelphia, Blanchard & Lea, 1853.

JOHN HUNTER: *Essays and Observations on Natural History, Physiology, Psychology, and Geology*, edited by Richard Owen, 2 Vols. London, John Van Voorsh, 1861.

WILLIAM HUNTER: "Further Observations upon a Particular Species of Aneurysm," *Medical Observations and Inquiries*, Vol. 1, pp. 390–414, 1762.

F. WOOD JONES: "John Hunter's Unwritten Book," *Lancet*, Vol. 2, pp. 788–790, 1951.

F. WOOD JONES: "John Hunter as a Geologist," *Annals of the Royal College of Surgeons of England*, Vol. 12, pp. 219–245, 1953.

G. M. LLOYD: "The Life and Works of Percivall Pott," *St. Bartholomew's Hospital Report*, Vol. 46, pp. 290–336, 1933.

Sir T. LONGMORE: *Richard Wiseman, Surgeon and Sergeant-Surgeon to Charles II*, A Biographical Study. London, Longmans, Green and Company, 1891.

PETER LOWE: *A Discourse on the Whole art of Chyrurgerie*. London, T. Purfoot, 1596.

PETER LOWE: *A Discourse on the Whole Art of Chyrurgery*. London, R. Hodgkinsonne, 1654.

GEORGE MACILWAIN: *Memoirs of John Abernethy*. New York, Harper and Brothers, 1853.

ALEXANDER MILES: *The Edinburgh School of Surgery before Lister*. London, A. & C. Black, Ltd., 1918.

ALEXANDER MONRO, JR.: *Observations on Crural Hernia*. Edinburgh, Longman, Rees and Laing, 1803.

JANE M. OPPENHEIMER: *New Aspects of John and William Hunter*. London, William Heinemann, 1946.

STEPHEN PAGET: *John Hunter, Man of Science and Surgeon* (1728–1793). London, T. Fisher Unwin, 1897.

PERCIVALL POTT: *The Chirurgical Works of Percivall Pott, F.R.S. A new edition with his last corrections to which are added a Short Account of the Life of the Author by* Sir James Earle, F.R.S., 3 Vols. London, for Johnson *et al.*, 1808.

S. C. THOMPSON: "The Great Windmill Street School," *Bulletin of the History of Medicine*, Vol. 12, pp. 377–391, 1942.

JOHN L. THORNTON: *John Abernethy, a Biography*. London, printed for the author, distributed by Simpkin Marshall, Ltd., 1953.

Sir JAMES WALTON: "The Hunterian Ideal Today," *British Journal of Surgery*, Vol. 35, pp. 1–6, 1947.

RICHARD WISEMAN: *Severall chirurgicall treatises*. London, R. Royston, 1676.

RICHARD WISEMAN: *Eight Surgical Treatises*, 2 Vols. London, 1734.

VII. EMINENT PRE-LISTERIANS

WILLIAM BEAUMONT: *Experiments and Observations on the Gastric Juice and the Physiology of Digestion*. Facsimile of the original edition of 1833, together with a biographical essay, "A Pioneer American Physiologist," by Sir William Osler. New York, Dover Publications, Inc., 1959.

BENJAMIN BELL: *A Treatise on the Theory and Management of Ulcers*. Edinburgh, C. Elliot, 1778.

BENJAMIN BELL: *A System of Surgery*, 6 Vols. Edinburgh, C. Elliot, 1782–1787.

Sir CHARLES BELL: *A System of Operative Surgery*, 2 Vols. London, Longman, 1807–1809.

Sir CHARLES BELL: *Illustrations of the Great Operations of Surgery*. London, A. and R. Spottiswoode, 1821.

Sir CHARLES BELL: *The Nervous System of the Human Body.* Edinburgh, Adam and Charles Black, 1836.

Sir CHARLES BELL: *Institutes of Surgery.* Edinburgh, Adam and Charles Black, 1838.

JOHN BELL: *The Principles of Surgery,* 3 Vols. Edinburgh, T. Cadell & W. Davies, 1801–1808.

JOHN BELL: *Letters on the Education of a Surgeon,* quoted in *History of Scottish Medicine* by John D. Comrie, Vol. I. London, The Wellcome Historical Medical Museum, 1932.

XAVIER BICHAT: *Oeuvres chirurgicales, ou éxposé de la doctrine et la pratique de P. J. Desault,* par Xav. Bichat, 3 Vols. Paris, Mequignon, 1801.

R. C. BROCK, *The Life and Work of Astley Cooper.* Edinburgh, E. & S. Livingstone, Ltd., 1952.

Sir ASTLEY PASTON COOPER: *Illustrations of the Diseases of the Breast.* London, Longman, Rees & Company, 1829.

Sir ASTLEY PASTON COOPER: *The Principles and Practice of Surgery,* edited by Alexander Lee, 2 Vols. London, E. Cox, 1837.

Sir ASTLEY PASTON COOPER: *The Anatomy and Surgical Treatment of Abdominal Hernia.* Philadelphia, Lea & Blanchard, 1844.

Sir ASTLEY PASTON COOPER: *The Anatomy and Diseases of the Breast, with Surgical Papers.* Philadelphia, Lea & Blanchard, 1845.

Sir ASTLEY PASTON COOPER AND BENJAMIN TRAVERS: *Surgical Essays,* 2 Vols. Philadelphia, James Webster, 1821.

BRANSBY B. COOPER: *The Life of Astley Cooper,* 2 Vols. London, John W. Parker, 1843.

PIERRE DIONIS: *Cours d'opération de chirurgie démontrées au Jardin Royal* par M. Dionis, edited by G. de la Fayo, 4th edition, 2 Vols. Paris, chez D'Houry, 1746.

LEROY DUPRÉ: *Memoir of Baron Larrey, Surgeon-in-Chief of Grande-Armée,* translated from the French, 2nd edition. London, Henry Renshaw, 1862.

GUILLAUME BARON DUPUYTREN: *Lectures on Clinical Surgery* delivered in the *Hôtel-Dieu* of Paris, by Baron Dupuytren, collected and published by an association of physicians, translated from the French, for the Register and Library of Medical and Chirurgical Science. Washington, stereotyped and published by Duff Green, 1835.

GUILLAUME BARON DUPUYTREN: *On the Injuries and Diseases of Bones,* translated by F. Le Gros Clark. London, The Sydenham Society, 1847.

GUILLAUME BARON DUPUYTREN: *On Lesions of the Vascular System, Diseases of the Rectum, and other Surgical Complaints,* selections from the Collected Edition of the Clinical Lectures of Baron Dupuytren, translated and edited by F. Le Gros Clark. London, printed for The Sydenham Society, 1854.

Sir GORDON GORDON-TAYLOR AND E. W. WALLS: *Sir Charles Bell: His Life and Times.* Edinburgh, E. & S. Livingstone, Ltd., 1958.

SAMUEL D. GROSS: *Lives of Eminent American Physicians and Surgeons of the Nineteenth Century.* Philadelphia, Lindsay and Blakiston, 1861.

SAMUEL D. GROSS: *Autobiography,* 2 Vols. Philadelphia, George Barrie, 1887.

SEALE HARRIS: *Woman's Surgeon.* New York, The Macmillan Company, 1950.

HOWARD A. KELLY AND WALTER L. BURRAGE: *American Medical Biographies.* Baltimore, The Norman Remington Company, 1920.

THOMAS E. KEYS: *The History of Surgical Anesthesia.* New York, Dover Publications, Inc., 1963.

Baron DOMINIQUE-JEAN LARREY: *Memoirs of Military Surgery and Campaigns of the French Armies,* from the French of D. J. Larrey by Richard Willmott Hall, 2 Vols. Baltimore, Joseph Cushing, 1814.

ANTOINE LOUIS: *Eloges lus dans les séances de l'Académie royale de chirurgie de 1750–1792.* Paris, J.-B. Baillière et fils, 1859.

W. S. MIDDLETON: "Philip Syng Physick," *Annals of Medical History*, Vol. 1, pp. 562–582, 1929.

ACHILLE MONTI: *Antonio Scarpa* in Scientific History and his Role in the Fortunes of the University of Pavia, translated by Frank L. Loria. New York, The Vigo Press, 1957.

FRANCIS R. PACKARD: *Guy Patin* and the Medical profession in Paris in the 17th Century. New York, Paul B. Hoeber, Inc., 1925.

JEAN LOUIS PETIT: *Oeuvres complètes*. [Paris] 1837.

AMÉDÉE PICHOT: *The Life and Labours of Sir Charles Bell*. London, Richard Bentley, 1860.

Sir BENJAMIN WARD RICHARDSON: "Antonio Scarpa, F.R.S., and Surgical Anatomy," Vol. 1, in *Disciples of Aesculapius*, 2 Vols. London, Hutchinson & Company, 1900.

MARY YOUNG RIDENBOUGH: *The Biography of Ephraim McDowell*. New York, Charles L. Webster, 1890.

J. ROCHARD: *Histoire de la chirurgie française au XIXe Siècle*. Paris, J.-B. Baillière et Fils, 1875.

ANTONIO SCARPA: *Saggio di osservazioni e d'esperienze sulle principali malattie degli occhi*. Pavia, B. Comino, 1801.

ANTONIO SCARPA: *A Treatise on the Anatomy, Pathology, and Surgical Treatment of Aneurism*, translated from the Italian with notes by John Henry Wishart. Edinburgh, Mundell, Doig & Stevenson, 1808.

ANTONIO SCARPA: *A Treatise on Hernia*, translated by John Henry Wishart. Edinburgh, Longman, Hurst, Rees *et al.*, 1814.

AUGUST SCHACHNER: *Ephraim McDowell*, *"Father of Ovariotomy" and Founder of Abdominal Surgery*. Philadelphia and London, J. B. Lippincott & Company, 1921.

J. MARION SIMS: "Two Cases of Vesico-Vaginal Fistula, Cured," *New York Medical Gazette*, Vol. 5, No. 1, pp. 1–7, 1854.

JAMES MARION SIMS: *Clinical Notes on Uterine Surgery*. New York, William Wood and Company, 1869.

J. MARION SIMS: "Remarks on Cholecystotomy in Dropsy of the Gall-Bladder," *The British Medical Journal*, Vol. 1, pp. 811–812, 1878.

JAMES MARION SIMS: *The Story of My Life*, edited by his son, H. Marion-Sims. New York, D. Appleton and Company, 1886.

J. J. SUE: *Écoles de chirurgie*, discours prononcé aux écoles de chirurgie par M. Sue, le Jeune, prévot du Collège. [Paris] 1774.

P. TRIAIRE: *Dominique Larray et les campagnes de la Révolution et de l'Empire, 1768–1842*. Tours, Mame, 1902.

VIII. LORD LISTER

CUTHBERT DUKES: *Lord Lister*. London, Leonard Parsons, 1924.

Sir RICKMAN JOHN GODLEE: *Lord Lister*, 3rd edition, revised. Oxford, at the Clarendon Press, 1924.

DOUGLAS GUTHRIE: *Lord Lister, His Life and Doctrine*. Edinburgh, E. & S. Livingstone, Ltd., 1949.

JOHN RUDD LEESON: *Lister as I Knew Him*. New York, William Wood and Company, 1928.

JOSEPH LISTER: "On a New Method of Treating Compound Fracture, Abscess, etc., with Observations on the Conditions of Suppuration," *Lancet*, Vol. I, pp. 326, 357, 387, 507; Vol. II, p. 95, 1867.

JOSEPH LISTER: *The Collected Papers of Joseph, Baron Lister*, 2 Vols. Oxford, at the Clarendon Press, 1909.

RHODA TRUAX: *Joseph Lister, Father of Modern Surgery*. Indianapolis, The Bobbs-Merrill Company, 1944.

A. LOGAN TURNER: *Joseph, Baron Lister*, Centenary Volume, 1827–1927. Edinburgh, Oliver and Boyd, 1927.

IX. MODERN SURGERY

EDUARD BASSINI: "Über die Behandlung des Leistenbruches," *Archiv für klinische Chirurgie* Berlin, Vol. 40, pp. 429–476, 1890.

THEODOR BILLROTH: *Historische Studien über die Beurtheilung und Behandlung der Schusswunden vom fünfzehnten Jahrhundert bis auf die neuste Zeit.* Berlin, G. Reimer, 1859.

THEODOR BILLROTH: *Lectures on Surgical Pathology and Therapeutics*, translated from the 8th edition, 2 Vols. London, The New Sydenham Society, 1877.

THEODOR BILLROTH: *Briefe*, achte veränderte auflage. Hannover und Leipzig, Hahnsche Buchhandlung, 1910.

THEODOR BILLROTH: *The Medical Sciences in the German Universities; a study in the history of civilization*, translated from the German of Theodor Billroth with an introduction by William H. Welch. New York, The Macmillan Company, 1924.

THEODOR BILLROTH: *Historical Studies on the Nature and Treatment and Gunshot Wounds* from the fifteenth century to the present time, translated by C. P. Rhoads. New Haven, Nathan Smith Medical Club, 1933.

HELEN BUCKLER: *Doctor Dan*, [Daniel Hale Williams] *Pioneer in American Surgery*. Boston, Little, Brown & Company 1954.

Sir ZACHARY COPE: *Pioneers in Acute Abdominal Surgery*. London, H. Milford, Oxford University Press, 1939.

HARVEY CUSHING: *From a Surgeon's Journal*. Boston, Little, Brown & Company, 1936.

DAVID FERRIER: *The Functions of the Brain*. London, Smith, Elder & Company, 1886.

GEORG FISCHER: *Chirurgie vor 100 Jahren, Historische Studie*. Leipzig, F. C. W. Vogel, 1876.

JOHN F. FULTON: "Arnold Klebs and Harvey Cushing at the 1st International Neurological Congress at Berne in 1931," *Bulletin of the History of Medicine*, Vol. VIII, No. 3, p. 345, 1940.

ROBERT GERSUNY: *Theodor Billroth*. Wien, Rikola, 1922. (Meister der Heilkunde, Band IV)

W. R. GOWERS AND VICTOR HORSLEY: "A Case of Tumor of the Spinal Cord. Removal; Recovery," *Medico-Chirurgical Transactions*, Royal Medical and Chirurgical Society, London, Vol. LXXI, p. 376 ff., 1888.

W. GRÖBLY: "Errinerungen an Theodor Kocher zur hundertsten Wiederkehr seines Geburtstages: am 25, August 1941," *Schweizerische medizinische Wochenschrift*, Vol. 22, pp. 1028–1031, 1941.

WILLIAM S. HALSTED: "The Operative Story of Goiter," *The Johns Hopkins Hospital Reports*, Vol. XIX, pp. 71–257, 1919.

GEORGE W. HEUER: "Dr. Halsted," Suppl. to *Bulletin of the Johns Hopkins Hospital*, Vol. 90, No. 2, 1952.

LEW A. HOCHBERG: *Thoracic Surgery before the 20th Century*. New York, Washington, Hollywood, Vantage Press, 1960.

GILBERT HORRAX: *Neurosurgery: a historical sketch*. Springfield, Illinois, Charles C Thomas, 1952.

Sir VICTOR HORSLEY AND MARY D. STURGES: *Alcohol and the Human Body*. London, Macmillan & Company, 1911.

THEODOR KOCHER: "Zur Pathologie und Therapie des Kropfes," *Deutsche Zeitschrift für Chirurgie*, Vol. 4, pp. 417–440, 1874.

THEODOR KOCHER: "Über Kropfextirpation und ihre Folgen," *Archiv für klinische Chirurgie*, Vol. XXIX, pp. 254–337, 1883.

W. G. MACCALLUM: *William Stewart Halsted*. Baltimore, The Johns Hopkins Press, 1930.

CHARLES H. MAYO AND HENRY S. PLUMMER: *The Thyroid Gland*, Beaumont Foundation [Annual Lecture Course IV, 1925]. St. Louis, C. V. Mosby Company, 1926.

Max Neuburger: "Some Relations between British and German Medicine in the first half of the Eighteenth Century," *Bulletin of the History of Medicine*, Vol. XVII, pp. 217–228, 1945.

Rudolph Nissen and Roger Wilson: *Pages in the History of Chest Surgery.* Springfield, Illinois, Charles C Thomas, 1960.

Stephen Paget: *Sir Victor Horsley: A Study of His Life and Work.* London, Constable & Company, Ltd., 1919.

August Gottlieb Richter: *Abhandlung von den Brüchen.* Göttingen, Johann Christian Dieterich, 1785.

August Gottlieb Richter: *Medical and Surgical Observations*, translated from the German. Edinburgh, T. Duncan, 1794.

Ferdinand Sauerbruch: "Zur Pathologie des offenen Pneumothorax und die Grundlagen meines Verfahrens zu seiner Ausschaltung," *Mitteilungen aus den Grenzgebieten der Medizin und Chirurgie*, Vol. 13, pp. 399–482, 1904.

Ferdinand Sauerbruch: "Über die Auschaltung der schädlichen Wirkung des Pneumothorax bei intrathorakalen Operationen," *Zentralblatt für Chirurgie*, Vol. 31, pp. 146–149, 1904.

Ferdinand Sauerbruch: *Das War Mein Leben.* Bad Wörishofen, Kindler und Schiermeyer Verlag, 1951.

Ferdinand Sauerbruch: *Master Surgeon: Ferdinand Sauerbruch*, translated by Fernand G. Renier and Anne Cliff. New York, Thomas Y. Crowell Company, 1954.

Friedrich Trendelenberg: *Die ersten 25 Jahre der deutschen Gesellschaft für Chirurgie.* Berlin, J. Springer, 1923.

E. Robert Wiese and Judson E. Gilbert: "Theodore Kocher," *Annals of Medical History*, Vol. 3 [N.S.], pp. 521–529, 1931.

Leo M. Zimmerman: "Henry O. Marcy, Pioneer of Hernial Surgery," *Quarterly Bulletin*, Northwestern University Medical School, Vol. 23, pp. 501–509, 1949.

Leo M. Zimmerman and Richard E. Heller: "Edoardo Bassini: His Role in the Development of Hernial Surgery," *Surgery, Gynecology, and Obstetrics*, Vol. 64, pp. 971–973, 1937.

Index